T0336843

Big Data Management, Technologies, and Applications

Wen–Chen Hu
University of North Dakota, USA

Naima Kaabouch
University of North Dakota, USA

A volume in the Advances in Data Mining
and Database Management (ADMDM)
Book Series

Information Science
REFERENCE
An Imprint of IGI Global

Managing Director:	Lindsay Johnston
Production Manager:	Jennifer Yoder
Publishing Systems Analyst:	Adrienne Freeland
Development Editor:	Allyson Gard
Acquisitions Editor:	Kayla Wolfe
Typesetter:	Lisandro Gonzalez
Cover Design:	Jason Mull

Published in the United States of America by
Information Science Reference (an imprint of IGI Global)
701 E. Chocolate Avenue
Hershey PA 17033
Tel: 717-533-8845
Fax: 717-533-8661
E-mail: cust@igi-global.com
Web site: http://www.igi-global.com

Library of Congress Cataloging-in-Publication Data

Big data management, technologies, and applications / Wen-chen Hu and Naima Kaabouch, editors.
     pages cm
 Includes bibliographical references and index.
   ISBN 978-1-4666-4699-5 (hardcover) -- ISBN 978-1-4666-4700-8 (ebook) -- ISBN 978-1-4666-4701-5 (print & perpetual access) 1. Big data. 2. Database management. I. Hu, Wen Chen, 1960- II. Kaabouch, Naima, 1959-
 QA76.9.D32B49 2014
 005.74--dc23
                                2013027713

This book is published in the IGI Global book series Advances in Data Mining and Database Management (ADMDM) (ISSN: 2327-1981; eISSN: 2327-199X)

British Cataloguing in Publication Data
A Cataloguing in Publication record for this book is available from the British Library.

For electronic access to this publication, please contact: eresources@igi-global.com.

Advances in Data Mining and Database Management (ADMDM) Book Series

David Taniar
Monash University, Australia

ISSN: 2327-1981
EISSN: 2327-199X

MISSION

With the large amounts of information available to businesses in today's digital world, there is a need for methods and research on managing and analyzing the information that is collected and stored. IT professionals, software engineers, and business administrators, along with many other researchers and academics, have made the fields of data mining and database management into ones of increasing importance as the digital world expands. The **Advances in Data Mining & Database Management (ADMDM) Book Series** aims to bring together research in both fields in order to become a resource for those involved in either field.

COVERAGE

- Cluster Analysis
- Customer Analytics
- Data Mining
- Data Quality
- Data Warehousing
- Database Security
- Database Testing
- Decision Support Systems
- Enterprise Systems
- Text Mining

IGI Global is currently accepting manuscripts for publication within this series. To submit a proposal for a volume in this series, please contact our Acquisition Editors at Acquisitions@igi-global.com or visit: http://www.igi-global.com/publish/.

Titles in this Series

For a list of additional titles in this series, please visit: www.igi-global.com

Big Data Management, Technologies, and Applications
Wen-Chen Hu (University of North Dakota, USA) and Naima Kaabouch (University of North Dakota, USA)
Information Science Reference • copyright 2014 • 342pp • H/C (ISBN: 9781466646995) • US $175.00 (our price)

Innovative Approaches of Data Visualization and Visual Analytics
Mao Lin Huang (University of Technology, Sydney, Australia) and Weidong Huang (CSIRO, Australia)
Information Science Reference • copyright 2014 • 373pp • H/C (ISBN: 9781466643093) • US $200.00 (our price)

Data Mining in Dynamic Social Networks and Fuzzy Systems
Vishal Bhatnagar (Ambedkar Institute of Advanced Communication Technologies and Research, India)
Information Science Reference • copyright 2013 • 412pp • H/C (ISBN: 9781466642133) • US $195.00 (our price)

Ethical Data Mining Applications for Socio-Economic Development
Hakikur Rahman (University of Minho, Portugal) and Isabel Ramos (University of Minho, Portugal)
Information Science Reference • copyright 2013 • 359pp • H/C (ISBN: 9781466640788) • US $195.00 (our price)

Design, Performance, and Analysis of Innovative Information Retrieval
Zhongyu (Joan) Lu (University of Huddersfield, UK)
Information Science Reference • copyright 2013 • 508pp • H/C (ISBN: 9781466619753) • US $195.00 (our price)

XML Data Mining Models, Methods, and Applications
Andrea Tagarelli (University of Calabria, Italy)
Information Science Reference • copyright 2012 • 538pp • H/C (ISBN: 9781613503560) • US $195.00 (our price)

Graph Data Management Techniques and Applications
Sherif Sakr (University of New South Wales, Australia) and Eric Pardede (LaTrobe University, Australia)
Information Science Reference • copyright 2012 • 502pp • H/C (ISBN: 9781613500538) • US $195.00 (our price)

Advanced Database Query Systems Techniques, Applications and Technologies
Li Yan (Northeastern University, China) and Zongmin Ma (Northeastern University, China)
Information Science Reference • copyright 2011 • 410pp • H/C (ISBN: 9781609604752) • US $180.00 (our price)

Knowledge Discovery Practices and Emerging Applications of Data Mining Trends and New Domains
A.V. Senthil Kumar (CMS College of Science and Commerce, India)
Information Science Reference • copyright 2011 • 414pp • H/C (ISBN: 9781609600679) • US $180.00 (our price)

DISSEMINATOR OF KNOWLEDGE

www.igi-global.com

701 E. Chocolate Ave., Hershey, PA 17033
Order online at www.igi-global.com or call 717-533-8845 x100
To place a standing order for titles released in this series, contact: cust@igi-global.com
Mon-Fri 8:00 am - 5:00 pm (est) or fax 24 hours a day 717-533-8661

Table of Contents

Foreword xviii

Preface xx

Acknowledgment xxviii

Section 1
Big Data Technologies, Methods, and Algorithms

Chapter 1
Technologies for Big Data 1
Kapil Bakshi, Cisco Systems Inc., USA

Chapter 2
Applying the K-Means Algorithm in Big Raw Data Sets with Hadoop and MapReduce 23
Ilias K. Savvas, TEI of Larissa, Greece
Georgia N. Sofianidou, TEI of Larissa, Greece
M-Tahar Kechadi, University College Dublin, Ireland

Chapter 3
Synchronizing Execution of Big Data in Distributed and Parallelized Environments 47
Gueyoung Jung, Xerox Research Center Webster, USA
Tridib Mukherjee, Xerox Research Center India, India

Chapter 4
Parallel Data Reduction Techniques for Big Datasets 72
Ahmet Artu Yıldırım, Utah State University, USA
Cem Özdoğan, Çankaya University, Turkey
Dan Watson, Utah State University, USA

Section 2
Big Data Storage, Management, and Sharing

Chapter 5
Techniques for Sampling Online Text-Based Data Sets 95
Lynne M. Webb, University of Arkansas, USA
Yuanxin Wang, Temple University, USA

Chapter 6
Big Data Warehouse Automatic Design Methodology 115
Francesco Di Tria, Università degli Studi di Bari Aldo Moro, Italy
Ezio Lefons, Università degli Studi di Bari Aldo Moro, Italy
Filippo Tangorra, Università degli Studi di Bari Aldo Moro, Italy

Chapter 7
Big Data Management in the Context of Real-Time Data Warehousing 150
M. Asif Naeem, Auckland University of Technology, New Zealand
Gillian Dobbie, University of Auckland, New Zealand
Gerald Weber, University of Auckland, New Zealand

Chapter 8
Big Data Sharing Among Academics 177
Jeonghyun Kim, University of North Texas, USA

Section 3
Specific Big Data

Chapter 9
Scalable Data Mining, Archiving, and Big Data Management for the Next Generation
Astronomical Telescopes 196
Chris A. Mattmann, California Institute of Technology, USA
Andrew Hart, California Institute of Technology, USA
Luca Cinquini, California Institute of Technology, USA
Joseph Lazio, California Institute of Technology, USA
Shakeh Khudikyan, California Institute of Technology, USA
Dayton Jones, California Institute of Technology, USA
Robert Preston, California Institute of Technology, USA
Thomas Bennett, SKA South Africa Project, South Africa
Bryan Butler, National Radio Astronomy Observatory (NRAO), USA
David Harland, National Radio Astronomy Observatory (NRAO), USA
Brian Glendenning, National Radio Astronomy Observatory (NRAO), USA
Jeff Kern, National Radio Astronomy Observatory (NRAO), USA
James Robnett, National Radio Astronomy Observatory (NRAO), USA

Chapter 10

Efficient Metaheuristic Approaches for Exploration of Online Social Networks 222
Zorica Stanimirović, University of Belgrade, Serbia
Stefan Mišković, University of Belgrade, Serbia

Chapter 11

Big Data at Scale for Digital Humanities: An Architecture for the HathiTrust Research Center 270
Stacy T. Kowalczyk, Dominican University, USA
Yiming Sun, Indiana University, USA
Zong Peng, Indiana University, USA
Beth Plale, Indiana University, USA
Aaron Todd, Indiana University, USA
Loretta Auvil, University of Illinois, USA
Craig Willis, University of Illinois, USA
Jiaan Zeng, Indiana University, USA
Milinda Pathirage, Indiana University, USA
Samitha Liyanage, Indiana University, USA
Guangchen Ruan, Indiana University, USA
J. Stephen Downie, University of Illinois, USA

Chapter 12

GeoBase: Indexing NetCDF Files for Large-Scale Data Analysis 295
Tanu Malik, University of Chicago, USA

Chapter 13

Large-Scale Sensor Network Analysis: Applications in Structural Health Monitoring 314
Joaquin Vanschoren, University of Leiden, The Netherlands
Ugo Vespier, University of Leiden, The Netherlands
Shengfa Miao, University of Leiden, The Netherlands
Marvin Meeng, University of Leiden, The Netherlands
Ricardo Cachucho, University of Leiden, The Netherlands
Arno Knobbe, University of Leiden, The Netherlands

Section 4
Big Data and Computer Systems and Big Data Benchmarks

Chapter 14

Accelerating Large-Scale Genome-Wide Association Studies with Graphics Processors 349
Mian Lu, Institute of High Performance Computing, A*STAR, Singapore
Qiong Luo, Hong Kong University of Science and Technology, Hong Kong

Chapter 15
The Need to Consider Hardware Selection when Designing Big Data Applications Supported
by Metadata 381
 Nathan Regola, University of Notre Dame, USA
 David A. Cieslak, Aunalytics, Inc., USA
 Nitesh V. Chawla, University of Notre Dame, USA

Chapter 16
Excess Entropy in Computer Systems 397
 Charles Loboz, Microsoft Corporation, USA

Chapter 17
A Review of System Benchmark Standards and a Look Ahead Towards an Industry Standard
for Benchmarking Big Data Workloads 415
 Raghunath Nambiar, Cisco Systems, Inc., USA
 Meikel Poess, Oracle Corp., USA

Compilation of References 433

About the Contributors 462

Index 476

Detailed Table of Contents

Foreword...xviii

Preface..xx

Acknowledgment...xxviii

Section 1
Big Data Technologies, Methods, and Algorithms

Chapter 1

Technologies for Big Data 1
    Kapil Bakshi, Cisco Systems Inc., USA

Unstructured data represents one of major challenges in the Big Data field. Unstructured data is information that either does not have a predefined data model or does not fit well into any relational database tables. Examples include imagery, sensor data, telemetry data, video, documents, log files, and email files. The challenge is not only to store and manage this vast mix of data, but also to analyze and extract meaningful value from it and do so within a reasonable timeframe and at a reasonable cost. This chapter presents an overview and analysis of the most accepted technologies used for collecting, storing, processing, and analyzing Big Data. The processing technologies discussed are Map-Reduce, NOSQL technology, Massively Parallel Processing, and In-Memory Databases. For each of these, the chapter covers several aspects, including history and genesis, problem set solving using the technology for Big Data analytics, components, technical architecture, and operations. These descriptions are followed by close examination of their technical operations and infrastructures (compute, storage, and network), design considerations, and performance benchmarks. Finally, the author provides an integrated approach to address the aforementioned Big Data challenge in Big Data.

Chapter 2

Applying the K-Means Algorithm in Big Raw Data Sets with Hadoop and MapReduce 23

Ilias K. Savvas, TEI of Larissa, Greece

Georgia N. Sofianidou, TEI of Larissa, Greece

M-Tahar Kechadi, University College Dublin, Ireland

The authors shed light on the impact of Big Data on data mining and how to address the problem using a combined technique. Data Mining is a process used for extracting useful information from bigger datasets. As these datasets are very large, the time complexity for most Data Mining techniques becomes very high. The major collection of raw data requires a fast and accurate mining process in order to extract the most useful information. The authors explore the possibility of using Hadoop's MapReduce framework and Hadoop Distributed File System to implement a popular clustering technique in a distributed fashion. MapReduce is a software framework used for the distributed computing of large data sets. The Apache Hadoop software library is a framework used for the distributed processing of large data sets, while the Hadoop Distributed File System is a distributed file system that provides high-throughput access to data-driven applications. Comparisons between the theoretical and experimental results of the combined technique are discussed and a conclusion is drawn, proving its efficiency.

Chapter 3

Synchronizing Execution of Big Data in Distributed and Parallelized Environments 47

Gueyoung Jung, Xerox Research Center Webster, USA

Tridib Mukherjee, Xerox Research Center India, India

This chapter focuses on the synchronous parallelization of big data analytics over a distributed system environment to optimize performance. Recently, the proliferation of many loosely coupled, distributed computing infrastructures (e.g., modern public, hybrid clouds, high performance computing clusters, and grids) have allowed high computing capability to be offered for large-scale computation. This advancement has allowed the execution of big data analytics to achieve a greater use across organizations and enterprises. However, even with such high computing capability, it is a major challenge to efficiently extract valuable information from vast astronomical data. The authors provide one solution of how to maximally leverage high computing capabilities from the aforementioned loosely coupled distributed infrastructure (e.g., modern public, private, hybrid clouds, high performance computing clusters, and grids) and ensure fast and accurate execution of big data analytics.

Chapter 4

Parallel Data Reduction Techniques for Big Datasets 72

Ahmet Artu Yıldırım, Utah State University, USA

Cem Özdoğan, Çankaya University, Turkey

Dan Watson, Utah State University, USA

This chapter discusses data reduction techniques and their importance in the analysis of big datasets. Data reduction is one of the most critical processes to implement when retrieving information from big data (i.e., petascale-sized data) with many data-mining techniques. This reduction process saves time and bandwidth and enables users to deal with larger datasets even in minimal resource environments, such as for desktop or small cluster systems. The authors describe several basic reduction techniques and their advantages and disadvantages. In addition, the chapter covers signal processing techniques used for mining big data through discrete wavelet transformation and server-side data reduction techniques. Finally, a general discussion is included on parallel algorithms for data reduction, with a special emphasis put on parallel wavelet-based, multi-resolution data reduction techniques for distributed memory systems, using MPI and shared memory architectures on GPUs. The discussion adds a demonstration of this improvement in performance and scalability with a case study.

Section 2
Big Data Storage, Management, and Sharing

Chapter 5

Techniques for Sampling Online Text-Based Data Sets 95

Lynne M. Webb, University of Arkansas, USA
Yuanxin Wang, Temple University, USA

The Internet has made very large comprehensive data sets readily available, including publicly available, textual, and online data. Such data sets offer richness and potential insights into human behavior, but they can be labor intensive and costly when it comes to mining, screening, and analyzing the data. Therefore, there is a need for effective sampling techniques in order to manage the sheer size of the data set, its complexity, and perhaps most importantly, its ongoing growth. In this chapter, the authors provide an overview of traditional sampling techniques and suggested adaptations that are relevant to big data studies of text downloaded from online media, including email messages, online gaming, blogs, micro-blogs (e.g., Twitter), and social networking Websites (e.g., Facebook).

Chapter 6

Big Data Warehouse Automatic Design Methodology 115

Francesco Di Tria, Università degli Studi di Bari Aldo Moro, Italy
Ezio Lefons, Università degli Studi di Bari Aldo Moro, Italy
Filippo Tangorra, Università degli Studi di Bari Aldo Moro, Italy

There is a growing need for more efficient techniques to address the problems that arise when dealing with big data traditional data warehouse design. Traditional data warehouse design methodologies are based on two opposite approaches: data-oriented and requirement-oriented. The data-oriented approach aims to realize the data warehouse mainly through a re-engineering process of the well-structured data sources solely, while minimizing the involvement of end users. The requirement-oriented approach aims to realize the data warehouse only on the basis of business goals as expressed by end users, with no regard for the information obtainable from the data sources. These approaches do not address the problems that arise when dealing with big data. Hybrid methodologies can deal with big data but require a more complex design process. In this chapter, the authors present a methodology based on a hybrid approach, which adopts a graph-based multidimensional model. In order to automate the whole design process, the methodology is implemented using logical programming.

Chapter 7

Big Data Management in the Context of Real-Time Data Warehousing 150

M. Asif Naeem, Auckland University of Technology, New Zealand
Gillian Dobbie, University of Auckland, New Zealand
Gerald Weber, University of Auckland, New Zealand

Accessing the latest information from big data warehouse repositories is important to businesses as they make timely and effective decisions. To keep these repositories up to date, real-time data integration is required. An important phase of real-time data integration is data transformation where a high volume of the updates stream is merged with large disk-based master data. Mesh Join (MESHJOIN) is a well-known algorithm that is used to process stream data with disk-based master data that uses limited memory. However, MESHJOIN is not very selective, and its performance is always inversely proportional to the size of the master data table. As a consequence, resource consumption is sub optimal in certain situations.

In this chapter, the authors describe an algorithm, Cache Join (CACHEJOIN), which performs better than MESHJOIN in realistic scenarios, particularly when parts of the master data are used with different frequencies. The authors provide a good comparison of both algorithms, using a synthetic dataset with known skewed distribution as well as TPC-H and real-life datasets.

Chapter 8

Big Data Sharing Among Academics 177
Jeonghyun Kim, University of North Texas, USA

Data sharing has recently become a hot topic in the scientific community. Promoting effective sharing of data is an increasing part of national and international scientific discourse and indeed essential to the future of science. This chapter explores the practice of big data sharing among academics and discusses the issues related to such sharing. It discusses four issues that future research should address in terms of sharing data via disciplinary repositories. The chapter is divided into several parts. The first part gives an overview of the literature on big data-sharing practices and the technologies used. The second part presents case studies on disciplinary data repositories in terms of their requirements and policies. These are described and compared at disciplinary repositories in three areas: Dryad for life science, Interuniversity Consortium for Political and Social Research (ICPSR) for social science, and the National Oceanographic Data Center (NODC) for physical science.

Section 3
Specific Big Data

Chapter 9

Scalable Data Mining, Archiving, and Big Data Management for the Next Generation
Astronomical Telescopes 196
Chris A. Mattmann, California Institute of Technology, USA
Andrew Hart, California Institute of Technology, USA
Luca Cinquini, California Institute of Technology, USA
Joseph Lazio, California Institute of Technology, USA
Shakeh Khudikyan, California Institute of Technology, USA
Dayton Jones, California Institute of Technology, USA
Robert Preston, California Institute of Technology, USA
Thomas Bennett, SKA South Africa Project, South Africa
Bryan Butler, National Radio Astronomy Observatory (NRAO), USA
David Harland, National Radio Astronomy Observatory (NRAO), USA
Brian Glendenning, National Radio Astronomy Observatory (NRAO), USA
Jeff Kern, National Radio Astronomy Observatory (NRAO), USA
James Robnett, National Radio Astronomy Observatory (NRAO), USA

Astronomy telescopes generate high volumes of data, ranging from a near terabyte (TB) per day to hundreds of TB of data per second. This chapter highlights the challenges in constructing data management systems for these astronomical instruments, specifically the challenge of integrating legacy science codes; handling data movement and triage; building flexible science data portals and user interfaces; allowing for flexible technology deployment scenarios, and automatically and rapidly mitigating the difference between science data formats and metadata models. The authors discuss these challenges and suggest open-source solutions based on software from the Apache Software Foundation, including Apache

Object Oriented Data Technology (OODT), Tika, and Solr. They leverage these solutions effectively and expeditiously to build many precursor and operational software systems to handle big data from astronomical instruments and better prepare for the coming data deluge from the future systems. These proposed solutions are not only applicable to the astronomical domain, but they are already applicable to a number of science domains, including earth science, planetary research, and biomedicine.

Chapter 10

Efficient Metaheuristic Approaches for Exploration of Online Social Networks 222
    Zorica Stanimirović, University of Belgrade, Serbia
    Stefan Mišković, University of Belgrade, Serbia

Big data presents major challenges in analytics. Developing adequate big data analysis techniques can improve the decision-making processes and minimize risks by unearthing invaluable insights that would otherwise remain hidden. This chapter describes a new approach for social network analytics that applies mathematical models and optimization techniques to analyze big data that is being obtained from different social sites in an efficient manner. The chapter starts by providing an overview of methods of social network analytics, followed by a section that describes the mathematical models for the efficient search of big data collected from social networks. The section that follows offers a detailed description of the metaheuristic methods developed for solving the considered problems. Finally, results are presented and analyzed, and conclusions are drawn, along with possibilities for future efforts and further research successes.

Chapter 11

Big Data at Scale for Digital Humanities: An Architecture for the HathiTrust Research Center 270
    Stacy T. Kowalczyk, Dominican University, USA
    Yiming Sun, Indiana University, USA
    Zong Peng, Indiana University, USA
    Beth Plale, Indiana University, USA
    Aaron Todd, Indiana University, USA
    Loretta Auvil, University of Illinois, USA
    Craig Willis, University of Illinois, USA
    Jiaan Zeng, Indiana University, USA
    Milinda Pathirage, Indiana University, USA
    Samitha Liyanage, Indiana University, USA
    Guangchen Ruan, Indiana University, USA
    J. Stephen Downie, University of Illinois, USA

Big Data is also expected to revolutionize humanities research and its processes. This chapter describes the most recent research in the humanities and the infrastructure related to Big Data. The authors discuss the HathiTrust Research Center (HTRC). HTRC is a cyberinfrastructure center that serves and supports researchers on big humanities data. Its purpose is to make that content easy to find, its research tools efficient and effective, allow researchers to customize their environment and combine their own data with that of the HTRC, and further, contribute to the development of new tools. The architecture offers multiple layers of abstraction to provide a secure, scalable, extendable, and generalizable interface for both human and computer users.

Chapter 12

GeoBase: Indexing NetCDF Files for Large-Scale Data Analysis 295
Tanu Malik, University of Chicago, USA

Scientists are increasingly dealing with big data issues but are not equipped with appropriate tools to manage it. In geosciences, large amounts of data are now available, but its analysis is limited by non-scalable access methods that affect analysis and visualization methods. This chapter describes an end-to-end system, GeoBase, which enables querying over scientific data by improving end-to-end support through two integrated, native components: a linearization based index to enable rich scientific querying on multi-dimensional data and a plugin that interfaces key-value stores with array-based binary file formats. The chapter first covers related work and describes the problems in designing an end-to-end system for geoscience applications. This is followed by a description of the GeoBase system. Experimental results of the extensive evaluation of the system and given and discussed.

Chapter 13

Large-Scale Sensor Network Analysis: Applications in Structural Health Monitoring..................... 314
Joaquin Vanschoren, University of Leiden, The Netherlands
Ugo Vespier, University of Leiden, The Netherlands
Shengfa Miao, University of Leiden, The Netherlands
Marvin Meeng, University of Leiden, The Netherlands
Ricardo Cachucho, University of Leiden, The Netherlands
Arno Knobbe, University of Leiden, The Netherlands

Sensors generate impressive amounts of all types of data, including images and signals. As the volume and complexity of such data continues to increase, their effectiveness in actual use becomes more challenging and more time consuming. Therefore, efficient techniques are needed both on a technical and a scientific level. Founded on several real-world applications, this chapter discusses the challenges involved in large-scale sensor data analysis and describes practical solutions to address them successfully. The chapter focuses on subsequence clustering, multi-scale analysis, scale-space decomposition, and modeling the interaction between various types of sensors in a network. Particularly, it focuses on key underlying types of processing such as convolution, smoothing, computing derivatives, and Fourier transforms for MapReduce-based implementations.

Section 4
Big Data and Computer Systems and Big Data Benchmarks

Chapter 14

Accelerating Large-Scale Genome-Wide Association Studies with Graphics Processors 349
Mian Lu, Institute of High Performance Computing, A*STAR, Singapore
Qiong Luo, Hong Kong University of Science and Technology, Hong Kong

Large-scale Genome-Wide Association Studies (GWAS) use and process a great deal of data that has high computation intensity. Genomic data analytics include sequence alignment, Single-Nucleotide Polymorphism (SNP) detection and Minor Allele Frequency (MAF) computation. MAF computation is the most time consuming task for GWAS. In this chapter, a technique based on a Graphical Processing Unit (GPU) that speeds up the processing of MAF is described. The authors first describe their methodology for using a GPU for such MAF computation and its implementation. Then, they describe a GPU-based technique to use for sequence alignment and SNP detection. Finally, experimental results are offered and discussed, and a conclusion regarding GPU processing time is drawn.

Chapter 15

The Need to Consider Hardware Selection when Designing Big Data Applications Supported
by Metadata 381

Nathan Regola, University of Notre Dame, USA
David A. Cieslak, Aunalytics, Inc., USA
Nitesh V. Chawla, University of Notre Dame, USA

Selecting the right hardware/software to support big data systems is a challenging task. Big data systems can have many component systems, such as a MapReduce cluster that processes data, analytics, and reporting applications that need to access large datasets to operate, and algorithms that can effectively operate on large datasets, or even basic scripts that will produce a needed result by leveraging data. For these reasons, it can be difficult to create a universal, representative benchmark that approximates a "big data" workload. Along with the trend toward utilizing large datasets and sophisticated tools to analyze big data, the cloud computing trend has emerged as an effective way to lease computing time. This chapter explores the issues that rest at the intersection of virtualized computing, metadata storage, and big data.

Chapter 16

Excess Entropy in Computer Systems 397

Charles Loboz, Microsoft Corporation, USA

Modern data centers house tens of thousands of servers in complex layouts. This scenario requires sophisticated reporting to turn available terabytes of data into information. The classical approaches can handle only a small number of connected computers. There is a need to identify problematic groups of servers, strange load patterns, and changes in composition, and do so with minimal human involvement. This chapter shows how a single concept, entropy, can describe multiple aspects of system use. The authors use several variants of entropy to address the problem, Excess Entropy (EE), normalized Excess Entropy (nEE), and Composite Excess Entropy (CEE). The EE is introduced as a way to describe various aspects of imbalance or concentrations of resource use in computer systems, both large and small. The nEE enables a comparison of imbalance between different systems, even when these systems have a different number of elements. CEE on the other hand allows for hierarchical composition and the decomposition of imbalance in subsystems into an imbalance in the overall system.

Chapter 17

A Review of System Benchmark Standards and a Look Ahead Towards an Industry Standard
for Benchmarking Big Data Workloads 415

Raghunath Nambiar, Cisco Systems, Inc., USA
Meikel Poess, Oracle Corp., USA

This chapter discusses the standards for measuring the performance of platforms for Big Data. Historically, industry standard benchmarks have produced a healthy competition that results in product improvements and the creation of new technologies. This scenario has also become a significant driving force behind the development of faster, less expensive, and/or more energy efficient system configurations. The authors envision new standards evolving from initiatives such Workshop on Big Data Benchmarking (WBDB) and further enhancements to existing standards from standard bodies like the Transaction Processing Performance Council (TPC). They believe that these standards can help customers compare performance, cost, and the energy efficiency of Big Data platforms. Standardized workloads and metrics can also help researchers develop and enhance new relevant technologies for Big Data applications.

Compilation of References 433

About the Contributors 462

Index 476

Foreword

In the information age, data is generated explosively. For example, everyday there are 230 million tweets sent, 294 billion emails delivered, and 100 terabytes of data uploaded to Facebook according to IDC (2012). Important and useful information such as crime prevention and customer buying patterns could be buried inside the huge amount of unstructured data. How to effectively manage and use the big data is a big headache for organizations. Many IT researchers and scholars and organizations are working on this problem. Even the Obama Administration (White House, 2012) announced a "Big Data Research and Development Initiative." Several US Federal departments and agencies have pledged more than $200 million for this big data initiative. The departments and agencies and their big data themes include:

- **Together National Science Foundation (NSF) and the National Institutes of Health (NIH):** Core Techniques and Technologies for Advancing Big Data Science and Engineering.
- **National Science Foundation (NSF):** Including funding the big data solicitations, keeping with its focus on basic research, and implementing a comprehensive, long-term big data strategy.
- **Department of Defense (DOD):** Data to Decisions.
- **National Institutes of Health (NIH):** 1000 Genomes Project Data Available on Cloud.
- **Department of Energy (DOE):** Scientific Discovery through Advanced Computing.
- **US Geological Survey (USGS):** Big Data for Earth System Science.

Big data is critical and popular, but not many books about big data are available at this moment (2013) because big data research just began to attract attention. This book, *Big Data Management, Technologies, and Applications*, is a timely and urgently needed publication. It is unique among those available big-data books because of its great depth and technical approach. It consists of four practical themes:

1. **Big Data Technologies, Methods, and Algorithms:** Which gives various big data methods.
2. **Big Data Storage, Management, and Sharing:** Which covers the issues related to storing, managing, and sharing big data.
3. **Specific Big Data:** Which discusses big data in specific areas like social networks.
4. **Big Data and Computer Systems and Big Data Benchmarks:** Which explains the roles of big data in computer systems and introduces the benchmarks for big data.

Unlike most big data books, it covers big data from a technological perspective. Readers can actually apply the methods learned from this book to real-world problems.

Big data is everywhere now and valuable information is hiding in it. In the past, this information was simply ignored and opportunities were missed. Realizing the great importance of big data, organizations scramble to find hidden information buried in big data and try to make the best use of it. This book, *Big Data Management, Technologies, and Applications*, provides the most up-to-date, crucial, and practical information for big data management, technologies, and applications. If any IT students, researchers, scholars, and workers have big data in mind, they should not miss this book because it will help them understand various big data issues and apply the proposed big data methods to their problems. It is a great book contributed by sixty world-renowned big data researchers and scholars. I trust you will enjoy reading it.

Wen-Chang Fang
National Taipei University, Taiwan
June 15, 2013

Wen-Chang Fang *is a professor in the Department of Business Administration, National Taipei University. He received his Ph.D. from Northwestern University, USA. His research focuses mainly on electronic commerce and network externalities. He is also chief editor of Electronic Commerce Studies, a quarterly academic journal in Taiwan. His research papers have been published in the Journal of Management, Journal of Information Management, Management Review, Chiao Da Management Review, Journal of Management & Systems, Sun Yat-Sen Management Review, Asia Pacific Management Review, Entrepreneurship & Regional Development, CyberPsychology and Behavior, Industrial Marketing Management, Expert Systems with Applications, Journal of Business Ethics, and Technological Forecasting and Social Change.*

REFERENCES

IDC. (2012, March 7). *IDC releases first worldwide big data technology and services market forecast, shows big data as the next essential capability and a foundation for the intelligent economy.* Retrieved May 4, 2013, from http://www.idc.com/getdoc.jsp?containerId=prUS23355112

White House. (2012, March 29). *Obama administration unveils "big data" initiative: Announces $200 million in new R&D investments.* Retrieved February 13, 2013, from http://www.whitehouse.gov/sites/default/files/microsites/ostp/big_data_press_release_final_2.pdf

Preface

This book collects high-quality research papers and industrial and practice articles in the areas of big data management, technologies, and applications from academics and industries. It includes research and development results of lasting significance in the theory, design, implementation, analysis, and application of big data, and other critical issues. Seventeen excellent chapters from sixty world-renowned scholars and industry professionals are included in this book, which covers four themes: (1) big data technologies, methods, and algorithms, (2) big data storage, management, and sharing, (3) specific big data, and (4) big data and computer systems and big data benchmarks. This preface presents this book, gives essential big data management, technologies, and applications, introduces each section and chapter of this book, and summarizes the discussions.

INTRODUCTION

The growth of information size is not linear, but exponential. For example, at least one million Web pages are added to the Internet every day, a massive amount of genetic data is created from various genome projects, or vast astronomical data is recorded after studying numerous galaxies. Big data is one of the hottest IT topics these days because many opportunities and great revenue are behind it based on the following reports:

- Big data is a major driver of IT spending these days; for example, $232 billion will be spent on IT including information management and analytics infrastructure from 2012 through 2016 according to Gartner (Beyer, Lovelock, Sommer, & Adrian, 2012).
- IDC (2012) predicted the worldwide market of big data technology and services will grow from $3.2 billion in 2010 to $16.9 billion in 2015, which represents a CAGR (Compound Annual Growth Rate) of 40%. For example, it reported big data storage had the strongest growth rate, growing at 61.4% annually.
- Two observations from Kelly, Floyer, Vellante, and Miniman (2013) are (1) factory revenue generated by the sale of big data-related hardware, software, and services growing by 59% in 2012 over 2011, and (2) the total big data market having an average 31% CAGR over the five-year period from 2012 ($11.4 billion) to 2017 ($47 billion).

Even though the future of big data is bright, traditional IT technologies such as files and relational databases are not able to handle this kind of data anymore because of its vast size, constant changes, and high complication. Other technologies have to be created or used to manage big data, which is complex, unstructured, or semi-structured. Therefore, IT workers and students look forward to books that can help them understand big data and learn effective big data methods. Unfortunately, very few big data books are able to meet the readers' needs at this moment. This is a just-in-time book. It discusses various issues related to big data management, technologies, and applications from a technological perspective. Readers learn fundamental big data knowledge from this book and are able to apply the learned knowledge to their big data problems.

Big data exists in a wide variety of data-intensive areas such as atmospheric science, genome research, astronomical studies, and network traffic monitor. This book does not target any specific areas. It is a generic big data book. Therefore, a broader audience could benefit from this book. The intended audience includes IT industrialists, students, educators, and researchers with big data in mind. It especially benefits the IT personnel of the big corporations, which face a great influx of data. This book will help IT workers smoothly build efficient and effective big data systems based on their traditional IT knowledge. It could be used for a textbook of an advanced IT (or related disciplines) course and could be a reference book for IT professionals and students. Since this book covers the big data subject systematically, it is also for people desiring to learn the big data topics on their own.

This book provides rich topics of big data management, technologies, and applications. This preface is to introduce this book and suggest essential big data management methods, technologies, and applications. The rest of this preface is organized as follows:

Section 2 - Essential Big Data Management, Technologies, and Applications: This section discusses the essential big data management, technologies, and applications. It includes the following steps: (1) big data generation, capturing, and collection, (2) big data storage and preservation, (3) big data analytics, management, visualization, and sharing, and (4) big data applications and other related topics. Each step and its corresponding topics will be introduced in this section.

Section 3 - Organization of this Book: This book consists of seventeen chapters divided into four sections: (1) big data technologies, methods, and algorithms, (2) big data storage, management, and sharing, (3) specific big data, and (4) big data and computer systems and big data benchmarks. Each section and chapter will be briefly introduced in this section.

Section 4 - Summary: The last section summarizes the management, technologies, and applications of big data discussed in this preface.

ESSENTIAL BIG DATA MANAGEMENT, TECHNOLOGIES, AND APPLICATIONS

Big data covers a wide variety of subjects and methods. This section tries to introduce essential big data management, technologies, and applications by using the following steps: (1) big data generation, capturing, and collection, (2) big data storage and preservation, (3) big data analytics, management, visualization, and sharing, and (4) big data applications and other related topics as shown in Figure 1. Each step is explained next.

Figure 1. A flowchart of generic big data management

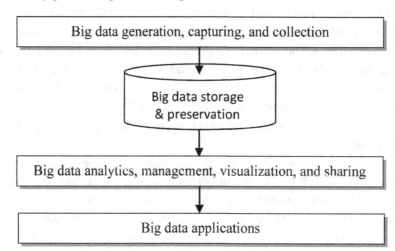

Big Data Generation, Capturing, and Collection

This is the first step of big data management including three actions: big data generation, capturing, and collection, which are briefly introduced as follows:

- **Big Data Generation:** During the time when computers were not popular, big data was rare. Since the number of (embedded) computers was greatly increased in the '80s, data is generated explosively. Big data can be generated from many sources; for example, all kinds of sensors, customer purchasing data, astronomical data, and texting messages.
- **Big Data Capturing:** Big data may be generated continuously (like steady satellite image transmission) or abruptly (during the peak hours). Compared to continuously generated big data, capturing abruptly generated big data is a challenge.
- **Big Data Collection:** Not all captured data is worth collection because of limited storage and processing power. For example, the size of videos of traffic monitor could be huge. Instead of saving the whole videos, specific video frames are selected and saved.

Big Data Storage and Preservation

After collecting big data, the next step is to store and preserve it. Because of its high volume, velocity, and variety, it is not a trivial task of storing and preserving big data. Big data storage and preservation are shortly explained below:

- **Big Data Storage:** The size of big data is huge and large scalable storage is required for storing it. Many times datacenters and warehousing are used and data structures are tailored for specific big data.
- **Big Data Preservation:** Big data has three key features: large volume, great variety, and high velocity. The feature of high velocity makes big data preservation volatile and complicated.

Big Data Analytics, Management, Visualization, and Sharing

Before big data can be put into use, it might need to be processed first. Various big data processing methods are available. Four major ones are analytics, management, visualization, and sharing introduced as follows:

- **Big Data Analytics:** It is to examine big data and uncover its hidden information. Examples of using the uncovered information include weather forecasts and economic indicators. Tools for big data analytics include NoSQL databases, Hadoop, and MapReduce.
- **Big Data Management:** After big data is collected, it needs to be well managed and maintained. There are many kinds of big data management methods. Some of them are organizing, searching, processing, mining big data.
- **Big Data Visualization:** Reading big data item by item is not feasible. Visualization tools or functions must be provided so data can be searched, viewed, and managed easily and collectively.
- **Big Data Sharing:** Many issues, like privacy and security, are related to big data sharing. Additionally, big data sharing is considered a hard problem because of its huge size. Cloud computing may relieve this problem.

Big Data Applications and Other Related Issues

Results of big data processing can be applied to many areas like businesses and sciences and can be used in many ways like increasing revenue and inventing new drugs. Other related critical big data issues worth mentioning such as privacy and security are given as follows:

- **Big Data Applications:** Most data-intensive areas could be the candidates for big data applications. Some of the examples are (1) data from various sensors for weather forecasts, (2) data from numerous traffic monitors for transportation control, and (3) customer purchasing patterns for revenue discovery.
- **Big Data Privacy and Security:** Without rigorous privacy and security control, big data could not flourish. Strict privacy encourages big data collection and high security assures the safety of big data.
- **Big Data Standards, Policies, and Benchmarks:** Big data is a fairly new research subject. Therefore, its standards, policies, and benchmarks are still developing and investigated.
- **Cloud, Green, and Mobile Computing for Big Data:** Many newest computing paradigms could be used by big data. Among them are (1) cloud computing for sharing big data, (2) green computing for saving time and energy, and (3) mobile computing for accessing big data from anywhere and anytime.

ORGANIZATION OF THE BOOK

This book provides timely, critical management methods, technologies, and applications of big data to IT workers and students. It contains seventeen chapters divided into four sections: (1) big data technologies, methods, and algorithms, (2) big data storage, management, and sharing, (3) specific big data, and (4) big data and computer systems and big data benchmarks. Each section and chapter is briefly introduced next.

Big Data Technologies, Methods, and Algorithms

Various technologies, methods, and algorithms are available for big data. This section discusses some of them including a survey, the K-means algorithm, synchronizing execution, and data reduction:

Chapter 1 - Technologies for Big Data: The author, Kapil Bakshi from Cisco Systems, Inc., gives a review and analysis of several key big data technologies including: MapReduce, NOSQL, MPP (Massively Parallel Processing), and in memory databases.

Chapter 2 - Applying the K-Means Algorithm in Big Raw Data Sets with Hadoop and MapReduce: The authors propose a distributed version of the K-means clustering algorithm for big data mining. It is based on three kinds of software: (1) Apache Hadoop software library, a framework for distributed processing of large data sets, (2) Hadoop Distributed File System (HDFS), a distributed file system that provides high-throughput access to data-driven applications, and (3) MapReduce, a software framework for distributed computing of large data sets.

Chapter 3 - Synchronizing Execution of Big Data in Distributed and Parallelized Environments: In order to ensure fast and accurate execution of big data analytics, the computing capability of loosely-coupled distributed infrastructure needs to be maximally leveraged. This chapter discusses synchronous parallelization of big data analytics over a distributed environment to optimize performance.

Chapter 4 - Parallel Data Reduction Techniques for Big Datasets: The major mission of data reduction is to save time and bandwidth in enabling users to deal with larger datasets even in minimal resource environments. This chapter first examines the importance of data reduction techniques for the analysis of big datasets and then presents several basic reduction techniques in detail, stressing on the advantages and disadvantages of each.

Big Data Storage, Management, and Sharing

Three themes, storage, management, and sharing, are critical to big data. How to store and share big data is challenging because of its high volume. Furthermore, the potentials of big data cannot be fully discovered if it is not properly managed. This section discusses various issues related to the three themes including sampling, warehouse design, warehousing, and sharing:

Chapter 5 - Techniques for Sampling Online Text-Based Data Sets: The chapter first reviews traditional sampling techniques and then suggests adaptations relevant to big data studies of text downloaded from online media such as email messages, online gaming, blogs, micro-blogs like Twitter, and social networking Websites like Facebook.

Chapter 6 - Big Data Warehouse Automatic Design Methodology: This chapter presents a data warehouse design methodology based on a hybrid approach, which adopts a graph-based multidimensional model. In order to automate the whole design process, the methodology has been implemented using logical programming.

Chapter 7 - Big Data Management in the Context of Real-Time Data Warehousing: In order to make timely and effective decisions, businesses need the latest information from big data warehouse repositories. A well-known algorithm called Mesh Join (MESHJOIN) is to process stream data with disk-based master data, which uses limited memory. This chapter presents an algorithm called Cache Join (CACHEJOIN), which performs asymptotically at least as well as MESHJOIN but performs better in realistic scenarios, particularly if parts of the master data are used with different frequencies.

Chapter 8 - Big Data Sharing among Academics: The first part of this chapter reviews literature on big data sharing practices using current technology. The second part presents case studies on disciplinary data repositories in terms of their requirements and policies. It describes and compares such requirements and policies at disciplinary repositories in three areas: Dryad for life science, Interuniversity Consortium for Political and Social Research (ICPSR) for social science, and the National Oceanographic Data Center (NODC) for physical science.

Specific Big Data

Big data is prevailing. Each application has its unique big data and requires a particular method to process it. This section covers five specific kinds of big data: astronomical telescopes, social networks, digital humanities, geography, and sensor networks:

Chapter 9 - Scalable Data Mining, Archiving, and Big Data Management for the Next Generation Astronomical Telescopes: This chapter first discusses the big data challenges in constructing data management systems for astronomical instruments and then suggests open source solutions to them based on software from the Apache Software Foundation including Apache Object-Oriented Data Technology (OODT), Tika, and Solr.

Chapter 10 - Efficient Metaheuristic Approaches for Exploration of Online Social Networks: This study focuses on big data analytics techniques. Developing adequate big data analysis techniques may help to improve the decision-making process and minimize risks by unearthing valuable insights that would otherwise remain hidden. An automated decision-making software can be provided by using big data analytics to automatically fine-tune inventories in response to real-time sales.

Chapter 11 - Big Data at Scale for Digital Humanities: An Architecture for the HathiTrust Research Center: The HathiTrust Research Center (HTRC) is a cyberinfrastructure to support humanities research on big humanities data including the following functions: to make the content easy to find, to make the research tools efficient and effective, to allow researchers to customize their environment, to allow researchers to combine their own data with that of the HTRC, and to allow researchers to contribute tools. The architecture has multiple layers of abstraction providing a secure, scalable, extendable, and generalizable interface for both human and computational users.

Chapter 12 - GeoBase – Indexing NetCDF Files for Large-Scale Data Analysis: The author, Tanu Malik, proposes the GeoBase, which enables querying over scientific data by improving end-to-end support through two integrated, native components: a linearization-based index to enable rich scientific querying on multi-dimensional data and a plugin that interfaces key-value stores with array-based binary file formats.

Chapter 13 - Large-Scale Sensor Network Analysis – Applications in Structural Health Monitoring: Based on several real-world applications, this chapter discusses the challenges involved in large-scale sensor data analysis, and describes practical solutions to address them. Due to the sheer size of the data, and the large amount of computation involved, these are clearly "Big Data" applications.

Big Data and Computer Systems and Big Data Benchmarks

Big data is complicated and its size is huge. It requires the services from high performance computer systems. The first three chapters in this section are related to computer systems, including graphics processors, hardware selection, and excess entropy. The last chapter, benchmarking big data workloads, does not belong to any topics of the four sections and is put here. The four chapters are briefly described as follows:

Chapter 14 - Accelerating Large-Scale Genome-Wide Association Studies with Graphics Processors: Large-scale Genome-Wide Association Studies (GWAS) are a big data application due to the great amount of data to process and high computation intensity and Graphics Processors (GPUs) have been used to accelerate genomic data analytics like Minor Allele Frequency (MAF) computation. This chapter proposes techniques of accelerating MAF computation by using GPUs.

Chapter 15 - The Need to Consider Hardware Selection When Designing Big Data Applications Supported by Metadata: The selection of hardware to support big data systems is complex. The trend of cloud computing has emerged as an effective method of leasing compute time and metadata enables many applications and users to access datasets and effectively use them without relying on extensive knowledge from humans about the data. This chapter explores some of the issues at the intersection of cloud computing, metadata, and big data.

Chapter 16 - Excess Entropy in Computer Systems: Entropy is well researched in physics and used in economics. This research applies it to large computer systems. The author, Charles Loboz, shows how entropy, a single concept, can identify problematic groups of servers, strange patterns in load, and changes in composition with minimal human involvement.

Chapter 17 - A Review of System Benchmark Standards and a Look Ahead Towards an Industry Standard for Benchmarking Big Data Workloads: Transaction Processing Performance Council (TPC) and the Standard Performance Evaluation Corporation (SPEC) have developed several industry standards for performance benchmarking for various applications, including big data applications. This chapter looks into various techniques and measures the effectiveness of hardware and software platforms dealing with big data.

SUMMARY

Big data has existed for a long time, but it did not catch great attention until recently because it did not prevail. However, owing to the high popularity of computers and great IT advancements, big data is everywhere. A tremendous amount of data is generated every day, everywhere, from fields such as businesses, research, and sciences. The high volume, velocity, and variety of data cause a great headache to people because the traditional methods are no longer working for this kind of data. A book covering big data from a technological perspective is in need. Unfortunately, not many books about big data are available at this moment (2013). This book, *Big Data Management, Technologies, and Applications*, is unique among those big-data books because of its great depth and technical approach. It consists of four themes: (1) big data technologies, methods, and algorithms, (2) big data storage, management, and sharing, (3) specific big data, and (4) big data and computer systems and big data benchmarks. It is a timely and urgently needed publication, and it provides the most up-to-date, crucial, and practical information for big data management, technologies, and applications. It is a must-read book for IT students, researchers, scholars, and workers with big data in mind.

This book covers various important issues of big data from fundamental knowledge to advanced algorithms. There are many advantages provided by this unique, much needed big data book. Some of the advantages are (1) covering various critical issues related to big data management, technologies, and applications, (2) helping IT students and workers gain essential knowledge of big data, (3) assisting researchers and professionals to master big data technologies, and (4) providing a just-in-time textbook for a course of big data. Additionally, it could be used as a reference book for data-intensive workers and students, who are interested in big data. Overall, this book will help readers better understand big data and apply the methods learned from this book to real world problems. Hope you enjoy reading it.

Wen-Chen Hu
University of North Dakota, USA

Naima Kaabouch
University of North Dakota, USA

REFERENCES

Beyer, M. A., Lovelock, J.-D., Sommer, D., & Adrian, M. (2012, October 12). *Big data drives rapid changes in infrastructure and $232 billion in IT spending through 2016*. Retrieved June 12, 2013, from http://www.gartner.com/id=2195915

IDC. (2012, March 7). *IDC releases first worldwide big data technology and services market forecast, shows big data as the next essential capability and a foundation for the intelligent economy*. Retrieved May 4, 2013, from http://www.idc.com/getdoc.jsp?containerId=prUS23355112

Kelly, J., Floyer, D., Vellante, D., & Miniman, S. (2013, April 17). *Big data vendor revenue and market forecast 2012-2017*. Retrieved May 22, 2013, from http://wikibon.org/wiki/v/Big_Data_Vendor_Revenue_and_Market_Forecast_2012-2017

Acknowledgment

The editors thank the authors for their quality works and great efforts in revising their works based on the reviewers' comments. The reviewers, who provided such helpful feedback and detailed comments, are particularly appreciated. Special thanks go to the staff at IGI Global, especially to Allyson Gard, Mehdi Khosrow-Pour, and Jan Travers. Finally, the biggest thanks go to our family members for their love and supports throughout this project.

Wen-Chen Hu
University of North Dakota, USA

Naima Kaabouch
University of North Dakota, USA
June 15, 2013

Section 1
Big Data Technologies, Methods, and Algorithms

Chapter 1
Technologies for Big Data

Kapil Bakshi
Cisco Systems Inc., USA

ABSTRACT

This chapter provides a review and analysis of several key Big Data technologies. Currently, there are many Big Data technologies in development and implementation; hence, a comprehensive review of all of these technologies is beyond the scope of this chapter. This chapter focuses on the most popularly accepted technologies. The key Big Data technologies to be discussed include: Map-Reduce, NOSQL technology, MPP (Massively Parallel Processing), and In Memory Databases technologies. For each of these Big Data technologies, the following subtopics are discussed: the history and genesis of the Big Data technologies, problem set that this technology solves for Big Data analytics, the details of the technologies, including components, technical architecture, and theory of operations. This is followed by technical operation and infrastructure (compute, storage, and network), design considerations, and performance benchmarks. Finally, this chapter provides an integrated approach to the above-mentioned Big Data technologies.

INTRODUCTION: THE CHALLENGE OF BIG DATA

The amount of data in the world is being collected and stored at unprecedented rates. A study by IDC Gantz & Reinsel, (2011) indicates that the world's information is doubling every two years. Also the IDC study by Gantz & Reinsel (2011), mentions that the world created a staggering 1.8 zettabytes of information (a zettabyte is 1000 exabytes), and projections suggest that by 2020, we'll generate will generate 50 times that amount.

Big Data has been defined as, when data sets get so large, that traditional technologies,

DOI: 10.4018/978-1-4666-4699-5.ch001

techniques, and tools for extracting insights are no longer useful in a reasonable timeframe and cost-effective manner. This has spawned a new generation of technologies and corresponding considerations. Desai, Kommu & Rapp (2011) examine the cause of this explosion of Big Data, the following factors dominate:

- **Mobility trends:** Mobile devices and sensor proliferation;
- **New data access:** Internet, interconnected systems, and social networking;
- **Open source model:** Major changes in the information processing model and the availability of an open source framework.

What distinguishes Big Data from data in the past, however, is not just its vast volume. The defining features of Big Data are also its variety—the sources and types of data being collected—and its velocity, the speed at which the data is flowing through the networked systems. Studies like Cisco Virtual Networking Index by Barnett, (2011) estimate that in 2016, global IP traffic will reach 1.3 zettabytes per year or 110.3 exabytes per month. Moreover, it is anticipated that there will be 19 billion networked devices by 2016.

One of the most interesting aspects about Big Data is that that unstructured data is the fastest growing type of data. Unstructured data refers to information that either does not have a predefined data model or does not fit well into relational database tables. Examples of unstructured data include imagery, sensor data, telemetry data, video, documents, log files, and email files. The challenge is not only to store and manage this vast mix, but to analyze and extract meaningful value from it—and to do so in a reasonable timeframe and at a reasonable cost.

Fortunately, a new generation of technologies has emerged for collecting, storing, processing, and analyzing Big Data. This chapter provides a survey of these technologies, including implementation and operational details:

- MapReduce framework, including Hadoop Distributed File System (HDFS);
- NoSQL (Not Only SQL) data stores;
- MPP (Massively Parallel Processing) databases;
- In-memory database processing.

MAPREDUCE AND HADOOP DISTRIBUTED FILE SYSTEM

In 2003, Google published a paper on Google File Systems (GFS) by Ghemawat, Gobioff & Leung (2003). and a subsequent paper on the MapReduce Dean & Ghemawat (2004) model to address processing large unstructured data sets. Hadoop, an open source framework developed by the Apache Foundation, is an outgrowth of the concepts presented by Google in these papers. The Hadoop project has both a distributed file system, called HDFS (Hadoop Distributed File System) modeled on GFS and a distributed processing framework using MapReduce concepts. This chapter will review Big Data Analytics technologies with the Hadoop project as a backdrop.

To get a big-picture understanding of the technology innovations embodied in Hadoop, let's start with the MapReduce programming model. The model, whose name comes from the map and reduces functions, uses a large number of computer nodes, connected via network interconnect, in a cluster fashion, to perform parallel processing across huge data sets.

Four characteristics —parallelism, fault tolerance, scalability, and data locality—are, in fact, the defining features of MapReduce systems, by White (2012):

- **Parallelism:** Breaking the large data sets into smaller compute and storage units makes it possible to perform analytics in parallel and therefore more efficiently. In addition, mappers and reducers do not communicate individually, so they can run in parallel and on distinct compute nodes. Mappers pass on the data to reducers for further processing and this can be done iteratively;

- **Fault Tolerance:** Because processor, storage, and memory in each compute node is leveraged independently, MapReduce systems support greater fault tolerance. For instance, MapReduce can re-execute and reschedule failed tasks on healthy compute nodes in the cluster. Also, the underlying file system has inherent replication of data for data protection;
- **Scalability:** The MapReduce model also fosters scalability. Additional compute nodes can be added to the cluster in a non-intrusive manner, with MapReduce applications taking advantage of the added compute and storage capacity;
- **Data Locality:** MapReduce can also take advantage of locality of data, processing data on or near the storage assets to decrease transmission times for data? In the MapReduce system, we bring the compute resources to the data instead of the other way around.

If we study MapReduce and its operational nature, several salient aspects can be discussed. To start with, the unit of work is always the task, and it either completes successfully or it fails completely. From a development point of view, one focuses on programming to process the data records only. Map functions operate on these records and produce intermediate key-value pairs. The reduce function then operates on the intermediate key-value pairs, providing an output result. Hence, MapReduce provides a framework, including Application Programming Interfaces (APIs), to process these records in a distributed, fault tolerant fashion. The logic of the analytics task is written in programming language like Java or C, which leverages the MapReduce framework.

Additionally, MapReduce is a batch-oriented system and assumes that jobs will run in a finite amount of time. It is designed to sequentially process data and not for random and low latency processing. Moreover, MapReduce is not a high-level language like Structured Query Language (SQL). Hence, basic SQL-like queries may be cumbersome to develop in MapReduce. Finally, not all workload processing can be parallelized, hence not all problems can be solved by MapReduce.

The MapReduce framework is similar to many distributed systems, in that it is based on a master/slave architecture. JobTracker (master role) and TaskTracker (slave role) processes perform the master and slave nodes functions. The JobTracker is the master process, responsible for accepting, scheduling, and coordinating tasks for the slave nodes. It also provides administrative tasks, such as health and task progress monitoring to the cluster. There is one JobTracker per MapReduce cluster and it usually runs on reliable hardware since a failure of the master will result in the failure of all running jobs.

TaskTrackers inform the JobTracker as to their current health and status via a heartbeat mechanism. Clients and TaskTrackers communicate with the JobTracker by way of Remote Procedure Calls (RPC). The information on the jobs is stored in the JobTracker process memory and is updated via the heartbeat process from TaskTracker. The JobTracker also performs task scheduling in which it manages the resource allocation and sharing for the cluster. The TaskTracker executes the user application locally on the node and reports back to JobTracker periodically. A single TaskTracker is assigned to a compute node. Each TaskTracker is configured with a specific number of map and reduce task slots that indicate how many of each type of task it is capable of executing in parallel. A TaskTracker executes map and reduce tasks in parallel, typically more map tasks than reduce tasks.

The Four Stages of MapReduce

The MapReduce model works in four stages: job submission and input phase, map task execution phase, shuffle and sort phase, and reduce task execution phase.

The Job Submission and Input Phase

The input to the MapReduce function is a set of key-value pairs. The MapReduce framework includes APIs for submitting jobs and enabling interaction with the cluster. The framework also plays an important role in managing input data. It decides how to split the input data set into input splits, which is distributed and processed in parallel. As discussed previously, the master process, called the JobTracker in Hadoop MapReduce, is responsible for accepting these submissions.

The Map Execution Phase

The map program takes an input pair list and produces a set of intermediate key-value pairs. For Example, map(key1,value) -> list<key2,value2>. For each input split data, a map task is executed on each record in the split. Map tasks are executed in parallel on various compute nodes and are queued and executed in the order the framework deems best. The output of the map phase is an intermediate key-value pair. These key values are further partitioned via a partitioner component. In Hadoop MapReduce, the default partitioner implementation is a hash partitioner that takes a hash of the key, modulo the number of configured reducers in the job, to get a partition number. Hence, the intermediate data is only logically partitioned, for the next phase.

The Shuffle and Sort Phase

This stage ensures that all the reducers receive the intermediate key-value pairs in a sorted order for each of the keys. This intermediary key-value pair is passed on to the reducer function, which is also written by the user. Each reducer is assigned one of the partitions on which it should process. This requires intermediate data to be copied over the network to the reducer nodes. This operation can utilize significant amounts of network resources and time, depending on the nature and size of data. To minimize the total runtime of the job, the framework begins copying intermediate data from completed map tasks as soon as they are finished. Since reducer processes expect a single list of sorted key-value pairs, a merge sort is performed before the reduce stage.

The Reduce Execution Phase

The reduce function merges together these values to the smaller set of values required. For example, reduce(key2, list<value2>) -> list<value3>. The reduce function is also invoked by distributing the intermediate data into sizable splits. The processed data is produced in output file format in HDFS for storage in separate files so that reducers do not have to coordinate access to a shared file.

Figure 1 demonstrates the stages of MapReduce for a word count example. The goal of this sample is to count the words in the initial record.

There are time complexity considerations when looking at the phases of MapReduce. When the map operation outputs its pairs they are already available in memory. To increase efficiency and reduce time complexity, it may make sense to leverage a combiner class to perform a reduce-type function.

If a combiner is used then the map key-value pairs are not immediately written to the output. Instead they are collected in lists, one list per each key value. When a certain number of key-value pairs have been written, this buffer is flushed by passing all the values of each key to the combiner's reduce method and outputting the key-value pairs of the combine operation as if they were created by the original map operation.

Figure 1. Phases of MapReduce

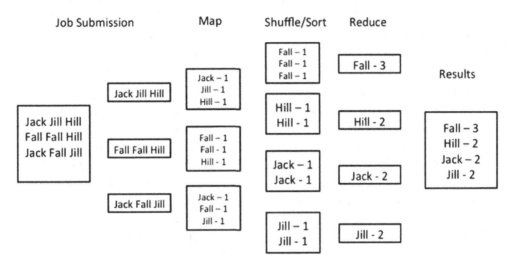

For example, a word count MapReduce application whose map operation outputs (word, 1) pairs as words are encountered in the input can use a combiner to speed up processing. A combine operation will start gathering the output in memory, one list per word. Once a certain number of pairs are output, the combine operation will be called once per unique word with the list available as an iterator. The combiner then emits pairs just like a map function, but there should be far fewer pairs output to disk and read from disk.

The combine function is typically used to reduce the network traffic. Notice that the input to the combine function must look the same as the input to the reducer function and the output of the combine function must look the same as the output of the map function.

A Closer Look at Hadoop Distributed File System (HDFS)

The Hadoop Distributed File System (HDFS) is designed for large data sets with typical file size ranging from gigabytes to terabytes in distributed nodes in a compute cluster. A distinguishing feature of HDFS is that it provides high throughput access to application data. HDFS was built with several goals and assumptions in mind. For one, HDFS is tuned to support large number of files (millions) in a high aggregate data bandwidth, with scale to thousands of nodes in a single cluster. HDFS is also designed more for batch processing rather than transactional processing. The goal is to provide high throughput of data access rather than low latency of data access. Applications that run on HDFS need streaming access to their data sets and typically have an I/O characterization of write-once-read-many.

Typically, a HDFS consists of a large number of compute and data nodes, which implies that the hardware failure is a norm and not an exception. Hence, detection of faults and consequent recovery from failures is an important feature of HDFS. When storing and processing on a large data set, it is efficient to move computation closer to data, rather than moving data to compute where the application is running. This optimizes the system, helping prevent network congestion and increasing the overall throughput of the system.

HDFS behaves like a traditional file system, where files are stored as blocks and metadata keeps track of the filename to support block mapping, directory tree structure, and permissions. Each node in a cluster stores a subset of the data that makes up the complete file system. File system metadata is stored on a central node, acting as a directory of block data and providing a global picture of the file system.

HDFS is also a user space file system, where code runs in the user space as opposed to kernel space of the operating systems. HDFS also allocates data in much larger block sizes, typically of 64 (default), 128, 256 or 1024 MB. Large block sizes means data will be written in larger contiguous chunks on disk, which optimizes for sequential I/O. HDFS can be used independently of MapReduce to store large data sets. MapReduce takes advantage of how the data in HDFS is split on ingestion into blocks and enables data locality.

Figure 2 illustrates the HDFS architecture.

As illustrated in figure 2, HDFS architecture consists of master/slave components, namely Name Node (NN) and Data Nodes (DN). The Name Node acts as a master server that manages the file system namespace and polices the access to files by clients. The Name Node maintains the file system namespace. The Name Node executes file system namespace operations like opening, closing, and renaming files and directories. It also stores the mapping of blocks to Data Nodes. The Name Node is the arbitrator and repository for all HDFS metadata and all arbitration is out of band

of user data flows. Name Node High Availability (or HA) is deployed as an active/passive pair of Name Nodes. The passive Name Node is called Secondary Name Node.

The Data Nodes (DN) manage the storage units attached to the nodes. A data file is split into one or more blocks and these blocks are stored on Data Nodes. The Data Nodes are responsible for serving read and write requests from the file system's clients. The Data Nodes also perform block creation, deletion, and replication operations. Adding more Data Nodes with additional disk capacity, or even adding disks to existing Data Nodes can add storage to a cluster.

HDFS supports a traditional hierarchical file organization in which a user or an application can create directories and store files inside these directories. An application can also specify the number of replicas of a file that should be maintained by HDFS. The Name Node makes all decisions regarding replication of blocks. HDFS Data Nodes store each file as a sequence of blocks; all blocks in a file except the last block are the same size. The blocks of a file are replicated for fault tolerance. The block size and replication factor are configurable per file. Name Node periodically receives a Heartbeat and a Blockreport, a list of all blocks, from each of the DN in the cluster.

Figure 2. HDFS architecture

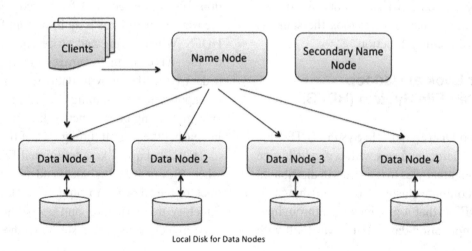

Local Disk for Data Nodes

For the common case, when the replication factor is three, HDFS's placement policy is to put one replica on one node in the local rack, another on a node in a different (remote) rack, and the last on a different node in the same remote rack. This policy cuts out the inter-rack write traffic, which generally improves write performance. Having multiple replicas means multiple data node failures are easily tolerated, but there are also advantages to reading data from a data node closest to an application on the network. HDFS actively tracks and manages the number of available replicas of a block as well.

The chance of rack failure is far less than that of node failure; this policy does not impact data reliability and availability guarantees; however, it does reduce the aggregate network bandwidth used when reading data since a block is placed in only two unique racks rather than three. With this policy, the replicas of a file do not evenly distribute across the racks. One third of replicas are on one node, two thirds of replicas are on one rack, and the other third are evenly distributed across the remaining racks. This policy improves write performance without compromising data reliability or read performance. To minimize global bandwidth consumption and read latency, HDFS tries to satisfy a read request from a replica that is closest to the reader. If replica exists on the same rack as the reader node, then that replica is preferred to satisfy the read request.

NoSQL DATABASE SYSTEMS

In a Big Data environment, the requirements for data storage and retrieval are quite different from those in a traditional database system. With large data quantities, often in an unstructured format, you need very high-speed insert and retrieval. Even if the data is structured, this may be of minimal importance: what really matters is the ability to store and retrieve great quantities of data, and not the relationships between the elements.

These requirements for highly efficient storage and retrieval have inspired a new class of database systems called as NoSQL. There are several approaches adopted by NoSQL for storing and managing unstructured data, also referred to as *nonrelational data*. These systems, which are sometimes also called *key-value stores*, share the goals of massive scaling "on demand," data model flexibility, and simplified application development and deployment.

All NoSQL database system implementations share some common attributes: distributed and fault tolerant architecture, schema-free design and Atomicity, Consistency, Isolation, Durability (ACID) properties.

NoSQL employs a distributed architecture, with the data held in a redundant manner on several nodes. As described in paper by DeCandia, Hastorun, Jampani, Kakulapati, Lakshman, Pilchin, Sivasubramanian, Vosshall & Vogels (2007), the system can easily scale out by adding more servers, and failure of a server can be tolerated. This type of database typically scales horizontally and is used for managing large amounts of data. The high availability aspects of NoSQL are enhanced by creating replicas of data, making them resilient to partition failures and mitigating single points of failure.

NoSQL also takes into consideration ACID aspects. NoSQL typically does not maintain complete consistency across distributed nodes, because of the burden this places on databases, particularly in distributed systems. As described in paper by Gilbert & Lynch (2002). The Consistency, Availability, Partition (CAP) Theorem states that with consistency, availability, and partitioning tolerance, only two can be optimized at any time. Traditional relational databases enforce strict transactional semantics to preserve consistency, but many NoSQL databases have more scalable architectures that relax the consistency requirement. Relaxing consistency is often called eventual consistency. This permits much more scalable distributed storage systems where writes can occur without using phased commits or system-wide locks. Relaxing consistency can lead to the possibility of conflicting writes and inconsistent reads. When multiple nodes can accept modifications without expensive lock coordination, concurrent writes can occur in conflict. However, it is inevitably the responsibility of the application to deal with these conflicts.

Most NoSQL databases can also be called schema-free databases. As described in paper by Chang, Dean, Ghemawat, Hsieh, Wallach, Burrows, Chandra, Fikes & Gruber (2006), the key advantage of schema-free design is that it enables applications to quickly upgrade the structure of data without table rewrites. It also allows for greater flexibility in storing heterogeneously structured data.

The HBase Implementation of NoSQL

Let's now review the details of an open source NoSQL data store implementation, namely HBase. HBase is a NoSQL data store, as opposed to a relational database. It lacks advanced relational data base features like typed columns, secondary indexes, triggers, advanced query languages, and many more. Hence, HBase is usually suitable for large data sets with millions and billons of records, with a scale-out infrastructure configuration. Typically, relational database applications cannot be ported to HBase systems without some reengineering.

The basic components for HBase are client library, master server, and region server. Just like Map Reduce and HDFS, HBase is also has a master-slave architecture. The HBase master server provides all the metadata for HBase region servers, which act as the slave servers. The master server also uses a distributed coordination service to facilitate the assigning of regions to a region server. In HBase, tables are partitioned into regions, which are the units that get distributed over the HBase region servers. Region servers are Java processes that are typically collocated with HDFS Data Nodes. The master server also handles the load balancing of regions across the region servers.

The most commonly used file system with HBase is HDFS; however, other file systems can also be used. In addition, major Linux operating systems can be leveraged for HBase.

Internally, the files are data blocks with indexes at the end. The files are stored in HDFS, which provides scalability and highly availability via replica store mechanisms. The basic operations like write, read, and delete happen in the following fashion: All writes are first written to a log for commit called Write Ahead Log (WAL) and then stored in memory (memstore). The data in memory is flushed into files on disk, after a threshold value. While the system is flushing, it can continue to serve readers and writers. Reading data is essentially merging what is stored in files and what may be contained in the memory store. WAL is used only for recovery purposes and not for reading. Delete operations are handled by writing a delete marker in the files, as you cannot remove key-value pairs.

Figure 3 illustrates some of these details by George (2011).

Let's now review the data model aspect of HBase NoSQL data store. In HBase, a table consists of rows and columns. One or more columns form a row that is addressed uniquely by a row key. Each column may have multiple versions, time stamped, with each distinct value contained in a separate cell. Rows are composed of columns, and those, in turn, are grouped into column families. All columns in a column family are stored together in the same low-level storage file, called an HFile. Columns are often referenced with a family qualifier with the qualifier being specific for the column family in array of bytes. One could have a very large number of columns in a column

Figure 3. Hbase NoSQL key value pair store architecture

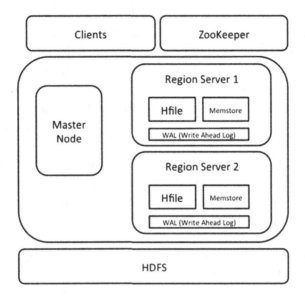

family, and a preset number of column families. Every column value, or cell, either is time stamped implicitly by the system or can be set explicitly by the user. This can be used, for example, to save multiple versions of a value as it changes over time. All data model operations in HBase return data in sorted order, first by row, then by column family, followed by column qualifier, and finally, timestamp. One example of a key-value pair for a table could read as follows:

(RowKey, Family, Column, Timestamp) -> Value

One can address the cell value with precision by all the tuples mentioned above. Also, one can drop the tuples and then address the maps to columns or families of row keys. All the primary data model operations of get, put, scan, and delete are done on the key-value pair basis. There is no transactional feature that spans multiple rows or across tables. Typical relational database operations like joins are not supported in HBase, but can be facilitated by the client application but not inherently in the database. Moreover, it does not support SQL query language, secondary indexing.

MapReduce and HBase Integration

There are three different ways of integrating HBase NoSQL data stores and MapReduce applications. HBase can be used as: A data source at the initiation of MapReduce job, as a data sink at the end of a job, or as a shared resource for intermediate jobs.

NoSQL data stores like HBase are designed for MapReduce interaction; it provides a TableMapper and TableReducer classes to integrate with MapReduce applications. Just like in a map job, the data files on HDFS can be scanned and key-value pairs can be read. Similarly, HBase provides classes for consuming data from tables. As mentioned by Dimiduk & Khurana (2012), when mapping over data in HBase, the same mechanism can be used. Internally, the scan operation is broken into pieces and distributed to all the map workers. Hence, TableMapper allows the MapReduce application to easily read data directly out of HBase.

Similarly, TableReducer makes it easy to write data back to HBase from MapReduce. A join in MapReduce means joining on data spread across multiple nodes. There are a two of different variations of each type, but a join implementation is either map-side or reduce-side. They are referred as map- or reduce-side, because that's the task where records from the two sets are linked. It's also possible to interact with the HBase key-value API from within the map and reduce Steps. This is helpful for situations where all the tasks need random access to the same data.

The other area of integration of MapReduce and NoSQL HBase is the file systems. As mentioned before, HBase is a database built on top of HDFS. HBase can, however, work on top of any distributed file system. One of the reasons that HBase is scalable and fault tolerant is that it persists its data onto a distributed file system that provides it a single namespace. This is one of the key factors that allows HBase to be a fully consistent data store. HBase region servers are typically collocated with HDFS Data Nodes (and Task Trackers) on the same cluster node, as they should be able to access HDFS.

Hence, MapReduce and HBase integration occurs not only at the run time level, but also at the data storage layer.

Complex Event Processing

So far in this section, we have discussed technologies that allow for batch processing or enable batch-oriented systems. Big Data is also closely associated with Complex Event Processing (CEP) models in which real-time information from highly dynamic sources is collected and analyzed.

Complex Event Processing (CEP) is a method of tracking and processing streams of data about events and creating actionable, situational knowledge from additional distributed message-based systems like databases and applications in real time or near real time. CEP can provide the capability to define, manage, and predict events, situations, exceptional conditions, opportunities, and threats in complex, heterogeneous networks. Hence, CEP systems can be used to identify meaningful events from a flood of events, and then take action on those events in real time.

Common examples of CEP include: sensors provide data in an aircraft which is collected and analyzed for an event anomaly in real time to warn or advise the pilot to take action; analyzing a constant stream of financial market data and analyzing it in real time to derive predictable event of the trading markets; collecting real-time scientific data from experiments or natural occurrences to monitor and predict events; and a network management-related CEP application correlating events using a stateful, high-speed rules engine for SNMP trap and logfile data.

One such CEP system is called Storm, which was developed by Twitter (not open source), to operate on not just static data, but also streaming data that is expected to be continuous. As described in the book by Leibiusky, Eisbruch & Simonassi (2012), Storm implements a data flow model in which data flows continuously through a network of transformation entities. The input stream of a Storm cluster is handled by a component called a *spout*, which is an unbounded sequence of tuples. Streams originate from spouts, which flow data from external sources into the Storm topology. The tuple structure represents standard data types, like ints, floats, byte arrays, and user-defined types. The spout passes the data to a component called a *bolt*, which transforms data.

Hence with Storm, one can develop CEP systems with a variety of data connectors, complex and distributed topologies, reliable messaging capabilities, and at the same time implement traditional MapReduce functionality or more complex actions like filtering, aggregations, or communication with external entities such as a database.

Planning for MapReduce, HDFS and NoSQL Operations

In order to plan for an operational environment of MapReduce, HDFS and related services, one has to consider several aspects of the hardware and software elements. This operational environment can be considered as a foundation for the applications and data elements to be developed, stored, and analyzed on top of it. Let's review some of the operational considerations.

Software Considerations

MapReduce and HDFS software can be obtained from several sources. Apache Foundation's Hadoop project is a good source of the latest innovation in the open source community. There are several other commercial sources, which have leveraged the open source projects and provide value-added elements to the distribution of Apache Hadoop.

Most of these software distribution options have similar operational considerations. Additionally, most of the implementations of MapReduce and HDFS are in Java and run on Linux. Most of the popular distributions of Linux are supported for these environments. Consequently, most of the Linux-based file systems, like ext3/ext5/xfs, are also commonly used for HDFS deployments. In addition, Linux services like cron, Network Time Protocol (NTP), Secure Shell (SSH) and rsync are commonly used software services.

Compute and Storage Hardware Considerations

The hardware design guidelines should be considered with the time state, as hardware elements, including CPU, memory, network, and disk constantly improve and revise. The compute (with storage) hardware selection can be categorized into master and slave configurations. The master configuration is for the functions of JobTracker, Name Node, and Secondary Name Node. Master nodes are typically more robust for running critical cluster services and managing hardware failures. Loss of a master almost certainly means some kind of service disruption.

On the other hand, slave nodes are expected to fail regularly. This directly impacts the type of hardware, as well as the amount of money, spent on these two classes of hardware. Typical compute nodes for master nodes have higher redundancy considerations, including dual power supplies, multiple bonded Network Interface Cards (NICs), and RAID 1+0 disk storage. In general, master nodes tend to be RAM intensive. Name Node and JobTracker also generate verbose log files, hence adequate disk space should be allocated.

For the Data Nodes, there are typically 8 or 12 CPU cores per node, with the number of cores equal or slightly larger than the number of spindles. The total number of mappers and reducers is the total number of CPU hyperthreads minus 2 (2 is for daemons and OS processing). The importance of CPU power increases with CPU-intensive jobs and when using more compute-intensive workloads.

The memory requirements for Name Node depend on the amount of metadata it is managing. HBase is a very memory-intensive application. Each region server in HBase keeps a number of regions in memory, assuming that caching parameters are enabled. Typically, a single region server can handle a few regions by allocating up to 2GB of memory. The memory requirement is usually at least 4GB per region server, but depends significantly on application load and access pattern. The master nodes can have anywhere from 48–96 GB of memory. For JobTracker nodes, one should allocate between 1-2 GB of memory per task in addition to the memory allocated for HBase for large clusters. Both HBase and MapReduce memory swapping are discouraged and can degrade the overall system performance.

MapReduce disk planning guidelines recommend at least two locations to store MapReduce intermediate files and the HDFS files. These files can be spread across the disk partition for parallelism. Regarding HDFS, the replication factor of 3 is set by default, and an additional 25 percent of the disk storage is typically required for intermediate shuffle files. In summary, four times the raw size of the data is required for HDFS store. HBase stores the regions in HFiles, which typically require a 30-50 percent overhead of free storage space. MapReduce is storage intensive and seek efficient, but it does not require fast, expensive hard drives. As pointed out by Sammer (2012) Typically slave systems is recommended to have 12 hard disk drives, typically SATA (2 or 3 TB capacity) and a collective capacity of 24 or 36 TB/node.

Network Considerations

Each node in a MapReduce and NOSQL cluster needs a high throughput data network. Moreover, the Name Node needs to be connected in a highly available fashion to avoid delisting the Data Nodes. A typical configuration connects the nodes into racks with 1-2 Gigabit network interfaces on the top of rack switches. For higher bandwidth workloads, a 10 Gigabit network interface is typically recommended.

Large MapReduce clusters are usually arranged in racks. Network traffic between different nodes within the same rack is much more desirable than network traffic across the racks. There are several network topology considerations, pointed out by Sammer (2012). MapReduce and NoSQL traffic is heavy on east-west pattern and this plays into the topology considerations, as follows:

- The first type of network is the tree topology. A tree may have multiple tiers and each tier aggregates nodes or branches from a downstream tier. Hosts are connected to access switches, which uplink to the next tier and the next tier uplinks to the next level tier. The number of tiers required to build a network depends on the total number of hosts that need to be supported;
- The second type of network topology is spine-leaf topology. In a spine-leaf topology, hosts are connected to leaf switches, just as in the tree topology, and each leaf switch has uplinks to spine switches. A routing protocol such as IS-IS, OSPF, or

EIGRP is run with Equal Cost Multipath (ECMP) routes so that traffic has multiple path options and takes the shortest path between two hosts. This topology provides a much denser host topology and can scale rapidly. Also, since all leaves have equidistant access to all others via the spine, bandwidth is not sacrificed. Figure 4 (below) illustrates a sample spine-leaf topology. This topology is gaining popularity.

Benchmarks for MapReduce

The benchmark for Big Data analytics is an emerging topic; however, there are a few benchmarks that can be reviewed for MapReduce, HDFS and NoSQL applications.

Benchmarks for MapReduce include the following:

- **Word Count Benchmark:** This benchmark counts the occurrences of each word in a large collection of documents. This benchmark simulates business intelligence types of workloads, where a large amount of data (terabytes) is presented to the mappers and a small amount (megabytes) is produced as result of the analysis by the reducers. This benchmark is intensive on the map process, but less intensive on the shuffle and reduce phases. This benchmark is CPU intensive, with low traffic spikes during the shuffle phase, with short-lived flows, representing traffic received from multiple mapper nodes;
- **TeraSort Benchmark:** This set of benchmarks focuses on workloads that have similar size data sets for input and output, which are typical of Extract, Transform, and Load (ETL) processes, where data must be converted to another format for consumption. The goal of TeraSort is to sort large (TB/PB) amounts of data, as quickly as possible. As pointed out by O'Malley (2008).

Figure 4. Big Data network topology with leaf and spine design

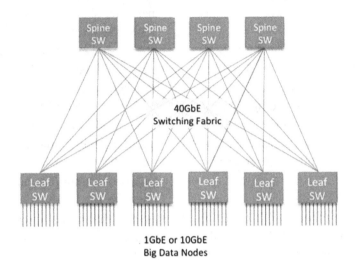

It is a benchmark that combines testing the HDFS and MapReduce layers;

- **Name Node Benchmark (nnbench):** This benchmark is useful for load testing the Name Node system configurations. It generates a lot of HDFS-related requests with small data sets to exercise the HDFS management on the Name Node. The benchmark can simulate requests for creating, reading, renaming, and deleting files on HDFS, as mentioned by White (2009);

- **MapReduce Benchmark (mrbench):** This benchmark is complementary to the large scale TeraSort benchmark. By design, it executes smaller jobs a number of times and checks to see whether they are responsive. It exercises the MapReduce layer and demonstrates a workload with low requirements on HDFS, as mentioned by White (2009);

- **Gridmix Benchmark:** A typical MapReduce Cluster can host a wide range of applications from a diverse set of functional groups. This benchmark tool stresses the framework at scale by supporting broader ranges of workload deployments and job mixes. As mentioned by Douglas &

Tang (2012), this benchmark is designed to model a realistic cluster workload by mimicking a variety of data access patterns seen in practice. The Gridmix benchmark tool can also be used to simulate job of one cluster on another. Hence to run Gridmix, one needs a MapReduce job trace describing the job mix for a given cluster. Gridmix also requires input data from which the synthetic jobs will serve as input. In order to emulate the load of production jobs from a given cluster on the same or another cluster, one needs to locate and build the job history and load it in Gridmix to benchmark the cluster.

Benchmark for NoSQL

One of the key benchmarks of NoSQL databases is Yahoo! Cloud Serving Benchmark (YCSB), it is detailed by Cooper, Silberstein, Tam, Ramakrishnan & Sears (2010). YCSB defines the data set, loads it into the database, and then execute operations against the data set while measuring performance. As a benchmark took, YCSB highlights online read/write access to data. It measures, for example, the reads and writes to the database that is carried out as part of the page construction and delivery as the web user waits for a web page to load.

YCSB focuses on two properties of NoSQL systems: performance and elasticity. Performance refers to the usual metrics of latency and throughput, with the ability to scale out by adding capacity. Elasticity refers to the ability to add capacity on demand to a running deployment. YCSB can also be extended to include availability and replication as properties to measure.

YCSB is focused on serving systems, as opposed to batch systems (although YCSB can be used for both types of workloads). Unlike traditional databases benchmarks, YCSB focuses on large number of extremely simple queries, which is typical of a NoSQL workload. For example, a serving workload runs a large number of simple queries on a random set of records, whereas as a batch workload runs one or small set of jobs on a large number of records. Hence, YCSB is suited for assessing serving NoSQL workloads.

MPP (Massively Parallel Processing) Databases

MPP Database Systems are becoming an important part of the Big Data technologies collection. The typical size of a MPP database system ranges from a few terabytes to a few petabytes of structured data. The following section will discuss the motivation and review mechanics of a MPP databases.

MPP Databases Motivation for Big Data

A survey of database systems reveals three major infrastructure models of databases: shared everything, shared disk, and shared nothing. General purposes databases are architected for high volumes of small transactional queries, like Online Transaction Processing (OLTP) systems. These OLTP workloads require fast access and updates to a small set of data records. The queries are performed in a local sector of disks, with a smaller number of parallel processes.

Architecturally, OLTP database systems are either shared everything or shared disk architectures. A shared everything architecture is constrained to a single large server, with Symmetric Multi Processors (SMP) with all the processors, memory, and disk scalability and performance limitations within the large compute node. A shared disk architecture consists of a system composed of multiple compute nodes connected to Storage Area Network (SAN) or other shared storage. Shared disk architectures can also be effective for OLTP because each compute node can take a subset of the queries and process them independently, while ensuring consistency through the shared disk subsystem. This architecture is typically a performance bottleneck to a shared disk subsystem. These general purpose shared disk architectures are can be hard to configure, manage, scale, and tune for performance for large Big Data-level jobs.

Figure 5 depicts the architectures for MPP databases.

Shared everything and shared disk architectures can be performance-constrained by the full table scans, multiple complex table joins, sorting, and aggregation operations against vast volumes of data that are typical of Big Data analytical workloads. These architectures aren't designed for the levels of parallel processing required to execute complex analytical queries, and tend to bottleneck as a result of failures of the query planner to leverage parallelism, lack of aggregate I/O bandwidth, and inefficient movement of the data between nodes.

MPP Database Operations

As discussed, traditional relational databases systems are for OLTP workloads. MPP databases are for data warehousing and Business Intelligence (BI) analytical workloads are fundamentally

Figure 5. Architecture layout for MPP databases

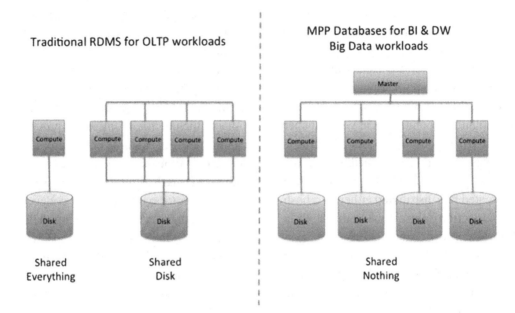

different from OLTP transaction workloads and therefore require a profoundly different architecture. MPP databases are based on share nothing architecture, where the compute nodes have dedicated disk subsystems for data storage and retrieval and these compute-disk pairs are connected via a network interconnect.

MPP database systems also have of master-slave nodes architecture, where the slave nodes store/process data and are interconnected via high bandwidth and latency sensitive links. Queries are planned at a master node and split into pieces that are executed in parallel across the cluster, with all communication happening over a high-bandwidth network interconnect. The slave nodes process every query in a parallel manner, performing on all disks connections in parallel, and enabling data flow between slaves as query plans dictate. MPP shared nothing databases automatically distribute data and make query workloads parallel across all available hardware. A unique aspect of this architecture is that each node has an independent high-speed channel to its local disks, simplifying

the architecture and providing highly scalable parallel scan and query processing performance.

Traditional relational databases have data stored in rows, as a sequence of tuples in which all the columns of each tuple are stored together on disk. This row based storage method is typical for OLTP systems and have advantages in OLTP environments. MPP analytics and databases, however, tend to have different access patterns than OLTP systems. Instead of seeing many single-row reads and writes, analytical databases must process larger, more complex queries that scan larger volumes of data, with scanning reads and infrequent batch appends of data. Thus, column-oriented stores are adopted for MPP databases, to serve the data warehouse and BI queries. Tabular data is vertically partitioned and each column is stored in a series of blocks that can be efficiently compressed. This provides performance advantages for those workloads suited to column-store, where MPP databases scan only those columns required by the query; it doesn't have the overhead of per-tuple IDs.

MPP databases also scale linearly to a certain extent. One of the key reasons MPP can achieve such high linear scalable performance is because it is able to utilize the full local disk I/O bandwidth of each system and overall I/O bandwidth can be increased linearly by simply adding nodes without any concerns about saturating a SAN/shared-storage backplane. As pointed out in Vertica paper by Loshin (2010), in addition, no special tuning is required to ensure that data is distributed across nodes for efficient parallel access. Typically, when a table is created it is distributed either by a hash distribution function or by a random distribution method. For each row of data inserted, the system computes the hash of these column values to determine the node in the MPP system. Once the data is in the MPP database, scanning a table is dramatically faster than in other architectures, because it eliminates single node bottlenecks. All MPP nodes work in parallel and scan their portion of the table, allowing the entire table to be scanned in a fraction of the time. The need for aggregates and indexes may also be minimized, but can be leveraged for if required.

The query planning and query optimizer are also implemented with parallelism methods. For example, in a typical commercial MPP database system, the parallel query optimizer is responsible for converting SQL or MapReduce into a physical execution plan. It performs this process using a cost-based optimization algorithm in which it evaluates a vast number of potential plans and selects the one that it believes will lead to the most efficient query execution. This query optimizer takes a global view of execution across the cluster and factors in the cost of moving data between nodes in any candidate plan. The resulting query plans contain traditional physical operations of scans, joins, sorts, aggregations, as well as parallel data motion operations that describe when and how data should be transferred between nodes during query execution. It delivers messages, moves data, collects results, and coordinates work among the segments in the system. Within the execution of each node in the query plan, multiple relational operations are processed by pipelining. Pipelining is the ability to begin a task before its predecessor task has completed, and this ability is key to increasing basic query parallelism.

Modern MPP databases also make provisions to include the MapReduce process in their architecture. An example of this provision by described by Abouzeid, Bajda-Pawlikowski, Abadi, Silberschatz & Rasin (2009). This is either done via a connector method, which connects a MPP structured data set to an unstructured data set for analytics in MapReduce; it can also be done in the part of the MPP parallelism engine, which connect data sets in each node. You can also put together a SQL-MapReduce framework to work with MapReduce.

In summary, the MPP database approach is a prudent consideration for querying, storing, and analyzing large structured data sets.

In-Memory Database and Data Processing

This section will look at the in-memory data processing aspect of Big Data. There are several trends and technologies in this space. We will review not only motivation, concepts and techniques, but also summarize implementation specifics of in-memory database technology.

Compute and memory architectures are continuously changing, including multi-core architectures and less expensive main memory. These new innovations bring real-time analytics and quick response times to systems with large datasets. Thus, the existing database management system must be adapted to keep pace with these developments.

As data sets grow, Relational Databases Management Systems (RDMS) are no longer able to efficiently service the analytics demands, in particular the ad-hoc queries on the entire transactional database, in a timely manner. One of the reasons for this is that typical transactional systems have normalized data which is not ideal for fast analytics. Hence, Online Analytics Processing (OLAP) systems were developed, which had to extract data out of transaction systems and transform the data to a fast query schema system. The limitation of this approach is that it is unable to do real-time analytics on the latest transactions and is done on a copy of data.

The other reason current RDMS cannot perform the queries fast enough is because of the disk subsystem bottlenecks. The main memory access time is on the order of 100 nanoseconds, whereas disk seek time is 5 milliseconds. Main memory database systems have existed for a several decades; however, they have now been adopted due to inexpensive memory systems and achievable fast query times, without the need for separate OLAP systems. In-memory databases systems based on the latest hardware can provide this missing capability. Coupled with memory innovations, multicore processers are also very prevalent with a new CPU-memory architecture—namely, Non Uniform Memory Architecture (NUMA), where each processor has a dedicated channel to its memory. Thus, if an application can be parallelized to take advantage of the multiple core and data be localized to each processor's memory, great performance benefits can be obtained.

To take advantage of an In-Memory Database (IMDB) System, it is preferable to host the entire database in a single compute node with a large memory footprint. Even the largest current computer nodes base on the Intel x86 processor architecture, however, are incapable of doing this. This shortcoming has created a need for multiple compute nodes, where the nodes are interconnected by a network fabric. The necessary prerequisite for this distributed architecture is a data partitioning strategy and the ability to distribute data across compute nodes, each with larger memory footprint. Precaution have to be taken to organize data so that the queries do not go over the interconnect very often. In case of the failure of a node, the stand-by node can takeover the function.

A good way to classify the in-memory database system is "shared nothing," but in a compute node local is a share-memory architecture. These compute nodes can connect to a shared persistent storage via Network Attached Storage (NAS) and Storage Area Network (SAN), however, the primary copy of data is held in memory and not on the persistent storage. An in-memory system takes full advantage of parallelism at all points of multicore and distributed architectures, namely, distributed query architecture on the compute nodes, parallel query processing on the cores of the CPU, and data partitioning in each compute memory. In addition to parallelism, latency between CPU cores and the storage hierarchy of CPU cache, main memory, flash-based storage, and non-volatile persistent storage has to be factored in for any in-memory system design.

Since most of the existing systems managing large data sets in an enterprise are relational databases systems, in-memory systems for RDMS are a good fit for an enterprise use case. As discussed, the relational storage is stored in the main memory and provides much faster performance than the disk-based systems, hence removing a key bottleneck.

Figure 6 provides a conceptual overview of an in-memory RDMS implementation as illustrated by Plattner & Zeier (2012).

As seen the figure above, active data is kept in the main memory, with the main store consisting of column- or row-oriented store, a differential store and indexes to data. The passive data is kept in non-volatile persistent storage disks. The data distribution layer is made up of traditional RDMS constructs of data interface sessions, session management, and distributed query processing.

Each of the compute nodes of this distributed in-memory database runs a server process, with which clients connect to access the in-memory

Figure 6. Architecture layout for In-Memory database

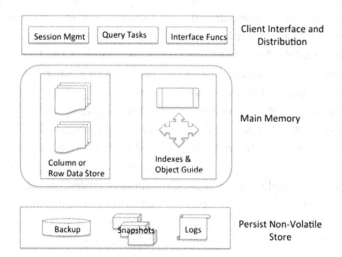

store. The server process also keeps track of client connections and session parameters. The interface service provides the SQL interface, stored procedures, and APIs to forward incoming requests to clients and server processes. This service is also responsible for managing metadata handling, transaction management, distributed transaction processing, and distributed query processing. The metadata contains information about the storage location of tables and their partitions. The in-memory system cluster replicates and synchronizes data across all server processes. Since the data is partitioned on all the compute nodes, IMDB provides a distributed transaction and distributed query processing.

Data values are either stored in row or column fashion in databases. Traditionally, row-based systems are implemented, with row data in adjacent blocks, which are efficient for fast reading for single tuples. A column-oriented store, where columns are stored in adjacent blocks, is more suited for reading a set of results from a single column. This is typical of scan performance and a good choice for OLAP systems and hence column-oriented DBMS are also suitable for this use case.

The drawback of columnar DBMS is that they are not suitable for reading or writing complete tuples. Hence, some IMDBs implement a combined column approach, where certain frequently queried columns are stored together, thereby providing fast read, with good write performance.

Data compression techniques are still beneficial for managing large datasets in IMDB. Compression also minimizes the amount of data that needs to be transferred between disk-based persistent memory and main memory. Typically, IMDB do not store the data values in memory directly, they store references to a compressed, sorted dictionary containing the distinct column values. Write performance can be poor if new values need to be added to the dictionary. To solve this issue for write performance, IMDB employs a write-optimized data structure called differential store. The differential store holds data that has been inserted into the IMDB, but in the main store. Hence, a differential store with the main store represents the current state of the database. A merge process is employed to move data from the differential store to the main store and queries are directed to both the stores.

CONCLUSION

To conclude of this chapter, we'll illustrate how the above-discussed Big Data technologies integrate and come together in a consumable fashion. There are many ways these technologies can be leveraged in a Big Data use case. The legacy and traditional methods of managing large data sets are still valid and continue be of use. These methods are not scalable to the increasingly massive data sets and also to the new types of data sets.

Let's analyze how large data sets are gathered and analyzed in an enterprise environment. This is only a sample use case to show a transition point to Big Data technologies; there are many other such examples.

Typically, enterprise sources of data are from transactional and operation sources. These data sets are gathered, collected, and processed through a Extract, Transform and Load (ETL) process, which typically ran either in a centralized system, with the end goal of transforming data to a state where it could be loaded into an Enterprise Data Warehouse (EDW). EDW systems are typically large Symmetric Multi Processing (SMP) systems

used to store and analyze these large datasets. The typical maximum size of an EDW is usually a few hundred Terabytes. These EDW would process queries and other analytics requests and deliver the analytical results to end users to consume.

There are several potential challenges to this current approach. First, the data source is no longer just from operational and transactional system; it is also from newer sources like machine-generated sources. Second, the data sets have grown so much in size and complexity that the transformation process is no longer trivial in terms of complexity and the timeframe involved. Third, the cost of storing this data in an EDW environment is no longer sustainable. Hence, a new approach with the above mentioned Big Data technologies has to be adopted.

Figure 7 illustrates an integrated approach to the above-discussed Big Date challenges.

The new approach tackles these challenges and addresses them with the Big Data technologies under discussion in this chapter and illustrated in the figure above. Let's walk through this new approach with Big Data technologies. The new and large data sources can be transformed

Figure 7. Integrated approach to Big Data challenges

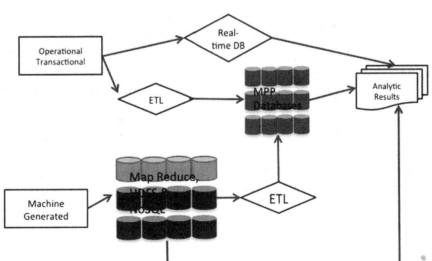

with traditional ETL techniques or via iterative MapReduce process, specifically the transform state. Users then query and run analytics data directly from the MapReduce cluster and No-SQL key-value pair data stores. Consecutively, one can take the traditional transformed data and load it into a MPP database for scale and performance. Additionally, an in-memory compute system with in-memory database could also be deployed to provide real time analytics.

All these new Big Data technologies are interconnected to address the challenges that a traditional method could not manage. Hence, in conclusion, the Big Data technologies can work together to provide a comprehensive approach to large integrated structured and unstructured data sets.

REFERENCES

Abouzeid, A., Bajda-Pawlikowski, K., Abadi, D., Silberschatz, A., & Rasin, A. (2009). HadoopDB: An architectural hybrid of MapReduce and DBMS technologies for analytical workloads. In *Proceedings of VLDB 2009*. VLDB.

Barnett, T. (2011). Cisco visual networking index: The zettabyte era. *Cisco Systems Inc*. Retrieved August 2012 from http://www.cisco.com/en/US/solutions/collateral/ns341/ns525/ns537/ns705/ns827/VNI_Hyperconnectivity_WP.html

Chang, F., Dean, J., Ghemawat, S., Hsieh, W., Wallach, D., & Burrows, M. ... Gruber, R. (2006). Bigtable: A distributed storage system for structured data. In *Proceeding of 7th Conference on Usenix Symposium on Operating System Design and Implementation*, (vol. 7). Usenix. Retrieved from http://citeseer.ist.psu.edu/viewdoc/summary?doi=10.1.1.101.9822

Cooper, B., Silberstein, A., Tam, E., Ramakrishnan, R., & Sears, S. (2010). Benchmarking cloud serving systems with YCSB. In *Proceedings of the ACM Symposium on Cloud Computing*. ACM. Retrieved January 2010 from http://research.yahoo.com/node/3202

Dean, J., & Ghemawat, S. (2004). MapReduce: Simplified data processing of large clusters. *OSDI*. Retrieved from http://research.google.com/archive/mapreduce.html

DeCandia, G., Hastorun, D., Jampani, M., Kakulapati, G., Lakshman, K., & Pilchin, A. ... Vogels, W. (2007). Dynamo: Amazon's highly available key-value store. In *Proceedings of 21st ACM SIGOPS Symposium on Operating Systems Principles*, (pp. 205-220). ACM. Retrieved December 2007 from http://dl.acm.org/citation.cfm?id=1294281

Desai, N., Kommu, S., & Rapp, J. (2011). Big data in the enterprise: Network design considerations. *Cisco Systems Inc*. Retrieved November 2011 from http://www.cisco.com/en/US/prod/collateral/switches/ps9441/ps9670/white_paper_c11-690561.html

Dimiduk, N., & Khurana, M. (2012). *HBase in action*. Shelter Island, NY: Manning Publication Inc..

Douglas, C., & Tang, H. (2012). Gridmix3-emulating Apache workload for Apache Hadoop. *Yahoo Developer Network*. Retrieved April 2012 from http://developer.yahoo.com/blogs/Hadoop/posts/2010/04/gridmix3_emulating_production/

Gantz, J., & Reinsel, D. (2011). The 2011 digital universe study: Extracting value from chaos. *IDC iView Research*. Retrieved June 2011 from http://www.emc.com/collateral/analyst-reports/idc-extracting-value-from-chaos-ar.pdf

George, L. (2011). *HBase: The definitive guide.* Sebastopol, CA, USA: O'Reilly Media Inc..

Ghemawat, S., Gobioff, H., & Leung, H. (2003). The Google file systems. In *Proceedings of the 19th ACM Symposium on Operating Systems Principles.* ACM. Retrieved October 2003 from http://research.google.com/archive/gfs.html

Gilbert, S., & Lynch, N. (2002). Brewer's conjecture and the feasibility of consistent. *ACM SIGACT, 33*(2), 51–59. doi:10.1145/564585.564601.

Leibiusky, J., Eisbruch, G., & Simonassi, D. (2012). *Getting started with storm.* Sebastopol, CA: O'Reilly Media Inc..

Loshin, D. (2010). *The Vertica analytic database technical overview white paper.* Vertica Systems Inc. Retrieved March 2010 from http://www.vertica.com/wp-content/uploads/2011/01/VerticaArchitectureWhitePaper.pdf

O'Malley, O. (2008). TeraByte sort on Apache Hadoop. *Yahoo.* Retrieved May 2008 from http://sortbenchmark.org/YahooHadoop.pdf

Plattner, H., & Zeier, A. (2012). *In-memory data management: Technology and applications.* New York: Springer.

Sammer, E. (2012). *Hadoop operations.* Sebastopol, CA: O'Reilly Media Inc..

White, T. (2009). *How to benchmark a Hadoop cluster.* O'Reilly Media Inc. Retrieved October 2009 from http://answers.oreilly.com/topic/460-how-to-benchmark-a-hadoop-cluster/

White, T. (2012). *Hadoop: The definitive guide.* Sebastopol, CA: O'Reilly Media Inc..

ADDITIONAL READING

Dimiduk, N., & Khurana, M. (2012). *HBase in action.* Shelter Island, NY: Manning Publication Inc..

Flach, P. (2012). *Machine learning: The art and science of algorithms that make sense of data.* Cambridge, UK: Cambridge University Press. doi:10.1017/CBO9780511973000.

George, L. (2011). *HBase: The definitive guide.* Sebastopol, CA: O'Reilly Media Inc..

Holmes, A. (2012). *Hadoop in practice.* Shelter Island, NY: Manning Publication Inc..

Janert, P. (2012). *Data analysis with open source tools.* Sebastopol, CA: O'Reilly Media Inc..

Plattner, H., & Zeier, A. (2012). *In-memory data management: Technology and applications.* New York: Springer.

White, T. (2012). *Hadoop: The definitive guide* (3rd ed.). Sebastopol, CA: O'Reilly Media Inc..

KEY TERMS AND DEFINITIONS

Big Data: Big Data refers to the notion when the data sets get so large that traditional tools and techniques to manage and analyze data are not longer valid and newer approaches need to be developed.

Map-Reduce: Map Reduce is a programming paradigm that enables scaling of data analytics on distributed set of computer systems, by breakup the datasets for analytics and also combining the results.

HDFS: Hadoop Distributed File System is a distributed filesystem which can store large amounts of data on local compute node filesystems and enables mapreduce jobs.

NoSQL: Not Only SQL, is an approach to data management and database design that is primarily utilized in very large sets of distributed data.

Key-Value Pair: Key-Value Pair is a data representation method of attribute followed by value, for data store and management systems, most commonly used in several NoSQL systems.

Complex Event Processing: CEP refers to processing, filtering and correlating real time flow of data for analytical decisions.

MPP Databases: Massively Parallel Databases partitions data across multiple servers with each node having memory/processors to process data locally. Additionally, all communication is via a network interconnect, with no disk-level sharing or contention.

In-Memory Databases: In-memory databases (IMDB) are database management systems that utilizes main memory of a server to store and manage data. IMDBs perform faster than disk-optimized databases because manipulating data in the main memory.

Chapter 2
Applying the K–Means Algorithm in Big Raw Data Sets with Hadoop and MapReduce

Ilias K. Savvas
TEI of Larissa, Greece

Georgia N. Sofianidou
TEI of Larissa, Greece

M-Tahar Kechadi
University College Dublin, Ireland

ABSTRACT

Big data refers to data sets whose size is beyond the capabilities of most current hardware and software technologies. The Apache Hadoop software library is a framework for distributed processing of large data sets, while HDFS is a distributed file system that provides high-throughput access to data-driven applications, and MapReduce is software framework for distributed computing of large data sets. Huge collections of raw data require fast and accurate mining processes in order to extract useful knowledge. One of the most popular techniques of data mining is the K-means clustering algorithm. In this study, the authors develop a distributed version of the K-means algorithm using the MapReduce framework on the Hadoop Distributed File System. The theoretical and experimental results of the technique prove its efficiency; thus, HDFS and MapReduce can apply to big data with very promising results.

INTRODUCTION

Big data refers to data sets whose size is beyond the capabilities of most current hardware and software technologies in order to be managed and processed within a reasonable response time. In addition, data may have different structures, heterogeneous, or may be completely unstructured (e.g., multi-media and text documents). The management of extremely large and always growing volumes of data has been since many years a challenge for all fields of science. For example, by 2014, the

DOI: 10.4018/978-1-4666-4699-5.ch002

Large Synoptic Survey Telescope (LSST, 2011) will produce 20 terabytes each night while by 2019 it is anticipated that the Square Kilometre Array radio telescope is planned to produce 7 petabytes of raw data per second (SKA, 2011). Facebook uploads six billion photos per month for a total of about 72 petabytes per annum. In addition, the vast amount of digital information that is now available should make easier the investigation of criminal activities, however the enormous size of the available data created a new challenge of how can we extract evidence within a reasonable processing time.

With Data Intensive Computing, organizations can progressively filter, transform and mine massive data volumes into information that can help the users make better decisions quicker. Data Mining is the process for extracting useful information from large datasets. As the datasets are very large, the time complexity of most Data Mining techniques is very high. One common method to overcome the complexity problem is to reduce the initial dataset size by using a representative sample and then use this small sample to extract the knowledge. The challenge here lies in identifying the representative sample, as its choice impacts directly on the final results. Another method is to distribute the dataset among a set of processing nodes and perform the calculation in Single Program Multiple Data (SPMD) paradigm (in parallel). It can be implemented by using threads, MPI or MapReduce. The choice of an appropriate implementation strategy is based on the size of the dataset, the complexity of the computational requirements, synchronisation, and the hardware profile.

The Apache Hadoop software library provides useful and efficient tools for the distributed computing of large datasets. HDFS is a distributed file system that provides high-throughput access to data-driven applications and MapReduce is a programming model for distributed processing of large datasets. Typical MapReduce computations involve many terabytes of data on thousands of machines. MapReduce usually divides the input dataset into disjoint subsets (chunks). The number of subsets depends on the size of the dataset and the number of processing nodes available. The users may specify a mapping function that processes (key, value) pairs to generate a set of intermediate (key, value) pairs, and a reduce function that merges all intermediate values associated with the same intermediate key.

The purpose of this chapter is to explore the possibility of using Hadoop's MapReduce framework and Hadoop Distributed File System to implement a popular clustering technique in a distributed fashion. The experimental results obtained are very promising and showed good performance of the proposed technique. In addition, the theoretical analysis of the algorithm's complexity is in line with the experimental results, and the approach scales very well and outperforms the sequential version.

RELATED WORK

There have been extensive studies on various clustering methods; and especially the k-means clustering has been given a great attention. However, there is very little on the application of k-means to the MapReduce. Since its early development, the k-means clustering (Lloyd, 1982) has been identified to have a very high complexity and significant effort has been spent to tune the algorithm and improve its performance. While k-means is very simple and straightforward algorithm, it has two main issues: 1) the choice of the number of clusters and of the initial centroids. 2) the iterative nature of the algorithm which impacts heavily on its scalability as the size of the dataset increases. Many researchers have come up with various algorithms that:

- Improve the accuracy of the final clusters;
- Help in choosing appropriate initial centroids;

- Reduce the number of iterations;
- Handle well the outliers.

In the case of K-means, the effectiveness of clustering depends on the initial centroids. The right set of initial centroids will lead to compact and well-formed clusters. In Jin et. al. (2006) the authors presented a new algorithm called the Fast and Exact K-means clustering. This algorithm uses sampling technique to create the initial cluster centres and thereafter requires one or a small number of passes on the entire dataset to adjust the cluster centres. The study has shown that this algorithm produces the same cluster centres as the original k-means algorithm. The algorithm has also been tested on distributed system of loosely coupled machines.

In McCallum et. al. (2000), the authors explained how the number of iterations can be reduced by partitioning the dataset into overlapping subsets and iterating only over the data objects within the overlapping areas. This technique is called Canopy Clustering and it uses two different similarity measures. First, a simple and approximate similarity measure is used to create the canopy subsets and then a more and accurate measure is used to cluster the objects. This reduces the total number of distance calculations and, therefore, the number of iterations (Guba et.al., 1998).

While the above studies largely concentrated on improving the k-means algorithm and reducing the number of iterations, there have been many other studies about its scalability. Recently, more research has been done on MapReduce framework. The paper from Zhao et. al. (2009) presented Parallel k-means clustering based on MapReduce. It has been shown that the k-means clustering algorithms can scale well and can be parallelized. The authors concluded that MapReduce can efficiently process large datasets on commodity hardware.

Some researchers have conducted comparative studies of various MapReduce frameworks available in the market and studied their effectiveness in the area of clustering big data. In (Ibrahim et. al. 2009), the authors have analysed the performance benefits of Hadoop on virtual machines, and it was shown that MapReduce is a good tool for cloud based data analysis. There have been also developments with Microsoft product DryadLINQ to perform data intensive analysis and compared the performance of DryadLINQ with Hadoop implementations (Ekanyake et. al. 2009). In another study, the authors have implemented a slightly enhanced model and architecture of MapReduce called the Twister (Ekanyake et. al. 2009). They have compared the performance of Twister with Hadoop and DryadLINQ with the aim of expanding the applicability of MapReduce for data-intensive scientific applications. According to their study, Twister is well suited for iterative, long running MapReduce jobs as it uses streaming to send the output of the map functions directly to reduce function instead of local writes by the mappers and read by the reducer. Two important observations can be made from this study. First, for computation intensive workload, threads and processes did not show any significant difference in performance. Second, for memory intensive workload, processes are 20 times faster than threads. In Jiang et. al. (2009) a comparative study of Hadoop MapReduce and Framework for Rapid Implementation of data mining Engines has been performed. According to this study, they have concluded that Hadoop is not well suited for modest-sized databases. However, when the datasets are large, there is a good performance benefit in using Hadoop.

There are many open source projects that work on MapReduce based algorithms. Apache Mahout is an Apache project that aims at building distributed and scalable machine learning algorithms on Hadoop (AM, 2012). Apache Mahout has a ready suite of algorithms for clustering, classification and collaborative filtering that work on top of Hadoop MapReduce framework. Disco is another open source MapReduce runtime that has been developed using Erlang, a functional programming language (DP, 2012 and EPL 2012). While Disco stores the intermediate results of map tasks in local files similar to Google and Hadoop MapReduce architectures, it employs HTTP to access this data for the reduce tasks. It also differs from HDFS in that it does not support a distributed file system but expects the files to be distributed initially over multiple disks of the computing platform. In the following we give a detailed description of MapReduce and explain how it can be used for data mining applications.

HADOOP DISTRIBUTED FILE SYSTEM (HDFS)

Hadoop can run large data intensive and distributed applications and can be installed on commodity Linux clusters (AH, 2012). Hadoop comes with its own file system called the Hadoop Distributed File System (HDFS) and a strong infrastructure support for very large datasets management and analysis. Each HDFS cluster consists of one unique server called the *Namenode*. *Namenode* manages the namespace of the file system, determines the mapping of blocks to *Datanodes*, and regulates file access (HDFS, 2012). Each node in the HDFS cluster is a *Datanode* that manages the storage attached to it. *Datanode*s are responsible for read and write requests from the clients and perform block creation, deletion and replication instructions from the *Namenode*.

The main HDFS goal is to deal with extremely large files by breaking them into blocks and replicating them across the network. The common policy is to replicate each file three times. HDFS places two replicas on two different nodes on the same rack and places the third replica on a different node in a different rack. This ensures reliability even without a RAID backup. However, HDFS is based on the Google File System model that follows the write-once-read-many access model that are not meant for continuous updates of data (Figure 1).

The Hadoop support infrastructure is built around the assumption that data will be distributed among the nodes (machines) that will fail. Therefore, when tasks are run on multiple nodes concurrently, Hadoop can automatically detect task failures and restart failed tasks on other healthy nodes. When a block or a node is lost, it automatically creates a copy of the missing data from the available replicas. The only single point of failure is the presence of a single *Namenode* for the entire HDFS. Even though HDFS supports an optional secondary *Namenode*, it does not provide real redundancy. The secondary *Namenode* connects to the primary *Namenode* from time to time to take a snapshot of the directory information. The function of the secondary *Namenode* is to facilitate a quick recovery and restart the primary *Namenode* if necessary. A real Backup *Namenode* would enhance the availability of HDFS.

Hadoop places emphasis on high throughput over low latency and is ideal for batch processing. Hadoop also works on the premise that it costs less to move the computation than data. Therefore, HDFS provides interfaces to move the applications closer to the data either on the same node as the data or the same rack and thereby improving I/O bandwidth.

There are many open source projects built on top of Hadoop. Hive is a data warehouse (AH, 2012) used for ad-hoc querying and complex analysis. It is designed for batch processing. Pig (AP, 2012) is a data flow and execution framework that produces a sequence of MapReduce programs. Mahout (AM, 2012) is used to build scalable machine learning libraries that focus on clustering, classification, mining frequent itemsets and evolutionary programming. Pydoop is a python package that provides an API for Hadoop MapReduce and HDFS. MapReduce is best suited to deal with large datasets and therefore ideal for mining in Big Data (which does not fit entirely in a physical memory). Most common use of MapReduce is for tasks of additive nature. However, we can adapt it to suit other tasks.

Figure 1. Architecture of HDFS

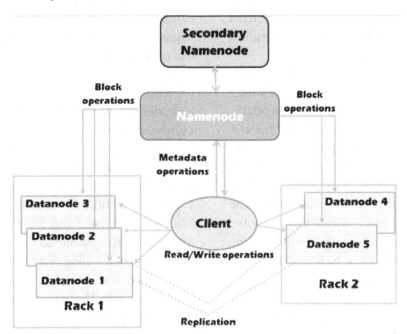

How to Install and Use the HDFS

Installing HDFS first of all requires to download and unpack a stable version form Apache mirrors. There is documentation and detailed instructions in hadoop.apache.org in order to configure the cluster.

The MapReduce Programming Model

MapReduce is a programming model with an associated implementation for processing and generating large data sets (HMT, 2012). A typical MapReduce computation performs many terabytes of data on thousands of machines. MapReduce usually divides the input dataset into disjoint chunks (subsets). The number of subsets depends on the size of the dataset and the number of nodes available. Users specify a map function that processes a (key, value) pair to generate a set of intermediate (key, value) pairs, and a reduce function that merges all intermediate values as-sociated with the same intermediate key (Dean, J. and Ghemawat, S., 2008).

There are separate Map and Reduce steps. Each step is executed in parallel on sets of (key, value) pairs. Thus, the whole process consists of two main stages: a Map stage and a Reduce stage. The two stages are separated by data exchange between nodes of the cluster. The Map stage takes in a function and a section of data values as input, applies the function to each value in the input set and generates an output set. The Map output is a set of records in the form of (key, value) pairs stored on the nodes. The records for any given key could be spread across many nodes. The framework, then, sorts the outputs from the Map functions and inputs them into a Reducer. This involves data exchange between the Mappers and the Reducer. The values are aggregated at the Reducer's node for that key. The Reduce stage produces another set of (key, value) pairs as the final output. The Reduce stage can only start when all the data from the Map stage is transferred to the appropriate nodes. MapReduce requires the input as a (key, value) pair that can be serialized and, therefore, restricted to tasks and algorithms that use (key, value) pairs.

A MapReduce process has a single master node, the *Job Tracker* and multiple slave/worker nodes, the *Task Trackers* (Figure 2). Potentially, each node in the cluster can be a *Task Tracker*. The master manages the input data partitioning over the nodes and node failures, schedules the tasks, reassigns failed tasks, controls the inter-node communications and monitors the task status. The slaves execute the tasks assigned by the master. Both input and output are stored in the file-system. The single *Job Tracker* can be a single point of failure in this framework.

Small Description of the Python Programming Language

Python (PPL, 2013), is not an acronym (or a moccasin..), but named after the BBC show "Monty Python's Flying Circus". Python started 1989, and designed by Guido van Rossum (National Research Institute for Mathematics and Computer Science, Amsterdam, The Netherlands). It is a compiled / interpreted mid-level object oriented language. Python is both simple and powerful and runs on Linux/Unix, Windows, and Mac OS operating systems (www.python.org). One of the most important features of Python is the data types that use, namely, Strings, Lists, Tuples, and Dictionaries, all of them supported by methods but tuples. Lists are dynamic, ordered and heterogeneous collection of data, while the tuples are similar to lists but they have no methods. Finally, the dictionaries consist of <value, key> objects and they are also like the list data type, heterogeneous, dynamic and mutable.

Another interesting feature of Python is the built in functions, between them, the map and reduce functions. The syntax of the map function is map(function, iterable) and returns a list of values after applying the function on each one of them. For example, to compute the cubes of numbers in the range 1,2,...,100 and having define the cube function (for example def cube(a): return a*a*a) the call of the map function: map(cube, range(1,101)) will return [1, 8, 27, ..., 1000000]. On the other hand, the reduce function returns a single value

Figure 2. Architecture of MapReduce

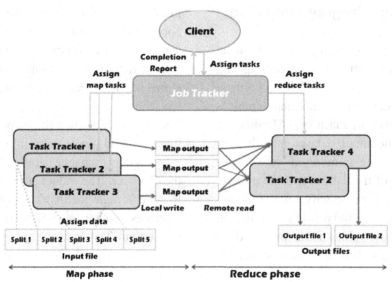

applying a binary function on a set of values. The syntax of the reduce function is: reduce(function, sequence) and applies the function on the first two items of the values, then on the result and the third item of the sequence, and so on. For example the reduce call: reduce(cube, range(1,101)) will return the value 13+23+33+...+1003.

Example: Word Counting

A very common use of the map and reduce functions is the word counting problem. Having a text file <test.txt> consisting of words, for example, "aaa bbb ccc ddd aaa aaa bbb qqq www eee rrr ttt yyy yyy eee aaa", the program Program 1, <map_user.py> will produce a new text file <test_out.txt> consisting of a a list of the words of the text file of the type <word, 1>, i.e. < aaa 1 bbb 1 ccc 1 ddd 1 aaa 1 aaa 1 bbb 1 qqq 1 www 1 eee 1 rrr 1 ttt 1 yyy 1 yyy 1 eee 1 aaa 1>.

Applying the reducer program (Program 2) to the <test_out.txt> the final output will be another text file <test_final.txt> where each word will appear with the corresponding total number of its appearance in the original file, i.e. < www 1, aaa 4, yyy 2, bbb 2, ttt 1, qqq 1, eee 2, rrr 1, ccc 1, ddd 1>.

Applying the above programs to HDFS and to the Apache MapReduce technique they are executed in parallel since MapReduce is dividing the work load across the distributed system. Thus, it takes advantage of the parallel processing power of the HDFS distributed system, and also reduces network bandwidth as the program is passed around to where the data lies, rather than a potentially huge dataset transferred to the client program. This makes the MapReduce technique extremely useful in manipulating Big Data schemas. The data is spread across the multiple hosts of the HDFS and the role of MapReduce is just

Program 1. map_user

```
#!/usr/bin/env python
import sys
import time
# the input from text file
fin = open ("C:\\Python\\test.txt","r")
fout = open ("C:\\Python\\test_out.txt","w")
start = time.time()
for line in fin:
    # split the line into words
    words = line.split()
    # map each word to 1
    for word in words:
        #print '%s\t%s' % (word, 1)
        value = word + "\t1\n"
        fout.write(value)
end = time.time()
print 'Elapsed time (in seconds) is: %10.4f' % (end-start)
# close the files
fin.close()
fout.close()
```

Program 2. reduce_user

```python
#!/usr/bin/env python
import sys
import time

# maps words to their counts
word_counter_array = {}
# input comes from text file
fin = open ("C:\\Python\\test_out.txt","r")
fout = open ("C:\\Python\\test_final.txt","w")
start = time.time()
for line in fin:
    # assign words to <word> and 1 to count (from the input produced by map_user.py
    word, count = line.split("\t", 1)
    print '%s\t%s' % (word, count)
    # count works only with integers
    count = int(count)
    word_counter_array[word] = word_counter_array.get(word, 0) + count

# write the results to STDOUT (standard output)
for word, count in word_counter_array.items():
    print '%s\t%s' % (word, count)
# write the results to text file
for word, count in word_counter_array.items():
    value = word + "\t" + str(count) + "\n"
    fout.write(value)
end = time.time()
print 'Elapsed time (in seconds) is: %10.4f' % (end-start)
# close the files
fin.close()
fout.close()
```

to transfer the program where data lives and after that to execute in parallel the program's instructions. Assuming that we want to count the words that appear into the text of Iliad by Homer (Gutenberg E-Books) the typical Linux commands of applying the MapReduce (after of course downloading the Iliad from http://www.gutenberg.org/ebooks/6130), are the following:

1. Copy the files into a <test> directory within the hadoop directory;
2. Copy the directory to hdfs: $ bin/hadoop fs -put test test;
3. Are the files there? $ bin/hadoop fs -ls test;
4. Apply map_user/reduce_user.py to them: $ bin/hadoop jar mapred/contrib/streaming/hadoop.21.0-streaming.jar -file ./

mapp_user.py -mapper ./mapp_user.py -file ./reduce_user.py -reducer ./reduce_user.py -input test/* -output test-output;

5. Check if the result is successfully stored in HDFS directory: $ bin/hadoop fs -ls test-output;

6. Display the results: $ bin/hadoop fs -cat test-output/part-00000 | more;

7. Or copy/move them to the local file system: $ bin/hadoop fs -get test-output test-output;

8. Search the results to see how many times Homer used the name of Jupiter: $ grep -w -i "Achilles" part-00000;

9. And stop the services: $ bin/stop-all.sh.

DATA MINING

Nowadays, automated data collection tools like radio telescopes and the mature database technology lead to tremendous amounts of data stored in databases, warehouses, and other information repositories, or in other words we have to deal with big data. We are drowning in data but on the other hand we are starving for information. One potential solution to this problem is data mining. The goal of data mining is to extract knowledge like patterns, rules, etc. for large datasets. Data mining techniques can solve a wide range of problems ranging from Astronomy and Sports to Economy, Risk Analysis and so on. For example, the Palomar Observatory discovered 22 quasars thanks to data mining. The data was lying there but the knowledge was absent. Besides the pure scientific applications, data mining has very profitable real world uses. Large companies and even many governments already perform data mining as part of their planning and analysis. The data explosion problem or in other words big data can be easily manipulated by data mining techniques in order to extract interest information (Jain and Dubes 1988, Han and Kamber 2006, Pertner 2007, and Larose 2005).

Cluster analysis is an important tool for data mining. It has been applied in a variety of scientific and engineering disciplines such as biology, marketing, medicine and so on. Cluster analysis organizes data by abstracting underlying structure either as object grouping or as a hierarchy of groups. A cluster can be considered as a set of similar objects. Different clusters contain different objects. In order to extract from big data similar objects it is essential to define the similarity measure which in turn will define which objects are similar according this metric to which others. As an example, the Euclidean distance (or norm) is a good paradigm of similarity measure if the objects can be defined as a set of parameters - attributes. These attributes can represent an N-dimensional space and the distance between any two of them can easily be defined as their norm. One of the most important techniques for clustering data is the K-means algorithm.

K-means algorithm is implemented in four simple steps. Given the number k of desired clusters, the technique partitions the objects of the dataset to k sets. Then, the centroid of each cluster is computed (centroid is the center or mean point of the participated objects). After that, each point is reassigned to the cluster with the nearest centroid. If no objects change cluster the algorithm terminates otherwise the new centroids are recalculated (since objects changed clusters, the centroids may change either) and so on. The advantage of K-means is its relative efficiency (its computational complexity is $O(kNM)$ where k, N, and M represent the number of cluster, data objects, and iterations, respectively), but on the other hand there are certain disadvantages mainly the beforehand knowledge of K, the number of clusters.

Transforming the K-Means Clustering Algorithm to Meet the MapReduce Requirements

The sequential k-means algorithm starts by choosing k initial centroids, one for each cluster and assigns each object of the dataset to the nearest centroid. Then, the technique recalculates the centroid of each cluster based on its member objects and goes through again each data object and assigns it to its closest centroid. This step is repeated until there is no change in the centroids (same centroids will attract the same data objects). In this work we transformed the original k-means algorithm to meet the MapReduce requirements. The chosen programming language was Python. Two versions of the technique was developed and examined, the first version which consists of two parts: a mapper, and a reducer, and the improved second version which again consists of two parts, a mapper with a combiner, and a reducer with a combiner.

The MapReduce Version of K-Means

The input dataset is distributed across the mappers. The initial set of centroids is either placed in a common location and accessed by all the mappers or distributed on each mapper. The centroid list has identification for each centroid as a key and the centroid itself as the value. Each data object in the subset $\{x_1, x_2, ..., x_m\}$ is assigned to its closest centroid by the mapper. We use the Euclidean distance to measure proximity of data objects; the distances between a data object and the centroids. The data object is assigned to the closest centroid. When all the objects are assigned to the centroids, the mapper sends all the data objects and the centroids they are assigned to, to the reducer (Algorithm 1).

After the execution of the mapper, the reducer takes as input the mapper outputs, $\big($key, value$\big)$ pairs, and loops through them in order to calculate the new centroid values. For each centroid, the reducer calculates a new value based on the objects assigned to it in that iteration. This new centroid list is sent back to the start-up program (Algorithm 2).

In the MapReduce model, the output of the map function is written to the disk and the reduce function reads it. In the meantime, the output is sorted and shuffled. In order to reduce the time overhead between the mappers and the reducer, Algorithm 1 was modified to combine the map outputs in order to reduce the amount of data that the mappers have to write locally and the reducer to read it. The proposed combiner reads the mapper outputs locally, and calculates the local centroids. After that, the reducer reads the output produced by the mappers (which is only the local centroids instead of the entire dataset) and calculates the global centroids. This method reduces dramatically the read/write operations. The mappers and reducer now are using the combiner, which are described in Algorithms 3 and 4 respectively.

SIMULATIONS

To evaluate the proposed MapReduce K-means technique, a cluster of 21 nodes were used. One of the nodes was defined as *Namenode* and Job Tracker (Intel Pentium IV cpu of 3.4 GHz and 4GB of main memory). The remaining nodes were defined as *Datanode*s and Task Trackers; (Intel dual Core cpu of 2.33 GHz and 2 GB of main memory). The network had a bandwidth of 1 Gbps. All nodes ran Red Hat version 4.1.2-48 and 32bit operating system 5.5. We used Java Runtime version 1.6.0_16, Python 2.4.3 and Hadoop 0.21.0.

In addition we used spatial data for testing for many reasons. The distance measure, Euclidian distance, is well suited for such data, the spatial dimensions are very complex, as their combination with the Euclidian distance, define spheri-

Algorithm 1. Mapper

```
1.  Begin
2.  requirements:
    a. Subset of m-dim objects {x₁,x₂,...,xₙ} in each mapper
    b. Initial set of centroids C = {c₁,c₂,...,cₖ}
3.  M ← {x₁,x₂,...,xₙ}
4.  Current_centroids ← C
5.  Output_List ← ∅
6.  // Cluster assignment for each object in the set
7.  for all xᵢ ∈ M do
    a. Best_Centroid ← ∅  // Initialise the best centroid for the object
    b. Min_Dist ← ∞
    c. // Checking the distance of the object and each centroid in the list
    d. for all c ∈ Current_centroid // While loops through each centroid in the list.
        i.   Dist ← ‖xᵢ,c‖
        ii.  if ( Best_Centroid = ∅ or Dist < Min_Dist )
             1. Min_Dist ← Dist
             2. Best_Centroid ← c
        iii. end if
    e. end for
8.  // Create an output list with each object and the Centroid cluster it belongs to
    a. Output_List ← Output_List ∪ (Best_Centroid, xᵢ)
9.  end for
10. Return Output_List // this output list consists of the centroid and their objects.
11. End
```

cal shapes, which are not always desirable. We generated datasets containing clusters of different shapes, densities and noise. So, the primary dimensions are the spatial dimensions. We generated about 10G data objects of 2d and 3d (see Table 1).

The datasets before clustering is shown in Figures 3 and 4.

Table 1. Size of the sample data set

Data points (in millions)	10	12	100	500	1000
2d (size in MB)	75	90	750	3748	7500
3d (size in MB)	110	132	1100	5510	11000

As a first step of the k-means algorithm we have considered various methods, from random choice of centroids to canopy clustering, to generate initial centroids. Because the quality of the final clusters in k-means depends highly on the first step (initial generation of centroids), we decided against random choice. Instead, we chose a more dependable approach of the density distribution of the data objects. This worked well for our study as our aim was not to optimise the choice of initial set of centroids but to analyse the effectiveness of MapReduce to cluster. The final clustered 2-d and 3-d data points are shown in Figures 5, and 6 respectively.

Algorithm 2. Reducer

```
1.  Begin
2.  Input: (key,value) where key = Best_Centroid and value = objects assigned to the centroids by the mappers
3.    Output_List ← Output_List  // from mappers
4.    v ← ∅
5.    New_CentroidList ← ∅
6.  for all y∈Output_List do
    a.  Centroid ← y.key
    b.  Object ← y.value
    c.  v_Centroid ← Object
7.  end for
8.  for all Centroid∈ v do
    a.  NewCentroid ← ∅
    b.  SumOfObjects ← 0
    c.  NumOfObjects ← 0
    d.  for all Object∈ v do
        i.   SumOfObjects ← SumoOfObjects + Object
        ii.  NumOfObjects ← NumOfObjects + 1
    e.  end for
    f.  NewCentroid ← (SumOfObjects / NumOfObjects )
    g.  NewCentroidList ← NewCentroidList ∪ NewCentroid
9.  end for
10. Return  NewCentroidList
11. End
```

Algorithm 3. Mapper with Combiner

```
1. Begin
2. As Algorithm 1 and in addition calculation of the set of LocalCentroids as in Algorithm 2 lines 8, 9
3. Return LocalCentroids
4. End
```

Algorithm 4. Reducer with Combiner

```
1. Begin
2. As Algorithm 3 but having the information of the set of LocalCentroids, calculates
   straight forward the NewCentroidList
3. Return NewCentroidList
2. End
```

Figure 3. 2d dataset

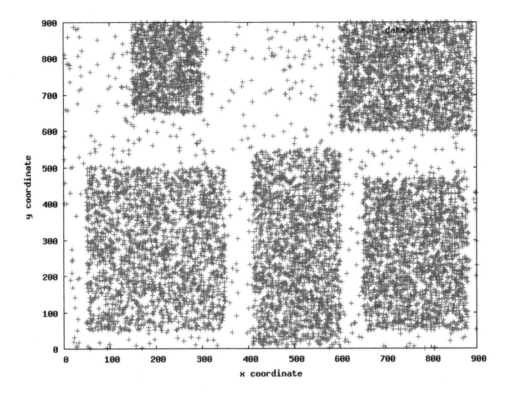

Figure 4. 3d dataset

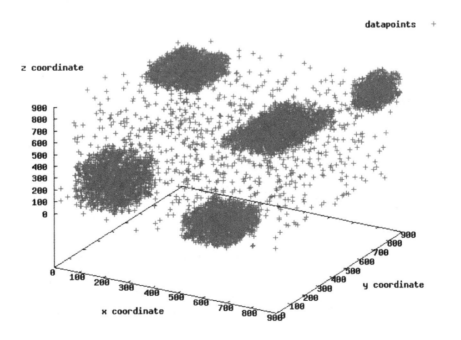

Figure 5. Final clusters of 2d data

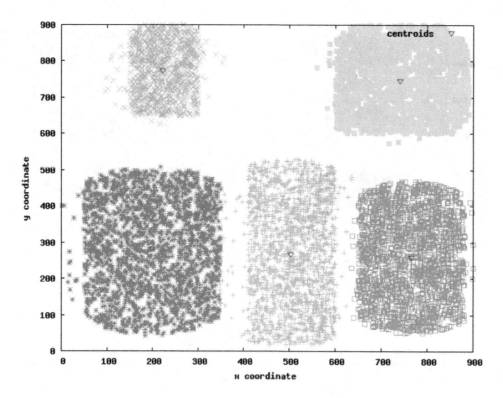

Figure 6. Final clusters of 3d data

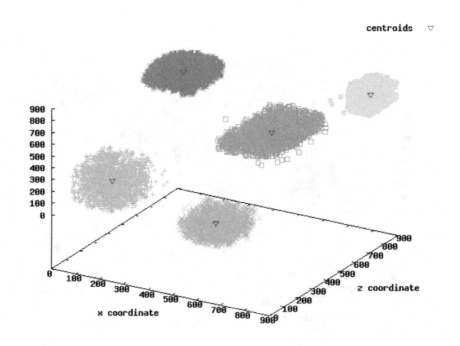

With the Hadoop characteristics in mind, we have improved the clustering response time. We also studied the effect of the number of nodes on the speed of convergence of the clustering technique. So we used the same set of data objects and perform the MapReduce with just one node. Gradually, we increased the number of nodes while keeping the same datasets.

The times needed to cluster the same dataset using 1, 2, 3, and 4 nodes are presented in Figure 7 and we continued to increase the number of nodes up to 21 nodes. As the number of nodes increases, the MapReduce version of k-means algorithm convergences faster. For example, a dataset of 100K data objects, it takes about 110 seconds with one node to converge and 71 seconds with 4 nodes. It is far from an ideal speedup but it is an improvement of 35%. The setup conditions and communications are still significant in this case.

Another very interesting point is the behavior of the technique when the number of clusters, k, varies. As we can see in Table 2 increasing the number of clusters, the performance of the proposed technique is also increasing. For example,

for k=2, the simple MapReduce algorithm needs at least 8 participating nodes in order to outperform the sequential algorithm when the number of data objects is about 10 million, and only 2 nodes when k=10. Basically, more k is bigger more the technique needs to be distributed, because more computations are required in order to assign the objects to their corresponding clusters, and therefore, the overhead of the MapReduce procedure becomes less important.

Table 2. Number of nodes needed to outperform the sequential technique

N	k=2		k=4		k=10	
	MR	MRC	MR	MRC	MR	MRC
10	>20	6	7	2	2	2
20	8	2	8	2	2	2
40	9	2	9	2	2	2
60	10	2	10	2	2	2
80	10	2	10	2	2	2
100	11	2	10	2	2	2
500	16	2	16	2	2	2
1000	>20	2	20	3	2	2

Figure 7. Comparative plot: Time to cluster 2d and 3d points

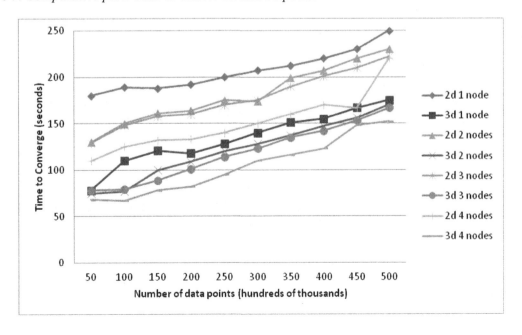

More precisely, in Figures 8, 9, and 10 we can see the behavior of the proposed technique with 3 different numbers of clusters. The number of participating nodes varied from 1 to 21 while keeping constant the number of data objects to 10 million. As the number of the clusters k and the number of nodes increase, the efficiency of MapReduce k-means increases also.

We performed the same tests again, but this time by increasing the number of data objects to 1G and the results are presented in Figures 11, 12, and 13. We can notice that the performance of the new technique improved significantly with the size of the computations and data. Thus, we can conclude that both MapReduce and the new k-means technique are scalable.

Figure 8. Time to cluster 10 million 3d points, number of clusters k=2

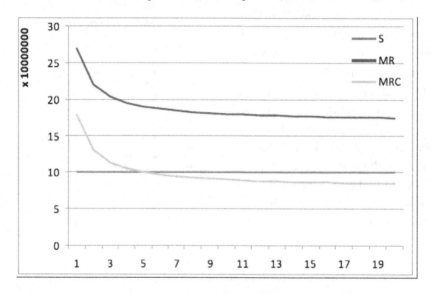

Figure 9. Time to cluster 10 million 3d points, number of clusters k=4

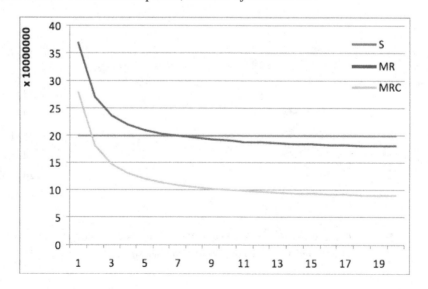

Figure 10. Time to cluster 10 million 3d points, number of clusters k=10

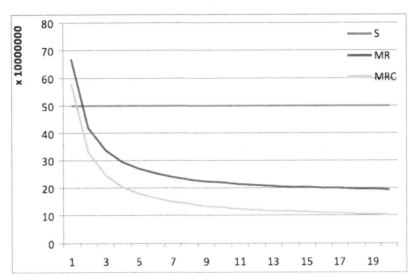

Figure 11. Time to cluster 1 billion 3d points, number of clusters k=2

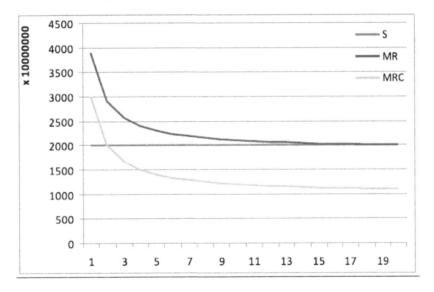

Finally, we perform the same experiment with 1G data objects on a fixed number of participating nodes 4 and 20 (Figures 14, and 15 respectively). We varied the number of clusters from 2 to 10. We can see that the performance of the new technique increases as the number of clusters (and therefore the computational work) increases. The simple MapReduce algorithm needs k>5 in order to outperform the sequential algorithm, while the MapReduce with Combiner outperforms the sequential even for k>2 and the number of nodes of 4. On the other hand, when the number of nodes is 20 the MapReduce with Combiner needs just k=2 while the simple MapReduce technique requires k >3.

Figure 12. Time to cluster 1 billion 3d points, number of clusters k=4

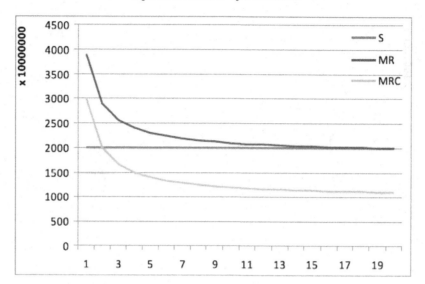

Figure 13. Time to cluster 1 billion 3d points, number of clusters k=10

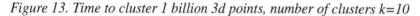
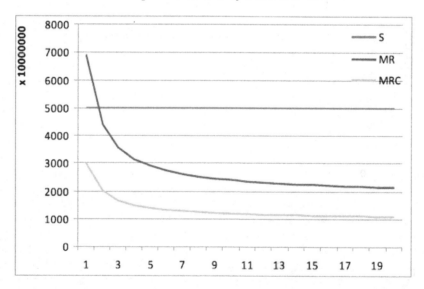

COMPLEXITY AND COMPARISONS

In this section we validate theoretically the experimental results obtained in the previous section.

In the sequential k-means clustering, we iterate through the dataset of size N for each centroid by calculating the distance between each data object and each centroid and it is affected to the closest centroid. After that, the new centroids are recalcu-lated and the distances between each data object and the new centroids is calculated and assigned to the closest one. This procedure is repeated for a number of M times until convergence. So, the complexity of a simple assignment is given by the Equation 1:

$$T_s\left(N\right) = MkN \tag{1}$$

Figure 14. N=1,000,000, and x=4

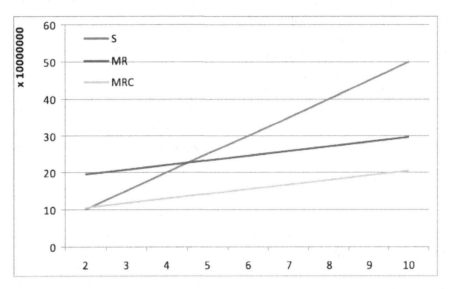

Figure 15. N=1,000,000, and x=20

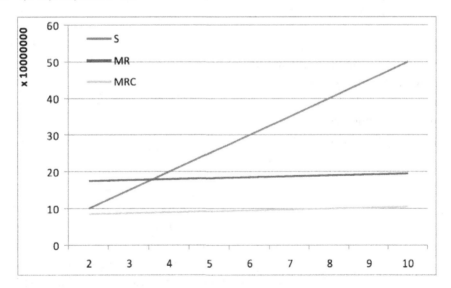

where k is the number of clusters, N is the number of data objects, and M is the number of iterations.

On the other hand, before using MapReduce for clustering, we need to partition the input data objects into x subsets, where x is the number of available mappers. In each mapper, we iterate through N/x data objects and for each centroid in the k clusters, for calculating the distance between them and assign for each object its corresponding centroid. So, the complexity of the mapper is expressed by the following equation:

$$T_M\left(N\right) = \frac{MkN}{x} \tag{2}$$

In the reducer, we iterate through the output from x mappers for assigning each object and its corresponding centroid into a dictionary type variable for further processing. We then iterate through each centroid k, by cumulating and counting the data objects in that cluster and calculate a new centroid. Therefore, the complexity of this operation is given by equation:

$$T_R(N) = M\left(N + k\frac{N}{k}\right) = 2MN \tag{3}$$

We repeat the MapReduce process M times until convergence. So, according to Equations 2 and 3, the total complexity for the MapReduce algorithm is as follows:

$$T_{MR}(N) = T_M(N) + T_R(N) = MN(\frac{k}{x} + 2) \tag{4}$$

In the contrary, when using the combiner, in the mapper, we iterate through all the N/x data objects for each centroid to calculate the distances between them while the combiner calculates the k centroids each time the mappers terminate their process. Therefore, the complexity now is as follows:

$$T_{MC} = \frac{MkN + N}{x} \tag{5}$$

In the reducer (using the combiner), we iterate through k outputs from the x mappers in order to calculate the global centroids. So the complexity can be expressed as:

$$T_{RC}(N) = N + k \tag{6}$$

We repeat the entire process for M iterations until convergence. Thus, the total complexity of the MapReduce with Combiner algorithm according Equations 5 and 6, is as follows:

$$T_{MRC}(N) = T_{MC}(N) + T_{RC}(N)$$
$$= \frac{MkN + N}{x} + N + k \tag{7}$$

where x is the number of nodes assigned for the MapReduce k-means process.

Comparing now the performance of the sequential versus the simple MapReduce technique, from Equations 1 and 4 we can derive the following:

$$\frac{MkN}{x} + 2MN \leq MkN, \forall \ (k > 2 \wedge x > 3)$$

Thus, for any k>2 and the number of the participating nodes is greater than 3 then the MapReduce k-means version outperforms the sequential one.

In addition, from Equations 4, and 7 we can derive the following:

$$\frac{N}{x} + N + k \leq 2MN, \forall \ (x \geq 1 \wedge M > 1)$$

Therefore, the MapReduce with Combiner technique outperforms the simple MapReduce technique even with one processing node and the number of iterations is more than 2. We can also notice that the experimental results are in line with the theoretical analysis. The only difference is that for smaller sizes of the input datasets, the overhead due to the MapReduce setup and communications is so significant that one cannot get any benefit for using it. However, for large datasets, the MapReduce version is at least 35% better than the sequential version and more importantly it is scalable.

More precisely, the overhead is due to two main issues:

1. The time taken for the read/write operations which in turn depend on the size of the data and on the latency of the secondary memory (disks). The latency of a secondary storage can be expressed as follows (Liu et. al. 2013):

$$v = \frac{v_{min} - v_{max}}{(v_{min} - v_{max})^{e^{rt}} + + v_{max}}$$

where r represents in each second the value of lost speed. So, the MapReduce with the combiner has very small overhead compared to the simple MapReduce technique, which transfers the total number of the data objects:

2. The time taken by the mappers to shuffle and sort the output data.

The above two issues have not been considered in the theoretical complexity of the algorithms. However, with reasonably large datasets and large number of the clusters, the overhead due to the previous two reasons is not significant and therefore the experimental performance matches the theoretical ones.

DISCUSSION AND CONCLUSION

In this study, we have adapted the MapReduce technique to the k-means clustering algorithm. We described the new techniques and discussed its theoretical complexity. We validated our implementation by experiments on a cluster of workstations. We can conclude that the k-means clustering technique can be successfully parallelised and run on a cluster of commodity hardware given that the MapReduce framework can be used. The results also show that the clusters formed using MapReduce are identical to the clusters formed using the sequential algorithm.

Our experimental results also show that the overheads generated by the MapReduce algorithm and the intermediate read and write between the mapper and reducer jobs is significant for smaller datasets but its efficiency increases when the amount of data increase. We also showed that by adding a combiner between Map and Reduce jobs improves the performance by decreasing the

amount of intermediate read/write. In addition, the number of available nodes for the map tasks affect significantly the performance of the system. More nodes we use for the algorithm the better is the performance. In this case the MapReduce is a valuable tool for clustering large datasets.

As near future work we would like to; 1) Evaluate the performance of the proposed techniques on a very large number of heterogeneous computing resources (nodes) since one of the main problems of the MapReduce is that all the mappers have to finish their jobs before starting the reduce phase. This is a bottleneck if there are nodes with different CPU speed, disk speed, etc. 2) Express explicitly the overhead produced from both the MapReduce technique and the read/write operations as a function of the size of the input dataset and the number of the nodes ($T_0 = f(N, x)$).

REFERENCES

AH. (2011). *Apache Hadoop*. Retrieved from http://hadoop.apache.org/

AH. (2012). *Apache Hive*. Retrieved from http://hive.apache.org/

AM. (2012). *Apache Mahout*. Retrieved from http://mahout.apache.org/

AP. (2012). *Apache Pig*. Retrieved from http://pig.apache.org/

Dean, J., & Ghemawat, S. (2008). Mapreduce: Simplified data processing on large clusters. *Communications of the ACM, 51*(1), 107–113. doi:10.1145/1327452.1327492.

Dean, J., & Ghemawat, S. (2008). Mapreduce: Simplified data processing on large clusters. *Communications of the ACM, 51*(1), 107–113. doi:10.1145/1327452.1327492.

DP. (2012). *Disco project*. Retrieved from http://discoproject.org/

Ekanayake, J., Gunarathne, T., Fox, G., Balkir, A. S., Poulain, C., Araujo, N., & Barga, R. (2009). Dryadlinq for scientific analyses. In *Proceedings of the Fifth IEEE International Conference on e-Science* (E-SCIENCE '09), (pp. 329–336). IEEE.

Ekanayake, J., Li, H., Zhang, B., Gunarathne, T., Bae, S., Qiu, J., & Fox, G. (2010). Twister: A runtime for iterative mapreduce. In *Proceedings of the 19th ACM International Symposium on High Performance Distributed Computing*, (pp. 810–818). ACM.

EPL. (2012). *Erlang programming language*. Retrieved from http://www.erlang.org/

Guba, S., Rastogi, R., & Shim, K. (1998). Cure: An efficient clustering algorithm for large databases. In *Proceedings of the ACM SIGMOD International Conference on Management of Data*, (pp. 73–84). ACM.

Han, J., & Kamber, M. (2006). *Data mining: Concepts and techniques*. San Francisco, CA: Morgan Kaufmann.

HMR. (2011). *Hadoop MapReduce*. Retrieved form http:// hadoop.apache.org/mapreduce/

Ibrahim, S., Jin, H., Lu, L., Qi, L., Wu, S., & Shi, X. (2009). Evaluating mapreduce on virtual machines: The hadoop case. In *Proceedings of the 1st International Conference on Cloud Computing*, (vol. 5931, pp. 519-528). Berlin: Springer.

Jain, A. K., & Dubes, R. C. (1988). *Algorithms for clustering data*. Hoboken, NJ: Prentice Hall.

Jiang, W., Ravi, V., & Agrawal, G. (2009). Comparing map-reduce and freeride for data-intensive applications. In *Proceedings of the IEEE International Conference on Cluster Computing and Workshops*, (pp. 1–10). IEEE.

Jin, R., Goswami, A., & Agrawal, G. (2006). Fast andexact out-of-core and distributed k-means clustering. *Knowledge and Information Systems*, *10*(1), 17–40. doi:10.1007/s10115-005-0210-0.

Larose, D. T. (2005). *Discovering knowledge in data: An introduction to data mining*. Hoboken, NJ: Wiley. doi:10.1002/0471687545.

Liu, Y. et al. (2013). Hsim: A mapreduce simulator in enabling cloud computing. *Future Generation Computer Systems*, *29*(1), 300–308. doi:10.1016/j.future.2011.05.007.

LLoyd, S. P. (1982). Least squares quantization in PCM. *IEEE Transactions on Information Theory*, *28*, 129–137. doi:10.1109/TIT.1982.1056489.

LSST. (2011). *Large synoptic survey telescope*. Retrieved from http://www.lsst.org/

McCallum, A., Nigam, K., & Ungar, L. H. (2000). Efficient clustering of high-dimensional data sets with application to reference matching. In *Proceedings of the ACM SIGKDD International Conference on Knowledge Discovery and Data Mining*, (pp. 169–178). ACM.

P. Pertner (Ed.). (2007). *Advances in data mining: Theoritical aspects and applications*. Academic Press. doi:10.1007/978-3-540-73435-2.

PPL. (2013). *Python programming language*. Retrieved from http://www.python.org/

Savvas, I. K., & Kechadi, M. T. (2012). Mining on the cloud: K-means with MapReduce. In *Proceedings of the International Conference on Cloud Computing and Services Science* (CLOSER), (pp. 413–418). CLOSER.

SKA. (2011). *Square kilometer array*. Retrieved from http://www.skatelescope.org/

Zhao, W., Ma, H., & He, Q. (2009). Parallel k-means clustering based on mapreduce. In *Proceedings of the 1st International Conference on Cloud Computing*, (vol. 5931, pp. 674-679). Berlin: Springer.

ADDITIONAL READING

Aggarval, N., & Aggarval, K. (2012). *An improved k-means clustering algorithm for data mining*. Lambert Academic Publishing.

Amorim, R. C. (2012). *Feature weighting for clustering using k-means and the Minkowski metric*. Lambert Academic Publishing.

Beazley, D. M. (2009). *Python essential reference*. Upper Saddle River, NJ: Pearson Education, Inc..

Bramer, M. (2013). *Principles of data mining*. London: Elsevier. doi:10.1007/978-1-4471-4884-5.

Dean, J., & Ghemawat, S. (2004). *MapReduce: Simplified data processing on large data clusters*. Google Research Publications.

Ghemawat, S., Gobioff, H., & Leung, S. T. (2003). *The Google file system*. Google.

Han, J., Kamber, M., & Pei, J. (2012). *Data mining: Concepts and techniques*. London: Elsevier.

Holmes, A. (2012). *Hadoop in practice*. Manning Publications Co..

Jain, A. K., & Dubes, R. C. (1998). *Algorithms for clustering data*. Englewood Cliffs, NJ: Prentice Hall.

Kaufman, L., & Rousseeuw, P. J. (2005). *Finding groups in data: An introduction to cluster analysis*. Hoboken, NJ: Wiley.

Knowlton, J. (2008). *Python: Create - modify – reuse*. Hoboken, NJ: Wiley Technology Pub..

Kogan, J. (2007). *Introduction to clustering large and high dimensional data*. Cambridge, UK: Cambridge University Press.

Lutz, M. (2001). *Programming Python*. Sebastopol, CA: O'Reilly.

Manyika, J. et al. (2011). *Big data: The next frontier for innovation, competition, and productivity*. Washington, DC: McKinsey Global Institute.

Mayer-Schonberger, V., & Cukier, K. (2013). Big data: A revolution that will transform how we live, work and think. London: John Murray (Publishers) An Hachette UK Company.

McKinney, W. (2013). *Python for data analysis*. Sebastopol, CA: O'Reilly.

Miner, D., & Shook, A. (2012). *MapReduce design patterns: Building effective algorithms and analytics for Hadoop and other systems*. Sebastopol, CA: O'Reilly.

Mirkin, B. (2005). *Clustering for data mining: A data recovery approach*. New York: Chapman & Hall/CRC, Taylor and Francis Group. doi:10.1201/9781420034912.

Perera, S., & Gunarathne. (2013). *Hadoop MapReduce*. Packt Publishing.

Shvachko, K., Kuang, H., Radia, S., & Chansler, R. (2010). *The Hadoop distributed file system*. Washington, DC: IEEE.

Solem, J. E. (2012). *Programming computer vision with Python*. Sebastopol, CA: O'Reilly.

Summer, E. (2012). *Hadoop operations*. Sebastopol, CA: O'Reilly.

Vassilivtskii, S. (2007). *K-means: Algorithms, analyses, experiments*. Palo Alto, CA: Stanford University.

White, T. (2007). *Hadoop: The definitive guide*. Sebastopol, CA: O'Reilly.

KEY TERMS AND DEFINITIONS

Big Data: Data sets whose size is beyond the capabilities of most current hardware and software technologies in order to be managed and processed within a reasonable response time. In addition, data may have different structures, heterogeneous, or may be completely unstructured (e.g., multimedia and text documents).

Clustering: The technique that organizes data either as a grouping of individuals or as a hierarchy of groups. Ay object of the data is characterized as a set of attributes which in turn define the dimensionality of the data space. Objects that belong on the same cluster are alike, and objects of different clusters are no alike.

Data Mining: The process to extract valuable information from data sets. In other words, data analysis that can be used to increase the knowledge extracting and transforming the data of the data set.

Hadoop: Apache Hadoop is an open source software which provides a distributed file system (the Hadoop Distributed File System - HDFS) and a framework for the analysis and transformation of very large data sets (Big Data) using the MapReduce paradigm.

HDFS: The Hadoop Distributed File System is a scalable distributed file system (based on Google File System – GFS) developed for the Hadoop framework. One of the main characteristics (and difference) with other distributed file systems is that HDFS is designed to be deployed on commodity low cost hardware.

K-means: An algorithm which divides the objects of a data set to K different subsets subject to their similarity. The similarity can be measured in many ways and depends on the application. For example, the distance between objects could represent the similarity metric.

MapReduce: A programming model for parallel / distributed processing large amounts of data. Operates on two phases, the map and the reduce phase. During the map phase the problem to be solved is divided into smaller sub-problems which are executed in parallel. Then, the reduce phase combines the results derived from the map phase and this results the answer of the problem.

MPI: Message Passing Interface is a standardized API used for parallel or distributed computing. MPI implementations consist of a set of routines callable from C, C++, Java, FORTRAN, C#, Python etc.

SPMD: The Single Program Multiple Data (SPMD) is a parallel technique where the same set of instructions (program) is executed using different data sets (multiple data). The MapReduce technique is of this type where the same Map function is executed on different computer nodes containing different data sets. Then, the same Reduce function combines the results obtained by the Map function in order to solve the original problem.

Chapter 3
Synchronizing Execution of Big Data in Distributed and Parallelized Environments

Gueyoung Jung
Xerox Research Center Webster, USA

Tridib Mukherjee
Xerox Research Center India, India

ABSTRACT

In the modern information era, the amount of data has exploded. Current trends further indicate exponential growth of data in the future. This prevalent humungous amount of data—referred to as big data—has given rise to the problem of finding the "needle in the haystack" (i.e., extracting meaningful information from big data). Many researchers and practitioners are focusing on big data analytics to address the problem. One of the major issues in this regard is the computation requirement of big data analytics. In recent years, the proliferation of many loosely coupled distributed computing infrastructures (e.g., modern public, private, and hybrid clouds, high performance computing clusters, and grids) have enabled high computing capability to be offered for large-scale computation. This has allowed the execution of the big data analytics to gather pace in recent years across organizations and enterprises. However, even with the high computing capability, it is a big challenge to efficiently extract valuable information from vast astronomical data. Hence, we require unforeseen scalability of performance to deal with the execution of big data analytics. A big question in this regard is how to maximally leverage the high computing capabilities from the aforementioned loosely coupled distributed infrastructure to ensure fast and accurate execution of big data analytics. In this regard, this chapter focuses on synchronous parallelization of big data analytics over a distributed system environment to optimize performance.

DOI: 10.4018/978-1-4666-4699-5.ch003

INTRODUCTION

Dealing with the execution of big data analytics is more than just a buzzword or a trend. The data is being rapidly generated from many different sources such as sensors, social media, click-stream, log files, and mobile devices. Recently, collected data can exceed hundreds of terabytes and moreover, they are continuously generated from the sources. Such big data represents data sets that can no longer be easily analyzed with traditional data management methods and infrastructures (Jacobs, 2009; White, 2009; Kusnetzky, 2010). In order to promptly derive insight from big data, enterprises have to deploy big data analytics into an extraordinarily scalable delivery platform and infrastructure. The advent of on-demand use of vast computing infrastructure (e.g., clouds and computing grids) has been enabling enterprises to analyze such big data using with low resource usage cost.

A major challenge in this regard is figuring out how to effectively use the vast computing resources to maximize the performance of big data analytics. Using loosely coupled distributed systems (e.g., clusters in a data center or across data centers; public cloud with the internal clusters as hybrid cloud formation) is often better choice to parallelize the execution of big data analytics compared to using local centralized resources. Big data can be distributed over a set of loosely-coupled computing nodes. In each node, big data analytics can be performed on the portion of the data transferred to the node. This paradigm can be more flexible and has obvious cost benefits (Rozsnyai, 2011; Chen, 2011). It enables enterprises to maximally utilize their own computing resources and effectively utilize external computing resources that are further optimized for the big data processing.

However, contrary to common intuition, there is an inherent tradeoff between the level of parallelism and performance of big data analytics. This tradeoff is primarily caused by the significant delay for big data to get transferred to computing nodes. For example, when a big data analytics is run on a pool of inter-connected computing nodes in hybrid cloud (i.e., the mix of private and public clouds), it is often experienced that an extended period of data transfer delay is comparable or even higher than the time required to data computation itself. Additionally, the heterogeneity of computing nodes on computation time and data transfer delay can make the tradeoff issue being further complicated. The data transfer delay mostly depends on the location and network overhead of each computing node. A fast transfer of data chunks to a relatively slow computing node can cause data overflow, whereas a slow transfer of data chunks to a relatively fast computing node can lead to underflow causing the computing node to be idle (hence, leading to low resource utilization of the computing node).

This chapter focuses on optimally parallelizing big data analytics over such distributed heterogeneous computing nodes. Specifically, this chapter will discuss how to improve the advantage of parallelization by considering the time overlap *across computing nodes* as well as *between data transfer delay and data computation time* in each computing node. It should be noted here that the data transfer delay may be reduced by using data compression techniques (Plattner, 2009; Seibold, 2012). However, even with such reduction, overlapping the data transfer delay with the execution can reap benefits in the overall turnaround of the big data analytics. Ideally, the parallel execution should be designed in such a way that the execution of big data analytics at each computing node, including such data transfer and data computation, completes at near same time with other computing nodes.

This chapter will 1) discuss the performance issue of big data analytics in loosely-coupled distributed systems; 2) describe some solution approaches to address the issue; and 3) introduce a case study to demonstrate the effectiveness of the solution approaches using a real world big data analytics application on hybrid cloud environments. Readers of this chapter will have a clear picture of the importance of the issue, various approaches to address the issue, and a practical application of parallelism on the state-of-art management and processing of big data analytics over distributed systems. Specific emphasis of this chapter is on addressing the tradeoff between the performance and the level of parallelism of big data analytics in distributed and heterogeneous computing nodes separated by relatively high latencies. In order to optimize the performance of big data analytics, this chapter addresses the following concerns:

- **Autonomous Determination of Computing Nodes:** "How many" and "which" computing nodes in distributed environment such clouds should be used for parallel execution of big data analytics;
- **Synchronized Completion:** How to do opportunistic apportioning of big data to those computing nodes to ensure fast and synchronized completion (i.e., finishing the execution of all workload portions at the near same time) for best-effort performance;
- **Autonomous Determination for Data Serialization:** How to determine a sequence of data chunks (from the ones apportioned to each computing node) so that transfer of one chunk is overlapped as much as possible with the computation of previous chunks.

While unequal loads (i.e., data chunks) may be apportioned to the parallel computing nodes, it is important to make sure that outputs are produced at the near same time. Any single slow computing node should not act as a bottleneck of the overall execution of big data analytics. This chapter will demonstrate the synchronous parallelization with the aid of real experiences from a case study using a parallel frequent pattern mining task as a specific type of big data analytics. The input to the frequent

pattern mining is huge but outputs are far small. Parallel data mining typically consumes a lot of computing resources to analyze large amounts of unstructured data, especially when they are executed with a time constraint. The case study involves a deployment of the analytics on small multiple Hadoop MapReduce clusters in multiple heterogeneous computing nodes in clouds, where we consider each cluster and cloud as a computing node. Hadoop MapReduce is a typical and most commonly used programming framework to host big data analytics tasks over clouds. The case study would help readers further understand the concept, definitions, and approaches presented in this chapter.

The remainder of this chapter is organized as follows. First, the chapter will introduce some background for readers on loosely coupled distributed systems, scheduling and load balancing methodologies to apportion workload in distributed computing nodes, and handling big data over distributed systems. Second, the chapter will discuss the performance issues and key tradeoffs tackled in this chapter. Third, the chapter will describe how load balancing methodologies can be used toward synchronous parallelization. Fourth, the case study will be described to illustrate the approach. Finally, future research directions in this area will be outlined before the conclusion.

BACKGROUND

Loosely Coupled Distributed Systems

Loosely coupled distributed systems is a general term for collection of computers (a.k.a. nodes) interconnected by some networks. A node can be a single server, a cluster of servers (e.g., a Hadoop MapReduce cluster) in a data center, a data center with multiple clusters, or an entire cloud infrastructure (with multiple data centers) depending on the scale of the system. There are various different examples of loosely coupled distributed systems, and we provide a list of such systems to name a few in order to provide the proper context:

- **Computing Grids:** A federation of whole computers (with CPU, disk, memory, power supplies, network interfaces, etc.) used toward performing a common goal to solve single task. Such systems are special type of parallel computation systems, where the computing units can be heterogeneous, geographically far apart, and/or can transcend beyond a single network domain. It can be used to have parallelized processing of large-scale tasks as well as scavenging CPU cycles from resources shared as part of grid for large scientific tasks;
- **Computing Clusters:** Sets of loosely-connected or in many case tightly connected computers working together such that a cluster can itself be viewed as a single computing node. Computing clusters are more tightly coupled compared to computing grids. In most cases, a cluster is designed in a single rack (or across set of racks) in a single data center;
- **Computing Clouds:** Federations of computing servers hosted in a single data center or across multiple data centers that are offered to users based on virtualization middleware for remote access. Clouds can be private (i.e., the infrastructure is inside an enterprise and the offering are to the internal users), public (i.e., the infrastructure is available to all users through pay-per-use service offerings), or hybrid (i.e., a combination of private and public clouds);
- **Parallel Computing Systems:** Allow simultaneous execution of multiple tasks. All the aforementioned systems can be a form of parallel computing systems. However, by definitions parallel computing systems are typically tightly coupled (e.g., multi-core or multi-processor systems) where computing units (processors) may not be inter-connected through a networking interface. A most prominent example of parallel computing system can be found in High Performance Computing systems (HPC).

The major advantage of aforementioned systems is the amount of computation capability it can provide for any large-scale computation such as big data analytics. This chapter focuses on how to effectively use the computation capability in loosely couple distributed systems to optimize performance of big data analytics.

Loosely coupled distributed systems can be further homogeneous (i.e., all the inter-connected nodes having same configuration and capabilities) or heterogeneous (i.e., the inter-connected nodes can differ in configuration and/or capabilities). An example of homogeneous system can include a Hadoop MapReduce cluster comprising of same type of servers with same processor, memory, disk, and network configurations. An HPC system or a computing cloud with a set of such clusters can also be considered as a homogeneous system, since each cluster will be identical in their configuration and capabilities. The cluster can become heterogeneous if it does not consist of the same type of servers. Similarly, a cloud can be heterogeneous with different underlying clusters in it.

Many enterprises are recently focusing on building their cloud-based IT infrastructures by integrating multiple heterogeneous clouds including their own private clouds into a hybrid cloud, rather than relying on a single cloud. This hybrid cloud can be one of the most practical approaches for enterprises, since it can reduce the inherited risk of losing service availability and further improve cost-efficiency. In order to optimize the performance in such parallel heterogeneous environments, task or job schedulers with load balancing techniques have indeed become a recent norm (Maheswaran, 1999; Kailasam, 2010; Kim,

2011). Such techniques will be further discussed in the following sections. This chapter will then discuss how load balancing can be used for big data analytics. For general discussions, from now on we will assume heterogeneous systems over loosely coupled distributed environments. However, all the problems, issues, and approaches discussed can also be applicable to homogeneous systems over either loosely coupled or tightly coupled environments.

Task Scheduling in Distributed Systems

Distributing workload among nodes and executing big data analytics in parallel in loosely coupled distributed systems can obviously reap performance benefits. However, such benefits are contingent upon how effectively the big data workload is distributed across the nodes. This section reviews scheduling of workload (i.e., deciding in which order the incoming tasks need to be served) and in the following section, the assignment of load (i.e., deciding in which node tasks would be assigned) will be discussed.

Workload scheduling has been an on-going research topic in parallel and distributed systems for many decades. There are many various scheduling algorithms in distributed computing system. It is not feasible to enumerate all these scheduling algorithms, but the main focus of this chapter is to provide an account of the main operating principles and intuitions used. Many variations of the algorithms exist for different types of execution environments. However, the basic principle of assigning tasks to suitable nodes in suitable order remains similar. According to a simple classification, scheduling algorithms can be categorized into two main groups - batch scheduling algorithms and online algorithms. It should be noted that scheduling and allocation problems are generally NP-hard in nature, and heuristics solutions are more of a norm in practical system settings.

In either batch or online scheduling algorithms, tasks are queued and collected into a set when they arrive in the system. The scheduling algorithm executes in fixed intervals. Examples of such algorithms include First-Come-First-Served (FCFS), Round Robin (RR), Min–Min algorithm, Max–Min algorithm, and priority-based scheduling. In FCFS, task in queue which comes first is served first. This algorithm is simple and fast. In the round robin scheduling, processes are dispatched in a FIFO manner but are given a limited amount of time called a time-slice or a quantum. If a process does not complete before its time-slice expires, the task is preempted and the node is given to the next process waiting in the queue. The preempted task is then placed at the back of the queue. Min–Min algorithm chooses smaller tasks to be executed first. This however may incur long delays for large tasks. Max–Min algorithm goes to the other extreme and chooses larger tasks to be executed first; thus delaying the smaller tasks.

Most of these algorithms can be generalized into priority-based scheduling. The main intuition is to assign priority to tasks and the order of them as per their priority. In FCFS, the job coming first gets higher priority. Similarly in Max-Min algorithm, the larger tasks have higher priority. Big data scheduling can be thought of as a specialized batch scheduling algorithm, where the batch is the set of data (i.e., the big data) and the scheduling problem boils down to which data chunk to be activated upon first to optimize performance. For online scheduling, the decision making boils down to which nodes the tasks (or data) need to be assigned to and there are various algorithms in the literature (e.g., first-fit as assigning to first available node, and best-fit as assigning to the best available node based on some performance criteria).

In some distributed systems (e.g., computing grids), a hierarchical scheduling structure is employed with two main schedulers, local and grid schedulers. The local schedulers work in computational nodes mostly having homogeneous environment (Sharma, 2010), whereas grid schedulers (a.k.a. meta-schedulers) reside at the top level to orchestrate nodes managed by their respective local schedulers (Huedo, 2005). Scheduling can further be static or dynamic. In static scheduling, tasks are typically executed without interruption in the nodes where they are assigned. On the other hand, tasks may get rescheduled in dynamic scheduling; tasks' executions can be interrupted and they can be migrated to different nodes based on dynamic information on the workload and the nodes (Chtepen, 2005).

Load Balancing

Distribution of load across nodes, normally referred as load balancing, has been explored for all the systems mentioned in the previous section. Indeed, load balancing is a common research problem for parallel processing of workload in loosely coupled distributed systems (Li, 2005; Miyoshi, 2010; Patni, 2011; Tsafrir, 2007; Liu, 2011).

Load balancing generally involves distribution of service loads (e.g., application tasks or workload) to computing nodes to maximize performance (e.g., task throughput). Various algorithms have been designed and implemented in a number of studies (Casavant, 1994; Xu, 1997; Zaki, 1996). Load balancing decisions can be made a-priori when resource requirements for tasks are estimated. On the other hand, a multi-core computer with dynamic load balancing allocates resources at runtime based on no a-priori information. (Brunner, 1999) proposed a load balancing scheme to deal with interfering tasks in the context of clusters of workstations.

(Grosu, 2005) and (Penmatsa, 2005) considered static load balancing in a system with servers and computers where servers balance load among all computers in a round robin fashion. (Kamarunisha, 2011) discussed about load balancing

algorithm types and policies in computing grids. A good description of customized load balancing strategies for a network of workstations can be found in (Zaki, 1996). (Houle, 2002) focuses on algorithms for static load balancing assuming that the total load is fixed. (Yagoubi, 2006) and (Kumar, 2011) presented dynamic load balancing strategy for computing grids. (Patni 2011) provided an overview of static and dynamic load balancing mechanisms in computing grids.

The problem of both load balancing and scheduling in distributed systems can be formulated into a bin-packing problem. Bin-packing is a well-known combinatorial optimization problem that has been applied to many similar problems in computer science. The main idea of the bin-packing problem is to pack multiple objects of different volumes into a finite number of bins (or buckets) of same or different capacity in a way that minimizes the number of bins used. The bin-packing problem is known as NP-hard in nature, and there is no optimal solution with polynomial time to solve the problem. A task allocation problem can be generally reduced to the bin-packing problem, and usually heuristics algorithms are developed to address the problem in various settings. Depending on the objective to be optimized, bins (or buckets) along with their respective capacities (i.e., bucket sizes) and objects to be packed to bins need to be designed carefully to cater to the specific problem settings. We will discuss how the data apportioning problem can be reduced to the bin-packing problem later in this chapter.

(Buyya, 1999) described load balancing for HPC clusters. Cloud friendly load balancing of HPC applications has been explored in (Sarood, 2012). Although the term of load balancing may suggest that equal amount of workload is distributed across the computing nodes, it is not the case often. (Sarood, 2012) used different parameters to distribute workload. This chapter focuses on distributing big data workload among distributed nodes based on performance and network parameters. Such distribution may incur cost and delay overheads in many systems.

Impact of Data Communication

Impact of the data transfer delay on performance, when loads are redirected to multiple computing nodes, has been considered to be an important problem recently (Fan, 2011; Andreolini, 2008). (Foster, 2008) compared the cloud and grid computing with light of how data transfer can become an issue for loosely coupled distributed systems because of the communication overhead. The problem further gets exacerbated when loads involve big data. This chapter provides an account on the distribution of big data over distributed computing nodes that can be separated far apart. In this setting, the overhead of the data transfer can be significant, since network latencies may be high between computing nodes due to the amount of data being transferred. Hence, the conventional notion of performance improvement through parallelization may not hold once the data transfer becomes a bottleneck.

It is beneficial if the data transfer to a computing node can be serialized, when some previous data is being processed in the computing node, to improve performance. Serialization of data transfers with instruction execution is an important feature for many-core architectures (Miyoshi, 2010). However, such serialization is restricted by a pre-defined order of instruction sets. Meanwhile, overlapping of data transfer and data computation has been identified as an important requirement for load balancing in computing clusters (Reid, 2000). Data compression techniques (Plattner, 2009; Seibold, 2012) can be used to reduce data transfer and associated overhead. However, the overlapping of data transfer and computation can still be beneficial in order to reduce the impact of any transfer delay on the end-to-end execution or turn-around time.

Platforms for Parallel Processing of Big Data

There are various existing platforms to execute big data applications on distributed systems. Google introduced the MapReduce programming model (Dean, 2004) for processing big data. MapReduce enables splitting of big data across multiple parallel map tasks, and the outputs are later merged by reduce tasks. Often map and reduce tasks are executed across massively distributed nodes for performance benefits (Chen, 2011; Huang, 2011). Apache implemented the MapReduce model in the Hadoop open source and free distribution. Another related framework is Apache GoldenOrb, which allows massive-scale graph analysis and built upon Hadoop. Open source Storm framework has also been developed at Twitter. It is often referred to as real-time Hadoop since it is a real-time, distributed, fault-tolerant, computation system; whereas Hadoop generally relies on batch processing.

Hadoop implementation operates on a distributed file system that stores the big-data and its intermediate data in the big-data processing. Many scheduling strategies for MapReduce cluster have been integrated (e.g., FIFO scheduler (Bryant, 2007), LATE scheduler (Zaharia, 2008), Capacity scheduler and Fair scheduler). Fair scheduling is a method of assigning resources to tasks such that all tasks get, on average, an equal share of resources over time. Fair-scheduling has also been used in Hadoop. Unlike the default scheduler of Hadoop, which forms a queue of tasks, fair scheduling lets short tasks complete within a reasonable time without starving long-running tasks. A major issue in all these frameworks is how to effectively reduce the impact of large data transfer delay (caused by communication overhead of big data across nodes) in the overall execution time of tasks.

One way to address the high data transfer latency is using only local cluster having high computation power with dynamic resource provisioning (Alves, 2011). However, distribution among federated private and public clouds can be more flexible and has obvious cost benefits (Rozsnyai, 2011; Chen, 2011). This chapter discusses how load balancing can be precisely used for the distributed parallel applications dealing with potentially big data such as the continuous data stream analysis (Chen, 2011) and the life pattern extraction for healthcare applications in federated clouds (Huang, 2011). To achieve the optimal performance of big data analytics, it is imperative to determine "how many" and "which computing nodes" are required, and then, how to apportion given big data to those chosen computing nodes.

PROBLEMS IN DEALING WITH BIG DATA OVER DISTRIBUTED SYSTEMS

The input big data to an analytics algorithm (e.g., a log file containing users' web transactions) is typically collected in a central place over a certain period (e.g., daily, weekly, monthly, or yearly), and is processed by the analytics algorithm to generate an output (e.g., frequent user behavior patterns). To execute analytics algorithm in multiple computing nodes for given big data, the big data needs to be first divided into a certain number of data chunks

(e.g., log files of individual user groups), and those data chunks are transferred to computing nodes separately. Before discussing on how to select computing nodes and how to apportion big data to these computing nodes, we first discuss some fundamental problems in this section.

Performance and Parallelism Tradeoff

Intuitively, as the number of computing nodes increases, the overall data computation time can decrease. However, as the amount of data chunks to be transferred to computing nodes increases, the overall data transfer delay can increase. As shown in Figure 1, the overall execution time, which consists of the data computation time and the data transfer delay, can start to increase if we use more than a certain number of computing nodes. This is because the delay taken to transfer data chunks starts to dominate the overall execution time.

The problem can be addressed by identifying the optimal number of computing nodes through exploration from a single computing node, and increasing the number of computing nodes one at a time. At each step, the best set of computing

Figure 1. The change of the overall execution time as the number of parallel computing nodes increases

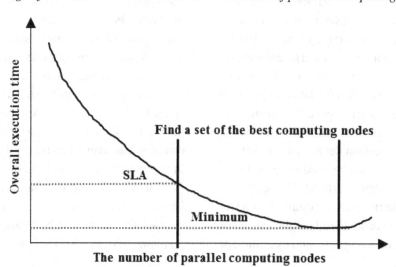

nodes among all possible combinations of computing nodes can be identified by estimating the data transfer delay and the data computation time of each computing node for given big data. The problem can however be even more exacerbated if the data executed in parallel needs to be synchronized at the end. The performance in such a case will depend on the slowest computing node.

To minimize the impact of data synchronization toward optimizing performance, it is needed to understand the characteristics of the input data before designing the parallel process. For example, in case of mining frequent user behavior patterns from web transaction log files, the input data is usually in temporal order and mixed with many users' web transaction activities. To generate frequent behavior patterns of each individual user (i.e., extract personalized information from the big data), the given big data can be divided into *user groups as a set of data chunks*. Distributing and executing individual user data in different computing nodes, which have different computing and network capacities, can reduce the data synchronization, since these data chunks are usually *independent* of each other. Then, the problem can be casted into a typical load balancing problem

as shown in Figure 2 that maximizes the time overlap across computing nodes and thereby, completes the execution at the near same time (i.e., synchronization).

Performance Bottlenecks: Data Overflow and Data Underflow

Capabilities of network channels and computing nodes determine if there is any performance bottleneck while parallelizing big data analytics. It should be noted that a fast transfer of data chunks to a relatively slow computing node can cause *data overflow*, whereas a slow transfer of data chunks to a relatively fast computing node can lead to *data underflow* causing the computing node to be idle over the time.

Overlapping between the data transfer delay and the data computation time as much as possible is thus imperative while distributing data chunks to computing nodes. As shown in Figure 3, ideally, the goal should be to select a data chunk that takes the same amount of delay to be transferred to a computing node with the computation time of the computing node with the previous data chunk.

Figure 2. Data allocation to computing nodes in clouds having different capacities

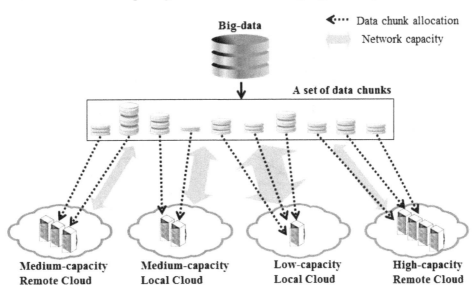

Figure 3. Ideal time overlap between data transfer and data computation in a single computing node

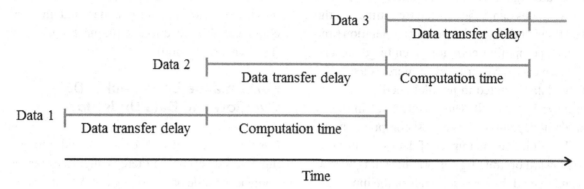

Practically, this overlap can be maximized by ensuring that the difference between the data computation time and the data transfer time (of following data chunk) is as low as possible. This chapter discusses how the performance can be optimized by maximizing the time overlap not only across computing nodes via a load balancing technique, but also between the data transfer delay and the data computation time in each computing node, simultaneously.

SYNCHRONOUS PARALLELIZATION THROUGH LOAD BALANCING

In the problem of the big data load distribution to parallel computing nodes as shown in Figure 4, each individual data chunk (i.e., L_i) is considered as the object to be packed, and the capacity of each computing node (i.e., n_i) including *both computation and network capacities* is considered as the bin.

Figure 4. Bin-packing with different sizes of data chunks and computing nodes

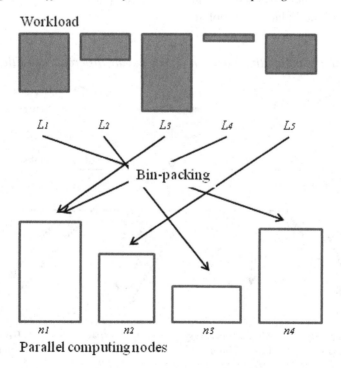

More specifically, the principal objective to maximize the performance using a federation of heterogeneous computing nodes would be to minimize the execution time difference among computing nodes by optimally apportioning given data chunks into these computing nodes. In other words, the time overlaps across these computing nodes need to be maximized when a big data analytics is performed. A heuristic bin-packing algorithm can be used for data apportioning in federated computing nodes by incorporating: weighted load distribution, which involves loading to a computing node based on its overall delay (i.e., the computing node with lower delay gets more data to handle); and delay-based computing node preference to ensure larger data chunks are assigned to a computing node with larger bucket size (i.e., with lower overall delay) so that individual data chunks get fairness in their overall delay.

It is imperative to have good estimates of data transfer delay and data computation time in each computing node to efficiently perform the apportioning. Many estimation techniques have been introduced for the data computation time and the data transfer delay such as response surface model (Kailasam, 2010) and queuing model (Jung, 2009). The data computation time of each computing node can be profiled to create an initial model, which can then be tuned based on observations over the time. The data transfer delay between different computing nodes can be more dynamic than the data computation time because of various factors such as network congestions and re-routing due to network failures. Estimating data transfer delay can be performed using auto-regressive moving average (ARMA) filter (Jung, 2009; Box, 1994) by periodically profiling the network latency. Periodic injection of a small size of unit data to the target computing node and recording the corresponding delay can allow for reasonable and up to date profiling of the network latency. We also assume that the larger data chunk needs the more computation

time and data transfer delay in this chapter. As mentioned in (Tian, 2011), this assumption can be applicable to many big data analytics applications. For some special cases, these estimates must be carefully modeled to improve the accuracy of the overall approach.

Based on the estimates of the data transfer delay and the data computation time in each computing node, there are two steps for maximizing performance through parallelization over federated computing nodes:

- **Maximal Overlapping of Data Processing:** Involves decision makings on "how many" and "which" computing nodes are used for data apportioning; and
- **Maximal Overlapping of Data Transfer & Data Computation:** Involves decision making on how to apportion data in the selected computing nodes so that overall performance is maximized through serializing of data transfer with data computation in each computing node.

The following sections discuss these two steps in detail.

Maximal Overlapping of Data Processing

A set of parallel computing nodes are chosen that have shorter execution time d than other candidate computing nodes. Figure 5 shows how those computing nodes are selected from a set of candidate computing nodes, based on estimates of the data transfer delay t to each computing node and the computing node's computation time e for the data assigned. The estimation is assumed to be using the unit of data (i.e., a fixed size of data) periodically. Those candidate computing nodes are sorted by the total estimate (i.e., $t + e$), and each computing node is added to the execution pool N if required. The procedure starts by considering the execution time with a single computing

Figure 5. The overview of computing node selection procedure

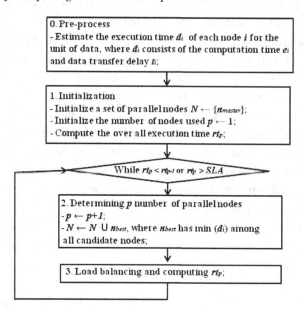

node n_{master}, which can be the central computing node where the big data is initially submitted for processing. One extreme case can be only using n_{master} if the estimated execution time meets the exit condition.

If Service Level Agreement (SLA) exists to specify the goal such as a low-bound of execution time, SLA can be used for the exit condition. Otherwise, an optimal execution time can be used for the condition. More specifically, if SLA cannot be met using the current set of parallel computing nodes (i.e., $rt_p > SLA$), or the overall execution time can be further reduced by utilizing more nodes (i.e., $rt_p < rt_{p-1}$), then the level of parallelization is increased by adding one computing node into the pool N. The newly added computing node is the best computing node that has the minimum delay (i.e., $t + e$ which is estimated periodically) among all candidate computing nodes. Once the set of parallel computing nodes is determined from the above step, one of load balancing techniques mentioned in the prior section can be applied to the distribution of given big data. In this chapter, a specific load balancing technique using a bin-packing algorithm, referred to as Maximally Overlapped Bin-packing (MOB), is performed that attempts to maximize the time overlap across these computing nodes and the time overlap between data transfer delay and data computation time in each computing node.

Figure 6 illustrates two main steps for data distribution to computing nodes:

- **Data Apportioning:** This involves: (a) the determination of bucket size for each computing node; (b) sorting of data chunks in descending order of their sizes; and (c) sorting computing node buckets in descending order of their sizes. The buckets' sizes are determined in a way that a computing node with higher delay will have lower bucket size. Then sorting of buckets essentially boils down to giving higher preference to computing nodes which have lower delay. The sorted list of data chunks are assigned to computing node buckets in a way that larger data chunks are handled by computing nodes with lower delay (i.e., higher preference). Any fragmentation of the bucket is handled in this step;

Figure 6. Steps to allocate data chunks to computing nodes

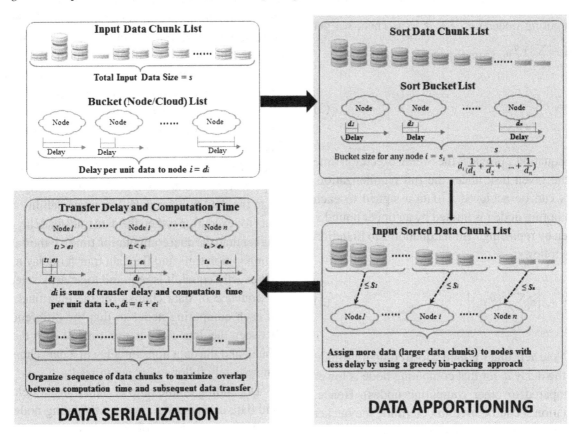

- **Serialization of Apportioned Data:** After the data chunks are assigned to the buckets, this step organizes the sequence of data chunks for each bucket such that the data transfer delay and data computation time are overlapped maximally.

Specifically, in data apportioning step, this approach intends to parallelize the given task by dividing input big data to multiple computing nodes. If the delay of the task for a unit of data on a computing node i is denoted as d_i then the overall delay of a data s_i (that is provided to node i for the given task) would be: *delay per unit data to the node* multiplied by *amount of data assigned to the node* (i.e., $s_i d_i$). Ideally, in order to ensure parallelization, for the set of computing nodes, $1, 2, \ldots, n$, the size of data to be assigned to each computing node, $s_1, s_2, \ldots, s_n$ should be, $s_1 d_1 = s_2 d_2 = s_3 d_3 = \ldots = s_n d_n$, where $d_1, d_2, \ldots, d_n$ are the delay per unit of data at each computing node, respectively. The delay per unit data is defined as the turnaround time (including data transfer and computation) when one data unit is assigned to a computing node. After such assignment, if the overall turnaround time of the given task (i.e., for all data assigned to a node) is assumed to be r, then the size of data assigned to each computing node would be as follows:

$$s_i = r / d_i, \text{ where } 1 \le i \le n \quad (1)$$

assuming full parallelization (i.e., the apportioning of data is ideal and all the nodes will be synchronous and complete execution together after the time r). Now, let s be the total amount of n input data, which are distributed to each computing node (i.e., $s = \sum_{i=1}^{n} s_i$). Then, we get $s = r \cdot \sum_{i=1}^{n} 1/d_i$ from Equation 1, and:

$$r = s / \sum_{i=1}^{n} 1/d_i \qquad (2)$$

Equation 2 provides the overall execution time of the given task under the full parallelization. This can be achieved if data assigned to each computing node i is limited by an upper bound s_i given by replacing r from Equation 2 to Equation 1 as follows:

$$s_i = s / \left(d_i \sum_{i=1}^{n} (1/d_i) \right) \qquad (3)$$

Note here that s_i is higher for a computing node i if the delay d_i for that computing node is lower (compared to other computing nodes). Hence, Equation 3 can be used to determine the bucket size for each computing node in a way where higher preference is given to computing nodes with lower delay. Once the bucket sizes are determined, the next step involves assigning the data chunks to the computing node buckets. A greedy bin-packing approach can be used where the largest data chunks are assigned to computing nodes with lowest delay (hence, reducing the overall delay), as shown in Figure 6. To reduce fragmentation of buckets, the buckets are completely filled one at a time (i.e., the bucket with lowest delay will be first exhausted followed by the next one and so on). This approach also enables to fill more data to computing nodes with lower delay.

Once data chunks are apportioned for computing nodes, our approach organizes the sequence of data chunks to each computing node. The previous step achieves the parallelization of the given task over a large set of data chunks. However, the delay d_i for unit of data to run on computing node

i can be explained by data transfer delay from the central computing node to computing node i and actual data computation time on computing node i. Therefore, it is possible to further reduce the overall execution time by transferring data to a computing node in parallel with execution on a different data chunk. Ideally, the data transfer delay of a data chunk should be exactly equal to the data computation time on previous data chunk. Otherwise, there can be a delay incurred by queuing (when the data computation time is higher than the data transfer delay) or unavailability of data for execution (when the data transfer delay is higher than the data computation time). If the data computation time and the data transfer delay are not exactly equal, it is required to smartly select a sequence of data chunks for the data bucket of each computing node, so that the difference between the data computation time of each data chunk and the data transfer delay of a data chunk immediately following is minimized.

Depending on the ratio of data transfer delay and data computation time, a computing node i can be categorized as follows:

- **Type 1:** For which the data transfer delay t_i per a unit of data is higher than the data computation time e_i per a unit of data;
- **Type 2:** For which the data computation time e_i per a unit of data is higher than the data transfer delay t_i per a unit of data.

It is important to understand the required characteristics of the sequence of data chunks sent to each of these types of computing nodes. If s_{ij} and $s_{i(j+1)}$ are the size of data chunk j and $(j+1)$ assigned to computing node i, then for complete parallelization of the data transfer of chunk $(j+1)$ and the data computation of j, it can said that $s_{i(j+1)}t_i = s_{ij}e_i$. It should be noted here that if $t_i \geq e_i$, then ideally $s_{i(j+1)} < s_{ij}$. Thus, data chunks in the bucket for type 1 computing node should be in descending order of their sizes. Similarly, it can be concluded that for a computing node of type 2, data chunks should be in ascending order, as shown in the last step in Figure 6 and ensured at the end of the approach (where descending order of data chunks is reversed to make the order ascending in case $t_i < e_i$).

The following pseudo code (Algorithm 1) summarizes the above data apportioning and data serialization with the heuristic bin-packing approach (i.e., MOB).

CASE STUDY

This section shows the efficacy of the solution approach (presented in previous section) using a case study where a frequent pattern mining task with big data is deployed into a federation of four different computing nodes, three of which are local clusters located in the northeastern part of US, and one is a remote cluster located in the mid-western part of US. We first describe details of the frequent pattern mining application and the federated computing nodes followed by some evaluation results in details.

Frequent Pattern Mining Application

Frequent pattern mining (Srikant, 1996) aims to extract frequent patterns from log files. A typical example of the log file is a web server access log, which contains a history of web page accesses from users. Enterprises need to analyze such web server access logs to discover valuable information such as web site traffic patterns and user behavior patterns in web sites by time of day, time of week, time of month, or time of year. These frequent patterns can also be used to generate rules to predict future activity of *a certain user* within a certain time interval based on the user's past patterns.

Algorithm 1. Maximal Overlapped Bin-packing

```
Sort DataChunkList by descending order of data chunk size
Determine bucket size, s_1, s_2, s_3, ..., s_n (Equation 1)
Sort BucketList by descending order of bucket size
Repeat
    For i = 1 to n do
        Remove first element from DataChunkList
        Insert the element to tail of BucketList[i]
        For j = 1 to remaining number of DataChunks do
            If (BucketList[i] is not empty) and (first element in DataChunkList can fit in BucketList[i]) then
                Remove first element from DataChunkList
                Insert the element to tail of BucketList[i]
            End if
        End for
    End for
Until all the BucketLists are full
For i = 1 to number of Computing nodes do
    If t_i < e_i then
        Reverse order of data chunks in BucketList[i]
    End if
End for
```

In the scenario, we further combine a phone call log obtained from a call center with the web access log on a human resource system (HRS) accessed by more than a hundred of thousands of users. The log contains data for a year including several millions of user activities, and the data size is up to 1.2 TB. The frequent pattern mining obtains patterns of each user's activities in the mix of the exploration on HRS web site and phone calls for HR issues such as 401K and retirement plan. As such, the log can be first divided into a set of user log files, each of which is the data chunk representing the log of a single HRS user and then, these user log files can be executed in parallel over the federation of heterogeneous computing nodes.

A Federation of Heterogeneous Computing Nodes

One local computing node, referred to as a Low-end Local Central (LLC) node, is used as a central computing node, where big data is submitted for frequent pattern mining task. This computing node consists of 5 virtual machines (VMs), each of which has two 2.8 GHz CPU cores, 1 GB memory, and 1 TB hard drive. The data computation time is high in LLC than other computing nodes, while there is no data transfer delay. Another local computing node, referred to as a Low-end Local Worker (LLW) node, has the similar configuration and data computation time with LLC. We have set up LLW to simulate the data transfer delay between LLC and LLW by intentionally injecting a delay. The third local computing node, referred to as a High-end Local Worker (HLW) node, is a cluster that has 6 non-virtualized servers, each of which has 24 2.6 GHz CPU cores, 48 GB memory, and 10 TB hard drive. HLW is shared by other three data mining tasks other than the frequent pattern mining task. HLW has the lowest data computation time among all the computing nodes, and the data transfer delay

between LLC and HLW is very low. The remote computing node, referred to as a Mid-end Remote Worker (MRW) node, has 9 VMs, each of which has two 2.8 GHz CPU cores, 4 GB memory, and 1 TB hard drive. MRW has a lower data computation time than LLC. However, the overall execution time is similar to LLC due to the large data transfer delay. Hadoop MapReduce is deployed into each of these computing nodes. Figure 7 shows each computing node's performance characteristics in the context of data computation time and data transfer delay. We have measured those values by deploying the frequent pattern mining into each computing node and executing it with the entire log files. For example, to figure out the ratio of data computation time and transfer delay in MRW, we have measured the data transfer delay by moving the entire log files into MRW, and measured the data computation time by executing the frequent pattern mining only in MRW. As shown in Figure 7, MRW has higher transfer delay than other computing nodes, and it is very close to the data computation time of MRW (but slightly lower than the data computation time).

Parallel Processing for Frequent Pattern Mining

Figure 8 outlines the main phases of the parallel pattern mining. For given big data (i.e., log files of HRS web site access log and HRS call center

Figure 7. Performance characteristics of different computing nodes

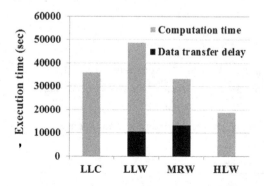

Figure 8. The overview of parallel patterning mining phases

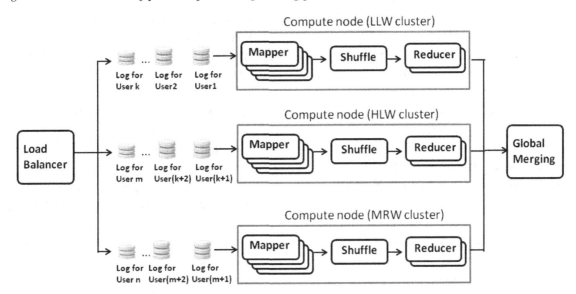

log), the load balancer divides it into multiple data chunks, each of which represents a log file containing a single user's site access log and phone call log. In the phase of parallel data processing, data chunks are sent to MapReduce system in each computing node one by one and executed in the node. Since each data chunk contains a single user log data, all data chunks can be independently processed in parallel in computing nodes. Therefore, in this case, we need a single global merging phase to combine all patterns of individual users and generate the overall view of patterns. However, since the number of data chunks is much larger than the number of computing nodes, we can also combine multiple data chunks into a single larger data chunks and then, MapReduce system in each computing node processes the data chunk in parallel. In this case, we need a local merging phase at the end of each MapReduce process. We omit this local merging in Figure 8.

Impact of Data Transfer Delay on Overall Execution Time

As shown in Figure 9, the execution time increases exponentially as the data size increases. This ex-

Figure 9. Impact of data transfer delay on the overall execution time

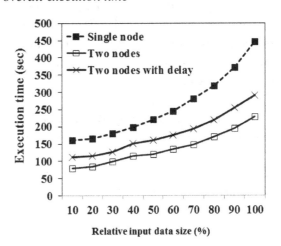

plains the need of parallel execution of such big data analytics to improve the performance. When using two computing nodes (i.e., LLC and LLW in this case) without the data transfer delay, the execution time decreases by almost half. However, when the frequent pattern mining is executed with the data transfer delay (when transfer delays are injected into LLW), the execution time is higher, and the difference in execution time increases as the data size increases. Therefore, it is important to deal with the data transfer delay carefully. To control the data size in this experiment, we have used the different amount of each individual data chunk (i.e., selected 10% to 100% of each original data chunk). This experiment also explains that the size of data chunk can be strongly related to the data transfer delay and data computation time in the pattern mining algorithm.

Effectiveness of Federated Heterogeneous Computing Nodes

As shown in Figure 10, the execution time decreases as computing nodes are added. However, the execution time is not significantly improved by using all four computing nodes compared to using two computing nodes (i.e., LLC and HLW). This is because the contributions of MRW and LLW to the performance are small, and the data transfer delays of MRW and LLW starts to impact the overall execution time. Therefore, using two computing nodes can be better choice rather than using four computing nodes that needs higher resource usage cost.

Comparison of MOB with Other Load Balancing Approaches

We run the frequent pattern mining task using Maximally Overlapped Bin-packing (MOB) and other three different methods that have been used in many prior load balancing approaches (Miyoshi, 2010; Fan, 2011; Andreolini, 2008; Reid, 2000; Kim, 2011) and then, compare the results. Methods used in this comparison are as follows:

- **Fair Division:** This method divides the input big data into data chunks and equally distributes those data chunks to computing nodes. We use this as a naive method to show as a baseline performance;
- **Computation-Based Division:** This method only considers the data computation power of each computing node when it performs load balancing (i.e., distributes data chunks to compute nodes based on the computation time of each computing node), rather than considering both data computation time and data transfer delay;
- **Delay-Based Division:** This method considers both data computation time and data transfer delay in load balancing. However, it does not consider the time overlap between the data transfer delay and the data computation time.

Figure 11 shows the result when we run the frequent pattern mining task in HLW and MRW. As evident from the results in Figure 11, MOB can

Figure 10. Impact of using multiple computing nodes on execution time

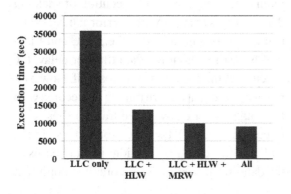

Figure 11. Comparison of MOB with different load balancing approaches

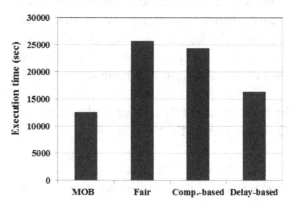

achieve at least 20% (and up to 60%) improvement compared to the other approaches. Since MRW has large data transfer delay, the execution time of Computation-based division is very close to the Fair division. Although Computation-based division considers the data computation powers of MRW and HLW for load balancing, MRW becomes a bottleneck due to its large data transfer delay. Delay-division considers both the data computation time and the data transfer delay. This significantly reduces the bottleneck. However, small data chunks are cumulated in the queues of computing nodes, until data computation of previous large data chunk is completed. Additionally, while large data chunks are transferred to MRW, small data chunks are computed earlier and then, MRW is often idle. This may incur a significant extra delay. MOB considers the maximal overlapping of data transfer delay and data computation time and thereby, achieves further reduction in execution time.

We have also conducted another experiment to see the impact of the data chunk size on the overall execution time. The size of data chunk is determined by the number of combined log files (i.e., the original data chunks) in this experiment. This can be empirically determined and then, user can provide the right number as a parameter of the system. As shown in Figure 12, the execution time slightly increases as the size increases. This is because the effectiveness of load balancing decreases as the load balancing gets coarser grained. Moreover, this coarse granularity makes the impact of overflow and underflow on execution time being even worse in Fair and Delay-based approaches, since the size difference between data chunks increases. However, it does not significantly affect the execution time of MOB, since the size difference in MOB is less than one in Fair and Delay-based approaches. When the small size of data chunk is used, the execution time slightly increases as well in MOB and Delay-based approaches. This is because a small amount of delay incurs when each data chunk is transferred to the node, and the node prepares the data execution. As the size of data chunk decreases, the number of data chunks transferred increases.

FUTURE RESEARCH DIRECTIONS

Load balancing techniques such as Maximally Overlapped Bin-packing (MOB) algorithm can efficiently handle data-intensive tasks (e.g., big

Figure 12. Impact of the number of combined log files on the overall execution time

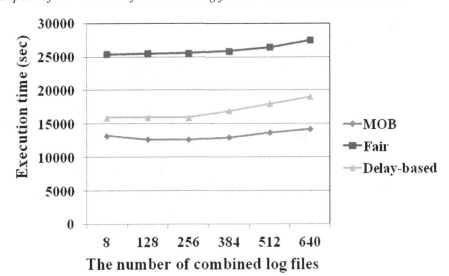

data analytics) that typically require special platforms and infrastructures (e.g., Hadoop MapReduce cluster) and especially, can run in parallel, when the target task can be divided into a set of independent identical sub-tasks. For the frequent pattern mining task used in the case study, the input big data can be divided into a set of data chunks. Then, each data chunk can be run independently in parallel computing nodes without the need for any synchronization until the task is completed. However, if the big data may not be divided into fully independent data chunks, such tasks may require an iterative algorithm, where data transfer should occur just once from a central node to computing nodes but the data computation is run multiple times on the same data chunk. In this case, those tasks may require multiple times of data transfer among computing nodes. Running these tasks across federated computing nodes in clouds may not be practical, since these tasks may require considerable synchronization among computing nodes and thereby, require considerable delay for transferring data before being completed (e.g., merging and redistributing intermediate results iteratively). Extending the performance benefits through parallel processing for such tasks is an open research issue.

The decision making of MOB is based on the current status of network and computation capacities. However, the status can change dynamically due to various unexpected events such as computing node failures and network congestions, while sorting computing nodes based on the earlier status. One of possible solutions can be that MOB periodically checks the available data computation capacities and network delays of computing nodes. Another possible solution can be that distributed monitoring systems can push events into MOB, when the status is significantly changed. In either case, the status change triggers MOB to re-sort computing nodes and re-target the sequence of remaining data chunks into the next available computing nodes.

CONCLUSION

In this chapter, we have described how the performance of big data analytics can be maximized through synchronous parallelization over federated, heterogeneous computing nodes in clouds that are a loosely-coupled and distributed computing environment. More specifically, this chapter have discussed: (a) how many and which computing nodes in clouds should be used; (b) an approach for the opportunistic apportioning of big data to these computing nodes in a way to enable synchronized completion; and (c) an approach for the sequence of apportioned data chunks to be computed in each computing node so that the transfer of a data chunk is overlapped as much as possible with the data computation of the previous data chunk in the computing node. Then, we have showed the efficacy of the solution approach using a case study, where a frequent pattern mining task with big data is deployed into a federation of heterogeneous computing nodes in clouds.

REFERENCES

Alves, D., Bizarro, P., & Marques, P. (2011). Deadline queries: Leveraging the cloud to produce on-time results. In *Proceedings of International Conference on Cloud Computing* (pp. 171–178). IEEE.

Andreolini, M., Casolari, S., & Colajanni, M. (2008). Autonomic request management algorithms for geographically distributed internet-based systems. In *Proceedings of International Conference on Self-Adaptive and Self-Organizing Systems* (pp. 171–180). IEEE.

Box, G., Jenkins, G., & Reinsel, G. (1994). *Time series analysis: Forecasting and control*. Upper Saddle River, NJ: Prentice Hall.

Brunner, R. K., & Kale, L. V. (1999) Adapting to load on workstation clusters. In *Proceedings of the Symposium on the Frontiers of Massively Parallel Computation* (pp. 106–112). IEEE.

Bryant, R. E. (2007). *Data-intensive supercomputing: The case for DISC[R]* (CMU Technical Report CMU-CS-07-128). Pittsburgh, PA: Department of Computer Science, Carnegie Mellon University.

Buyya, R. (1999). *High performance cluster computing: Architectures and systems* (Vol. 1). Upper Saddle River, NJ: Prentice Hall.

Casavant, T. L., & Kuhl, J. G. (1994). A taxonomy of scheduling in general purpose distributed computing systems. *Transactions on Software Engineering*, *14*(2), 141–153. doi:10.1109/32.4634.

Chen, Q., Hsu, M., & Zeller, H. (2011). Experience in continuous analytics as a service. In *Proceedings of International Conference on Extending Database Technology* (pp. 509-514). IEEE.

Chtepen, M. (2005). Dynamic scheduling in grids system. In *Proceedings of the PhD Symposium*. Ghent, Belgium: Faculty of Engineering, Ghent University.

Dean, J., & Ghemawat, S. (2004). MapReduce: Simplified data processing on large clusters. In *Proceedings of the Symposium on Operating System Design and Implementation* (pp. 107-113). ACM.

Fan, P., Wang, J., Zheng, Z., & Lyu, M. (2011). Toward optimal deployment of communication-intensive cloud applications. In *Proceedings of International Conference on Cloud Computing* (pp. 460–467). IEEE.

Foster, I., Zhao, Y., Raicu, I., & Lu, S. (2008). Cloud computing and grid computing 360-degree compared. In *Proceedings of the Grid Computing Environments Workshop* (pp. 1-10). IEEE.

Grosu, D., & Chronopoulos, A. T. (2005). Noncooperative load balancing in distributed systems. *Journal of Parallel and Distributed Computing*, *65*(9), 1022–1034. doi:10.1016/j.jpdc.2005.05.001.

Houle, M., Symnovis, A., & Wood, D. (2002). Dimension-exchange algorithms for load balancing on trees. In *Proceedings of International Colloquium on Structural Information and Communication Complexity* (pp. 181–196). IEEE.

Huang, Y., Ho, Y., Lu, C., & Fu, L. (2011). A cloud-based accessible architecture for large-scale ADL analysis services. In *Proceedings of International Conference on Cloud Computing* (pp. 646–653). IEEE.

Huedo, E., Montero, R. S., & Llorente, I. M. (2005). The GridWay framework for adaptive scheduling and execution on grids. *Scalable Computing: Practice and Experience*, *6*, 1–8.

Jacobs, A. (2009). *The pathologies of big data*. Retrieved July 1, 2009, from http://queue.acm.org/detail.cfm?id=1563874

Jung, G., Joshi, K., Hiltunen, M., Schlichting, R., & Pu, C. (2009). A cost sensitive adaptation engine for server consolidation of multi-tier applications. In *Proceedings of International Conference on Middleware* (pp. 163–183). ACM/IFIP/USENIX.

Kailasam, S., Gnanasambandam, N., Dharanipragada, J., & Sharma, N. (2010). Optimizing service level agreements for autonomic cloud bursting schedulers. In *Proceedings of International Conference on Parallel Processing Workshops* (pp. 285–294). IEEE.

Kamarunisha, M., Ranichandra, S., & Rajagopal, T.K.P. (2011). Recitation of load balancing algorithms in grid computing environment using policies and strategies an approach. *International Journal of Scientific & Engineering Research, 2*.

Kim, H., & Parashar, M. (2011). CometCloud: An autonomic cloud engine. In *Cloud Computing: Principles and Paradigms*. Hoboken, NJ: Wiley. doi:10.1002/9780470940105.ch10.

Kumar, U.K. (2011). A dynamic load balancing algorithm in computational grid using fair scheduling. *International Journal of Computer Science Issues, 8*.

Kusnetzky, D. (2010). *What is big data?* Retrieved February 16, 2010, from http://blogs.zdnet.com/virtualization/?p=1708

Li, Y., & Lan, Z. (2005). A survey of load balancing in grid computing. *Computational and Information Science, 3314*, 280–285. doi:10.1007/978-3-540-30497-5_44.

Liu, Z., Lin, M., Wierman, A., Low, S., & Andrew, L. (2011). Greening geographical load balancing. In *Proceedings of SIGMETRICS Joint Conference on Measurement and Modelling of Computer Systems* (pp. 233–244). ACM.

Maheswaran, M., Ali, S., Siegal, H., Hensgen, D., & Freund, R. (1999). Dynamic matching and scheduling of a class of independent tasks onto heterogeneous computing systems. In *Proceedings of Heterogeneous Computing Workshop* (pp. 30–44). IEEE.

Miyoshi, T., Kise, K., Irie, H., & Yoshinaga, T. (2010). Codie: Continuation based overlapping data-transfers with instruction execution. In *Proceedings of International Conference on Networking and Computing* (pp. 71-77). IEEE.

Patni, J. C., Aswal, M. S., Pal, O. P., & Gupta, A. (2011). Load balancing strategies for Grid computing. In *Proceedings of the International Conference on Electronics Computer Technology* (Vol. 3, pp. 239–243). IEEE.

Penmatsa, S., & Chronopoulos, A. T. (2005). Job allocation schemes in computational Grids based on cost optimization. In *Proceedings of 19th International Parallel and Distributed Processing Symposium*. IEEE.

Plattner, H. (2009). A common database approach for OLTP and OLAP using an in-memory column database. In *Proceedings of the SIGMOD Conference*. ACM.

Reid, K., & Stumm, M. (2000). *Overlapping data transfer with application execution on clusters*. Paper presented at the meeting of Workshop on Cluster-based Computing. Santa Fe, NM.

Rozsnyai, S., Slominski, A., & Doganata, Y. (2011). Large-scale distributed storage system for business provenance. In *Proceedings of International Conference on Cloud Computing* (pp. 516-524). IEEE.

Sarood, O., Gupta, A., & Kale, L. V. (2012). Cloud friendly load balancing for HPC applications: Preliminary work. In *Proceedings of International Conference on Parallel Processing Workshops* (pp. 200–205). IEEE.

Seibold, M., Wolke, A., Albutiu, M., Bichler, M., Kemper, A., & Setzer, T. (2012). Efficient deployment of main-memory DBMS in virtualized data centers. In *Proceedings of International Conference on Cloud Computing* (pp. 311-318). IEEE.

Srikant, R., & Agrawal, R. (1996). Mining sequential patterns: Generalizations and performance improvements. In *Proceedings of International Conference on Extending Database Technology* (pp. 3–17). IEEE.

Tian, F., & Chen, K. (2011). Towards optimal resource provisioning for running MapReduce programs in public clouds. In *Proceedings of International Conference on Cloud Computing* (pp. 155-162). IEEE.

Tsafrir, D., Etsion, Y., & Feitelson, D. (2007). Backfilling using system generated predictions rather than user runtime estimates. *Transactions on Parallel and Distributed Systems, 18,* 789–803. doi:10.1109/TPDS.2007.70606.

White, T. (2009). *Hadoop: The definitive guide.* Sebastopol, CA: O'Reilly.

Xu, C. Z., & Lau, F. C. M. (1997). *Load balancing in parallel computers: Theory and practice.* Boston: Kluwer.

Yagoubi, B., & Slimani, Y. (2006). Dynamic load balancing strategy for grid computing. *Transactions on Engineering. Computing and Technology, 13,* 260–265.

Zaharia, M., Konwinski, A., & Joseph, A. D. (2008). Improving MapReduce performance in heterogeneous environments. In *Proceedings of Symposium on Operating Systems Design and Implementation* (pp. 29-42). USENIX.

Zaki, M. J., Li, W., & Parthasarathy, S. (1996). Customized dynamic load balancing for a network of workstations. In *Proceedings of International Symposium on High Performance Parallel and Distributed Computing* (pp. 282–291). IEEE.

ADDITIONAL READING

Armbrust, M., Fox, A., Grith, R., Joseph, A. D., Katz, R. H., & Konwinski, A. … Zaharia, M. (2009). *Above the clouds: A Berkeley view of cloud computing* (Technical Report UCB/EECS-2009-28). Berkeley, CA: EECS Department, University of California, Berkeley.

Babu, S. (2010). Towards automatic optimization of MapReduce programs. In *Proceedings of Symposium on Cloud Computing* (pp. 137–142). ACM.

Bennett, C. (2010). MalStone: Towards a benchmarking for analytics on large data clouds. In *Proceedings of Conference on Knowledge, Discovery, and Data Mining* (pp. 145-152). ACM.

Boyd, S., & Vandenberghe, L. (2004). *Convex optimization.* Cambridge, UK: Cambridge University Press. doi:10.1017/CBO9780511804441.

R. Buyya, J. Broberq, & A. M. Goscinski (Eds.). (2011). *Cloud computing: Principles and paradigms.* Hoboken, NJ: Wiley. doi:10.1002/9780470940105.

Buyya, R., Yeo, C., & Venugopal, S. (2009). Market-oriented cloud computing: Vision, hype, and reality for delivering IT services as computing utilities. In *Proceedings of International Symposium on Cluster Computing and the Grid* (pp. 1-10). ACM.

Dean, J., & Ghemawat, S. (2008). MapReduce: Simplified data processing on large clusters. In *Proceedings of Symposium on Operating Systems Design and Implementation* (pp. 107-113). ACM.

Foster, I., Zhao, Y., Raicu, I., & Lu, S. (2008). Cloud computing and grid computing 360-degree compared. In *Grid Computing Environments Workshop,* (pp. 1 – 10). IEEE.

Fraser, S., Biddle, R., Jordan, S., Keahey, K., Marcus, B., Maximilien, E. M., & Thomas, D. A. (2009). Cloud computing beyond objects: Seeding the cloud. In *Proceedings of Conference on Object-Oriented Programming Systems, Languages, and Applications* (pp. 847-850). ACM.

Gupta, S., Fritz, C., de Kleer, J., & Wittevenn, C. (2012). *Diagnosing heterogeneous Hadoop clusters.* Paper presented at the Meeting of International Workshop on Principles of Diagnosis. Great Malvern, UK.

Jiang, D., Ooi, B., Shi, L., & Wu, S. (2010). The performance of MapReduce: An in-depth study. In *Proceedings of Very Large Databases Conference* (pp. 472-483). ACM.

Jung, G., Hiltunen, M. A., Joshi, K. R., Schlichting, R. D., & Pu, C. (2010). Mistral: Dynamically managing power, performance, and adaptation cost in cloud infrastructures. In *Proceedings of International Conference on Distributed Computing Systems* (pp. 62-73). IEEE.

Kailasam, S., Gnanasambandam, N., Dharanipragada, J., & Sharma, N. (2010). Optimizing service level agreements for autonomic cloud bursting schedulers. In *Proceedings of International Conference on Parallel Processing Workshops* (pp. 285-294). IEEE.

Kambatla, K., Pathak, A., & Pucha, H. (2009). Towards optimizing Hadoop provisioning in the cloud. In *Proceedings of Workshop on Hot Topics in Cloud Computing*. ACM.

Kayulya, S., Tan, J., Gandhi, R., & Narasimhan, P. (2010). An analysis of traces from a production MapReduce cluster. In *Proceedings of International Conference on Cluster Cloud and Grid Computing* (pp. 94-103). IEEE.

Lai, K., Rasmusson, L., Adar, E., Zhang, L., & Huberman, B. A. (2005). Tycoon: an implementation of a distributed, market-based resource allocation system. *Multiagent and Grid Systems*, *1*(3), 169–182.

Lenk, A., Klems, M., Nimis, J., Tai, S., & Sandholm, T. (2009). What's inside the cloud? An architectural map of the cloud landscape. In *Proceedings of Workshop on Software Engineering Challenges of Cloud Computing* (pp. 23-31). IEEE.

Mannila, H., Toivonen, H., & Verkamo, A. I. (1997). Discovery of frequent episodes in event sequences. *Data Mining and Knowledge Discovery*, *1*(3), 259–289. doi:10.1023/A:1009748302351.

Morton, K., Friesen, A., Balazinska, M., & Grossman, D. (2010). Estimating the progress of MapReduce pipelines. In *Proceedings of International Conference on Data Engineering* (pp. 681-684). IEEE.

Panda, B., Herbach, J. S., Basu, S., & Bayardo, R. J. (2009). Planet: Massively parallel learning of tree ensembles with MapReduce. In *Proceedings of Very Large Databases Conference* (pp. 1426-1437). ACM.

Paylo, A., Paulson, E., Rasin, A., Abadi, D. J., DeWitt, D. J., Madden, S., & Stonebraker, M. (2009). A comparison of approaches to large-scale data analysis. In *Proceedings of International Conference on Management of Data* (pp. 165-178). ACM.

Pei, J., Han, J., Morazavi-Asl, B., & Pinto, H. (2001). PrefixSpan: Mining sequential patterns efficiently by prefix-projected pattern growth. In *Proceedings of International Conference on Data Engineering* (pp. 215-224). IEEE.

Seibold, M., Wolke, A., Albutiu, M., Bichler, M., Kemper, A., & Setzer, T. (2012). Efficient deployment of main memory DBMS in virtualized data centers. In *Proceedings of International Conference on Cloud Computing* (pp. 311-318). IEEE.

Sotomayor, B., Montero, R. S., Llorente, I. M., & Foster, I. (2009). Virtual infrastructure management in private and hybrid clouds. *IEEE Internet Computing*, *13*(5), 14–22. doi:10.1109/MIC.2009.119.

Thusoo, A., Shao, Z., Anthony, S., Borthakur, D., Jain, N., & Sen Sarma, J. … Liu, H. (2010). Data warehousing and analytics infrastructure at Facebook. In *Proceedings of International Conference on Management of Data* (pp. 1013-1020). ACM.

Zaharia, M., Konwinski, A., Joseph, A. D., Katz, R., & Stoica, I. (2008). Improving MapReduce performance in heterogeneous environments. In *Proceedings of Symposium on Operating Systems Design and Implementation* (pp. 29-42). ACM.

KEY TERMS AND DEFINITIONS

Big Data: A collection of data that has so large volume, increases with a high velocity, and has a wide variety of data. Due to those characteristics, it becomes difficult to process it using traditional database management tools and traditional data processing approaches.

Data Mining: A computational process to extract information and patterns from a large data set and then, transform information into an understandable structure for further use. Typically, it involves a wide variety of disciplines in mathematics and computer science such as artificial intelligence, machine learning, statistics, and database systems.

Federated Cloud: The combination of multiple cloud computing services (i.e., infrastructures, platforms, and software from multiple cloud providers) to match business needs. Typically, it forms the deployment and management of hybrid cloud that consists of internal and external clouds.

Load Balancing: A method for improving the performance of computing tasks by distributing workload across multiple computers or a computer cluster, networks, or other resources. It is designed to achieve optimal resource utilization, maximize throughput, minimize task execution time, and avoid some overload of computing resources.

MapReduce: A programming model for processing large data sets in parallel. It has been created and implemented by Google. MapReduce is typically used to deal with big data with distributed computing on clusters of computing nodes. A popular free implementation is Apache Hadoop.

Optimization: A procedure or a selection of a best case with regard to some criteria from a set of available alternatives. Typically, an optimization problem can be defined as a mathematical function and then, it aims at maximizing or minimizing the function by systematically choosing input values from a set and computing the value of the function.

Parallelization: A method of computing tasks with multiple computing nodes that are carried out simultaneously. Typically, it divides a large problem into smaller problems and then, solves those smaller problems concurrently.

Synchronization: Two distinct but related concepts, synchronization of processes and synchronization of data. Synchronization of processes indicates that multiple parallel processes are to join at a certain point before going forward. Synchronization of data is for keeping multiple copies of a data in coherence with one another or maintaining data integrity.

Chapter 4
Parallel Data Reduction Techniques for Big Datasets

Ahmet Artu Yıldırım
Utah State University, USA

Cem Özdoğan
Çankaya University, Turkey

Dan Watson
Utah State University, USA

ABSTRACT

Data reduction is perhaps the most critical component in retrieving information from big data (i.e., petascale-sized data) in many data-mining processes. The central issue of these data reduction techniques is to save time and bandwidth in enabling the user to deal with larger datasets even in minimal resource environments, such as in desktop or small cluster systems. In this chapter, the authors examine the motivations behind why these reduction techniques are important in the analysis of big datasets. Then they present several basic reduction techniques in detail, stressing the advantages and disadvantages of each. The authors also consider signal processing techniques for mining big data by the use of discrete wavelet transformation and server-side data reduction techniques. Lastly, they include a general discussion on parallel algorithms for data reduction, with special emphasis given to parallel wavelet-based multi-resolution data reduction techniques on distributed memory systems using MPI and shared memory architectures on GPUs along with a demonstration of the improvement of performance and scalability for one case study.

DOI: 10.4018/978-1-4666-4699-5.ch004

INTRODUCTION

With the advent of information technologies, we live in the age of data – data that needs to be processed and analyzed efficiently to extract useful information for innovation and decision-making in corporate and scientific research labs. While the term of 'big data' is relative and subjective and varies over time, a good working definition is the following:

- **Big Data:** Data that takes an excessive amount of time/space to store, transmit, and process using available resources.

One remedy in dealing with big data might be to adopt a distributed computing model to utilize its aggregate memory and scalable computational power. Unfortunately, distributed computing approaches such as grid computing and cloud computing are not without their disadvantages (e.g., network latency, communication overhead, and high-energy consumption). An "in-box" solution would alleviate many of these problems, and GPUs (Graphical Processing Units) offer perhaps the most attractive alternative. However, as a cooperative processor, GPUs are often limited in terms of the diversity of operations that can be performed simultaneously and often suffer as a result of their limited global memory as well as memory bus congestion between the motherboard and the graphics card. Parallel applications as an emerging computing paradigm in dealing with big datasets have the potential to substantially increase performance with these hybrid models, because hybrid models exploit both advantages of distributed memory models and shared memory models.

A major benefit of data reduction techniques is to save time and bandwidth by enabling the user to deal with larger datasets within minimal resources available at hand. The key point of this process is to reduce the data without making it statistically indistinguishable from the original data, or at least to preserve the characteristics of the original dataset in the reduced representation at a desired level of accuracy. Because of the huge amounts of data involved, data reduction processes become the critical element of the data mining process on the quest to retrieve meaningful information from those datasets. Reducing big data also remains a challenging task that the straightforward approach working well for small data, but might end up with impractical computation times for big data. Hence, the phase of software and architecture design together is crucial in the process of developing data reduction algorithm for processing big data.

In this chapter, we will examine the motivations behind why these reduction techniques are important in the analysis of big datasets by focusing on a variety of parallel computing models ranging from shared-memory parallelism to message-passing parallelism. We will show the benefit of distributed memory system in terms of memory space to process big data because of the system's aggregate memory. However, although many of today's computing systems have many processing elements, we still lack data reduction applications that benefit from multi-core technology. Special emphasis in this chapter will be given to parallel clustering algorithms on distributed memory systems using the MPI library as well as shared memory systems on graphics processing units (GPUs) using CUDA (Compute Unified Device Architecture developed by NVIDIA).

GENERAL REDUCTION TECHNIQUES

Significant CPU time is often wasted because of the unnecessary processing of redundant and non-representative data in big datasets. Substantial speedup can often be achieved through the elimination of these types of data. Furthermore, once non-representative data is removed from large datasets, the storage and transmission of these datasets becomes less problematic.

There are a variety of data reduction techniques in current literature; each technique is applicable in different problem domains. In this section, we provide a brief overview of sampling – by far the simplest method in implementation but not without intrinsic problems – and *feature selection* as a data reduction technique, where the goal is to find the best representational data among all possible feature combinations. Then we examine *feature extraction* methods, where the aim is to reduce numerical data using common signal processing techniques, including discrete Fourier transforms (DFTs) and discrete wavelet transforms (DWTs).

Sampling and Feature Selection

The goal of sampling is to select a subset of elements that adequately represents the complete population. At first glance, sampling may appear to be overly simplistic, but these methods are nonetheless a very usable class of techniques in data reduction, especially with the advent of big data. With the help of sampling, algorithms performed on the sampled population retain a reasonable degree of accuracy while yielding a significantly faster execution.

Perhaps the most straightforward sampling method is simple *random sampling* (Figure 1), in which sample tuples are chosen randomly using a pseudorandom number generator. In simple random sampling, the original big data population is randomly sampled, and those sampled

units are added to the (initially empty) sampled population set with (or without) replacement. With replacement, as sampled units are placed into the sampled population set, if an identical unit already exists in that set, it is replaced by the sampled unit. Thus, one unit is randomly selected first with probability of $1/N$ where N is the size of population, and there are no duplicate elements in the sampled population. Without replacement, sampled units are added to the sampled population set without prejudice, and thus identical elements may exist in the resulting set. In simple random sample without replacement, because there are $C(N, n)$ possible samples, where n is sample size, the probability of selecting a sampled unit is $1 / C(N, n)$ (Lohr, 1999).

It is worth noting that random number generation on parallel computers is not straightforward, and care must be taken to avoid exact duplication of the pseudorandom sequence when multiple processing elements are employed. The reader is directed for further reader on parallel pseudorandom number generation to Aluru et al., 1992, Bradley et al., 2011; and Matteis & Pagnutti, 1990).

Another sampling method is *systematic sampling*, illustrated in Figure 2. The advantage of this method over simple random method is that systematic sampling does not need a parallel random number generator. Let $k = N/n$ and R be a random number between 1 and k, then every i^{th} tuple, $0 \le i < n$, in database is selected according to the equation $R + i \times k$. Because systematic sampling performs selection of the sampled units in a

Figure 1. Simple random sampling algorithm

Input: Set of tuples X, size of samples n
Output: Set of sample tuples S
1: $S \leftarrow \varnothing$
2: **for** $i = 1 \to n$ **do**
3: $\quad x \leftarrow selectRandomTuple(X)$
4: $\quad S \leftarrow S \cap \{x\}$
5: **end for**

Figure 2. Systematic sampling algorithm

Input: Set of tuples X, size of population N, size of samples n
Output: Set of sample tuples S
1: $S \leftarrow \varnothing$
2: $k \leftarrow N/n$
3: $R \leftarrow randomNumber(1, k)$
4: **for** $i = 0 \to n - 1$ **do**
5: $\quad x \leftarrow X(R + i \times k)$
6: $\quad S \leftarrow S \cap \{x\}$
7: **end for**

well-patterned manner, the tuples must be stored in a random fashion in the database; otherwise, systematic sampling may introduce unwanted bias into the sampled set. For example, as a web server records the information of the visitors, the order of information stored in the database might produce bias if the employment status of the visitors affects this ordering because of heterogeneous characteristics of the population. See Figure 3 for sampling illustrations using both simple random sampling and systematic sampling.

In *stratified sampling*, shown in Figure 4, population units are divided into disjoint, homogeneous groups, called *strata* in which a sampling technique such as simple random sampling or systematic sampling is applied on those strata independently. One of the advantages of stratified sampling is to minimize estimation error. For example, suppose the manager of a web site wishes to obtain sampled users represented fairly in a sampled population, and that the information of gender proportions is known in advance. Therefore, the group (strata) consisting of all males are sampled together, and then the same sampling operation is applied on the remaining portion of database tuples (i.e., females), independently.

While sampling techniques are straightforward and efficient in reducing data, they may introduce a biased result, because the sampled set does not represent the population fairly. Thus, *feature subset selection* (FSS) techniques come up as a promising way to deal with this problem. A *Feature* is defined as an attribute of the data specifying one of its distinctive characteristics. The objective of an FSS is to find the feature subset with size d representing the data "best" among

Figure 3. Sampling illustrations on 2D domain: (a) Simple random sampling, (b) Systematic sampling

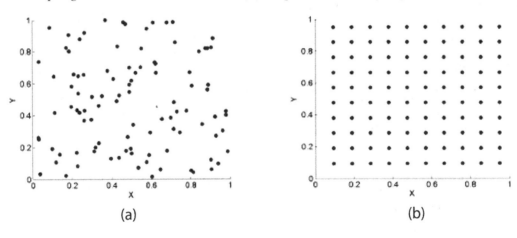

(a)   (b)

Figure 4. Stratified sampling algorithm

Input: Set of tuples X, size of population N, size of strata h, set of strata
$\quad Z = \{z_1, z_2, \ldots, z_h\}$
Output: Set of sample tuples S
1: $S \leftarrow \emptyset$
2: **for all** $z_i \in Z$ **do**
3: $\quad X' \leftarrow \sigma_{z_i = true}(X)$
4: $\quad S' \leftarrow applySampling(X')$
5: $\quad S \leftarrow S \cap S'$
6: **end for**

all possible feature set combinations, $C(n, d)$, over n features. To measure how well the selected feature subset represents the data, an objective function is used to evaluate the "goodness" of the candidate subset. Let set of features of the data be $X = \{x_i \mid i \in \mathbb{N} \text{ and } i \leq n\}$ and the feature subset be $Y = \{y_j \mid j \in \mathbb{N} \text{ and } j < n\}$ where $Y \subset X$. Then feature subset Y maximizes the objective function $J(Y)$.

Exhaustive search, shown in Figure 5, is one straightforward way to find the optimum feature subset of size d. This algorithm is able to obtain the optimal feature set of size d over all possible feature subsets. The algorithm is considered a "top-down" approach where starts from an empty feature subset and incrementally finds the solution. The most optimal feature set is the set having maximum goodness value. While exhaustive search guarantees the best solution, it is obvious that it exhibits poor performance due to its exponential algorithm complexity of $O(J(Y_i)) \times O(C(n, d)) =$ $O(J(Y_i) \times C(n,d))$. Therefore, exhaustive search can be used only in practice if the data has a small number of features. The search space of exhaustive search is illustrated in Figure 6 where every leaf node is traversed to find the optimum solution.

In contrast to the exhaustive search approach, the branch and bound algorithm for future subset selection (Narendra & Fukunaga, 1977) finds the optimal feature set in a "bottom-up" manner using a tree structure. Hence, the algorithm discards m features to find the feature subset with d dimensions where $m = n - d$. The monotonicity property of feature subsets with respect to objective function, J, is satisfied at each iteration in which only one feature is discarded. Thus, the objective function is maximized at each iteration as shown in Equation 1:

$$J_1(Y_{i_1}) \leq J_2(Y_{i_1}, Y_{i_2})$$
$$\leq \cdots \leq J_m(Y_{i_1}, Y_{i_2}, \ldots, Y_{i_n}) \tag{1}$$

Figure 5. Exhaustive feature selection algorithm

Input: Set of features X, size of feature set n, size of target feature subset d,
   set of possible feature subsets, F, of X where each subset is of size d
Output: Optimum feature subset Y_{opt} of size d
1: $Y_{opt} \leftarrow \varnothing$
2: $G_{opt} \leftarrow -\infty$
3: **for all** $Y_i \in F = \{Y_0, Y_1, \ldots, Y_k\} \mid k = \binom{n}{d}$ **do**
4:    $G_i \leftarrow J(Y_i)$
5:    **if** $G_i > G_{opt}$ **then**
6:       $Y_{opt} \leftarrow Y_i$
7:       $G_{opt} \leftarrow G_i$
8:    **end if**
9: **end for**

Figure 6. Search space of exhaustive search where $n = 4$ and $d = 3$

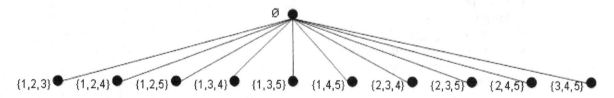

The search space of the *branch and bound algorithm* is illustrated as a tree structure form in Figure 7. The tree has $m + 1$ levels where $0 \leq i \leq m$. Each leaf node represents a candidate feature subset. The label near each node indicates the feature to be discarded. Traversing begins from the root node and switches to the next level. When the goodness-of-fit value of the feature set is less than the current maximum value or there are no nodes left to be visited at level i, the algorithm backtracks up to the previous level. The maximum goodness-of-fit value is calculated when the leaf node is reached for the corresponding candidate feature set. The algorithm finishes when it backtracks to level zero and the candidate feature set with highest goodness-of-fit value is considered the optimal feature set.

Although the branch and bound algorithm is superior to exhaustive search algorithm in terms of algorithmic efficiency, the objective function is invoked not only for the leaf nodes, but also for other nodes in the tree. In addition, there is no guarantee that every node is visited. In order to alleviate this problem, Somol et al. (2000) introduced *fast branch and bound algorithm* (FBB) for optimal subset selection. The FBB algorithm uses a prediction mechanism to save the computation time of excessive invocation of objective function by monitoring goodness-of-fit changes.

Another data reduction approach is to use heuristic feature selection algorithms such as *sequential forward selection* (SFS, shown in Figure 8) and *sequential backward selection* (SBS, shown in Figure 9), which employ a greedy approach by respectively adding or removing the best features in an incremental fashion. The SFS algorithm starts with an empty set and then adds features one by one, whereas the SBS algorithm starts with all feature sets and then yield a suboptimum feature set by incrementally discarding features. Because heuristic algorithms substantially reduce the search space (for example by three orders of

Figure 7. Search space of branch and bound algorithm where $n = 5$ and $d = 2$. The sample traversed path is shown by dashed lines.

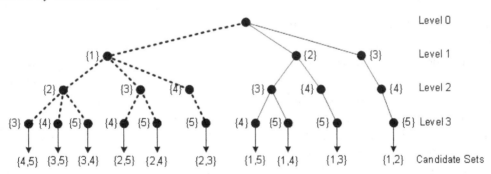

Figure 8. Sequential forward feature selection algorithm

Input: Set of features $X = \{x_0, x_1, \ldots, x_n\}$, size of feature set n, size of target feature subset d
Output: Suboptimum feature subset Y_{subopt} of size d
1: $Y_{subopt} \leftarrow \varnothing$
2: **for** $j = 1 \rightarrow d$ **do**
3: $\quad x \leftarrow \max(J(Y_{subopt} \cap \{x_i\})) \mid x_i \in X \ and \ x_i \notin Y_{subopt}$
4: $\quad Y_{subopt} \leftarrow Y_{subopt} \cap \{x\}$
5: **end for**

Figure 9. Sequential backward feature selection algorithm

Input: Set of features $X = \{x_0, x_1, \ldots, x_n\}$, size of feature set n, size of target feature subset d

Output: Suboptimum feature subset Y_{subopt} of size d

1: $Y_{subopt} \leftarrow X$
2: **for** $j = 1 \rightarrow n - d$ **do**
3: $\quad x \leftarrow \min(J(Y_{subopt} - \{x_i\})) \mid x_i \in X$ and $x_i \in Y_{subopt}$
4: $\quad Y_{subopt} \leftarrow Y_{subopt} - \{x\}$
5: **end for**

magnitude when $n = 20$, $d = 10$ (Whitney, 1971)), they are considered faster than exhaustive search at the expense of optimality. Furthermore, because forward selection starts with small subsets and then enlarges them, while backward selection starts with large subsets and then shrinks them, experiments show that forward selection is typically faster than backward selection because of the computational cost in repetitively processing large subsets (Jain & Zongker, 1997). As a forward selection approach, FOCUS by Almuallim & Dietterich (1991) is a quasi-polynomial algorithm that starts searching from bottom when the size of candidate feature subsets is one, then increments the size until the minimum goodness is satisfied.

The drawback of those heuristic algorithms is a problem called *nesting*, in which the operation of adding (SFS) or removing (SBS) cannot be undone once the operation is finished. This situation is a primary cause of a suboptimal solution. To overcome the nesting problem, some algorithms have been proposed, such as the *Plus-L-Minus-R* introduced by Stearns (1976) in which the algorithm performs l adding operations and r removing operations. If $l > r$, it functions like the forward

selection algorithm, otherwise it functions like the backward selection algorithm. One drawback of the Plus-L-Minus-R algorithm is that the parameters of l and r must be determined to obtain the best feature set. To compensate for this problem, a floating search method is proposed in which the algorithm changes l and r values at run time to maximize the feature set optimality (Pudil et al., 1994).

As stated by John et al. (1994), the approach of any data reduction algorithm falls into two models for selecting relevant feature subsets. The first is the *filter model* (see Figure 10) in which the phase of feature selection algorithm is applied independently of the induction algorithm as a preprocessing step. This is contrasted with the *wrapper model* (see Figure 11), which "wraps" the induction algorithm into the feature selection step. In the wrapper model, the evaluation phase of the goodness function for the feature subset is performed according to the induction algorithm. Each model has its own strengths and weaknesses; the filter model may introduce irrelevant features that may impose performance problems on the induction algorithm because of its separate

Figure 10. Flow of the filter model

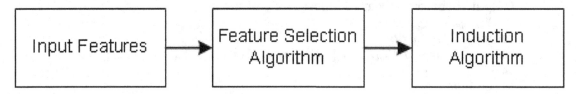

Figure 11. Flow of the wrapper model with cross validation

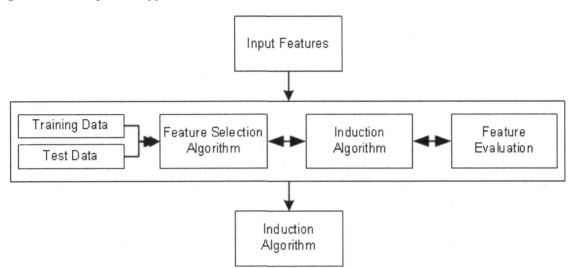

existence but still performs relatively faster than the wrapper model. Even so, the wrapper model has the ability to find more relevant subsets at a reasonable cost to performance.

The wrapper model utilizes an *n*-fold cross validation technique where the input feature set is divided into *n* partitions of equal sizes. Using those partitions, the algorithm uses *n – 1* partitions as training data and performs a validation operation on one partition. This operation is repeated *n* times for each of the other partitions and the feature subset with the maximum averaged goodness-of-fit value is regarded as the best solution. Cross validation can also avoid the phenomena of over-fitting; the problem of fitting noise into the model. While the wrapper model may not be ideal for big data due to its performance inefficiencies, some feature pruning techniques or sampling techniques applied to training data may yield faster execution times.

Data Reduction using Signal Processing Techniques

Another way to reduce big data to a manageable size is to use contemporary signal processing techniques. Although those methods fall into the class of feature extraction methods in the context of dimensionality reduction (Pudil et al., 1998), they are considered here as an alternative approach to feature selection techniques. Feature extraction methods reduce the dimensionality by mapping a set of elements in one space to another; however, feature selection methods perform this reduction task by finding the "best" feature subset. Additionally, because feature selections methods require an objective function to evaluate the goodness of the subset, the output of the reduction operation therefore depends on the objective function. By contrast, feature extraction methods solve the reduction problem on another space on transformed data without using objective function. Because of the fact that signal processing techniques do not work on non-numerical data, they require a quantization step to process non-numerical data as a preprocessing step before applying the signal processing technique.

The *Discrete Fourier Transform* (DFT) method is used in many signal-processing studies that are seeking a reduction in data, for example in reducing time series data (that naturally tends toward large amounts of data) without sacrificing trend behavior (Faloutsos et al., 1994). The main aim of applying a DFT is to convert a series of data from the time domain into the frequency domain by decomposing the signal into a number of sinusoidal components. The DFT extracts f features from sequences in which each feature in the transformed feature space refers to one DFT coefficient.

While DFTs are useful tool for analyzing signal data, it often fails to properly analyze non-stationary data that might be frequently encountered in time series data. To overcome this problem, another signal processing technique, the *Discrete Wavelet Transform* (DWT) can be employed to analyze the components of non-stationary signals (Sifuzzaman et al., 2009). Moreover, while DFTs transform the signal from the time/space domain into frequency domain, DWTs transform the signal into time/frequency domain. Thus, DWTs are beneficial to preserve spatial property of the data on the transformed feature space unlike DFTs. Wu et al. (2000) show that the DWT is a better tool than the DFT for the application of time series analysis because DWTs reduce the error of distance estimates on the transformed data. Additionally, the DWT (like the DFT), produces no false dismissal (Chan & Fu, 1999). This important property allows us to use wavelet transform for data reduction.

DWTs decompose signals into high-frequency and low-frequency components using filtering techniques. The low-frequency component represents a lower resolution approximation of the original feature space on which the data-mining algorithm is applied to obtain (upon re-application of the DWT on the low-frequency component) solutions at different scales from fine (as in the case of the original dataset) to coarse as in the case of multiple applications of the DWT). IN addition, a lookup table can be used to map the units from the transformed feature space back to a unit in the original feature space, providing a useful indexing capability of the resulting units in the transformed space.

As implied above, wavelet transforms can be applied to the input data multiple times on the low-frequency component in a recursive manner, creating a multi-resolution sampling of the original feature set. This recursive operation of decomposing the signal is called a *filter bank*. Each operation of wavelet transform constitutes half-sized objects in the transformed feature space for each dimension as compared to previous dimension of the feature space.

Figure 12 illustrates the low-frequency component extracted from the image of A. Lincoln. As shown in the Figures, as the scale level of the wavelet transform increases, we obtain coarser representation of the original data in which typically a data-mining algorithm is applied to

Figure 12. Illustration of "Low-frequency Component" in Art: (a) Original image, (b) Low-Frequency Component (scale level = 3), (c) Low-Frequency Component (scale level = 4), (d) "Low-frequency Component" in Art, mosaic painting of A. Lincoln by Leon Harmon, which is small in "resolution" and a coarser representation of the original image

(a)   (b)   (c)   (d)

extract the information from this reduced data. For example, in Figure 12(b), DWT is applied three times on the low-frequency component (scale level is 3), and in Figure(c), DWT is applied one more time using Figure 12(b), so the scale level becomes four. Thus, the reduced data in Figure 12(c) has half-sized cells as compared to the Figure 12(b) and Figure 12(c) has coarser representation of the input data as compared to the previous low-frequency component (Figure 12(b)). For comparison, Figure 12(d) is actually a rather famous illustration by Leon Harmon (1973) created to illustrate his article on the recognition of human faces.

There are many popular wavelet algorithms including Haar wavelets, Daubechies wavelets, Morlet wavelets and Mexican Hat wavelets. As stated by Huffmire & Sherwood (2006), Haar wavelets (Stollnitz et al., 1995) are used in many studies because of their simplicity and their fast and memory-efficient characteristics. It should also be noted that it is necessary to scale source datasets linearly to power of two for each dimension, because the signal rate decreases by a factor of two at each level. If we let $X = \{x_1, x_2,...,x_n\}$ be an input data of size n, then the low frequency component of the data can be extracted via simple averaging operation as shown below:

$$\begin{pmatrix} 0.5 & 0.5 & 0 & 0 & 0 & 0 & \cdots & 0 & 0 \\ 0 & 0 & 0.5 & 0.5 & 0 & 0 & \cdots & 0 & 0 \\ \vdots & \vdots & \vdots & \vdots & \vdots & \vdots & \ddots & \vdots & \vdots \\ 0 & 0 & 0 & 0 & 0 & 0 & \cdots & 0.5 & 0.5 \end{pmatrix}$$

$$\bullet \begin{pmatrix} x_1 \\ x_2 \\ \vdots \\ x_n \end{pmatrix} = \begin{pmatrix} \dfrac{x_1 + x_2}{2} \\ \dfrac{x_3 + x_4}{2} \\ \vdots \\ \dfrac{x_{n-1} + x_n}{2} \end{pmatrix} \qquad (2)$$

Where each object in the low-frequency component of the feature space W_φ^j, is also contained in the low-frequency component of the previous transformed feature space W_φ^{j-1}. Hence, the feature spaces are nested (Stollnitz et al., 1995). That is:

$$W_\varphi^j \subset W_\varphi^{j-1} \subset W_\varphi^{j-2} \subset \ldots \subset W_\varphi^0 \qquad (3)$$

Popivanov & Miller (2002) list the main advantages of using DWTs over DFTs:

- DWTs are able to capture time-dependent local properties of data, whereas DFTs can only capture global properties;
- The algorithmic complexity of DWTs is linear with the length of data, which is superior to even Fast Fourier Transforms with *O(nlogn)* complexity;
- While DFTs provide the set of frequency components in the signal, DWTs allows us to analyze the data at different scales. The low-frequency component of the transformed space represents the approximation of the data in another scale;
- Unlike DFTs, DWTs have many wavelet functions. Thus, they provide access to information that can be obscured by other methods.

PARALLEL DATA REDUCTION ALGORITHMS

Despite substantial an continuing improvements in processor technology in terms of speed, data reduction algorithms may still not complete the required task in a reasonable amount of time for big data problems. Besides, there may not be enough available memory resources to hold all the data on a single computer. One of the most promising approaches for overcoming those issues is to make use of parallel computing systems and algorithms (Hedberg, 1995). Parallel processing techniques are extensively used in divide-and-conquer approaches in which the task is divided into smaller subtasks, all of which are then executed simultaneously, to cope with memory limits and to decrease the overall execution time of a given task.

In this section, we briefly overview parallel processing as applied to big data. Then, we present studies in the literature that examine the task of data reduction on data centers in parallel. As a case study, we investigate the parallel WaveCluster algorithm on distributed memory systems using the Message-Passing Interface (MPI) model and on GPUs as an instance of the shared memory system using CUDA. WaveCluster algorithms employ DWTs to reduce the dimension of the data before finding clusters on dataset, and so are well-suited to this discussion.

Parallel Processing

Parallel computer architectures can be classified according to the memory sharing models. The first of these is the *Distributed Memory System* (DMS) model in which independent processors or nodes, each with their own memory and address space, are connected to each other by means of high-speed network infrastructure. In this model, data is shared among nodes via explicit message-passing, either between individual nodes, or via a broadcast mechanism. Typically, program written for DMS systems using library function calls such as those provided by the Message Passing Interface (MPI) libraries (Gropp et al., 1994) to construct the communication patterns among the processors by sending/receiving messages.

An alternative parallel architecture model is the Shared Memory System (SMS) model. Under the SMS model, there is a single address space

– and thus the appearance of a shared memory bank – into which any of the nodes may read or write at any time. Data sharing among processors occurs without any explicit message passing; each node simply reads from or write to the shared space, which is immediately available to all other processors. In practice, SMS systems are usually built out of individual processing elements that each contain their own private memory, and the appearance of a shared address is created with a set of protocols that are often written for DMS-type systems. One notable exception to this (as discussed below) is in the realm of GPUs, which often contain some mix of shared and distributed memory hierarchies.

Each memory model has its own advantages over another model. One advantage of SMS over DMS is that there is no need to store duplicate items in separate memory. Additionally, SMS provides much faster communication among the processors. On the other hand, distributed memory architectures fully utilize the larger aggregate memory that allows us to solve larger problems, which typically imply large memory needs. Hybrid memory models represent a combination of the shared and distributed memory models. With an increasing number of clusters with hybrid architectures, the MPI library is used to achieve data distribution between GPU nodes whereas CUDA functions as "main computing engine" (Karunadasa & Ranasinghe, 2009). Hence, they have been considered complementary models in order to maximally utilize system resources.

As a distributed memory system, MapReduce (Dean & Ghemawat, 2008) has the potential to provide a novel way of dealing with big data. In this model, the programmer is not required to specify the parallelism in code. At its core, there are only two functions: *map* and *reduce. Map* processes key/value pairs and divides the data into a group of sub-data where each sub-data is represented by a key. The sub-data, which are collectively known as intermediate values, are stored in a distributed file system. *Reduce* then merges all the intermediate values across the distributed file system associated with the same key. In the starting phase of a job, the library splits the input files into M pieces of typically from 16 megabytes to 64 megabytes per piece. It then starts up the many copies of the program on a cluster. The implementation has been developed based on master/worker model. Master node makes assignments of map and reduces tasks to available worker jobs. Each worker writes the intermediate results of map and reduce operations to local disks which can be accessed by all nodes in the cluster.

One of the characteristics of the map-reduce model is that processors are not allowed to communicate with each other directly. Thus, while this strategy has been criticized as being too low-level, the model provides us with scalability to support ever-growing datasets. It also ensures fault-tolerance by storing intermediate files on distributed file system and by taking advantage of its dynamic job scheduling system. One popular implementation of map-reduce framework is Apache Hadoop which provides for the distributed processing of large data sets across clusters of computers. Hodoop implements a distributed file system to provide high-throughput data access. Although Hadoop's byte-stream data model

leads to inefficiencies in data access for highly structured data, Sci-Hadoop, a Hadoop plugin, attenuates this effect by allowing users to specify logical queries over array-based data models (Buck et al, 2011). See Figure 13 for an illustration of the map-reduce model.

There are many programming model choices for shared memory systems. *Threading* is one way to run concurrent processes on multi-core processors where each thread may run on different cores within a single process. Threads share the process address space and can access other process resources, as well. Another choice is OpenMP (Chapman et al., 2007), as an application-programming interface (API), OpenMP provides the programmer flexibility, ease of use and transparency in the creation of CPU threads, which speed up the loops by using pragma directives.

Recent work in big data processing coincides with the advent of many-core *graphical processing units* (GPUs), which are used for general-purpose computation as a co-processor of the CPU (in addition to its traditional usage of accelerating the graphic rendering). In 2008, NVIDIA introduced CUDA (Compute Unified Device Architecture) (Nickolls et al., 2008) to enable general-purpose computations on NVIDIA GPUs in an efficient

Figure 13. Illustration of map-reduce model where the number of pieces, M = 6

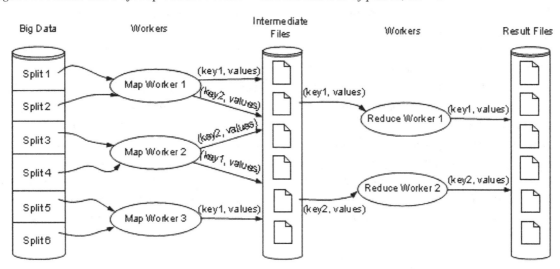

way. In CUDA programming, the programmer must partition the problem into sub problems that can be solved independently in parallel on GPU cores. In practice, the programmer writes a function named a *kernel* and accesses the data using thread IDs in a multidimensional manner. The advantage of this model is that once the parallel program is developed, it can scale transparently to hundreds of processor cores independently on any CUDA-capable NVIDIA graphic processor.

There are three main stages in CUDA program flow. First, input data is copied from local memory (RAM) to the global memory of the graphic processor so that processing cores can access the input data in a fast manner. Second, the CUDA machine executes the parallel program given. Third, the data that reside on the global memory of graphic processor is transferred from global memory back to local memory (RAM). Thus, the main disadvantage of this model is that this mechanism may incur performance bottlenecks due to the extra memory copy operations, eventually decreasing the speedup ratio of the parallel program when compared to the sequential one. The other disadvantage is that the CUDA kernel does not allow accessing the disk and calling the functions of the operating system or libraries compiled for CPU execution.

Because GPU hardware implements the SIMD (Single Instruction stream, Multiple Data stream) parallel execution model, each control unit in the GPU broadcasts one instruction among all the processor units inside the same processor group in which the instruction is executed. This architectural difference from the traditional CPU architecture requires non-trivial parallel programming models. It also comes with its own intrinsic restrictions in developing a parallel program such as the synchronization issue among the GPUs and the complications of having different levels of memory models. Furthermore, most of the classical programming techniques such as recursion

might not be applied in GPU computing. Thus, GPU programs have to be developed in accordance with the underlying architectures.

Server-Side Parallel Data Reduction Methods for Data Centers

Due to massive bandwidth requirements, the task of moving of data between hosting datacenters and workstations requires a substantial amount of time. One remedy is to run data reduction application on the data center to take advantage of data locality. Wang et al. (2007) introduced the Script Workflow Analysis for MultiProcessing (SWAMP) system. In SWAMP system, the user is required to write a shell script and then the script is submitted to the OpenDAP data server using Data Access Protocol (DAP). The SWAMP parser has ability to recognize netCDF options and parameters. The execution engine of SWAMP manages the script execution and builds dependency trees. The SWAMP engine can then potentially exploit parallel execution of the script when possible.

Today, map-reduce frameworks are beginning to see increased use to reduce big data for further processing. Singh et al. (2009) introduced parallel feature selection algorithm to quickly evaluate billions of potential features for very large data sets. In the mapping phase, each map worker iterates over the training records of the block and produces intermediate data records for each new feature. Then, each reduce worker computes an estimated coefficient for each feature. Finally, post-processing is performed to aggregate the coefficients for all features in the same feature class.

Another map-reduce study is presented by Malik et al. (2011) to accelerate the performance of subset queries on raster images in parallel. Inherently, geographic information data consists of a collection of multidimensional petabyte-sized data that are becoming more common. To fetch subsets of data from geographic information database efficiently, each of the spatial, time and weather variables of data are stored in a column-oriented storage format, instead of in a row-oriented storage format where multidimensional data is stored as a single record. Column-oriented storage format leads to performance benefit by allowing each subset to be loaded into memory without loading unnecessary data when subset query is issued. The algorithm indexes data in Hilbert order (Song et al., 2000) to take advantage of data locality.

Parallel WaveCluster Algorithm

WaveCluster Algorithm

Clustering is a common data mining technique that is used for data retrieval by grouping similar objects into disjoint classes or clusters (Fayyad et al., 1996). There has been an explosive growth of very large or big datasets in scientific and commercial domains with the recent progress in data storage technology. Because cluster analysis has become a crucial task for the mining of the data, a considerable amount of research is focused on developing sequential clustering analysis methods. Clustering algorithms have been highly utilized in various fields such as satellite image segmentation (Mukhopadhyay & Maulik, 2009), unsupervised document clustering (Surdeanu et al., 2005) and clustering of bioinformatics data (Madeira & Oliveira, 2004). The WaveCluster algorithm is a multi-resolution clustering algorithm introduced by Sheikholeslami et al. (1998). The algorithm is designed to perform clustering on very large spatial datasets by taking advantage of discrete wavelet transforms. Thus, the algorithm has the ability to detect arbitrary shape clusters at different scales and can handle dataset noise in an appropriate way.

The WaveCluster algorithm contains three phases. In the first phase, the algorithm quantizes the feature space and then assigns objects to the units. This phase also affects the performance of clustering for different values of interval size. In the second phase, the discrete wavelet transform is applied on the feature space multiple times. Discrete wavelet transforms are a powerful tool for time-frequency analysis that decomposes the signal into average subband and detail subbands using filtering techniques. The WaveCluster algorithm gains the ability to remove outliers with wavelet transforms and detects the clusters at different levels of accuracy (multi-resolution property) from fine to coarse by applying the wavelet transform multiple times. Following the transformation, dense regions (clusters) are detected by finding connected components and labels are assigned to the units in the transformed feature space.

In the second phase, a lookup table is constructed to map the units in the transformed feature space to original feature space.

In the third and last phase, WaveCluster algorithm assigns the cluster number of each object in the original feature space. In Figure 14, the effect of the wavelet transformation on source dataset is demonstrated.

Figure 14. WaveCluster algorithm multi-resolution property: (a) Original source dataset, (b) ρ and 6 clusters are detected, (c) $\rho = 3$ and 3 clusters are detected (where ρ is the scale level)

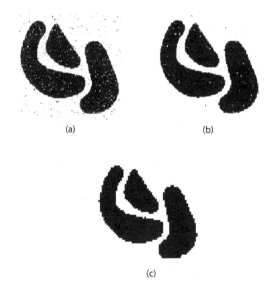

(a)

(b)

(c)

The results of the WaveCluster algorithm for different values of ρ are shown in Figure 14; where ρ (scale level) represents how many times wavelet transform is applied on the feature space. There are 6 clusters detected with $\rho = 2$ (Figure 14(b)) and 3 clusters are detected with $\rho = 3$ (Figure 14(c)). In the performed experiments, connected components are found on average sub bands (feature space) using a classical two-pass connected component labeling algorithm (Shapiro & Stockman, 2001) at different scales.

Parallel WaveCluster Algorithm on the Distributed Memory System

We reported our developed parallel WaveCluster algorithm based on the message-passing model using MPI library (Yıldırım & Özdoğan, 2011). The algorithm scales linearly with the increasing number of objects in the dataset. One may conclude that it makes mining big datasets possible via the parallel algorithm on distributed memory systems, without having restrictions such as dataset size and other relevant criteria.

In the message-passing approach, each copy of the single program runs on processors independently, and communication is provided by the manner of sending and receiving messages among nodes. We followed master-slave model in implementation. Each processor works on a specific partition of the dataset and executes discrete wavelet transform and connected component labeling algorithm. The obtained results from each processor are locally correct, but might not be globally correct. Therefore, processors exchange their local results and then check for correctness. This operation is achieved simply by sending the border data of the local results to the parent node, called master node. This border data consists of transformed values and their corresponding local cluster numbers. After processors send the border data to the parent node, the parent node creates a merge table for all processors with respect to the global adjacency property of all cells. This require-

ment for sustaining consistency in effect creates a barrier primitive. Accordingly, all processors wait for the parent node to receive merged table. Then, all processors update the cluster numbers of the units on local feature space. Lastly, processors map the objects of the original feature space to the clusters using lookup table. In the lookup table, each entry specifies the relationships of one unit in the transformed feature space to the corresponding units of the original feature space. The flow of the algorithm is depicted in Figure 15.

Experiments for this technique were conducted and obtained performance behaviors were presented for 1, 2, 4, 8, 16 and 32 core cases on a cluster system having 32 cores with a 2.8 GHz clock speed and fast Ethernet (100 Mbit/sec) as underlying communication. Our experiments have shown that the cluster shape complexity of the dataset has minimal impact on the execution time of the algorithm. Datasets below are named as DS32 (1073741824 objects) and DS65 (4294967296 objects) according to the dataset size. The DS 65 case is beyond the limit of data-

Figure 15. Parallel WaveCluster algorithm for Distributed Memory Systems

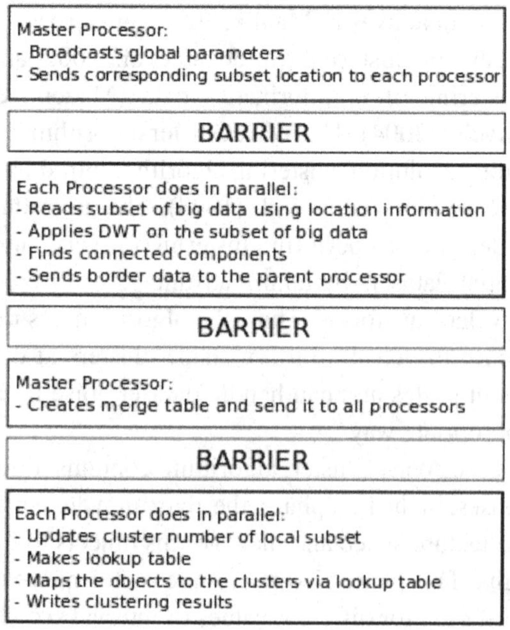

set size that fits into the memory of a single processor within the available hardware, and is studied by running that dataset with 8, 16 and 32 processors.

Table 1 shows execution times and speed-up ratios with respect to the number of objects in the dataset for varied numbers of processors. Analysis of the dataset DS65 is only possible at or above the size of eight processors in our computer cluster system. The benefit of the distributed memory system is easily observed above in processing big data. Experimental results have shown that this parallel clustering algorithm provides supe-

Table 1. Execution times and speed-up ratios for varying dataset sizes and number of processors (np)

Dataset	np = 1	np = 2	np = 4	np = 8	np = 16	np = 32
Execution Times (in seconds)						
DS65	-	-	-	17.59	9.70	5.21
DS32	35.19	17.96	9.15	4.41	2.50	1.30
Speed-up Ratios						
DS65	-	-	-	1	1.81	3.37
DS32	1	1.95	3.84	7.97	14.07	27.06

rior speed-up and linear scaling behavior (time complexity) and is useful in overcoming space complexity constraints via aggregate memory of the cluster system.

Parallel WaveCluster Algorithm on the Shared Memory System

The parallel implementation of WaveCluster algorithm on GPUs is presented in (Yıldırım & Özdoğan, 2011). In this study, we used a Haar wavelet, because of its initial small window width and easy implementation. Then, a lookup table is built which maps more than one unit in the original dataset to one unit in the transformed dataset. After this phase, the connected component labeling algorithm is performed on the low-frequency component to find the connected units and the resulting units are transformed back to the original space using look-up table. In the WaveCluster algorithm, a cluster is defined as a group of connected units in the transformed feature space.

Figure 16 shows the pseudo-code of the extraction of the low-frequency component on the CUDA

Figure 16. CUDA algorithm of Low-Frequency Component Extraction

Input: $W_\varphi^{j-1}, islastscale, TH$
Output: W_φ^j
1: **declare** $I[dim.y * 2][dim.x * 2]$ in shared memory
2: **declare** $H[dim.y * 2][dim.x]$ in shared memory
3: **load** thread-related disjoint 2x2 points of V^j into buffer I
4: **apply** one-dimensional wavelet transform to each column of points of 2x2 field and store values into buffer H
5: **apply** one-dimensional wavelet transform to each row of points over H and store approximation value in local memory m
6: **if** $islastscale = true$ **then**
7:     **if** $val > TH$ **then**
8:         $m \leftarrow MAXFLOAT$
9:     **else**
10:         $m \leftarrow threadindex$
11:     **end if**
12: **end if**
13: $W_\varphi^j[threadindex] \leftarrow m$

machine. The kernel is invoked j times and each invocation results in the extraction of coarser component. W_{φ}^{j} is the low-frequency component of scale j and the previous component W_{φ}^{j-1} is the input of the following CUDA kernel. The kernel also removes outliers on the transformed feature space in which the threshold value *TH* is chosen as arbitrary. Each CUDA thread is responsible for finding one approximation value extracted from the feature space of 2x2 size. Before kernel invocation, the input feature space is transferred from host memory to the CUDA global memory and the output buffer is allocated in the device memory to store the transformed feature space. Because the input data is 2-dimensional, the wavelet transform is applied twice for each dimension. Each CUDA thread applies a one-dimensional wavelet transform to each column of the local feature space and stores the intermediate values in the shared memory buffer *H*. The final approximation value is eventually calculated by applying a second one-dimensional discrete wavelet transform for each row on *H*. Hence, buffer *H* is used to store temporal results. To facilitate the data access operation, the algorithm takes advantage of shared memory located on the CUDA machine.

We implemented the CUDA-based algorithms of the wavelet transform, connected component labeling and look-up phases and then evaluated the performance of each CUDA kernel on very large synthetic datasets. CUDA experiments were conducted on a Linux workstation with 2 GB RAM, Intel Core2Duo processor (2 Cores, 2.4 GHz, 4MB L2 Cache) and an NVIDIA GTX 465 GPU(1 GB memory, 352 computing cores, each core runs at 1.215 GHz) with compute capability 2.0 and runtime version 3.10. In this section, we present the extraction phase of the low frequency component as a data reduction algorithm on GPUs. In the experiments, two-dimensional fog datasets (DataSet1; DS1 and DataSet2; DS2) have been used. These datasets were obtained from the web

site of NASA Weather Satellite Imagery Viewers (2011). As a distinctive property, DS1 has more clusters than DS2, but the size of clusters is bigger in DS2. The larger datasets (DS(1 or 2) with the size of 4096, 2048, 1024 and 512) have been obtained by scaling the datasets linearly.

Execution times (in microseconds) and corresponding kernel speed-up values for the low-frequency extraction algorithm are presented in Table 2.

The obtained results indicate achievement of up to a 165.01x kernel speed-up ratio in dataset DS1 with the size 4096 in the kernel of low-frequency extraction. We obtain high speed-up ratios as the number of points increase in the dataset. This result indicates that the operation of signal component extraction in the wavelet transform is suitable to be executed on CUDA devices.

Detected numbers of clusters (K) for varying scale level ρ are depicted in Figure 17. As shown in the figures, there is a negative correlation between scale level, ρ, and number of clusters K. Because resizing the dataset results in a coarser representation of the original dataset, the number of clusters is decreasing with the increasing scale level ρ. This phenomenon is the natural consequence of applying wavelet transforms on the low-frequency component of the original signal.

Table 2. Performance results of CUDA and CPU versions of Low-Frequency Component Extraction for scale level one on datasets (DS1 & DS2); times in microseconds

Dataset	Number of Points	Execution Time (CPU)	Execution Time (GPU)	Kernel Speed-Up
DS1_4096	16777216	121286	735	165.01
DS1_2048	4194304	30739	228	134.82
DS1_1024	1048576	7742	94	82.36
DS1_512	262144	1958	52	37.65
DS2_4096	16777216	121267	735	164.98
DS2_2048	4194304	30406	230	132.20
DS2_1024	1048576	7710	95	81.15
DS2_512	262144	1956	54	36.22

Figure 17. Application of WaveCluster approach on fog datasets: (a) DS1 dataset, (b) ρ = 3 and K = 35 for DS1, (c) ρ = 4 and K = 15 and for DS1, (d) DS2 dataset, (e) ρ = 3 and K = 21 for DS2, (f) ρ = 4 and K = 6 for DS2 (where ρ is the scale level and K is the number of clusters detected)

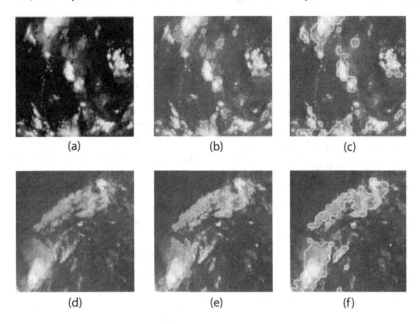

CONCLUSION

In this chapter, we have investigated the study of data reduction methodologies for big datasets both from the point of theory as well as application with special emphasis on parallel data reduction algorithms. Big datasets need to be processed and analyzed efficiently to extract useful information for innovation and decision-making in corporate and scientific research. However, because the process of data retrieval on big data is computationally expensive, a data reduction operation can result in substantial speed up in the execution of the data retrieval process. The ultimate goal of the data reduction techniques is to save time and bandwidth by enabling the user to deal with larger datasets within minimal resources without sacrificing the features of the original dataset in the reduced representation of the dataset at the desired level of accuracy.

Despite substantial improvements on processor technology in terms of speed, data reduction algorithms may still not complete the required task in a reasonable amount of time at big data. Additionally, there may not be enough available memory resources to hold all the data on a single computer. One of the possible solutions to overcome those issues and efficiently mine big data is to make utilization of parallel algorithms (Hedberg, 1995). Parallel processing techniques are extensively used by dividing the task into smaller subtasks and then executing them simultaneously to cope with memory limits and to decrease the execution time of given task.

Graphical processing units (GPUs) are regarded as co-processors of the CPU and have tremendous computational power. NVIDIA introduced CUDA, providing a programming model for parallel computation on GPUs. In this chapter, we have presented a CUDA algorithm of wavelet transform that is used in the WaveCluster algorithm for reducing the original dataset. The WaveCluster approach first extracts the low-frequency component from the signal using wavelet transform and then performs connected component labeling on the low-frequency component to find the clusters present on the dataset. The algorithm has a multi-resolution feature. Thus, the algorithm has the ability of detecting arbitrarily-shaped clusters at different scales and can handle noise in an appropriate way.

Due to limited memory capacity of the video cards, CUDA device may not be a remedy to all problems in processing big data. Much larger datasets could be mined on distributed memory architectures with the aggregate memory of the system using message passing APIs such as MPI. We have also implemented the WaveCluster algorithm for distributed memory models using MPI (Yıldırım & Özdoğan, 2011) in which a master-slave model and replicated approach are followed. A dataset that does not fit into the available memory is processed by taking advantage of the aggregate memory on the distributed memory system.

Each parallel memory architecture has intrinsic advantages over the other model. With the increasing hybrid architectures, MPI model (or map-reduce model) can be used to achieve data distribution between GPU nodes whereas CUDA functions as "main computing engine" (Karunadasa & Ranasinghe, 2009). Hence, they have been considered complementary models in order to utilize the system resources at maximum.

REFERENCES

Almuallim, H., & Dietterich, T. G. (1991). Learning with many irrelevant features. In *Proceedings of the Ninth National Conference on Artificial Intelligence (AAAI-91)*, (vol. 2, pp. 547–552). Anaheim, CA: AAAI Press.

Aluru, S., Prabhu, G. M., & Gustafson, J. (1992). A random number generator for parallel computers. *Parallel Computing*, *18*(8), 839–847. doi:10.1016/0167-8191(92)90030-B.

Bradley, T., Toit, J. D., Tong, R., Giles, M., & Woodhams, P. (2011). Parallelization techniques for random number generators. In W. Hwu (Ed.), GPU Computing Gems Emerald Ed., (pp. 231–246). Boston: Morgan Kaufmann.

Buck, J. B., Watkins, N., LeFevre, J., Ioannidou, K., Maltzahn, C., Polyzotis, N., & Brandt, S. (2011). SciHadoop: Array-based query processing in Hadoop. In *Proceedings of 2011 International Conference for High Performance Computing, Networking, Storage and Analysis* (SC '11). ACM.

Chan, K.-P., & Fu, A. W.-C. (1999). Efficient time series matching by wavelets. [IEEE.]. *Proceedings of Data Engineering*, *1999*, 126–133.

Chapman, B., Jost, G., & Ruud, R. V. D. P. (2007). *Using OpenMP: Portable shared memory parallel programming*. Cambridge, MA: The MIT Press.

de Matteis, A., & Pagnutti, S. (1990). A class of parallel random number generators. *Parallel Computing*, *13*(2), 193–198. doi:10.1016/0167-8191(90)90146-Z.

Dean, J., & Ghemawat, S. (2008). Mapreduce: Simplified data processing on large clusters. *Communications of the ACM*, *51*(1), 107–113. doi:10.1145/1327452.1327492.

Faloutsos, C., Ranganathan, M., & Manolopoulos, Y. (1994). Fast subsequence matching in time-series databases. *SIGMOD Record*, *23*(2), 419–429. doi:10.1145/191843.191925.

Fayyad, F., Piatetsky-Shapiro, G., & Smyth, P. (1996). From data mining to knowledge discovery in databases. *AI Magazine*, *17*, 37–54.

Gropp, W., Lusk, E., & Skjellum, A. (1999). *Using MPI: Portable parallel programming with the message-passing interface*. Cambridge, MA: MIT Press.

Harmon, L. D. (1973). The recognition of faces. *Scientific American, 229*(5), 71–82. doi:10.1038/scientificamerican1173-70 PMID:4748120.

Hedberg, S. R. (1995). Parallelism speeds data mining. *IEEE Parallel & Distributed Technology Systems & Applications, 3*(4), 3–6. doi:10.1109/88.473600.

Huffmire, T., & Sherwood, T. (2006). Wavelet-based phase classification. In *Proceedings of the 15th International Conference on Parallel Architectures and Compilation Techniques* (pp. 95–104). New York, NY: ACM.

Jain, A., & Zongker, D. (1997). Feature selection: Evaluation, application, and small sample performance. *IEEE Transactions on Pattern Analysis and Machine Intelligence, 19*(2), 153–158. doi:10.1109/34.574797.

John, G. J., Kohavi, R., & Pfleger, K. (1994). Irrelevant features and the subset selection problem. In *Proceedings of the International Conference on Machine Learning* (pp. 121–129). IEEE.

Karunadasa, N. P., & Ranasinghe, D. N. (2009). Accelerating high performance applications with cuda and mpi. In *Proceedings of the Industrial and Information Systems (ICIIS),* (pp. 331–336). ICIIS.

Lohr, S. L. (1999). *Sampling: Design and analysis.* Duxbury Press.

Madeira, S. C., & Oliveira, A. L. (2004). Biclustering algorithms for biological data analysis: A survey. *IEEE/ACM Transactions on Computational Biology and Bioinformatics, 1,* 24–45. doi:10.1109/TCBB.2004.2 PMID:17048406.

Malik, T., Best, N., Elliott, J., Madduri, R., & Foster, I. (2011). Improving the efficiency of subset queries on raster images. In *Proceedings of the ACM SIGSPATIAL Second International Workshop on High Performance and Distributed Geographic Information Systems* (HPDGIS '11). ACM.

Mukhopadhyay, A., & Maulik, U. (2009). Unsupervised satellite image segmentation by combining sa based fuzzy clustering with support vector machine. In *Proceedings of the Advances in Pattern Recognition,* (pp. 381–384). IEEE.

Narendra, P. M., & Fukunaga, K. (1977). A branch and bound algorithm for feature subset selection. *IEEE Transactions on Computers, 26*(9), 917–922. doi:10.1109/TC.1977.1674939.

NASA Earth Science Office. (2011). *Interactive weather satallite imagery viewers.* Retrieved from http://weather.msfc.nasa.gov/GOES/goeseasthurrir.html

Nickolls, J., Buck, B., Garland, M., & Skadron, K. (2008). Scalable parallel programming with CUDA. *Queue, 6*(2), 40–53. doi:10.1145/1365490.1365500.

Popivanov, I., & Miller, R. J. (2002). Similarity search over time-series data using wavelets. [IEEE.]. *Proceedings of Data Engineering, 2002,* 212–221.

Pudil, P., & Novovičová, J. (1998). Novel methods for feature subset selection with respect to problem knowledge. In *Feature Extraction, Construction and Selection* (pp. 101–116). New York: Springer. doi:10.1007/978-1-4615-5725-8_7.

Pudil, P., Novovičová, J., & Kittler, J. (1994). Floating search methods in feature selection. *Pattern Recognition Letters, 15*(11), 1119–1125. doi:10.1016/0167-8655(94)90127-9.

Shapiro, L. G., & Stockman, G. C. (2001). *Computer vision.* Englewood Cliffs, NJ: Prentice Hall.

Sheikholeslami, G., Chatterjee, S., & Zhang, A. (1998). Wavecluster: A multi-resolution clustering approach for very large spatial databases. In *Proceedings of the International Conference on Very Large Data Bases* (pp. 428-439). IEEE.

Sifuzzaman, M., Islam, M. R., & Ali, M. Z. (2009). Application of wavelet transform and its advantages compared to Fourier transform. *The Journal of Physiological Sciences; JPS, 13*, 121–134.

Singh, S., Kubica, J., Larsen, S., & Sorokina, D. (2009). Parallel large scale feature selection for logistic regression. In *Proceedings of the SIAM International Conference on Data Mining (SDM)*. SDM.

Somol, P., Pudil, P., Ferri, F. J., & Kittler, J. (2000). Fast branch & bound algorithm in feature selection. In B. Sanchez, M. J. Pineda, & J. Wolfmann, (Eds.), *Proceedings of SCI 2000: The 4th World Multiconference on Systemics, Cybernetics and Informatics* (pp. 646–651). Orlando, FL: IIIS.

Song, Z., & Roussopoulos, N. (2000). Using Hilbert curve in image storing and retrieving. In *Proceedings of the 2000 ACM Workshops on Multimedia* (MULTIMEDIA '00). ACM.

Stearns, S. D. (1976). On selecting features for pattern classifiers. In *Proceedings of the 3rd International Conference on Pattern Recognition* (ICPR 1976) (pp. 71–75). Coronado, CA: ICPR.

Stollnitz, E. J., DeRose, T. D., & Salesin, D. H. (1995). Wavelets for computer graphics: A primer, part 1. *IEEE Computer Graphics and Applications, 15*(3), 76–84. doi:10.1109/38.376616.

Surdeanu, M., Turmo, J., & Ageno, A. (2005). A hybrid unsupervised approach for document clustering. In *Proceedings of the Eleventh ACM SIGKDD International Conference on Knowledge Discovery in Data Mining* (pp. 685–690). New York, NY: ACM.

Wang, D. L., Zender, C. S., & Jenks, S. F. (2007). Server-side parallel data reduction and analysis. *Advances in Grid and Pervasive Computing, 4459*, 744–750. doi:10.1007/978-3-540-72360-8_67.

Whitney, A. W. (1971). A direct method of nonparametric measurement selection. *IEEE Transactions on Computers, 20*(9), 1100–1103. doi:10.1109/T-C.1971.223410.

Wu, Y., Agrawal, D., & Abbadi, A. E. (2000). A comparison of DFT and DWT based similarity search in time-series databases. In *Proceedings of the Ninth International Conference on Information and Knowledge Management*, CIKM '00 (pp. 488–495). New York, NY: ACM.

Yıldırım, A. A., & Özdoğan, C. (2011). Parallel WaveCluster: A linear scaling parallel clustering algorithm implementation with application to very large datasets. *Journal of Parallel and Distributed Computing, 71*(7), 955–962. doi:10.1016/j.jpdc.2011.03.007.

Yıldırım, A. A., & Özdoğan, C. (2011). Parallel wavelet-based clustering algorithm on GPUs using CUDA. *Procedia Computer Science, 3*, 396–400. doi:10.1016/j.procs.2010.12.066.

KEY TERMS AND DEFINITIONS

Big Data: Data that takes an excessive amount of time/space to store, transmit, and process using available resources.

Clustering: A common data mining technique that is used for data retrieval by grouping similar objects into disjoint classes or clusters.

CUDA (Compute Unified Device Architecture): A parallel programming model that is used for general-purpose computation on NVIDIA GPUs (Graphical Processing Units).

Distributed Memory System (DMS) model: A model in which independent processors or nodes, each with their own memory and address space, are connected to each other by means of high-speed network infrastructure.

Feature Selection Technique: As a data reduction technique, where the goal is to find the best representational data among all possible feature combinations.

Feature Extraction Technique: A technique that solves the reduction problem by transforming input data into another space in which the task is performed using reduced transformed data.

Parallel Processing Techniques: Techniques that are extensively used in divide-and-conquer approaches in which the task is divided into smaller subtasks, all of which are then executed simultaneously to decrease the overall execution time of a given task.

Shared Memory System (SMS) model: A model that there is a single address space – and thus the appearance of a shared memory bank – into which any of the nodes/processors may read or write at any time.

Section 2
Big Data Storage, Management, and Sharing

Chapter 5
Techniques for Sampling Online Text-Based Data Sets

Lynne M. Webb
University of Arkansas, USA

Yuanxin Wang
Temple University, USA

ABSTRACT

The chapter reviews traditional sampling techniques and suggests adaptations relevant to big data studies of text downloaded from online media such as email messages, online gaming, blogs, micro-blogs (e.g., Twitter), and social networking websites (e.g., Facebook). The authors review methods of probability, purposeful, and adaptive sampling of online data. They illustrate the use of these sampling techniques via published studies that report analysis of online text.

INTRODUCTION

Studying social media often involves downloading publically-available textual data. Based on studies of email messages, Facebook, blogs, gaming websites, and Twitter, this essay describes sampling techniques for selecting online data for specific research projects. As previously noted (Webb & Wang, (2013); Wiles, Crow, & Pain, 2011), research methodologies for studying online text tend to follow or adapt existing research methodologies,

including sampling techniques. The sampling techniques discussed in this chapter follow well-established sampling practices, resulting in representative and/or purposeful samples; however, the established techniques have been modified to apply to sampling online text—where unusually large populations of messages are available for sampling and the population of messages is in a state of constant growth. The sampling techniques discussed in this chapter can be used for both qualitative and quantitative research.

DOI: 10.4018/978-1-4666-4699-5.ch005

Rapidly advancing internet technologies have altered daily life as well as the academic landscape. Researchers across disciplines are interested in examining the large volumes of data generated on internet platforms, such as social networking sites and mobile devices. Compared to data collected and analyzed through traditional means, big data generated around-the-clock on the internet can help researchers identify latent patterns of human behavior and perceptions that were previously unknown. The richness of the data brings economic benefits to diverse data-intensive industries such as marketing, insurance, and healthcare. Repeated observations of internet data across time amplify the size of already large data sets; data-gathered across time have long interested academics. Vast-sized data sets, typically called "big data," share at least four shared traits: The data are unstructured, growing at an exponential rate, transformational, and highly complicated.

As more big data sets become available to the researchers through the convenience of internet technologies, ability to analyze the big data sets can weaken. Many factors can contribute to a deficiency in analysis. One major obstacle can be the capability of the analytical systems. Although software developers have introduced multiple analytical tools for scholars to employ with big data (e.g., Hadoop, Storm), the transformational nature of big data requires frequent software updates as well as increases in relevant knowledge. In other words, analyzing big data requires specialized knowledge. Another challenge is selecting an appropriate data-mining process. As Badke (2012, p.47) argued, seeking "specific results for specific queries" without employing the proper mining process can further complicate the project instead of helping manage it. Additionally, data of multi-petabyte which include millions of files from heterogeneous operating systems might be too large to back up through conventional computing methods. In such a case, the choice of the

data mining tool becomes critical in determining the feasibility, efficiency, and accuracy of the research project.

Many concerns raised regarding big data collection and analysis duplicate concerns surrounding conventional online data collection:

- **Credibility of Online Resources:** Authors of the online text often post anonymously. Their responses, comments, or articles are susceptible to credibility critiques;

- **Privacy Issues:** Internet researchers do not necessarily have permission of the users who originally generated the text. Users are particularly uncomfortable when data generated from personal information, such as Facebook posts or text messages on mobile devices, are examined without their explicit permission. No comprehensive legal system currently exists that draws a clear distinction between publically available data and personal domains;

- **Security Issues:** When successful online posters, such as bloggers, enjoy the free publicity of the internet, they also can be victimized by co-option of their original work and thus violation of their intellectual property rights. It is difficult for researchers to identify the source of a popular Twitter post that is re-tweeted thousands of times, often without acknowledging the original author. Therefore, data collected from open-access online sources might infringe authors' copyrights.

Despite these concerns, researchers and entrepreneurs collect large data sets from the internet and attempt to make sense of the trends contained therein. Howe et al. (2008) issued a call to action for scientists to assist in coping with the complexities of big data sets. Bollier (2010) observed that "small samples of large data sets can be entirely reliable proxies for big data" (p. 14). Furthermore, boyd (2010) raised serious questions about representative sampling of big data sets. Indeed, such incredibly large and complex data sets cry out for effective sampling techniques to manage the sheer size of the data set, its complexity, and perhaps most importantly, its on-going growth. In this essay, we review multiple sampling techniques that effectively address this exact set of issues.

BACKGROUND

Because millions of internet venues exist, containing thousands of posts with an ever increasing number of messages, a sampling plan is essential for any study of new media. Indeed, this wealth of data awaiting harvest can be bewildering in its complexity (Hookway, 2008) and thus studies of online textual data require methodical planning and procedures for sampling. We adopt Thompson's definition of sampling as "selecting part of a population to observe so that one may estimate something about the whole population" (2012, p. 1). In this section, we describe well-established sampling practices that are widely used in the social sciences and explain how internet researchers working with big data can employ such practices to produce representative and/or purposeful samples.

Population, Census, and Sampling

In an ideal world, every research project would conduct a census of its objects of study. That is, in an ideal world, the researcher would examine the entire population and report the findings. We define population as every instance of the phenomenon under study to which the researcher desires to generalize (e.g., all Twitter posts about a new product during the week following its launch). A census (sampling all relevant instances of a phenomenon) eliminates any concerns about

whether a sample is representative versus biased or inaccurate, because all instances are examined.

On rare occasion, an approximation of a census is possible. For example, Webb, Hayes, Chang, & Smith (2012) examined every blog post on the topic of brides or weddings that appeared in the five longest threads of conversation on every fan website of AMC's drama *Mad Men* ($n = 11$) to describe how fans interpret and describe the weddings that appeared on the TV show across its first three seasons. Note, however, that Webb, Hayes et al. approximated a census. They examined only the five longest threads of conversation. Furthermore, they did not examine all fan websites—only those surrounding one television program. Finally, the researchers did not examine every mention of brides or weddings on *all* fan websites. Because their sample, even though comprehensive in certain ways, examined only the fan websites for one object of fandom, *Mad Men,* they can generalize their findings only to what they sampled, fans of this one television show who posted on fan websites during the first three seasons. Such is the dynamic relationship between samples, populations, and generalizations—the researcher's results only apply to the given sample; however, if the sample is comprehensive or representative, an argument can be made for generalizing beyond the sample to the larger population.

In the real world of research, censuses are rarely attempted, as time and budgets limit the number of incidences examined. Additionally, researchers often employ analyses so detailed that only a finite number of incidences can be subjected to analysis for the project to be completed in a timely manner. For this reason, researchers might sample the population of incidents to select a limited number of incidences for analysis. The subset selected for analysis is called "the sample." The set of all incidences of the object of study from which the sample is selected is called "the population."

SAMPLING AND BIG DATA SETS

The Question of Sample Size

Whenever a researcher draws a sample, the question of sample size arises. Researchers desire to draw samples large enough to represent the diversity in the population, but no larger than necessary. Each sample draw requires time, effort, and potentially money to both gather and analyze the data. Thus, efficient researchers aspire to draw samples of sufficient size, but no larger. What is the ideal sample size? Exact formulas exist for calculating appropriate sample size for *quantitative analyses*, depending on three factors: population size, statistics of interest, and tolerance for error (see, for example, Chapter 4 in Thompson, 2012). Appropriate sample size for *qualitative analyses* is determined typically by the saturation process. When no new themes emerge from qualitative analyses of the data set, then the analyses are considered complete and the sample is determined. The difficulty, of course, with using saturation as a guideline for sampling internet data is that by the time the researcher knows that more data is needed for inclusion in the sample, the time of data collection can be long past. Therefore, as a practical matter, most qualitative researchers rely on previously published reports of sample size as a guideline for how much data to download. As the researcher conducts the relevant literature review, a mean sample size employed in previous studies can be ascertained by taking special notice of the sample sizes in previous studies of similar phenomena using similar methods. In addition to the typical sample size employed in published work on similar objects of study, cautious researchers add a cushion of an additional 10 – 20% of incidences in case saturation comes later than usual in the given sample.

Sampling Techniques

The techniques the researcher employs to select incidences from the population and into the sample have received intense scholarly scrutiny (Daniel, 2012; Kalton, 1983; Scheaffer, Mendenhall, Ott, & Gerow, 2012; Thompson, 2012). Any acceptable sampling technique must be carefully selected and defended using the principles discussed in this section of the chapter. The goal of all sampling techniques is to obtain a representative sample (i.e., a sample in which the incidences selected accurately portray the population). Of course, obtaining a representative sample from a big-data set is especially challenging, given its ever changing and ever growing nature as well as its potential complexity. However, widely-accepted methods for obtaining a representative sample are multiple; the most common techniques are discussed below.

Critical Decision Point: Probability vs. Convenience Sampling

The first choice before the researcher is whether to employ a probability sample or a convenience sample. An argument can be made that both kinds of samples are representative of their respective populations; however, the argument relies on the phenomenon under study.

"Sample designs based on planned randomness are called probability samples" (Schaeffer et al., 2012, p. 10). In probability sampling, each element has a known, nonzero probability of inclusion into the sample (Kalton, 1983). In the case where every instance has an equal probability of selection into the sample (simple random sampling), the researcher can offer a statistical argument for the representativeness of the sample. The argument is based primarily on two points: "selection biases are avoided" (Kalton, 1983, p. 7), and statistical theory allows for the prediction that the sample is likely to be representative of the population from which it was drawn.

In convenience sampling, the researcher includes easy-to-access incidences in the sample, thus saving time and money involved in drawing a probability sample. "The weakness of all non-probability sampling is its subjectivity" (Kalton, 1983, p. 7). Conversely, convenience sampling is always the best choice when a compelling argument can be made that the phenomenon under study is likely to be equally represented in all incidences of the object of study. For example, the studies to determine human body temperature were not conducted with random samples of the human population, but rather with the incidences "at hand," specifically medical residents and students as well as nurses and nursing students. The researchers reasoned that if human beings as a species retain an average body temperature, it does not matter which human specimens were included in the sample; the average temperature of any sample of humans would serve as an accurate approximation for the average temperature in the population. Given the tremendous diversity of internet text, researchers examining this object of study rarely have the opportunity to argue for the universality of the phenomenon under study and thus typically employ probability rather than convenience sampling.

Probability Sampling

How do researchers engage in probability sampling? Such sampling involves two steps described in detail below: (a) selection of the population and sampling frame as well as (b) choosing the sampling technique that selects incidences for inclusion in the sample.

Selecting a Population and Sample Frame

The researcher must decide on a population to study. For example, will a study of political blogs examine a sample drawn from all political blogs in the world or in a given nation? Will the study examine only filter blogs, campaign blogs, popular blogs, political party blogs, or another type of blog of interest?

Most sampling experts describe selecting a population as a "first step" in methodological design (e.g., Kalton, 1983, p. 6). In reality, for most research projects, the selected population under study exists in a dynamic relationship to its sampling frame. That is, researchers often define the population via the sampling frame and visa-versa. The term sampling frame refers to a list of all incidences in the population—all the incidences available for sampling (Scheaffer et al., 2012). For example, Waters and Williams (2011) defined their population and their sampling frame as all U. S. government agencies; they reported randomly selecting from this sampling frame 60 government agencies to examine their recent tweets.

Given the dynamic nature of internet texts, discovering an accurate sampling frame can prove challenging. Researchers may employ convenience sampling when "there is no single systematic register from which to select randomly" (Thewall & Stuart, 2007, p. 530). This practice was more common in early studies on online text (e.g., Bar-Ilan, 2005). Contemporary researchers can select among multiple techniques to address this problem:

- Rely on pre-existing services and companies to provide sampling frames. As Tremayne, Zheng, Lee, and Jeong (2006) noted, "A number of websites provide rankings of blogs, usually according to the total number of web links pointing to each blog" (p. 296). Thus, help is available to identify existing sampling frames. For example, Thelwall, Buckley and Paltoglou (2011) "downloaded from data company Spinn3r as part of their (then) free access program for researchers" (p. 410). Similarly, Xenos (2008) captured blog discussion on topics of interest using "an early incarnation of the Blogrunner (also known as the Annotated *New York Times*)" (p. 492). Alternatively, Subrahmanyam et al. (2009) used a simple Google search to locate blog-hosting websites that were then examined for adolescent blogs; the Goggle search results provided their sampling frame. Finally, Huffaker and Calvert (2005) retrieved their sampling frame "using two weblog search engines, as well as from *Blogspot* and *LiveJournal* (p. 4);

- Rely on features built into online technologies, such Twitter's key-word search feature (e.g., Cheng, Sun, Hu, & Zeng, 2011). Websites typically contain search features that allow both random sampling as well as purposeful sampling by key word. For example, Webb, Wilson, Hodges, Smith, and Zakeri (2012) reported using a Facebook feature that provides on request a random page from the user's network. Similarly, Ji and Lieber (2008) reported sampling profiles on a dating website by using its search feature. Some blog host sites require researchers to join the blogging community and establish an empty blog to access the search feature, but the service is typically free with open access after joining;
- Use commercial software packages with sampling functions. For example, Greer and Ferguson (2011) report using Webpage Thumbnailer "to capture digital

pictures of Web pages from a batch list" (p. 204) and then sampling the captured pages. See Boulos, Sanflippo, Corley, and Wheeler (2010) for detailed descriptions and reviews of multiple social web mining applications;

- Define the population quite narrowly such that a census or near census is possible and/or a sampling frame can be readily ascertained (e.g., Webb, Hayes, et al., 2012);
- Define the population as the sampling frame. For example, Thoring (2011) defined her population as the Twitter feeds of "all UK trade publishers that were members of the Publishers Association (PA) and/or Independent Publishers Guild (IPC) at the time of surveying" (p. 144-145);
- Employ multiple, overlapping sampling frames that are likely to capture the vast majority of the population. For example, Hale (2012) reported using three overlapping search engines to locate blogs for sampling and analysis;
- Define the population and sampling frame, in large part, by a given time frame that might or might not be tied to the phenomenon understudy. For example, Ifukor (2010) sampled blog posts during three time periods: pre-, during, and post-election. Alternatively, Thelwall, Buckley, and Paltoglou examined Twitter posts between February 9, 2010 and March 9, 2010; they identified "the top 30 events from the 29 selected days using the time series scanning method" (2011, p. 410);
- Sampling across time (see Intille, 2012 for three options). For example, to correlate Twitter mood to stock prices, Bollen, Mao, and Zeng (2011), collected all tweets posted across a 9.5 month period and then used a software text analytic tool "to generate a six-dimensional daily time series of public mood" (p. 2);

- Systematic sampling at fixed-intervals (e.g., every day at noon for 2 weeks). For example, McNeil et al. (2012) collected tweets via keyword searches each day at one specific time across a seven day period.

Selecting a Probability Sampling Technique

After a sampling frame is identified, the researcher can engage in "pure random sampling" meaning numbers can be drawn from a random number table and used as the basis for selecting incidences into the sample. For example, Waters and Williams (2011) defined their population and their sampling frame as all U. S. government agencies; they reported randomly selecting from this sampling frame 60 government agencies to examine their recent tweets. Random number tables appear in the back of most statistics book; they are available free of charge on the internet and can be discovered via a Google search. Using a random number table is equivalent to assigning numbers to all incidences in the sampling frame, printing the numbers on individual pieces of paper, tossing the pieces of papers into a bowl, thoroughly mixing the pieces of paper, and then drawing the numbers from the bowl. "To reduce the labor of the selection process and to avoid such problems as pieces of paper sticking together, the selection is more commonly made using a random number table" (Thompson, 2012, p. 11). In random sampling, each incidence has the same or an equal probability of inclusion into the sample (Scheaffer et al., 2012).

Simple Random Sampling

Researchers employ simple random sampling when the sampling frame is stable and can be examined at a fixed point in time, such as customers' incoming email messages during the first week following the launch of a new product. In simple random sampling, each incident has an equal probability of inclusion in the sample and that probability is based on population size. For example, if the researcher identified 963 tweets containing a key word sent on a given day, simple random sampling of those tweets would allow each tweet a 1 in 963 chance of selection into the sample. Fullwood, Sheehan, and Nicholls (2009) reported randomly selecting open My Space pages for analysis. Similarly, Williams, Trammell, Postelnicu, Landreville, and Martin (2005) downloaded the front page of the Bush and Kerry campaign websites every day after the conventions, and then randomly sampled blog posts from the downloaded pages for analysis.

Simple random sampling can be done *with or without replacement*—meaning a researcher can either allow or fail to allow an incident to be selected more than once. With larger samples, replacement seems unnecessary, as many incidences are available for selection. Also, the more diverse the population, the more each incident potentially represents a unique set of characteristics, the less the researcher would desire to include multiple copies of that unique set of characteristics in any given incidence, and thus the less likely the researcher would employ replacement sampling. For example, McNeil, Brna, and Gordon (2012) collected data via keyword searching Twitter posts, but excluded re-tweets and duplications to avoid skewing the data. Random sampling with and without replacement can be conducted within a large data set via standard statistical analysis software packages such as SPSS and SAS.

Systematic Sampling

When a population is quite fluid, such as tweets posted about a product recall, the researcher might employ a *systematic sample*, also called a "1 in K." "In general, systematic sampling involves random selection of one element from the first k elements and then selection of every kth element thereafter" (Scheaffer et al., 2012, p. 219). For example, a researcher could elect to analyze all email messages generated in a given organization during a given week by sampling every 12th email message generated from 12:00 AM Sunday to 11:59 PM the following Saturday. Usually the researcher uses a random number table to select a number representing a small portion of the population, typically between one and ten per cent and samples every *k*th incident. For example, if a collection of comments on a gaming website contain a total of 997 posts, a researcher could calculate that 10% of 997 is 10, then select a random number between 0 and 9 from a random number table. If we assume that selected number was 6, then the researcher samples posts number 6, 16, 26, 36, etc. until post number 996. In this way the researcher will randomly sample 99 posts or 10% of the population. Vandoorn, vanZoonen, and Wyatt (2007) reported employing a systematic sampling technique in their examination of online gender identifiers displayed in Dutch and Flemish weblogs: From their sample frame, "every 11th, 12th, and 13th weblog was searched. On this basis, 97 weblogs were selected" (p. 148).

Systematic sampling has multiple advantages that simple random sampling does not share (Kalton, 1983)—advantages that can make it more useful for big data research:

- A sample frame listing each member of the population is not necessary;
- The population size can be unknown;
- The population can be fluid and contain fluctuations in time, space, and frequency that would make random sampling difficult. For example, in their research on adolescent blogging, Subrahmanyam et al. (2009) examined "the last three entries posted between April 15 and May 15" in each identified blog" (p. 226) regardless of how many posts each blog contained. Similarly, Greer and Ferguson (2011) analyzed the first page of Twitter accounts, thus reading the latest post and reports by account holders;

- Compared to random sampling from a random number table, a sample can be selected with little effort or complexity;
- Systematic sampling is easy to apply and thus involves no complex mathematics or training for the sample selector;
- Systematic sampling can "yield more precise estimates than a simple random sample" (Schaeffer, 2012, p. 11). For example, in attempting to identify a network of bloggers who regularly post about the Iraq War, Tremayne et al. (2006) "used a systematic sample to isolate posts from each political blog" discussing the War. Specifically, they selected posts from 16 days for coding, because "a Lexis-Nexis search revealed these months to be higher than average for war in Iraq news, which served as assurance that a considerable number of [relevant] post would be found " (p. 296).

Cluster Sampling

"A cluster sample is a probability sample in which each sampling unit is a collection, or cluster, of elements" (Scheaffer et al., 2012, p. 252). For example, a researcher might desire to sample the longest strings of conversation on fan blogs—a sting composed of an original post and all subsequent commentary (e.g., Webb, Chang et al., 2012).

How does the researcher draw a cluster sample? "The population is partitioned into primary units, each primary unit being composed of secondary units. Whenever a primary unit is included in the sample, every secondary unit within it is observed.... Even though the actual measurement may be made on secondary units, it is the primary units that are selected" (Thompson, 2012, p. 157). For example, Webb, Chang et al. (2012) observed 11 fansites, discovered all strings on each fansite, and then downloaded all elements within the five longest strings on each fansite. As with any form of sampling, the first step is to specify the population and sampling frame—in this case, appropriate clusters. Typically, incidences within a cluster are "close" in some way (e.g., geographically, chronologically, emotively) and "hence tend to have similar characteristics" (Scheaffer et al., 2012, p. 253). Indeed, on fansites, all elements in a string of conversation appear next to one another in reverse chronological order and tends to discuss the same topic. Cluster sampling is preferable under two conditions: (1) when the phenomenon under study cannot be easily sampled any other way such as looking at email messages in a trail, given that the messages appear attached to one another and (2) when the phenomenon under study can only be observed in clusters such as blog interaction which is by definition comprised of clusters of posts.

Multi-Staged Designs

Big data sets easily accommodate multi-staged designs, in which sampling occurs in a repeated fashion across time. "If, after selecting a sample of primary units, a sample of secondary units is selected from each of the primary units selected, the design is referred to as *two-stage sampling*. If in turn a sample of tertiary units is selected from each selected secondary unit, the design is *three-stage sampling*. Higher-order *multi-stage designs* are also possible" (Thompson, 2012, p. 171). For example, Subrahmanyam et al. (2009) used a simple Google search to locate blog-hosting websites ($N=9$) that were then examined for adolescent blogs ($N=201$). The Google search results provided the sampling frame. After adolescent blogs were located within the blog-hosting websites, the team harvested the three most recent three entries within a 3 month time frame from each adolescent blog as their data for analysis ($N=603$ entries). Multi-staged designed are a useful alternative for digging into a complex data set to find exact incidences of the phenomenon under study.

Critical Decision Point 2: Balancing the Goals of Representativeness vs. Indecent-Rich Sampling

The second choice before the researcher is how to balance the competing goals of drawing a representative sample but also a purposeful (incident rich) sample. The researcher's ultimate desire is a representative sample, but the object of study can relatively rare (e.g., How does a researcher locate the Facebook pages of pre-adolescents among the sea of open Facebook pages available for examination?). Within a set of big data, access can be difficult to obtain (e.g., Pre-adolescents might be quite secretive about their Facebook posts and thus send updates to friends only, thus effectively blocking parental viewing as well as researcher viewing of their posts). In such cases, the researcher might opt for an in-depth analysis of an incident rich sample without a known probability. To ameliorate the concerns of representativeness raised with a nonprobability sample, researchers often select incidences in a way that infuses the sample with diversity that they believe exists in the population. For example, Subrahmanyam, Garcia, Harsono, Li, and Lipana (2009) gathered adolescent blogs from nine hosting sites in the belief that different hosting sites attract different kinds/types of adolescent bloggers. When researchers employ non-probability samples, they often acknowledge in the limitations section of their discussion that the generalizability of the study's conclusion remain unknown.

Purposeful Sampling

How does a researcher go about carefully selecting incidences that illustrate a rare phenomenon under study and thus create an incident-rich study? Multiple sampling techniques exist for such purposes:

- Samples can account for the *rate of message production and/or number of views*. For example, Ferguson and Greer (2011) desired to sample "normally active" Twitter feeds and therefore dropped from their sample frame twitter feeds from accounts they considered inactive and over-active, as defined by the number of tweets per day;

- Samples can be defined by *time frames*. For example, Sweetser Trammell (2007) analyzed blog posts aimed at young votes on campaign websites during the intense period of campaigning (Labor Day through Election Day 2004). Similarly, Gilpin (2010) studied blog posts and Twitter messages within "two financial quarters, an important unit of measure for publically traded companies" (p. 271);

- The *object of study can be defined so narrowly* that *all incidences* of the phenomenon can be included in the sample. For example, Gilbert, Bergstrom, and Karahalios (2009) sampled authoritative blogs, defined by "the number of distinct blogs linking to each indexed blog over the last six months" (*N*=100; p. 7). Similarly, Subrahmanyam et al. (2009) used a simple Google search to locate blog-hosting websites (*N*=9) that were then examined for adolescent blogs (*N*=201);

- The *object of study can be defined so narrowly* that the researcher creates a sample by systematically *excluding incidences* from the study. For example, Hassid (2012) captured 2198 blog updates written in Chinese and posted in a given time period; then he carefully screened them to exclude posts from areas outside of mainland China. Alternatively, when an organization had multiple twitter feeds, Burton and Soboleva (2011) examined only organizations' most visible and central Twitter feed;

- Samples can be defined *in response to user initiatives*. For example, Trammell (2006) examined only those campaign blog posts

that mentioned the opponent, issues, or political matters directly. Similarly, Hardey (2008) examined conversational threads relating to eDating on "23 public English language newsgroups that were hosted by UK websites from April to June 2005" (p. 1114) and ignored the vast majority of conversational threads that failed to discuss the online dating website eDating;

- Samples can be defined by the *web location itself*. Because Schiffer (2006) examined new coverage of one political incident and desired to learn which journalists broke which parts of the story when, he purposefully sampled text from blogs known for cutting edge reporting—blog posts on "ten of the leading Weblogs and the Daily Kos diaries" (p. 498);

- *Exemplar sampling* allows the researcher to select *information-rich internet text* to serve as case studies. For example, Hayes (2011) carefully selected one mommy blog to examine in depth to explain how the blogger and her readers created a sense of community through the expression of identity and discussion on the blog. Hayes chose one specific blog for analysis exactly because its posts and comments provided clear examples of the notions she discussed. Similarly, Keating and Sunakawa (2010) observed online interactions between two carefully-selected gaming teams as a case study of co-ordinated online activities;

- *Context-sensitive sampling* is "purposive sampling in response to automatically detected user behavior, context, or physiological response, as measured passively or semi-automatically using sensors" (Intille, 2012, p. 268). Examples include key words relative to weather, place, proximity to others relevant phenomenon (e.g., blogroll). The sampling can be two-tiered in that detection of an occurrence of an initial keyword can trigger searches for additional and/or secondary key words, such as rain-lightening, sale-discount, Republication-Romney.

Adaptive Sampling: Using Probability Techniques to Obtain Purposeful Samples

Researchers often use probability sampling techniques within studies of narrowly defined or rare phenomenon to obtain incident-rich samples that are generalizable because they have known probabilities. Such techniques are called adaptive sampling because they employ either systematic or random sampling techniques that "depend on observed values of the variable of interest" (Thompson, 2012, p. 6). We consider adaptive sampling an ideal sampling choice for big data sets when a researcher desires to study a specific aspect of a data set but also to generalize the findings to a population. Adaptive sampling offers the advantages of both probability sampling and purposive sampling with the disadvantages of neither. Below we discuss multiple techniques for adaptive sampling:

- *Creating comparison groups* based on characteristics of interest. Creating comparison groups is essential when the researcher desires to examine contrasts such as the differences between popular versus unpopular websites or males versus female authored texts. For example, Reese, Rutigliano, Hyun, and Jeong (2007) used Technorati ratings to locate the most popular conservative political blogs and the most popular liberal political blogs to analyze text from blogs with opposing viewpoints and thus likely capture national discussion on political issues. Alternatively,

Burton and Soboleva (2011) examined the Twitter feeds of multi-national businesses in two English-speaking countries to discover differing uses of the interactive features of Twitter to accommodate the culturally-different expectations of consumers. Finally, Jansen, Zhang, Sobel, and Chowdury (2009) examined tweets about representative companies from segments of major industries; their created groups were the segments of industry.

Stratified Random Sampling

"In stratified sampling, the population is partitioned into regions or strata, and a sample is selected by some design within each stratum" (Thompson, 2012, p. 141). Strata are defined in such a way that they function as nonoverlapping groups; the researcher selects specific incidences from each strata into the sample typically via random sampling (Scheaffer et al., 2012). For example, Boupha, Grisso, Morris, Webb, & Zakeri (2013) reported randomly selecting open Facebook pages from each U. S. state; their 50 strata were the 50 United States. Alternatively, Trammell, Williams, Postelnicu, and Landreville (2006) analyzed blog posts from the 10 Democratic primary presidential candidates in the 2004 election; they stratified their sampling across time by gathering posts from 14 target days spanning the beginning of the primary season (Labor Day 2003) through the Iowa caucus (January 2004). Stratified random sampling can be conducted within a large data set using standard statistical analysis software packages such as SPSS and SAS, if each sample entry is coded for the strata of interest. This sampling technique is appropriate when researchers desire to compare multiple groups or strata across variables of interest.

Stratified Sampling at Random Times Across a Fixed Period (e.g., 12 Randomly Selected Times Across a 48 Hour Period)

This sampling technique is appropriate when researchers desire to compare multiple groups or strata across variables of interest—and across time; researchers use this technique to observe how the comparisons between the strata change across time. For example, Williams, Trammell, Postelnicu, and Martin examined hyperlinks posted in a stratified random sample of "10% of the days in the hot phase of the general election period, from Labor Day through Election day 2004" (2005, p. 181). In another study of candidates' 2004 websites, Trammell, Williams, Postelnicu, and Landreville (2006) examined blog posts from ten Democratic presidential candidates' websites during the 2004 primary campaigns. The researchers reported that using a stratified sampling method, specifically "10% of the days spanning the beginning of the primary season (Labor Day 2003) through the Iowa caucuses (January 2004)" (p. 29); thus, they identified a total of 14 target days (or 14 strata) for analysis.

Sampling Nodes Based on Attributes of Interest (e.g., Location, Activity, Longevity)

For example, Thelwall, Buckley, and Paltoglou examined Twitter posts between February 9, 2010 and March 9, 2010. Then "the top 30 events from the 29 selected days were identified using the time series scanning method" (2011, p. 410). The researchers then employed a "3-hour burst method" (p. 410) to identify topics that sustained increases in commentary for three-consecutive hours. Tweets about such topics were inclusion in the sample. This technique is especially appropriate for complex phenomenon that occur in nodes or clusters based on location, activity, or longevity.

Critical Decision Point 3: Balancing the Goals of Representing Typical, Popular, and Rare Phenomena

A third choice before the researcher is whether to examine (a) typical phenomena, view-points, media, and texts or (b) popular occurrences, or (c) rare and unusual occurrence. All three objects of study are worthy of examination and represent important segments of the human experience. Big data sets contain sufficient numbers of incidences to allow for random sampling to reveal typical phenomena as well as careful sampling of the unusual. More challenging is operationally defining popularity. Researchers have assessed website popularity via the number of links to the page, Google PageRank, number of hits, and number of unique page views (Webb, Fields, Boupha, & Stell, 2012). Researcher can select and defend choices based on conceptual thinking or simply employ multiple assessment techniques in the given study. For example, Webb, Fields et al. (2012) measured blog popularity in two ways: number of comments and number of hits. Their analyses yielded two paths to popularity; one set of variables was associated with popularity as assessed by number of comments (length of homepage and number of comments opportunities), whereas a different set of characteristics were associated with popularity as assessed by number of hits (number of tabs, link, and graphics as well as the website's internal accessibility). Thus, the operationalization of popularity is no small matter, as it can influence sampling decisions and ultimately the results of the study.

Managing and Analyzing Samples of Big Data

As big data became gradually available to web researchers, major methodological concerns emerged such as how to store and analyze such large quantities of data simultaneously—even samples carefully drawn from such large data pools. Specific technologies and software emerged to address these concerns. Big data technology includes big data files, database management, and big data analytics (Hopkins & Evelson, 2011).

One of most popular and widely available data management systems for dealing with hundreds of gigabytes or petabytes data simultaneously is the Hadoop programming model popularized by Google. Its strengths include providing reliable shared online storage for large amounts of multiple-sourced data through the Hadoop Distributed Filesystem (HDFS), analysis through MapReduce (a batch query processer that abstracts the problem from disk reads and writes), and transforming data into a map-and-reduce computation over sets of keys and values (White, 2012). MapReduce works well with unstructured or semi-structured data because it is designed to interpret the data at processing time (Verma, Cherkasova, & Campbell, 2012). While the MapReduce system is able to analyze a whole "big data" set and large samples in batch fashion, the Relational Database Management System (RDBMS) shows more strength in processing point queries where the data is structured into entities with defined format (i.e., structured data) as may occur in key-word or key-characteristic sampling (White, 2012). Different from MapReduce's linear scalable programming that is not sensitive to the change of data size and cluster, RDBMS is a nonlinear programming which allows complex functions such as quadratic or cubic terms (Sumathi & Esakkirajan, 2007) in the model. RDBMS could be retrieved from http://mysql-com.en.softonic.com/. Google's success in text processing and their embrace of statistical machine learning was decoded as an endorsement that facilitated Hadoop's wide-spread adoption (Cohen, Dolan, Dunlap, Hellerstein, & Welton, 2009). Hadoop, the open-source software can be downloaded from http://hadoop.apache.org/releases.html.

On the other hand, additional technologies and software are available for use with big data sets and samples. They represent reasonable alternatives to Hadoop, especially when data sets display unique characteristics that can be best addressed with specialized software. Such alternatives include the following:

- High Performance Computing (HPC) and Grid Computing also are designed to process large-scale data. This system works well for compute-intensive jobs, but becomes problematic when the compute nodes need to access larger data volumes (White, 2012), making it a good candidate for complex analyses of smaller samples of big data;

- A competitive pool of analytical tools for big data is provided by a diversity of software developers. For example, Ayasdi launched its Topological Data Analysis to seek the fundamental structure of massive data sets in 2008. This software could be used in the areas of life sciences, oil and gas, public sector, financial services, retail, and telecom (Empson, 2013) and works well with large and small samples;

- SAS also provides a Web-based solution that leverages SAS high-performance analytics technologies, SAS Visual Analytics, to explore huge volumes of data by showing the correlations and patterns within big data sets and samples, thus identifying opportunities for further analysis (Troester, 2012). Such software is quite useful in exploratory analyses;

- More commonly used in social science research are software programs that specialize in analyzing the statistical patterns of big data, after the sampling process. For example, the U. S. computer technology company Oracle released a version of R integrated into its database and big data appliance (Harrison, 2012);

- For those who are not familiar with syntax-based statistical tools such as STATA, SAS, or R and are handling a relatively small dataset, Minitab and IBM SPSS could be a more practical choice. However, it is important to note that Minitab allows a maximum of 150 million cells, or a maximum of 4,000 columns and 10 million rows; while SPSS, on the other hand, holds up to 2 billion cases in dataset. Thus, SPSS can process larger samples than Minitab.

Solutions and Recommendations

This chapter reviewed a wide variety of sampling options and techniques applicable to big data sets of text harvested from the internet. Based on studies of email messages, Facebook, blogs, gaming websites, and Twitter, the chapter described sampling techniques for selecting online data for specific research projects. We considered the essential characteristics of big data generated from diverse online resources—that the data might be unstructured, transformational, complicated, and growing in fast pace—as we discussed sampling options. Rationale for the use of each technique were offered as the options were presented through an examination of important sampling principles including representativeness, purposefulness, and adaptively. Three critical decision points were reviewed and multiple examples of successful sampling were presented. This information can assist the researcher in making an informed and appropriate choice of sampling techniques, given the goals of the research project and its object of study. However, because of the ever-changing nature of the online data sets, it is necessary to update our understanding and analytical techniques for big data in an on-going way. Additionally, issues regarding privacy, credibility, and security must be carefully monitored during the online data collection process.

FUTURE RESEARCH DIRECTIONS

As future researchers continue to publish reports of analyses of big data sets, many positive developments are likely to occur: Researchers examining internet text are likely to:

- Provide an ever *increasing set of excellent examples* of sampling frames for big data sets;
- Develop *new and innovative sampling techniques* not yet invented and thus not discussed in this chapter. Such innovative techniques are likely to be based on the time-honored set of sampling principles reviewed above;
- Develop a set of *sampling conventions* to effectively manage big data sets. As these conventions are repeatedly replicated, they will become normative and sampling big data sets could become simplified;
- Demonstrate a more *comprehensive understanding* of the core traits of the online data;
- Optimize the existing analytic tools for big data to *increase the capability of dealing with large-size data*;
- With improved sampling techniques, *examine smaller and smaller data sets* to gain a deeper understanding of the latent patterns in big data sets;
- *Define big data differently* based on differing academic disciplines and research goals.

CONCLUSION

The development of internet technology has made large comprehensive data sets readily available, including publically-available, textual, online data. Such data sets offer richness and potential insights into human behavior, but can be costly to harvest, store, and analyze as huge data sets can translate into big labor and computing costs for mining, screening, cleansing, and textual analysis. Incredibly large and complex data sets cry out for effective sampling techniques to manage the sheer size of the data set, its complexity, and perhaps most importantly, its on-going growth. In this essay, we review multiple sampling techniques that effectively address this exact set of issues.

No sampling method works best in all studies. This chapter assists researchers in making critical decisions that result in appropriate sample selections. Discovering feasible and appropriate sampling methods can assist the researcher in discovering otherwise invisible patterns of human behavior available for discovery in big data sets.

Big data sets present sampling challenges that can be addressed with a working knowledge of sampling principles and a "tool box" of sampling techniques reviewed in this chapter. The chapter reviewed traditional sampling techniques and suggested adaptations relevant to big data studies of text downloaded from online media such as email messages, online gaming, blogs, micro-blogs (e.g., Twitter), and social networking websites (e.g., Facebook). Specifically, we reviewed methods of probability, purposeful, and adaptive sampling of online data. We illustrated the use of these sampling techniques via published studies that report analysis of online text. As more big data analyses are published, sampling conventions are likely to emerge that will simplify the decision-making process; the emergent conventions are likely to follow the guiding principles of sampling discussed in this chapter.

REFERENCES

Badke, W. (2012). Big search, big data. *Online, 36*(3), 47–49.

Bar-Ilan, J. (2005). Information hub blogs. *Journal of Information Science, 31*, 297–307. doi:10.1177/0165551505054175.

Bollen, J., Mao, H., & Zeng, X. J. (2011). Twitter mood predicts the stock market. *Journal of Computational Science, 2*(1), 1–8. doi:10.1016/j.jocs.2010.12.007.

Bollier, D. (2010). *The promise and peril of big data*. Retrieved from http://www.thinkbiganalytics.com/uploads/Aspen-Big_Data.pdf

Boulos, M. N. K., Sanfilippo, A. P., Corley, C. D., & Wheeler, S. (2010). Social web mining and exploitation for serious applications: Technosocial predictive analytics and related technologies for public health, environmental and national security surveillance. *Computer Methods and Programs in Biomedicine, 100*, 16–23. doi:10.1016/j.cmpb.2010.02.007 PMID:20236725.

Boupha, S., Grisso, A. D., Morris, J., Webb, L. M., & Zakeri, M. (2013). How college students display ethnic identity on Facebook. In R. A. Lind (Ed.), *Race/gender/media: Considering diversity across audiences, content, and producers* (3rd ed.), (pp. 107-112). Boston, MA: Pearson. boyd, d. (2010, April). *Privacy and publicity in the context of big data*. Retrieved from http://www.danah.org/papers/talks/2010/WWW2010.html

Burton, S., & Soboleva, A. (2011). Interactive or reactive? Marketing with Twitter. *Journal of Consumer Marketing, 28*(7), 491–499. doi:10.1108/07363761111181473.

Cheng, J., Sun, A., Hu, D., & Zeng, D. (2011). An information diffusion-based recommendation framework for micro-blogging. *Journal of the Association for Information Systems, 12*, 463–486.

Cohen, J., Dolan, B., Dunlap, M., Hellerstein, J. M., & Welton, C. (2009). *MAD skills: New analysis practices for big data*. Lyon, France: Paper Presented at Very Large Data Base.

Daniel, J. (2012). *Sampling essentials: Practical guidelines for making sampling choices*. Thousand Oaks, CA: Sage.

Empson, R. (2013). *DARPA-backed Ayasdi launches with $10m from Khosla, Floodgate to uncover hidden value in big data.* Retrieved from http://techcrunch.com/2013/01/16/darpa-backed-ayasdi-launches-with-10m-from-khosla-floodgate-to-uncover-the-hidden-value-in-big-data/

Ferguson, D. A., & Greer, C. F. (2011). Local radio and microblogging: How radio stations in the U.S. are using Twitter. *Journal of Radio & Audio Media, 18*, 33–46. doi:10.1080/1937652 9.2011.558867.

Fullwood, C., Sheehan, N., & Nicholls, W. (2009). Blog function revisited: A content analysis of Myspace blogs. *CyberPsychology & Behavior, 12*(6), 685-689. doi: 10. 1089/cpb.2009.0138

Gilbert, E., Bergstrom, T., & Karahalios, K. (2009). Blogs are echo chambers: Blogs are echo chambers. In *Proceedings of the 42ⁿᵈ Hawaii International Conference on System Sciences.* IEEE. Retrieved http://comp.social.gatech.edu/papers/hicss09.echo.gilbert.pdf

Gilpin, D. (2010). Organizational image construction in a fragmented online media environment. *Journal of Public Relations Research, 22*, 265–287. doi:10.1080/10627261003614393.

Greer, C. F., & Ferguson, D. A. (2011). Using Twitter for promotion and branding: A content analysis of local television Twitter sites. *Journal of Broadcasting & Electronic Media, 55*(2), 198–214. doi:10.1080/08838151.2011.570824.

Hale, S. A. (2012). Net increase? Cross-lingual linking in the blogosphere. *Journal of Computer-Mediated Communication, 17*, 135–151. doi:10.1111/j.1083-6101.2011.01568.x.

Harrison, G. (2012). Statistical analysis and R in the world of big data. *Data Trends & Applications, 26*(3), 39.

Hassid, J. (2012). Safety valve or pressure cooker? Blogs in Chinese political life. *The Journal of Communication, 62*, 212–230. doi:10.1111/j.1460-2466.2012.01634.x.

Hayes, M. T. (2011). Parenting children with autism online: Creating community and support online. In M. Moravec (Ed.), *Motherhood online: How online communities shape modern motherhood* (pp. 258–265). Newcastle upon Tyne, UK: Cambridge Scholars Publishing.

Hookway, N. (2008). Entering the blogosphere: Some strategies for using blogs in social research. *Qualitative Research, 8*, 91–113. doi:10.1177/1468794107085298.

Hopkins, B., & Evelson, B. (2011). *Expand your digital horizon with big data.* Washington, DC: Forrester Research, Inc..

Howe, D., Costanzo, M., Fey, P., Gojobori, T., Hannick, L., & Hide, W. et al. (2008). Biddata: The future of bio-curation. *Nature, 455*(4), 47–50. doi:10.1038/455047a PMID:18769432.

Huffaker, D. A., & Calvert, S. L. (2005). Gender, identity, and language use in teenage blogs. *Journal of Computer-Mediated Communication, 10*. Retrieved September 10, 2008, from http://www3.interscience.wiley.com/cgi-bin/fulltext/120837938/HTMLSTART

Ifukor, P. (2010). Elections or selections? Blogging and twittering the Nigerian 2007 general elections. *Bulletin of Science, Technology & Society, 30*(6), 398–414. doi:10.1177/0270467610380008.

Intille, S. S. (2012). Emerging technology for studying daily life. In M. R. Mehl, & T. S. Conner (Eds.), *Handbook of research methods for studying daily life* (pp. 267–283). New York, NY: Guilford Press.

Jansen, B. J., Zhang, M., Sobel, K., & Chowdury, A. (2009). Twitter power: Tweets as electronic word of mouth. *Journal of the American Society for Information Science and Technology, 60*(11), 2169–2188. doi:10.1002/asi.21149.

Ji, P., & Lieber, P. S. (2008). Emotional disclosure and construction of the poetic other in a Chinese online dating site. *China Media Research, 4*(2), 32–42.

Kalton, G. (1983). *Introduction to survey sampling*. Newbury Park, NJ: Sage.

Keating, E., & Sunakawa, C. (2010). Participation cues: Coordinating activity and collaboration in complex online gaming worlds. *Language in Society, 39*, 331–356. doi:10.1017/S0047404510000217.

McNeil, K., Brna, P. M., & Gordon, K. E. (2012). Epilepsy in the Twitter era: A need to re-tweet the way we think about seizures. *Epilepsy & Behavior, 23*(2), 127–130. doi:10.1016/j.yebeh.2011.10.020 PMID:22134096.

Reese, S. D., Rutigliano, L., Hyun, K., & Jeong, J. (2007). Mapping the blogosphere: Professional and citizen-based media in the global news arena. *Journalism, 8*, 235–261. doi:10.1177/1464884907076459.

Scheaffer, R. L., Mendenhall, W. III, Ott, R. L., & Gerow, K. G. (2012). *Elementary survey sampling* (7th ed.). Boston, MA: Brooks/Cole.

Schiffer, A. J. (2006). Blogsworms and press norms: News coverage of the Downing Street memo controversy. *Journalism & Mass Communication Quarterly, 83*, 494–510. doi:10.1177/107769900608300302.

Subrahmanyam, K., Garcia, E. C., Harsono, L. S., Li, J. S., & Lipana, L. (2009). In their words: Connecting on-line weblogs to developmental processes. *The British Journal of Developmental Psychology, 27*, 219–245. doi:10.1348/026151008X345979 PMID:19972670.

Sumathi, S., & Esakkirajan, S. (2007). *Fundamentals of relational database management systems*. New York, NY: Springer. doi:10.1007/978-3-540-48399-1.

Sweetser Trammell, K. D. (2007). Candidate campaign blogs: Directly reaching out to the youth vote. *The American Behavioral Scientist, 50*, 1255–1263. doi:10.1177/0002764207300052.

Thelwall, M., Buckley, K., & Paltoglou, G. (2011). Sentiment in Twitter events. *Journal of the American Society for Information Science and Technology, 62*(2), 406–418. doi:10.1002/asi.21462.

Thelwall, M., & Stuart, D. (2007). RUOK? Blogging communication technologies during crises. *Journal of Computer-Mediated Communication, 12*, 523–548. doi:10.1111/j.1083-6101.2007.00336.x.

Thompson, S. K. (2012). *Sampling* (3rd ed.). Hoboken, NJ: Wiley. doi:10.1002/9781118162934.

Thoring, A. (2011). Corporate tweeting: Analysing the use of Twitter as a marketing tool by UK trade publishers. *Public Relations Quarterly, 27*, 141–158. doi:10.1007/s12109-011-9214-7.

Trammel, K. D. (2006). Blog offensive: An exploratory analysis of attacks published on campaign blog posts from a political public relations perspective. *Public Relations Review, 32*, 402–406. doi:10.1016/j.pubrev.2006.09.008.

Trammel, K. D., Williams, A. P., Postelnicu, M., & Landreville, K. D. (2006). Evolution of online campaigning: Increasing interactivity in candidate web sites and blogs through text and technical features. *Mass Communication & Society, 9*, 21–44. doi:10.1207/s15327825mcs0901_2.

Tremayne, M., Zheng, N., Lee, J. K., & Jeong, J. (2006). Issue publics on the web: Applying network theory to the war blogosphere. *Journal of Computer-Mediated Communication, 12*, 290–310. doi:10.1111/j.1083-6101.2006.00326.x.

Troester, M. (2012). *Big data meets big data analytics: Three key technologies for extracting real-time business value from the big data that threatens to overwhelm traditional computing architectures.* SAS Institute. Retrieved from www.sas.com/resources/whitepaper/wp_46345.pdf

van Doorn, N., van Zoonen, L., & Wyatt, S. (2007). Writing from experience: Presentations of gender identity on weblogs. *European Journal of Women's Studies, 14*, 143–159. doi:10.1177/1350506807075819.

Verma, A., Cherkasova, L., & Campbell, R. H. (2012). *Two sides of a coin: Optimizing the schedule of MapReduce jobs to minimize their makespan and improve cluster performance.* Paper presented at 2012 IEEE 20th International Symposium on Modeling, Analysis and Simulation of Computer and Telecommunication System. Arlington, VA.

Webb, L. M., Chang, H. C., Hayes, M. T., Smith, M. M., & Gibson, D. M. (2012). Mad men dot com: An analysis of commentary from online fan websites. In J. C. Dunn, J. Manning, & D. Stern (Eds.), *Lucky strikes and a three-martini lunch: Thinking about television's Mad Men* (pp. 226–238). Newcastle upon Tyne, UK: Cambridge Scholars Publishing.

Webb, L. M., Fields, T. E., Boupha, S., & Stell, M. N. (2012). U. S. political blogs: What channel characteristics contribute to popularity? In T. Dumova, & R. Fiordo (Eds.), *Blogging in the global society: Cultural, political, and geographic aspects* (pp. 179–199). Hershey, PA: IGI Global.

Webb, L. M., Thompson-Hayes, M., Chang, H. C., & Smith, M. M. (2012). Taking the audience perspective: Online fan commentary about the brides of Mad Men and their weddings. In A. A. Ruggerio, (Ed.), *Media depictions of brides, wives, and mothers* (pp. 223-235). Lanham, MD: Lexington.

Webb, L. M., & Wang, Y. (2013). Techniques for analyzing blogs and micro-blogs. In N. Sappleton (Ed.), *Advancing research methods with new technologies* (pp. 183-204). Hershey, PA: IGI Global.

Webb, L. M., Wilson, M. L., Hodges, M., Smith, P. A., & Zakeri, M. (2012). Facebook: How college students work it. In H. S. Noor Al-Deen & J. A. Hendricks (Eds.), *Social media: Usage and impact* (pp. 3-22). Lanham, MD: Lexington.

White, T. (2012). *Hadoop: The definitive guide* (3rd ed.). Sebastopol, CA: O'Reilly Media.

Wiles, R., Crow, G., & Pain, H. (2011). Innovation in qualitative research methods: A narrative review. *Qualitative Research, 11*, 587–604. doi:10.1177/1468794111413227.

Williams, A. P., Trammell, K. P., Postelnicu, M., Landreville, K. D., & Martin, J. D. (2005). Blogging and hyperlinking: Use of the web to enhance viability during the 2004 US campaign. *Journalism Studies, 6*, 177–186. doi:10.1080/14616700500057262.

Xenos, M. (2008). New mediated deliberation: Blog and press coverage of the Alito nomination. *Journal of Computer-Mediated Communication, 13*, 485–503. doi:10.1111/j.1083-6101.2008.00406.x.

ADDITIONAL READING

C. C. Aggarwal (Ed.). (2011). *Social network data analytics*. Hawthorne, NY: IBM Thomas J. Watson Research Center. doi:10.1007/978-1-4419-8462-3.

Daniel, J. (2012). *Sampling essentials: Practical guidelines for making sampling choices*. Thousand Oaks, CA: Sage.

Davis, K., & Patterson, D. (2012). Ethics of big data: Balancing risk and innovation. Sebastopol, CA: O' Reilly.

Eastin, M. S., Daugherty, T., & Burns, N. M. (2011). *Handbook of research on digital media and advertising: User generated content consumption*. Hershey, PA: IGI Global.

Franks, B. (2012). *Taming the big data tidal wave: Finding opportunities in huge data streams with advanced analytics*. Hoboken, NJ: John Wiley & Sons.

C. Hine (Ed.). (2005). *Virtual methods: Issues in social research on the internet*. Oxford, UK: Berg.

Janert, P. K. (2010). Data analysis with open source tools. Sebastopol, CA: O' Reilly Media.

Kolb, J. (2012). *Business intelligence in plain language: A practical guide to data mining and business analytics*. Chicago, IL: Applied Data Labs.

Marin, N. (2011). *Social media: Blogging, social networking services, microblogging, wikis, internet forums, podcasts, and more*. New York, NY: Webster's Digital Services.

Milton, M. (2009). Head first data analysis: A learner's guide to big numbers, statistics, and good decisions. Sebastopol, CA: O' Reilly Media.

Miner, G., Elder, J. IV, Hill, T., Nisbet, R., & Delen, D. (2012). *Practical text mining and statistical analysis for non-structured text data applications*. Waltham, MA: Elsevier.

Presll, C. (2012). *Social network analysis: History, theory & methodology*. Thousand Oaks, CA: SAGE.

Russell, M. A. (2011). Mining the social web: Analyzing data from Facebook, Twitter, LinkedIn, and other social media sites. Sebastopol, CA: O' Reilly Media.

Scheaffer, R. L., Mendenhall, W. III, Ott, R. L., & Gerow, K. G. (2012). *Elementary survey sampling* (7th ed.). Boston, MA: Brooks/Cole.

Smolan, R., & Erwitt, J. (2012). The human face of big data. Sausalito, CA: Against all odds.

Thompson, S. K. (2012). *Sampling* (3rd ed.). Hoboken, NJ: Wiley. doi:10.1002/9781118162934.

White, T. (2012). Hadoop: The definitive guide. Sebastopol, CA: O' Reilly Media.

KEY TERMS AND DEFINITIONS

Articulated Networks: A social networking source where large data sets could be retrieved by recording interactions between users who are connected by explicitly announced relationships, for example, a public friend list on Facebook.

Behavioral Networks: A social networking source for collecting large data sets by extracting reply relations between user comments. Behavioral networks also are called behavior-driven networks. Example of behavioral networks include instant message service and texting message through mobile devices.

Big Data: Diverse and complex data in rapidly expanding volume drawn from an unusually large population. Big data sets are usually produced by and harvested from new media technology such as the Internet.

Big Search: The behavior of locating or generating big amount of data to bring a wide scope of results for one single query.

Blog: A medium established through the Internet, which enables people to publish their personal stories, opinions, product reviews and many other forms of texts in real time.

Blog Audience: Boyd (2010) introduced four analytical of blog's audiences. First, the intended audience which comprises a blogger's general idea of the audience she or he wants to address. Second, the address audience comprises those people that are addressed in a specific blog posting, which can be the same as the intended audience in general but can also be a specific subset. The third category contains the empirical audience who actually take notice of any given posting or tweet. The final category includes the potential audience who are determined by the technological reach of a blog within the wider context of network by communication.

Blogosphere: The totality of all blogs and its interconnections which implies that blogs are connected to each other in a virtual community.

Convenience Sample: A sample containing easy to access incidences in the sample with no known probability of inclusion.

Front-End Approach to Big Search: A method used to carry out a big search by throwing large amount of data into the search query and allowing themes to emerge.

Micro-Blog: An online medium inheriting all the features from the traditional blogging, and differing from traditional blogging by imposing limit on the number of characters in a single posting (140 characters) and facilitating a more instant updating speed, through more flexible forms of platforms (web, text messaging, instant messaging and other third-party application).

Random Sampling: Every instance in the sampling frame has an equal probability of selection into the sample.

RSS: A standardized format that automatically syndicates blog content into summarized text and is sent to the readers who subscribed to the blog. RSS is often dubbed Really Simple Syndication.

Representative Sample: A sample in which the incidences selected accurately portray the population.

Semi-Structured Data: Raw data arranged with hierarchies or other signs of distinctness within the data, but does not conform to formal structure which is widely accepted in other data. Examples of semi-structured data include email messages and other text based online data.

Structured Data: Highly organized data retrieved from databases or other sources which process and manage large quantity of data. Data listed in Google search results could be regarded as structured data.

Social Networking Service: An online platform that builds social structures among people sharing common interests, activities, and other social connections. The term is often presented in abbreviation as SNS.

Un-Structured Data: Raw data directly extracted from online applications without being organized into effective formats. Examples of un-structured data include mobile text data and mp3 files.

Web 2.0: A combination of different web applications that facilitates participatory information sharing and collaborating in a social media dialogue (such as social networking sites, blogs sites) in a virtual community.

Chapter 6
Big Data Warehouse Automatic Design Methodology

Francesco Di Tria
Università degli Studi di Bari Aldo Moro, Italy

Ezio Lefons
Università degli Studi di Bari Aldo Moro, Italy

Filippo Tangorra
Università degli Studi di Bari Aldo Moro, Italy

ABSTRACT

Traditional data warehouse design methodologies are based on two opposite approaches. The one is data oriented and aims to realize the data warehouse mainly through a reengineering process of the well-structured data sources solely, while minimizing the involvement of end users. The other is requirement oriented and aims to realize the data warehouse only on the basis of business goals expressed by end users, with no regard to the information obtainable from data sources. Since these approaches are not able to address the problems that arise when dealing with big data, the necessity to adopt hybrid methodologies, which allow the definition of multidimensional schemas by considering user requirements and reconciling them against non-structured data sources, has emerged. As a counterpart, hybrid methodologies may require a more complex design process. For this reason, the current research is devoted to introducing automatisms in order to reduce the design efforts and to support the designer in the big data warehouse creation. In this chapter, the authors present a methodology based on a hybrid approach that adopts a graph-based multidimensional model. In order to automate the whole design process, the methodology has been implemented using logical programming.

DOI: 10.4018/978-1-4666-4699-5.ch006

1. INTRODUCTION

Big data warehousing refers commonly to the activity of collecting, integrating, and storing (very extra) large volumes of data coming from data sources, which may contain both structured and unstructured data. However, volume alone does not imply big data. Further and specific issues are related to the velocity in generating data, and their variety and complexity.

The increasing volume of data stored in data warehouses is mainly due to their nature of preserving historical data, for performing statistical analyses and extracting significant information, hidden relationships, and regular patterns from data. Other factors that affect the size growth derive from the necessity of integrating several data sources, each of them provides a different variety of data that contribute to enrich the types of analyses, by correlating a large set of parameters. Furthermore, some data sources—such as Internet transactions, networked devices and sensors, for example—generate billions of data very quickly. These data should update the data warehouse as soon as possible, in order to gain fresh information and make timely decisions (Helfert & Von Maur, 2001).

These issues affect the design process, because big data warehouses must integrate heterogeneous data to be used to perform analyses that consider many points of view, and to produce complex schemas having cubes with high number of dimensions. Furthermore, they must be capable of quickly integrating new data sources through a minimal data modelling process.

To summarize this, new aspects for data warehouses supporting analyses of Big Data have been stated in Cohen *et al.* (2009). Big data warehouses have to be (i) *magnetic* for they must attract all the data sources available in an organization; (ii) *agile* for they should support continuous and rapid evolution; and (iii) *deep* in that they must support analyses more sophisticated that traditional OLAP functions.

1.1. Background Approaches to Automatic Design

In the mentioned scenario, traditional design methodologies, which are based on two opposite approaches—data-oriented and requirement-oriented— (Romero & Abelló, 2009), are not able to solve problems when facing big data.

In fact, methodologies adopting a data-oriented approach are devoted to define multidimensional schemas on the basis of the remodelling of the data sources. These data must be strongly structured, since functional dependencies are taken into account in the remodelling phase (dell'Aquila *et al.*, 2009). Then, these methodologies are not able to create a multidimensional schema from non-structured data sources. Furthermore, in presence of a high number of data sources, the process of solving semantic and syntactical inconsistencies among the different databases can be a very hard task without using an ontological approach. This reengineering process is individually executed by the designer who minimizes the involvement of end users and, consequently, goes towards a possible failure of their expectations. In the worst case, the data warehouse is completely useless and the design process must be revised.

On the opposite side, methodologies adopting a requirement-oriented approach define multidimensional schemas using business goals resulting from the decision makers' needs. The data sources are considered later, when the Extraction, Transformation, and Loading (ETL) phase is addressed. In the feeding plan, concepts of the complex multidimensional schema (such as facts, dimensions, and measures) have to be mapped on the data sources, in order to define the procedures to populate the data warehouse by cleaned data. At this point, the definition of these procedures can be very difficult and, in the worst case, it may happen that the designer discovers that the needed data are not currently available at the sources. On the other hand, some data sources containing interesting information, albeit available, may have been omitted or not exploited.

However, each of these two approaches has valuable advantages. So, the necessity emerged to adopt a hybrid methodology which takes into account their best features (Di Tria *et al.*, 2012; Di Tria *et al.*, 2011; Mazón & Trujillo, 2009; Mazón *et al.*, 2007; Giorgini *et al.*, 2008; Bonifati *et al.*, 2001). As a counterpart, hybrid methodologies are more complex because they need to integrate and to reconcile both the requirement and the data oriented approaches.

Nonetheless, the advantages in adopting hybrid methodologies justify the higher efforts to be spent in the multidimensional design. For these reasons, the current research is devoted to introduce automatisms able to reduce the design efforts and to support the designer in the data warehouse design (Romero & Abelló, 2010a; Phipps & Davis, 2002). On the basis of automatic methodologies, we may be able to include and to integrate new data sources on the fly.

The emergent method to manage such integration is based on the ontological approach (Jiang *et al.*, 2011; Thenmozhi & Vivekanandan, 2012). Indeed, ontologies represent a common and reusable base to compare and align data sources in a fast manner.

1.2. On the Content of the Paper and Its Organization

The contribution of the paper is a hybrid methodology for big data warehouse design, whose steps are completely automatic. It is based on our previous methodology devoted to hybrid multidimensional modelling. Here, we extend the previous work and present the complete methodology. First, integration of different data sources, both structured and non-structured, is based on an ontological approach. Then, the conceptual design is performed by formal rules that modify an integrated schema according to users' require-

ments. At last, the conceptual schema is validated against a workload before transforming it into a logical schema.

The paper is organized as follows. Section 2 reports related papers on the use of ontologies in the multidimensional design. Section 3 presents an overview of our methodology, focusing on the underlying multidimensional model. Then, a detailed description of the steps of the methodology follows. Section 4 shows how the users' requirements are investigated and represented. Section 5 describes the ontological approach for data sources integration. Section 6 contains the description of the conceptual design. The case study illustrated in Section 7 shows a real example of data sources integration and conceptual design. Finally, Section 8 draws future research and Section 9 concludes the paper with some our remarks.

2. RELATED WORK

At present, a lot of effort is devoted to designing a data warehouse automatically. Many steps can be done using algorithms and inference rules. Nonetheless, the process of integration of data sources is far from being solved, due to the semantic heterogeneity of the components and means. In fact, to solve semantic inconsistencies among conceptual schemas, techniques derived from artificial intelligence must be used (Chen, 2001). So, the current trend in data warehouse design relies on the ontological approach, which is widely used in the semantic web (Sure *et al.*, 2002).

An important work is described in (Hakimpour & Geppert, 2002). The authors' approach is based on local ontologies for designing and implementing a single data source, inherent to a specific domain. Next, the data warehouse design process aims to create a global ontology coming from the integration of the local ontologies. Finally, the global ontology is used along with the logical schemas of the data sources to produce an integrated and reconciled schema, by mapping each local concept to a global ontological concept automatically. However, the integration of the local ontologies must be manually done. Moreover, the global ontology needs to be modified each time a data source must be integrated. On the contrary, as we shall see, in our approach the ontology is pre-existing and never changes.

The work of Romero and Abelló (2010b) is also based on an ontological approach but it skips the integration process and directly considers the generation of a multidimensional schema starting from a common ontology, namely Cyc. In this case, the approach is semi-automatic since it requires a user validation to solve inconsistencies.

In (Bakhtouchi *et al.*, 2011), the authors propose a methodology to integrate data sources using a common ontology, enriched with a set of functional dependencies. These constraints support the designer in the choice of primary keys for dimension tables and allow the integration of similar concepts using common candidate keys. To show this, the authors consider relations $R_1(id,$ *name, address, telephone*), $R_2(id,$ *name, telephone*), and $R_3($*telephone, name, address*), and dependencies *id→name, id→address, id→telephone, telephone→name*, and *telephone→address*. Then, the *name* and *address* data integration is possible using *telephone*, which represents the common candidate key.

An interesting proposal to automatically reconcile user requirements and data sources in early stages using ontologies is presented in (Thenmozhi & Vivekanandan, 2012). First, each source is converted into OWL format. Then, a global ontology is obtained by mapping and integrating local concepts. On the other hand, user requirements, represented as information requirements in normal text, are converted from natural language to a logical format. At this point, concepts of interest for analysis are discovered, by matching information requirements against concepts in the global ontology and extracting those with high similarity values. Finally, the discovered concepts are tagged as multidimensional elements using reasoning.

This last proposal is very close to our approach, since we share the opinion that converting sentences from natural language to a logical format, such as clauses of predicate calculus, can be useful for matching concepts on the basis of similarity metrics.

To summarize, we use ontology because this allows us to integrate many different data sources by detecting the similarity of concepts automatically.

3. METHODOLOGY

Here, we present a hybrid methodology for data warehouse design. The core is a multidimensional model providing a graph-based representation of a data source. In this way, the traditional operations performed in the reengineering process (such as adding and removing attributes, or modifying functional dependencies) correspond to basic operations on graphs (such as adding and removing nodes). Nevertheless, this remodelling activity relies on a set of constraints that have to be derived from the requirement analysis, avoiding the oversight of business needs. Using these constraints, it is possible to perform the remodelling activity in a supervised and automatic way. Moreover, the conceptual schema is automatically validated against a preliminary workload before proceeding with further design phases. Also the workload is obtained from the requirements analysis. All the automatic phases of the methodology have been implemented using the logical programming, in order to define a system able to support the designer by producing schemas.

The data warehouse design methodology we propose is depicted in Figure 1 and it is based on *GrHyMM* model (Graph-based Hybrid Multidimensional Model) (Di Tria *et al.*, 2011). In the figure, the phases that are done automatically and the artifacts that are automatically-produced have been highlighted.

In detail, the complete *GrHyMM*'s framework is composed of the following phases:

Figure 1. Data warehouse design methodology

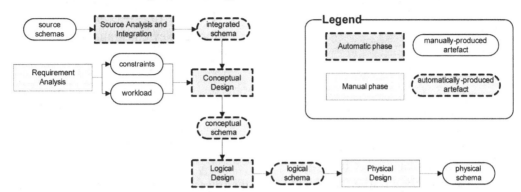

1. **Requirement Analysis:** Decision makers' business goals are represented using the *i** framework for data warehousing (Mazón *et al.*, 2005). The designer has to detect the information requirements and to translate them into a *workload*, containing the typical queries that allow the extraction of the required information. Then, the goals of the data warehouse must be transformed into a set of *constraints*, defining facts and dimensions to be considered in the multi-dimensional schema. To this aim, both the workload and constraints must be given in input to *Conceptual Design*;

2. **Source Analysis and Integration:** The schemas and metadata of the different data sources must be analyzed and then reconciled, in order to obtain a global conceptual schema. The integration strategy is based on an ontological approach and, therefore, we need to work at the conceptual level. To this end, a reverse engineering from data sources to a conceptual schema is necessary, in order to deal with the concepts, when considering structured data sources. On the other hand, metadata are taken into account, when considering unstructured data sources. The conceptual schema that results from the integration process must then be transformed into a relational schema, which constitutes the input to the *Conceptual Design*;

3. **Conceptual Design:** This phase is based on the multidimensional model that provides a graph-oriented representation of relational databases. In particular, it aims to build attribute trees representing facts pointed out in the integrated data source (dell'Aquila *et al.*, 2009) and to automatically remodel those attribute trees on the basis of the *constraints* derived from the *Requirement Analysis*. Finally, the resulting attribute trees are checked in order to verify whether they are able to support the defined *workload* (dell'Aquila *et al.*, 2010);

4. **Logical Design:** The conceptual schema is transformed into a relational schema—for instance, a snow-flake schema—considering each attribute tree present in the conceptual schema as a cube, having the root as the fact and the branches as the dimensions, possibly structured in hierarchies;

5. **Physical Design:** The design process ends with the definition of the physical properties of the database on the basis of the specific features provided by the database system, such as indexing, partitioning, and so on.

3.1. Multidimensional Model

The multidimensional model aims to represent a relational schema using a tree-based representation. This schema can be then remodelled on the basis of traditional operations on graphs in order to obtain a multidimensional schema.

Let:

$G = (N, E)$ be a tree

where:

- $N = \{A_1, A_2, \ldots, A_n\}$ is a set of n nodes;
- $E = \{(A_i, A_j) \mid \text{oriented edge from } A_i \in N \text{ to } A_j \in N, i \neq j\} \subset N \times N$ is a set of oriented edges; and
- A_1 is the root of G.

Assumption 1: Let $R(X_1, \ldots, X_n)$ be a relation, and let $G = (N, E)$ be a tree. We assume $X_i \in N$, $\forall i = 1, \ldots, n$. We assume also $(X_i, X_j) \in E$, if X_i is the primary key of R and $i \neq j$. We say that $G = (N, E)$ is the *attribute tree* obtained from the relation R, where X_i is the root of G.

On the basis of Assumption 1, the edge (X_i, X_j) indicates the presence of the non trivial $(i \neq j)$ functional dependency $X_i \rightarrow X_j$ that holds on R (in this case, established by a primary key constraint). It is worth noting that, for the sake of simplicity, we assume the primary key is composed of only one attribute:

Assumption 2: Let $R(X_1, \ldots, X_n)$ and $S(Y_1, \ldots, Y_m)$ be relations, and let $G = (N, E)$ be a tree. We assume $(X_i, Y_j) \in E$, if:
- Y_j is the primary key of the relation S; and
- X_i is a foreign key referencing Y_j.

On the basis of Assumption 2, an edge can also indicate the presence of a functional dependency established by a foreign key constraint:

Assumption 3: (*Tree Minimization*) Let $R(X_1, \ldots, X_n)$ and $S(Y_1, \ldots, Y_m)$ be relations, and let $G = (N, E)$ be a tree. Now, let w be a real function $w: N \times N \rightarrow \mathbb{R}$ such that $w(u, v) = 1$ for all $(u, v) \in E$. Then, we can use the foreign key constraint *to minimize* the tree G as follows:
- $X_i \rightarrow X_j$;
- X_j is not (part of) the primary key of R; and
- X_j is a foreign key referencing the primary key Y_s of the relation S,

then the tree $G' = (N', E')$ obtained from G, where:

- $N' \subseteq N$;
- $(X_i, Y_s) \in E'$;
- $(X_i, X_j) \notin E'$; and
- $(X_j, Y_s) \notin E'$,

is the *minimization* of G.

Example 1: With reference to the relational schema depicted in Figure 2(a), the attribute tree shown in Figure 2(b) is the tree obtained on the basis of Assumption 1 and Assumption 2, while the attribute tree shown in Figure 2(c) is the minimized tree obtained on the basis of Assumption 3.

Until now we have considered relational schemas composed of one or two relations. Hereafter, we will be concerned with complex schemas composed of several relations. For this end, we introduce the *tree(R)* function that builds an attribute tree starting from the relation R. In fact, the topology of the attribute tree depends on the relation taken as the starting point to navigate in the schema:

Assumption 4: Let $R_1(X_{11}, \ldots, X_{1h1})$, $R_2(X_{21}, \ldots, X_{2h2})$, ..., $R_r(X_{r1}, \ldots, X_{rhr})$, and $T(Z_1, \ldots, Z_p)$ be $r + 1$ relations:
- T is the starting relation;
- X_{ij} is the primary key of the relation R_i, $i = 1, 2, \ldots, r$;

Figure 2. (a) Relational schema; (b) Attribute tree; (c) Minimized attribute tree

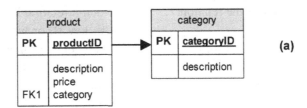

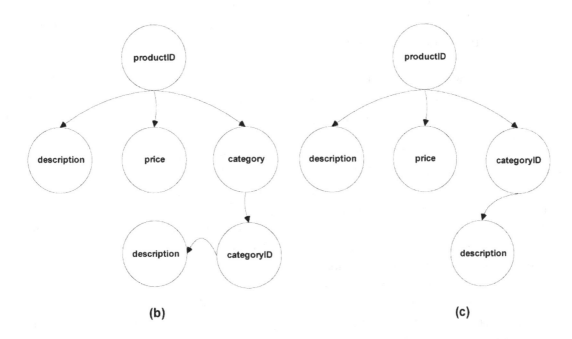

(b)   **(c)**

- $\circ$ $\exists\, Z_{t1}, \ldots, Z_{tr} \in T$ such that:
  - $\forall i = 1, \ldots, r$, Z_{ti} is a foreign key referencing X_{ij}; and
  - Attribute $Z = (Z_{t1}, \ldots, Z_{tr})$ is the primary key of the relation T,

then the tree $\mathbf{G} = (N, E)$ is defined so:

- $\circ$ $N = \{T\} \cup \{X_{ij} \mid X_{ij} \in R_i; i = 1, \ldots, r\}$;
- $\circ$ T is the root node of the tree $\mathbf{G}$;
- $\circ$ $(X_{ij}, X_{il}) \in E, \forall j \neq l$;
- $\circ$ $(T, X_{ij}) \in E, \forall i = 1, \ldots, r$; and
- $\circ$ $(T, Z_{tv}) \in E, Z_{tv} \in T$ and $Z_{tv} \notin Z$.

Assumption 4 allows to build an attribute tree when a relation representing a many-to-many n-ary relationship is taken as the starting point:

Assumption 5: Let $R_1(X_{11}, \ldots, X_{1h1})$, $R_2(X_{21}, \ldots, X_{2h2})$, $\ldots, R_r(X_{r1}, \ldots, X_{rhr})$, and $T(Z_1, \ldots, Z_p)$ be $r + 1$ relations:

- $\circ$ R_i is the starting relation, $1 \leq i \leq r$;
- $\circ$ X_{ij} is the primary key of the relation R_i, $i = 1, 2, \ldots, r$;
- $\circ$ $Z_{t1}, \ldots, Z_{tr} \in T$ such that:
  - $\forall i = 1, \ldots, r$, Z_{ti} is a foreign key referencing X_{ij}; and

- Attribute $Z = (Z_{t1}, ..., Z_{tr})$ is the primary key of the relation T,

then the tree $\mathbf{G} = (N, E)$ is defined so:

- X_{ij} is the root node of $\mathbf{G}$;
- $(X_{ij}, T) \in E$;
- $(T, X_{kj}) \in E$, for $k = t_1, t_2, ..., t_r$ and $k \neq i$; and
- $(T, Z_v) \in E, \forall v = 1, ..., p$ and $v \neq t_1, t_2, ..., t_r$.

Assumption 5 allows to build an attribute tree when a relation representing a many-to-many n-ary relationship is encountered while navigating in the schema:

Example 2: With reference to the relational schema in Figure 3(a), we can build four different attribute trees, according to the relation chosen as the starting point. Figure 3(b) shows the attribute tree obtained by invoking the *tree*(*product*) function. Notice that Assumption 5 has been applied and the double-head arrow "↠" represents a multi-valued dependency, that is, one *productID* points out many occurrences of the *sale* relation. Figure 3(c) shows the attribute tree obtained by invoking the *tree*(*sale*) function—Assumption 4 is applied here—while Figures 3(d) and 3(e) show those obtained by invoking *tree*(*order*) and *tree*(*category*), respectively. Assumption 5 is applied again in Figure 3(d) to navigate from *order* to *sale*.

3.1.1. Operations on the Graph

In what follows, in reference to attributes A and B, *A* and *B* denote the nodes representing the corresponding attributes, and $A \to B$ the edge existing from the node *A* to the node *B*. In the case of branches between nodes *A*, *B* simultaneously

referring each other (as an example, this happens when a relation has primary key A and alternative key B, or when two relations are mutually referencing each other via the respective foreign keys A and B), the "loop" $A \leftrightarrows B$ is solved algorithmically by a node-splitting and renaming (*A*, for example). That is, the loop $A \leftrightarrows B$ generates the (sub-)tree $A \to B \to A'$.

The basic operations it is possible to execute on a graph are:

1. `create_root (A)`, creating the root *A*;
2. `create_node (A)`, creating the node *A*;
3. `delete_node (A)`, deleting the node *A*;
4. `create_edge (A,B)`, adding an edge from *A* to *B*; and
5. `delete_edge (A,B)`, removing the edge from *A* to *B*.

However, complex operations could also be defined:

6. `prune (A)`, removing the *A* node with all its children;
7. `graft (A)`, removing the *A* node and adding its children to its parent; and
8. `change_parent (A,B,C)`, for the edge $B \to C$ and node *A*, *change parent of C from B to A* means: (a) `delete_edge(B,C)`, and (b) `create_edge(A,C)`.

Accordingly, the four basic operations defined on the tree correspond respectively to: creating attribute A, deleting attribute A, adding the functional dependency $A \to B$, and removing the functional dependency $A \to B$. Moreover, the change parent operation is very useful to modify hierarchical dimensional levels. Therefore, the basic operations allow performing a reengineering of schemas using a completely data-driven approach. So, if we manually remodel the attribute tree not on

Figure 3. (a) Relational Schema. Attribute trees obtained by (b) Tree(product); (c) Tree(sale); (d) Tree(order); and (e) Tree(category).

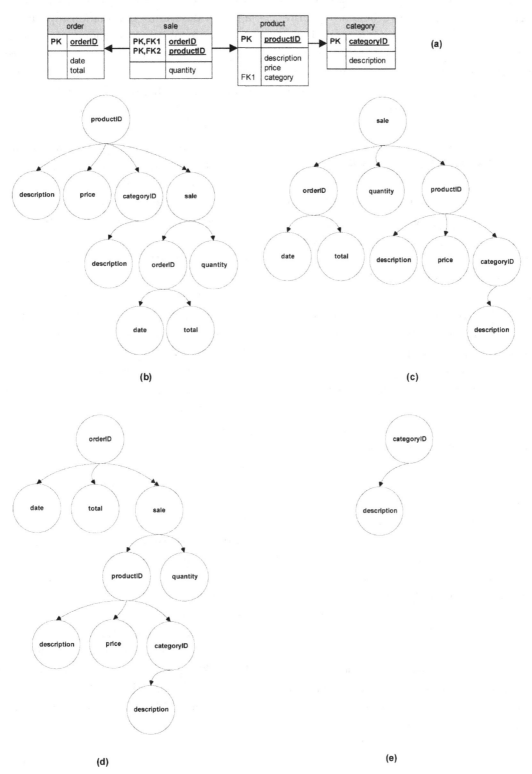

the basis of the designer's experience and choice, but considering also user needs coming from the requirement analysis, then we obtain a hybrid approach. As a further evolution, if we define a set of rules that apply the defined operations on a graph on the basis of a set of constraints derived from the requirement analysis, we can remodel an attribute tree automatically.

4. REQUIREMENT ANALYSIS

In phase 1 of the methodology (*cf*, Figure 1), the needs of the decision makers are investigated. To this aim, we adopt the *i** framework, which allows to explicitly represent business goals in reference to the actors considered in the system. In the application to data warehousing, we can observe two main categories of actors: the decision makers and the data warehouse itself. Each actor performs specific tasks, in order to achieve his/her own goals.

The detailed steps of the *Requirement Analysis* are:

1. **Business Goals Representation:** Representing the tasks and the goals of the different actors using the *i** framework;
2. **Workload Representation:** Translating the tasks of the decision makers into a preliminary workload;
3. **Constraints Representation:** Translating the goals and the tasks of the data warehouse into a set of constraints.

4.1. Business Goals Representation

In the *i** framework, user requirements, alias business goals, are exploded into a more detailed hierarchy of nested goals: (a) *strategic goals*, or high-level objectives to be reached by the organization; (b) *decision goals*, to answer how strategic goals can be satisfied; and (c) *information goals*,

to define which information is needed for decision making. To do this, the designer must produce a model describing the relationships among the main actors of the organization, along their own interests. This model is the so-called *strategic dependency* model and aims to outline how the data warehouse helps decision makers to achieve business goals.

Each actor in a strategic dependency model is further detailed in a *strategic rationale model* that shows the specific tasks the actor has to perform in order to achieve a given goal.

Then, strategic rational models are used to create a workload and a set of constraints.

4.2. Workload Representation

The workload contains a set of queries to be manually derived from the tasks of the decision makers and it helps the designer to identify the information the final users are interested in. In a few words, it includes the typical queries that will be executed by decision makers in the analytical processing.

The grammar for a high-level possible representation of the queries of the workload is shown in Algorithm 1.

Here, *constant* is a number or string from the *attribute* domain, and *identifier* is a user-defined name corresponding to any valid variable (the name of a table or column, for example).

Other authors (*e.g.*, Phipps & Davis, 2002) utilize a workload representation based on SQL statements, in order to select a schema, among the set of conceptual schemas designed by an algorithm, which best supports user requirements. Also Romero & Abelló (2010a) use SQL statements for the workload representation, but their aim is to detect the role played by each model element—that is, whether a table is a dimension or a fact table, for example—and assign it a label accordingly. The grammar we use is based on that introduced in (Golfarelli & Rizzi, 2009), which allows to

Algorithm 1. Grammar for a high-level possible representation of the queries of workload

```
<query>                ::-<function>(<fact_pattern>);
<fact_pattern>         ::-<fact>[<aggreg_pattern>;<sel_clause>].<measure>
<aggreg_pattern>       ::-<level> | <aggreg_pattern>,<level>
<sel_clause>           ::-<attribute> <comp_op> <constant> |
                          <sel_clause> <logical_op> <sel_clause>
<function>             ::-avg | sum | count
<logical_op>           ::-and | or
<comp_op>              ::-≥ | ≤ | < | > | =
<fact>                 ::-<identifier>
<measure>              ::-<identifier>
<level>                ::-<identifier>
<attribute>            ::-<identifier>
```

represent queries at conceptual level. Then, we have a coherent level of abstraction between the workload and the schema we intend to validate. Moreover, it allows checking a conceptual schema before proceeding to the next logical design.

4.3. Constraints Representation

For each resource needed from decision makers, the data warehouse must provide adequate information by achieving its own goals. Moreover, a goal must have measures that are resources to be used in order to provide the information required for decision making. Therefore, a fact is generated in order to allow the data warehouse to achieve its own goal. At last, for each measure, a context of analysis must be provided by a task of the data

warehouse. So, starting from measures and dimensions emerged from data warehouse's goals, it is possible to define some constraints the designer must necessarily consider.

The grammar for a high-level representation of constraints is shown in Algorithm 2.

5. SOURCE ANALYSIS AND INTEGRATION

In phase 2, the preliminary step is the source analysis, devoted to the study of the source databases. If necessary, the designer has to produce, for each data source, a conceptual schema along with a data dictionary, storing the description in natural language of the concepts modelled by the

Algorithm 2. Grammar for a high-level representation of constraints

```
<constraint>      ::-<fact>[<dimensions>].[<measures>];
<dimensions>      ::-<dimension> | <dimensions>;<dimension>
<dimension>       ::-<level> | <dimension>,<level>
<measures>        ::-<measure> | <measures>,<measure>
<level>           ::-<identifier>
<measure>         ::-<identifier>
<fact>            ::-<identifier>
```

database. Then, the integration process proceeds incrementally using a binary operator that, given two conceptual schemas as operands, produces a new conceptual schema:

Assumption: Given the conceptual schemas S_1, S_2,..., S_n, $n \geq 2$, we assume the following recurrence:

$G_1 = integration\ (S_1, S_2)$; and

$G_i = integration\ (G_{i-1}, S_{i+1})$, for $i = 2, ..., n-1$.

In detail, the integration process of two databases S_i and S_j is composed of the following steps:

1. **Ontological Representation:** In this step, we consider an ontology describing the main concepts of the domain of interest. If such ontology does not exist, it must be built by domain experts. The aim is to build a shared and reusable *ontology*;

2. **Predicate Generation:** For each concept in the ontology, we introduce a unary predicate. The output of this step is a set of *predicates*, which represents a vocabulary to build definitions of concepts using the first-order logic;

3. **Ontological Definition Generation:** For each concept in the ontology, we also introduce a definition on the basis of its semantic relationships. This definition is the description of the concept at the ontological level (that is, the common and shared definition). The output of this step is a set of *ontological definitions*;

4. **Entity Definition Generation:** For each entity present in the data sources and described in the data dictionary, we introduce a definition using the predicates. Therefore, an entity definition is a logic-based description of a concept in the database. The output of this step is a set of *entity definitions*;

5. **Similarity Comparison:** Assuming that similar entities have a very close description, we can detect whether (a) entities that have different names refer to the same concept, and (b) entities that have the same name refer to different concepts. To do so, we utilize a set of inference rules, the so-called *similarity comparison rules*, to analyze the logic-based descriptions and a metric to calculate the pairwise similarity of entity definitions. In detail, given two schemas S_i $(A_i^1, A_i^2, ..., A_i^k)$ and S_j $(A_\varphi^1, A_\varphi^2, ..., A_\varphi^m)$, where A_τ^h is the h-th entity of schema S_t, we compare the logic definition of A_i^h (for $h = 1, ..., k$) with that of A_φ^q (for $q = 1, ..., m$). For each comparison, we calculate a similarity degree d and an output list L. The output list contains the possible ontological concepts shared by both the logic definitions. Assuming that we can compare the logical definitions of entities A_i^h and A_φ^q and calculate both the similarity degree d and the output list L, we can observe one of the following cases: A_i^h is *equivalent* to A_φ^q, if $d \geq x$, where x is a fixed threshold value. For convenience, we fixed x at 0.70:

   a. A_i^h is a *generalization* of A_i^q, if the definition of A_φ^q is part of the definition of A_i^h (or *vice versa*);

   b. A_i^h and A_φ^q are both *specializations* of a concept present in the ontology, if $0 < d \leq x$ and $L \neq \emptyset$;

   c. A_i^h and A_φ^q are *linked* via a relationship γ present in the ontology;

   d. A_i^h and A_φ^q are distinct entities, if $d \leq x$ and $L = \emptyset$.

6. **Integrated Logical Schema Generation:** An intermediate *global conceptual schema* G_u is built using the results obtained from the similarity comparison process and ap-

plying some generation rules. In detail, we have $G_u(A_v^1, A_v^2, ..., A_v^p)$, where, for $s = 1, ..., p$:

a. $A_v^s = A_i^h \approx A_j^q$, if we observe case 2.5(a). In this case, all the distinct attributes are merged in A_v^s;

b. $A_v^s = \{A_i^h, A_\varphi^q\}$, if we observe case 2.5(b). In this case, all the common attributes are associated to A_i^h (resp., A_φ^q);

c. $A_v^s = \{L, A_i^h, A_\varphi^q\}$, if we observe case 2.5(c). In this case, all the common attributes are associated to L;

d. $A_v^s = \{\gamma, A_i^h, A_\varphi^q\}$, if we observe case 2.5(d). In this case, all the entities preserve their own attributes;

e. $A_v^s = \{A_i^h, A_\varphi^q\}$, if we observe case 2.5(e). In this case, all the entities preserve their own attributes.

As concerns the cardinality constraints, we adopt the following assumptions:

- If a new relationship γ is added, then we use the 0:N cardinality for each entity A which participates to γ. Indeed, this is the most general cardinality;

- If entities A_i and A_j are merged, then we use the minimum of the respective minimum cardinality constraints and the maximum of the respective maximum cardinality constraints for each relationship in which A_i and/or A_j participate;

- In all the other cases, the original cardinalities are maintained.

It is worth noting that both attributes and cardinality constraints are retrieved from the *Data Dictionary* without any elaboration. Only entity definitions are converted into predicates for comparison.

The graphical representation of the whole integration process is shown in Figure 4.

When a further schema S_w has to be integrated, the integration process starts from step 2.4, using the previous result of step 2.6 and schema S_w.

At last, the *global conceptual schema G_u* is translated into an integrated logical schema by applying the well-known mapping algorithms (Elmasri & Navathe, 2010).

Figure 4. Integration process of (two) databases

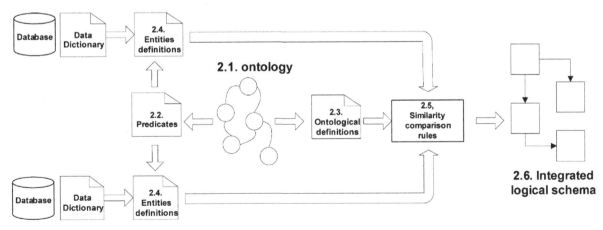

5.1. Representation of the Integrated Logical Schema

In order to represent the integrated logical schema, we need to define a *metamodel*. Such a metamodel describes how to organize the so-called *metadata*, that is, the data we can use to describe any relational schema.

The description of a relational schema is based on the following statements:

- A schema is composed of a set of tables;
- Each table is composed of a set of fields;
- A field can be (part of) a primary key;
- A field can be (part of) a foreign key;
- A foreign key points to the primary key of another table.

The language we used for the definition of the metamodel is the *Predicate Calculus*. In particular, our metamodel consists of the following four predicates:

1. `table (X)`. The predicate states that X is a table;

2. `field (X,Y)`. The predicate states that Y is an attribute (field) of X. As X must be a table, we can use the AND logical operator in order to impose this constraint. For instance, the expression *field*$(X,Y) \land$ *table*(X) states that Y must be an attribute of the table X;

3. `key (X,K)`. The predicate states that K is (part of) the primary key of X, where X must be a table and K must be a field of X (for instance, *key*$(X,K) \land$ *field*$(X,K) \land$ *table*(X)). Moreover, the predicate allows us to model logical schemas where the primary key is composed of more than one field;

4. `fkey(X1,FK1,X2,K2)`. The predicate states that *FK*1 is a foreign key. Moreover, *FK*1 is an attribute of $X1$ and references (*i.e.*, points to) the attribute $K2$. The constraints on the predicate are that *FK*1 must be an attribute of the table $X1$, and $K2$ must be the primary key of the table $X2$.

6. CONCEPTUAL DESIGN

Phase 3 is based on the multidimensional model and aims to automatically produce a data ware-

Figure 5. Steps of the conceptual design

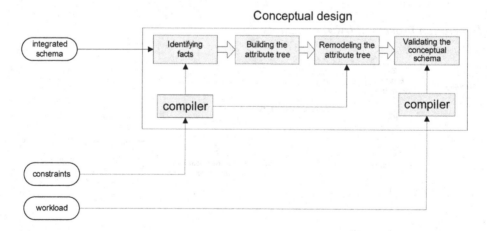

house conceptual schema. In fact, this phase has been implemented as a logical program, able to simulate the behaviour and the reasoning of a designer.

In order to use the constraints and the workload in the conceptual design, we need to preliminarily transform these manually-produced artifacts into predicates to be given in input to the logical program. To this end, we realized two compilers, as depicted in Figure 5.

The steps to be performed in this phase are:

1. *Compiling* the artifacts into predicates;
2. *Identifying* facts present in the integrated logical schema on the basis of the constraints;
3. *Building* an attribute tree for each correctly-identified fact;
4. *Remodelling* each attribute tree on the basis of the constraints;
5. *Validating* the data warehouse conceptual schema, by verifying whether all the remodelled trees agree with the workload.

6.1. Compiling the Artifacts

In this sub-Section, we show how both the input artifacts are transformed into predicates by a compilation process. Each compiler is composed of a Syntactical Analyzer (SA) that, on turn, uses a Lexical Analyzer (LA) for string pattern recognition.

The SA is a parser that verifies the syntactical structure of a statement. The SA has been developed using Bison (Levine, 2009), which is a tool that (a) reads a grammar-file, and (b) generates a C-code program. This C-code program represents the SA. In particular, the grammar-file contains the declaration of a set of terminal symbols (*tokens*) and a set of *grammar rules*, expressed according to the Backus Naur Form.

To define a grammar, tokens must be first defined. The tokens include literals (*i.e.*, string

constants), identifiers (*i.e.*, string variables), and numeric values.

Examples of tokens in Bison are:

```
%token DOT "."

%token COMMA ","

%token SEMICOL ";"
```

which represent string constants; and

```
%token VAR
```

which represents a string variable.

Then, grammar rules must be defined in the following form:

<result>: <components> { <statement> };

where *<result>* is a non-terminal symbol, *<components>* is a set of terminal and/or non-terminal symbols, and *<statement>* is the C-code statement to be executed when the rule is applied.

The LA is the component used by the SA, in order to obtain an ordered sequence of tokens. The tokens are recognized by the LA inside a string (*i.e.*, pattern matching on text) and, then, passed to the SA. The LA has been developed using Flex (Paxson *et al.*, 2007), which is a tool that (a) uses the tokens defined for the SA program, (b) reads a rule-file, and (c) generates a C-code program. This C-code program represents the LA. In particular, the rule-file is composed of two sections: (a) definition, and (b) rules. The definition section includes the tokens already defined with Bison, plus further identifiers. The identifiers define how to perform the matching between a sequence of alphanumeric characters and a token.

As an example, the statement:

```
UVAR [a-z][a-z0-9]*
```

creates an identifier named UVAR which represents any string that starts with an alphabetic character, followed by an arbitrary number of alphabetic characters or digits 0 to 9. Then, some examples of rules for string pattern matching follow:

```
[;] {return SEMICOL;}

{UVAR} {return VAR;}
```

The first rule states that, whenever the constant ";" is recognized inside the input string, the token SEMICOL must be returned. In fact, when the LA recognizes an identifier, it returns the corresponding token to the SA. Accordingly, when the SA recognizes the identifier UVAR returns the token VAR to the SA. At last, when the LA encounters the end-of-file symbol, it stops the string scanning. So, using the sequence of tokens returned by the LA, the SA is able to check whether a statement is well-formed against the given grammar.

6.1.1. Compiling the Constraints

In order to transform the constraints coming from the Requirement analysis into predicates, we describe the metamodel used to represent a starting multidimensional schema. On the basis of this assumption, the constraints define an "ideal" multidimensional schema and the logical program has to create a final multidimensional schema that properly satisfies these constraints:

1. cube (C). The predicate states that C must be a table;
2. measure (M,C). The predicate states that M must be a measure of C;
3. dimension_level (D,N,E,C,T). The predicate states that E is a dimension level of cube C. Here, D indicates the dimension number and N the hierarchical level

number inside the dimension. T indicates whether E is a time dimension or not.

6.1.2. Compiling the Workload

Also the queries included into the workload must be transformed into a set of predicates using the following query model, used to represent a query to be checked against the final multidimensional schema:

1. query (C,A,S,M). The predicate states that C is the cube involved in the query, A is the aggregation pattern, S is the selection pattern, and M is the measure.

6.2. Identifying Facts

As stated before, we developed a logical program able to construct an attribute tree. The logical program contains the metadata of the relational schema and the navigation rules. It uses the rules for navigating in a recursive way through a logical schema, starting from an initial table marked as a cube.

Indeed, the main difficulty in this step is to correctly map the multidimensional concepts to the integrated schema. For example, in a relational schema, the designer must face the problem to identify which relations can be considered as cubes or dimension tables.

In our methodology, we mainly deal with the correct identification of facts, as these are the starting point to build the initial attribute tree.

We consider the facts involved in the constraints coming from the requirement analysis. Given a fact F_1 in a constraint, we choose a candidate fact F_2 in the integrated schema such that F_2 corresponds to F_1:

Rule 1: tree(C) $\Leftarrow$ table(C) $\wedge$ cube(C) $\wedge$ create_root(C) $\wedge$ navigate(C).

The rule, which is based on a syntactical matching, builds an attribute tree from the table C, if C is marked as a cube in the requirements. If so, the rule asserts that C is the root for that attribute tree and, then, the navigation starts. (Notice that create_root(C) is the function introduced in sub-Section 3.1.1. We will use these functions also in the next).

6.3. Building the Attribute Tree

The complete attribute tree is now constructed by navigation rules. These rules allow to navigate in the logical schema via join paths, defined by foreign key constraints. The nodes of the constructed tree are the fields of the tables. Therefore, the tree represents the structure of the database according to the multidimensional model introduced in Section 3.1.:

Rule 2: navigate(X1) ⇐ table (X1) ∧ field(X1,C1) ∧ fkey(X1,C1,X2,C2) ∧ table(X2) ∧ key(X2,C2) ∧ navigate(X2)

This first rule allows to navigate from table $X1$ to table $X2$, via a foreign key constraint, when there is a one-to-many relationship between $X1$ and $X2$:

Rule 3: navigate(X1) ⇐ table(X1) ∧ key(X1,C1) ∧ fkey(T,CX1,X1,C1) ∧ fkey(T,CX2,X2,C2) ∧¬(X1=X2) ∧ table(X2) ∧ key(X2,C2) ∧ table(T) ∧ key(T,CX1) ∧ key(T,CX2) ∧ create_double_edge(C1,T) ∧ create_edge(T,C2) ∧ navigate(X2)

This second rule allows to navigate from table $X1$ to table $X2$, via a foreign key constraint, when there is a many-to-many relationship between $X1$ and $X2$. T is the intermediate table. Here, an edge with a double harrow is created from $C1$ to T and a simple edge from T to $C2$.

As concerns rule I, the logical program needs to distinguish whether a table is the root, *i.e.*, the starting fact table, and whether the foreign key is defined on a primary key. The differentiation can be done on the basis of the first navigation rule, by creating three specialized rules. The main difference consists of the creation of the edge. The specialized rules are the following:

- ¬ root (X1) ∧¬ key(X1,C1) ∧ create_edge(K,C2).

If $X1$ is not the root and the foreign key is not defined on its primary key, then an edge must be created between K and $C2$, where K is the primary key of $X1$ and $C2$ is the primary key of the target relation $X2$; create_edge(K,C2) is a function, which asserts that an edge exists between K and $C2$:

- ¬ root (X1) ∧ key(X1,C1) ∧ create_edge(C1,C2).

If $X1$ is not the root and the foreign key is defined on its primary key, then an edge must be created between $C1$ and $C2$, where $C1$ is the primary key of $X1$:

- root(X1) ∧ create_edge(X1,C2).

If $X1$ is the root, then an edge must be created between $X1$ and $C2$.

At last, every time a table has been reached, a new node is created—using create_node(A) function—and its own fields are listed, by creating edges among the primary key and fields; thus, these fields form a set of leaf nodes.

The final output of the logical program is a set of assertions, which defines the tree **G**:

- root (C) : C is the root of **G**;
- node (N) : N is a node of **G**;
- edge (A,B) : An edge exists between nodes A and B, *ie* $A \rightarrow B$.

6.4. Remodelling the Attribute Tree

In this step, an attribute tree is modified in a supervised way using all the constraints coming from requirements.

We denote with (A, B):- C the fact that the attribute C can be computed using A and B, that is, C is a derived measure. As an example, (*price, quantity*):- *amount* means that there exists an (algebraic) expression to compute *amount* using *price* and *quantity*.

Let us consider a tree **G** and a constraint coming from the user requirements. In informal way, we create as many root children as many measures there are in the constraint. Moreover, we add a root child for each first dimensional level in the constraint. In a recursive way, the other dimensional levels are added as children nodes of their own predecessor levels. In general, when we add a new node B to a parent node A, the node B can be created *ex novo* or can be already present in the tree. In the latter case, the edge between B and the old parent of B must be deleted and a new edge between B and the new parent A must be created; this is the so-called *change parent* operation.

Remodelling rules are reported here:

- Adding measures:
    - ```
      add_measures() ⇐
      measure(M,C)   ∧   root(C)
      ∧   ¬        edge(C,M)   ∧
      edge(Z,M)   ∧   node(Z)   ∧
      change_parent(C,Z,M).
      ```
    - ```
      add_measures()            ⇐
      measure(M,C)   ∧ root(C) ∧
      ¬   edge(C,M) ∧ (M_1,...,M_n):-
      M   ∧   edge(Z_i,M_i)   ∧   node(Z_i)
      ∧delete_edge(Z_i,M_i)
      ∧ create_node(M)   ∧   create_
      edge(C,M).
      ```

For each measure M which is not a root child but is a child of another node Z, a change parent operation is done. Similarly, if M is not a root child but can be derived from a set of nodes M_i, for $i=1, ..., n$, then nodes M_i are deleted, a new node M is added, and an edge between the root and M is created. In the other cases, the program fails:

- Adding dimensions:
    - ```
      add_dimensions()  ⇐ dimen-
      sion_level(D,1,E,C,false)
      ∧   root(C)   ∧   table(E)∧
      key(K,E)   ∧   ¬    edge(C,K)
      ∧ edge(Z,K)   ∧ node(Z)   ∧
      change_parent(C,Z,K)     ∧
      add_description(K).
      ```

For each first dimensional level E, which is not a time dimension and whose primary key K is not a root child but is a child of another node Z, a change parent operation of K from Z to C is done. If such a dimensional level E does not exist, then the program fails. In this rule, `add_description(K)` is the function that creates a node as a descriptive attribute of K, if necessary:

- ```
  add_time_dimensions()  ⇐   dimen-
  sion_level(D,1,E,C,true)   ∧   cre-
  ate_node(E) ∧ root(C) ∧ create_
  edge(C,E).
  ```

This rule adds a time dimension to C having E as terminal level, if imposed in the requirements:

- Adding hierarchical levels:
    - ```
      add_levels()   ⇐   dimension_
      level(D,N,E,C,false) ∧ dimen-
      sion_level(D,N-1,E',C,false)
      ∧table(E)∧key(K,E)∧table(E')
      ∧ key(K',E')  ∧  ¬ edge(K,K')
      ∧ edge(Z,K)  ∧  node(Z)   ∧
      ```
      ```

```
change_parent(K',Z,K)      ∧
add_description(K).
```

For each *n*-th dimensional level *E*, whose primary key *K* is not a child of the primary key of the *n*−1-th dimensional level *E'* but is a child of another node *Z*, a change parent operation of *K* from *Z* to *K'* is done. If such a dimensional level *E* does not exist, then the program fails:

- ```
  add_time_levels() ⇐ dimension_
  level(D,N,E,C,true) ∧ dimension_
  level(D2,N-1,E',C,true) ∧ create_
  node(E) ∧ create_edge(E',E).
  ```

For each *n*-th time dimensional level present in the requirements a node is created as a child of the *n*−1-th time dimensional level:

- Deleting attributes:

```
del_nodes() ⇐ node(P)
∧¬ dimension_level(D,N,P,C,T) ∧prune(P)
```

In the end, all the remaining nodes that do not represent dimensional levels are deleted.

The resulting graph represents a multidimensional schema where:

- The root node is the cube and the children of the root represent the measures of the fact table;
- The non-leaf nodes represent dimensional attributes, *i.e.*, entities that represent levels of aggregation. The number of dimensional attributes linked to the root establishes the dimensionality of the data cube. The dimensional attributes linked each other by an edge form a hierarchy;
- The leaf nodes represent the descriptive attributes of a dimensional attribute.

6.5. Validating the Data Warehouse Conceptual Schema

The workload is now used in order to perform the validation process. If all the queries of the workload can be effectively executed over the schema, then such a schema is assumed to be validated and the designer can safely translate it into the corresponding logical schema. Otherwise, the conceptual design process must be revised.

We define the following issues related to the validation of a conceptual schema in reference to the queries included into the preliminary workload:

- A query involves a cube that has not been defined as such;
- A query requires a measure that is not an attribute of the given cube;
- A query presents an aggregation pattern on levels that are unreachable from the given cube;
- A query requires an aggregation on a field that has not been defined as a dimensional attribute;
- A query requires a selection on a field that has not been defined as a descriptive attribute.

A query is assumed to be validated if there exists at least an attribute tree such that the following conditions hold: (a) the fact is the root of the tree; (b) the measures are the children nodes of the root; (c) for each level in the aggregation pattern, there exists a path from the root to a node X, where X is a non-leaf node representing the level; and (d) for each attribute in the selection clause, there exists a path from the root to a node Y, where Y is a leaf node representing that attribute.

If all the queries are validated, then each attribute tree can be considered as a cube, where
```

the root is the fact, non-leaf nodes are aggregation levels, and leaf nodes are descriptive attributes belonging to a level. So, the conceptual design ends and the designer can transform the conceptual schema into a logical one. On the other hand, if a query cannot be validated, then the designer has to opportunely modify the tree. For example, if an attribute of the selection clause is not in the tree, then the designer can decide to add a further node.

In reference to these issues, a set of tests to be performed has been designed.

The conceptual schema validation is executed by the logical program, via an inferential process that allows verifying the issues pointed out above. At the end of the inferential process, the logical program states whether the conceptual schema is valid, on the basis of a given preliminary workload and the produced attributes trees.

The rules are checked in that order given below:

- Cube test:

```
cube_test() ⇐ query(C,A,S,M)
∧ root(C) ∧ write('...')
```

```
cube_test()⇐query(C,A,S,M)∧¬root(C)∧fail
```

If *C* is a cube, then a successful message is shown and the test is accomplished. So, further tests follow. Otherwise, if *C* is not a cube, then the logical program fails and the schema is not validated:

- Measure test:

```
measure_test() ⇐ query(C,A,S,M)
∧ edge(M,C) ∧ write('...')
```

```
measure_test() ⇐ query(C,A,S,M)
∧¬ edge(M,C) ∧ fail
```

When performing this rule, the cube test is terminated and, therefore, we have the assurance that *C* is a cube. So, this rule only verifies whether *M* is a measure of the cube *C*. If *M* is not a measure of the cube *C*, then the logical program fails and the schema is not validated:

- Path test:

```
path_test(C,D) ⇐ root(C)
∧ child(C,D) ∧ write('...')
```

```
path_test(C,D) ⇐ root(C) ∧¬ child(C,D)
∧ child(W,D) ∧ path_test(C,W)
```

This test recursively scans the list *A* of the aggregation pattern, defined inside the query query(C,A,S,M). (The ending condition is represented by the empty list). For each element *D* extracted from the head of *A*, this rule checks whether *D* is a root child or there is a path from *C* to *D*. If a path from *C* to *D* is found, then a successful message is shown and the test is accomplished:

- Aggregation test:

```
aggregation_test(D) ⇐ node(D)
∧ child(D,F) ∧ write('...')
```

```
aggregation_test(D) ⇐ node(D)
∧¬ child(D,F) ∧ fail
```

Also this test first recursively scans the list *A*, but this rule checks whether all the elements of the list are dimensional attributes. If an element *D* of the list does not have a child node *F*, then the logical program fails. The underlying assumption is that each dimensional attribute must be equipped with at least one descriptive attribute:

- Selection test:

```
selection_test(D) ⇐ node(D)
∧¬ child(D,R) ∧ write('...')
```

selection_test(D) ⇐ node(D)∧child(D,R)∧fail

This test recursively scans the list S of the selection pattern, defined inside the query query(C,A,S,M). For each element D extracted from the head of S, this rule first performs the *path test* from C to D, then checks whether all the elements of the list are descriptive attributes. If an element D of the list is not a descriptive attribute—*ie*, a leaf node—then the logical program fails. To accomplish this test, D must have no child.

7. CASE STUDY

The case study aims at illustrating the application of the methodology in a context where the designer has to create a data warehouse, adopting a hybrid approach supporting automatic steps.

7.1. Requirement Analysis

In this case study, we assume there is only one decision maker, who manages a company that sells many products, also using e-commerce tools.

7.1.1. Business Goals Representation

The manager is interested in increasing the selling of the products. So, this represents the strategic goal.

From this high level goal, the decision goal is "make promotions", which establishes how to boost selling. To this aim, the information that is necessary to satisfy this goal is "identify the most sold products". Then, we represent the information requirements as tasks of the decision maker. In this case, the task is "analyze the quantity of sold products per month, region, and category in the last year". For the sake of simplicity, we omitted the other goals and tasks of the decision maker.

On the other hand, we have to represent also the tasks of the data warehouse, in reference to the information to be provided. For the given requirements, the task is "provide information about selling per time, location, and products". This task includes *quantity* as a measure. Furthermore, it is possible to define complete *time* and *location* hierarchies on the given dimensions.

7.1.2. Workload Representation

From the task of the decision maker, we define the following query string:

```
"sales[month, category, region;
 year='2012'].quantity"
```

which is well-formed and is devoted to the aggregation on quantity measure by month, region, and category, considering only products sold in 2012.

7.1.3. Constraints Representation

From the task of the data warehouse, we define the following constraint:

```
"sales[product,category; day,month,year;
 city,region].[quantity]"
```

which is well-formed and states that the we must have a sales cube, having a quantity measure and three dimensions. In the example, the first dimension is composed of two hierarchical levels: `product`, which is the first level, and `category`, the second. The second dimension is a time dimension, composed of three levels: namely `day`, `month` and `year`. The third dimension is a geographical dimension, composed of two levels: namely `city` and `region`.

7.2. Source Analysis and Integration

In this Section, we provide a complete example of source analysis and integration, in order to highlight how the ontology supports the designer in the data warehouse conceptual design when considering a broad variety of data sources.

7.2.1. Ontological Representation

We built our ontology starting from OpenCyc, the open source version of Cyc (Reed & Lenat, 2002; Foxvog, (2010). To this end, we extracted from OpenCyc the concepts of interest related to the business companies and sales activity, which is the most frequent domain in data warehousing. The relationships considered are *isA*(*X*, *Y*) to indicate that *X* is a specialization of *Y*, and *has*(*X*, *Y*) to indicate that *X* has an instance of *Y*. To make

this cleaner, we provide an oriented graph. The ontology is partially shown in Figure 6.

7.2.2. Predicate Generation

Using the ontology previously introduced, first we defined the predicates to be used as a vocabulary for the logical definitions of database entities. Each predicate corresponds to a concept present in the ontology. A subset of the predicates is reported below:

- `socialBeing (X)`: *X* is a social being;
- `individualAgent (X)`: *X* is an individual agent;
- `person (X)`: *X* is a person;
- `document (X)`: *X* is a document;
- `legalForm (X)`: *X* is a document having a legal value.

7.2.3. Ontological Definition Generation

For each ontological concept, we also provide an extended definition, using the predicate previously introduced. So, we obtained a logical definition for each ontological concept. In what follows, instead of using the *isA*(*X*,*Y*) relationship, we adopt the *prolog* notation, in order to state that *X*

Figure 6. Part of the ontology

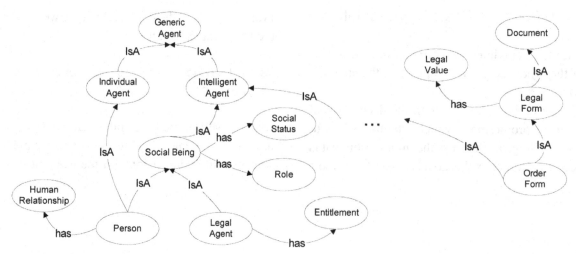

is a social being if *X* is an intelligent agent and *X* has both a social status and a role. A number of the ontological definitions of concepts follow:

- **Social Being:** `socialBeing(X)` $\Leftarrow$ `intelligentAgent(X)` $\wedge$ `has(X,Y)` $\wedge$ `has(X,Z)` $\wedge$ `socialStatus(Y)` $\wedge$ `role(Z)`.
- **Person:** `person(X)` $\Leftarrow$ `socialBeing(X)` $\wedge$ `individualAgent(X)` $\wedge$ `has(X,Y)` $\wedge$ `humanRelationship(Y)`.

7.2.4. Entity Definition Generation

The case study aims to integrate two relational databases, a web log, and social data:

1. **MusicalInstruments** (*see,* Figure 7a);
2. **Fruit&Vegetables** (*see,* Figure 7b);
3. **MusicalInstrumentsWebLog** (*see,* Figure 7c); and
4. **SocialWebData** (*see,* Figure 7d).

For both databases (1) and (2), we provide their essential conceptual schemas.

MusicalInstruments is the database used by an on-line shop, in order to manage the sales of musical instruments and accessories. *Fruit&Vegetables* is the database used by a farm, in order to manage the wholesale of fruit and vegetables. *MusicalInstrumentsWebLog* is the log file generated by the web server of the e-commerce software. *SocialWebData* is the dataset that can be obtained from most popular social networks.

For each database entity, we created a definition using the predicates we had previously generated. Indeed, such predicates represent the vocabulary for the construction of the concepts using the first-order logic. Part of the data dictionary along with the logical definitions of database entities is shown in Table 1.

Notice that these definitions often disagree with the ontological ones. In fact, entities are always defined without considering common and shared concepts, since entities represent local concepts. This means we assume that the database designer ignores the ontology.

As concerns the web log, it must be transformed into a structured data source, composed of entities related by relationships. Also for these entities, definitions must be provided. The last data source is represented by social networks, providing interesting information about users' trend.

So, starting from S_1(*client, order, product, company, category*), S_2(*customer, order, product, vegetable, package, price*), S_3(*product, visit*), and S_4(*product, page*), we have to create $G_1 = integration(S_1, S_2)$, by comparing each entity of S_1 with each entity of S_2. Then, we have to create $G_2 = integration(G_1, S_3)$, by mapping the concepts in S_3 to the corresponding database entities. Finally, the global schema G_3 is obtained by integrating also S_4.

7.2.5. Similarity Comparison

The comparison is done automatically using inference rules defined in *first order logic*. These rules check the similarity degree between two lists L_1 and L_2 containing a logical definition of a database entity (Ferilli *et al.*, 2009).

The similarity degree *d* is given by:

$$d(n,l,m) = 0.5 \times \frac{l+1}{l+n+2} + (1-0.5) \times \frac{l+1}{l+m+2}$$

where:

- *l* is the number of common predicates;
- *n* is the number of predicates *p* such that $p \in L_1$ and $p \notin L_2$; and

Figure 7. Data sources

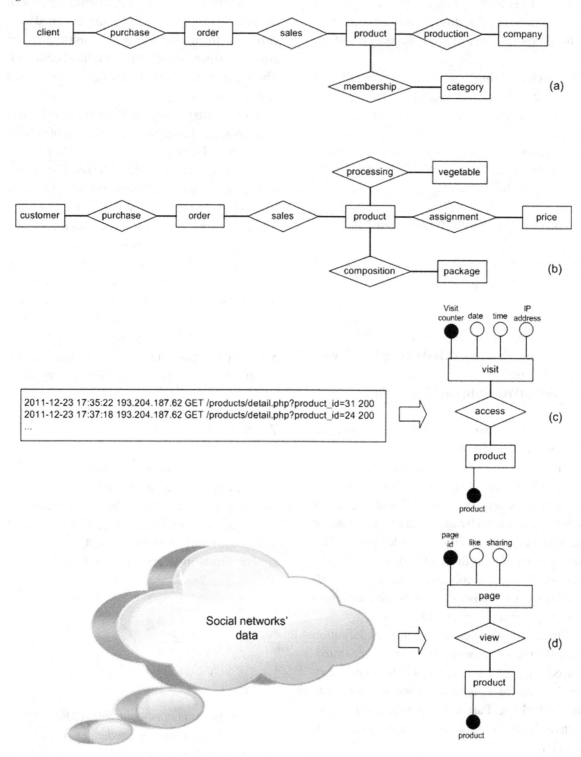

Table 1. (Part of) the data dictionary

Database	Entity	Description	Entity Fefinition

MusicalInstruments	*Client*	"client" is a person who has an account to interact with the system.	`client(X) ⇐`
			`socialBeing(X) ∧ individualAgent(X) ∧`
			`has(X,Y) ∧ userAccount(Y).`

MusicalInstruments	*Product*	"product" is an item to be sold, which has a producer and a price.	`product(X) ⇐`
			`physicalDevice(X) ∧ goods(X) ∧ has(X,Y) ∧`
			`producer(Y) ∧ has(X,Z) ∧ monetaryValue(Z).`

...	...	...	...
Fruit&Vegetables	*Customer*	"customer" is a legal agent who has a shop.	`customer(X) ⇐` `legalAgent(X) ∧ has(X,Y) ∧ shop(Y).`

Fruit&Vegetables	*Product*	"product" is an edible item to be sold. It has an assigned price.	`product(X) ⇐`
			`goods(X) ∧ partiallyTangible(X) ∧`
			`has(X,Y) ∧ monetaryValue(Y).`

...	...	...	...

- m is the number of predicates p such that $p \notin L_1$ and $p \in L_2$.

As an example, we show the comparison process between the entities *client* of S_1 and *customer* of S_2. These entities were previously defined as:

- `client (X) ⇐ socialBeing(X) ∧ individualAgent(X) ∧ has(X,Y) ∧ userAccount(Y);`
- `customer (X) ⇐ legalAgent(X) ∧ has(X,Y) ∧ shop(Y).`

First, we bind the variable X of *client* to the variable X of *customer*, and then we create two lists L_1 and L_2 using the predicates present in each logic definition, which, for readability reasons, we informally represent as:

$L_1 = \{socialBeing(X), individualAgent(X), has(X,Y), userAccount(Y)\}$

$L_2 = \{legalAgent(X), has(X,Y), shop(Y)\}$

Then, we compare each unary predicate in L_1 with all unary predicates in L_2, considering the bound variables.

To do the comparison, we introduce the mapping operator ↔. When we map one predicate to another, we obtain:

- 1 for a successful mapping, if the predicates are the same or have a generalization in common in the ontology; or
- 0 for a failure, if the predicates have no ontological relationship.

In the first case, we add the common concept to the generalization list L (cf., Section 5, step 2.5.):

1. **First Mapping:** $socialBeing(X) \leftrightarrow legalAgent(X) = 1$, because the predicates can be successfully mapped. In fact, *socialBeing* is a generalization of *legalAgent* in the ontology. Therefore, a common predicate has been found and we can increment l. Each successfully-mapped predicate can be safely removed from both the lists L_1 and L_2.

So, we have these partial results: $l = 1$, $n = 0$, $m = 0$, $L = \{socialBeing(X)\}$:

2. **Second Mapping:** $individualAgent(X) \leftrightarrow shop(Y) = 0$, because $X \neq Y$ and, therefore, the predicates cannot be compared. So, we increase n because $individualAgent(X) \in L_1$ and $individualAgent(X) \notin L_2$;

3. **Third Mapping:** $userAccount(Y) \leftrightarrow shop(Y) = 0$, because there is no ontological relationship between the concepts. So, we increment n because $userAccount(Y) \in L_1$ and $userAccount(Y) \notin L_2$. Moreover, we increase m because $shop(Y) \notin L_1$ and $shop(Y) \in L_2$.

At the end, we have $l = 1$, $n = 2$, $m = 1$, and $L = \{socialBeing(X)\}$.

Now, we compare each binary predicate in L_1 with all binary predicates in L_2.

The only binary predicate in both lists L_1 and L_2 is $has(X,Y)$. In order to explicitly show this binary relationship and the involved entities, we consider the bound variables and make the substitutions: (i) $has(client, userAccount)$ that means that a client is a social being having a user account, and (ii) $has(customer, shop)$ that means that a customer is a social being having a shop.

So, $has(client, userAccount) \leftrightarrow has(customer, shop) = 0$, and $l = 1$, $n = 3$, $m = 2$, and $L = \{socialBeing(X)\}$ is the final result of the comparison. Therefore, $d = 0.36$ is the similarity degree and $L = \{socialBeing(X)\}$ is the list containing the common concept(s).

Since $0 < 0.36 \leq 0.70$ and $L = \{socialBeing(X)\} \neq \varnothing$, the two entities *client* and *customer* do not refer to the same concept, but present a common ontological concept (*cf.*, case 2.5(c) of Section 5). This means that both client and customer are social beings.

The complete result of the case study is reported in Table 2. For each comparison between entities, both the similarity degree d (in the top cell) and the generalization list L (in the bottom cell) are reported. (The symbol "$\approx$" means that the entities are *equivalent*).

7.2.6. Integrated Logical Schema Generation

Now we examine the results of the similarity comparison. We note that client and customer are always used as synonyms. However, the comparison results indicate that the client and customer have not been defined identically and, therefore,

Table 2. Results of the similarity comparison

		Fruit&Vegetables					
		Customer	Order	Product	Vegetable	Package	Price
Client	0.367	0.128	0.166	0.183	0.183	0.25
		{socialBeing}	∅	∅	∅	∅	∅
Order	0.155	0.888	0.252	0.284	0.311	0.222
		∅	≈	∅	∅	∅	∅
Product	0.162	0.118	0.583	0.325	0.287	0.229
		∅	∅	{goods}	∅	∅	∅
Company	0.2	0.155	0.183	0.2	0.2	0.266
		∅	∅	∅	∅	∅	∅
Category	0.225	0.18	0.385	0.417	0.225	0.291
		∅	∅	∅	∅	∅	∅

MusicalInstruments (row group label on the left)

they refer to different database entities. In fact, the similarity degree is different from zero but lower that the threshold (fixed at 0.70, *cf,* rule 2.5a in Section 5), and they present a common ontological concept.

This suggests introducing into the global schema G_1 the *SocialBeing* entity and two specializations corresponding to a client who is a social being with an account (that is, a registered user) and a client who is a social being with a legal title (that is, a company having a shop). This has been obtained by applying rule 2.6(c) in Section 5.

Another generalization that has been detected is that between *product* in *MusicalInstruments* and *product* in *Fruit&Vegetables*. Even if there is a syntactical concordance, the terms refer to very different items: the former refers to an instrument, the latter to a fruit or a vegetable. However, these are both items having a monetary value and are produced to be sold. Then, we created a generalization, namely *product*, which is an item having an assigned price. The specific products have been introduced as specializations,

each with its own relationships. For example, an instrument is produced by a company whereas the producer of vegetables is missing information in the *Fruit&Vegetables* database. This has also been obtained by applying rule 2.6(c) in Section 5.

Finally, it is worth noting that the *order* entity has been defined in the same way in both databases because their similarity degree *d* is greater than the threshold. So, they do not present a generalization because they refer to the same concept. This is the only overlapping concept. This has been obtained by applying rule 2.6(a) in Section 5.

The final global conceptual schema G_3 is shown in Figure 8. Notice that descriptive attributes are not shown in the figure.

After we have obtained the final global conceptual schema representing an integrated data source, we proceed to the elimination of hierarchies and the transformation of this schema into a relational one, in order to use it in our hybrid data warehouse design methodology. This transformation is based on algorithms present in literature and produces a set of relational metadata.

Figure 8. Global conceptual schema

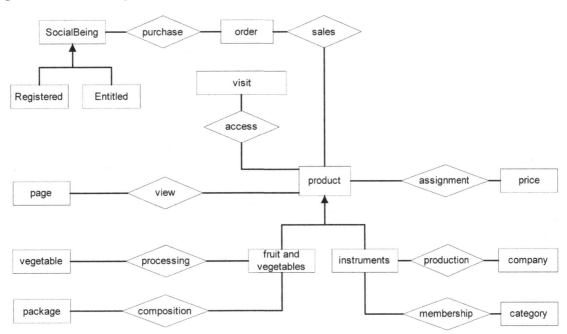

Part of the metadata describing the relational schema is reported below (see the metamodel introduced in sub-Section 5.1):

```
table(product)
table(page)
key(product, productID)
key(page, pageID)
fkey(product, page, page, pageID)
...
table(sales)
key(sales, productID)
key(sales, orderID)
fkey(sales, product, product, productID)
```

7.3. Conceptual Design

In this section, we show the core of the methodology, which relies on the graph-based multidimensional model for representing the integrated global schema. This schema will be remodelled according to the requirements emerged from business goals.

7.3.1. Compiling the Artifacts

First, we consider all the queries included in the workload. As an example, the query:

"sales[month, category, region; year='2012'].quantity".

is translated into the following predicate to be submitted later to the logical program, when validating the data warehouse conceptual schema:

```
query(sales, [month, category, region], [year='2012'], quantity).
```

Then, we consider the constraints. Given the constraint:

"sales[product, category; day, month, year; city, region].[quantity]".

the compiler produces the following predicates:

```
cube(sales).
measure(quantity, sales).
dimension_level(1, 1, product, sales, false).
dimension_level(1, 2, category, sales, false).
dimension_level(2, 1, day, sales, true).
dimension_level(2, 2, month, sales, true).
dimension_level(2, 3, year, sales, true).
dimension_level(3, 1, city, sales, false).
dimension_level(3, 2, region, sales, false).
```

These predicates are used to identify facts in data source and to remodel the attribute tree automatically.

7.3.2. Identifying Facts

At this point, the metadata describing the global schema are considered. The *tree* function searches for a table *C* in data source such that *C* has been marked as a cube in the requirements. In this running example, *C* is *sales* and this table is also asserted as the root of the tree to be build. Then, the navigation through the logical schema starts from the *sales* table.

7.3.3. Building the Attribute Tree

The attribute tree built by navigation rules is depicted in Figure 9(a).

The *sales* table, which has the *quantity* attribute, is linked to two tables via foreign keys: the one is *product*, whose primary key is *productID*, and the other is *order*, whose primary key is *ordereID*. On turn, *order* is related to *customer*, because each order is made by a customer. Each of these tables has its own descriptive attributes, such as *price* and *category*. Further nodes not relevant for the running example, are not reported in the figure.

7.3.4. Remodelling the Attribute Tree

The attribute tree resulting by remodelling rules is depicted in Figure 9(b) and it has been obtained on the basis of next operations.

Since *quantity* is already a root child, no operations are necessary to add measures. Then, dimensions must be defined.

The first dimension is *product*, which is a root child; therefore, no operation is done. The second dimension is *city*, which is a *customer*'s descriptive attribute; in this case, a *change parent* operation is done, in order to add the *city* dimension to the root. Since *city* must be a dimensional attribute—*i.e.*, a non-leaf node—also

a descriptive attribute is added (not shown in the figure due to tree readability) and a surrogate key is used for this dimension. As an example, given a tuple t_1 in the *customer* relation such that $t_1[customerID, city] = <A1, Rome>$, we should create a tuple $s_1[city, description] = <1, Rome>$. The third dimension is *time*. So, a *day* node is added to the root, as specified in the requirements.

Now, hierarchies must be introduced. To this end, a change parent operation is done to make *region* a *city*'s child. As concerns *category*, it is already a child of *productID*, but a descriptive attribute is added and a surrogate key is used. Finally, a complete *time* dimen-

Figure 9. (a) Part of the attribute tree of sales fact; (b) Part of the remodelled attribute tree of sales fact; (c) Logical schema

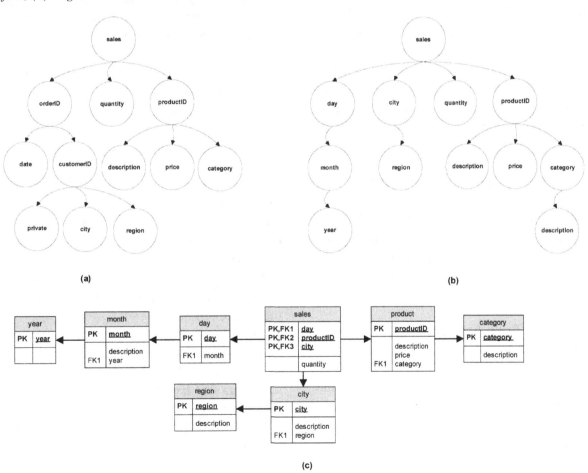

sion is built. At the end, remaining nodes can be safely deleted.

7.3.5. Validating the Conceptual Schema

In order to exemplify validation, we consider the query included in the workload:

```
query(sales, [month, category, region],
[year='2012'], quantity)
```

The aim is to check whether this query can be executed against the conceptual schema depicted in Figure 9(b).

The *Cube test* is accomplished for *sales* is the root of the tree. Also, the *Measure test* is accomplished because *quantity* is a root child.

The aggregation pattern is represented by the list [month, category, region]. Therefore, we have to check whether a path from the root to each element of the list exists. In the tree, paths exist from *sales* to *month*, *category*, and *region*. Then, the *Path test* is accomplished. Moreover, all these are non-leaf nodes. (We recall that *region* has its own descriptive attribute). For this reason, also the *Aggregation test* is accomplished. At last, the *Selection test* is accomplished because *year* is a leaf-node reachable from the root. So, the given attribute tree can be safely transformed into a logical schema during the next logical design phase (see, Figure 9(c)). It is worth noting that rules to transform a conceptual schema into a logical schema are not discussed here, since they are quite intuitive.

7.3.6. On Agile Aspects of the Methodology

The main aspect of agile methodologies is the ability to address the frequent changes in user requirements (Collier & Highsmith, 2004), such to have the minimum impact on the design process.

We note that it is possible to observe three kinds of changes in user requirements:

1. **Addition of Information:** Usually, this kind of change is not incoherent with pre-existing requirements, but simply implies the creation of new cubes, or the addition of further dimensions to a cube, new levels/hierarchies to a dimension, or further attributes to a dimensional level;

2. **Deletion of Information:** This case requires the deletion of existing attribute(s), dimension(s), or cube(s). To our knowledge, this is the most unusual case, as data warehouse are normally used to preserve historical data;

3. **Modification of Requirements:** This kind of change implies the complete revision of the conceptual/logical schemas, as it may involve specifications eventually in contradiction with the produced artifacts.

Now, let us assume we have a physical data warehouse schema and that new user requirements are available. If we observe case b), then we can directly jump to phase 2—that is, the *conceptual design*—using the produced *logical schema* as a source schema. So, applying to this schema the rules for building the attribute tree, we are able to reverse to the conceptual schema. As an example, applying the constraints (reported at the end of section 7.3.1) to the schema in Figure 9(c), we obtain the tree shown in Figure 9(b). At this point, the new requirements (in the form of new constraints) imply the deletion of nodes.

On the other hand, if we observe case a) or c), then we have to restart the complete design process from the beginning, since we may need some data that have been discarded. However, since the methodology is completely automatic, this does not represent a drawback of the proposed approach.

8. FUTURE RESEARCH

One of the hot words in Big Data is Velocity. This refers not only to the rate at which data are produced, but mainly to the capacity of the system to process them for information delivery. This capacity requires that a new data source should be integrated in the system in a scalable way, that is, quickly and without affecting the pre-existing system.

The integration process is composed of two issues: schema integration, that is addressed in the data warehouse design phase, and data integration, that is addressed in the ETL design phase.

While the roadmap for schemas integration is planned and it should be based on an ontological approach, only few authors focus their attention on the automatic generation of ETL plans.

In (Romero *et al.*, 2011) a semi-automatic process is presented. The explained strategy aims to identify necessary operators for populating the target schema, after a multidimensional tagging has correctly identified each required concept and mapped it to the data source. Although the paper presents an interesting method to define a preliminary ETL plan, some questions arise—for example, how the right aggregate function is chosen, when an aggregation operation must be executed. So, when dealing with complex schemas or when finding an algorithmic solution is a hard task, a manual participation is needed.

Another automatic method for ETL design is presented in (Muñoz *et al.*, 2009). It is devoted to the code generation, by transforming a conceptual ETL plan into platform-dependent procedures. The method has the merit of being based on well-known standards—such as UML and QVT. Furthermore, if a new ETL process must be added to feed a different target system, only transformations must be created once. However, the starting conceptual plan must be manually defined by the designer. Therefore, the aim of creating ETL procedures using only a source schema and a target schema still remains unresolved.

Hence, future trends must address the problem of automatically generating the ETL procedures, in order to minimize the time necessary for effectively including a new data source into the data warehouse system.

9. CONCLUSION

We have presented a hybrid methodology for big data warehouse design. The core of the methodology is a graph-based model, aiming at producing multidimensional schemas automatically. To this end, the inputs of the conceptual design are a global schema and a set of user requirements.

The global schema is obtained through an integration process of data sources, which can be structured or unstructured. In order to solve syntactic and semantic inconsistencies present in data sources, we used ontology for representing in a formal way the domain's concepts, along their relationships. The integration strategy aims to detect similar or identical concepts defined in different data sources and to identify common ontological concepts.

User requirements, which consist in a set of constraints and a workload, are respectively used to perform the reengineering process of the global schema in a supervised way, and the validation of the resulting multidimensional schema.

REFERENCES

Bakhtouchi, A., Bellatreche, L., & Ait-Ameur, Y. (2011). Ontologies and functional dependencies for data integration and reconciliation. In O. De Troyer, C. Bauzer Medeiros, R. Billen, P. Hallot, A. Simitsis, & H. Van Mingroot (Eds.), *Advances in Conceptual Modeling. Recent Developments and New Directions, (LNCS)* (Vol. 6999, pp. 98–107). Berlin: Springer. doi:10.1007/978-3-642-24574-9_13.

Bonifati, A., Cattaneo, F., Ceri, S., Fuggetta, A., & Paraboschi, S. (2001). Designing data marts for data warehouses. *ACM Transactions on Software Engineering and Methodology*, *10*, 452–483. doi:10.1145/384189.384190.

Chen, Z. (2001). *Intelligent data warehousing: From data preparation to data mining*. Boca Raton, FL: CRC Press. doi:10.1201/9781420040616.

Cohen, J., Dolan, B., Dunlap, M., Hellerstein, J. M., & Welton, C. (2009). Mad skills: New analysis practices for big data. *Proceedings of the VLDB Endowment*, *2*(2), 1481–1492.

Collier, K., & Highsmith, J. A. (2004). Agile data warehousing: Incorporating agile principles. *Business Intelligence Advisory Service Executive Report*, *4*(12).

dell'Aquila, C., Di Tria, F., Lefons, E., & Tangorra, F. (2009). Dimensional fact model extension via predicate calculus. In *Proceedings of the 24th International Symposium on Computer and Information Sciences* (pp. 211-217). IEEE Press.

dell'Aquila, C., Di Tria, F., Lefons, E., & Tangorra, F. (2010). Logic programming for data warehouse conceptual schema validation. In T. B. Pedersen, M. K. Mohania, & A. M. Tjoa (Eds.), *Data Warehousing and Knowledge Discovery (LNCS)* (Vol. 6263, pp. 1–12). Berlin: Springer. doi:10.1007/978-3-642-15105-7_1.

Di Tria, F., Lefons, E., & Tangorra, F. (2011). GrHyMM: A graph-oriented hybrid multidimensional model. In O. De Troyer, C. Bauzer Medeiros, R. Billen, P. Hallot, A. Simitsis, & H. Van Mingroot (Eds.), *Advances in Conceptual Modeling. Recent Developments and New Directions (LNCS)* (Vol. 6999, pp. 86–97). Berlin: Springer. doi:10.1007/978-3-642-24574-9_12.

Di Tria, F., Lefons, E., & Tangorra, F. (2012). Hybrid methodology for data warehouse conceptual design by UML schemas. *Information and Software Technology*, *54*(4), 360–379. doi:10.1016/j.infsof.2011.11.004.

Elmasri, R., & Navathe, S. B. (2010). *Fundamentals of database systems* (6th ed.). Reading, MA: Addison-Wesley.

Ferilli, S., Basile, T. M. A., Biba, M., Di Mauro, N., & Esposito, F. (2009). A general similarity framework for horn clause logic. *Fundamentals of Informatics*, *90*(1-2), 43–66.

Foxvog, D. (2010). Cyc. In *Theory and Applications of Ontology: Computer Applications* (pp. 259–278). Berlin: Springer. doi:10.1007/978-90-481-8847-5_12.

Giorgini, P., Rizzi, S., & Garzetti, M. (2008). GRAnD: A goal-oriented approach to requirement analysis in data warehouses. *Decision Support Systems*, *45*, 4–21. doi:10.1016/j.dss.2006.12.001.

Golfarelli, M., & Rizzi, S. (2009). *Data warehouse design: Modern principles and methodologies*. New York: McGraw-Hill Osborne Media.

Hakimpour, F., & Geppert, A. (2002). Global schema generation using formal ontologies. In S. Spaccapietra, S. T. March, & Y. Kambayashi (Eds.), *ER (LNCS)* (Vol. 2503, pp. 307–321). Berlin: Springer.

Helfert, M., & Von Maur, E. (2001). A strategy for managing data quality in data warehouse systems. In E. M. Pierce & R. Katz-Haas (Eds.), *Sixth Conference on Information Quality* (pp. 62-76). Cambridge, MA: MIT.

Jiang, L., Xu, J., Xu, B., & Cai, H. (2011). An automatic method of data warehouses multi-dimension modeling for distributed information systems. In W. Shen, J.-P. A. Barthès, J. Luo, P. G. Kropf, M. Pouly, J. Yong, Y. Xue, & M. Pires Ramos (Eds.), *Proceedings of the 2011 15th International Conference on Computer Supported Cooperative Work in Design* (pp. 9-16). IEEE.

Levine, J. (2009). *Flex & bison text processing tools*. Sebastopol, CA: O'Reilly Media.

Mazón, J. N., & Trujillo, J. (2009). A hybrid model driven development framework for the multidimensional modeling of data warehouses. *SIGMOD Record, 38*, 12–17. doi:10.1145/1815918.1815920.

Mazón, J. N., Trujillo, J., & Lechtenbörger, J. (2007). Reconciling requirement-driven data warehouses with data sources via multidimensional normal forms. *Data & Knowledge Engineering, 63*, 725–751. doi:10.1016/j.datak.2007.04.004.

Mazón, J. N., Trujillo, J., Serrano, M., & Piattini, M. (2005). Designing data warehouses: From business requirement analysis to multidimensional modeling. In K. Cox, E. Dubois, Y. Pigneur, S. J. Bleistein, J. Verner, A. M. Davis, & R. Wieringa (Eds.), *Requirements Engineering for Business Need and IT Alignment* (pp. 44–53). Wales Press.

Muñoz, L., Mazón, J. N., & Trujillo, J. (2009). Automatic generation of ETL processes from conceptual models. In I.-Y. Song & E. Zimànyi (Eds.), *DOLAP 2009, ACM 12th International Workshop on Data Warehousing and OLAP* (pp. 33-40). ACM.

Phipps, C., & Davis, K. C. (2002). Automating data warehouse conceptual schema design and evaluation. In L. V. S. Lakshmanan (Ed.), *DMDW: CEUR Workshop Proceedings, Design and Management of Data Warehouses* (pp. 23-32). CEUR.

Reed, S. L., & Lenat, D. B. (2002). Mapping ontologies in Cyc. In *Proceedings of AAAI 2002 Conference Workshop on Ontologies for the Semantic Web*. Edmonton, Canada: AAAI.

Romero, O., & Abelló, A. (2009). A survey of multidimensional modeling methodologies. *International Journal of Data Warehousing and Mining, 5*, 1–23. doi:10.4018/jdwm.2009040101.

Romero, O., & Abelló, A. (2010a). Automatic validation of requirements to support multidimensional design. *Data & Knowledge Engineering, 69*(9), 917–942. doi:10.1016/j.datak.2010.03.006.

Romero, O., & Abelló, A. (2010b). A framework for multidimensional design of data warehouses from ontologies. *Data & Knowledge Engineering, 69*(11), 1138–1157. doi:10.1016/j.datak.2010.07.007.

Romero, O., Simitsis, A., & Abelló, A. (2011). GEM: Requirement-driven generation of ETL and multidimensional conceptual designs. In A. Cuzzocrea, & U. Dayal (Eds.), *Data Warehousing and Knowledge Discovery (LNCS)* (Vol. 6862, pp. 80–95). Berlin: Springer. doi:10.1007/978-3-642-23544-3_7.

Sure, Y., Erdmann, M., Angele, J., Staab, S., Studer, R., & Wenke, D. (2002). OntoEdit: Collaborative ontology development for the semantic web. In I. Horrocks & J. A. Hendler (Eds.), *International Semantic Web Conference* (LNCS), (Vol. 2342, pp. 221-235). Berlin: Springer.

Thenmozhi, M., & Vivekanandan, K. (2012). An ontology-based hybrid approach to derive multidimensional schema for data warehouse. *International Journal of Computers and Applications, 54*(8), 36–42. doi:10.5120/8590-2343.

ADDITIONAL READING

Abadi, D. J., Madden, S., & Hachem, N. (2008). Column-stores vs. row-stores: How different are they really? In J. Tsong-Li Wang (Ed.), *SIGMOD Conference* (pp. 967-980). ACM.

Agrawal, D., Bernstein, P., Bertino, E., Davidson, S., Dayal, U., Franklin, M., et al. (2012). *Challenges and opportunities with big data*. Retrieved October 25, 2012, from http://cra.org/ccc/docs/init/bigdatawhitepaper.pdf

Bellatreche, L., Ait Ameur, Y., & Pierra, G. (2010). Special issue on contribution of ontologies in designing advanced information systems. *Data & Knowledge Engineering, 69*(11), 1081–1083. doi:10.1016/j.datak.2010.08.002.

Bellatreche, L., Cuzzocrea, A., & Benkrid, S. (2010). A methodology for effectively and efficiently designing parallel relational data warehouses on heterogenous database clusters. In T. Bach Pedersen, M. K. Mohania, & A. M. Tjoa (Eds.), *Data Warehousing and Knowledge Discovery (LNCS)* (Vol. 6263, pp. 89–104). Berlin: Springer. doi:10.1007/978-3-642-15105-7_8.

Buitelaar, P., Olejnik, D., & Sintek, M. (2003). OntoLT: A protege plug-in for ontology extraction from text. In *Proceedings of the International Semantic Web Conference*. IEEE.

Cuzzocrea, A. (2011). Pushing artificial intelligence in database and data warehouse systems. *Data & Knowledge Engineering, 70*(8), 683–684. doi:10.1016/j.datak.2011.03.005.

Cuzzocrea, A. (2011). Data warehousing and knowledge discovery from sensors and streams. *Knowledge and Information Systems, 28*(3), 491–493. doi:10.1007/s10115-011-0440-2.

Giunchiglia, F., Shvaiko, P., & Yatskevich, M. (2007). Semantic matching: Algorithms and implementation. In S. Spaccapietra, P. Atzeni, F. Fages, M.-S. Hacid, M. Kifer, & J. Mylopoulos, et al. (Eds.), *Journal of Data Semantics IX (LNCS)* (Vol. 4601, pp. 1–38). Berlin: Springer. doi:10.1007/978-3-540-74987-5_1.

Hakimpour, F., & Geppert, A. (2005). Resolution of semantic heterogeneity in database schema integration using formal ontologies. *Information Technology Management, 6*(1), 97–122. doi:10.1007/s10799-004-7777-0.

Kalfoglou, Y., & Schorlemmer, M. (2003). Ontology mapping: The state of the art. *The Knowledge Engineering Review Journal, 18*(1), 1–31. doi:10.1017/S0269888903000651.

Khouri, S., & Bellatreche, L. (2010). A methodology and tool for conceptual designing a data warehouse from ontology-based sources. In I.-Y. Song & C. Ordonez (Eds.), *ACM 13th International Workshop on Data Warehousing and OLAP* (pp. 19.24). ACM.

Khouri, S., Boukhari, I., Bellatreche, L., Sardet, E., Jean, S., & Baron, M. (2012). Ontology-based structured web data warehouses for sustainable interoperability: Requirement modeling, design methodology and tool. *Computers in Industry, 63*(8), 799–812. doi:10.1016/j.compind.2012.08.001.

March, S., & Hevner, A. (2007). Integrated decision support systems: A data warehousing perspective. *Decision Support Systems, 43*(3), 1031–1043. doi:10.1016/j.dss.2005.05.029.

Prat, N., Akoka, J., & Comyn-Wattiau, I. (2006). A UML-based data warehouse design method. *Decision Support Systems, 42*(3), 1449–1473. doi:10.1016/j.dss.2005.12.001.

Queralt, A., Artale, A., Calvanese, D., & Teniente, E. (2012). OCL-lite: Finite reasoning on UML/OCL conceptual schemas. *Data & Knowledge Engineering, 73*, 1–22. doi:10.1016/j.datak.2011.09.004.

Rull, G., Farré, C., Teniente, E., & Urpí, T. (2009). MVT: A schema mapping validation tool. In M. L. Kersten, B. Novikov, J. Teubner, V. Polutin, & S. Manegold (Eds.), *ACM International Conference Proceeding Series* (vol. 360, pp. 1120-1123). ACM.

Skoutas, D., & Simitsis, A. (2007). Ontology-based conceptual design of ETL processes for both structured and semi-structured data. *International Journal on Semantic Web and Information Systems*, *3*(4), 1–24. doi:10.4018/jswis.2007100101 PMID:18974854.

Song, I., Khare, R., & Dai, B. (2007). SAMSTAR: A semi-automated lexical method for generating STAR schemas from an ER diagram. In I.-Y. Song & T. Bach Pedersen (Eds.), *Proceedings of ACM 10th International Workshop on Data Warehousing and OLAP* (pp. 9-16). ACM Press.

Vassiliadis, P., Simitsis, A., Georgantas, P., Terrovitis, M., & Skiadopoulos, S. (2005). A generic and customizable framework for the design of ETL scenarios. *Information Systems*, *30*(7), 492–525. doi:10.1016/j.is.2004.11.002.

Weininger, A. (2002). Efficient execution of joins in a star schema. In M. J. Franklin, B. Moon, & A. Ailamaki (Eds.), *SIGMOD Conference* (pp. 542-545). ACM.

Yu, B., Cuzzocrea, A., Jeong, D., & Maydebura, S. (2012). On managing very large sensor-network data using bigtable. In *Proceedings of the 12th IEEE/ACM International Symposium on Cluster, Cloud and Grid Computing* (pp. 918-922). IEEE.

KEY TERMS AND DEFINITIONS

Business Goals: User requirements derived from the needs of decision makers.

Conceptual Representation: A local representation of concepts, along with their relationships, that are true only in a given context.

Data-Driven Approach: A data warehouse design strategy that aims to produce multidimensional schemas, by detecting facts and dimensions in structured data sources.

Hybrid Approach: A multidimensional design strategy that takes into account both user requirements and data sources.

Logical Program: A program composed of facts and deductive rules, expressed according to the *Predicate Calculus*.

Ontological Representation: A formal, general and widely shared representation of concepts, along with their relationships in a specific domain.

Reengineering Process: The process that modifies a relational schema by introducing and/or deleting attributes and functional dependencies.

Requirement-Driven Approach: A data warehouse design strategy that aims to produce multidimensional schemas, by transforming information requirements in multidimensional concepts.

Schemas Integration: The process that aims to define a global and reconciled schema, by solving syntactical and semantic inconsistencies in data sources.

Workload Validation: The process that allows to check whether a schema is able to support a set of queries representing the analytical workload.

Chapter 7
Big Data Management in the Context of Real-Time Data Warehousing

M. Asif Naeem
Auckland University of Technology, New Zealand

Gillian Dobbie
University of Auckland, New Zealand

Gerald Weber
University of Auckland, New Zealand

ABSTRACT

In order to make timely and effective decisions, businesses need the latest information from big data warehouse repositories. To keep these repositories up to date, real-time data integration is required. An important phase in real-time data integration is data transformation where a stream of updates, which is huge in volume and infinite, is joined with large disk-based master data. Stream processing is an important concept in Big Data, since large volumes of data are often best processed immediately. A well-known algorithm called Mesh Join (MESHJOIN) was proposed to process stream data with disk-based master data, which uses limited memory. MESHJOIN is a candidate for a resource-aware system setup. The problem that the authors consider in this chapter is that MESHJOIN is not very selective. In particular, the performance of the algorithm is always inversely proportional to the size of the master data table. As a consequence, the resource consumption is in some scenarios suboptimal. They present an algorithm called Cache Join (CACHEJOIN), which performs asymptotically at least as well as MESHJOIN but performs better in realistic scenarios, particularly if parts of the master data are used with different frequencies. In order to quantify the performance differences, the authors compare both algorithms with a synthetic dataset of a known skewed distribution as well as TPC-H and real-life datasets.

DOI: 10.4018/978-1-4666-4699-5.ch007

INTRODUCTION

Real-time data warehouse deployments are driving an evolution to more aggressive data freshness service levels. The tools and techniques for delivering against these new service levels are rapidly evolving (Karakasidis, Vassiliadis, & Pitoura, 2005)(Naeem, Dobbie, & Weber, 2008). In the beginning, most data warehouses fully refreshed all content during each load cycle. However, due to rapid growth in the size of warehouses and the increasing demand of information freshness, it became infeasible to meet the business needs. Thus the data acquisition mechanism in warehouses changed from full refresh to an incremental refresh strategy, in which new data is added to the warehouse without requiring a complete reload (Labio & Garcia-Molina, 1996)(Labio, Yang, Cui, Garcia-Molina, & Widom, 1999). Although this strategy is more efficient than the traditional one, it is still batch-oriented; a fraction of the data is propagated to the warehouse after a particular timestamp.

In order to overcome update delays, these batch-oriented and incremental refresh strategies are being replaced with a continuous refresh strategy (Golab, Johnson, Seidel, & Shkapenyuk, 2009)(Zhang & Rundensteiner, 2002) (Zhuge, García-Molina, Hammer, & Widom, 1995). In such strategies, end user data from data sources is being captured and propagated to the data warehouse in real-time in order to support high levels of data freshness. This leads to a stream processing approach. Stream processing is natural for todays Big Data, since no intermediate storage has to be considered. This can lead to an architecture that is even simpler than batch processing and at the same time delivers a distinctly new quality of service.

One important research area in the field of data warehousing is data transformation, since the updates coming from the data sources are often not in the format required for the data warehouse. In the field of real-time data warehousing where data arrives in the form of an infinite stream and a continuous transformation from a source to a target format is required, such tasks become more challenging. In the ETL (Extract-Transform-Load) layer, a number of transformations are performed such as the detection of duplicate tuples, identification of newly inserted tuples, and the enriching of some new attribute values from master data. One common transformation is the key transformation. The key used in the data source may be different from that in the data warehouse and therefore needs to be transformed into the required value for the warehouse key. To explain the transformation phase further we consider an example shown in Figure 1 that implements one of the above features called enrichment. In the example we consider the source updates with attributes *product_id*, *qty*, and *date* that are extracted from data sources. At the transformation layer in addition to key replacement (from source key *product_id* to warehouse key *s_key*) some information such as vendor information and sales price are needed to calculate the total amount. In the figure this information with attribute names *s_key*, *s_price*, and *vendor*

Figure 1. An example of content enrichment

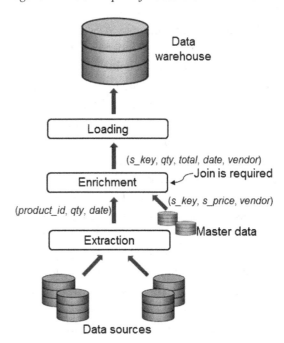

are extracted at run time from the master data and are enriched into source updates. This transformation can be obtained by implementing a join operation between the update tuples and a lookup table. One important factor related to the join is that both inputs of the join come from different sources with different arrival rates. The input from the data sources is in the form of an update stream, which is fast, while the access rate of the lookup table is comparatively slow due to disk I/O cost. A research challenge here is to amortize the expensive I/O cost over the fast stream of data.

In the past, the algorithm MESHJOIN (Neoklis Polyzotis, Skiadopoulos, Vassiliadis, Simitsis, & Frantzell, 2008) (N Polyzotis, Skiadopoulos, Vassiliadis, Simitsis, & Frantzell, 2007) was proposed for joining a stream with a slowly changing table with limited main memory requirements. This algorithm is an interesting candidate for a resource-aware system setup. The MESHJOIN algorithm also has few requirements with respect to the organization of the master data table. However, the problem that we are addressing is that the MESHJOIN performance is directly coupled to the size of the master data table, and its performance is inversely proportional to the size of the master data table. This is an undesired behavior if the master data becomes very large, and our analysis will show that it is indeed an unnecessary behavior. The problem becomes obvious if we consider that the master data table could contain a large part that is never joined with the stream data. In MESHJOIN, if one contiguous half of the master data is unused, the presence of this master data halves the performance. This situation can easily arise if the master data table is storing data for long-term availability and in the current business process only a fraction is used. A typical scenario would be catalogue data for seasonal products. This is undesirable, especially where the aim is to minimize resource consumption, since the algorithm still uses the same resources for half the performance. This would put the burden on the administrator to meticulously clean

the master data, in order to optimize system performance. Therefore it would be a great advantage if we have an algorithm that shares the advantages of MESHJOIN, but adapts itself to certain situations, for example if the algorithm is more sensitive to the usage of the master data.

In this chapter we present a new algorithm, CACHEJOIN, which is able to utilize differences in the access frequency of master data. CACHEJOIN's performance is not affected, if a large set of unused data is added to the master data table. We are interested in understanding the relative performance of the MESHJOIN and CACHEJOIN algorithms. As we have said before CACHEJOIN will be unaffected by contiguous unused master data, therefore it is easy to create data sets where CACHEJOIN is arbitrarily better than MESHJOIN. However, in order to test our algorithm in a scenario that is not biased against any algorithm, we were looking for characteristics of data that are considered ubiquitous in real world scenarios. A Zipfian distribution of the foreign keys in the stream data matches distributions that are observed in a wide range of applications (Anderson, 2006). We therefore created a data generator that can produce such a Zipfian distribution. The exponent of the underlying power law parameterizes a Zipfian distribution. In different scenarios, different exponents are observed, and determine whether the distribution is considered to have a short tail or a long tail. Distributions with a short tail would be more favourable for CACHEJOIN from the outset; therefore we decided not to use a distribution with a short tail in order to not bias our experiment towards CACHEJOIN. Instead we settled on the most natural exponent that is observed in a variety of areas, including the original Zipf's Law in linguistics (Knuth, 1998) that gave rise to the popular name of these distributions. The main result of our analysis is that CACHEJOIN performs better on a synthetic skewed data set that follows a Zipfian distribution as is found frequently in practice. For our analysis we do not consider joins on categorical attributes in master data, e.g. we do not consider equijoins solely on attributes such as gender.

CACHEJOIN outperforms MESHJOIN with skewed data, which is a common characteristic of real-world applications. CACHEJOIN performs at most a constant factor worse than MESHJOIN in one case only when the key distribution is completely uniform and no adaptive approach is needed. This is because MESHJOIN eliminates seek times by reading the master data sequentially.

RELATED WORK

In this section, we present an overview of the previous work that has been done in this area, focusing on those, which are closely related to our problem domain.

The Symmetric Hash Join (SHJ) algorithm (Wilschut & Apers, 1991)(Wilschut & Apers, 1990) extends the original hash join algorithm in a pipeline fashion. In the symmetric hash join, there is a separate hash table for both input relations. When a tuple t of one input arrives, SHJ probes the hash table of the other input, generates the result (if any) and then stores t into the hash table of its own stream. SHJ can produce results before reading either input relation entirely; however, it stores both relations in memory. The Double Pipelined Hash Join (DPHJ) (Ives, Florescu, Friedman, Levy, & Weld, 1999), XJoin (Urhan & Franklin, 2000) and Early Hash Join (EHJ) (Lawrence, 2005) are further extensions of SHJ for the pipeline execution of join. Hash-Merge Join (HMJ) (Mokbel, Lu, & Aref, 2004) is also one from the series of symmetric joins. This is based on push technology and consists of two phases, hashing and merging.

MJoin (Viglas, Naughton, & Burger, 2003), a generalized variant of XJoin, extends the symmetric binary join operators to handle multiple inputs. MJoin uses a separate hash table for each input. On the arrival of a tuple from an input, it is stored in the corresponding hash table and

is probed in the rest of the hash tables. It is not necessary to probe all the hash tables for each arrival, as the sequence of probing stops when a probed tuple does not match in a hash table. The methodology for choosing the correct sequence of probing is determined by performing the most selective probes first. The algorithm uses a coordinated flushing technique that involves flushing the same partition on the disk for all inputs. To identify the duplicate tuples, MJoin uses two timestamps for each tuple, the arrival time and the departure time from memory.

Another join operator called Adaptive, Hash-partitioned Exact Window Join (AH-EWJ) (Chakraborty & Singh, 2010) has been introduced to produce accurate results for sliding window joins over data streams. This approach can also be used in the scenario where a stream joins with disk-based data. However, the focus of this approach is on the accuracy of the join output rather than on performance optimization while considering the non-uniform characteristic on the stream data.

A novel algorithm Mesh Join (MESHJOIN) (Neoklis Polyzotis et al., 2008)(N Polyzotis et al., 2007) has been designed especially for joining a continuous stream with a disk-based relation, like the scenario in active data warehouses. The MESHJOIN algorithm is a hash join, where the stream serves as the build input and the disk-based relation serves as the probe input. A characteristic of MESHJOIN is that it performs a staggered execution of the hash table build in order to load in stream tuples more steadily. The algorithm makes no assumptions about data distribution and the organization of the master data. The MESHJOIN authors report that the algorithm performs worse with skewed data.

R-MESHJOIN (reduced Mesh Join) (Naeem, Dobbie, Weber, & Alam, 2010) clarifies the dependencies among the components of MESHJOIN. As a result the performance has been improved slightly. However, R-MESHJOIN implements the same strategy as in the MESHJOIN algorithm for accessing the disk-based relation.

The X-HYBRIDJOIN (Naeem, Dobbie, & Weber, 2011) algorithm is an extension of R-MESHJOIN. This algorithm has been designed particularly to address real market conditions. Although this is an adaptive algorithm and performs better than other similar approaches, there are some limitations at the architectural level that need to be explored further. Also the algorithm assumes the master data is sorted in the order of access frequency.

The Optimized X-HYBRIDJOIN (Naeem, Dobbie, & Weber, 2012) algorithm is an improved form of X-HYBRIDJOIN. The algorithm removes the unnecessary architectural limitations of X-HYBRIDJOIN. Consequently, it improves the performance of the algorithm however Optimized X-HYBRIDJOIN also assumes the master data is sorted.

Another approach to improve MESHJOIN has been a partition-based join algorithm (Chakraborty & Singh, 2009) which can also deal with stream intermittence. It uses a two-level hash table in order to attempt to join stream tuples as soon as they arrive, and uses a partition-based waiting area for other stream tuples. For the algorithm in (Chakraborty & Singh, 2009), however, the time that a tuple is waiting for execution is not bounded. We are interested in a join approach where there is a time guarantee for when a stream tuple will be joined, and therefore a guarantee that our algorithm is asymptotically as fast as MESHJOIN.

Another recent approach Semi-Streaming Index Join (SSIJ) (Bornea, Deligiannakis, Kotidis, & Vassalos, 2011) has been developed to process the stream data with the disk-based data. In general the algorithm is divided into three phases, namely the pending phase, the online phase and the join phase. In the pending phase the stream tuples wait in a buffer until the size of the buffer is less than the predefined threshold limit or the stream ends. Once the size of the buffer crosses the threshold limit, the algorithm starts its online phase. In the online phase stream tuples from the input buffer are looked-up in cache-based disk

blocks. If the required disk tuple exists in cache, the join is executed and the algorithm produces an output. In the case when the required disk tuple is not available in cache, the algorithm flushes the stream tuple into a stream buffer where it waits for the join phase. The algorithm implements another threshold on the stream buffer and during the join phase the disk invoke is performed if the size of the stream buffer is greater than the threshold value. In the join phase the algorithm joins the tuples from the stream buffer with the tuples in the invoked disk block. The algorithm implements a utility counter for each disk block that determines which disk blocks need to be retained in memory.

Although SSIJ is a feasible approach for processing stream data, the algorithm uses a page level cache i.e. stores the entire disk pages in cache while it is possible that all the tuples in these pages may not be frequent in the stream. As a result the algorithm can perform suboptimally. Also, because the algorithm does not include the mathematical cost model, it makes the criteria for calculating threshold parameters unclear.

EXISTING MESHJOIN

In this section we present an overview of the existing MESHJOIN algorithm. At the end of the section we outline the observations that we focus on later in this chapter.

MESHJOIN was designed to support streaming updates over persistent data in the field of real-time data warehousing. The algorithm reads the disk-based relation sequentially in partitions. Once the last partition is read, it again starts from the first partition. The algorithm contains a buffer, called the disk buffer, to store each disk partition in memory one at a time. The algorithm uses a hash table to store the stream tuples, while the key attribute for each tuple is stored in the queue. All partitions in the queue are equal in size. The total number of partitions is equal to the number of partitions on the disk while the size of each partition on the disk is equal to the size of the disk buffer. There is a stream buffer of negligible size that is used to hold the fast stream if required.

In each iteration the algorithm reads one disk partition into the disk buffer and loads a chunk of stream tuples into the hash table while also placing their key attributes in the queue. After loading the disk partition into memory it joins each tuple from the disk buffer to the stream hash table using a hash function. Before the next iteration the oldest stream tuples are removed from the hash table with their key attribute values from the queue. All chunks of the stream in the queue are advanced by one step. In the next iteration the algorithm replaces the current disk partition with the next one, loads a chunk of new stream tuples into the hash table and places their key attribute's values in the queue, and repeats the above procedure.

The crux of the algorithm is that the total number of partitions in the stream queue must be equal to the total number of partitions on the disk and that number can be determined by dividing the size of the disk-based relation R by the size of the disk buffer b (i.e. $k=N_R/b$). This constraint ensures that a stream tuple that is loaded into memory is matched against the entire disk relation before it expires.

An overview of MESHJOIN is presented in Figure 2 where we consider only three partitions in the queue, with the same number of partitions on disk. At any time t, for example when disk partition p_3 is in memory the status of the stream tuples in memory can be explained. In the queue w_1 tuples have already joined with disk partition p_1 and p_2 and therefore after joining with partition p_3 they will be dropped out of memory. While tuples w_2 have joined with partition p_2 only and therefore, after joining with partition p_3 they will advance one step in the queue. Finally, tuples w_3 have not joined with any disk partition and they will also advance one step in the queue after joining with partition p_3. Once the algorithm

Figure 2. Example of MESHJOIN when disk partition p_3 is in memory

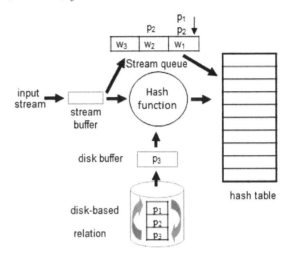

completes the cycle of R, it starts loading sequentially again from the first partition.

The MESHJOIN algorithm amortizes the fast arrival rate of the incoming stream by executing the join of disk partitions with a large number of stream tuples. However there are still some further issues that exist in the algorithm. Firstly due to the sequential access of R, the algorithm reads the unused or less used partitions of R into memory with equal frequency, which increases the *processing time* for every stream tuple in the queue due to extra disk I/O. *Processing time* is the time that every stream tuple spends in the join window from loading to matching without including any delay due to the low arrival rate of the stream.

To determine the access rate of disk partitions of R we performed an experiment using a benchmark that is based on Zipf's Law to model commercial applications (Knuth, 1998)(Anderson, 2006). In this experiment we assumed that R is sorted in ascending order with respect to the frequency of access of a join attribute in memory and we measure the rate of use for the pages at different locations of R. From the results shown in Figure 3 it can be seen that the rate of page-use

Figure 3. Measured rate of page-use at different locations of R while the size of total R is 16000 pages

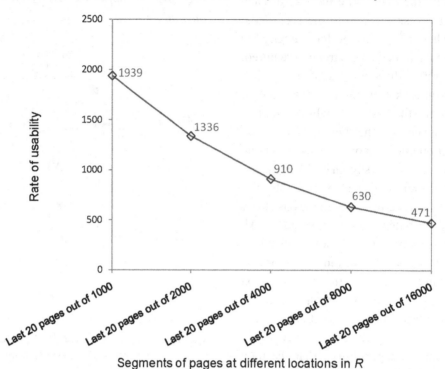

decreases towards the end of *R*. The MESHJOIN algorithm does not consider this factor and reads all disk pages with the same frequency.

Secondly, MESHJOIN cannot deal with bursty input streams effectively. In MESHJOIN a disk invocation occurs when the number of tuples in the stream buffer is equal to or greater than the stream input size *w*. In the case of intermittent or low arrival rate (λ) of the input stream, the tuples already in the queue need to wait longer due to disk invocation delay. This *waiting time* negatively affects the performance. *Waiting time* is a time that each stream tuple stays in the stream buffer.

In summary, the problems that we addresses in this chapter are: (a) to make the performance independent from the size of the master data especially when a large part of the master data is unused or less used, (b) dealing with intermittency in stream data effectively.

CACHEJOIN

In this chapter, we propose a new algorithm, CACHEJOIN, which overcomes the issues stated above. In order to allow CACHEJOIN to access the disk-based relation *R* selectively, an index is needed. However, a non-clustered index is sufficient, if we consider equijoins on a foreign key element that is stored in the stream.

This section gives a high level description of CACHEJOIN, and a detailed walkthrough can be found in the section named Algorithm. The CACHEJOIN algorithm possesses two complementary hash join phases, somewhat similar to Symmetric Hash Join. One phase uses *R* as the probe input; the largest part of *R* will be stored in tertiary memory. We call it the disk-probing phase. The other join phase uses the stream as the probe input, but will deal only with a small part of relation *R*. We call it the stream-probing phase. For each incoming stream tuple, CACHE-JOIN first uses the stream-probing phase to find a match for frequent requests quickly, and if no match is found, the stream tuple is forwarded to the disk-probing phase.

The execution architecture for CACHEJOIN is shown in Figure 4. The largest components of CACHEJOIN with respect to memory size are two hash tables, one storing stream tuples denoted by H_S and the other storing tuples from the disk-based relation denoted by H_R. The other main components of CACHEJOIN are a disk buffer, a queue and a stream buffer. Relation R and stream S are the external input sources. Hash table H_R, for R contains the most frequently accessed tuples of R and is stored permanently in memory.

CACHEJOIN alternates between the stream-probing and disk-probing phases. According to the procedure described above, the hash table H_S is used to store only that part of the stream which

does not match tuples in H_R. A stream-probing phase ends if H_S is completely filled or if the stream buffer is empty. Then the disk-probing phase becomes active. The length of the disk-probing phase is determined by the fact that a few disk pages of R have to be loaded at a time in order to amortize the costly disk access. In the disk-probing phase of CACHEJOIN, the oldest tuple in the queue is used to determine the partition of R that is loaded for a single probe step. In this way, in CACHEJOIN it is guaranteed that every probe step processes at least one stream tuple, while in MESHJOIN there is no such guarantee. This can be extended to an argument that CACHEJOIN performs asymptotically at least as well as MESHJOIN. This is also the step where CACHEJOIN needs an index on table R in order to find the partition in R that matches the oldest stream tuple. After one probe step, a sufficient number of stream tuples are deleted from H_S, so

Figure 4. Data structures and architecture of CACHEJOIN

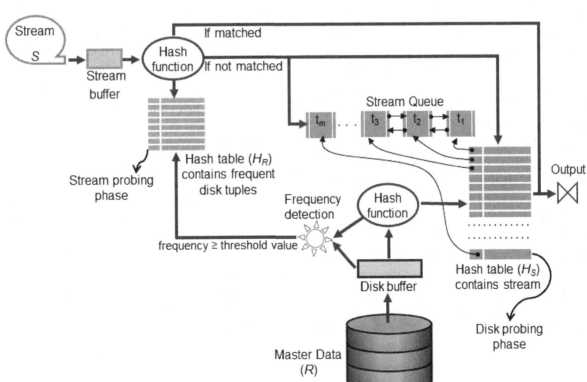

the algorithm switches back to the stream-probing phase. One phase of stream-probing with a subsequent phase of disk-probing constitutes one outer iteration of CACHEJOIN. The disk-probing phase could work on its own; without the stream-probing phase.

Therefore, in performance experiments, we will also run the algorithm with the stream-probing phase switched off. This further simplifies the architecture, and the memory used for the stream-probing phase should be reassigned, giving a new intermediate algorithm that we call HYBRIDJOIN. We restrict the cost model and tuning to the full CACHEJOIN algorithm, but we provide experimental results for CACHEJOIN as well as HYBRIDJOIN. The experimental results allow us to study which contribution is made by the disk-probing phase alone (HYBRIDJOIN) and by both phases together. An analysis of our proposed algorithm is presented in the following subsections.

The stream-probing phase is used to boost the performance of the algorithm by quickly matching the most frequent master data. The question of where to set the threshold arises, i.e. how frequently must a stream tuple be used in order to get into this phase, so that the memory sacrificed for this phase really delivers a performance advantage. In the cost model section we give a precise and comprehensive analysis that shows that a remarkably small memory sacrifice in the stream-probing phase can deliver a substantial performance gain. In fact, CACHEJOIN will be tuned to a provably optimal distribution of memory between the two phases, and the components within the phases. In order to corroborate this theoretical model, we will present experimental performance measurements that show high accuracy of the model. For determining very frequent tuples in R and loading them into H_R, the frequency detection process is required. The detail of the process is presented in the algorithm section. The disk buffer stores the

swappable part of R and for each iteration it loads a particular segment of R into memory. The other component queue is based on a doubly-linked-list, and is used to store the values for the join attribute. Each node in the queue also contains the addresses of its one step neighbour nodes. The reason for choosing this data structure is to allow random deletion from the queue. The stream buffer is included in the diagram for completeness, but is in reality always a tiny component and it will not be considered in the cost model.

Asymptotic Runtime Analysis

In the performance experiments we have focused on a data set that has a skewed distribution but without extreme imbalances. In particular there are no large unused master data areas. We provide a theoretical result for the most general characterization of CACHEJOIN.

We compare the asymptotic runtime of CACHEJOIN with that of MESHJOIN based on the processing time for a stream section. For such a time measure, smaller values are better. We denote the time needed to process a stream prefix s as $MEJ(s)$ for MESHJOIN and as $CHJ(s)$ for CACHEJOIN. Every stream prefix represents a binary sequence, and by viewing this binary sequence as a natural number, we can apply asymptotic complexity classes to the functions. Note therefore that the following theorem does not use functions on input lengths, but on concrete inputs encoded as binary strings. We assume that the setup for CACHEJOIN and for MESHJOIN is such that they have the same number h_S of stream tuples in the hash table and in the queue accordingly:

- **Theorem:** $CHJ(s) = O(MEJ(s))$;
- **Proof:** To prove the theorem, we have to show CACHEJOIN performs no worse than MESHJOIN. The cost of MESHJOIN is dominated by the number of accesses to

R. For asymptotic runtime, random access of disk pages is as fast as sequential access (seek time is a constant factor, see below for a further discussion of the constant factor). For MESHJOIN with its cyclic access pattern for *R*, every page of *R* is accessed exactly once after every h_S stream tuples. We have to show that for CACHEJOIN no page is accessed more frequently. For that we look at an arbitrary page *p* of *R* at the time it is accessed by CACHEJOIN. The stream tuple at the front of the queue has some position *i* in the stream. There are h_S stream tuples currently in the hash table, and the first tuple of the stream that is not yet read into the hash table has position $i+h_S$ in the stream. All stream tuples in the hash table are joined against the disk-based master data tuples on *p*, and all matching tuples are removed from the queue. We now have to determine the earliest time that *p* could be loaded again by CACHEJOIN. For *p* to be loaded again, a stream tuple must be at the front of the queue, and has to match a master data tuple on *p*. The first stream tuple that can do so is the previously mentioned stream tuple with position $i+h_S$, because all earlier stream tuples that match data on *p* have been deleted from the queue. This proves the theorem.

In this asymptotic argument we make use of the fact that we abstract from constant factors, particularly the influence of seek time. Our experimental results show that CACHEJOIN does not perform much worse than MESHJOIN even on uniform data.

Algorithm

The pseudo-code for CACHEJOIN is shown in Algorithm 1. The outer loop of the algorithm is an endless loop, which is common in stream processing algorithms (line 2). The body of the outer loop

has two main parts, the stream-probing phase and the disk-probing phase. Due to the endless loop, these two phases alternate.

Lines 3 to 11 comprise the stream-probing phase. The stream-probing phase has to know the number of empty slots in H_S. This number is kept in variable $h_S available$. At the start of the algorithm, all slots in H_S are empty (line 1). The stream-probing phase has an inner loop that continues while stream tuples as well as empty slots in H_S are available (line 3). In the loop, the algorithm reads one input stream tuple *t* at a time (line 4). The algorithm looks up *t* in H_R (line 5). In the case of a match, the algorithm generates the join output without storing *t* in H_S (line 6). In the case where *t* does not match, the algorithm loads *t* into H_S along with enqueuing its key attribute value in the queue (line 8). The counter of empty slots in H_S has to be decreased (line 9).

Lines 12 to 28 comprise the disk-probing phase. At the start of this phase, the algorithm reads the oldest key attribute value *g* from the queue and finds the relative index value in *R*. If the relative index value does not exist, the algorithm deletes *g* from the queue and jumps back to line 12. Otherwise the algorithm loads a segment of *R* into the disk buffer using *g* as an index (lines 12 to 17). In an inner loop, the algorithm looks up one-by-one all tuples *r* from the disk buffer in hash table H_S. In the case of a match, the algorithm generates the join output (lines 18 to 20). Since H_S is a multi-hash-map, there can be more than one match, and the number of matches is *f* (line 21). The algorithm removes all matching tuples from H_S while also deleting the corresponding nodes from the queue (line 22). This creates empty slots in H_S (line 23).

Lines 24 to 26 are concerned with frequency detection. In line 24 we test whether the matching frequency *f* of the current tuple is larger than a pre-set threshold. If it is, then this tuple is entered into H_R. If there are no empty slots in H_R the algorithm overwrites an existing tuple in H_R (lines 24 to 26).

Cost Model

In this section we develop the cost model for our proposed CACHEJOIN. The main objective for developing our cost model is to interrelate the key parameters of the algorithm, such as input size w, processing cost c_{loop} for these w tuples, the available memory M and the service rate μ. It is intuitively clear that there is a trade-off between the memory consumption of the various components. We will use the equations of the cost model in the tuning process to find the optimal size for each component of the algorithm by using calculus of variations. The details of the tuning process are presented in

Algorithm 1. CACHEJOIN

```
Input: A disk based relation R with index on join attribute and a stream of updates S
Output: R ⋈ S
Parameters: w (where w=w_s+w_N) tuples of S and k number of pages of R
Method:
1.   h_s available ← h_s
2.   while (true) do
3.       while (stream available AND h_s available > 0) do
4.           read a stream tuple t from stream buffer
5.           if t ∈ H_R then
6.               output t ⋈ H_R
7.           else
8.               add stream tuple t into H_s and also place its join attribute value into Q.
9.               h_s available ← h_s available-1
10.          end if
11.      end while
12.      read the oldest join attribute value g from Q
13.      if g does not match with index value in R then
14.          delete g from Q
15.          go to line 12
16.      end if
17.      read a segment of R into the disk buffer using g as an index look-up
18.      for each tuple r in disk buffer do
19.          if r ∈ H_s then
20.              output r ⋈ H_s
21.              f ← number of matching tuples found in H_s
22.              delete all matching tuples from H_s along with the corresponding nodes from Q
23.              h_s available ← h_s available+ f
24.              if f ≥ thresholdvalue then
25.                  switch the tuple r into hash table H_R
26.              end if
27.          end if
28.      end for
29. end while
```

the tuning section. The cost model presented here follows the style used in the original MESHJOIN. Equation 1 represents the total memory used by the algorithm (except the stream buffer), and Equation 2 describes the processing cost for each iteration of the algorithm. The notations we use in our cost model are given in Table 1:

- **Memory Cost:** The major portion of the total memory is assigned to the hash table H_S together with the queue while a comparatively much smaller portion is assigned

to H_R and the disk buffer. The memory for each component can be calculated as follows:

Memory for the disk buffer (bytes) $= k.v_P$

Memory for H_R (bytes) $= l.v_P$

Memory for H_s (bytes) $= \alpha \, [M - (k + l)v_P]$

Memory for the queue (bytes) $= (1 - \alpha)[M - (k + l)v_P]$

Table 1. Notations used in cost estimation of CACHEJOIN

Parameter Name	Symbol
Total allocated memory (bytes)	M
Service rate (processed tuples/sec)	μ
Number of stream tuples processed in each iteration through H_R	w_N
Number of stream tuples processed in each iteration through H_S	w_S
Stream tuple size (bytes)	v_S
Disk page size (bytes)	v_P
Size of disk tuple (bytes)	v_R
Disk buffer size (pages)	k
Disk buffer size (tuples)	$d=k(v_P/v_R)$
Size of H_R (pages)	l
Size of H_R (tuples)	$h_R=l(v_P/v_R)$
Size of H_S (tuples)	h_S
Disk relation size (tuples)	R_t
Memory weight for the hash table	α
Memory weight for the queue	$1-\alpha$
Cost to read k disk pages into the disk buffer (nanosecs)	$c_{I/O}(k.v_P)$
Cost to look-up one tuple in the hash table (nanosecs)	c_H
Cost to generate the output for one tuple (nanosecs)	c_O
Cost to remove one tuple from the hash table and the queue (nanosecs)	c_E
Cost to read one stream tuple into the stream buffer (nanosecs)	c_S
Cost to append one stream tuple in the hash table and the queue (nanosecs)	c_A
Cost to compare the frequency of one disk tuple with the threshold value (nanosecs)	c_F
Total cost for one loop iteration (secs)	c_{loop}

By aggregating the above, the total memory for CACHEJOIN can be calculated as shown in Equation 1:

$$M = (k+l)v_P + \alpha\left[M - (k+l)v_P\right]$$
$$+ (1-\alpha)\left[M - (k+l)v_P\right] \quad (1)$$

Currently, the memory for the stream buffer in not included because it is small (1 MB is sufficient in our experiments):

- **Processing Cost:** In this section we calculate the processing cost for the algorithm. To make it simple we first calculate the processing cost for individual components and then sum these costs to calculate the total processing cost for one iteration:

Cost to read k pages into the disk buffer $= c_{I/O}(k.v_P)$

Cost to look-up w_N tuples in $H_R = w_N . c_H$

Cost to look-up all the disk buffer tuples in $H_S = d.c_H$

Cost to compare the frequency of all the tuples in the disk buffer with the threshold value $= d.c_F$

Cost to generate the output for w_N tuples $= w_N.c_O$

Cost to generate the output for w_S tuples $= w_S.c_O$

Cost to read w_N tuples from the stream buffer $= w_N.c_S$

Cost to read w_S tuples from the stream buffer $= w_S.c_S$

Cost to append w_S tuples into H_S and the queue $= w_S.c_A$

Cost to delete w_S tuples from H_S and the queue $= w_S.c_E$

By aggregating the above costs the total cost of the algorithm for one iteration can be calculated using Equation 2:

$$c_{loop}(secs) = 10^{-9}[c_{I/O}(k.v_P) + d(c_H + c_F)$$
$$+ w_S(c_O + c_E + c_S + c_A) + w_N(c_H + c_O + c_S)] \quad (2)$$

Since in c_{loop} seconds the algorithm processes w_N and w_S tuples of stream S, the service rate μ can be calculated using Equation 3:

$$\mu = \frac{w_N + w_S}{c_{loop}} \quad (3)$$

Tuning

We have outlined in the introduction that CACHE-JOIN can operate in limited available resources. In this case the components of the algorithm face a trade-off with respect to memory distribution. Assigning more memory to one component means assigning equally less memory to some other components. Therefore, to utilize the available memory optimally, tuning of the join components is important. If the size of R and the overall memory size M are fixed, the equation is a function of two parameters, the size for the disk buffer and the size of hash table H_R.

The tuning of the algorithm uses the cost model that we have derived. Therefore we decided to use the tuning of the algorithm to experimentally validate the cost model. We provide a theoretical approach to tuning, based on calculus of variations. We first approximate optimal tuning settings using an empirical approach, by considering a sample of values for the sizes of the disk buffer and hash table H_R. Finally we compare the experimentally obtained tuning results with the results obtained based on the cost model:

- **Experimental Setup:** Before proceeding to the tuning results it is first necessary to describe the hardware and software specifications for our experiments. The same settings will be used for later experiments;

- **Hardware Specifications:** We accomplished our experiment on a *Pentium-i5* with main memory of 8GB and secondary storage of 500GB. We implemented our experiments in *Java* using *Eclipse*. We also used built-in plugins, provided by the *Apache* and *Java API*, to measure the memory and processing time respectively. As the join attribute value can be duplicated in stream data, it needs to store multiple values in the hash table against one value of master data. However the hash table provided by the Java API does not support this feature therefore, we used Multi-Hash-Map, provided by Apache, as the hash table in our experiments. For MESHJOIN as the implementations were not available on request, we implemented MESHJOIN ourselves;

- **Measurement Strategy:** The performance or service rate of the join is measured by calculating the number of tuples processed in a unit second. In each experiment both algorithms first complete their warm-up phase before starting the actual measurements. These kinds of algorithms normally need a warm-up phase to tune their components with respect to the available memory resources so that each component can deliver maximum performance. In our experiments, for each measurement we calculate the confidence interval by considering 95% accuracy, but sometimes the variation is very small. The calculation of the confidence interval is based on 4000 measurements for one setting. Moreover, during the execution of the algorithm no other application is running in parallel. We use constant stream arrival rate throughout a run in order to measure the service rate for both algorithms:

- **Data Specification:** We analyze the performance of the algorithms using synthetic, TPC-H, and real-life datasets. The relation *R* is stored on disk using a *MySQL* database with a non-clustered index on the join attribute. Both the algorithms read master data from the database. To measure the I/O cost more accurately we set the fetch size for *ResultSet* equal to the disk buffer size. A further description of our datasets is give below;

- **Synthetic Data:** The stream dataset we used is based on the Zipfian distribution. We test the performance of both algorithms by varying the skew value from 0 (fully uniform) to 1 (highly skewed). The detailed specifications of our synthetic dataset are shown in Table 2;

- **TPC-H:** We also analyze the performance of both algorithms using the TPC-H dataset which is a well-known decision support benchmark. We create the datasets using a scale factor of 100. More precisely, we use table Customer as our master data table and table Order as our stream data table. In table Order there is one foreign key attribute *custkey* which is a primary key in Customer table. So the two tables are joined using attribute *custkey*. Our Customer table contains 20 million tuples while the size of each tuple is 223 bytes. The Order table also contains the same number of tuples with each tuple of 138 bytes. The plausible scenario for such a join is to add customer details corresponding to the order before loading it into the warehouse;

- **Real-Life Data:** Finally, we also compare the performance of both algorithms using a real-life dataset[1]. This data set basically contains cloud information stored in summarized weather reports format. The same dataset was also used with the original MESHJOIN algorithm. The master data table contains 20 million tuples, while the stream data is infinite. The size of each tuple in both the master data table and the streaming data is 128 bytes. Both the tables are joined using a common attribute, *longitude (LON)*, and the domain for the join attribute is the interval [0,36000];

- **Empirical Tuning:** This section focuses on obtaining samples for the approximate tuning of the key components. Since, the performance is a function of two variables, the size of the disk buffer, d, and the size of hash table H_R, h_R. We tested the performance of the algorithm for a grid of values for both components, i.e. for each setting of d the performance is measured against a series of values for h_R.

The performance measurements for the grid of d and h_R are shown in Figure 5. It is worth following the data along the h_R axis, i.e. for a fixed d we look at all values for h_R. This will show that a stream-probing phase is useful if it remains within a certain size. This is so, because in the beginning the performance increases rapidly with an increase in h_R. Then, after reaching an optimum the performance decreases. The explanation is

Table 2. Data specifications for synthetic dataset

Parameter Name	Value
Size of disk-based relation R	100 million tuples ($\approx$11.18GB)
Total allocated memory M	1% of R ($\approx$0.11GB) to 10% of R ($\approx$1.12GB)
Size of each disk tuple	120 bytes
Size of stream	in terabytes
Size of each stream tuple	20 bytes
Size of each node in the queue	12 bytes
Data set	based on Zipf's law (skew value from 0 to 1)

that when h_R is increased beyond this value, it does not make any significant difference to the stream matching probability due to the characteristics of the skewed distribution. On the other hand it reduces the memory for hash table H_S. Similarly we can follow the data along the d axis. Initially the performance increases, since the costly disk access is amortized for a larger number of stream tuples. This effect is actually of crucial importance, because it is this gain that gives the algorithm an advantage over a traditional index-based join. It is here that H_S is used in order to match more tuples than just the one that was used in order to determine the partition that was loaded. After attaining a maximum, the performance decreases because of the increase in I/O cost for loading more of R at one time in a non-selective way.

From the figure the optimal memory settings for both disk buffer and hash table H_R can be determined by considering the intersection of the values of both components at which the algorithm individually performs at a maximum:

- **Tuning Based on Cost Model:** We now show how the cost model for CACHEJOIN can be used to (theoretically) obtain an optimal tuning of the components. Equation 1 and 2 represents the memory and processing cost respectively for the algorithm. On the basis of these equations the performance of the algorithm can be calculated using Equation 3.

The algorithm can be tuned to perform optimally using Equation 3 by knowing w_N, w_S and c_{loop}. The value of c_{loop} can be calculated from Equation 2 if we know w_N and w_S:

- **Mathematical Model to Calculate w_N:** CACHEJOIN has two separate phases, the stream-probing phase and the disk-probing phase. The stream tuples that are matched in the stream-probing phase are joined

Figure 5. Tuning of CACHEJOIN using measurement approach

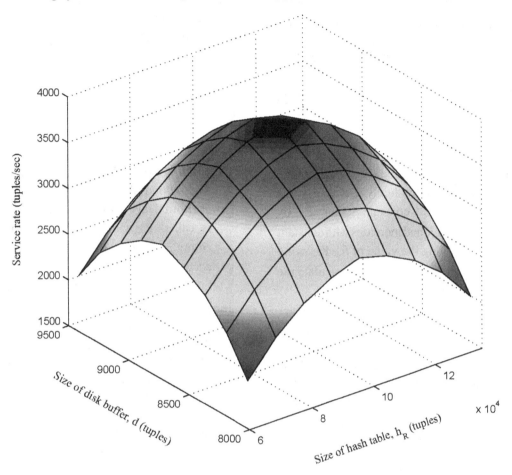

straight away without storing them in H_S. The number of tuples processed through this phase per outer iteration is denoted by w_N.

The main components that directly affect w_N are the size of the master data on disk and the size of H_R. To calculate the effect of both components on w_N we assume that R_t is the total number of tuples in R while h_R is the size of H_R in terms of tuples. We now use our assumption that the stream of updates S has a Zipfian distribution with skew parameter value equal to one. In this case the matching probability for S in the stream-probing phase can be determined using Equation 4. The

denominator is a normalization term to ensure all probabilities sum up to 1:

$$p_N = \frac{\sum_{x=1}^{h_R} \frac{1}{x}}{\sum_{x=1}^{R_t} \frac{1}{x}} \qquad (4)$$

Each summation in the above equation generates the harmonic series which can be summed up using formula $\sum_{x=1}^{k} \frac{1}{x} = \ln k +^3 + \epsilon_k$ (Abramowitz & Stegun, 1964), where γ is Euler's constant whose value is approximately equal to 0.5772156649 and ϵ_k is another constant which is $\approx \frac{1}{2k}$. The value of ϵ_k approaches 0 as k goes to ∞ (Abramowitz & Stegun, 1964). In our case the value of $\frac{1}{2k}$ is small so we ignore it. Hence Equation 4 can be written as shown in Equation 5:

$$p_N = \frac{\ln h_R}{\ln R_t} \tag{5}$$

Now using Equation 5 we can determine the constant factors of change in p_N by changing the values of h_R and R_t individually. Let us assume that p_N decreases with constant factor φ_N by doubling the value of R_t and increases with constant factor ψ_N by doubling the value of h_R. Knowing these constant factors we are able to calculate the value of w_N. Let us assume the following:

$$p_N = R_t^y h_R^z \tag{6}$$

where y and z are the unknown constants whose values need to be determined.

Determination of y: We know that by doubling R_t, the matching probability p_N decreases by a constant factor φ_N therefore, Equation 6 becomes:

$$\varphi_N p_N = (2R_t)^y h_R^z$$

Dividing the above equation by Equation 6 we get $2^y = \varphi_N$ and therefore, $y = \log_2(\varphi_N)$.

Determination of z: Similarly we also know that by doubling h_R the matching probability p_N increases by a constant factor ψ_N therefore, Equation 6 can be written as:

$$\psi_N p_N = R_t^y (2h_R)^z$$

By dividing the above equation by Equation 6 we get $2^z = \psi_N$ and therefore, $z = \log_2(\psi_N)$. After substituting the values of constants y and z into Equation 6 we get:

$$p_N = R_t^{\log_2(\varphi_N)} h_R^{\log_2(\psi_N)}$$

Now if S_n is the total number of stream tuples that are processed (through both phases) in n outer iterations then w_N can be calculated using Equation 7:

$$w_N = \frac{\left(R_t^{\log_2(\varphi_N)} h_R^{\log_2(\psi_N)}\right) S_n}{n} \tag{7}$$

- **Mathematical Model to Calculate w_S:** The second phase of the CACHEJOIN algorithm deals with the rest of R. This part is called $\acute{R}$, with $\acute{R} = R - h_R$. The algorithm reads $\acute{R}$ in segments. The size of each segment is equal to the size of the disk buffer d. In each iteration the algorithm reads one segment of $\acute{R}$ using an index on the join attribute and loads it into the disk buffer. Since we assume a skewed distribution, the matching probability is not equal, but decreases in the tail of the distribution, as shown in Figure 6. We calculate the matching probability for each segment by summing over the discrete Zipfian distribution separately and then aggregating all of them as shown below:

$$\sum_{x=h_R+1}^{h_R+d} \frac{1}{x} + \sum_{x=h_R+d+1}^{h_R+2d} \frac{1}{x} + \sum_{x=h_R+2d+1}^{h_R+3d} \frac{1}{x}$$
$$+ \ldots + \sum_{x=h_R+(n-1)d+1}^{h_R+nd} \frac{1}{x}$$

We simplify this to:

$$\sum_{x=h_R+1}^{h_R+nd} \frac{1}{x} \quad \Rightarrow \quad \sum_{x=h_R+1}^{R_t} \frac{1}{x}$$

From this we can obtain the average matching probability $\bar{p}_S$ in the disk-probing phase, which we need for calculating w_S. Let N be the total number of segments in $\acute{R}$. In the denominator, we

Figure 6. Matching probability of R in stream

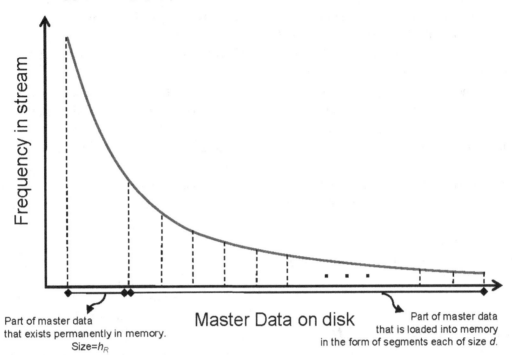

have to use the same normalization term as in Equation 4:

$$\bar{p}_S = \frac{\sum_{x=h_R+1}^{R_t} \frac{1}{x}}{N\sum_{x=1}^{R_t} \frac{1}{x}}$$

We again use the summation formula (Abramowitz & Stegun, 1964):

$$\bar{p}_S = \frac{\ln\left(R_t\right) - \ln(h_R + 1)}{N[\ln\left(R_t\right) + \gamma]} \qquad (8)$$

To determine the effects of d, h_R and R_t on $\bar{p}_S$, a similar argument can be used as in the case of w_N. Let's suppose we double d in Equation 8, then N will be halved and the value of $\bar{p}_S$ increases by a constant factor of θ_S. Similarly, if we double h_R or R_t respectively, then the value of $\bar{p}_S$ decreases by

some constant factor of ψ_S or φ_S respectively. Using a similar argument for w_N, we get:

$$\bar{p}_S = d^x h_R^y R_t^z \qquad (9)$$

The values for the constants x, y and z in this case will be $x = \log_2(\theta_S)$, $y = \log_2(\psi_S)$ and $z = \log_2(\varphi_S)$ respectively. Therefore by replacing the values with constants Equation 9 will become:

$$\bar{p}_S = d^{\log_2(\theta_S)} h_R^{\log_2(\psi_S)} R_t^{\log_2(\varphi_S)}$$

Now if h_S are the number of stream tuples stored in the hash table then the average value for w_S can be calculated using Equation 10:

$$w_S(average) = d^{\log_2(\theta_S)} h_R^{\log_2(\psi_S)} R_t^{\log_2(\varphi_S)} h_S \qquad (10)$$

Once the values of w_N and w_S are determined, the algorithm can be tuned using Equation 3:

- **Comparison Between Tuning Approaches:** We can now compare the tuning results obtained through measurements with the tuning results that we calculated using the cost model. Figure 7(a) shows the empirical and the mathematical tuning results for the disk buffer size *d*. One can say that the results in both cases are reasonably similar, with a deviation of only 2.5%.

Figure 7(b) shows the empirical and the mathematical tuning results for the hash table size H_R. Again we think it is fair to say that the results in both cases are reasonably similar, with a deviation of only 2.1%. This is a corroboration of the accuracy of our cost model.

PERFORMANCE EXPERIMENTS

In this section we present a series of experimental comparisons between CACHEJOIN and MESH-JOIN using synthetic, TPC-H, and real-life data. In order to understand the difference between the algorithms better, we included two other algorithms that we have mentioned. First we included R-MESHJOIN, which is a slight modification of MESHJOIN. It introduces an additional degree of freedom for the optimization of MESHJOIN. Then we included HYBRIDJOIN, as explained before, CACHEJOIN becomes HYBRIDJOIN if its stream-probing phase is switched-off. By including HYBRIDJOIN we can understand better, where the difference in performance comes from.

In our experiments we perform three different analyses. In the first analysis, we compare service rate, produced by each algorithm, with respect to the externally given parameters. In the second analysis, we present time comparisons, both processing and waiting time, for all approaches.

Finally, in our last analysis we validate our cost models for each algorithm.

External Parameters Analysis

We identify three parameters, for which we want to understand the behavior of the algorithms in the case of different memory settings. The three parameters are: the total memory available *M*, the size of the master data table *R*, and the skew in the stream data. For the sake of brevity, we restrict the discussion for each parameter to a one dimensional variation, i.e. we vary one parameter at a time:

- **Analysis by Varying Size of Memory *M*:** In our first experiment we compare the service rate produced by all four algorithms by varying the memory size *M* from 1% to 10% of *R* while the size of *R* is 100 million tuples ($\approx$11.18GB). The results of our experiment are presented in Figure 8(a). From the figure it can be noted that CACHEJOIN performs up to 5 times faster than MESHJOIN in the case of a 10% memory setting. While in the case of a limited memory environment (1% of *R*) CACHEJOIN still performs up to 4 times better than MESHJOIN that makes it an adaptive solution for memory constraint applications. R-MESHJOIN performs slightly better than MESHJOIN due to an optimal memory distribution among the join components. HYBRIDJOIN, using an efficient strategy to access *R*, performs considerably better than MESHJOIN but due to the absence of a cache module it performs significantly worse than CACHEJOIN;

Figure 7. Tuning Comparisons: Empirical approach vs analytical approach: (a) Tuning comparison for the disk buffer, (b) Tuning comparison for hash table H_R

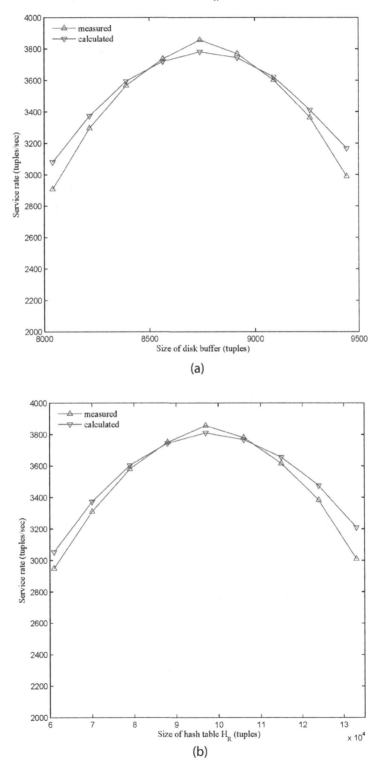

(a)

(b)

Figure 8. Service rate analysis by varying external parameters: (a) Service rate vs memory, (b) Service rate vs size of R, (c) Service rate vs skew, (d) TPC-H dataset, (e) Real-life dataset

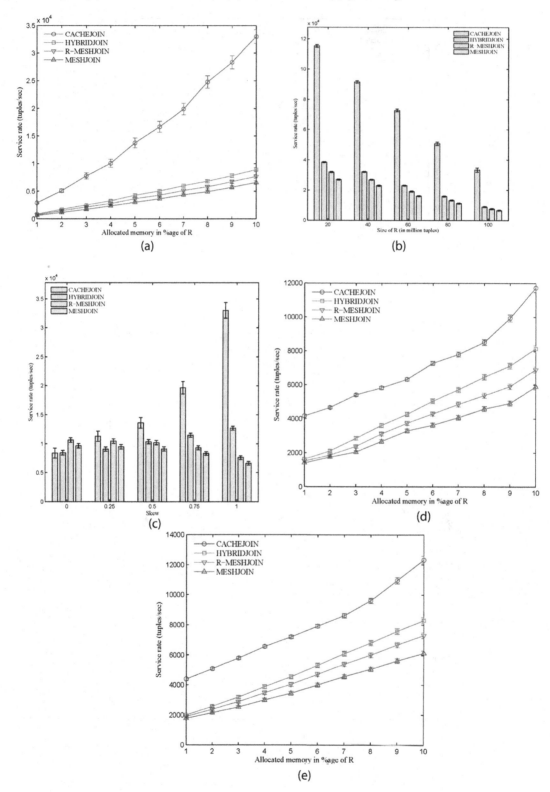

- **Analysis by Varying Size of *R*:** In this experiment we compare the service rate of CACHEJOIN with the other three algorithms at different sizes of *R* under fixed memory size, ≈1.12GB (10% of *R*). We also fix the skew value equal to 1 for all settings of *R*. The results of our experiment are shown in Figure 8(b). From the figure it can be seen that CACHEJOIN performs up to 4 times better than MESHJOIN when the size of *R* is 20 million tuples. This improvement increases up to 5 times when the size of *R* is 100 million tuples. One important fact that can be concluded here is that by increasing the size of *R* the service rate does not decrease inversely as in MESHJOIN. On the other hand if we compare the performance of CACHEJOIN with HYBRIDJOIN and R-MESHJOIN, it also performs significantly better than both of the algorithms under all the settings of *R*;

- **Analysis by Varying Skew Value:** In these experiments we compare the service rate of all the algorithms by varying the skew value in the streaming data. To vary the skew, we vary the value of the Zipfian exponent. In our experiments we allow it to range from 0 to 1. At 0 the input stream *S* is completely uniform while at 1 the stream has a larger skew. We consider the sizes of two other parameters, memory and *R*, to be fixed. The size of *R* is 100 million tuples (≈11.18GB) while the available memory is set to 10% of *R* (≈1.12GB). The results presented in Figure 8(c) show that CACHEJOIN again performs significantly better among all approaches even for only moderately skewed data. Also this improvement becomes more pronounced for increasing skew values in the streaming data. At skew value equal to 1, CACHEJOIN performs about 5 times better than MESHJOIN. Contrarily, as MESHJOIN and R-MESHJOIN do not exploit the data skew in their algorithms,

their service rates actually decrease slightly for more skewed data, which is consistent to the original algorithms findings. Although HYBRIDJOIN considers the feature of skew in stream data, due to missing the stream-probing phase, there is room to improve the performance of the algorithm. We do not present data for skew value larger than 1, which would imply short tails. However, we predict that for such short tails the trend continues. CACHEJOIN performs slightly worse than MESHJOIN only in a case when the stream data is completely uniform. In this particular case the stream-probing phase does not contribute considerably while on the other hand random access of *R* influences the seek time;

- **TPC-H and Real-Life Datasets:** We also compare the service rate of all the algorithms using TPC-H and real-life datasets. The details of both datasets have already been described under heading experimental setup. In both experiments we measure the service rate produced by all four algorithms at different memory settings. The results of our experiments using TPC-H and real-life datasets are shown in Figure 8(d) and Figure 8(e) respectively. From Figures 8(d) and 8(e) it can be noted that the service rate of the CACHEJOIN is about twice that of MESHJOIN. It is also obvious from the figures that CACHEJOIN performs remarkably better than R-MESHJOIN and HYBRIDJOIN under all memory settings.

Time Analysis

A second kind of performance analysis besides service rate refers to the time an algorithm takes to process a tuple. In this section we analyze both waiting time and processing time. The terms waiting time and processing time have already been described in the section named existing MESH-

JOIN. We measure the waiting time taken by both of the algorithms at different stream arrival rates.

The experiment, shown in Figure 9(a), presents the comparisons with respect to the processing time. From the figure it is clear that the processing time in the case of CACHEJOIN is significantly smaller than the other three algorithms. This difference becomes even more as we increase the size of *R*. The plausible reason for this is that in CACHEJOIN a big part of stream data is directly processed through the stream-probing phase without joining it with the whole relation *R* in memory. Contrarily, both MESHJOIN and R-MESHJOIN bring the whole *R* into memory. Furthermore, both the algorithms load all pages of *R* into memory with the same frequency without prioritizing the most and least useful pages. As a consequence, this increases the processing time for each stream tuple in memory.

In the experiment shown in Figure 9(b) we compare the waiting time for each of the algorithms. It is obvious from the figure that the waiting time in the case of CACHEJOIN is sig-

nificantly smaller than the other three algorithms. The reason behind this is that in CACHEJOIN since there is no constraint to match each stream tuple with the whole of *R*, each disk invocation is not synchronized with the stream input. This also supports our argument that CACHEJOIN can deal with intermittency in stream data effectively. However, if we observe the overall behavior, for all the algorithms the waiting time decreases as the stream arrival rate increases up to a certain limit. After that limit if we further increase the stream arrival rate, the waiting time also starts increasing. The plausible reason behind this is that initially, when the stream arrival rate is quite low, an algorithm needs to wait more until the accumulating stream tuples (in the stream buffer) become equal to the input size of the algorithm. Later, when the stream arrival rate continuously grows the waiting time of the algorithm starts reducing. The algorithm can support up to one maximum level of stream arrival rate, and after that level further incrementing the stream arrival

Figure 9. Time analysis: (a) Processing time, (b) Waiting time

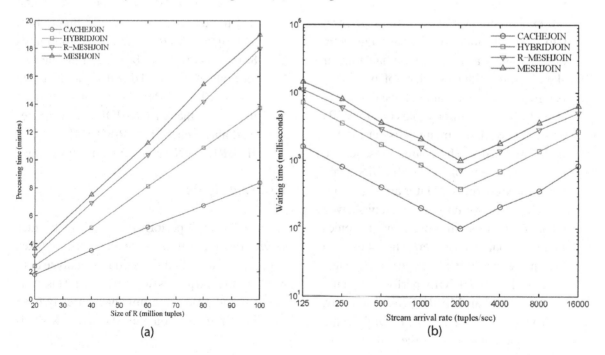

rate causes each stream tuples in the stream buffer to wait, creating a backlog.

Cost Analysis

The cost models for all the algorithms have been validated by comparing the estimated cost with the measured cost. Figure 10 presents the comparisons of both costs for each algorithm. The results presented in the figure show that for each algorithm the estimated cost closely resembles the measured cost, which proves the correctness of our cost models.

SUMMARY

In this chapter we discuss a new stream-based join called CACHEJOIN that can be used to join a stream with a disk-based, slow changing master data table. We compare it with MESHJOIN, an algorithm that can be used in the same context. CACHEJOIN is designed to make use of skewed, non-uniformly distributed data as found in real-world applications. In particular we consider a Zipfian distribution of foreign keys in the stream data. Contrary to MESHJOIN, CACHEJOIN stores these most frequently accessed tuples of *R* permanently in memory saving a significant disk I/O cost and accelerating the performance of the algorithm. CACHEJOIN uses two phases,

Figure 10. Cost validation

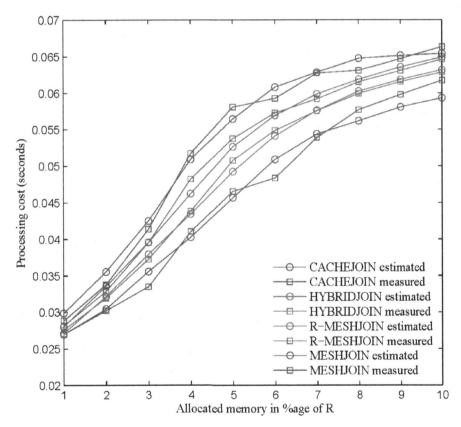

which is reminiscent of Symmetric Hash Join. The contributions of the work are the following. We have provided a cost model of the new algorithm and validated it with experiments. We have used the cost model to precisely tune the relative size of the components of the algorithm. We have provided an extensive experimental study showing an improvement of CACHEJOIN over the earlier MESHJOIN and other related algorithms.

In the future we plan to design an adaptive semi-stream join algorithm in which memory allocated to each component of the algorithm will be assigned dynamically. In this way each component of the algorithm will perform optimally under all sizes of available memory resources. Another objective that we want to achieve is to design a generalized semi-stream algorithm that can process both uniform and non-uniform stream data efficiently.

REFERENCES

Abramowitz, M., & Stegun, I. A. (1964). *Handbook of mathematical functions with formulas, graphs, and mathematical tables* (9th ed.). New York: Dover.

Anderson, C. (2006). *The long tail: Why the future of business is selling less of more*. New York: Hyperion.

Bornea, M. A., Deligiannakis, A., Kotidis, Y., & Vassalos, V. (2011). Semi-streamed index join for near-real time execution of ETL transformations. In *Proceedings of the IEEE 27th International Conference on Data Engineering (ICDE'11)* (pp. 159–170). IEEE. doi:10.1109/ICDE.2011.5767906

Chakraborty, A., & Singh, A. (2009). A partition-based approach to support streaming updates over persistent data in an active datawarehouse. In *Proceedings of the 2009 IEEE International Symposium on Parallel & Distributed Processing* (pp. 1–11). Washington, DC: IEEE Computer Society. doi:http://dx.doi.org/10.1109/IPDPS.2009.5161064

Chakraborty, A., & Singh, A. (2010). A disk-based, adaptive approach to memory-limited computation of windowed stream joins. In *Proceedings of the 21st International Conference on Database and Expert Systems Applications: Part I* (pp. 251–260). Berlin: Springer-Verlag. Retrieved from http://portal.acm.org/citation.cfm?id=1881867.1881892

Golab, L., Johnson, T., Seidel, J. S., & Shkapenyuk, V. (2009). Stream warehousing with DataDepot. In *Proceedings of the 35th SIGMOD International Conference on Management of Data* (pp. 847–854). New York, NY: ACM. doi:http://doi.acm.org/10.1145/1559845.1559934

Ives, Z. G., Florescu, D., Friedman, M., Levy, A., & Weld, D. S. (1999). An adaptive query execution system for data integration. *SIGMOD Record, 28*(2), 299–310. doi:http://doi.acm.org/10.1145/304181.304209

Karakasidis, A., Vassiliadis, P., & Pitoura, E. (2005). ETL queues for active data warehousing. In *Proceedings of the 2nd International Workshop on Information Quality in Information Systems* (pp. 28–39). New York, NY: ACM. doi:http://doi.acm.org/10.1145/1077501.1077509

Knuth, D. E. (1998). The art of computer programming: Vol. 3. *Sorting and searching* (2nd ed.). Redwood City, CA: Addison Wesley Longman Publishing Co., Inc..

Labio, W., & Garcia-Molina, H. (1996). Efficient snapshot differential algorithms in data warehousing. In *Proceedings of the 22th International Conference on Very Large Data Bases (VLDB '96)* (pp. 63–74). San Francisco, CA: Morgan Kaufmann Publishers Inc.

Labio, W., Yang, J., Cui, Y., Garcia-Molina, H., & Widom, J. (1999). Performance issues in incremental warehouse maintenance. In *Proceedings of the 26th International Conference on Very Large Data Bases (VLDB'00)*. Cairo, Egypt: VLDB.

Lawrence, R. (2005). Early hash join: A configurable algorithm for the efficient and early production of join results. In *Proceedings of the 31st International Conference on Very Large Data Bases* (pp. 841–852). VLDB Endowment.

Mokbel, M. F., Lu, M., & Aref, W. G. (2004). Hash-merge join: A non-blocking join algorithm for producing fast and early join results. In *Proceedings of the 20th International Conference on Data Engineering*. Washington, DC: IEEE Computer Society.

Naeem, M. A., Dobbie, G., & Weber, G. (2008). An event-based near real-time data integration architecture. In *Proceedings of the 2008 12th Enterprise Distributed Object Computing Conference Workshops* (pp. 401–404). Washington, DC: IEEE Computer Society. doi:http://dx.doi.org/10.1109/EDOCW.2008.14

Naeem, M. A., Dobbie, G., & Weber, G. (2011). X-HYBRIDJOIN for near-real-time data warehousing. In *Proceedings of the 28th British National Conference on Advances in Databases* (pp. 33–47). Berlin: Springer-Verlag. Retrieved from http://dl.acm.org/citation.cfm?id=2075914.2075919

Naeem, M. A., Dobbie, G., & Weber, G. (2012). Optimised X-HYBRIDJOIN for near-real-time data warehousing. In *Proceedings of the Twenty-Third Australasian Database Conference (ADC 2012)*. Melbourne, Australia: CRPIT.

Naeem, M. A., Dobbie, G., Weber, G., & Alam, S. (2010). R-MESHJOIN for near-real-time data warehousing. In *Proceedings of the ACM 13th International Workshop on Data Warehousing and OLAP*. Toronto, Canada: ACM. doi:http://dx.doi.org/10.1109/IPDPS.2009.5161064

Polyzotis, N., Skiadopoulos, S., Vassiliadis, P., Simitsis, A., & Frantzell, N. (2008). Meshing streaming updates with persistent data in an active data warehouse. *IEEE Transactions on Knowledge and Data Engineering, 20*(7), 976–991. doi:10.1109/TKDE.2008.27.

Polyzotis, N., Skiadopoulos, S., Vassiliadis, P., Simitsis, A., & Frantzell, N. E. (2007). Supporting streaming updates in an active data warehouse. In *Proceedings of the 23rd International Conference on Data Engineering* (pp. 476–485). Istanbul, Turkey: IEEE.

Urhan, T., & Franklin, M. J. (2000). XJoin: A reactively-scheduled pipelined join operator. *A Quarterly Bulletin of the Computer Society of the IEEE Technical Committee on Data Engineering, 23*.

Viglas, S. D., Naughton, J. F., & Burger, J. (2003). Maximizing the output rate of multi-way join queries over streaming information sources. In *Proceedings of the 29th International Conference on Very Large Data Bases* (pp. 285–296). VLDB Endowment.

Wilschut, A. N., & Apers, P. M. G. (1990). Pipelining in query execution. In *Proceedings of the International Conference on Databases, Parallel Architectures and Their Applications (PARBASE 1990)*. Los Alamitos, CA: IEEE Computer Society Press.

Wilschut, A. N., & Apers, P. M. G. (1991). Dataflow query execution in a parallel main-memory environment. In *Proceedings of the first International Conference on Parallel and Distributed Information Systems* (pp. 68–77). Los Alamitos, CA: IEEE Computer Society Press.

Zhang, X., & Rundensteiner, E. A. (2002). Integrating the maintenance and synchronization of data warehouses using a cooperative framework. *Information Systems*, *27*(4), 219–243. doi:10.1016/S0306-4379(01)00049-7.

Zhuge, Y., García-Molina, H., Hammer, J., & Widom, J. (1995). View maintenance in a warehousing environment. In *Proceedings of the 1995 ACM SIGMOD International Conference on Management of Data* (pp. 316–327). New York, NY: ACM. doi:http://doi.acm.org/10.1145/223784.223848

ENDNOTES

[1] This dataset is available at: http://cdiac.ornl.gov/ftp/ndp026b/

Chapter 8
Big Data Sharing Among Academics

Jeonghyun Kim
University of North Texas, USA

ABSTRACT

The goal of this chapter is to explore the practice of big data sharing among academics and issues related to this sharing. The first part of the chapter reviews literature on big data sharing practices using current technology. The second part presents case studies on disciplinary data repositories in terms of their requirements and policies. It describes and compares such requirements and policies at disciplinary repositories in three areas: Dryad for life science, Interuniversity Consortium for Political and Social Research (ICPSR) for social science, and the National Oceanographic Data Center (NODC) for physical science.

INTRODUCTION

The September 2009 issue of *Nature* included an interesting special section on data sharing. An opinion article in the section discussed the Toronto International Data Release Workshop, where attendees "[recommended] extending the practice to other biological data sets" (Birney et al., 2009, p. 168) and developing a set of suggested best practices for funding agencies, scientists, and journal editors. The February 2011 issue of *Science*

compiled several interesting articles to provide a broad look at the challenges and opportunities posed by the data deluge in various areas of research, including neuroscience, ecology, health, and social science, where there is a demand for the acquisition, integration, and exchange of vast amounts of research data.

The term *big data* is a current buzzword. It is a loosely defined term to describe massive and complex data sets largely generated from recent and unprecedented advancements in data recording

DOI: 10.4018/978-1-4666-4699-5.ch008

and storage technology (Diebold, 2003). Explosive growth means that revolutionary measures are needed for data management, analysis, and accessibility. Along with this growth, the emergence of a new "fourth paradigm" (Gray, 2009) for scientific research, where "all of the science literature is online, all of the science data is online, and they interoperate with each other" (Howe et al., 2008, p. 47), has created many opportunities. Therefore, the activity of organizing, representing, and making data accessible to both humans and computers has become an essential part of research and discovery.

Given the significance of this context, data sharing has become a hot topic in the scientific community. Data is a classic example of a public good in that shared data do not diminish in value. In particular, scientific data have long underpinned the cycle of discovery and are the dominant vehicles by which scientists earn credit for their work. So shared data have served as a benchmark that allows others to study and refine methods of analysis, and once collected, they can be creatively repurposed indefinitely by many hands and in many ways (Vision, 2010). Sharing data not only reinforces open scientific inquiry but also promotes new research and expedites further discovery (Fienberg, 1994). As science has become more data intensive and collaborative, data sharing has become more important.

Promoting the effective sharing of data is an increasing part of national and international scientific discourse and essential to the future of science (National Science and Technology Council, 2009). Today, many U.S. government agencies recognize that scientific, biomedical, and engineering research communities are undergoing a profound transformation in regard to access to and reuse of large-scale and diverse data sets; as such, these agencies have developed policies that mandate and/or encourage data sharing. For instance, the National Science Foundation (NSF) expects grantees to share their primary data, samples, physical collections, and other supporting materials created or gathered in the course of work under the grant.[1] The National Institutes of Health (NIH) has had a data-sharing policy since 2003; the policy states that any investigator submitting a grant application seeking direct costs of $500,000 or more in any single year is expected to include a plan to address data sharing in the application or state why data sharing is not possible.[2]

To support these needs, infrastructure is being built to store and share data for researchers as well as educators and the general public. In 2008, the NSF awarded nearly $100 million over 5 years to data preservation and infrastructure development projects under the DataNet initiative.[3] DataONE[4] is one of the awards, which is dedicated to large-scale preservation and access to multiscale, multidiscipline, and multinational data in biology, ecology, and the environmental sciences. Recently, the White House announced a $200 million initiative to create tools to improve scientific research by making sense of the huge amount of data now available. Programs like these are needed to improve the technology required to work with large and complex sets of digital data.[5]

Researchers and scientists in academia, industry, and government may choose to store and share their data in a number of ways. Among the various means, data repositories often appear to offer the best method of ensuring that data are preserved and presented in a high-quality manner and made available to the largest number of people. Data repositories are constructed with the chief goal of storage and preservation and emphasize use/reuse. In other words, the implementation of data repositories is constrained by not only the needs of data sharing but also concurrent data access. They have data as its primary focus and are often shared by a scientific community.

The goal of this chapter is to explore the practice of big data sharing among academics and issues related to this sharing. The background section of this chapter reviews literature on researchers' practices and trends with regard to data sharing and access. The main section reviews disciplinary data repositories in the areas of social science, life science, and physical science, and describes and compares the requirements and policies at disciplinary repositories. It also examines recommended and accepted file formats and data structure repositories, metadata, and specifications and guidelines on data access and sharing.

DATA SHARING PRACTICES AND TRENDS

Data sharing has been a critical issue in scientific research for some time. Since the National Academy of Sciences published the book *Sharing Research Data* in 1985, the benefits of sharing data have been discussed widely and data sharing has been a regular practice in many academic disciplines. While researchers may share a relatively low volume of data via emails or disks, the rate of data produced in many academic disciplines has now exceeded the growth of computational power predicted by *Moore's law*; the enormous amount of data that scholars and researchers generate now can easily overwhelm their computers. As the size of data sets grow, managing heterogeneous data sets that contain different formats, data types, and descriptions can be burdensome. This leads to difficulties sharing and reusing data as well. The explosion in the amount of data available means researchers need better tools and methods for handling, analyzing, and storing data.

As a result, cloud computing has become a popular solution for storing, processing, and sharing data because it integrates networks, servers, storage, applications, and services, enabling convenient and on-demand access to a shared pool of configurable computing resources. Additionally, cloud computing offers other benefits: cost efficiency as it reduces investment in generic hardware systems; faster implementation of features of new products and systems; flexible provisioning and resource scalability of systems; and a pay-as-you-go service model (Agrawal, Das, & Abbadi,

2011). Currently, cloud computing services are provided by commercial vendors, such as Amazon and Microsoft, as well as academic centers and government agencies. Such cloud computing services may be suitable for sharing certain types of data and offer immediate scalability of storage resources necessary to successfully facilitate a big data sharing project, but they are not recommended for data that may be confidential because of the issue of individual privacy (Wang, 2010). In addition, users need to be aware that they do not control where data are ultimately stored.

As scientific research endeavors are increasingly carried out by researchers collaborating across disciplines, laboratories, institutions, and geographic boundaries, additional tools and services are needed. Because collaboration involves geographically distributed and heterogeneous resources such as computational systems, scientific instruments, databases, sensors, software components, and networks, information and computing technology, popularly called "eScience," plays a vital role in large-scale and enhanced scientific ventures; as such, grid computing has become an emerging infrastructure for eScience applications by integrating large-scale, distributed, and heterogeneous resources. In their foundation paper "The anatomy of grid," Foster, Kesselman, and Tuecke (2001) distinguished grid computing from conventional distributed computing or cloud computing by its focus on large-scale resource sharing, innovative applications, and in some cases, high-performance orientation. Scientific communities, such as high-energy physics, gravitational-wave physics, geophysics, astronomy, and bioinformatics, are utilizing grids to share, manage, and process large data sets (Taylor, Deelamn, Gannon, & Shields, 2006).

A Virtual Research Environment (VRE), a platform which allows multiple researchers in different locations to work together in real time without restrictions, has been developed from this context (e.g., De Roure, Goble, & Stevens, 2009; Neuroth, Lohmeier, & Smith, 2011; Avila-

Garcia, Xiong, Trefethen, Crichton, Tsui, & Hu, 2011). VREs include access to data repositories and grid computation services, but also collaboration tools, such as e-mail, wikis, virtual meeting rooms, tools for sharing data, and the ability to search for related information. The key issue of a VRE is the development and implementation of an information and data-sharing concept. It should be noted that such VREs require significant setup and maintenance costs, and are usually mono-institutional. Consequently, many researchers are not comfortable with their features and may still resort to sharing data via email and/or online file-sharing services.

The following section reviews the impact of big data in four different academic disciplines and changes in their data-sharing practices.

Arts and Humanities

Researchers in the arts and humanities often prefer to publish considered works in monographs. There has been a slow adoption of digital publishing in the field, because there has been a general reluctance to experiment with new technologies and a distrust of online dissemination. Nevertheless, networked access to information sources in the field has increased since the early 1990s (American Council of Learned Society, 2006). Examples include Project MUSE,[6] which provides online access to 500 full-text journals and 15,000 full-text e-books from 200 nonprofit publishers in the humanities; JSTOR,[7] a full-text archive of journal articles in many academic fields, including arts, literature, and humanities; and ARTStor,[8] which holds hundreds of thousands of images contributed by museums, archaeological teams, and photo archives.

Blanke, Dunn, and Dunning (2005) foresee that research in the humanities is becoming data-centric, with a large amount of data available in digital formats and that this trend will change the landscape of humanities research. The increasing availability of massive collections of digitized books, newspapers, images, and audio, combined with the development of accessible tools for analyzing those materials, means computationally based approaches are growing in the field. Recently, a number of initiatives have been taken; for instance, Digging Into Data[9] is an initiative that shows the importance of big data in the humanities and social sciences.

Compared with other disciplines, researchers in the arts and humanities do not produce a great deal of research data. However, a critical mass of information is often necessary for understanding both the context and the specifics of an artifact or event. Thus, the field has used primary sources and data from manuscripts, early printed editions of classical texts, ancient inscriptions, excavated artifacts, and images of classical art objects, among many other types of sources. Nevertheless, some disciplines produce data that carry complex interoperability and semantic challenges. For instance, researchers in the field of archaeology, epigraphy, and art history produce lexica, edited catalogs, and statistical data. They have long been proponents of data sharing and reuse because of the unrepeatable nature of the work. Open access collections of primary archaeological data, such as the Archaeology Data Service[10] and the Archaeobotanical Database,[11] bring large quantities of raw data directly to the researcher's fingertips.

Social Sciences

The social sciences tend to be more dependent on technology. In particular, quantitative social science researchers have long used mainframes and personal computers for statistical analysis and other types of data processing even though they have dealt with smaller samples. Social scientists have also expressed interest in using technology to improve access to conference papers, unpublished research, and technical reports (American Council of Learned Society, 2006). Data have often been shared in many different ways, ranging from informal dissemination with known peers to formal archives. However, as Crosas (2011) asserted, traditional approaches to storing and sharing data sets in social sciences have been either inadequate or unattractive to many researchers.

There have been few clear guidelines on data sharing in the social sciences as data collection and use are bound by rules or agreements relating to confidentiality and legal and ethical considerations. These factors have been significant barriers to the sharing and reuse of research data. Yet, the value of data sharing has become apparent to the social science field because of massive increases in the availability of informative social science data (King, 2011). The urgent need to understand complex, global phenomena leveraging the deluge of data arising from new technologies is driving an agenda in the social sciences.

The social science research community, in fact, was among the first to recognize the benefits of archiving digital data for use and reuse. Since the advent of survey research in the 1930s, many data archives, most of them nationally funded, have been established around the world to preserve social science data resources (Vardigan & Whiteman, 2007). Data archive and data library development in the field has been discussed since the late 1960s (Heim, 1982). In the United States, a set of archives with ties to major research universities has emerged, including the Roper Center for Public Opinion Research at the University of Connecticut;[12] the Howard W. Odum Institute for Research in Social Science at the University of North Carolina at Chapel Hill;[13] the Henry A. Murray Research Archive[14] and the Harvard-MIT Data Center at the Institute for Quantitative Social Science,[15] Harvard University; and the ICPSR at the University of Michigan.[16]

Life Sciences

The research process in the life sciences often involves the use of data produced from a range of sources, with data generated in the laboratory being complemented by imported data. The quantity of data created in the life sciences is certainly growing at an exponential rate and the size of individual data sets is increasing massively. Large-scale data sets from genomics, physiology, population genetics, and neuroimaging are rapidly driving research. Today, genomics technologies enable individual labs to generate terabyte- or even petabyte-scale data. At the same time, computational infrastructure is required to maintain and process such large-scale data sets and to integrate them with other large-scale sets. Furthermore, interdisciplinary collaborations among experimental biologists, theorists, statisticians, and computer scientists have become key to making effective use of data sets (Stein, 2008). However, existing data storage systems and data analysis tools are not adapted to handle large data sets and have not been implemented on platforms that can support such big data sets.

It should be noted that there is no single data culture for the life sciences because the field ranges in scope and scale from the field biologist whose data are captured in short-lived notebooks as a prelude to a narrative explanation of observations to the molecular biologist whose data are born digital in near terabyte quantities and are widely shared through data repositories (Thessen & Patternson, 2011). Nevertheless, the life sciences have had a stronger culture of open data publication and sharing than other disciplines. Researchers in the field have participated in collaborative environments that allow data to be annotated, such as EcoliWiki[17] or DNA Subway.[18] Some journal publications have data-sharing policies that encourage their authors to archive primary data sets in an "appropriate" public data repository. In the biosciences, the mandatory deposits of sequence data to GenBank[19] or the Protein Data Bank[20] is well established; these repositories have highly structured data, rich metadata, and analytical capabilities uniquely tailored to their contents (Scherle et al., 2008). All large funding bodies, such as NIH, now make data sharing a requirement of support for all projects and have created data repositories for the funded research data. For instance, the National Database for Autism Research,[21] an NIH-funded research data repository, aims to accelerate progress in autism research through data sharing, data harmonization, and the reporting of research results.

Physical Sciences

The physical sciences, which are an aggregation of astronomy, astrophysics, chemistry, computer sciences, mathematics, and physics, deal with more data other disciplines. The field is also experiencing an unprecedented data avalanche due to the fast advance and evolution of information technology that enables capture, analysis, and storage of huge quantities of data. Astronomy, for example, has a long history of acquiring, systematizing, and interpreting large quantities of data but has become a very data-rich science, driven by the advances in telescope, detector, and computer technology (Brunner, Djorgovski, Prince, & Szalay, 2002). It was one of the first disciplines to embrace data-intensive science with the Virtual Observatory,[22] enabling highly efficient access to data and analysis tools at a centralized site.

Physicists have long enjoyed the tradition of sharing their research ideas and results with their peers in the format of preprint through an online archive database, arXiv,[23] operated by Cornell University. The astronomy community also has a well-established culture of data sharing that was pioneered by the National Aeronautics and Space Administration (NASA) space missions. Many astronomical observatories and institutes have important data archives and databases that contain large amounts of data. Data discovery, access, and reuse are common in astronomy; the Space Telescope Science Institute (STScI) reports that more papers are published with archived data sets than with newly acquired data (Space Telescope Science Institute, 2012). Climate and environmental science is another field that ben-efits from the existence of centrally funded data archives, such as National Climate Data Center (NCDC)[24] and GEONGrid Portal.[25]

CASE STUDIES: DISCIPLINARY REPOSITORIES

A repository is defined as "a networked system that provides services pertaining to a collection of digital objects" (Bekaert & Sompel, 2006, p.4). A repository, in general, provides services for the management and dissemination of data by making it discoverable, providing access, protecting its integrity, ensuring long-term preservation, and migrating data to new technologies (Lynch, 2003).

Disciplinary repositories, often called domain repositories or subject-based repositories, are thematically defined to serve specific community users and store and provide access to the scholarly output of a particular academic domain, field, or specialty. Their scope is often specialized; they are often community endorsed, conform to established standards, serve the needs of researchers in the discipline, and bring together research from multiple institutions and/or funders. In contrast to institutional repositories, these repositories accept work from scholars across institutions. They have specialized knowledge of approaches to data in a specific scientific field, such as domain-specific metadata standards, and have the ability to give high-impact exposure to research products. These disciplinary repositories can also act as stores of research data sets related to a particular discipline. Financial support for such repositories may come from a variety of sources; grant funding often covers the start-up costs, institutions provide pro bono services, and volunteers often serve as editors. Universities are sometimes motivated to host and manage a disciplinary repository to reflect and build upon a center of excellence. There are a number of repositories run by federal agencies, such as NASA.

As the preservation and reuse of data through data sharing has become a strategic issue, various discussions on disciplinary repositories have been presented in several publications. Green and Gutmann (2007) differentiated institutional repositories and disciplinary repositories; they asserted that institutional repositories do not fully support the scientific research lifecycle as they often focus on capturing final or near-final forms of scholarly productivity and partner less with researchers during the initial process and phase of a typical research project. In a survey of data repositories, Marcial and Hemminger (2010) found that a significant majority of the data repositories they identified on the open Web are funded or directly affiliated with individual universities. In addition, most of those repositories are described as highly domain specific. Johnson and Eschenfelder (2011), in their preliminary report of the study on access and use control in data repositories, reported some interesting differences in repositories; repositories in biology and the social sciences cited privacy as a reason for restricting access to data as they deal with human subject data, whereas repositories in social science mentioned intellectual property as a concern.

The following section reviews disciplinary repositories from three disciplines: Dryad for life science, ICPSR for social science, and the National Oceanographic Data Center (NODC) for physical science. Each repository's requirements and policies are explored. In addition, recommended and accepted file formats and data structure repositories, metadata, and policies regarding data access and sharing are examined.

Dryad

Dryad[26] is an international, open, cost-effective data repository for the preservation, access, and reuse of scientific data and objects underlying published research in the field of evolutionary biology, ecology, and related disciplines. The re-pository is designed specifically to enable authors to archive data upon publication and to promote the reuse of that data.

Dryad, named after tree nymphs in Greek mythology, was initially designed in 2007 as a "response to a 'crisis of data attrition' in the field of evolutionary biology" (Greenberg, 2009, p. 386) by the National Evolutionary Synthesis Center and Metadata Research Center at the School of Information and Library Science, University of North Carolina at Chapel Hill. Today it is operated as a nonprofit organization, governed by its member organizations, including journals, publishers, scientific societies, funding agencies, and other stakeholders.[27] In particular, it has been supported by a number of grants, including the Institute for Museum and Library Services (USA), the Joint Information Systems Committee (UK), and the National Science Foundation (USA); these grants and others have allowed continued development of the repository and ensured its sustainability. The repository, initially developed to help support the coordinated adoption of a policy by a number of leading ecology and evolution journals, would require all authors to archive their data at the time of publication.[28]

The scientific, educational, and charitable mission of Dryad is to promote the availability of data underlying findings in the scientific literature for research and educational reuse. It welcomes data files associated with any published article in the biosciences, as well as software scripts and other files important to the article. The repository software is based on DSpace, which allows Dryad to leverage a technology platform being used by hundreds of organizations, and is maintained by a large and active open-source software community. Dryad accepts data in any format, from spreadsheets or other tables, images, and alignments to video files. All data files in Dryad are available for download and reuse, except those under a temporary embargo period, as permitted by editors of the relevant journals. Primary access to Dryad is through its Web interface, where users most commonly search on authors, titles, subjects, and other metadata elements. As of May 23, 2013, Dryad contains 3,287 data packages and 9,446 data files, associated with articles in 223 journals (Dryad, n.d.).

For submissions, Dryad recommends authors use nonproprietary file formats wherever possible and use descriptive file names to reflect the contents of the file. Authors are also asked to provide documentation to help ensure proper data reuse and additional keywords to make the data easier to discover. The documentation, in the form of ReadMe files, consists of a file name, a short description of what data it includes, how data are collected, who collected the data, and whom to contact with questions. Once data are submitted, the data files are given a digital object identifier (DOI), which is a permanent, unique, and secure identifier that should be used whenever referring to data in Dryad. All data deposited to Dryad is released to the public domain under Creative Commons Zero (CC0), which reduces legal and technical impediments to the reuse of data by waiving copyright and related rights to the extent permitted by law.

Specifically, Dryad focuses on providing thorough metadata to allow new access to the unique data types generated by its constituents (Greenberg, White, Carrier, & Scherle, 2009; Vision, 2010). Dryad's metadata application profile supports basic resource and data discovery, with the goal of being interoperable with other data repositories used by evolutionary biologists. The application profile has been developed in compliance with the Dublin Core Metadata Initiative's guidelines, including the Singapore Framework. The application profile Version 3.0 consists of three modules: 1) a publication module for representing an article associated with content in Dryad; 2) a data package module for representing a group of data files associated with a given publication; and 3) a data file module for representing

a deposited bitstream (Dryad Development Team, 2012). The profile (Table 1) includes 19 properties.

ICPSR

As one of the oldest and largest archives of digital social science data in the world, ICPSR[29] was

Table 1. Dryad application profiles: Property names and definitions

Property Name	Definition
Type	The nature or genre of the resource
Status	Status of the metadata record
Article Publication	Publication status of the associated article
Author	The entity or entities who created the resource being described
Title	Descriptive title of the article, data package, or data file
Rights Statement	Statement regarding rights held over the resource
Description	Human-readable description of the resource; an abstract or summary
Keywords	Subject keywords describing the data
Scientific Name	The full name of the lowest level taxon to which the organism has been identified in the most recent accepted determination
Spatial Coverage	The spatial description of the data specified by a geographic description and/or geographic coordinates
Temporal Coverage	The temporal description of the data, as geologic time span
Date of Issuance	Date of formal issuance (e.g., publication) of the resource
Deposit Date	An automatic time-stamped date when a depositor finalizes their submission
Data Available	Date when the Dryad metadata records becomes public
Embargo Date	A date after which the data itself will be made public and available for download
File Format	The format in which the data file is stored Can also represent software format
File Size	The size of the file storage
Provenance	Information related to the origin and integrity of the file

originally started as a partnership among 21 universities in 1962. It has served as the long-term steward and a primary channel for sharing a vast archive of social science data.

As a part of the Institute of Social Research at the University of Michigan, ICPSR is a consortium of 700 academic institutions and research organizations worldwide.[30] This consortium has served the social science community's need for capturing data and has evolved its practices through the technology transitions from punch cards, floppy disks, and compact discs (CDs) to today's electronic submissions (Rockwell, 1994; Vardigan & Whiteman, 2007). Each entity provides representation to a council that manages "administrative, budgetary, and organizational policies and procedures" (Beattie, 1979, p. 354) of the consortium. The member institutions of a consortium pay annual dues that enable faculty, staff, and students free and direct access to the full range of data resources and services provided by ICPSR.

The mission of ICPSR is to "provide leadership and training in data access, curation, and methods of analysis for a diverse and expanding social science research community" (ICPSR, n.d.). ICPSR has collected and made available the data sets of many major government studies in their entirety, along with polls and surveys conducted by organizations and individual researchers. The repository data span many disciplines, including sociology, political science, criminology, history, education, demography, gerontology, international relations, public health, economics, and psychology; it maintains a data archive of more than 500,000 files of research in such disciplines. Most of the data sets in the ICPSR are raw data from surveys, censuses, and administrative records. Furthermore, ICPSR has collaborated with a number of funders, including U.S. statistical agencies and foundations, to widen its vast archive of social science data for research and instruction; as a result, it hosts 23 specialized collections of data thematically arranged by topics, including education, aging, criminal justice, substance abuse, and terrorism.

Data submissions at ICPSR are initiated in various ways (Vardigan & Whiteman, 2007). The data deposit may be voluntary and unsolicited; for instance, a researcher who understands the importance of long-term preservation of digital data may decide to deposit his or her data for future generations of scholars to use. In other cases, data are submitted as a requirement of a grant or sponsoring agency agreement with ICPSR. Deposits are made using a secure data deposit form to describe the data collection and upload content. ICPSR accepts data related to the social sciences for research and instructional activities, but selectively accepts data that fit within the scope of its collection and would be of potential future interest to its members based on their appraisal criteria in collection development policy (ICPSR, 2012). ICPSR accepts both quantitative data for standard statistical software packages and qualitative data, including transcripts and audiovisual media for preservation and dissemination. Increasingly, however, ICPSR seeks out researchers and research agencies to identify content for acquisition through a wide variety of means, including press releases and published reports announcing results of a study, and papers presented at professional meetings and scholarly conferences (Gutmann, Schürer, Donakowski, & Beedham, 2004).

Archival work at ICPSR begins by teaming staff members with the researcher to ensure that ICPSR understands the data that the investigator wishes to deposit and to identify any constraints on future access to data (Albright & Lyle, 2010). Once the data are received, they are reviewed for confidentiality risks, errors, and internal consistency issues; direct and/or indirect identifiers, such as name, Social Security number, or telephone number, are removed and level of access is determined. At this point in the process, data with a proprietary data format, such as SPSS, are transformed into a more appropriate software-independent archival format, specifically raw ASCII text data with SPSS "setup" files that enable a user to read in the raw data to re-create the proprietary SPSS format. Additionally, ICPSR creates high-level metadata about the study using data documentation initiative (DDI) markup, an international standard for documenting social science research, using information provided by data depositors and other sources (Table 2). A DOI is assigned to each study held, and ICPSR encour-

ages the use of DOI for journal publications and other articles to make it easier for researchers to find relevant work.

Access to data is determined by multiple factors. All documentation files associated with ICPSR data sets are available to the general public. Studies funded by federal agencies are usually available for access and download for the general public through the Web site. To download data sets, all general public users must register with a MyData account or log in with their Facebook or Google account. Some data are only

Table 2. Important Metadata Elements for ICPSR

Elements	Definition
Principal Investigator	Principal investigator name(s) and affiliation(s) at time of data collection
Title	Official title of the data collection
Funding Sources	Names of funders, including grant numbers and related acknowledgments
Data Collector	Persons or organizations responsible for data collection, and the date and location of data production
Project Description	A description of the project and its intellectual goals and indicates how the data articulate with related data sets
Sample and Sampling Procedure	A description of the target population investigated and the methods used to sample it
Weighting	Information on weight variables
Coverage of the Data Collection	Descriptions of topics covered, time period, and location
Data Source	Citations to the original sources or documents from which data were obtained
Unit of Analysis	A description of who or what is being studied
Variables	The exact question wording or the exact meaning of the datum; The text of the question integrated into the variable text; Universe information; Exact meaning of codes; Missing data codes; Unweighted frequency distribution or summary statistics; Imputation and editing information; Details on constructed and weight variables; Location in the data file; Variable groupings
Related Publications	Citations to publications based on the data, by the principal investigators or others
Technical Info on Files	Information on file formats, file linking, and similar information
Data Collection Instruments	Copies of the original data collection forms and instruments
Flowchart of the Data Collection Instrument	A graphical guide to the data collection
Index or Table of Contents	A list of variables either in alphabetical order or organized into variable groups
List of Abbreviations and Other Conventions	Variable names and variable labels often contain abbreviations
Interviewer Guide	Details on how interviews were administered
Coding Instrument	A document that details the rules and definitions used for coding the data

available to users at ICPSR member institutions. The search box can be found on the "Find & Analyze Data" page of the Web site. The current search interface allows users to search title, author/ investigator, and summary fields and browse by topic, series, geography, and investigator. Certain data sets are restricted use with specified use policies as there is a risk that the identity of research participants could be disclosed. To request access to restricted-use data materials, an application for restricted data, a data protection plan, a restricted data-use agreement, and a supplemental agreement with research staff are required. Once such requests are reviewed and approved, the data are sent to researchers through the mail via CD (ICPSR, n.d.).

NODC

The NODC[31] is one of three national environmental data centers operated by the National Oceanic and Atmospheric Administration (NOAA) of the U.S. Department of Commerce.[32] As the world's largest collection of publicly available oceanographic data, it provides scientific and public stewardship for national and international marine environmental and ecosystem data and information.

Established in 1961, the NODC was originally an interagency facility administered by the U.S. Naval Hydrographic (later Oceanographic) Office. The NODC was transferred to NOAA in 1970 when NOAA was created by Executive Order of the President of the United States. The mission of the NODC is to enhance oceanographic services and promote further marine research by making ocean data and products available in real and non-real time to policymakers and marine communities for the efficient management and sustainable development of coastal and marine resources. Since May 2011, the NODC has served as the NOAA Ocean Acidification Program (OAP) data management focal point through its Ocean Acidification Data Stewardship (OADS) project (NODC, n.d.).

NODC holdings include in situ and remotely sensed physical, chemical, and biological oceanographic data from coastal and deep ocean areas; they were originally collected for a variety of operational and research missions by federal, state, and local organizations, including the Department of Defense, universities and research institutions, international data exchange partners, and industry. It also offers climatology products, ocean profile data, fisheries closure data, coastal ecosystem maps, ocean currents data, satellite data, as well as a selected bibliography (Collins & Rutz, 2005). Most digital data in the NODC are available to the general public in its original format at no cost or on customized media for the cost of distribution. For some types of digital data, a specialized product is available to subset and select or retrieve specific data from multiple sources. For example, the NODC World Ocean Database contains a collection of millions of temperature, salinity, and other parameter profiles that have been reformatted to a common format (Collins & Rutz, 2005).

The Federal Ocean Data Policy requires that appropriate ocean data and related information collected under federal sponsorship be submitted to and archived by designated national data centers. For data submission, depositors are required to provide proper data documentation, which includes complete descriptions of what parameters/observations were measured; how they were measured/collected; where and when they were collected (latitude, longitude, Greenwich mean time [GMT], depth[s], altitude[s]), and other geographic descriptions; the data collector or principal investigator; collecting institution/ agency and platforms; collecting/measuring instrumentation; data processing and analyses methodologies; description of units, precisions, and accuracies of measured parameters; descriptions of the data format, and the computer compatible media submitted. The NODC also solicits references to literature that have pertinence to the data, both published and gray literature.

Upon receipt and acceptance by the NODC, a unique accession number is generated for each data submission. Files are often converted into ASCII so they are readable for the long term. A copy of the original data and metadata files, as well as any relevant additional information about the original data, is placed in the archive. There are also "deep archive processes" that include the creation and validation of off-site copies intended for use in disaster recovery situations or when the local working archive copy is rendered temporarily unavailable due to equipment malfunction or other reasons (Collins, 2004). The system exports metadata into XML files. The metadata format follows the Federal Geographic Data Committee (FGDC) Content Standard for Digital Geospatial Metadata (CSDGM), which uses a controlled vocabulary for data set descriptions (Collins et al., 2003). Such data sets and metadata are periodically reviewed for completeness and correctness.

Most digital data in the NODC archival collection are available to a worldwide audience via the web in its original format for no cost or on customized media for the cost of distribution. For some types of digital data, a specialized product is available to subset and select or retrieve specific data from multiple sources; for instance, the NODC World Ocean Database contains a collection of millions of temperature, salinity, and other parameter profiles that have been reformatted to a common format. The Ocean Archive System (OAS) is the public web interface to the Archive Management and Metadata System and provides access to the original set of ocean data in the archive. Authority tables for people, projects, institutions, platforms, sea names, data types, instruments, and observation allow the user to locate search criteria. The NODC also provides a number of other search utilities for specific products, such as the NODC World Ocean Database.

Table 3. Metadata used in the NODC

Elements	Definition
Accession Number	Assigned by the NODC to identify individual data shipments or packets
Date Received	The date on which the NODC actually received the data from a particular source
Start Date	The date of the first or earliest observation within the data collection
End Date	The date of the last or latest observation within the data collection
Availability Date	The date when the NODC made the data collection available to the public
Abstract	A summary of the main points about the data accession
Submitter	The name of the scientist who submitted the data collection to the NODC
Geographical	West boundary; East boundary; North boundary; South boundary
Data Type	The parameters that are contained in the collection
Observation Type	Description of how the data observations were collected
Instrument Type	Description of the instrumentation that was used to collect the data
Sea Area	Based on the International Hydrographic Bureau's Limits of Oceans and Seas
Contributing Project	The names of the projects that were associated with the collection of the data
Submitting Institution	The institution that submitted the data collection to the NODC
Collecting Institution	The institution that was responsible for collecting the data
Platforms	The names of the platforms that were used when collecting the data
Title	The title of the FGDC record for a data collection

FUTURE RESEARCH DIRECTIONS AND CONCLUSION

The need for big data sharing in academic disciplines via publicly accessible repositories has been emphasized in this chapter. The remainder of this chapter discusses four issues that future study should address in terms of sharing data via disciplinary repositories.

First, as discussed, most disciplinary repositories exist to serve specific community users; they store and provide access to the scholarly output of their identified community. Community-based approaches to the challenge of high volume within the data domain have proven to be the most effective and efficient in the long term. In particular, community standards for data description and exchange are important because it facilitates data reuse by making it easier to import, export, and combine data (Lynch, 2008). Recognizing the importance of such standards, the NSF issued a call for proposals to support community efforts to provide for broad interoperability through the development of mechanisms, such as robust data and metadata conventions, ontologies, and taxonomies. Metadata is a critical factor in this area. It is important to provide rich metadata, which includes information about the context, content, quality, provenance, and/or accessibility of a set of data, and make it openly available to enable other researchers to understand the potential for further research and reuse of the data (Griffiths, 2009). Metadata, using appropriate standards, needs to be used to ensure adequate description and control over the long term. As a matter of fact, many academic disciplines have supported initiatives to formalize the metadata standards the community deems to be required for data reuse; they already have established metadata standards for describing and sharing data sets within the discipline. In disciplinary repositories, metadata standards generally are most usefully considered within the limits of their user communities' standard practices. For instance, the geospatial field has long utilized the Federal Geographic Data Committee's (FGDC) Content Standard for Digital Geospatial Metadata; the NODC's metadata requirements are based on this standard. Within the social science data community, a standard for describing the content of data files has been established through

the Data Documentation Initiative (DDI); ICPSR uses the DDI metadata specification in documenting its data holdings.

Second, the long-term sustainability of disciplinary repositories is contingent upon various aspects of management, such as maintaining the repository services, managing the repository budget, and coordinating activities of repository personnel. One way to promote such sustainability is to recognize and provide funding to support them. Funding is essential for the physical facilities, viable technological solutions for conducting data stewardship processes, programs to assess services, and programs to educate and train a skilled workforce. It is exemplary that the government is commiting long-term funding for a national data repository where researchers can deposit publicly funded research data, as such repositories can accept data sets that are too big to store locally at institutional repositories and provide convenient public access. There are a number of repositories hosted and managed by federal agencies, such as GenBank, Protein Data Bank, and National Nuclear Data Center. On the other hand, disciplinary repositories owned and managed by other agencies, such as libraries and research institutions, still need federal support and sponsorship. Green and Gutmann (2007) asserted, "[T]he next step in the evolution of digital repository strategies should be an explicit development of partnerships between researchers, institutional repositories, and domain-specific repositories" (p. 50). In a similar vein, Lynch (2008) viewed that challenges with big data in science can be overcome with a focused effort and collaboration among funders, institutions, and researchers in academia.

Third, a robust and scalable technical infrastructure is essential to support the collection, storage, retrieval, and sharing of data. Repositories have grown at a rapid pace over the past decade with open-source software, including EPrints, DSpace, and Fedora. In particular, DSpace and Fedora are two of the largest open-source software platforms for managing and providing access to digital content. DSpace[33] is a turnkey application for building digital repositories; its built-in structure consists of a pre-determined hierarchy that allows users to organize content easily. It provides an internal metadata schema based on Dublin Core for describing the content. It also includes a variety of preservation and management tools and a simple workflow for uploading, approving, and making content available via the web. The Dryad repository reviewed in this chapter is based on DSpace. Fedora (Flexible Extensible Digital Object Repository Architecture) Commons[34] is a flexible framework to manage, preserve, and link data of any format with corresponding metadata. It enables users to customize a pre-existing application designed to work with Fedora, such as Islandora or Libra, a variant of Hydra. It permits users to construct simple to complex object models representing any number of unique use cases for data preservation and archiving. Recently, considerable attention has been paid to iRODS, integrated Rule-Orientated Data-management System, a data grid software system developed by the Data Intensive Cyber Environments research group and collaborators. It supports collaborative research and, more broadly, the management, sharing, publication, and long-term preservation of data that are distributed. It also enables the management of large sets of computer files, which can range in size from moderate to a hundred million files totaling petabytes of data. A particular feature of iRODS is the ability to represent data management policies in terms of rules.

Last, implementing appropriate regulatory and legal frameworks is important. To this end, it may be ideal to mandate digital data deposits into disciplinary repositories. Even though several funding agencies have their own data-sharing requirements, some policies are ambiguous with respect to what must be released (Borgman, 2012). Furthermore, federal agencies can account for inherent differences between scientific disciplines and different types of digital data when developing data management policies by adopting a relatively general mandate for data sharing while requiring more specificity for the practices within each discipline. However, it should be noted that not all data is reusable or can be repurposed. Therefore, funding agencies should customize requirements based on the type of research proposed. Additionally, federal policy should give clear direction as to what data may be shared publicly to increase legal certainty for data users and producers. Such direction should be regulated by legal standards that ensure and promote free public access, discovery, and reuse.

REFERENCES

Agrawal, D., Das, S., & Abbadi, A. E. (2011). Big data and cloud computing: Current state and future opportunities. In *Proceedings of the 14th International Conference on Extending Database Technology* (pp. 530-533). IEEE.

Albright, J. J., & Lyle, J. A. (2010). Data preservation through data archives. *PS: Political Science & Politics*, *43*(1), 17–21. doi:10.1017/S1049096510990768.

American Council of Learned Society. (2006). *Our cultural commonwealth: The report of the American council of learned societies commission on cyberinfrastructure for the humanities and social sciences*. Retrieved from http://www.acls.org/cyberinfrastructure/ourculturalcommonwealth.pdf

Avila-Garcia, M. S., Xiong, X., Trefethen, A. E., Crichton, C., Tsui, A., & Hu, P. (2011). A virtual research environment for cancer imaging research. In *Proceedings of the IEEE Seventh International Conference on eScience* (pp. 1-6). IEEE.

Beattie, R. (1970). ICPSR: Resources for the study of conflict resolution: The inter-university consortium for political and social research. *The Journal of Conflict Resolution, 23*(2), 337–345. doi:10.1177/002200277902300207.

Bekaert, J., & Sompel, V. (2006). *Augmenting interoperability across scholarly repositories.* Retrieved from http://msc.mellon.org/Meetings/Interop/FinalReport/

Birney, E., Hudson, T. J., Green, E. D., Gunter, C., Eddy, S., & Rogers, J. et al. (2009). Prepublication of data sharing. *Nature, 461*, 168–170. doi:10.1038/461168a PMID:19741685.

Blanke, T., Dunn, S., & Dunning, A. (2006). Digital libraries in the arts and humanities – Current practices and future possibilities. In *Proceedings of the 2006 International Conference on Multidisciplinary Information Sciences and Technologies (INSciT 2006)*. INSciT.

Borgman, C. L. (2012). The conundrum of sharing research data. *Journal of the American Society for Information Science and Technology, 63*(6), 1059–1078. doi:10.1002/asi.22634.

Brunner, R. J., Djorgovski, S. G., Prince, T. A., & Szalay, A. S. (2002). Massive datasets in astronomy. In J. Abello, P. Pardalos, & M. Resende (Eds.), *Handbook of massive data sets*. Norwell, MA: Kluwer Academic Publishers.

Collins, D. W. (2004). US national oceanographic data center: Archival management practices and the open archival information system reference model. In *Proceedings of the 21st IEEE Conference on Mass Storage Systems and Technologies*. IEEE. Retrieved from http://storageconference.org/2004/Papers/39-Collins-a.pdf

Collins, D. W., & Rutz, S. B. (2005). The NODC archive management system: Archiving marine data for ocean exploration and beyond. In *Proceedings of MTS/IEEE Data of Conference*. IEEE. doi:10.1109/OCEANS.2005.1640202

Collins, D. W., Rutz, S. B., Dantzler, H. L., Ogata, E. J., Mitchell, F. J., Shirley, J., & Thailambal, T. (2003). Introducing the U.S. NODC archive management system: Stewardship of the nation's oceanographic data archive. *Earth System Monitor, 14*(1). Retrieved from http://www.nodc.noaa.gov/media/pdf/esm/ESM_SEP2003vol14no1.pdf.

Crosas, M. (2011). The dataverse network: An open-source application for sharing, discovering and preserving data. *D-Lib Magazine, 17*(1/2). Retrieved from http://www.dlib.org doi:10.1045/january2011-crosas.

De Roure, D., Goble, C., & Stevens, R. (2009). The design and realization of the myExperiment virtual research environment for social sharing of workflows. *Future Generation Computer Systems, 25*, 561–567. doi:10.1016/j.future.2008.06.010.

Diebold, F. X. (2003). Big data dynamic factor models for macroeconomic measurement and forecasting: A discussion of the papers by Reichlin and Watson. In M. Dewatripont, L. P. Hansen, & S. Turnovsky (Eds.), *Advances in Economics and Econometrics: Theory and applications*. Cambridge, UK: Cambridge Press. doi:10.1017/CBO9780511610264.005.

Dryad Development Team. (2010). *Dryad metadata application profile, version 3.0*. Retrieved from http://wiki.datadryad.org/wg/dryad/images/8/8b/Dryad3.0.pdf

Dryad. (n.d.). *Dryad digital repository*. Retrieved from http://datadryad.org/

Fienberg, S. E. (1994). Sharing statistical data in the biomedical and health sciences: Ethical, institutional, legal, and professional dimensions. *Annual Review of Public Health, 15*, 1–18. doi:10.1146/annurev.pu.15.050194.000245 PMID:8054076.

Foster, I., Kesselman, C., & Tuecke, S. (2001). The anatomy of the gird: Enabling scalable virtual organizations. *International Journal of High Performance Computing Applications, 15*(3), 200–222. doi:10.1177/109434200101500302.

Gray, J. (2009). Jim Gray on eScience: A transformed scientific method. In T. Hey, S. Tansley, & K. Tolle (Eds.), *The fourth paradigm: Data-intensive scientific discovery*. Redmond, WA: Microsoft Research.

Green, A. G., & Gutmann, M, P. (2007). Building partnerships among social science researchers, institution-based repositories and domain specific data archives. *OCLC Systems & Services, 23*(1), 35–53. doi:10.1108/10650750710720757.

Greenberg, J. (2009). Theoretical considerations of lifecycle modeling: An analysis of the dryad repository demonstrating automatic metadata propagation, inheritance, and value system adoption. *Cataloging & Classification Quarterly, 47*(3-4), 380–402. doi:10.1080/01639370902737547.

Greenberg, J., White, H., Carrier, S., & Scherle, R. (2009). A metadata best practice for a scientific data repository. *Journal of Library Metadata, 9*(3/4), 194–212. doi:10.1080/19386380903405090.

Griffiths, A. (2009). The publication of research data: Researcher attitudes and behaviors. *International Journal of Digital Curation, 4*(1), 46–56. doi:10.2218/ijdc.v4i1.77.

Gutmann, M., Schürer, K., Donakowski, D., & Beedham, H. (2004). The selection, appraisal, and retention of digital social science data. *Data Science Journal, 3*, 209–221. doi:10.2481/dsj.3.209.

Heim, K. M. (1982). Introduction. *Library Trends, 30*(3), 321–325.

Howe, D., Costanzo, M., Fey, P., Gojobori, T., Hannick, L., & Hide, W. et al. (2008). Big data: The future of biocuration. *Nature, 455*(7209), 47–50. doi:10.1038/455047a PMID:18769432.

ICPSR. (2012). *Guide to social science data preparation and archiving: Best practice throughout the data life cycle* (5th ed.). Retrieved from http://www.icpsr.umich.edu/files/ICPSR/access/dataprep.pdf

ICPSR. (n.d.). Retrieved from https://www.icpsr.umich.edu

Johnson, A., & Eschenfelder, K. (2011). *Managing access to and use of data collections: A preliminary report*. Retrieved from http://minds.wisconsin.edu/handle/1793/48205

King, G. (2011). Ensuring the data-rich future of the social science. *Science, 331*(6018), 719–721. doi:10.1126/science.1197872 PMID:21311013.

Lynch, C. (2008). How do your data grow? *Nature, 455*(7209), 28–29. doi:10.1038/455028a PMID:18769419.

Lynch, C. A. (2003). Institutional repositories: Essential infrastructure for scholarship in the digital age. *ARL: A Bimonthly Report, 226*. Retrieved from http://www.arl.org

Marcial, L., & Hemminger, B. (2010). Scientific data repositories on the web: An initial survey. *Journal of the American Society for Information Science and Technology, 61*(10), 2029–2048. doi:10.1002/asi.21339.

National Science and Technology Council. (2009). *Harnessing the power of digital data for science and society*. Retrieved from http://www.nitrd.gov/About/Harnessing_Power_Web.pdf

Neuroth, H., Lohmeier, F., & Smith, K. M. (2011). TextGrid – Virtual research environment for the humanities. *The International Journal of Digital Curation*, *2*(6), 222–231.

NODC. (n.d.). Retrieved from http://www.nodc.noaa.gov

Rockwell, R. C. (1994). An integrated network interface between the researcher and social science data resources: In search of a practical vision. *Social Science Computer Review*, *12*(2), 202–214. doi:10.1177/089443939401200205.

Scherle, R., Carrier, S., Greenberg, J., Lapp, H., Thompson, A., Vision, T., & White, H. (2008). Building support for a discipline-based data repository. In *Proceedings of the 2008 International Conference on Open Repositories*. Retrieved from http://pubs.or08.ecs.soton.ac.uk/35/1/submission_177.pdf

Space Telescope Science Institute. (2012). *HST publication statistics*. Retrieved from http://archive.stsci.edu/hst/bibliography/pubstat.html

Stein, L. D. (2008). Towards a cyberinfrastructure for the biological sciences: Progress, visions and challenges. *Nature Reviews. Genetics*, *9*, 677–688. doi:10.1038/nrg2414 PMID:18714290.

Taylor, I., Deelamn, E., Gannon, D., & Sheilds, M. (2006). *Workflows for e-science: Scientific workflows for grids*. London, UK: Springer-Verlag.

Thessen, A. E., & Patterson, D. J. (2011). Data issues in the life sciences. *Zookeys*, *150*, 15–51. doi:10.3897/zookeys.150.1766 PMID:22207805.

Vardigan, M., & Whiteman, C. (2007). ICPSR meets OAIS: Applying the OAIS reference model to the social science archive context. *Archival Science*, *7*(1), 73–87. doi:10.1007/s10502-006-9037-z.

Vision, T. J. (2010). Open data and the social contract of scientific publishing. *Bioscience*, *60*(5), 330. doi:10.1525/bio.2010.60.5.2.

Wang, H. (2010). Privacy-preserving data sharing in cloud computing. *Journal of Computer Science and Technology*, *25*(3), 401–414. doi:10.1007/s11390-010-9333-1.

ADDITIONAL READING

Erway, R. (2012). *Lasting impact: Sustainability of disciplinary repositories*. Dublin, OH: OCLC Research. Retrieved from http://www.oclc.org/research/publications/library/2012/2012-03r.html

Key Perspectives. (2010). *Data dimensions: Disciplinary differences in research data sharing, reuse, and long term viability: SCARP synthesis study*. Digital Curation Centre. Retrieved from http://www.dcc.ac.uk/sites/default/files/SCARP%20SYNTHESIS_FINAL.pdf

Kowlczyk, S., & Shanker, K. (2011). Data sharing in the sciences. *Annual Review of Information Science & Technology*, *45*, 247–294. doi:10.1002/aris.2011.1440450113.

KEY TERMS AND DEFINITIONS

Big Data: Data that requires massive computing power to process.

Cloud Computing: A model for enabling convenient, on-demand network access to a shared pool of configurable computing resources (e.g., networks, servers, storage, applications, and services) that can be rapidly provisioned and released with minimal management effort or service provider interaction.

Digital Object Identifier (DOI): A unique persistent identifier for a published digital object, such as an article or a study.

Grid Computing: A form of networking which, unlike conventional networks that focus on communication among devices, harnesses unused processing cycles of all computers in a network for solving problems too intensive for any standalone machine.

Metadata: Data about data, i.e., data about the content, quality, condition, and other characteristics of data.

Repository: A place where electronic data, databases, or digital files have been deposited, usually with the intention of enabling their access and dissemination over a network.

Virtual Research Environment (VRE): A platform dedicated to support collaboration whether in the management of a research activity, the discovery, analysis and curation of data or information, or in the communication and dissemination of research outputs.

ENDNOTES

[1] NSF data management plan requirements are found at http://www.nsf.gov/eng/general/dmp.jsp.

[2] NIH data sharing policy is found at http://grants.nih.gov/grants/policy/data_sharing/.

[3] http://www.nsf.gov/pubs/2007/nsf07601/nsf07601.htm

[4] http://www.dataone.org/

[5] http://www.whitehouse.gov/sites/default/files/microsites/ostp/big_data_press_release_final_2.pdf

[6] http://muse.jhu.edu/

[7] http://www.jstor.org/

[8] http://www.artstor.org/

[9] http://www.diggingintodata.org/

[10] http://archaeologydataservice.ac.uk/

[11] http://www.ademnes.de/

[12] http://www.ropercenter.uconn.edu/

[13] http://www.irss.unc.edu/odum/

[14] http://www.murray.harvard.edu/

[15] http://hmdc.harvard.edu/

[16] http://www.icpsr.umich.edu/

[17] http://ecoliwiki.net

[18] http://dnasubway.iplantcollaborative.org/

[19] http://www.ncbi.nlm.nih.gov/genbank/

[20] http://www.rcsb.org/pdb/home/home.do

[21] http://ndar.nih.gov/

[22] For example, U.S. National Virtual Observatory http://www.us-vo.org/

[23] http://arxiv.org/

[24] http://www.ncdc.noaa.gov/

[25] http://www.geongrid.org/

[26] http://datadryad.org

[27] Dryad members are found at http://www.datadryad.org/pages/members.

[28] Dryad journal archiving policy is found at http://www.datadryad.org/pages/jdap.

[29] http://www.icpsr.umich.edu/

[30] The ICPSR list of member institutions is found at http://www.icpsr.umich.edu/icpsrweb/membership/administration/institutions.

[31] http://www.nodc.noaa.gov/

[32] NOAA also operates two other data centers: National Climatic Data Center (NCDC) at http://www.ncdc.noaa.gov and National Geophysical Data Center (NGDC) at http://www.ngdc.noaa.gov/.

[33] http://www.dspace.org

[34] http://www.fedora-commons.org

Section 3
Specific Big Data

Chapter 9
Scalable Data Mining, Archiving, and Big Data Management for the Next Generation Astronomical Telescopes

Chris A. Mattmann
California Institute of Technology, USA

Andrew Hart
California Institute of Technology, USA

Luca Cinquini
California Institute of Technology, USA

Joseph Lazio
California Institute of Technology, USA

Shakeh Khudikyan
California Institute of Technology, USA

Dayton Jones
California Institute of Technology, USA

Robert Preston
California Institute of Technology, USA

Thomas Bennett
SKA South Africa Project, South Africa

Bryan Butler
National Radio Astronomy Observatory (NRAO), USA

David Harland
National Radio Astronomy Observatory (NRAO), USA

Brian Glendenning
National Radio Astronomy Observatory (NRAO), USA

Jeff Kern
National Radio Astronomy Observatory (NRAO), USA

James Robnett
National Radio Astronomy Observatory (NRAO), USA

DOI: 10.4018/978-1-4666-4699-5.ch009

ABSTRACT

Big data as a paradigm focuses on data volume, velocity, and on the number and complexity of various data formats and metadata, a set of information that describes other data types. This is nowhere better seen than in the development of the software to support next generation astronomical instruments including the MeerKAT/KAT-7 Square Kilometre Array (SKA) precursor in South Africa, in the Low Frequency Array (LOFAR) in Europe, in two instruments led in part by the U.S. National Radio Astronomy Observatory (NRAO) with its Expanded Very Large Array (EVLA) in Socorro, NM, and Atacama Large Millimeter Array (ALMA) in Chile, and in other instruments such as the Large Synoptic Survey Telescope (LSST) to be built in northern Chile. This chapter highlights the big data challenges in constructing data management systems for these astronomical instruments, specifically the challenge of integrating legacy science codes, handling data movement and triage, building flexible science data portals and user interfaces, allowing for flexible technology deployment scenarios, and in automatically and rapidly mitigating the difference in science data formats and metadata models. The authors discuss these challenges and then suggest open source solutions to them based on software from the Apache Software Foundation including Apache Object-Oriented Data Technology (OODT), Tika, and Solr. The authors have leveraged these solutions to effectively and expeditiously build many precursor and operational software systems to handle data from these astronomical instruments and to prepare for the coming data deluge from those not constructed yet. Their solutions are not specific to the astronomical domain and they are already applicable to a number of science domains including Earth, planetary, and biomedicine.

1. INTRODUCTION

The next generation of astronomical telescopes including MeerKAT/KAT-7 in South Africa (Jonas 2009), the Low Frequency Array (LOFAR) in Europe (De Vos, 2009), the Expanded Very Large Array (EVLA) in Socorro, New Mexico (Perley, 2011), the Atacama Large Millimeter Array (ALMA) in Chile (Wootten, 2003) and eventually over the next decade the cross-continental Square Kilometre Array (SKA) (Hall, 2004), and the Large Synoptic Survey Telescope (LSST) in northern Chile (Tyson, 2002) will generate unprecedented volumes of data, stretching from the near terabyte (TB) of data/day range for EVLA on the lower bounds to the 700 TB of data per second range for the SKA. These ground-based instruments will push the boundaries of *Big Data* (Lynch, 2008) (Mattmann, 2013) in several dimensions shown in Table 1. Table 1 represents the common challenges that users, educators, scientists, and other discipline users face when leveraging astronomical data, namely its size (volume, velocity); variety of

formats (complexity); the geographically distributed nature of these telescopes, and the limitations in bandwidth that prevents the wide dissemination of the information throughout the world's users who desire access to it. Big data is the buzzword of the day, used to define data sets so large and complex that traditional data management systems have difficulties handling them. There are three main challenges when dealing with big data: the amount of data collected (volume), the speed at which data must be analyzed (velocity), and the array of different data formats that is collected (complexity).

Engineering the data management, data mining, and archiving systems for these world-wide science assets is a complex (computer) scientific task in its own right, especially considering most of these telescopes are under construction from different funding agencies in the U.S. and abroad, each with different priorities and with different scientific end-user communities. Furthermore, each of the telescopes and their science foci have engendered highly complex data mining chal-

Table 1. Big data challenges and their mappings to upcoming or current astronomical instruments. Challenges are labeled as C1, C2 and C3.

Big Data Challenge		Description
C1	Volume	Across all science domains, the SKA will set the precedent in many ways when it sees first light in 2020 in terms of data volume. For example, it will generate exabytes (10^{18} bytes) in days, eclipsing the size of the current Internet in that same time span. LOFAR is already at the petabyte (10^{15} bytes) per day range. EVLA is generating hundreds of terabytes per experiment, and per month. ALMA will generate similar volumes.
C2	Velocity	Not only are these astronomical instruments generating large volumes, but also they are doing so in a rapid fashion. For example, the SKA will generate 700Tb/sec; LOFAR is already generating 138Tb/day, other instruments such as EVLA are generating on the order of terabytes per day. Some processing stages have larger data rates (e.g., data staging of raw instrument measurements), while others (data reduction) may have comparatively smaller rates.
C3	Complexity	Each of these ground-based instruments stores data in a number of different formats, and metadata models, for example, the EVLA and ALMA store data in a custom binary and metadata directory-based format called *Measurement Sets (MS)*, and also in the FITS format (Hanisch, 2001). Some of these communities, e.g., LOFAR and the SKA South Africa project have already made the transition to HDF-5 (Fortner, 1998) for their image cubes. The ability to automatically facilitate transformations between these different formats is also a characteristic of these projects as *Big Data*.

lenges, including data triage techniques for identification of important or interesting signal (e.g., fast radio transients, pulsars, etc.) amongst the fire hose of noise.

Our team at the Jet Propulsion Laboratory, California Institute of Technology (JPL) has been closely coordinating and working with the science data processing and operations teams from three of the world's largest astronomical telescopes. They are highlighted in bold text in the ensuing sentences. *The Square Kilometre Array (SKA) South Africa project and its MeerKAT/KAT-7 precursor array* have presented data management challenges focused on automatic file identification, curation and ingestion, along with data format heterogeneity (C3 from Table 1) – KAT-7 is amongst a newer set of telescopes that has standardized on the Hierarchical Data Format version 5 ("HDF-5") (Fortner, 1998), a popular Earth science data format, but different from the traditional astronomical Flexible Image Transport System (FITS) file format (Hanisch, 2001). The U.S. National Radio Astronomy Observatory (NRAO) is undergoing an upgrade and implementation refresh centered on providing more flexible science user-focused processing for the *Expanded*

Very Large Array (EVLA) and its science data and is preparing to coordinate data management and pipeline development (challenges C2 and C3 from Table 1) with the *Atacama Large Millimeter Array (ALMA) instrument*. These science-user pipelines will allow science users to dynamically tune parameters including calibration techniques and gain, and to interactively explore and search the EVLA and ALMA data using the Common Astronomical Software Applications (CASA) software package (McMullin, 2006), the next generation analysis software under development by the NRAO. So, the NRAO use case is more focused on workflow management, and dynamic user pipelines (challenges C2 and C3 from Table 1), than on file management (challenge C3 from Table 1) in comparison to SKA South Africa and the KAT-7 precursor. The aforementioned issues related to e.g., automatic file identification, curation, ingestion, data format heterogeneity, science user focused processing, and data management pipeline development are core research issues that our team is tackling, and that we report on in this paper.

We have worked with both SKA South Africa and NRAO through the Apache OODT project

(Mattmann, 2006) (Mattmann, 2009) the first software system developed by the National Aeronautics and Space Administration to be stewarded at the Apache Software Foundation (ASF). The ASF is the world's largest open source community, encompassing over 3000 developers world-wide, and with over 100 top level projects including some of the world's most pervasively deployed software such as the Apache HTTPD web server (53% of the World's Internet servers are estimated to run HTTPD), Apache Tomcat, and the Apache Hadoop (White, 2012) big data technology that powers much of the data warehouses of technology giants Amazon, EBay, Facebook, and Yahoo. Much of the current scientific research around Big Data involves a number of studies centered around extensions to existing Apache software that our team has principally contributed to, including Hadoop (Mattmann was one of the co-progenitors of Hadoop as a Nutch PMC member and committer), Tika (Mattmann progenitor), OODT, Solr/Lucene (Mattmann former PMC member of Lucene). We are investigating through this research effort the application of these technologies to astronomical big data problems, and thus are conducting ongoing research into the field of Big Data by applying these technologies to astronomical problems, culling feedback from the developers of these systems, and then using that feedback to improve these core products upstream at the Apache Software Foundation and in downstream derivative works.

Apache OODT is a system constructed over the last decade involving 100s of FTEs of investment across a number of funding agencies and projects (NIH/NCI, NASA, NSF, DoD/DARPA, Universities, etc.). The framework provides services for information integration and for complex science data processing and dissemination. It is these latter elements of Apache OODT that have caused its emergence as a disruptive *Big Data* technology within the Astronomy domain. File and metadata management, rapid science algorithm integration and workflow processing, and resource manage-

ment, coupled with automatic tools for remote file acquisition, and automatic file identification and ingestion have thrust Apache OODT forward as a next generation data management toolkit for these astronomical science instruments. In addition, we have also incorporated other software toolkits from Apache, including the Apache Tika toolkit for automatic file identification and text/metadata parsing and information retrieval, and the Apache Solr framework for faceted search, flexible queries, and access to data. We will describe the relationship between OODT, Tika and Solr briefly in Sections 2.11 and 2.12, and also later in Sections 4.3 and 4.5 respectively.

Besides the technology, the community model, governance mechanism and world-wide recognition of Apache have allowed the teams at JPL, SKA South Africa, and NRAO to independently collaborate on Apache technologies including OODT, Tika and Solr, to improve them, fix their bugs, and to deploy new code in each of our unique data management use cases, across time zones, continents and science use cases to the satisfaction of our customers and other constituents. Though organizational and managerial issues such as these are important in the Big Data domain, we restrict our focus in this chapter to technical issues related to Big Data.

This chapter will motivate the science and big data challenges for the three aforementioned astronomical telescopes described above in bold (Section 2), and will then describe in Section 3 the Apache *Big Data* technologies including Hadoop, OODT, Tika and Solr. Specific attention and focus will be given to the interoperability of Apache OODT with Apache Tika (for automatic, rapid file identification and processing), and Apache Solr (for data search). Section 4 will highlight five core issues that have emerged in the context of building out *Big Data* infrastructures for these astronomical instruments, they are: (1) integrating legacy scientific codes; (2) data movement; (3) data triage; (4) building flexible science data portals; and (5) automatic handling of data and metadata formats . Section 4 also will describe each of the deployments of Apache technologies for the MeerKAT/KAT-7 telescope and for the EVLA and ALMA telescopes, critically discussing the benefits of the solution, and the further improvements that our teams intend to undertake. The chapter rounds out with a set of concluding remarks (Section 5) to frame our future work.

2. SCIENCE AND BIG DATA CHALLENGES IN NEXT GENERATION ASTRONOMICAL INSTRUMENTS

Radio astronomy is the science of investigating space objects that emit radio waves, which are electromagnetic waves with a wavelength in the range of approximately 1 mm to 100 km (and corresponding frequencies between 300 GHz to 3 kHz). Examples of "exotic" space object that are strong radio-emitters include radio galaxies, quasars and pulsars. Radio astronomy started in the 1930s, when Karl Jensky from Bell Laboratories first detected radio waves originating from the center of our galaxy.

Radio waves from space are detected through very large antennas called "radio telescopes". Typically, a radio telescope is composed of a parabolic dish that focuses all incoming waves onto a single small central antenna located above its center, which then reflects the combined signal onto a high sensitivity detector. Because the resolution of a single telescope is proportional to the size of its dish, telescopes are built to be very large. Additionally, several radio telescopes can be pointed at the same source in the sky and their signals synchronized, to achieve a higher resolution that is proportional to the distance between antennas. Increasingly, these arrays of telescopes are built in very remote areas to minimize interference from terrestrial sources, and possibly on high mountains to minimize absorption and distortion of radio waves in the Earth atmosphere.

The next generation of radio telescope arrays that is currently under construction in various parts of the world is going to generate unprecedented amounts of data, both because of the increased number of instruments, the higher detection power of each antenna, and recent advances in fast signal pre-processing and storage. These data volumes will be among the largest in any scientific field, and comparable to the "big data" volumes currently managed by commercial companies such as Google, Facebook and Oracle. Additionally, data complexity is driving ever more resource-intensive processing requirements, and the collaboration between international partners is putting new emphasis on archiving and dissemination of data for global availability. In this section we highlight a few of the prominent next-generation radio astronomy instruments, describing their scientific goals and the *Big Data* challenges they face, and we enumerate a number of open source software technologies that have evolved in the last decade explicitly to facilitate interacting with massive data sets.

2.1. Expanded Very Large Array (EVLA)

The Expanded Very Large Array (EVLA) instrument consists of 27 antennas, each 25 meters in diameter, which features configurable baselines of between 35 meters and 36 kilometers. The EVLA is located in the high deserts of southern New Mexico, in the United States and provides high-resolution imaging in the long-millimeter to short-meter wavelengths. The instrument is operated by the U.S. National Radio Astronomy Observatory (NRAO) and provides an order of magnitude increase in sensitivity over the original Very Large Array (VLA) instrument.

EVLA is a prime example of how the data management needs of large modern radio astronomy experiments are growing exponentially. Early experiments on the EVLA instrument generated data at an average rate of approximately 12

Megabytes per second, or roughly 350 Gigabytes per normal 6-hour observation. When the EVLA begins full operations in 2013, its correlator data rate is expected to be roughly 1000 times that of standard correlator data rates from 2009, and the annual data output of the instrument will be on the order of Petabytes (challenges C1 and C2 from Table 1) (Butler, 2012).

2.2. Atacama Large Milimeter/ Sub-Milimeter Array (ALMA)

The Atacama Large Milimeter/sub-milimeter Array (ALMA) instrument is the result of an international partnership between the North America, Europe, East Asia, and Chile, and consists of 66 radio telescopes located in the desert region of northern Chile. The ALMA instrument's design, with a combination of 12- and 7-meter telescopes that can be dynamically re-positioned into different configurations, is expected to provide significantly greater sensitivity and higher resolution than existing alternatives. With measurement capabilities at wavelengths of between 0.3 and 9.6mm, it is expected that the ALMA instrument will provide new insights into planetary formation from protoplanetary disks, as well improve understanding of the process of star birth in the early universe.

As of early 2013, and several months before the instrument's expected inauguration, ALMA holds the distinction of being the largest astronomical project in existence. Estimates of the expected data volume from experiments utilizing this instrument have steadily increased over the years (Scott, 2002) (Luca, 2004) (Lacy, 2012). With the addition of the Alma Compact Array (ACA) whose correlator is capable of data rates in the range of 2 Gigabytes per second (challenge C2 from Table 1), the latest estimates put the upper end at between 700 Terabytes and 1 Petabyte annually (challenge C1 from Table 1), according to a detailed analysis by the North American Alma Regional Center (NAASC) – this includes both binary measurement set data and derived products

(challenge C3 from Table 1). The remote location of the instrument itself, the variety of scientific use cases it supports, and the expected interest in the generated data offer significant challenges for the storage and transfer of the volumes of data between the instrument and the global community of research scientists (Scott, 2002).

2.3. Low Frequency Array (LOFAR)

LOFAR, the Low Frequency Array telescope of ASTRON in the Netherlands, is a massive radio astronomy instrument consisting of 25,000 dipole antennas located in over forty stations across five countries in Northern Europe. By utilizing a BlueGene/P supercomputer, signals from thousands of antennas can be combined, forming a virtual observing dish with a diameter of almost 100 kilometers. The LOFAR instrument's low band antennas (LBA) observe at frequencies between 10 and 90 MHz, while its high-band antennas (HBA) record data at frequencies between 110 and 250 MHz. LOFAR is designed both to look back in time to observe events that took place very shortly after the Big Bang, and to assist with improving our understanding of local phenomena like the solar wind.

LOFAR's vast scale presents significant data processing challenges. Unlike traditional dish arrays, LOFAR can be thought of more as a distributed sensor network with thousands of antennas to integrate in real time, and correlator data rates exceeding 500 Gigabytes per second in some configurations. To support multiple processing pipelines and maintain a high level of configurability, the instrument makes use of software rather than customized hardware components to perform data correlation, and leverages a supercomputer to process the hundreds of gigabits per second of data generated by the antennas (challenge C2 from Table 1) (Romein, 2006).

In addition to the data volume and velocity challenges, LOFAR has also pushed the boundaries in terms of data formats – the project is exploring the use of HDF-5 (Anderson, 2010) to represent its data cubes, and is also collaborating with the SKA South Africa project, specifically the KAT-7 precursor discussed in Section 2.5 (challenge C3 from Table 1).

2.4. Square Kilometre Array (SKA)

The Square Kilometre Array (SKA) project represents the most ambitious radio astronomy project to date. A truly global initiative, the project is managed by the SKA Organisation, a multi-national cooperation headquartered at the Jodrell Bank Observatory near Manchester, UK and will feature observing stations to be spread across South Africa and Australia. The name is derived from the fact that the planned array, consisting of thousands of antennas, will represent a combined collecting area of one full square kilometer. Through the use of dishes and mid- and low-frequency aperture arrays, the SKA instrument will be able to observe within a range from 70 MHz to 10 GHz, and will be tasked with providing insight into phenomena such as the expansion of the early universe and the presence of complex molecules in space.

It is difficult to adequately communicate the planned scale of the SKA initiative. It will be the world's largest radio telescope by a large margin and the statistics regarding its construction and operation are in many cases several orders of magnitude beyond anything available today. For example, the length of optical fiber needed to connect the thousands of receptors that will make up the SKA would wrap around the Earth twice. Furthermore, the SKA is expected to generate over 900 Petabytes of data per day (challenges C1 and C2 from Table 1) at full bore. SKA pushes the limits in many dimensions, from data collection, to data storage and archiving, cataloging, processing and transfer/dissemination with a variety of data formats and models under consideration including FITS, to HDF-5, to custom binary (challenge C3 from Table 1). While the full SKA instrument

is expected to take over a decade to construct, a number of smaller precursor initiatives are underway that serve, in addition to being excellent instruments in their own right, as pathfinders for the larger SKA initiative. We detail three of these projects, the MeerKAT, KAT-7, and ASKAP radio telescopes, below.

2.5. MeerKAT

The MeerKAT Array is a radio telescope currently under construction in the Karoo region of South Africa. The planned 64-dish array, scheduled to be operational in 2016, is being developed in a cooperative effort between South African industry and education stakeholders with the support of the South African government. Ultimately, the MeerKAT dishes will make up one quarter of the first phase of the SKA's mid-frequency observing resources (challenge C1 from Table 1) scheduled to be built at the same location once MeerKAT is complete.

2.6. KAT-7

The Karoo Array Telescope (KAT-7) is a demonstration array of seven radio telescopes that was envisioned as a precursor to the full MeerKAT array. Construction of the 13.5-meter dishes, which hold the distinction of being the world's first fiberglass radio telescope dishes, was completed in 2010 and, as of the time of this writing, the instrument is in the process of being commissioned. In addition to providing scientific capabilities that are valuable in their own right, KAT-7 is proving helpful in identifying engineering challenges associated with both the construction of the MeerKAT dishes and with the data management challenges associated with collecting, archiving, and distributing observations (challenge C1 and C3 from Table 1) from this powerful instrument from its remote location in South Africa.

2.7. ASKAP

The Australian Square Kilometre Array Precursor (ASKAP) instrument is part of the Australia Telescope National Facility (ATNF) and is operated by Commonwealth Scientific and Industrial Research Organization (CSIRO), Australia's national science agency. ASKAP consists of 36 12-meter dishes that represent a total collecting area approaching 4,000 square meters. The array is being constructed at the future site of the Australian portion of the SKA telescope, the Murchison Radio-astronomy Observatory (MRO) in Western Australia. The cryogenically cooled ASKAP receivers operate at a temperature less than 50K and the array is capable of observing at frequencies between 700 MHz and 1.8 GHz. The instrument has been specially designed to carry out rapid surveys of the entire sky, and, at roughly 100 times more powerful than any predecessor survey telescope, is expected to provide significant assistance in improving our understanding of galaxy formation and the evolution of the early Universe (challenge C1 and C2 from Table 1).

2.8. Very Large Baseline Array (VLBA)

The Very Large Baseline Array (VLBA) instrument is a continent-scale interferometer operated by the U.S. National Radio Astronomy Observatory (NRAO). The instrument consists of ten identical antennas geographically distributed across the North American region from Hawaii to the Virgin Islands and derives its name from the nearly 8000 km baseline created by the separation of its component dishes.

The VLBA has made a sustained effort to maximize the considerable investment made in its construction by taking steps to improve its core capabilities and remain relevant to research scientists. These enhancements underscore the dramatic growth in radio astronomy data volumes that has occurred over the lifetime of the VLBA.

At its initial dedication in 1993, the instrument was capable of sustained recording rates of 128 Mb/s (challenge C1 from Table 1), with bursts up to 256 Mb/s. An upgrade to the instrument's sensitivity completed in 2011 increased that rate by a factor of 16, currently allowing for sustained recording rates of 4 Gb/s (challenge C1 from Table 1).

3. BIGDATA TECHNOLOGIES FROM THE APACHE SOFTWARE FOUNDATION

A wide variety of open source software technologies have evolved in recent years to address the challenges associated with indexing, manipulating, archiving, and distributing data at scale, and to deal with the challenges associated with C1, C2 and C3 from Table 1. In the following sections we touch upon several of these, describing each briefly and highlighting the potential role each may play in developing scalable data management systems for radio astronomy. Our focus in this section is restricted to technologies from the Apache Software Foundation, and on their applicability to astronomical challenges. For broader discussions of e.g., data warehousing, and product data management fields, we point the reader to (La Valle, 2011) (Berson, 1997) (Agrawal, 2011), and for and data system integration to literature cited on e.g., Apache OODT (Mattmann, 2006) (Mattmann, 2009).

3.1. Apache OODT

Apache Object Oriented Data Technology (OODT) is a suite of software components designed to facilitate the rapid construction of robust software systems for large-scale data management. Originally developed at the Jet Propulsion Laboratory (Mattmann, 2006) (Mattmann, 2009) with funding from the NASA Office of Space Science to reduce redundancy and overhead in the development of science data systems for NASA missions, OODT soon formed the basis for a software product line approach to developing mission software for data management. The success of early implementations of OODT led to broader recognition and an extension of the core set of components to support a greater range of data management and processing use cases. Despite this expansion, however, the architectural imperatives at the heart of OODT - that components be loosely coupled and leverage common protocols, that metadata be treated on equal footing with data itself, and an emphasis on sensible extension points and extensive configurability - remained intact and continue to define the software today. Apache OODT is the first NASA project to be selected by the open source Apache Software Foundation as a top level project, indicating its ability and sustainability as a software community; and its ability to make consistent software releases; have a diverse project community and to be released under the permissive Apache License, version 2 ("ALv2") license. Apache software projects represent a growing $1B industry* and significant market share in the Big Data community.

As the software matured, it became apparent that aspects of the framework were applicable to a wider set of situations involving the cataloging, processing, and dissemination of data and metadata. To facilitate development in this area, and in the interest of supporting the nascent community that was growing up around the framework, the decision was made to transition OODT to an open source project at the Apache Software Foundation (ASF). Since becoming a top-level project at the ASF, OODT has enjoyed significantly greater exposure, and has a robust developer community dedicated to the maintenance and enhancement of the framework.

OODT provides components that simplify the process of developing data archives and metadata catalogs, automating the acquisition and integration of information from disparate, heterogeneous sources, and the execution of processing pipelines

that leverage a common metadata model with full data provenance and accountability. OODT components can be leveraged individually to complement an existing data management infrastructure, or can be utilized in concert with each other to form the basis for a highly configurable system for a variety of high-volume, computationally intensive scenarios. We will describe in later sections the use of OODT on several fronts to handle the Data Volume (C1), Velocity (C2), and Complexity (C3) use cases from Table 1, and OODT's components as deployed in several astronomical telescopes including the VLBA, EVLA and ALMA and SKA South Africa projects.

3.2. Apache Hadoop

Apache Hadooop is an open source software framework that has gained prominence for its ability to support scalable distributed computing, and to do so reliably even when compute nodes are utilizing unreliable commodity hardware components. Hadoop is an open-source implementation of the MapReduce programming model first developed at Google (Dean, 2008) for achieving scalability through a two step process of distributing a small piece of a parallelizable computation to many nodes (the *map* step), and then aggregating the results from the nodes in some fashion to arrive at the final result (the *reduce* step).

The popularity of the MapReduce paradigm, and the accessibility of the Hadoop framework, has spawned an entire ecosystem of open-source software applications dedicated to simplifying, optimizing, and improving various aspects of working with extremely large datasets. Apache Hive (Thusoo, 2010) for instance, offers a petabyte-scale data warehouse capability built on top of Hadoop. Hive provides a higher level of abstraction, allowing users to issue queries in a familiar SQL-like language that are then transparently compiled into MapReduce jobs and executed on the underlying data store. Taken together, Hadoop and its offspring have significantly expanded the options and reduced the barriers to successfully working with massive data.

Hadoop and OODT are complementary technologies. As we will describe later in the Chapter (Section 5), Hadoop can provide a distributed file system with a single logical mount, simplifying the data movement and data staging requirements of the Apache OODT CAS-PGE algorithm wrapper.

3.3. Apache Tika

Apache Tika is an open source content detection and analysis toolkit that provides a framework for identifying and extracting information (including metadata and structured text) from a broad array of file types. Tika is highly extensible in that it provides the scaffolding for performing content detection and information extraction, but leaves the heavy lifting to a vast library of plug-ins that include parsers for many of the common file types. In this way, Tika can be extended to handle nearly any file type imaginable, provided a parser can be written that describes how to extract content and metadata from that format (Mattmann, 2011).

Tika, which was originally a sub-project of the Apache Lucene search engine project, is now a top-level project at the Apache Software Foundation, and is leveraged in a wide variety of scenarios to provide rapid understanding of heterogeneous catalogs of content and as a precursor tool to performing automated text mining, processing, and analysis.

Tika and OODT are highly complementary in nature. As will be explored later in Sections 4 and 5, OODT can call Tika-based metadata extractors, and leverage them for client side extraction (e.g., using Tika's support for FITS and HDF-5) and/or for metadata extraction and text extraction on the server side for analytic processing (e.g., using the information provided by Tika, such as number of basebands extracted from an input file, decide what processing to kick off in the OODT Workflow Manager). Furthermore, Tika provides

file classification facilities used by the OODT File Manager to delineate file types, and this functionality is also used by the OODT Crawler, and by the OODT Push Pull system in the same fashion for file-type or content-type based remote file acquisition and crawling.

3.4. Apache Solr

Apache Solr is an open source web application for metadata indexing and querying that is becoming increasing popular both in eScience and more general in eCommerce applications. Underneath, Solr is based on another Apache project, Lucene, which is a high performance engine optimized for text querying. Solr builds on top of Lucene by providing a RESTful web interface that allows users to index and query metadata through standard HTTP POST/GET requests, and by providing advanced capabilities such as faceted search (i.e. querying based on search categories), scoring and highlighting of results, query terms auto completion, and others.

Additionally, the Solr architecture offers options for scaling the system to tens and hundreds of millions of records, by supporting multiple cores, distributing queries to multiple shards, and replicating entire indexes. These solutions are particularly interesting for addressing the Big Data challenges emerging in radio astronomy, and will be discussed in detail later on in this chapter.

One of the main challenges is the use of Apache Solr as the front-end, user-facing search for Apache OODT systems. The Apache OODT File Manager provides a rudimentary search based on file catalog and pedigree/provenance and file staging queries. But its simplistic model is not nearly as flexible, or as adaptable as Solr's, which was designed for free-text, faceting, or forms-based search. So, we have developed technology that we are leveraging in these astronomical instrument projects, and that we will describe below, that easily dumps Apache OODT metadata information out of the File Management system, into Apache

Solr, and then makes that information available to flexible portal systems, which we will describe in Section 4.1.3.

4. MAIN FOCUS OF THE CHAPTER[1]

4.1. Focus Areas for Big Data

Our team at JPL has spent the better part of the past three years working closely with a number of astronomical instrument projects, both next generation and under construction (ALMA), and also those in early science operations (SKA South Africa, EVLA). In doing so, parts of the *Big Data* infrastructures that we have constructed have brought to our attention a number of pertinent focus areas that we believe require progress in to properly deal with the volume (C1), velocity (C2) and complexity (C3) challenges discussed in Table 1. We will discuss these focus areas in Sections 4.1.1 – 4.1.5 below, and also include solutions to these challenges that we have developed along the way.

4.1.1. Integrating Legacy Scientific Codes

Many astronomical instruments bring with them science codes written in a myriad of languages that are used to (1) correlate voltage data taken by multiple antennas; (2) perform various gain and filter operations on that data; (3) reduce the data, etc. Two often used software packages to perform these types of operations are the Astronomical Image Processing System (AIPS) (Wells, 1985) written primarily in C and in Fortran, and more recently the Common Astronomical Software Applications (CASA) software (McMullin, 2007), which is primarily written in Python (and thus often called "CASApy"). The U.S. National Radio Astronomy Observatory (NRAO) originally developed both of these packages.

Running these scientific codes independently of one another, one quickly realizes that they vary along a number of dimensions specifically:

1. **Input File Formats:** For example, AIPS takes in a particular file to specify various commands to apply to datasets, and to transform them in particular ways (e.g., switches for changing AMPLITUDE, commands to FLAG single pixels in baseband data, etc.). On the other hand, CASPy uses a Python oriented input file format, provides a different set of commands to do similar things, etc. These input must be generated in different ways, and typically from information collected by the *Big Data* system, e.g., by File Management, Catalogs, Workflow Management and Resource Management systems. Apache OODT collects much of this information through its substrate CAS services. Besides input file formats, some underlying algorithms require their inputs as environment variables, by command line switches, or even still by combinations of any of the above methods (challenge C3 from Table 1);

2. **Methods of Execution:** Running the algorithm may involve invocation of a particular command line program (such as the AIPS interpreter interactively) – it may involve execution of a program using iPython (in the case of CASA), etc. The setup and actual management of this execution is different depending upon the underlying algorithm (challenge C3 from Table 1);

3. **Production of Output Files and Metadata:** Each algorithm, depending on the selected processing steps may produce one or more output files and (optionally) metadata. In these cases, in astronomy we regularly deal with FITS files, and/or the emerging use of HDF-5 as an output file format, and each algorithm (AIPS, CASApy, etc.) may generate one or more of these files, depending on

what the input file generated. So we need ways of encapsulating both the file archiving and cataloging (for use in later downstream processing), and in metadata extraction. Apache OODT has facilities including the CAS-PGE wrapper that will manage the file cataloging and archiving, and the execution of a series of metadata extractors (possibly including Apache Tika) for this scenario (challenge C1, C2 and C3 from Table 1).

Over the last year with the NRAO, we have worked with the EVLA team to prototype integration of Apache OODT and CASA, as shown in Figure 1. To date, our team has provided the ability for CASApy-based algorithms (including continuum image generation and spectral line cube generation) to be executed in the Apache OODT context, which involved (1) generation of two different CASApy scripts with inputs fed into it from the OODT File Manager, and upstream ex-

Figure 1. Integration of Apache OODT with the CASApy algorithm suite at the U.S. National Radio Astronomy Observatory (NRAO). In the middle-left, data comes into the ELVA archive, Measurement Set (MS) data for the EVLA Summer School exercise and is cataloged by the OODT File Manager, and then made available for processing of two unique OODT workflows. In the upper one, we generate a spectral line cube using a particular CASApy script constructed by CAS-PGE; in the bottom one we construct a continuum image using a different CASApy script dynamically generated by CAS-PGE. Output "products" (sets of files), and metadata are generated by a combination of CASApy, and CAS-PGE calling OODT and Tika metadata extractors.

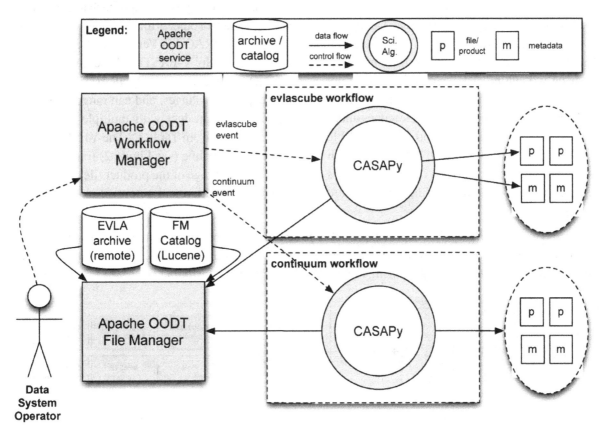

tracted metadata from raw Measurement Set (MS) data from the EVLA instrument; (2) execution of CASApy; and (3) automatic metadata extraction and generation using OODT and Apache Tika, helping to address many of the science algorithm integration challenges previously mentioned. In addition to NRAO, the science processing team for the MeerKAT/KAT-7 archive expects to heavily leverage CASApy in its data processing pipeline and is already actively collaborating with NRAO on Graphics Processing Unit (GPU) speed-ups in CASApy and on testing of parallel CASApy deployments in large cluster environments so this portion of our existing effort will ultimately be reusable in two *Big Data* projects for astronomical instruments in which we are actively participating.

In the next section, we will focus on the *Big Data* topic area concerned with data movement.

4.1.2. Data Movement

As discussed earlier, identification and archiving of interesting products from the overwhelming pool of collected data is going to become an increasingly daunting task, as collection rates are projected to increase several order of magnitudes with the new generation of radio telescopes under construction (challenges C1 and C2 from Table 1). This task will require a multi-faceted approach to the problem that combines a careful analysis of the full data processing pipeline, new software

architectures, and a product analysis strategy that leverages both human inspection and new data adapting, machine learning algorithms. In this section, we propose several techniques based on our successful experience with the V-FASTR project (Wayth, 2011), and other Big Data systems from other scientific domains such as the Planetary Data System (PDS) (Crichton, 2011) in planetary science and the Earth System Grid Federation (ESGF) (Cinquini, 2012) in climate science.

First of all, because data volumes are increasing faster than the capacity of the network to transmit them, careful attention must be paid to minimize data movement over non-local domains. This can be accomplished by both sub-selecting the amount of data for each product that needs to be moved, and by adopting a distributed system architecture where data is served and inspected from multiple locations, close to where the data are collected.

For example, the V-FASTR project employs a commensal (i.e. passive) approach to analyzing data collected for other primary scientific purposes by the U.S. NRAO-led Very Large Baseline Array (VLBA). In V-FASTR, the complete data products stored on disk at NRAO include the telescope raw voltages, and can range from 1 to 100GB for a product with multiple detections (challenge C1 from Table 1). The VFASTR data processing pipeline (see Figure 2) transfers only a small percentage of the product files (detection images, calibration and output files – challenge

Figure 2. The VFASTR project transfer reduced data products from NRAO to JPL, where product metadata is extracted and events are reviewed and tagged by a team of scientists on a web portal. Data mining algorithms use human assigned to identify similar events across the available pool.

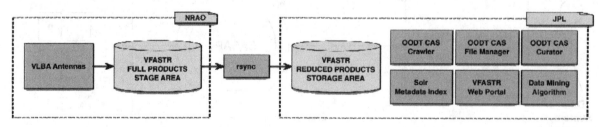

C3 from Table 1) to the data analysis system at JPL, where products are reviewed by a team of scientists and either disregarded, or tagged as interesting for further inspection. On average, each product transferred to JPL is about 50MB, thus three orders of magnitudes smaller than the full product stored at NRAO. After inspection, interesting products are archived in full at NRAO for further analysis.

At the same time, in systems where large amount of data are generated, collected or archived at multiple geographic locations, it makes sense to develop services that are able to search and analyze distributed repositories, as opposed to access only local storage. For example, ESGF is a federation of tens of data centers around the world that globally manages a distributed archive of climate datasets (model output and observations) consisting of several petabytes, or PB (see Figure 3 and challenge C1 from Table 1). The ESGF architecture employs federation-level ser-

vices that enable search, discovery and access of datasets across the whole federation, exposing the distributed data holdings to clients as if they were held in one single location. Similarly, the PDS is a system of several Discipline Nodes that manage planetary data of different kinds ("Imaging", "Small Bodies", "Rings", etc.). A small portion of the product metadata is harvested into a single location (the "Engineering Node"), where a high-level search service is exposed to clients. Individual search results contain links back to the Discipline Nodes, where the search parameters can be refined, or the data granules inspected and downloaded.

When data movement is unavoidable (for example, for reduced data products such as in the V-FASTR case, or for data replication as in ESGF), projects should establish data processing pipelines that combine high performance data transfer technologies with software components for automatic detection and processing of products. These

Figure 3. The Earth System Grid Federation architecture is based on web services that allow for searching and processing of data that are stored on geographically distributed archives, close to where the data were generated or collected.

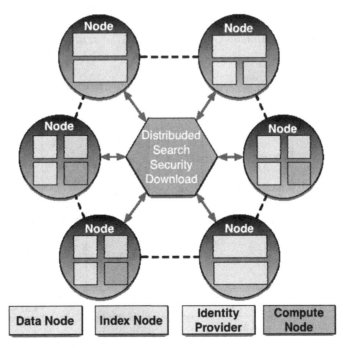

pipelines should be built from already existing, production ready software frameworks, as opposed to expensive and labor-intensive in-house solutions. For example, as already discussed, Apache OODT is a complete solution for scientific data management and processing that includes several components for data archiving, metadata extraction, cataloging and querying, and product retrieval. Several OODT components can be configured with swappable data transfer protocols to meet the specific project requirements for performance, security and easiness of deployment. The V-FASTR project uses an OODT-based pipeline (see again Figure 2) that includes the CAS Crawler (for automatic detection of new products at JPL), the CAS File Manager (for processing and archiving), and the CAS Curator (for metadata updates). Products are transferred from NRAO to JPL using *rsync*, a Unix utility that can be used to synchronize two remote directory trees with minimal human intervention. Rsync enables high performance data transfers because of its "delta encoding" algorithm (meaning that only file differences are transferred during successive executions) and optional compression.

Other data transfer technologies that offer significant performance advantages over traditional protocols such as FTP and *scp* include UDT (UDP-Based Data Transfer) (Gu, 2007) and Globus Online (Foster, 2011) (a hosted service based on the GridFTP protocol). All these new technologies combine different algorithms for data compression with parallel transfer streams and tunable buffer sizes. In general, projects should carefully evaluate the different tradeoffs that these technologies offer in terms of performance, configuration, installation and security.

The issue of data transfer and selecting the appropriate data movement technology has come to light in our recent work. Consider our team's prototype deployment of the Apache OODT Crawler framework and OODT File Manager for the KAT-7 SKA precursor, as demonstrated in the middle-right portions of Figure 4. Correlator data and correlator-specific sensor data is ingested by K7 Capture component and written into an HDF-5 file (Fortner, 1998) (Anderson, 2010) that is created in the data staging area (shown in the middle portion of Figure 4). After successfully writing the initial HDF-5 file, it

Figure 4. Prototype deployment of Apache OODT for the KAT-7 array

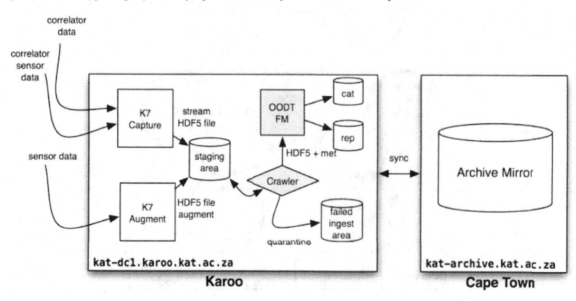

is augmented with relevant sensor data that is collected from the KAT sensor data store.

Once the augmentation process is complete, the HDF-5 file is made available to the OODT Crawler daemon. The OODT Crawler is a high-powered XML-RPC-based, a protocol that transports XML-encoded data via HTTP, component that uses Apache Tika (Mattmann, 2011) and its MIME, an internet readable standard for formatting non-text messages (e.g. images and video), detection capabilities to identify the HDF-5 file in the staging directory. MIME detection can be based on regular expressions; digital file signature bytes (also known as MIME "magic") and/or Byte Order Markers (BOM); file extension and "glob pattern"; and finally by XML schema and namespace checking if the file type is XML-based (see challenge C3 from Table 1).

Once the file is identified by Tika and by the OODT Crawler daemon, the crawler performs metadata extraction preconditions (e.g., has the file been ingested already?). If the preconditions are successfully evaluated, the crawler extracts metadata (that we describe further in Section 4.1.5) relevant for data search and retrieval and for data curation. Once metadata is available, the OODT

Crawler ingests the HDF-5 file into the OODT File Manager (middle-upper portion of Figure 4). This process involves recording the extracted metadata, file locations, and transfer status in a catalog (usually a DBMS, or search engine for example in our work we are using Apache Solr/Lucene), and transferring the original files from client to server using a pluggable data transfer component. All of the OODT components, and K7 Capture and Augment components are stored locally at the KAT-7 prototype in the Karoo region. A Cape Town based archive mirror (shown in the right sides of Figure 4) is located off site, in the SKA South Africa office in Pinelands.

In order to disseminate the MeerKAT, and KAT-7 data products from South Africa to JPL and then to U.S. scientists and students (as shown in the middle portion of Figure 5), we are evaluating several modern data movement technologies. In recent studies led by our team (Mattmann, 2007) (Tran, 2011) (Mattmann, 2010) (Mattmann, 2006) we have seen tremendous variation in the speed, capability, reliability and dependability of the technology. Broadly speaking, modern data movement technologies can be classified into two categories: (1) parallel TCP/IP-based, e.g.,

Figure 5. Building out the U.S. Based MeerKAT/KAT-7 archive. We augment our prototype deployment with a US node at JPL, and the OODT file manager web services (labeled as FM services) and the OODT curation component.

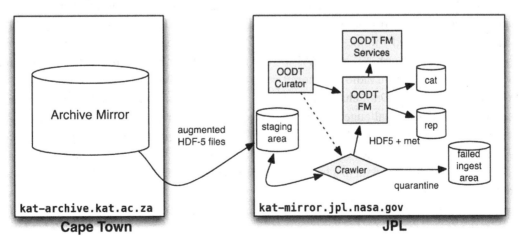

GridFTP, bbFTP, iRODS, Globus Connect; and (2) UDP-bursting-based, e.g., UDT, UFTP, Aspera, etc. Our research group has experience investigating these sets of technologies, and understanding the trade space for their optimal use. That space includes properties such as total volume (of data to deliver), number of delivery intervals, volume per interval, geographic distribution/network type (WAN/LAN), performance requirements, number of users, number of user types, number of data types and access policies.

Our current efforts with the SKA South Africa and KAT-7 project include the evaluation of data movement technologies to increase the efficiency and reliability of sending data from Cape Town to JPL.

Besides direct data push-based transfers from Cape Town to JPL, we are also exploring the use of the OODT Crawler extension point for data transfer, and plan to research pull-based transfers originating from JPL to Cape Town as well. In addition, data movement from the crawler to the file manager, and from the OODT File Manager to any data processing tasks that require already-ingested products is under investigation.

In the next section we will discuss the issue of Data Triage as a *Big Data* focus area.

4.1.3. Data Triage

The massive volumes of data expected over the next decade from the Square Kilometer Array (SKA) and Large Synoptic Survey Telescope (LSST), and before that the increased volumes from precursor projects such as MeerKAT and KAT-7 will almost by definition present radio astronomy with new unprecedented *Big Data* challenges as described in Table 1. These challenges will span the full lifecycle of standard data collection and analysis operations: from storing the raw antenna signals onto disk to moving the data to a location where they can be analyzed, from running CPU-expensive processing algorithms to insightful

inspection of millions of records along several defining characteristics. If the next generation of sky observing experiments is to yield new and valuable scientific results, a paradigm shift needs to occur in the way that radio and astronomical data is managed and analyzed.

In the past, a principal investigator would apply for observing time at a telescope, collect data on a transportable device, and then move the device to their own institution for an analysis that had no real time constraints. This approach is already inapplicable to sky survey projects such as EVLA and ALMA, where the sensors collect data at rates of ~GB/sec (challenge C2 from Table 1). At these rates, data must be pre-analyzed and reduced (i.e., *triaged*) even before it is written to disk, so to separate interesting records from background noise and interference. It is obviously absolutely critical that these pre-processing algorithms be able to correctly identify data with scientific value while rejecting the largest possible percentage of uninteresting events.

Once the data are stored onto disk, the expected volumes are still too large to be moved comfortably and inexpensively across large network distances. Rather, data will need to be processed and analyzed in place, preferably by flexible pipelines built out of reliable and high performance software components. The new trend in radio astronomy and other scientific fields is to "bring the computation to the data", and not vice versa. This paradigm requires data operations to be supported by a software architecture based on easily deployable services that can possibly operate on distributed data holdings by minimizing data transfers in between archives.

Over the past few years, some interesting new approaches have already emerged in the way that large astronomical datasets are processed and analyzed. The first revolutionary project of this kind was "SETI@Home" (dating back to 1999), a project that allowed ordinary people to download processing software on their personal computer to analyze a small portion of the data collected by the SETI radio telescopes, and upload back the results to a central location. Building on this idea, new "crowd-sourcing" projects are asking volunteers to either process radio-signals from objects of different kinds ("AstroPulse", the follow up to SETI@Home), or classify galaxy images according to a few pre-defined parameters ("GalaxyZoo" (Lintott, 2008)). Although these approaches are proving very valuable in providing a large pool of freely available computing resources, and in leveraging human intelligence, which still offers better insight than the most advanced computer programs, it is unlikely that these techniques alone will be able to successfully analyze the tens of millions of records expected from the SKA and LSST experiments. Rather, they will have to be combined with machine learning and data mining techniques which are able to apply the findings of human analysis to large catalogs of similar records.

A critical aspect of any data inspection and triaging procedure is represented by the ability to conduct efficient and powerful queries across the metadata stores. In the past decade, several new technologies have emerged (Lucene, Solr, NoSQL, MongoDB, etc.) that offer alternate solutions to traditional relational databases, and

potential advantages in terms of query capabilities, distributed deployments, and cost.

One of the most mature and popular such technology is Apache Solr, an open source, high performance web-enabled search engine based on Apache Lucene. Solr allows ingestion of generic metadata records (based on any custom-defined schema) and querying by free text or facets (i.e. search categories), including advanced features such as stemming, highlighting and scoring. Many of the aforementioned projects (e.g., KAT-7, V-FASTR, ESG and PDS) use Solr as the underlying search engine across *Big Data* metadata archives. What makes Solr particularly appealing for *Big Data* is the ability to scale to tens of millions of records by deploying it in different configuration architectures. First of all, each Solr installation can support multiple "cores", i.e. distinct indexes containing logically different metadata records (see Figure 6a) which can be queried separately for increased performance. This can be very useful to reduce the size of the index when the query patterns only target specific metadata fields. For example, V-FASTR records are logically divided into "job", "scan" and "event" metadata, which can be searched and retrieved separately. Similarly, most science data systems (such as ESGF and PDS)

Figure 6. Different architectures that can be used and combined to scale Apache Solr to be able to query indexes containing tens of millions of records: (a) Split metadata across multiple cores, (b) Distributing a single query across multiple shards, and (c) Routing separate queries to identical replicas

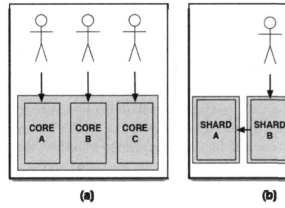 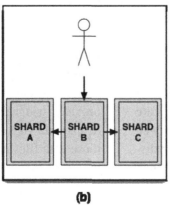 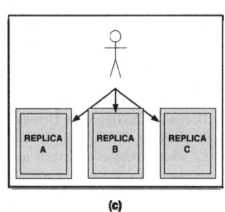

(a) (b) (c)

maintain a distinction between high-level collection metadata, and lower level granule information. Secondly, Solr allows a single query to span multiple "shards", i.e. indexes containing metadata records of the same type, but running on separate Solr engines, possibly installed on separate hardware (see Figure 6b). This architecture is useful to speed up performance of complex queries, which require considerable CPU, by spreading the query load across multiple servers. For example, ESGF uses sharding to execute multi-faceted metadata queries across all Index Nodes in the federation. Finally, Solr includes a replication algorithm, which allows both cores and shards to be automatically replicated across machines. Replication can be very useful when the system needs to support a high query rate, because distinct queries can be routed to different replicas of the same index (see Figure 6c). Replication can also be used to remove network latency in cases where queries would span geographically distributed shards.

Finally, the next generation of radio-astronomy data systems must employee event identification strategies that combine human insight with machine learning and data mining techniques. Already projects such as AstroPulse (von Korff, 2007) and Galaxy Zoo (Lintott, 2008) are using a social, collaborative approach to inspect and tag large archives of candidate events through the help of dedicated volunteers ("crowd-sourcing"). In the coming years, these archives will become too large to be completely analyzed by human scientists and amateurs. Yet, machine algorithms can be written that are seeded with events tagged by humans, and that can look for events with similar characteristics through the full available pool, possible on distributed metadata stores. Such a system is currently been developed and evaluated for the V-FASTR project. Here all events are made available for inspection through a web portal, where scientists login daily to either disregard the events, or tag them with pre-defined or custom labels. A self-training script is run periodically to query for all newly tagged candidates, retrieve their fundamental detection parameters, and discover similar events within the available pool. So far, preliminary results indicate that the V-FASTR algorithm is indeed capable of discovering reasonable candidates representing known cosmic signals such as pulsars, and flag local radio-frequency interferences.

We will explain the need for flexible portals and the *Big Data* topic area around it in the ensuing section.

4.1.4. Building Flexible Portals and Applications for Astronomy Data

Building flexible portals and applications for the EVLA, SKA South Africa and KAT-7, and most recently for the V-FASTR project has become more important than ever. Many of the astronomical instruments and their data systems that we have been involved in tend to evolve quickly, with no concrete requirements provided. Therefore, rapid prototyping, feedback cycles, and agile software development are vital to the success of new discoveries in astronomy. The constantly expanding astronomical data calls for efficient and ever evolving tools and services. Science teams desire visualization tools that help reduce the challenges in analyzing large volumes of data, and improve communication between teams.

Our work in this area has included the implementation of Apache OODT Balance, a generic, reusable web-based data system environment. Balance is a rapid prototyping framework of OODT services like File Manager or Workflow Manager for users, who desire to easily combine different concepts from those OODT *Big Data* services in unique ways. For example, Balance provides widgets that talk to the File Manager to list data files, and metadata, and then maps those data files and metadata to workflows that produced them, and display associated workflow information (data flow and control flow). Balance is a framework that provides a common codebase to quickly build PHP web applications utilizing Apache OODT.

There is a growing emphasis on web-based tools to enhance collaboration, but the large data volumes that astronomical projects possess directly conflict with web tool flexibilities. Challenges have emerged while presenting large amounts of information (challenges C1 and C2 from Table 1), for example the need to deal with transient-based data reduction as described previously for the V-FASTR project. Instead of pushing raw data to users, we first run intelligent software that assists in quickly identifying meaningful signals from radio frequency noise. This automated review method that combines a human-in-the-loop

model in which reviewers use our web portal was built using Apache OODT Balance as shown in Figure 8 in the right most portion of the diagram. Balance is the main driver in which users of the V-FASTR collaborative review portal interact with the backend OODT services, and data from the VLBA archive (shown in the upper left portion of Figure 8). Balance sits on top of the HTTPD web server as a suite of PHP modules, and extensions that include skins, CSS, and a request/rewrite and queuing framework for REST-ful URLs and service endpoints. Reviewers enter the Balance portal, and browse de-dispersion images as shown in Figure 7 and then classify those images as pulsar, saltandpepper, and other relevant tags that dictate the outcome for the relevant data, e.g., "triage the

Figure 7. Telescope signal processing, demonstrating time correlation of two fundamental components. De-dispersion (i.e. corrected for dispersion in interstellar medium) is shown in the right most series of graphs. Adaptive excision (some telescopes are disregarded based on self-learning algorithm) is shown in the left most portion.

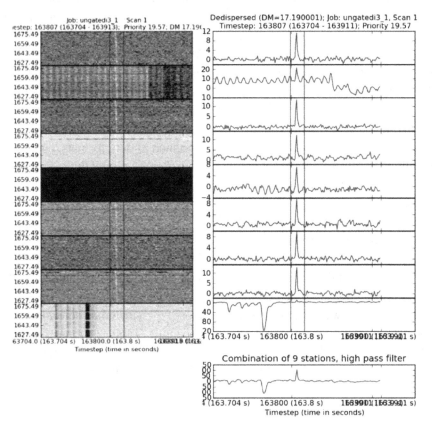

Figure 8. Data transfer process to help reduce data volume and make analysis more efficient. The dashed arrows show how reduced data is transferred from NRAO to JPL. Once end-users have completed a review and tagged events, the entries will be recorded by the Apache OODT Curator and transmitted over to Apache OODT File Manager – shown in the middle-left portion of figure with dashed arrows.

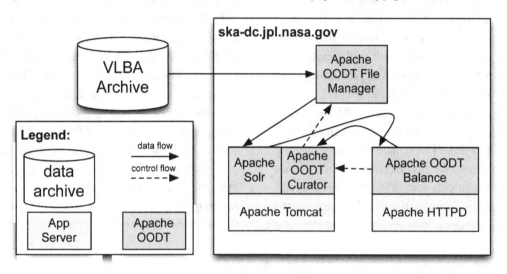

data for later exploration" or "ignore the data and do not save it". The tags are tied into the process of improving and training an automated system, and the tags can also be machine generated by the backend data tagging system. Thus in addition to human input, we have incorporated these automated results to assist the team in conducting their reviews.

One of the unique aspects of our Balance portal is the ease that it integrates with the flexible search capabilities of Apache Solr. We leverage an Apache OODT tool to dump metadata from the File Management service for V-FASTR into Apache Solr (shown in the middle portions of Figure 8), along with capabilities provided by the Apache OODT Curator component which provides web services for updating the File Manager catalog (and ultimately Solr on resync) based on the tagging and collaborative review that occurs using the V-FASTR portal.

Because Balance provides URL rewriting and REST-ful URLs, creating interoperability between

Balance, which runs on top of Apache HTTPD, and Apache Solr and Apache OODT Curator, which run on Apache Tomcat, is not difficult. Balance web pages reference URLs for Solr and Tomcat using front-end Javascript and AJAX, and as far as our users are concerned they are visiting a Balance portal page that presents them with the common tagging interface and URL.

In the next section, we will describe the importance of data formats, and our ability to deal with them as part of the perennial *Big Data* focus area, and challenge.

4.1.5. Data Formats

Though the data products and file types are still very much in development for KAT-7 and for MeerKAT, we are developing an understanding of those types, including core, and common metadata to capture. Table 2 demonstrates the thirteen core metadata elements and their definitions for the KAT-7 correlator-based products. These defini-

Table 2. Core Metadata to be curated for the KAT-7 correlator-based data products

Metadata Element	Definition
Observer	Observer for data capture.
Description	A short free-text explanation of the data being observed.
Start Time	The beginning date and time of the observation.
Duration	The length of the observation.
Antennas	The specific antennas used in the experiment.
Center Frequency	Center frequency of observation in Hz.
Correlator dump rate	Correlator dump rate in Hz.
Num freq. channels	Number of frequency channels the bandwidth is divided in to.
Targets	A list of targets that were observed.
Experiment ID	UUID fingerprint for identifying the specific experiment.
File Size	The size of the file(s) this metadata describes in bytes.
File Digest	An MD5 checksum for this (these) file(s).
File Type	The file type being ingested.

tions and elements are similar in scope to other projects that are considering the use of HDF-5 as a model and data format for their astronomical data products, for example the European Low Frequency Array (LOFAR) project, which is actively using HDF-5.

To date, three KAT-7 data types (or file type from Table 2) have been identified: KAT-7 correlator data (7-dish system); Fringe Finder (FF) correlator data (two dish system); and Holography data (single dish system). The KAT-7 and FF correlator data are persisted as HDF-5 format files on disk. The Holography data will include both a raw HDF-5 file, along with an accompanying directory of dataset and engineering information.

For MeerKAT, several data types are being considered, including VLBI data, pulsar timing, transient searching, continuum images, and spectral line cubes. We have experience curating and capturing these data types using Apache OODT, and not just on the KAT-7 environment, but also with respect to Extended Very Large Array (EVLA) data types. Drawing upon our own experience in the realm of Earth science (where the widespread use of HDF-5 originated) we expect that much of the metadata, indexing, and search code can be reused and leveraged in existing software including metadata extractors, curation policies, and metadata element definitions within Apache OODT, Apache Tika, and in Apache Solr. We have leveraged the parsing capabilities of Apache Tika, which includes support for HDF-5, and NetCDF scientific data file formats.

Support for the aforementioned file formats, and associated per-project, or per-discipline metadata models is an emerging field as many data system developers desire technology in the *Big Data* space such as Tika that automatically classifies these file representations, but also extracts metadata according to standard metadata models, and extracts data and text according to the file format specifications. We see this constantly as a challenge in *Big Data* and a focus area since astronomical instruments must deal with ever-growing amounts of these formats and models (challenge C3 from Table 1) yet most of the funding and interest in the area is related to Volume and Velocity (challenges C1 and C2 from Table 1).

5. FUTURE RESEARCH DIRECTIONS AND CONCLUSION

This chapter discussed the application and challenges within the *Big Data* domain for the next generation astronomical telescopes. We outlined a series of *Big Data* challenges in the areas of volume, velocity and complexity, and then mapped those challenges to several astronomical projects including projects led in part by the U.S. National Radio Astronomy Observatory (NRAO) and its Expanded Very Large Array (EVLA), and Atacama Large Milimeter/Sub-Milimeter Array (ALMA) projects, and with the SKA South Africa project and its precursor MeerKAT and the KAT-7 (first 7 dishes of MeerKAT) array.

We motivated a series of *Big Data* focus areas including rapid science algorithm integration, data movement, data triage, flexible science data portals, and automatic file identification and extraction. We described these focus areas, and then mapped them to the *Big Data* challenges, and described solutions to these focus areas using modern open source technologies from the Apache Software Foundation (ASF), including Apache OODT, Apache Tika, and Apache Solr.

The next generation astronomical telescope projects are already setting the bar in many of the *Big Data* dimensions such as volume and velocity, but also helping to drive the complexity challenges in dealing with proliferation of file formats, and standardization of metadata models (e.g., moving from FITS to HDF-5). We expect this trend to continue, but not to be unique to astronomy as more instruments become highly sensitive and data intensive across science domains.

Finally we believe our solutions and understanding of the *Big Data* problem space to be applicable across domains, as illustrated by our relation and description to projects in Earth Science (the ESGF), as well as planetary science (the PDS), and even including work in areas such as biomedicine and health care.

ACKNOWLEDGMENT

Parts of this research were carried out at the Jet Propulsion Laboratory, California Institute of Technology, under a contract with the National Aeronautics and Space Administration. © 2013. All rights reserved.

REFERENCES

Agrawal, D., Das, S., & El Abbadi, A. (2011). Big data and cloud computing: Current state and future opportunities. In *Proceedings of the 14th International Conference on Extending Database Technology* (pp. 530-533). ACM.

Berson, A., & Smith, S. J. (1997). *Data warehousing, data mining, and OLAP*. New York: McGraw-Hill, Inc..

Butler, B. J., & Chandler, C. J. (2012). Data management for the EVLA. In *Proceedings of SPIE Astronomical Telescopes+ Instrumentation* (pp. 84510A-84510A). International Society for Optics and Photonics.

Cinquini, L., Crichton, D., Mattmann, C., Harney, J., Shipman, G., Wang, F., & Schweitzer, R. (2012). The earth system grid federation: An open infrastructure for access to distributed geospatial data. In *Proceedings of E-Science* (e-Science), (pp. 1-10). IEEE.

Crichton, D. J., Mattmann, C. A., Hughes, J. S., Kelly, S. C., & Hart, A. F. (2011). A multidisciplinary, model-driven, distributed science data system architecture. In *Guide to e-Science* (pp. 117–143). London: Springer. doi:10.1007/978-0-85729-439-5_5.

de Vos, M., Gunst, A. W., & Nijboer, R. (2009). The LOFAR telescope: System architecture and signal processing. *Proceedings of the IEEE, 97*(8), 1431–1437. doi:10.1109/JPROC.2009.2020509.

Dean, J., & Ghemawat, S. (2008). MapReduce: Simplified data processing on large clusters. *Communications of the ACM, 51*(1), 107–113. doi:10.1145/1327452.1327492.

Fortner, B. (1998). HDF: The hierarchical data format. *Dr Dobb's J Software Tools Prof Program, 23*(5), 42.

Foster, I. (2011). Globus online: Accelerating and democratizing science through cloud-based services. *IEEE Internet Computing, 15*(3), 70–73. doi:10.1109/MIC.2011.64.

Gu, Y., & Grossman, R. L. (2007). UDT: UDP-based data transfer for high-speed wide area networks. *Computer Networks, 51*(7), 1777–1799. doi:10.1016/j.comnet.2006.11.009.

Hall, P. J. (2005). The square kilometre array: An international engineering perspective. In *The Square Kilometre Array: An Engineering Perspective* (pp. 5–16). Springer Netherlands. doi:10.1007/1-4020-3798-8_2.

Hanisch, R. J., Farris, A., Greisen, E. W., Pence, W. D., Schlesinger, B. M., Teuben, P. J., & Warnock, A. III. (2001). Definition of the flexible image transport system (FITS). *Astronomy & Astrophysics, 376*(1), 359–380. doi:10.1051/0004-6361:20010923.

Jonas, J. L. (2009). MeerKAT—The South African array with composite dishes and wide-band single pixel feeds. *Proceedings of the IEEE, 97*(8), 1522–1530. doi:10.1109/JPROC.2009.2020713.

Lacy, M., & Halstead, D. (n.d.). *NAASC memo 110: ALMA data rates and archiving at the NAASC.* Retrieved from https://science.nrao.edu/facilities/alma/naasc-memo-series/naasc-memos/110.naasc-data-rates

LaValle, S., Lesser, E., Shockley, R., Hopkins, M. S., & Kruschwitz, N. (2011). Big data, analytics and the path from insights to value. *MIT Sloan Management Review, 52*(2), 21–32.

Lintott, C. J., Schawinski, K., Slosar, A., Land, K., Bamford, S., Thomas, D., & Vandenberg, J. (2008). Galaxy zoo: Morphologies derived from visual inspection of galaxies from the Sloan digital sky survey. *Monthly Notices of the Royal Astronomical Society, 389*(3), 1179–1189. doi:10.1111/j.1365-2966.2008.13689.x.

Luca, R., Richer, J., Shepherd, D., Testi, L., Wright, M., & Wilson, C. (2004). *ALMA memo 501: Estimation of ALMA data rate.* National Radio Astronomy Observatory. Retrieved from https://science.nrao.edu/facilities/alma/aboutALMA/Technology/ALMA_Memo_Series/alma501/abs501

Lynch, C. (2008). Big data: How do your data grow? *Nature, 455*(7209), 28–29. doi:10.1038/455028a PMID:18769419.

Mattmann, C., & Zitting, J. (2011). *Tika in action.* Manning Publications Co..

Mattmann, C. A., Crichton, D. J., Hart, A. F., Kelly, S. C., & Hughes, J. S. (2010). Experiments with storage and preservation of NASA's planetary data via the cloud. *IT Professional, 12*(5), 28–35. doi:10.1109/MITP.2010.97.

Mattmann, C. A., Crichton, D. J., Medvidovic, N., & Hughes, S. (2006). A software architecture-based framework for highly distributed and data intensive scientific applications. In *Proceedings of the 28th International Conference on Software Engineering* (pp. 721-730). ACM.

Mattmann, C. A., Freeborn, D., Crichton, D., Foster, B., Hart, A., Woollard, D., & Miller, C. E. (2009). A reusable process control system framework for the orbiting carbon observatory and npp. sounder peate missions. In *Proceedings of Space Mission Challenges for Information Technology* (pp. 165–172). IEEE. doi:10.1109/SMC-IT.2009.27.

McMullin, J. P., Waters, B., Schiebel, D., Young, W., & Golap, K. (2007). CASA architecture and applications. In *Astronomical Data Analysis Software and Systems XVI* (Vol. 376, p. 127). ADASS.

Perley, R. A., Chandler, C. J., Butler, B. J., & Wrobel, J. M. (2011). The expanded very large array: A new telescope for new science. *The Astrophysical Journal Letters, 739*(1), L1. doi:10.1088/2041-8205/739/1/L1.

Romein, J. W., Broekema, P. C., van Meijeren, E., van der Schaaf, K., & Zwart, W. H. (2006). Astronomical real-time streaming signal processing on a blue gene/L supercomputer. In *Proceedings of the Eighteenth Annual ACM Symposium on Parallelism in Algorithms and Architectures* (pp. 59-66). ACM.

Scott, S., Myers, S., & Momose, M. (2002). *Data rates for the ALMA archive and control system.* ALMA Science Software Requirements Committee. Retrieved from http://www.iram.fr/~lucas/almassr/report-2/DataRates.pdf

Thusoo, A., Sarma, J. S., Jain, N., Shao, Z., Chakka, P., Zhang, N., & Murthy, R. (2010). Hive-a petabyte scale data warehouse using hadoop. In Proceedings of Data Engineering (ICDE), (pp. 996-1005). IEEE.

Tran, J. J., Cinquini, L., Mattmann, C. A., Zimdars, P. A., Cuddy, D. T., Leung, K. S., & Freeborn, D. (2011). Evaluating cloud computing in the NASA DESDynI ground data system. In *Proceedings of the 2nd International Workshop on Software Engineering for Cloud Computing* (pp. 36-42). ACM.

Tyson, J. A. (2002). Large synoptic survey telescope: overview. In *Astronomical Telescopes and Instrumentation* (pp. 10–20). International Society for Optics and Photonics.

Wayth, R. B., Brisken, W. F., Deller, A. T., Majid, W. A., Thompson, D. R., Tingay, S. J., & Wagstaff, K. L. (2011). V-FASTR: The VLBA fast radio transients experiment. *The Astrophysical Journal*, *735*(2), 97. doi:10.1088/0004-637X/735/2/97

Wells, D. C. (1985). Nrao'S astronomical image processing system (AIPS). In *Data Analysis in Astronomy* (pp. 195–209). New York: Springer US. doi:10.1007/978-1-4615-9433-8_18

White, T. (2012). *Hadoop: The definitive guide.* Sebastopol, CA: O'Reilly Media, Inc..

KEY TERMS AND DEFINITIONS

ALMA: Atacama Large Millimeter/submillimeter Array (ALMA) instrument is the result of an international partnership between the North America, Europe, East Asia, and Chile, and consists of 66 radio telescopes located in the desert region of northern Chile.

Apache Software Foundation: The Apache Software Foundation is a 501(c)3 non-profit charity that develops and delivers open source software to the public at no charge for the public good. Apache is home to the world's largest and most prolific software projects including the Apache HTTPD web server that powers over 50% of the Internet, and to a growing number of Big Data technologies as highlighted in this chapter.

Astronomy: The study of the Universe, our solar system, our planets, including early formulation questions, as well as new science questions like the Hydrogen Epoch of Reionization (HERA).

EVLA: The Expanded Very Large Array (EVLA), a network of 27 antennas, each 25 meters in diameter, which features configurable baselines of between 35 meters and 36 kilometers to provides high-resolution imaging in the long-millimeter to short-meter wavelengths.

Hadoop: The de facto *Big Data* technology, provides a computational platform, a distributed and replicated storage platform and an ecosystem of software projects that run on top of these kernel software added elastic and reliable data storage, complex workflow technologies, and column oriented information to the core of Hadoop.

OODT: Object Oriented Data Technology, the first NASA project to be stewarded at the Apache Software Foundation (ASF) is a flagship *Big Data* project that helps glue together existing file systems, repositories, catalogs, workflow systems, and science algorithms, allowing users to focus on developing and maintain execution flows, and allowing developers of data systems to easily glue together workhorse components to rapidly construct data systems.

SKA: The Square Kilometre Array, the next generation astronomical instrument whose 700 Tb/sec in many ways will drive the volume, velocity and complexity *Big Data* challenges for the next decade in computer science, hardware, physics, etc.

Solr: The de facto search engine technology that powers many *Big Data* projects. Easily allows free-text, faceted, and forms based search of information, providing schema, data type and a web service interface on top of Lucene. Solr is being used in an increasing number of astronomy, Earth and other science projects.

Tika: A content detection and analysis toolkit, providing metadata extractors, text extractors, and MIME type classification of all major file types both on the Internet, and increasingly in the science and *Big Data* domains.

V-FASTR: The VLBA fast radio transient experiment, and supporting infrastructure for the detection of radio transient events e.g., pulsars, etc.

ENDNOTES

[1] http://www.businessinsider.com/yahoo-hadoop-2011-4

Chapter 10
Efficient Metaheuristic Approaches for Exploration of Online Social Networks

Zorica Stanimirović
University of Belgrade, Serbia

Stefan Mišković
University of Belgrade, Serbia

ABSTRACT

This study presents a novel approach in analyzing big data from social networks based on optimization techniques for efficient exploration of information flow within a network. Three mathematical models are proposed, which use similar assumptions on a social network and different objective functions reflecting different search goals. Since social networks usually involve a large number of users, solving the proposed models to optimality is out of reach for exact methods due to memory or time limits. Therefore, three metaheuristic methods are designed to solve problems of large-scaled dimensions: a robust Evolutionary Algorithm and two hybrid methods that represent a combination of Evolutionary Algorithm with Local Search and Tabu Search methods, respectively. The results of computational experiments indicate that the proposed metaheuristic methods are efficient in detecting trends and linking behavior within a social network, which is important for providing a support to decision-making activities in a limited amount of time.

1. INTRODUCTION

The term *big data* refers to vast amounts of information that originates from variety of sources, such as transactional records, log files, social media, sensors, third parties, Web applications, etc. *Big data* should be distinguished from *large amount of data*, since big data is not just about giant data volumes. It's also about an extraordinary diversity of data types, delivered at various speeds and frequencies. There are two important issues concerning big data, which occupy attention of researchers in past several years.

DOI: 10.4018/978-1-4666-4699-5.ch010

- **Big Data Storage:** Big data is characteristically generated in large volumes per individual data set and in high frequency, meaning that information is collected at frequent time intervals. Additionally, big data is usually not nicely packaged in a spreadsheet or even a multidimensional database and often involves unstructured, qualitative information as well. Data warehouses are popular technologies for managing large volumes of data. However, they mostly rely on a relational format for storing data, which works fine for structured data, but not so successful for unstructured data. For example, relational databases are good for handling discrete packets of information, but they are less able to handle content such as video or sound files or emails, which do not necessarily conform to a rigid structure.

- **Big Data Analytics:** In contrast to traditional data, big data varies in terms of volume, frequency, variety and value. It is difficult to analyze big data with traditional data analytics tools that were not designed having these massive data sets in mind. With data volumes growing at an alarming rate, the importance of big data analytics has never been greater. For business enterprises, it is important to have a real time or near-real time information delivery that will allow analysts to quickly spot trends and avoid business problems. With the ability to comprehensively analyze large volumes of disparate and complex data, data analytics can help senior and board-level executives in better understanding and managing business opportunities.

In this study, we focus our attention to big data analytics techniques. The big data represents great challenges for analytics in general (Cuzzocrea et al., 2011). Developing adequate big data analysis techniques may help to improve decision making

process and minimize risks by unearthing valuable insights that would otherwise remain hidden. In some perspective, an automated decision making software can be provided by using big data analytics to automatically fine-tune inventories in response to real-time sales.

In the literature, clustering techniques are mainly used for big data analysis. Clustering is a process of organizing data into groups according to certain property or similarity. It is used for discovering natural groups or underlying structure of a given data set in many fields, for example in text mining (Dhillon et al., 2002), social network analysis (Sharma & Gupta, 2010), bioinformatics (Enright & Ouzounis, 2000), market research (Vakharia & Mahajan, 2000), etc. Parallel clustering technique showed to be an effective way to clustering big data (Jain et al., 1999). Recently, Chen et al. (2011) investigated parallel spectral clustering in distributed computing systems, and showed that a parallel clustering algorithm can effectively handle massive data problems.

Lin and Cohen (2010) introduced power iteration clustering (PIC), which replaces the eigendecomposition of the similarity matrix required by spectral clustering by a small number of matrix-vector multiplications, which leads to a great reduction in the computational complexity. They have demonstrated that the PIC algorithm outperformed several spectral clustering methods in terms of clustering accuracy. Yan at al. (2013) further expand PIC's data scalability by implementing a parallel power iteration clustering strategy (*p*-PIC). They propose a strategy to fit the data and its associated similarity matrix into memory, which makes the *p*-PIC algorithm appropriate for applications in big data analysis. Experimental results demonstrate that the parallel *p*-PIC implementation scales well, regarding the data size, and minimizes computation and communication costs.

Chiba and Sato-Ilic (2012) consider analysis of web survey data based on similarity of fuzzy clusters. The authors propose a method that captures the similarity of different clusters for the temporal evaluate data from web-based surveys, in order to capture similar groups of evaluators over time. The authors summarize obtained structure of evaluators by using a smaller number of groups, and capturing the changing situation of considered data over time. Presented simulation results and numerical examples show the capability of the proposed method when estimating the public opinion observed through web-based surveys.

In the literature, one can also find presentations of software for big data analytics. *Hadoop* is a MAD system (Cohen et al., 2009), which became popular for big data analytics. Handoop has two primary components: a *MapReduce* execution engine and a distributed file system (Hadoop MapReduce Tutorial, n.d.). Analytics with Hadoop consists of two phases: loading data as files into the distributed file system, and then running parallel MapReduce computations on the data. Herodotou et al. (2011) introduce *Starfish*, a self-tuning system for big data analytics, which is based on Hadoop software. Starfish is adapting to user needs and system workloads to provide good performance automatically, without any need for users to understand and manipulate the many tuning knobs in Hadoop.

In the paper by Demirkan and Delen (2012), the authors propose a conceptual framework for service-oriented support system (DSS in cloud), as an emerging alternative solution for big data storage and analysis. Data oriented cloud systems include storage and computing in a distributed and virtual environment. These solutions also come with many challenges, such as security, service level, data governance, etc. The authors in (Demirkan & Delen, 2012) offer the opportunity to bring analytical, computational, and conceptual modeling into the context of service science, service orientation, and cloud intelligence.

In this study, we focus our attention to analyzing the big data produced by social networks. We propose a new approach to social network analytics by developing mathematical models and optimiza-

tion techniques to analyze big data from different social site in an efficient manner. The remainder of this chapter is organized as follows. Section 2 provides an overview of methods of social network analytics. In Section 3, we propose mathematical models for efficient search of big data collected from social networks. Section 4 gives a detailed description of metaheuristic methods that are developed for solving the considered problems. In Section 5, we present and analyze the results of conducted computational experiments, while in section 6, we draw out conclusions and some possibilities for future work.

2. BIG DATA ANALYTIC IN SOCIAL NETWORKS

A social network is generally defined as a system with a set of social actors (users) and a collection of social relations (links) that specify how the users are connected (Wasserman & Faust, 1994; Adamic & Adar, 2005). The concept of network has been used in the literature for describing online friendships and connections between users of online social sites. The studies on Twitter (Huberman et al., 2009), blog sites (Highfield et al., 2011), Facebook and LinkedIn (Ryan & Xenos, 2011; Caers & Castelyns, 2011) use the model of network to represent the users of a social site, connections and interactions between them. Social networks may be open to everybody, or built around a particular group of people sharing the same interest or certain common characteristic (Boyd & Ellison, 2008; Malika & Malik, 2011).

Social networks have reached the point where they are a vital part of daily life. There are numerous social networking sites that are used daily to connect with friends, peers and colleagues, and their number is constantly growing. The most popular ones are: sites for instant messaging (IRC, AIM, MSN, Jabber, Skype), sharing sites (Flickr, Picassa, YouTube, Plaxo), blogs (Blogger, WordPress, LiveJournal), microblogs (Twitter,

Jaiku), social networks (MySpace, Facebook, Ning), collaboration networks (DBLP, Active Collab), etc. By using social network sites, we are generating an enormous amount of personal data that potentially provide a valuable material for demographics, examination of public opinion, and behavioral information for third party entities (Malika & Malik, 2011). Online social networks contain various types of information (text, pictures, video, audio, etc.), and the amount of data originating from social media sites is increasing daily. Enormous global popularity of online social network sites has initiated numerous studies and methods investigating different aspects of their use, such as analysis of social structures, social positions, role analysis, and many others (Rogers & Kincaid, 1981; Wasserman & Faust, 1994; Adamic & Adar, 2005; etc.).

However, most of the existing research is still focused on the inference of social processes in online social networks. Due to challenges associated with the analysis of social networks, there are not so many studies in the literature dedicated to the analysis of big data from social networks in real-life applications. Some examples that can be found in the literature arise from the areas of marketing (Domingos & Richardson, 2001), news spreading (Gruhl et al., 2004; Golder et al., 2007), network dynamics (Adar et al., 2004), and maximizing the spread of influence through a social network (Kempe et al., 2003).

Analyzing big data coming from social media can be used to spot trends that may benefit to sales, marketing, and finance teams' analysis. Companies are increasingly looking to extract values from mostly unstructured data to uncover the opportunities for the business that it contains. The big data collected from online social networks is a valuable source of information for understanding customers' behavior, purchasing trends and new sales opportunities. Communications and interactions between users (represented by nodes) can be used to identify a sub-network of the initial online social network, i.e. the group of

users sharing certain common interest. Segmenting populations is important for customizing actions of a company, so that products and services can be better tailored to meet actual customers' needs. For example, consumer goods and services companies can use big data analysis techniques to better target promotions and advertising.

This large amount and variety of data in a social network has gained the interest of business companies that want to advertise or sell products online. More and more advertisements and links to online stores are present on social media sites. Users exchanging information on these sites become evaluators of online products or stores (Couper & Miller, 2008; Manfreda et al., 2008). In order to use the information from such preference assessment of sites effectively, it is important to capture the hidden features of the information, categorize users based on their preferences, and identify captured features to categorized clusters (Schönemannand & Wang, 1979).

Beyond the commercial usage, big data analysis offers a number of other opportunities, such as improving threat detection capabilities of government agencies. The expanding use of the Internet and social networks caused a recent explosion of data, which can be mined to help in defending from growing threats coming from terrorists, hackers, and criminals in cyberspace. For example, web-organized revolutions and uprisings may be predicted by monitoring what people are searching for and how they are communicating online. By analyzing big data, governments will better understand various threats that they are facing, potential attacks and the actors who might perpetrate them.

One of the most important challenges related to the social network analysis is dealing with big data daily created within numerous social media sites. For example, both Facebook and Myspace produce more than a petabyte of social data per day ("MySpace Uses SQL Server Service Broker to Protect Integrity of 1 Petabyte of Data," n.d.; "Facebook Now Has 30 000 Servers," n.d). Only

Facebook's logging data excess 25 terabytes per-day ("Facebook Now Has 30 000 Servers," n.d). For such a large volume of data, it is almost impossible for humans to find useful information from the social networks data in limited amount of time. The processing of social network data in a timely manner remains a big challenge. Social network analysis tools have progressed little beyond data collection and presentation, according to (Malika & Malik, 2011).

Another issue of social network analysis is dealing with the unstructured, and in many cases, inconstant data. Non-text contents in the form of sound, music, pictures and video material, leave the basic data mining techniques ineffective. Another issue is the interpretation of the context, which is essentially semantic in nature. Given the level of slang and abbreviations on social networking sites, understanding recovered conversations, and captured content may be quite difficult. An intelligent interpretation and analysis of users' profiles contents and users' communication may contribute to crime prevention and detection, as well as greater public safety.

The expertise gained from various researches has been used in establishing frameworks for mining the social network data, which can be useful for various domains. However, they mainly involve traditional data mining techniques. Several software based on standard data mining techniques have been introduced for exploring online social networks: *Gephi* – an open source software for exploring and manipulating networks (Bastian et al., 2009), *SocSciBot* – a software designed to collect data on organizational hyperlink networks on the web ("SocSciBot: Web crawler and link analyser for the social sciences," n.d.), *IssueCrawler* – another software that enables the collection and analysis of hyperlink data, and is popular in the humanities and social sciences ("IssueCrawler," n.d.), etc.

As the big data changes rapidly and constantly, there is need for improved and more efficient methods. In this study, we use a novel approach to tackle big data from social media sites, in order to discover different interest groups or underlying structures of the considered social network. We use optimization methods to analyze online social networks by examining linking behaviors and information flow in social media sites. We develop three mathematical models using similar assumptions on the considered social network, but different objective functions that reflect different goals of the search. Since social networks usually involve large number of nodes (users), the proposed models can not be solved to optimality, due to memory or time limits. Therefore, it was necessary to develop optimization techniques tailored to the problems under consideration, which are capable to solve the cases of large-scale dimensions in acceptable amounts of running time.

2.1 Motivation and Related Work

Concepts and models from network-based studies in optimization theory and applications may be adapted for research into online networks, such as facility location models (ReVelle & Eiselt, 2005; Stanimirović et al., 2007; Matić et al., 2011), hub networks (Alumur & Kara, 2008; Kratica & Stanimirović, 2007; Stanimirović, 2010; Kratica et al., 2011), network flow models (Ahuja et al., 1993) and covering models (Schilling et al., 1993).

This study is inspired by the well-known vertex *p*-center problem, which has wide area of applications, including the design of telecommunication networks, service delivery networks, fast delivery systems, locating emergency facilities, etc (Drezner, 1995; Farahani & Hekmatfar, 2009). In the vertex *p*-center problem, the objective is to find the optimal locations of *p* nodes (facilities, switching centers), and to assign demand nodes to them, such that that the maximum distance of a demand node to its assigned center is minimized. Facilities may be located at the nodes of the network only, and each demand node may be assigned exactly to one located facility. It is assumed that established facilities have unlimited capacities. This problem was first formulated by Hakimi in (Hakimi, 1965), and later proved to be an NP-hard problem in (Kariv & Hakimi, 1979).

Various modifications of the p-center problem are presented in the literature up to now, see (Drezner, 1995) and (Farahani & Hekmatfar, 2009). We will mention only several variants that have a potential to be applied to the exploration of social networks. For example, the vertex p-center problem with demand-weighted distances was proposed in (Daskin, 1995). The assumptions and objective function are similar to the ones of the vertex p-center problem, except that demand nodes are weighted, and each node has certain demand to be satisfied. Özsoy and Pinar (2006) presented the capacitated vertex p-center problem, which involves limited service capacities of potential facilities (centers) to be located.

Burkand and Dollani were first to introduce positive or negative weights on nodes in the p-center problem (Burkand & Dollani, 2003). Friendly services to be located have positive weights, while the obnoxious services are assigned negative weights. The author consider the case $p = 1$ and try to minimize a linear combination of the maximum weighted distances of the located center to the vertices with positive weights and to the vertices with negative weights, respectively. The anti p-center problem was introduced for the first time in (Klein & Kincaid, 1994). All node weights in this case are negative, which means that we are dealing with location of p obnoxious centers (services). Therefore, instead of minimizing the maximum weighted distance between a demand node and its assigned center, in anti p-center problem, the objective is to maximize the minimum weighed distance between a demand node and its assigned center.

In paper (Puerto et al., 2008), the authors consider the p-center problem on tree graphs where customers are modeled as sub-trees. They address unweighted and weighted models, as well as distances with and without addends. They focus on the case that is relevant to most applications, where the number of facilities to be located - p is significantly smaller than the number of customers. Tamir in (Tamir, 2001) studies the p-facility k-centrum model, which generalizes and unifies the p-center and p-median problems (Kariv & Hakimi, 1979a). The objective of this unifying model is to minimize the sum of the k largest service distances. In this paper, Tamir also presents polynomial time algorithms for solving the p-facility k-centrum problem on path and tree graphs.

Hochbaum et al. in paper (Hochbaum et al., 1998) deal with a dynamically changing network, where the costs or distances between locations are different in each discrete time period. A typical example of this situation is an online social network. The authors consider the problem of locating a fixed number of permanent emergency services or control facilities, in order to minimize the maximum distance to any customer on the network across all time periods. This problem is named the k-network p-center problem in (Hochbaum et al., 1998). It is defined as the problem of locating p centers over k underlying networks corresponding to k periods of time.

Since social networks involve large number of user nodes exchanging large amounts of data of different types, it is impossible to implement a searching technique that will provide up to date information on the considered social network. Simple exhaustive search by using given keywords through all nodes and all network flow may take days or months, and when (and if) finally obtained, the information has already lost its timeliness, and becomes worthless. Therefore, it is important to provide simple, but efficient strategy on exploring the data flow in a social network, in order to provide the valuable information in short amount of time. We want to identify nodes that exchange information containing certain keywords, which further may indicate that identified nodes belong to the same interest group.

Suppose that we dispose the large amount of data that has been collected from an online social network within certain (usually small) amount of time Δt. As it was discussed above, in each second, the users of social networks exchange enormous quantity of data, containing files of various size and type (text, video and music clips, images, etc), which may be classified as big data. Therefore, we are dealing with the problem of searching and analysis of big data collected from an online social network within time period Δt, in order to provide new information on linking behaviors and information flow between user nodes in a timely manner.

Following the concept of the well-known vertex p-center problem, our idea is to choose exactly p nodes in a social network that will serve as control devices and to allocate each node to its nearest control device (in the sense of searching cost or searching time). These devices are searching through the data originating from user nodes looking for certain keywords. For example, a control device may be a computer station or server that is able to collect and process large amount of data in relatively short time. Each of the located control devices is servicing certain number of users with different amount of data flow consisting of various data types. The goal of the considered problem is to minimize the maximal load of an established control device, ensuring that the data search is provided within minimal amount of time. Another goal, which is considered in this study, is to ensure the load balance between the established p control devices, i.e. to minimize the difference between the maximal and minimal load of a control device. In this way, located control devices will be as equally loaded as possible, which will lead to minimizing the searching time. Similar idea of partial, but strategic exploration of a social network is used by Gupta et al. in (Gupta et al.,

2011), where the authors consider the problem of detecting the top k most significant shortest path distance changes between two snapshots of an evolving graph. The exploration of carefully chosen sub-network is used in cases when we are dealing with very large graphs and when the exploration of the whole graph would be extremely slow and impractical.

In this chapter, we propose three mathematical models, which start from the same input data derived from particular online social network. These models represent variants of the well-known vertex p-center problem and, to our knowledge, they have not been considered in the literature up to now. The proposed models have certain common assumptions with vertex p-center problem, which are reflected through several common constraints. The models will be presented and discussed in details in Section 3.

Since online social networks usually involve large number of users and large amount of data flow, exact methods fail to provide solution of the proposed models, due to memory or time limits. Therefore, we have developed three metaheuristic methods that are capable of solving large problem dimensions: a pure evolutionary algorithm (EA), a hybridization of the EA and a Local Search method (EA-LS) and a hybridization of the EA and a Tabu Search heuristic (EA-TS). The proposed models and metaheuristics may be used as a base of data analysis tools. They may further be hybridized with existing software for collecting data from the web, and professional databases that already contain necessary data.

The results of this study may be applied for exploration and analysis of big data originating from various social networks. The presented results may be used for the purposes of social behavior studies, market research, political marketing, but also in security purposes, such as discovering sexual harassment, child pornography, mobbing, bullying in the cyberspace, etc. Further applications may include efficient exploration of other large-scale networks, especially in telecommunication and transportation systems, computer and satellite networks, etc.

3. MATHEMATICAL MODELS

In all three models, we consider the same input data, obtained from an online social network. Let $I = \{1, 2, ..., m\}$ be the set of m user nodes in the network, and $J = \{1, 2, ..., n\}$ a set of n potential locations for establishing control devices. For each user node $i \in I$ and control device $j \in J$, we introduce $c_{ij} > 0$, which represents the costs of searching through the data originating from a user node i by a control device j. The searching costs c_{ij} may depend on the amount of time needed to explore one unit of data coming from i by device j, the distance between nodes i and j, the availability of user node i by control device j, the speed of internet connection between i and j, etc. In all three models, the goal is to choose exactly p locations from the given set J for installing control devices, and to assign users to one of more activated control devices in order to minimize the objective function value.

In the first model, denoted as Model 1, we choose exactly p locations for setting up control devices, and assign user nodes to located devices, such that the maximal load of an established control device is minimized. The load of an established control device is defined as the sum of searching costs through the data flow originating from all user nodes that are assigned to this control device. A single allocation scheme is assumed, which means that each user is assigned to exactly one, previously located control device. If a control device is located at a node, we will assume that this device is active. We put an additional condition on allocation of user nodes to control devices: it is required that each user node is assigned to an established control device that explores the out-

coming flow of a user node in the most efficient way, in respect to corresponding searching costs.

Model 1 involves decision binary variable $x_{ij} \in \{0, 1\}$, $i \in I$, $j \in J$, which takes the value of 1 if a user node i is assigned to a control device j and 0 otherwise. Variable $y_j \in \{0, 1\}$, $j \in J$, is equal to 1 if a control device j is active, and 0 otherwise. Non-negative variable z_{max} represents the maximum load of an active control device.

Using the notation mentioned above, Model 1 can be written as:

$$\min z_{max} \tag{1}$$

subject to:

$$\sum_{j \in J} y_j = p, \tag{2}$$

$$x_{ij} \leq y_j, \text{ for every } i \in I, j \in J, \tag{3}$$

$$\sum_{j \in J} x_{ij} = 1, \text{ for every } i \in I, \tag{4}$$

$$\sum_{k \in J} c_{ik} x_{ik} \leq c_{ij} + M(1 - y_j), \\ \text{for every } i \in I, j \in J, \tag{5}$$

$$\sum_{i \in I} c_{ij} x_{ij} \leq z_{max}, \text{ for every } j \in J, \tag{6}$$

$$y_j \in \{0, 1\}, \text{ for every } j \in J, \tag{7}$$

$$x_{ij} \in \{0, 1\}, \text{ for every } i \in I, j \in J, \tag{8}$$

$$z_{max} \geq 0. \tag{9}$$

By objective function (1) we minimize the maximal time needed to search the data coming from all user nodes assigned to an established control device. Constraint (2) indicates that exactly p control devices are established. Each user node is assigned to exactly one, previously established control device, which is ensured by constraints (3) and (4) respectively. By constraint (5) we require that each user node is assigned to an established control device with minimal exploration costs. In this constraint, we use a large positive constant $M > 0$ that satisfies $M > max\{c_{ij} \mid i \in I, j \in J\}$. Constraints (6) impose lower bounds on the value of objective variable z. Constraints (7) and (8) reflect the binary nature of decision variables y_j and x_{ij}, while (9) denotes that continuous variable z takes a non-negative value.

The second considered model, named Model 2 has a different objective function compared to Model 1. In Model 2, the goal is to locate exactly p control devices, and assign user nodes to them, in order to provide load balance among control devices. More precisely, the objective function in this model minimizes the difference between maximal and minimal load among established control devices. The load of an established control device is defined as in Model 1. Note that in Model 2, we impose the same set of constraints as in Model 1. Besides previously introduced decision variables x_{ij}, y_j and z_{max}, in Model 2 we also involve a non-negative variable z_{min}, representing the minimal load of an activated control device. By using this notation, Model 2 may be stated as:

$$\min(z_{max} - z_{min}) \qquad (10)$$

subject to conditions (2) – (9) and additional requirements

$$\sum_{i \in I} x_{ij}c_{ij} + K(1 - y_j) \geq z_{min}, \qquad (11)$$
for every $j \in J$,

$$z_{min} \geq 0. \qquad (12)$$

By objective function (10) we want to provide a load balance among established control devices, as much as possible. Upper bounds on the value of objective variable z_{min} are given by constraints (11), where $K > 0$ is a large positive constant satisfying

$$K > \max_{j \in J} \sum_{i \in I} x_{ij}c_{ij}.$$

By constraint (12), we ensure that decision variable z_{min} is continuous and takes non-negative values.

In the third model, referred as Model 3, we use different assumptions. Instead of allocating each user to exactly one control device (single allocation scheme), we allow that a user node may be assigned to more than one established control device. More precisely, a user node may split its outcoming data flow to several active control devices. Naturally, the sum of these flow parts must be equal to the outcoming flow of the considered user node. This strategy is known as multiple allocation scheme in the literature. The goal of the problem described by Model 3 is to choose exactly p locations for setting up the control devices and to split the outcoming flow of each user node to one of more to established devices. The objective is to minimize the maximal cost of exploring one fraction of flow coming from an user node by an established control device.

Differently from Models 1 and 2, in Model 3 decision binary variables x_{ij}, $i \in I$, $j \in J$ are continuous and take values between 0 and 1, due to assumed multiple allocation schemes. Variable x_{ij} represents the fraction of information flow originating from a user node i and explored by a control device j. Binary variable y_j, $j \in J$, has the same meaning as in Models 1 and 2. Non-negative variable z represents the maximal cost of exploring the part of data flow coming from an user node by an activated control device. Using this notation, Model 3 can be stated as:

$$\min z \qquad (13)$$

subject to (2) – (4) and additional conditions

$$c_{ij} x_{ij} \leq z, \text{ for every } i \in I, j \in J, \qquad (14)$$

$$0 \leq x_{ij} \leq 1, \text{ for every } i \in I, j \in J, \qquad (15)$$

$$z \geq 0. \qquad (16)$$

Objective (13) minimizes the maximal cost z of exploring the fraction of flow from an user node by a located control device. Lower bounds on decision variable z are set by constraint (14). Decision variables x_{ij} and z are continuous, which is provided by constraints (15) and (16) respectively.

3.1 Illustrative Example for Models 1–3

Let us consider a small network with $m = 10$ user nodes and $n = 6$ potential locations for establishing control devices, where $m = |I|$ and $n = |J|$. Suppose that exactly $p = 3$ control devices are to be established. Cost matrix $C = [c_{ij}]$, $i \in I, j \in J$, is of dimension 10×6, and we assume that each element c_{ij} is directly proportional to the size of the data transferred from i to j. Suppose that the values of c_{ij} are randomly chosen from two intervals: $c_{ij} \in [0, 500]$, in the case of lower costs (smaller data), and $c_{ij} \in [10\,000, 15\,000]$, in the case of higher costs (larger data).

In our example, we will consider three different cost matrices, denoted as C_1, C_2 and C_3, which reflect the nature of big data in the considered network.

Optimal solutions of the considered Models 1–3 for Cases 1–3 are presented in Table 1. The first two columns refer to the considered case and model, respectively. In the next column we present optimal choice of nodes for locating control devices, while the last column shows the corresponding objective function value.

Graphical illustration of optimal solutions of Models 1–3 are presented on Figures 1–3, respectively. On each figure we present three optimal solutions that correspond to considered Cases 1–3, respectively (from left to right on each figure). Note that user nodes are represented by white

Case 1. The matrix C_1 is chosen such that 2/3 of its elements $c_{ij}^{(1)}$, $i \in I$, $j \in J$, are randomly chosen from the interval [0, 500], while remaining 1/3 elements are random values from the interval [10 000, 15 000]. It means that 2/3 of smaller data and 1/3 of larger data are sent/received in the network. Matrix C_1, which is generated in this case, has the following form:

$$C_1 = \begin{bmatrix} 10\,163 & 14 & 73 & 489 & 14\,588 & 125 \\ 113 & 234 & 29 & 12\,365 & 12\,657 & 265 \\ 12\,050 & 12\,955 & 132 & 73 & 368 & 0 \\ 12\,114 & 12\,765 & 114 & 221 & 42 & 143 \\ 192 & 14\,245 & 122 & 13\,123 & 169 & 33 \\ 10\,533 & 12\,446 & 195 & 294 & 325 & 133 \\ 25 & 171 & 393 & 385 & 11\,333 & 10\,765 \\ 370 & 14\,645 & 116 & 292 & 14\,748 & 449 \\ 286 & 13\,273 & 245 & 14\,095 & 497 & 82 \\ 476 & 11\,263 & 187 & 124 & 14\,359 & 275 \end{bmatrix}$$

Case 2. In this case, matrix C_2 is randomly generated such that one half of $c_{ij}^{(2)}$, $i \in I$, $j \in J$, is randomly chosen from [0, 500], and the other half from [10 000, 15 000], i.e. smaller and larger data are equally present in the network. Matrix C_2 having this property is of the following form:

$$
C_2 = \begin{bmatrix}
45 & 480 & 11\,490 & 262 & 10\,547 & 12\,334 \\
261 & 13\,960 & 384 & 106 & 10\,252 & 12\,226 \\
11\,942 & 160 & 11\,929 & 11 & 14\,575 & 145 \\
13\,124 & 10\,496 & 303 & 340 & 394 & 14\,895 \\
13\,837 & 190 & 14\,982 & 13\,807 & 498 & 116 \\
13\,303 & 163 & 394 & 344 & 11\,273 & 13\,320 \\
191 & 13\,729 & 14\,365 & 16 & 461 & 14\,653 \\
10\,073 & 52 & 10\,031 & 398 & 13\,944 & 10 \\
12\,211 & 11\,570 & 282 & 98 & 14\,084 & 175 \\
12\,777 & 120 & 10\,623 & 14\,993 & 170 & 290
\end{bmatrix}
$$

Case 3. This case considers matrix C_3 with 1/3 elements $c_{ij}^{(3)}$, $i \in I$, $j \in J$, that are randomly chosen from the interval [0, 500], while 2/3 elements are random values from [10 000, 15 000]. This reflects a situation when the nodes send/receive 1/3 of smaller data and 1/3 of larger data. In this case, we generate matrix C_3 as follows:

$$
C_3 = \begin{bmatrix}
492 & 12592 & 12187 & 10022 & 191 & 12997 \\
11\,709 & 12\,863 & 11\,165 & 264 & 12\,988 & 270 \\
254 & 333 & 12\,616 & 12\,075 & 11\,743 & 13\,903 \\
14\,400 & 11\,056 & 79 & 355 & 13\,696 & 11\,565 \\
12\,592 & 151 & 273 & 11\,455 & 10\,264 & 11\,475 \\
13\,000 & 11\,312 & 482 & 11\,512 & 325 & 13\,286 \\
11\,164 & 12\,442 & 10\,705 & 108 & 417 & 14\,737 \\
10\,362 & 99 & 13\,976 & 11\,889 & 173 & 13\,872 \\
11\,724 & 10\,995 & 449 & 12\,936 & 12\,080 & 33 \\
13\,114 & 10\,535 & 283 & 10\,985 & 12\,421 & 413
\end{bmatrix}
$$

circles with a grey outline, while candidate nodes for establishing control devices are denoted by filled squares. Note that on Figures 1–2, which correspond to Models 1–2, the nodes that are chosen for establishing control devices are represented by black-filled squares, while nodes with no active control devices are presented as grey-filled squares. For Models 1 and 2, the lines connecting circles and black-filled squares represent allocations of user nodes to located control devices. Note that each user is assigned to exactly one control device, having in mind single allocation scheme imposed in Models 1–2. Since Model 3 involves multiple allocation scheme, the

Table 1. Optimal solutions of Models 1–3 through Cases 1–3

Case	Model	Control Devices	Objective
1	1	2, 4, 6	419
1	2	2, 4, 6	28
1	3	1, 3, 6	90.124
2	1	2, 3, 4	525
2	2	1, 2, 3	188
2	3	2, 4, 5	179.388
3	1	2, 3, 4	10 394
3	2	1, 4, 5	1 025
3	3	2, 3, 4	3 827.742

presentation of optimal solutions in Cases 1–3 of this model is different. In Figure 3, the nodes with established control devices are represented by squares filled with different colors (white, gray or black). The rectangles between user nodes and control devices show the percentage of exploration of data flow coming from an user node by each of the established control devices.

By analyzing optimal solutions in Cases 1–3 of Model 1, we notice that located control de-vices and corresponding allocations of user nodes are chosen such that as many nodes with smaller values of $c_{ij}^{(k)}$, $k = 1, 2, 3$, as possible are assigned to established control devices. In this way, the minimal value of the maximal load of an active control device will be achieved. Similar conclusions may be obtained in Cases 1–3 of Model 2, where the balance between minimal and maximal load among located control devices should be provided. The difference in maximal and minimal load of an established control device will generally be smaller, if the nodes with small values of $c_{ij}^{(k)}$, $k = 1, 2, 3$, are assigned to them. In the case that $c_{ij}^{(k)}$ have larger values, the difference between maximal and minimal load of an active control device will probably be larger. By considering Cases 1–3 of Model 3, we may observe that some user nodes almost equally distribute data/costs to the established control nodes, while other nodes have uneven data/cost distribution. The first case generally occurs for users i having the values of $c_{ij}^{(k)}$ from the same interval, and the second case otherwise.

Regarding objective function values in Cases 1–3, we may notice that the lowest objective values are obtained in Case 1 of Models 1-3. Higher ob-

Figure 1. Optimal solutions in Cases 1-3 of Model 1 (from left to right)

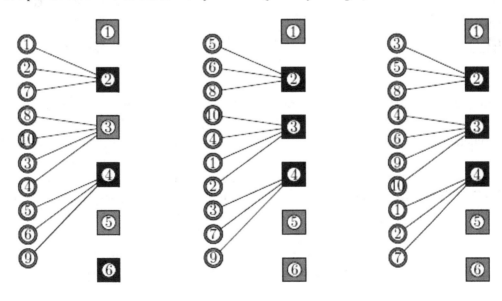

Figure 2. Optimal solutions in Cases 1-3 of Model 2 (from left to right)

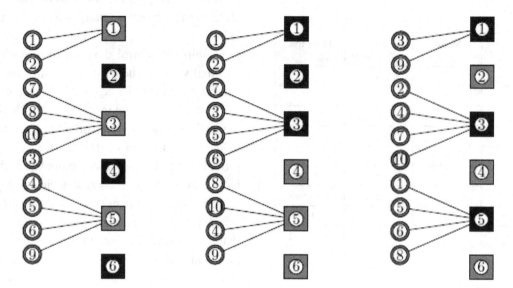

Figure 3. Optimal solutions in Cases 1-3 of Model 3 (from left to right)

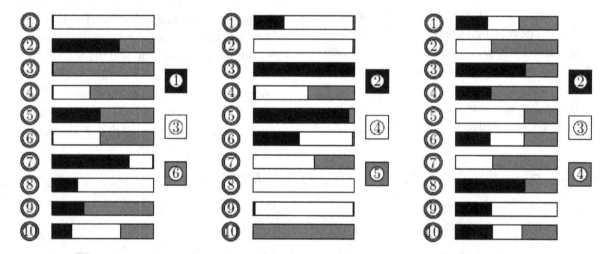

jective values are produced for Case 2, comparing to Case 1, while in Case 3 of all three models, the objective functions take the largest values.

4. PROPOSED METAHEURISTIC METHODS

Conducted computational experiments showed that all three considered models are very difficult to be solved to optimality. As it can be seen from Computational results section, the CPLEX 12.1 solver used in our tests was able to find optimal solutions for small size instances only. In order to solve instances of real-life dimensions, we have initially designed a pure evolutionary algorithm EA. The pure EA was further hybridized with Local Search method (LS) and Tabu Search heuristic (TS), resulting in two hybrid metaheuristics EA-LS and EA-TS, respectively. The proposed metaheurictics have several common elements when applied to solving the considered problems. However, each metaheuristic method had to be adapted to each particular problem, due to its specific properties. In this section, the proposed evolutionary method EA and hybrid metaheuristics EA-LS and EA-TS will be presented in details, and the differences in the proposed implementations when solving Models 1–3 will be highlighted.

We first designed a pure EA, an effective population-based metaheuristic, which is able to find good-quality solutions of the considered problems quickly. The elements of our EA implementation (encoding, objective function calculation, evolutionary operators, replacement, and diversification strategies) had to be adapted when solving each particular problem. The proposed EA was further combined with a Local Search strategy and a Tabu Search heuristic, resulting in two efficient hybrid metaheuristic methods EA-LS and EA-TS. The main motivation behind the hybridization of different algorithms is to exploit the complementary characteristics of different optimization strategies, in our case, population-based approach (EA), and single-solution improvement heuristics (LS or TS). At initialization part, the EA generally tries to capture a global picture of the search space, and later, during the search process, it successively focuses the search on more promising search regions. However, the EA may be not so effective, concerning the exploitation of the accumulated search experience, i.e., finding the best solutions in these high quality areas. Therefore, it was necessary to apply an efficient search strategy to give an impulse to the EA, and to help in preventing the EA convergence to a local optimum trap.

The basic scheme of the proposed metaheuristic approaches is presented in Algorithm 1. After generating initial population of solutions and their objective function calculation, evolutionary operators are iteratively applied until certain termination criterion is satisfied. A Local Search or a Tabu Search heuristic are further applied, in

Algorithm 1. The basic structure of the metaheuristic methods

```
Read Input()
Generate Initial Population()
while Termination() = false do
        Objective Function()
        Selection()
        Crossover()
        Mutation()
        Local Search()
        Tabu Search()
end while
Write Output()
```

order to improve the best solution obtained by the pure EA. Note that *Local Search()* and *Tabu Search()* steps are omitted in the pure EA method. In the EA-LS approach, we do not include *Tabu Search()*, while *Local Search()* is excluded from the EA-TS method.

4.1 Solution's Encoding and Objective Function Calculation

In the proposed algorithms for solving Models 1–3, we use binary encoding of solutions, which means that a potential solution of a problem is represented by a binary code (chromosome) of length n. Each bit in the chromosome corresponds to a potential location for a control device. If a bit on the j-th position in individual's code takes the value of 1, i.e., $chr[j] = 1$, it means that a control device is located at node j, which further implies the value of the corresponding binary variable $y_j = 1$. In case that $chr[j] = 0$, no control device is located at node j, and therefore, $y_j = 0$.

In the proposed metaheuristics, we apply efficient strategies for calculating objective function values. From the solution's code, we first obtain the locations of established devices (and consequently, the values of variables y_j), and then check whether the chromosome is correct or not.

A chromosome is labeled as *correct*, if there exists exactly p ones in the chromosome. Chromosomes that are not correct are excluded from the population by setting their fitness to infinity. In this way, a selection operator will prevent them to enter the new generation, and the feasibility of individuals in the population will be preserved through all generations.

Objective function calculation is usually the most time-consuming part of the EA. Since the objective function has to be calculated for each individual in each EA generation, this step may influence the total running time of the algorithm significantly. In order to provide the algorithm's efficiency, we have applied a greedy heuristic approach for calculating the objective function of an individual. Since the considered models involve different objectives, the proposed greedy approach has been adapted for each particular model, resulting in three slightly different greedy procedures for Models 1–3.

All three greedy procedures start from the set of installed control devices $S = \{j_1, ..., j_p\} \subseteq J$, obtained from an individual's chromosome. In the case of Models 1-2, for each user $i \in I$, we first try to find its best assignment to exactly one of the installed control devices $j_k \in S$, $k = 1, ..., p$ (single allocation scheme). In this way, we obtain the values of binary decision variables x_{ij}, $i \in I$, $j \in J$, that are used in Models 1-2. For each installed control device $j_k \in S$, $k = 1,...,p$, we calculate the sum of costs c_{ij_k} for searching the data coming from all users $i \in I$ assigned to a control device j_k, i.e., $x_{ij_k} = 1$. Let f_{max} and f_{min} denote the maximum and the minimum of these sums, respectively. More precisely,

$$f_{max} = \max_{j_k \in S} \sum_{i \in I, x_{ij_k}=1} c_{ij_k} \text{ and}$$

$$f_{min} = \min_{j_k \in S} \sum_{i \in I, x_{ij_k}=1} c_{ij_k}.$$

Obviously, the objective function value of Model 1 is equal to f_{max}, while objective function value of Model 2 is $f_{max} - f_{min}$. Pseudocodes of greedy procedures for calculating objective values for Model 1 and Model 2 are presented in Algorithm 2 and Algorithm 3, respectively. The array *sum* of length n stores the allocation costs for each control device. Matrix $C = [c_{ij}]$ of dimension $m \times n$ is the cost matrix introduced in the definition of the problem (see Section 3). Maximal and minimal loads of an established control device are stored in f_{max} and f_{min} respectively. In the array *best* of length m, we keep the index of established control device with the minimal search costs for each user node. A solution's code (chromosome) is stored in the binary array *chr* of length n. For each user, the proposed greedy procedures GP-M1 and GP-M2 find an established control device with minimal costs of search, and update the array *sum*. In addition, the values of f_{max} and f_{min} are updated in the GP-M2 procedure. Finally, the GP-M1 returns the objective value *obj*, which is equal to f_{min}, while the GP-M2 returns the objective value *obj*, calculated as $f_{max} - f_{min}$.

In order to calculate the objective function value of Model 3, for each user node $i \in I$, we first calculate

$$sum_i = \sum_{j_k \in S} 1 / c_{ij_k}.$$

We further use the following Proposition to show that objective value z is equal to $\max_{i \in I} (sum_i)^{-1}$.

Proposition 3.1: Let parameters m, n, p, and a cost matrix $C = [c_{ij}]_{1 \le i \le m, 1 \le j \le n}$ be defined as in Section 3. The objective function value z of Model 3 is equal to

$$\max_{1 \le i \le m} \left(\sum_{k=1}^{p} \frac{1}{c_{ij_k}} \right)^{-1},$$

Algorithm 2. Greedy procedure for calculating objective function value of Model 1 (GP-M1)

```
for all j∈{1, 2, ..., n} do
        sum[j] = 0
end for
for all i∈{1, 2, ..., m} do
        best[i] = 0
        for all j∈{1, 2, ..., n} do
                if chr[j] = 0 then
                        continue
                end if
                if best[i] = 0 then
                        best[i] = j
                else if c[i][j] < c[i][best[i]] then
                        best[i] = j
                end if
                sum[best[i]] = sum[best[i]] + c[i][best[i]]
        end for
end for
f_max = 0
for all j∈{1, 2, ..., n} do
        if chr[j] = 1 and sum[j] > f_max then
                f_max = sum[j]
        end if
end for
obj = f_max
return obj
```

where $j_1, j_2, ..., j_p$ are the indices of established control devices, and $j_k \in \{1, ..., n\}$, $1 \leq k \leq p$.

Proof: Let i, $1 \leq i \leq m$, be the index of an arbitrarily chosen user node. Let us denote by α_1, $\alpha_2, ..., \alpha_p$ the fractions of flow, originating from a user node i, which are searched by established control devices $j_1, j_2, ..., j_p$, respectively (see Figure 4). According to the problem definition (see Model 3), we have $\alpha_1 + \alpha_2 + ... + \alpha_p = 1$. Therefore, corresponding searching costs for the fractions of flow $\alpha_1, \alpha_2, ..., \alpha_p$ by using the assigned control devices $j_1, j_2, ..., j_p$, are equal to $\alpha_1 c_{ij_1}$, $\alpha_2 c_{ij_2}, ..., \alpha_p c_{ij_p}$, respectively.

Figure 4. Allocating the fractions of flow from a user node i to established control devices $j_1, ..., j_p$

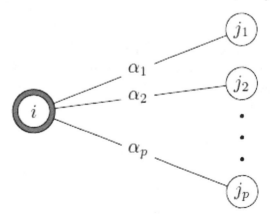

Algorithm 3. Greedy procedure for calculating objective function value of Model 2 (GP-M2)

```
for all j∈{1, 2, ..., n} do
        sum[j] = 0
end for
for all i∈{1, 2, ..., m} do
        best[i] = 0
        for all j∈{1, 2, ..., n} do
                if chr[j] = 0 then
                        continue
                end if
                if best[i] = 0 then
                        best[i] = j
                else if c[i][j] < c[i][best[i]] then
                        best[i] = j
                end if
                sum[best[i]] = sum[best[i]] + c[i][best[i]]
        end for
end for
f_max = 0
f_min = ∞
for all j∈{1, 2, ..., n} do
        if chr[j] = 1 and sum[j] > f_max then
                f_max = sum[j]
        end if
        if chr[j] = 1 and sum[j] < f_min then
                f_min = sum[j]
        end if
end for
obj = f_max - f_min
return obj
```

We will now prove that the best strategy is to divide the outcoming flow from a user node i to equal fractions, i.e., to choose $\alpha_1, \alpha_2, ..., \alpha_p$ such that

$$\alpha_1 c_{ij_1} = \alpha_2 c_{ij_2} = ... = \alpha_p c_{ij_p}.$$

We will prove this by contradiction. Suppose that there is a division of the outcoming flow from a user node i, defined by fractions $\beta_1, \beta_2, ..., \beta_p$,

such that $\beta_1 + \beta_2 + ... + \beta_p = 1$. Suppose that there exists t, $1 \le t \le p$, such that

$$\beta_t c_{ij_t} < \max\{\beta_k c_{ijk} \mid k = 1, 2, ..., p\}$$

holds. Let us choose parameters $\alpha_1, \alpha_2, ..., \alpha_p$ in the following way

$$\alpha_k = \frac{1}{c_{ij_k} \sum_{l=1}^{p} 1 / c_{ij_l}}, \quad 1 \le k \le p.$$

We further obtain

$$\sum_{k=1}^{p}\alpha_k = \alpha_1 + \alpha_2 + ... + \alpha_k$$

$$= \frac{1}{c_{ij_1}\sum_{l=1}^{p}1/c_{ij_l}} + \frac{1}{c_{ij_2}\sum_{l=1}^{p}1/c_{ij_l}}$$

$$+ ... + \frac{1}{c_{ij_p}\sum_{l=1}^{p}1/c_{ij_l}}$$

$$= \frac{1}{\sum_{l=1}^{p}1/c_{ij_l}}\left(\frac{1}{c_{ij_1}} + \frac{1}{c_{ij_2}} + ... + \frac{1}{c_{ij_p}}\right)$$

$$= \frac{1}{\sum_{l=1}^{p}1/c_{ij_l}}\sum_{l=1}^{p}1/c_{ij_l}$$

$$= 1.$$

Without any loss of generality, let us assume that we have

$$\beta_1 c_{ij_1} = \max_{1\le k\le p}\beta_k c_{ij_k}.$$

Then

$$\beta_1 c_{ij_1} \ge \beta_k c_{ij_k}$$

holds for $k = 1, 2, ..., p$, and, in particular, we have

$$\beta_1 c_{ij_1} \ge \beta_t c_{ij_t}.$$

Therefore, we conclude that inequalities

$$c_{ij_1}/c_{ij_k} \ge \beta_k/\beta_1$$

$k = 1, 2, ..., p$, and

$$c_{ij_1}/c_{ij_t} \ge \beta_t/\beta_1$$

hold. We further obtain

$$\beta_1 c_{ij_1}\left(\frac{1}{c_{ij_1}} + \frac{1}{c_{ij_2}} + ... + \frac{1}{c_{ij_p}}\right)$$

$$= \beta_1 + \beta_1\frac{c_{ij_1}}{c_{ij_2}} + \beta_1\frac{c_{ij_1}}{c_{ij_3}} + ... + \beta_1\frac{c_{ij_1}}{c_{ij_p}}$$

$$> \beta_1 + \beta_1\frac{\beta_2}{\beta_1} + \beta_1\frac{\beta_3}{\beta_1} + ... + \beta_1\frac{\beta_p}{\beta_1}$$

$$= \beta_1 + \beta_2 + \beta_3 + ... + \beta_p$$

$$= 1.$$

Finally, from the last inequality, we conclude

$$\beta_1 c_{ij_1} > \frac{1}{1/c_{ij_1} + 1/c_{ij_2} + ... + 1/c_{ij_p}}$$

$$= \alpha_1 c_{ij_1} = \alpha_1 c_{ij_2} = ... = \alpha_p c_{ij_p},$$

which is contradiction with our assumption. Therefore, the objective function value of Model 3 is equal to

$$z = (1/c_{ij_1} + 1/c_{ij_2} + ... + 1/c_{ij_p})^{-1}.$$

The pseudocode of the greedy procedure GP-M3 for calculating objective function value of Model 3 is presented in Algorithm 4. The Algorithm 4 uses the same notation as in Algorithms 2–3. The array *active* of length p stores the indices of established control devices. For each user node, the greedy procedure GP-M3 calculates

$$sum[i] = \sum_{j=1}^{p}\frac{1}{c[i][active[j]]}$$

and updates (if necessary) the value of f, which stores the maximum of $(sum[i])^{-1}$, $i = 1, ..., m$. Finally, the objective *obj* takes the value of f, and the value of *obj* is returned by the greedy procedure GP-M3.

Algorithm 4. Greedy procedure for calculating objective function value of Model 3 (GP-M3)

```
j = 0
for all i∈{1, 2, ..., m} do
        if chr[i] = 1 then
                j = j + 1
                active[j] = i
        end if
end for
f = 0
for all i∈{1, 2, ..., m} do
        sum[i] = 0
        for all j∈{1, 2, ..., p} do
                sum[i] = sum[i] + 1 / c[i][active[j]]
                if 1 / sum[i] > f then
                        f = 1 / sum[i]
                end if
        end for
end for
obj = f
return obj
```

4.2 Evolutionary Method EA

The proposed EA algorithm works over a population of individuals, where each individual corresponds to one potential solution to the problem. As it was explained in previous section, each individual in the population is encoded by a chromosome - binary string of length n. The initial population, numbering P individuals, is generated randomly by uniform distribution, which ensures good diversibility of the genetic material. In order to provide better quality of the genetic material, individuals in the initial population are created with exactly p ones in the genetic code. In generating an individual's code, we first choose a random value by uniform distribution $j_1 \in \{1, 2, ..., n\}$ and set the bit value at the position j_1 to 1. In the same way, we randomly choose $j_2 \in \{1, 2, ..., n\} \setminus \{j_1\}, j_3 \in \{1, 2, ..., n\} \setminus \{j_1, j_2\}, ..., j_p \in \{1, 2, ..., n\} \setminus \{j_1, ..., j_{p-1}\}$ by uniform distribution and set bit values at positions $j_2, ..., j_p$ to 1. Remaining $n - p$ bits in the individual's chromosome take the values of 0.

In the case of pure EA for solving Models 1–3, the population size is $P = 30$, while in the case of hybrid methods EA-LS and EA-TS, we use population with $P = 150$ individuals. Each individual in the population is evaluated by calculating objective function value (Section 3.1). After objective function calculation part, we iteratively apply evolutionary operators (selection, crossover and mutation) until certain stopping criteria are satisfied.

4.2.1 Evolutionary Operators

As a selection operator, we use the Fine Grained Tournament Selection (FGTS), which has different number of tournament participants involved. Instead of using an integer tournament size, as in the classic tournament selection, the FGTS operator depends on real parameter F representing the "desired tournament size" (Filipović, 2003; Kratica et al., 2005). In this HEA implementation, F takes the value of 5.4, while the size of each performed tournament is chosen from the set $\left\{\lfloor F \rfloor, \lceil F \rceil\right\}$.

Individuals that are tournament winners are further subjected to the modified crossover operator, which is implemented as follows. We randomly choose the pairs of parent-chromosomes that will exchange genetic material and produce two offspring-chromosomes. The exchange of genetic material of parent-chromosomes $chr1$ and $chr2$ is performed by repeating Steps 1–3 exactly $n/2$ times:

Step 1: Randomly choose a bit position $i \in \{1, 2, ..., n\}$, such that $chr1(i) = 1$ and $chr2(i) = 0$;
Step 2: Randomly choose a bit position $j \in \{1, 2, ..., n\}$, such that $chr1(j) = 0$ and $chr2(j) = 1$;
Step 3: Parent-chromosomes chr1 and chr2 exchange bits on the chosen positions i and j.

If no bit exchange occurs, offspring-chromosomes remain identical to their parents. Note that the proposed crossover operator preserves exactly p ones in the offspring's genetic codes and keeps the individuals correct.

The probability that a chosen pair of parent-chromosomes will exchange bits and create two offspring-chromosomes is set to constant $p_c = 0.85$ in the pure EA implementation. However, in the hybrid EA-LS and EA-TS methods, the crossover rate parameter is decreased and depends on the current number of iterations – k. The applied LS and TS procedures will lead the algorithm to promising regions of search space, and after certain number of iterations, we will have high-quality individuals in the population. As the algorithms progress, we do not need frequent intensive changes of individuals' codes. Therefore, we set crossover rates to

$$p_c = 0.85\sqrt[3]{k^2}$$

and

$$p_c = 0.85\sqrt[3]{k}$$

in the EA-LS and EA-TS approaches, respectively. These crossover rates, as well as and other EA, EA-LS and EA-TS parameters, are fine-tuned through the set of preliminary computation experiments, in order to determine parameter values that provide the best performance of the proposed algorithms.

Offspring individuals generated by modified crossover are further subjected to mutation operator. The role of mutation is to increase the diversity of individuals in the population and to help in restoring the lost subregions of the search space. In the hybrid EA-LS and EA-TS implementation, we have used simple mutation operator, which is performed by changing a randomly selected gene in the genetic code of the individual, with constant mutation rate $p_{mut} = 0.25/n$.

In the pure EA hybrid approach, which requires more effort to increase diversity of individuals, we have applied mutation operator with frozen bits (Stanimirović, 2008; Kratica & Stanimirović, 2006). If all individuals in the population have the same bit value on certain position, these bits are called *frozen*. If the number of frozen genes is l, the search space becomes 2^l times smaller, and the possibility of premature convergence rapidly increases. Applied selection and crossover operator can not change bit value of any frozen gene, while the basic mutation rate is often insufficiently small to restore the lost subregions of search space. Therefore, we increase the basic mutation rate of

$p_{mut} = 0.25/n$ for frozen bits only, by multiplying p_{mut} with factor 5.5, which results in the mutation rate of $p_{frozen} = 1.4/n$ for frozen bits.

Note that it may happen that mutated individuals are not correct, i.e. the number of ones in their chromosomes may be different from p. Infeasible mutated individuals are excluded from the population by setting their objective to infinity in the objective function calculation part.

4.2.2 Replacement and Diversification Strategies. Termination Criteria

As generation-replacement strategy, we used steady-state approach with elitist individuals (Michalewicz, 1996). During each generation, only the worst 1/3 of the population is replaced, while remaining 2/3 of the population are elite individuals that directly pass to the next generation. Elite individuals preserve highly fitted genes, and do not need recalculation of fitness function. The applied generation-replacement strategy provides additional time savings.

The objective values of duplicated individuals are set to infinity, and the selection operator disables them to enter the next generation. This strategy helps in preserving the diversity of genetic material, and in keeping the algorithm away from the local optimum trap.

Individuals with the same objective value, but different genetic codes may dominate in the population after certain number of iterations. If their codes are similar, this may cause a premature convergence of the GA. For that reason, we have limited the appearance of these individuals to some constant N_{rep}.

All three metaheuristic methods use a combination of two termination criteria. The algorithm stops if the maximal number of generations $- G_{max}$ is reached, or no improvement of the best individual is achieved through the maximal number of consecutive generations $- R_{max}$. We have used different combinations of termination criteria in applied heuristic methods when solving Models

1–3. These combinations are obtained experimentally, in order to provide the best performance of the proposed algorithms without prolonging running times unnecessarily. Parameters of stopping criteria for the EA, EA-LS, and EA-TS method are presented in Table 2.

4.3 Hybridization EA-LS

We have first combined the pure EA with a Local Search (LS) procedure, in order to achieve an improvement of the EA's solutions. The combination of the Evolutionary Algorithm and the Local Search results in the proposed hybrid EA-LS approach. Due to differences in the conditions of Models 1 – 3, the basic idea of LS strategy has to be adapted for each of the three considered models. The basic idea of the implemented Local Search is as follows. The LS procedure is applied on each individual in each EA generation, as long as some improvement of a solution is achieved. The LS strategy first tries to find a better set of active control devices by deactivating an established device, activating a non-established one, and determining the best assignments of user nodes to the new set of active control devices. Note that the objective function evaluations of newly created individuals within LS cycles is the most time-consuming part of the LS procedure, which may significantly affect the total running time of the EA-LS. Therefore, for each of the considered models, we apply efficient strategies for decreasing the computational complexity of

Table 2. Parameters of stopping criteria

Parameter	Model 1	Model 2	Model 3
G_{max} (EA)	50 000	20 000	50 000
G_{max} (EA-LS)	30 000	20 000	20 000
G_{max} (EA-TS)	20 000	20 000	20 000
R_{max} (EA)	2 000	1 000	5 000
R_{max} (EA-LS)	2 000	1 000	5 000
R_{max} (EA-TS)	2 000	1 000	2 000

Algorithm 5. LS algorithm for Model 1

```
termination = false
while termination = false do
        randomly choose l₀∈ [1, n] such that chr[l₀] = 1
        randomly choose l₁∈ [1, n] such that chr[l₁] = 0
        chr[l₀] = 0
        chr[l₁] = 1
        for all i∈{1, 2, ..., m} do
                if best[i] = l₀ then
                        for all j∈{1, 2, ..., n} do
                                if chr[j] = 0 then
                                        continue
                                end if
                                if best[i] = l₀ then
                                        best[i] = j
                                else if c[i][j] < c[i][best[i]] then
                                        best[i] = j
                                end if
                        end for
                else if c[i][l₁] < c[i][best[i]] then
                        best[i] = l1
                end if
        end for
        for all j∈{1, 2, ..., n} do
                sum[j] = 0
        end for
        for all i∈{1, 2, ..., m} do
                sum[best[i]] = sum[best[i]] + c[i][best[i]]
        end for
        f_max = 0
        for all j∈{1, 2, ..., n} do
                if chr[j] = 1 and sum[j] > f_max then
                        f_max = sum[j]
                end if
        end for
        if f_max < obj then
                obj = f_max
        else
                RestoreValues()
                termination = true
        end if
end while
```

calculating objective function values. Preliminary computational experiments showed that this strategy provides significant running time reductions.

Local Search procedure for solving Model 1, starts from a given chromosome *chr* of a solution, and its objective function *obj*, which is previously calculated. The procedure first randomly chooses indices l_0, $l_1 \in [1, n]$, $l_0 \neq l_1$, such that $chr[l_0] = 1$ (control device is located at node l_0), and $chr[l_1] = 0$ (control node is not located at l_1), and tries to exchange bit values of *chr* at l_0 and l_1, looking for an improvement. In other words, the LS tries to deactivate control device at position l_0, by setting $chr[l_0] = 0$, and to establish control node at l_1, by setting $chr[l_1] = 1$ at the same time.

Instead of recalculating objective function value, we go through the array of user nodes $i \in$ I and check if the newly established control node l_1 is more preferable for a user *j*, compared to the currently assigned control node. If the answer is positive, we assign *j* to l_1, and update objective function value. We also identify all users $j \in$ I previously assigned to a control node l_0 that is now closed. For each client *j* with such property, we try to find an established control device $k \in$ J, $chr[k] = 1$, which is the most suitable for *j*. We further assign client *j* to control device *k,* and update objective function value.

Finally, we calculate the objective function value f_{max} of the new solution with exchanged positions of control devices and re-assignments of user nodes. If the objective value f_{max} of a new solution is lower compared to the objective *obj* of the initial solution, the LS procedure for Model 1 returns new solution and its objective function value. Note that the implemented Local Search strategy is of *first-improvement* type, i.e., it will stop as soon as an improvement of the initial solution is obtained. The pseudocode of Local Search procedure applied to a single solution in the case of Model 1 is shown in Algorithm 5.

The Local Search algorithm implemented for Model 2 is similar to the LS procedure for Model 1, which is described above. After the bit ex-

change on positions $chr[l_0]$ and $chr[l_1]$, for each user node $i \in$ I we search for better allocation to one of the established control devices. The values of f_{min} and f_{max} are calculated for the new solution. If the new objective value $f_{max} - f_{min}$ is lower compared to the objective *obj* of the initial solution, the Local Search procedure stops and returns the new, improved solution, and the corresponding objective function value. Otherwise, all changes in locations of control nodes and allocations of user nodes are reset, and the Local Search tries to exchange another pair of bits on randomly chosen positions l_0 and l_1, such that $chr[l_0] = 1$ and $chr[l_1] = 0$ (see Algorithm 6).

The Algorithm 7 shows the concept of Local Search procedure for Model 3. The positions l_0 and l_1 for deactivating/activating control devices are randomly chosen from the interval [1, n]. After we obtain the new set of nodes with established control devices, we search for the possible reallocations of user nodes, which will provide better objective function value. As it can be seen from Algorithm 7, the Local Search procedure stops after the first improvement is found.

4.4 Hybridization EA-TS

The second hybrid method proposed in this study is based on a combination of the EA and a Tabu Search heuristic (EA-TS). The strength of the applied Tabu Search procedure is in its capability of quickly finding better solutions in the neighborhoods of the solution obtained by the pure EA. As in the case of Local Search, the Tabu Search heuristic is applied on every individual in every EA generation. In the implemented TS procedure, a *move* is defined as an exchange of an established control device with a non-established one. The re-assignments of user nodes to the new set of activated control devices are performed in an efficient manner to avoid unnecessary steps in evaluating a newly created individual. As in the case of Local Search, the Tabu Search algorithm is adapted to each of the considered models, re-

Algorithm 6. LS algorithm for Model 2

```
termination = false
while termination = false do
        randomly choose l₀ ∈ [1, n] such that chr[l₀] = 1
        randomly choose l₁ ∈ [1, n] such that chr[l₁] = 0
        chr[l₀] = 0
        chr[l₁] = 1
        for all i ∈ {1, 2, ..., m} do
                if best[i] = l₀ then
                        for all j ∈ {1, 2, ..., n} do
                                if chr[j] = 0 then
                                        continue
                                end if
                                if best[i] = l₀ then
                                        best[i] = j
                                else if c[i][j] < c[i][best[i]] then
                                        best[i] = j
                                end if
                        end for
                else if c[i][l₁] < c[i][best[i]] then
                        best[i] = l1
                end if
        end for
        for all j ∈ {1, 2, ..., n} do
                sum[j] = 0
        end for
        for all i ∈ {1, 2, ..., m} do
                sum[best[i]] = sum[best[i]] + c[i][best[i]]
        end for
        f_max = 0
        f_min = ∞
        for all j ∈ {1, 2, ..., n} do
                if chr[j] = 1 and sum[j] > f_max then
                        f_max = sum[j]
                end if
                if chr[j] = 1 and sum[j] < f_min then
                        f_min = sum[j]
                end if
        end for
        if f_max - f_min < obj then
                obj = f_max - f_min
        else
                RestoreValues()
                termination = true
        end if
end while
```

Algorithm 7. LS algorithm for Model 3

```
termination = false
while termination = false do
        randomly choose l₀ ∈ [1, n] such that chr[l₀] = 1
        randomly choose l₁ ∈ [1, n] such that chr[l₁] = 0
        chr[l₀] = 0
        chr[l₁] = 1
        f = 0
        for all i ∈ {1, 2, ..., m} do
                sum[i] = sum[i] + 1 / c[i][l₁] - 1 / c[i][l₀]
                if 1 / sum[i] > f  then
                        f = 1 / sum[i]
                end if
        end for
        if f < obj then
                obj = f
        else
                RestoreValues()
                termination = true
        end if
end while
```

sulting in three Tabu Search procedures. These TS procedures generally follow the same idea of exchanging two locations for control devices and performing necessary re-assignments of user nodes, trying to obtain improvements of the objective value. In this section, we will present Tabu Search algorithms for Models 1 – 3.

Tabu Search procedure for solving Model 1 (see Algorithm 8) starts from a given chromosome *chr* of a solution and its objective function *obj*, previously calculated. The procedure first randomly chooses an index $l_0 \in [1, n]$, such that $chr[l_0]$ = 1, meaning that a control device is located at node l_0. For each potential control node $j \in J$, the array *Tnum* stores the information in which TS iteration a control device is activated at node j, while in the array *Tsum* we keep the corresponding objective function increment when activating a device at node j. Short-term memory *TList* contains the list of nodes not to be established

within certain number of TS iterations. The index of control device l_1 to be established is chosen by a tournament selection from the indices stored in the array *Tnum*, regarding corresponding improvements from the list *Tsum*, i.e., $l_1 = Tour(Tnum, Tsum)$, such that $chr[l_1] = 0$. In order to increase the diversity when performing TS procedure, an index l_1 is chosen randomly with probability *prob* > 0.5, such that $chr[l_1] = 0$, $l_1 \notin TList$.

Once the indices l_0 and l_1 are chosen, the TS procedure tries to deactivate control device at position l_0, by setting $chr[l_0] = 0$, and to establish a control device at l_1, by setting $chr[l_1] = 1$ at the same time. As in the LS procedure, instead of recalculating objective function value, we search the array of user nodes $i \in I$, and if the newly established control node l_1 is more preferable for a user j, we assign j to l_1 and update the objective function value. If a user $j \in I$ was previously assigned to the device at l_0, which is now deactivated, we try to find an active control device $k \in$ J, $chr(k) = 1$, which is the most suitable for a user node j. We further assign a user j to the found control device k, and update the objective function value.

If the objective value of the new individual is less than the objective value of the initial initial, multiplied by some positive constant $C = 1 + \varepsilon$ ($\varepsilon = 0.01$ is fixed positive number close to zero), the individual and its objective value are updated. This is denoted as *aspiration criterion* in the TS procedure. Otherwise, the control device j is added in the tabu-list *TList*, which means that this device can not be activated in the current and the following TS iterations (*short-term memory*). The tabu-list is of a fixed length $w = 10$, and the TS procedure will stop when the maximal length of the tabu-list is reached.

Tabu Search procedures for Model 2 and Model 3 follow the same concept as in the case of Model 1. The differences in TS algorithms for Model 2 and Model 3 follow from the different way of calculating objective function value of the new solution with exchanged bits at chosen positions l_0 and l_1 (i.e. re-locations of control devices and re-allocations of users). These strategies are explained in details in LS algorithms for Model 2 and Model 3. Tabu Search procedures for Model 2 and Model 3 use the same parameter values as TS procedure for Model 1, with exception of constant ε, which takes the value of 0.003 in the case of Model 3.

Conducted computational experiments show that combination of the EA and TS outperformed both pure EA and the hybrid of EA and LS, in the sense of solution quality and running times. One of the reasons of successful application of Tabu Search in this context is that tabu conditions from the tabu-list are involved as additional constraints. This strategy results in directing the EA-TS algorithm to promising search regions and in avoiding the moves that are more likely to lead to less quality solutions. A time-savings strategy, which is additionally applied within the

TS, ensures that the total running time of the EA-TS is reasonably short, having in mind considered problem dimensions.

5. COMPUTATIONAL RESULTS

All computational experiments were carried out on an Intel Core i5-2430M on 2.4GHz with 8GB DDR3 RAM memory under Windows 7 operating system. The EA, EA-LS and EA-TS implementations were coded in C# programming language.

We have generated a set of test instances with up to 20 000 user nodes and 500 potential locations for establishing control devices. We have used the same data set for all three considered models. In the generated data set, we suppose that c_{ij}, $i \in$ I, $j \in$ J, represent the number of cost units (or equivalently, the number of data units), where a cost (data) unit is defined by user. The values of c_{ij} were randomly chosen by uniform distribution from three intervals: one third of c_{ij} was chosen from [0.001, 0.1], the second third of c_{ij} belongs to interval [1, 100], while the remaining values of c_{ij} were chosen from the interval [1.000, 100.000]. Different levels cost values are chose in order to reflect the nature of big data, which often varies in size and type.

5.1 Results and Comparisons on Smaller and Medium-Size Problem Instances

We have first considered smaller and medium-size problem instances. For smaller size instances, the number of nodes is $15 \leq m \leq 500$, the number of potential control devices is $5 \leq n \leq 75$, while the number of control devices to be located varies $3 \leq p \leq 25$. In the case of medium-size test instances parameters m, n and p take the following values: $1000 \leq m \leq 5000$, $100 \leq n \leq 250$ and $20 \leq p \leq 100$. The small-size instances were first subject to CPLEX 12.1 solver in order to solve the considered problems to optimality. The obtained results

Algorithm 8. TS algorithm for Model 1

```
termination = false
while termination = false do
        randomly choose l₀∈[1, n] such that chr[l₀] = 1
        randomly choose prob∈[1, n], prob∈ ℝ
        if prob < 0.5 then
                l₁ = Tour(Tnum, Tsum), chr[l₁] = 0
        else
                randomly choose l₁∈[1, n] such that chr[l₁] = 0, l₁∉ TList
        end if
        chr[l₀] = 0
        chr[l₁] = 1
        for all i∈{1, 2, ..., m} do
                if best[i] = l₀ then
                        for all j∈{1, 2, ..., n} do
                                if chr[j] = 0 then
                                        continue
                                end if
                                if best[i] = l₀ then
                                        best[i] = j
                                else if c[i][j] < c[i][best[i]] then
                                        best[i] = j
                                end if
                        end for
                else if c[i][l₁] < c[i][best[i]] then
                        best[i] = l₁
                end if
        end for
        for all j∈{1, 2, ..., n} do
                sum[j] = 0
        end for
        for all i∈{1, 2, ..., m} do
                sum[best[i]] = sum[best[i]] + c[i][best[i]]
        end for
        f_max = 0
        for all j∈{1, 2, ..., n} do
                if chr[j] = 1 and sum[j] > f_max then
                        f_max = sum[j]
                end if
        end for
        if f_max < 1.01 × obj then
                obj = f_max
                Tnum[l₁] = Tnum[l₁] + 1
```

continued on following page

Algorithm 8. Continued

```
                    Tsum[l₁] = Tsum[l₁] + (obj - f_max)
        else

                    RestoreValues()
                    add l₁ to TList
                    w = w + 1
                    if w = 10 then
                            termination = true
                            empty TList
                            w = 0
                    end if
        end if
end while
```

Algorithm 9. TS algorithm for Model 2

```
termination = false
while termination = false do
        randomly choose l₀∈ [1, n] such that chr[l₀] = 1
        randomly choose prob∈ [1, n], prob∈ ℝ
        if prob < 0.5 then
                l₁ = Tour(Tnum, Tsum), chr[l₁] = 0
        else
                randomly choose l₁∈ [1, n] such that chr[l₁] = 0, l₁∉ TList
        end if
        chr[l₀] = 0
        chr[l₁] = 1
        for all i∈{1, 2, ..., m} do
                if best[i] = l₀ then
                        for all j∈{1, 2, ..., n} do
                                if chr[j] = 0 then
                                        continue
                                end if
                                if best[i] = l₀ then
                                        best[i] = j
                                else if c[i][j] < c[i][best[i]] then
                                        best[i] = j
                                end if
                        end for
                else if c[i][l₁] < c[i][best[i]] then
                        best[i] = l₁
                end if
```

continued on following page

Algorithm 9. Continued

```
            end for
            for all j∈{1, 2, ..., n} do
                    sum[j] = 0
            end for
            for all i∈{1, 2, ..., m} do
                    sum[best[i]] = sum[best[i]] + c[i][best[i]]
            end for
            f_max = 0
            f_min = ∞
            for all j∈{1, 2, ..., n} do
                    if chr[j] = 1 and sum[j] > f_max then
                            f_max = sum[j]
                    end if
                    if chr[j] = 1 and sum[j] < f_min then
                            f_min = sum[j]
                    end if
            end for
            if f_max - f_min < 1.01 × obj then
                    obj = f_max - f_min
                    Tnum[l_1] = Tnum[l_1] + 1
                    Tsum[l_1] = Tsum[l_1] + (obj - (f_max - f_min))
            else
                    RestoreValues()
                    add l_1 to TList
                    w = w + 1
                    if w = 10 then
                            termination = true
                            empty TList
                            w = 0
                    end if
            end if
    end while
end while
```

showed that the CPLEX 12.1 solver provided optimal solutions only for small problem instances with up to 100 user nodes, while larger instances were out of its reach of CPLEX. The instances from the benchmark set were further subject to the proposed metaheuristic approaches. On each instance from the considered data set, each of the metaheuristic methods was run 15 times with different random seeds.

In Tables 3–5, we present the results of the CPLEX 12.1 solver and the results of the EA, EA-LS and EA-TS metaheuristics on the test data set. For each considered instance, we first give instance's parameters $m = |I|$, $n = |J|$, and p = number of control devices to be located. The next three columns contain the results of CPLEX 12.1 solver, in cases when it provided a solution: optimal solution obtained by CPLEX 12.1 solver

Algorithm 10. TS algorithm for Model 3

```
termination = false
while termination = false do
        randomly choose l₀ ∈ [1, n] such that chr[l₀] = 1
        randomly choose prob ∈ [1, n], prob ∈ ℝ
        if prob < 0.5 then
                l₁ = Tour(Tnum, Tsum), chr[l₁] = 0
        else
                randomly choose l₁ ∈ [1, n] such that chr[l₁] = 0, l₁ ∉ TList
        end if
        chr[l₀] = 0
        chr[l₁] = 1
        f = 0
        for all i ∈ {1, 2, ..., m} do
                sum[i] = sum[i] + 1 / c[i][l₁] - 1 / c[i][l₀]
                if 1 / sum[i] > f  then
                        f = 1 / sum[i]
                end if
        end for
        if f < 1.003 × obj then
                obj = f
                Tnum[l₁] = Tnum[l₁] + 1
                Tsum[l₁] = Tsum[l₁] + (obj - f)
        else
                RestoreValues()
                add l₁ to TList
                w = w + 1
                if w = 10 then
                        termination = true
                        empty TList
                        w = 0
                end if
        end if
end while
```

Opt.Sol, total CPLEX 12.1 running time *t* (in seconds), and the number of nodes needed to obtain optimal solution. In the remaining columns, we provide the results of the proposed EA, EA-LS and EA-TS approaches, respectively. For each metaheuristic we present:

- The best value of the proposed method *Best.Sol*, with mark Opt in cases when it coincides with the optimal solution *Opt. Sol*;
- Average running time *t* (in seconds);
- Average number of the generations *gen*;

Table 3. Experimental results for Model 1

Instance			CPLEX			EA				
m	*n*	*p*	*Opt.Sol*	*t*	*Nodes*	*Best.Sol*	*t*	*gen*	*agap*	*σ*
15	5	3	75.773	0.1	0	Opt	<0.1	2	0.0	0.0
15	7	4	2.904	0.1	0	Opt	<0.1	2	6.4	5.9
25	10	5	2.656	0.2	2	Opt	<0.1	3	3.1	0.0
25	12	7	1.505	0.2	6	Opt	<0.1	37	9.1	2.8
50	20	15	0.800	0.9	43	Opt	<0.1	11	3.9	0.0
100	30	15	1.080	8.8	1043	Opt	<0.1	113	8.4	5.0
200	50	20	–	–	–	1.306	0.4	419	8.5	1.1
300	50	25	–	–	–	1.369	2.6	1399	5.2	1.1
500	75	25	–	–	–	2.212	4.5	1807	3.7	1.1
1000	100	20	–	–	–	6.791	61.1	5945	4.3	0.5
1000	100	50	–	–	–	1.286	25.0	1588	9.1	4.5
1000	150	35	–	–	–	2.404	113.9	5538	11.8	1.0
2000	100	20	–	–	–	13.725	78.4	2322	4.6	1.0
2000	100	35	–	–	–	4.812	280.6	5268	4.7	0.8
2000	200	50	–	–	–	7.438	143.9	1955	3.8	2.2
2000	200	75	–	–	–	3.411	311.3	3625	3.8	1.9
5000	200	25	–	–	–	22.653	493.5	5273	6.1	0.1
5000	200	50	–	–	–	6.088	434.5	4095	4.2	0.6
5000	250	75	–	–	–	2.898	1047.8	10198	3.7	8.2
5000	250	100	–	–	–	2.724	459.7	4363	10.4	8.1
Average:			–	–	–	–	172.9	2698	5.7	2.3

Instance			EA-LS					EA-TS				
m	*n*	*p*	*Best.Sol*	*t*	*gen*	*agap*	*σ*	*Best.Sol*	*t*	*gen*	*agap*	*σ*
15	5	3	Opt	<0.1	1	0.0	0.0	Opt	<0.1	1	0.0	0.0
15	7	4	Opt	<0.1	2	0.0	0.0	Opt	<0.1	2	0.0	0.0
25	10	5	Opt	<0.1	2	0.0	0.0	Opt	<0.1	2	0.0	0.0
25	12	7	Opt	<0.1	5	0.0	0.0	Opt	<0.1	10	0.0	0.0
50	20	15	Opt	<0.1	14	0.0	0.0	Opt	<0.1	15	0.0	0.0
100	30	15	Opt	0.5	834	1.6	1.2	Opt	0.6	748	0.7	1.3
200	50	20	1.283	0.7	633	2.3	1.7	0.761	1.6	1357	1.4	1.3
300	50	25	1.347	1.6	1026	2.2	1.4	1.080	3.2	1918	1.2	1.2
500	75	25	2.107	5.6	1932	2.5	1.3	0.760	4.5	1433	1.3	1.2
1000	100	20	6.680	46.2	3368	1.6	0.5	1.550	37.3	2617	1.0	0.5
1000	100	50	1.262	79.8	7320	1.7	1.1	0.767	73.6	5524	1.7	1.4
1000	150	35	2.354	63.6	4082	2.1	1.1	1.007	120.0	6972	1.2	0.7
2000	100	20	13.561	99.2	2471	1.6	1.1	2.573	189.9	4189	1.4	1.1
2000	100	35	4.787	188.7	4923	1.3	0.8	0.805	207.2	5573	0.9	0.5

Table 4. Experimental results for Model 2

Instance			CPLEX			EA				
m	*n*	*p*	*Opt.Sol*	*t*	*Nodes*	*Best.Sol*	*t*	*gen*	*agap*	*σ*
15	5	3	14.185	0.1	5	Opt	<0.1	1	0.0	0.0
15	7	4	2.454	0.2	19	Opt	<0.1	15	0.0	0.0
25	10	5	1.605	0.2	29	Opt	<0.1	24	3.7	4.5
25	12	7	0.683	0.4	154	Opt	<0.1	68	4.2	3.7
50	20	15	0.685	0.7	348	Opt	0.1	123	2.0	2.4
100	30	15	–	–	–	0.632	0.2	174	9.3	4.3
200	50	20	–	–	–	0.701	6.7	1410	9.4	3.5
300	50	25	–	–	–	0.763	14.4	1768	7.8	1.7
500	75	25	–	–	–	0.758	47.2	2864	7.7	4.9
1000	100	20	–	–	–	1.346	383.7	5480	9.0	5.5
1000	100	50	–	–	–	0.486	1570.4	15110	5.1	3.7
1000	150	35	–	–	–	0.690	937.7	8370	5.5	3.5
2000	100	20	–	–	–	2.109	509.0	3606	7.5	3.1
2000	100	35	–	–	–	1.223	693.1	6245	6.7	2.7
2000	200	50	–	–	–	0.849	572.3	3097	7.1	2.7
2000	200	75	–	–	–	0.463	1593.1	6727	5.9	3.8
5000	200	25	–	–	–	2.669	630.2	1671	5.9	1.9
5000	200	50	–	–	–	1.237	2793.0	5708	5.5	4.0
5000	250	75	–	–	–	0.720	5078.3	7601	6.3	5.0
5000	250	100	–	–	–	0.528	7063.2	9185	3.6	2.2
Average:			–	–	–	–	1094.7	3962	5.6	3.2

Instance			EA-LS					EA-TS				
m	*n*	*p*	*Best.Sol*	*t*	*gen*	*agap*	*σ*	*Best.Sol*	*t*	*gen*	*agap*	*σ*
15	5	3	Opt	<0.1	1	0.0	0.0	Opt	<0.1	1	0.0	0.0
15	7	4	Opt	<0.1	2	0.0	0.0	Opt	<0.1	3	0.0	0.0
25	10	5	Opt	<0.1	4	0.0	0.0	Opt	<0.1	3	0.0	0.0
25	12	7	Opt	<0.1	16	0.0	0.0	Opt	<0.1	13	0.0	0.0
50	20	15	Opt	<0.1	48	0.0	0.0	Opt	<0.1	21	0.0	0.0
100	30	15	0.498	0.1	376	5.3	1.4	0.395	0.3	654	4.8	3.5
200	50	20	0.484	0.8	866	5.8	2.6	0.390	0.9	992	4.9	3.6
300	50	25	0.489	1.0	762	2.8	2.8	0.489	1.0	772	2.6	2.1
500	75	25	0.645	4.6	2088	3.3	1.3	0.593	3.2	1463	3.3	2.8
1000	100	20	0.964	31.4	3161	3.6	2.9	0.915	13.9	1361	3.9	3.5
1000	100	50	0.476	31.6	3842	3.7	2.1	0.445	59.4	7226	2.2	2.1
1000	150	35	0.649	69.7	6061	3.4	2.2	0.609	32.8	3179	2.3	2.1
2000	100	20	1.578	48.1	1982	3.9	2.3	1.481	44.5	2184	2.6	2.3
2000	100	35	1.025	53.2	3220	4.2	1.5	0.886	78.5	4544	3.3	2.6

continued on following page

Table 4. Continued

Instance			CPLEX					EA				
2000	200	50	0.639	81.9	3965	4.3	2.9	0.598	107.0	5323	3.3	2.7
2000	200	75	0.432	117.8	6541	3.5	1.7	0.403	131.8	6641	3.1	2.6
5000	200	25	2.123	118.4	1525	2.8	1.9	2.052	162.7	2102	3.0	2.6
5000	200	50	1.157	233.7	3830	3.1	1.7	1.079	267.9	4021	2.1	2.2
5000	250	75	0.657	606.3	9808	2.6	1.9	0.637	671.5	8150	2.9	2.5
5000	250	100	0.507	873.2	6625	3.3	2.5	0.487	561.3	8696	2.1	2.1
Average:			–	113.6	2736	2.8	1.6	–	106.9	2867	2.3	2.0

Table 5. Experimental results for Model 3

Instance			CPLEX			EA				
m	n	p	Opt.Sol	t	Nodes	Best.Sol	t	gen	agap	σ
15	5	3	57.680	<0.1	0	Opt	<0.1	40	0.0	0.0
15	7	4	0.855	<0.1	0	Opt	<0.1	83	0.0	0.0
25	10	5	0.610	0.1	0	Opt	<0.1	167	0.0	0.0
25	12	7	0.422	0.2	0	Opt	<0.1	209	0.0	0.0
50	20	15	0.165	0.4	84	Opt	0.1	282	0.0	0.0
100	30	15	0.136	375.6	11591	Opt	1.1	1800	1.0	1.2
200	50	20	–	–	–	0.096	3.3	2454	1.9	1.2
300	50	25	–	–	–	0.075	9.1	4025	1.5	0.4
500	75	25	–	–	–	0.084	23.8	6205	2.6	1.2
1000	100	20	–	–	–	0.159	180.4	12029	3.0	1.7
1000	100	50	–	–	–	0.033	374.8	13210	1.8	1.1
1000	150	35	–	–	–	0.059	167.8	9376	2.8	1.1
2000	100	20	–	–	–	0.205	147.8	6421	2.7	1.7
2000	100	35	–	–	–	0.067	424.2	10235	2.4	1.4
2000	200	50	–	–	–	0.036	989.1	18963	1.4	1.1
2000	200	75	–	–	–	0.019	646.9	14032	1.3	1.6
5000	200	25	–	–	–	0.161	1399.1	14198	2.2	1.8
5000	200	50	–	–	–	0.044	926.2	9042	1.5	1.0
5000	250	75	–	–	–	0.022	1507.4	10886	1.2	1.5
5000	250	100	–	–	–	0.014	2980.1	18389	1.4	1.4
Average:			–	–	–	–	489.1	7602	1.4	1.0

Instance			EA-LS					EA-TS				
m	n	p	Best.Sol	t	gen	agap	σ	Best.Sol	t	gen	agap	σ
15	5	3	Opt	<0.1	4	0.0	0.0	Opt	<0.1	5	0.0	0.0
15	7	4	Opt	<0.1	16	0.0	0.0	Opt	<0.1	4	0.0	0.0
25	10	5	Opt	<0.1	24	0.0	0.0	Opt	<0.1	201	0.0	0.0

continued on following page

Table 5. Continued

Instance			CPLEX					EA				
25	12	7	Opt	<0.1	87	0.0	0.0	Opt	<0.1	635	0.0	0.0
50	20	15	Opt	<0.1	111	0.0	0.0	Opt	0.2	1284	0.0	0.0
100	30	15	Opt	0.1	577	1.1	1.2	Opt	0.1	597	0.0	0.0
200	50	20	0.095	0.5	1786	1.5	1.0	0.094	0.4	1343	1.1	0.6
300	50	25	0.074	0.8	1877	0.3	0.4	0.074	0.9	1883	0.0	0.0
500	75	25	0.081	1.8	2497	2.5	1.2	0.080	1.7	2122	2.2	1.8
1000	100	20	0.154	13.9	4686	2.0	1.3	0.152	14.7	4656	1.6	1.5
1000	100	50	0.032	20.3	6876	1.1	1.2	0.032	20.5	6388	1.1	1.2
1000	150	35	0.055	18.7	6210	1.8	1.6	0.055	18.4	5695	1.8	1.5
2000	100	20	0.204	15.3	2489	2.0	1.1	0.199	39.9	5624	1.3	1.3
2000	100	35	0.066	39.7	6903	1.8	1.1	0.065	22.0	3303	1.6	1.3
2000	200	50	0.036	52.4	8370	1.5	1.1	0.036	37.0	4629	1.5	1.1
2000	200	75	0.019	72.0	11115	1.5	1.6	0.019	76.6	10616	0.0	0.0
5000	200	25	0.160	130.1	5053	1.9	1.5	0.160	169.6	6472	1.6	1.2
5000	200	50	0.043	287.8	11172	0.7	1.0	0.043	179.4	6405	0.9	1.1
5000	250	75	0.022	313.2	11337	0.8	1.3	0.022	301.5	8806	0.8	1.3
5000	250	100	0.014	231.6	8241	2.1	1.9	0.014	382.7	10897	1.2	1.7
Average:			–	59.9	4472	1.1	0.9	–	63.3	4078	0.8	0.8

- Average gap of the obtained solution from the optimal/best one – *agap* (in percents);
- Standard deviation of the obtained solution from the optimal/best one – σ (in percents).

Note that the optimal or best obtained results of all three metaheuristic methods are bolded through Tables 3–5.

Presented computational results show that the all three metaheuristic approaches quickly reach all optimal solutions obtained by CPLEX 12.1 solver. In general, all three proposed methods give solutions for larger problem dimensions in short CPU times, but the obtained solutions are of different quality. From the results presented in column *Best.Sol* in Tables 3–5, it is obvious that the EA-TS method showed significantly better performance compared to the pure EA and hybrid EA-LS approaches. For all three models, the EA-

TS produced the best results, while the EA-LS and the pure EA reached the best solutions obtained by EA-TS in several cases only.

From the values presented in columns *agap* and σ in Tables 3–5, we can see that the EA-TS method showed good stability through all 15 runs when solving instances from the benchmark set. Although the considered models involve different objective function and different set of conditions, the proposed EA-TS showed excellent performance in all three cases. Low values of average gap *agap* and standard deviation σ in Tables 3–5 clearly indicate good stability and reliability of the EA-TS approach for solving all three problems under consideration.

On Figures 5–7, we present the comparisons of average gap of EA, EA-LS and EA-TS for each of the considered Models 1–3. For each problem dimension *m*, we take the average values of *agap* over the subset of the considered instances with the same number of user nodes *m*. The values of average gap of the EA-TS on Figures 5–7 are obviously lower compared to corresponding values of average gap of the EA-LS and significantly lower compared to the case of the pure EA. These results indicate that the pure EA needs an additional impulse (Local Search or Tabu Search) to help in improving the solution and directing the algorithm to promising regions of the search space. In the case of the EA-TS method, the incorporated TS heuristic obviously successfully leads the algorithm to high quality solutions.

The TS heuristic was implemented in an efficient manner, such that running time savings are obtained as well. This can be seen from both average CPU times and average number of generations in Tables 3-5. The column *gen* shows that in most cases the EA-TS needed less generations to converge to its best solutions, compared to both EA-LS and the pure EA methods.

Regarding columns related to running times through Tables 3–5, we may notice that for Model 1, the EA method is generally slightly faster compared to the EA-LS and EA-TS (average CPU times are 172.9 s, 182 s and 180.3 s respectively),

Figure 5. Comparison of average gap values for Model 1

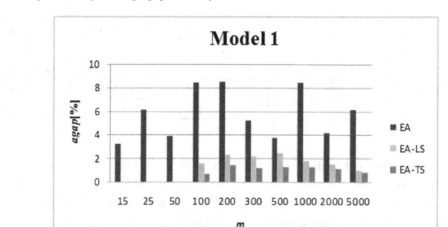

Figure 6. Comparison of average gap values for Model 2

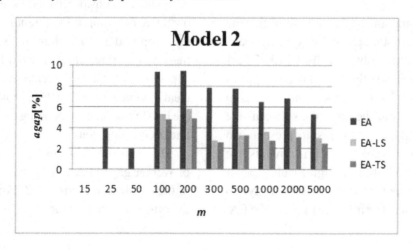

but the EA's solution quality is significantly lower. For Model 2, the EA-TS showed the best performance regarding running times; it reached its best solutions in slightly shorter CPU time compared to EA-LS, and around 10 times shorter time compared to the pure EA (in average). The corresponding average CPU times for EA-TS, EA-LS and EA are 1094.7 s, 113.6 s and 106.9 s, respectively. In the case of Model 3, the EA-LS and EA-TS have similar running times (in average), while the pure EA is around 8 times slower compared to other two methods (average CPU times are 489.1 s, 59.9 s and 63.3 s respectively). The running times of all three metaheuristics are reasonably short, having in mind the dimensions of considered problem instances. For the largest medium-size instance with 5000 users, 250 potential control devices, and 100 control devices to be located, the proposed EA-TS method produced its best solution within 579.4s, 561.3s and 382.7s for Models 1-3, respectively.

5.2 Results and Comparisons on Large-Scale Problem Instances

We further considered large-scale test instances including $6000 \le m \le 20\,000$ user nodes in the network and $200 \le m \le 500$ potential locations for control devices. The number of devices to be located – p is varied from 100 to 250. The results on small and medium size problem dimensions, presented in previous subsection, showed that the performance of the pure EA is much worse compared to the hybrid EA-LA and EA-TS approaches, regarding both running times and solutions' quality. Therefore, we have omitted the pure EA from the experiments with large-scale data set. Considering the results from Tables 3–5, it is obvious that benchmarking the pure EA on large-scale problem instances would take large amount of time. For this reason, we have tested only the hybrid EA-LS and EA-TS methods on problem instances with $6000 \le m \le 20\,000$ user nodes.

In Tables 6–8, we give the results of the EA-LS and EA-TS on large-scale test data set for Models 1 – 3 respectively. The results are presented in similar way as in Tables 4–5 and the same notation is used in table headings. For each considered test instance, the best solution obtained by EA-TS or EA-LS method is bolded.

The presented computational results show the superiority of the proposed EA-TS approach in the sense of solution quality, when compared to the EA-LS method. Only in the case of three instances, the EA-LS reached the best solution obtained by the EA-TS. The average gap and

Figure 7. Comparison of average gap values for Model 3

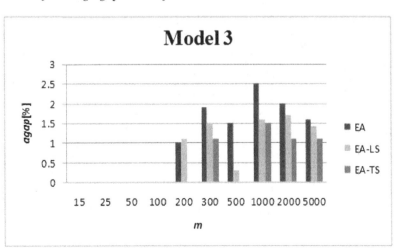

257

Table 6. Experimental results on large-scale instances for Model 1

Instance			EA-LS				
m	*n*	*p*	*Best.Sol*	*t*	*Gen*	*agap*	*σ*
6000	200	100	0.244	574.029	7447.3	1.174	1.418
6000	250	100	0.242	916.429	11039.5	2.053	1.284
7000	200	100	0.286	967.692	8920.8	1.912	1.618
7000	250	100	0.278	904.679	9518.1	1.791	1.271
8000	250	100	0.320	1483.836	13985.4	1.709	1.078
8000	300	100	0.320	660.975	6052.8	1.289	1.966
9000	250	100	0.357	1209.282	9659.1	1.199	1.336
9000	300	100	0.356	1712.420	13552.2	1.279	1.326
10000	300	100	0.399	904.844	6398.5	1.517	1.687
10000	300	150	0.206	1123.567	17781.2	1.151	1.219
11000	300	150	0.229	1241.342	8130.7	1.855	2.029
12000	300	150	0.246	1615.359	9918.1	1.379	1.098
13000	300	150	0.268	1974.083	10739.5	1.657	1.843
14000	350	150	0.287	1162.167	11317.8	2.091	1.565
15000	350	150	0.307	1220.980	10846.4	2.130	1.530
16000	400	200	0.215	1376.698	9579.5	1.663	1.638
17000	400	200	0.224	2854.165	17802.9	1.189	1.622
18000	450	200	0.241	1580.229	8560.3	1.845	1.406
19000	450	250	0.187	2516.983	13029.1	1.034	1.654
20000	500	250	0.194	3144.652	15558.6	1.776	1.430
Average:			–	1457.221	10991.9	1.585	1.501
Instance			EA-TS				
m	*n*	*p*	*Best.Sol*	*t*	*Gen*	*agap*	*σ*
6000	200	100	0.241	190.001	1621.9	0.972	1.097
6000	250	100	0.238	325.413	2668.3	1.848	1.271
7000	200	100	0.283	714.764	5971.0	1.796	1.231
7000	250	100	0.275	544.895	3684.2	1.563	1.050
8000	250	100	0.315	464.589	2958.9	1.486	0.645
8000	300	100	0.319	470.651	2716.0	1.178	1.853
9000	250	100	0.357	543.566	2959.6	1.185	1.261
9000	300	100	0.354	625.152	3405.1	0.953	1.260
10000	300	100	0.395	516.637	2353.1	1.358	1.201
10000	300	150	0.199	602.990	2183.4	0.791	0.819
11000	300	150	0.222	1025.812	3942.9	1.759	1.942
12000	300	150	0.244	1091.532	3843.4	1.254	0.860
13000	300	150	0.267	1956.224	6441.7	1.244	1.565
14000	350	150	0.287	1904.906	4363.8	1.718	1.439

continued on following page

Table 6. Continued

Instance			EA-LS				
15000	350	150	0.301	1441.032	6533.4	1.784	1.134
16000	400	200	0.212	1721.586	5717.6	1.188	1.155
17000	400	200	0.221	1945.627	6541.3	0.713	1.231
18000	450	200	0.237	1411.890	4264.2	1.686	0.927
19000	450	250	0.186	2966.232	6353.8	0.536	1.227
20000	500	250	0.193	1571.338	2356.1	1.389	1.421
Average:			–	1101.742	4044.0	1.320	1.229

Table 7. Experimental results on large-scale instances for Model 2

Instance			EA-LS				
m	*n*	*p*	*Best.Sol*	*t*	*gen*	*agap*	*σ*
6000	200	100	0.074	625.829	9129.3	1.172	1.840
6000	250	100	0.082	449.961	5793.6	0.943	1.991
7000	200	100	0.094	1058.071	10950.0	1.939	1.817
7000	250	100	0.084	1325.567	13223.7	1.629	1.425
8000	250	100	0.100	1371.286	11766.4	1.354	2.081
8000	300	100	0.095	1490.804	12897.2	1.308	0.949
9000	250	100	0.102	912.587	6626.8	1.163	1.840
9000	300	100	0.103	1526.602	11460.2	2.213	1.789
10000	300	100	0.112	937.905	5922.7	1.199	1.519
10000	300	150	0.081	1444.399	9968.9	1.851	1.807
11000	300	150	0.093	889.427	5176.5	1.706	1.080
12000	300	150	0.096	1447.676	16791.0	0.892	1.413
13000	300	150	0.099	1229.453	12360.9	1.514	1.510
14000	350	150	0.106	1383.773	12242.7	1.630	1.969
15000	350	150	0.115	1345.626	9760.3	1.332	1.313
16000	400	200	0.093	1191.237	7368.6	1.508	1.836
17000	400	200	0.106	2168.401	12198.4	1.880	1.369
18000	450	200	0.108	3145.288	14736.2	1.318	1.022
19000	450	250	0.100	2829.691	16693.2	1.788	1.698
20000	500	250	0.102	3667.747	20837.9	1.417	1.541
Average:			–	1522.066	11295.2	1.488	1.590
Instance			EA-TS				
m	*n*	*p*	*Best.Sol*	*t*	*gen*	*agap*	*σ*
6000	200	100	0.074	514.679	7226.4	0.820	1.436
6000	250	100	0.075	597.537	7723.3	0.460	1.670
7000	200	100	0.086	1005.027	11566.2	1.776	1.336

continued on following page

Table 7. Continued

Instance			EA-LS				
7000	250	100	0.079	1405.217	13640.4	1.247	1.072
8000	250	100	0.095	1181.581	9539.3	0.889	1.937
8000	300	100	0.090	1382.163	11612.7	1.211	0.655
9000	250	100	0.096	1061.766	15791.2	0.726	1.509
9000	300	100	0.098	1164.358	8471.6	2.190	1.555
10000	300	100	0.106	1524.476	9918.2	0.703	1.436
10000	300	150	0.078	930.662	5530.1	1.593	1.394
11000	300	150	0.089	1393.469	8074.8	1.434	0.715
12000	300	150	0.085	1457.200	7700.5	0.487	1.220
13000	300	150	0.096	1547.101	16216.6	1.360	1.025
14000	350	150	0.101	1884.356	7765.0	1.310	1.568
15000	350	150	0.111	1833.020	7133.3	0.952	1.058
16000	400	200	0.088	2329.437	17581.7	1.024	1.811
17000	400	200	0.099	1096.038	6741.8	1.515	1.173
18000	450	200	0.107	1228.724	6984.6	1.233	0.808
19000	450	250	0.092	2662.941	15046.7	1.614	1.678
20000	500	250	0.101	2104.738	9976.8	1.078	1.453
Average:			–	1415.225	10212.1	1.181	1.325

Table 8. Experimental results on large-scale instances for Model 3

Instance			EA-LS				
m	*n*	*p*	*Best.Sol* $\times 10^{-5}$	*t*	*gen*	*agap*	*σ*
6000	200	100	162.112	353.436	11162.9	1.400	1.494
6000	250	100	163.368	396.669	12247.7	1.083	1.605
7000	200	100	163.647	413.449	10716.4	1.338	1.595
7000	250	100	165.641	457.380	11998.3	1.104	2.244
8000	250	100	166.910	634.118	14334.5	1.959	1.486
8000	300	100	171.898	581.262	13109.6	2.092	2.143
9000	250	100	171.290	636.383	12831.5	1.829	1.813
9000	300	100	169.184	675.187	13419.6	1.676	0.870
10000	300	100	172.656	572.592	10188.3	1.576	1.768
10000	300	150	94.243	973.532	16786.5	1.576	2.015
11000	300	150	94.993	948.496	15221.8	1.655	1.368
12000	300	150	94.616	1322.068	19384.1	0.988	1.756
13000	300	150	99.658	1032.955	27899.1	1.854	1.763
14000	350	150	98.597	795.235	9231.8	2.082	1.201
15000	350	150	98.258	1897.109	20737.4	1.345	1.985

continued on following page

Table 8. Continued

Instance			EA-LS				
16000	400	200	66.810	1648.228	15824.9	1.208	1.871
17000	400	200	65.564	1044.429	9301.8	1.470	1.542
18000	450	200	66.827	1263.754	20654.6	1.115	1.718
19000	450	250	49.069	2009.992	31067.2	1.889	1.481
20000	500	250	49.380	1237.975	17539.0	1.320	1.464
Average:			–	944.712	15682.8	1.528	1.659
Instance			EA-TS				
m	*n*	*p*	*Best.Sol* $\times 10^{-5}$	*t*	*gen*	*agap*	σ
6000	200	100	160.266	323.091	8625.0	1.005	1.451
6000	250	100	162.103	737.468	19419.9	1.015	1.581
7000	200	100	163.010	493.212	11005.7	0.857	1.475
7000	250	100	164.010	855.156	19172.3	0.651	1.861
8000	250	100	166.825	614.896	11746.2	1.682	1.095
8000	300	100	164.042	692.461	13234.3	1.842	1.834
9000	250	100	170.518	605.609	9959.1	1.546	1.459
9000	300	100	166.650	491.412	7689.3	1.370	0.711
10000	300	100	172.136	1090.363	16220.8	1.544	1.446
10000	300	150	92.053	817.844	10743.2	1.401	1.553
11000	300	150	94.850	724.418	9237.2	1.520	1.116
12000	300	150	93.369	747.112	8304.1	0.493	1.596
13000	300	150	99.243	1397.783	14878.3	1.529	1.447
14000	350	150	97.348	848.849	7684.6	1.925	0.738
15000	350	150	97.208	913.082	7899.1	0.888	1.804
16000	400	200	64.816	1820.879	13390.0	1.015	1.708
17000	400	200	65.422	1762.630	13133.9	1.348	1.454
18000	450	200	65.395	1595.167	10328.0	0.683	1.318
19000	450	250	49.050	1573.847	9121.2	1.623	1.049
20000	500	250	49.379	1643.783	14939.6	1.194	1.066
Average:			–	987.453	11836.6	1.257	1.388

standard deviation of both EA-LS and EA-TS have relatively small values, indicating good stability of both proposed hybrid approaches. For Models 1–3, average gap and standard deviation of the EA-LS solutions are 1.585%, 1.488%, 1.528% and 1.501%, 1.590%, 1.659%, respectively. For the EA-TS method, corresponding values in the cases of Models 1–3 are 1.320%, 1.181%, 1.257% (average gap) and 1.229%, 1.325%, 1.388% (standard deviation).

Regarding the computational time, from the last row in Table 6, it can be seen that the EA-TS needed less time (in average) to reach its best solutions for Model 1, compared to the EA-LS. In the case of Models 2 and 3, the EA-TS was slightly slower (in average) than the EA-LS, but the EA-TS solution quality was better for all instances, with exception of one instance where both approaches reached the same solution for Model 2. Average CPU times of the EA-LS and EA-TS for solving large-scale problem instances of Models 1–3 are presented on Figures 8 and 9, respectively.

The presented results reflect the robustness and efficiency of both hybrid EA-TS and EA-LS approaches when solving the instances of real-life dimensions. In general, the EA-LS needed slightly shorter CPU time when solving large-scale problem dimensions, but the EA-TS provided better quality solutions for all tested instances (with exception of three cases only). The presented results indicate that the proposed hybrid metaheuristic may be successfully applied for analyzing big data originating from social networks.

6. CONCLUSION

This study considers the question of how to efficiently analyze and process the big data from a social network to discover useful information about users' behavior, and to provide better decision making. The analysis of social data in timely manner is a big challenge, since it is important to detect trends and patterns in order to support system management activities in limited time. In this study, mathematical models and adequate optimization methods are proposed for efficient exploration of big data flow within a social network. Three metaheuristic approaches are designed for solving large-scale dimensions of the proposed models: a robust Evolutionary Algorithm EA, which was further hybridized with Local Search and Tabu Search methods, resulting in two efficient hybrid metaheuristic approaches EA-LS and EA-TS.

Binary solution's encoding is used in all three methods, and efficient greedy strategies for calculating objective function are implemented. The constructive elements of the proposed metaheuristic approaches are adapted to problems under consideration. All three metaheuristics were subject to broad computational experiments on generated large-scale data set with up to 20 000 user nodes and 500 potential locations for control devices. The obtained results indicate that the hybrid EA-LS and EA-TS metaheuristics outperform the pure EA in the sense of both solutions' quality and running times. For large-scale problem instances, the EA-TS method shows excellent performance regarding solution quality and stability when solving all considered problem instances. In general, the EA-LS is slightly faster compared to the EA-TS, but its solution quality is lower, with exception of few cases.

The results of conducted computational experiments clearly indicate that the proposed hybrids EA-LS and EA-TS represent promising approaches for the three considered problems related to efficient analysis of the big data flow in social networks. The computational results show the stability and efficiency of the proposed methods, which indicate that this approach may be used in for real-time or near real-time information delivery to enable analysts to quickly spot trends and patterns in users' behavior within a social network.

The proposed mathematical models and hybrid metaheuristic methods may be used as additional tools for further research in this field. They can be applied for solving similar problems related to large-scale networks with big data flow. Future work will be directed to designing new mathematical models, which correspond to various problems related to big data from different large-scale networks, and implementing efficient optimization tools for solving them.

Figure 8. Time comparison for EA-LS on large-scale instances

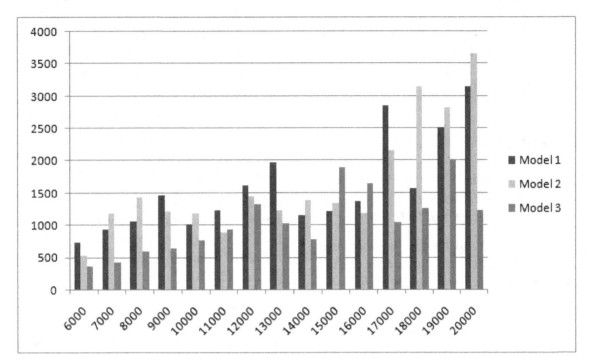

Figure 9. Time comparison for EA-TS on large-scale instances

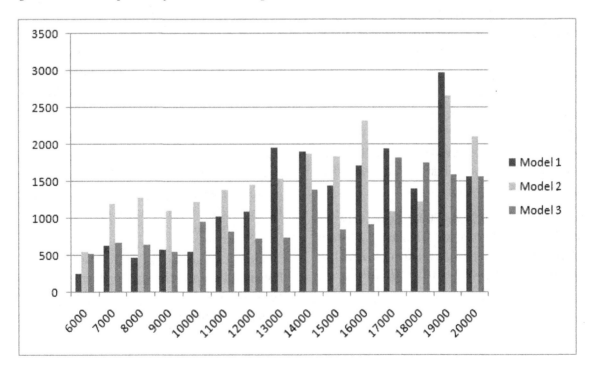

ACKNOWLEDGMENT

This research was supported by Ministry of Education, Science and Technological Development of the Republic of Serbia under the grants no. 174010, 47017 and 044006.

REFERENCES

Adamic, L. A., & Adar, E. (2005). How to search a social network. *Social Networks, 27*(3), 187–203. doi:10.1016/j.socnet.2005.01.007.

Adar, E. Zhang, L. Adamic, L. A., & Lukose, R. M. (2004). Implicit structure and the dynamics of blogspace. *Workshop on the Weblogging Ecosystem, 13*(1).

Ahuja, R. K., Magnanti, T. L., & Orlin, J. B. (1993). *Network flows*. Englewood Cliffs, NJ: Prentice Hall, Inc..

Alumur, S., & Kara, B. Y. (2008). Network hub location problems: The state of the art. *European Journal of Operational Research, 190*(1), 1–21. doi:10.1016/j.ejor.2007.06.008.

Bastian, M., Heymann, S., & Jacomy, M. (2009). Gephi: An open source software for exploring and manipulating networks. In *Proceedings of the 3rd International AAAI Conference on Weblogs and Social Media*. Retrieved January, 2013, from http://www.aaai.org/ocs/index.php/ICWSM/09/paper/view/154.

Boyd, D., & Ellison, N. B. (2008). Social network sites: Definition, history, and scholarship. *Journal of Computer-Mediated Communication, 13*, 210–230. doi:10.1111/j.1083-6101.2007.00393.x.

Caers, R., & Castelyns, V. (2011). LinkedIn and Facebook in Belgium: The influences and biases of social network sites in recruitment and selection procedures. *Social Science Computer Review, 29*, 437–448. doi:10.1177/0894439310386567.

Chen, W. Y., Song, Y., Bai, H., Lin, C., & Chang, E. Y. (2011). Parallel spectral clustering in distributed systems. *IEEE Transactions on Pattern Analysis and Machine Intelligence, 33*(3), 568–586. doi:10.1109/TPAMI.2010.88 PMID:20421667.

Chiba, R., & Sato-Ilic, M. (2012). Analysis of web survey data based on similarity of fuzzy clusters. In C. H. Dagli (Ed.), *Complex adaptive systems*. Procedia Computer Science. doi:10.1016/j.procs.2012.09.060.

Cohen, J., Dolan, B., Dunlap, M., Hellerstein, J. M., & Welton, C. (2009). MAD skills: New analysis practices for big data. *Proccedings of VLDB 2009, 2*(2).

Couper, M. P., & Miller, P. V. (2008). Web survey methods. *Public Opinion Quarterly, 72*(5), 831–835. doi:10.1093/poq/nfn066.

Cuzzocrea, A., Song, I. Y., & Davis, K. C. (2011). Analytics over large-scale multidimensional data: The big data revolution! In *Proceedings of DOLAP Conference*, (pp. 101-104). DOLAP.

Demirkan, H., & Delen, D. (2012). *Leveraging the capabilities of service-oriented decision support systems: Putting analytics and big data in cloud*. Decision Support Systems. Retrieved January, 2013, from http://dx.doi.org/10.1016/j.dss.2012.05.048.

Dhillon, I., Mallela, S., & Kumar, R. (2002). Enhanced word clustering for hierarchical text classification. In *Proceedings of the 8th ACM SIGKDD*. Edmonton, Canada: ACM.

Domingos, P., & Richardson, M. (2001). Mining the network value of customers. In *Proceedings of the Seventh ACM SIGKDD International Conference on Knowledge Discovery and Data Mining*. San Francisco, CA: ACM.

Enright, A., & Ouzounis, C. (2000). GeneRAGE: A robust algorithm for sequence clustering and domain detection. *Bioinformatics (Oxford, England)*, *16*, 451–457. doi:10.1093/bioinformatics/16.5.451 PMID:10871267.

Facebook Now Has 30 000 Servers. (n.d.). Retrieved January, 2013, from http://www.datacenterknowledge. com/archives/2009/10/13/facebook-now-has-30000-servers/

Filipović, V. (2003). Fine grained tournament selection operator in genetic algorithms. *Computing and Informatics*, *22*, 143–161.

Golder, S. A., Wilkinson, D. M., & Huberman, B. A. (2007). Rhythms of social interaction: Messaging within a massive online network. In *Proceedings of 3rd International Conference on Communities and Technologies* (pp. 41-66). IEEE.

Gruhl, D., Guha, R., Liben-Nowell, D., & Tomkins, A. (2004). Information diffusion through blogspace. In Proceedings *of the 13th International Conference on World Wide Web*. New York: IEEE.

Hadoop MapReduce Tutorial. (n.d.). Retrieved January, 2013, from http://hadoop.apache.org/common/docs/ r0.20.2/mapred_tutorial.html

Herodotou, H., Lim, H., Luo, G., Borisov, N., Dong, L., Cetin, F.-B., & Babu, S. (2011). Starfish: A self-tuning system for big data analytics. In *Proceedings of the 5th Biennial Conference on Innovative Data Systems Research (CIDR 2011)*. Asilomar, CA: CIDR.

Highfield, T., Kirchhoff, L., & Nicolai, T. (2011). Challenges of tracking topical discussion networks online. *Social Science Computer Review*, *29*(3), 340–353. doi:10.1177/0894439310382514.

Huberman, B. A., Romero, D. M., & Wu, F. (2009). Social networks that matter: Twitter under the microscope. *First Monday*, 14.

IssueCrawler. (n.d.). Retrieved January, 2013, from http://www.issuecrawler.net/

Jain, A., Murty, M., & Flynn, P. (1999). Data clustering: A review. *ACM Computing Surveys*, *31*(3), 264–323. doi:10.1145/331499.331504.

Kempe, D., Kleinberg, J., & Tardos, É. (2003). Maximizing the spread of influence through a social network. In *Proceedings of the Ninth ACM SIGKDD International Conference on Knowledge Discovery and Data Mining*. Washington, DC: ACM.

Kratica, J., Milanović, M., Stanimirović, Z., & Tošić, D. (2011). An evolutionary-based approach for solving a capacitated hub location problem. *Applied Soft Computing*, *11*(2), 1858–1866. doi:10.1016/j.asoc.2010.05.035.

Kratica, J., & Stanimirović, Z. (2006). Solving the uncapacitated multiple allocation p-hub center problem by genetic algorithm. *Asia-Pacific Journal of Operational Research*, *23*(4), 425–437. doi:10.1142/S0217595906001042.

Kratica, J., Stanimirović, Z., Tošić, D., & Filipović, V. (2005). Genetic algorithm for solving uncapacitated multiple allocation hub location problem. *Computing and Informatics*, *24*(4), 415–426.

Kratica, J., Stanimirović, Z., Tošić, D., & Filipović, V. (2007). Two genetic algorithms for solving the uncapacitated single allocation p-hub median problem. *European Journal of Operational Research*, *182*, 15–28. doi:10.1016/j. ejor.2006.06.056.

Lin, F., & Cohen, W. W. (2010). Power iteration clustering. In *Proceedings of the 27th International Conference on Machine Learning*. Haifa, Israel: IEEE.

Malika, H., & Malik, A. S. (2011). Towards identifying the challenges associated with emerging large scale social networks. In *Proceedings of the 2nd International Conference on Ambient Systems, Networks and Technologies*. Niagara Falls, Canada: Procedia Computer Science.

Manfreda, K. L., Bosnjak, M., Berzelak, J., Haas, I., & Vehovar, V. (2008). Web surveys versus other survey modes: A meta-analysis comparin response rates. *International Journal of Market Research, 50*(1), 79–104.

Matić, D., Filipović, V., Savić, A., & Staimirović, Z. (2011). A genetic algorithm for solving multiple warehouse layout problem. *Kragujevac Journal of Mathematics, 35*(1), 119–138.

Michalewicz, Z. (1996). *Genetic algorithms + data structures = evolution programs* (3rd ed.). Berlin: Springer-Verlag. doi:10.1007/978-3-662-03315-9.

MySpace Uses SQL Server Service Broker to Protect Integrity of 1 Petabyte of Data. (n.d.). Retrieved January, 2013, from http://www.techrepublic.com/whitepapers/myspace-uses-sql-server-service-broker-to-protect-integrity-of-1-petabyte-of-data/1097845

Puerto, J., Tamir, A., Mesa, J. A., & Pérez-Brito, D. (2008). Center location problems on tree graphs with subtree-shaped customers. *Discrete Applied Mathematics, 156*(15), 2890–2910. doi:10.1016/j.dam.2007.11.022.

ReVelle, C. S., & Eiselt, H. A. (2005). Location analysis: A synthesis and survey. *European Journal of Operational Research, 16*, 1–19.

Rogers, E. M., & Kincaid, D. L. (1981). *Communication networks: Toward a new paradigm for research*. New York: Free Press.

Ryan, T., & Xenos, S. (2011). Who uses Facebook? An investigation into the relationship between the big five, shyness, narcissism, loneliness, and Facebook usage. *Computers in Human Behavior, 27*, 1658–1664. doi:10.1016/j.chb.2011.02.004.

Schilling, D. A., Jayaraman, V., & Barkhi, R. (1993). A review of covering problems in facility location. *Location Science, 1*(1), 25–55.

Schönemannand, P. H., & Wang, M. M. (1979). An individual difference model for the multi-dimensional analysis of preference data. *Psychometrika, 37*(3), 275–309. doi:10.1007/BF02306784.

Sharma, S., & Gupta, R. K. (2010). Improved BSP clustering algorithm for social network analysis. *International Journal of Grid and Distributed Computing, 3*(3), 67–76.

SocSciBot. (n.d.). *Web crawler and link analyzer for the social sciences*. Retrieved January 2013, from http://socscibot.wlv.ac.uk/

Stanimirović, Z. (2008). An efficient genetic algorithm for the uncapacitated multiple allocation p-hub median problem. *Control and Cybernetics, 37*(3), 669–692.

Stanimirović, Z. (2010). A genetic algorithm approach for the capacitated single allocation p-hub median problem. *Computing and Informatics, 29*(1), 117–132.

Stanimirović, Z., Kratica, J., & Dugošija, D. (2007). Genetic algorithms for solving the discrete ordered median problem. *European Journal of Operational Research, 182*, 983–1001. doi:10.1016/j.ejor.2006.09.069.

Vakharia, A. J., & Mahajan, J. (2000). Clustering of objects and attributes for manufacturing and marketing applications. *European Journal of Operational Research, 123*(3), 640–651. doi:10.1016/S0377-2217(99)00103-4.

Wasserman, S., & Faust, K. (1994). *Social network analysis: methods and applications*. New York: Cambridge University Press. doi:10.1017/CBO9780511815478.

Yan, W., Brahmakshatriya, U., Xue, Y., Gilder, M., & Wise, B. (2013). p-PIC: Parallel power iteration clustering for big data. *Journal of Parallel and Distributed Computing*, *73*(3), 352–359. doi:10.1016/j.jpdc.2012.06.009.

ADDITIONAL READING

C. C. Aggarwal (Ed.). (2011). *Social network data analytics*. London: Springer. doi:10.1007/978-1-4419-8462-3.

Aggarwal, C. C., Ashish, N., & Sheth, A. (2013). The internet of things: A survey from the data-centric perspective. In *Managing and Mining Sensor Data*. London: Springer. doi:10.1007/978-1-4614-6309-2_12.

Aggarwal, C. C., Khan, A., & Yan, X. (2011). On flow authority discovery in social networks. In *Proceedings of SIAM Conference on Data Mining (SDM)*. SIAM.

Aggarwal, C. C., Lin, S., & Philip, S. Y. (2012). *On influential node discovery in dynamic social networks*. Retrieved January 2013, from http://charuaggarwal.net/dynamic-camera.pdf

Alumur, S., & Kara, B. Y. (2008). Network hub location problems: The state of the art. *European Journal of Operational Research*, *190*(1), 1–21. doi:10.1016/j.ejor.2007.06.008.

Bansal, N. K., Feng, X., Zhang, W., Wei, W., & Zhao, Y. (2012). Modeling temporal pattern and event detection using hidden Markov model with application to a sludge bulking data. *Procedia Computer Science*, *12*, 218–223. doi:10.1016/j.procs.2012.09.059.

Burkard, R. E., & Dollani, H. (2003). Center problems with pos/neg weights on trees. *European Journal of Operational Research*, *145*(3), 483–495. doi:10.1016/S0377-2217(02)00211-4.

Campbell, J. F., Ernst, A., & Krishnamoorthy, M. (2002). Hub location problems. In H. Hamacher, & Z. Drezner (Eds.), *Location Theory: Applications and Theory*. Berlin: Springer-Verlag.

Cross, R. L., & Parker, A. (2004). *The hidden power of social networks: Understanding how work really gets done in organizations*. Boston: Harvard Business Press.

Daskin, M. S. (1995). *Network and discrete location: Models, algorithms, and applications*. New York: Wiley-Interscience. doi:10.1002/9781118032343.

Drezner, Z. (1995). *Facility location: a survey of applications and methods*. Berlin: Springer Verlag. doi:10.1007/978-1-4612-5355-6.

Farahani, R. Z., & Hekmatfar, M. (2009). *Facility location: Concept, models, algorithms and case studies*. Berlin: Springer. doi:10.1007/978-3-7908-2151-2.

Fayyad, U. M., Wierse, A., & Grinstein, G. G. (2002). *Information visualization in data mining and knowledge discovery*. San Francisco, CA: Morgan Kaufmann Pub..

F. Glover, & G. A. Kochenberger (Eds.). (2003). *Handbook of metaheuristics*. Boston: Kluwer Academic Publishers.

Goloboff, P. A. (2005). Analyzing large data sets in reasonable times: Solutions for composite optima. *Cladistics*, *15*(4), 415–428. doi:10.1111/j.1096-0031.1999.tb00278.x.

Gui, H., & Roantree, M. (2012). A data cube model for analysis of high volumes of ambient data. *Procedia Computer Science*, *10*, 94–101. doi:10.1016/j.procs.2012.06.016.

Hakimi, S. L. (1965). Optimum distribution of switching centers in a communication network and some related graph theoretic problems. *Operations Research*, *13*(3), 462–475. doi:10.1287/opre.13.3.462.

Hang, C. W., Wang, Y., & Singh, M. P. (2009). Operators for propagating trust and their evaluation in social networks. In *Proceedings of the 8th International Conference on Autonomous Agents and Multiagent Systems*, (vol. 2, pp. 1025-1032). IEEE.

Hochbaum, D. S., & Pathria, A. (1998). Locating centers in a dynamically changing network, and related problems. *Location Science*, *6*(1), 243–256. doi:10.1016/S0966-8349(98)00048-5.

Inches, G., & Crestani, F. (2011). Online conversation mining for author characterization and topic identification. In *Proceedings of the 4th Workshop on Workshop for Ph. D. Students in Information & Knowledge Management*. New York: ACM.

Kariv, O., & Hakimi, S. L. (1979a). An algorithmic approach to network location problems: The *p*-centers. *SIAM Journal on Applied Mathematics*, *3*, 513–538. doi:10.1137/0137040.

Kariv, O., & Hakimi, S. L. (1979b). An algorithmic approach to network location problems: The *p*-medians. *SIAM Journal on Applied Mathematics*, *37*, 539–560. doi:10.1137/0137041.

Kinsella, S., Passant, A., Breslin, J. G., Decker, S., & Jaokar, A. (2009). The future of social web sites: Sharing data and trusted applications with semantics. *Advances in Computers*, *76*, 121–175. doi:10.1016/S0065-2458(09)01004-3.

Klein, C. M., & Kincaid, R. K. (1994). Technical note—The discrete anti-p-center problem. *Transportation Science*, *28*(1), 77–79. doi:10.1287/trsc.28.1.77.

Kossinets, G., & Watts, D. (2006). Empirical analysis of an evolving social network. *Science*, *311*, 88–90. doi:10.1126/science.1116869 PMID:16400149.

LaValle, S., Lesser, E., Shockley, R., Hopkins, M. S., & Kruschwitz, N. (2011). Big data, analytics and the path from insights to value. *MIT Sloan Management Review*, *52*(2), 21–32.

Özsoy, A. F., & Pınar, M. Ç. (2006). An exact algorithm for the capacitated vertex p-center problem. *Computers & Operations Research*, *33*(5), 1420–1436. doi:10.1016/j.cor.2004.09.035.

Paradis, R. D., Davenport, D., Menaker, D., & Taylor, S. M. (2012). Detection of groups in non-structured data. *Procedia Computer Science*, *12*, 412–417. doi:10.1016/j.procs.2012.09.095.

Ribeiro, C. C., & Hansen, P. (2002). *Essays and surveys in metaheuristics*. Boston: Kluwer Academic. doi:10.1007/978-1-4615-1507-4.

Tamir, A. (2001). The *k*-centrum multi-facility location problem. *Discrete Applied Mathematics*, *109*(3), 293–307. doi:10.1016/S0166-218X(00)00253-5.

Thomas, J. J., & Cook, K. A. (2006). A visual analytics agenda. *IEEE Computer Graphics and Applications*, *26*(1), 10–13. doi:10.1109/MCG.2006.5 PMID:16463473.

Zikopoulos, P., & Eaton, C. (2011). *Understanding big data: Analytics for enterprise class Hadoop and streaming data*. New York: McGraw-Hill Osborne Media.

KEY TERMS AND DEFINITIONS

Big Data Analytics: Collection of techniques and methods for analyzing big data, which must take into account its specific properties and issues (big data structure, type, variety, frequency, etc).

Evolutionary Algorithm: A methauristic method that is based on the principles of natural evolution of individuals in a population. The quality of individuals in the population is improved by iterative application of evolutionary operators: selection, crossover and mutation.

Hybrid Metaheuristic Method: Combination of two or more optimization methods, where one of them must be a metaheuristic method (for example combination metaheuristic-metheuristic and metaheuristics-heuristic).

Local Search: Single solution based heuristic method that tries to improve the current solution by exploring the solutions its smaller or bigger neighborhood, defined by user.

Metaheuristics: Techniques and methods used for solving various optimization problems, especially the large-scale ones. They efficiently provide a solution to the problem, but its optimality can not be proven.

*p***-Center Problem:** Well-known facility location problem of finding the optimal location of p nodes in a given network so that the maximum distance of a node to its nearest center is minimized.

Social Network: A system with a set of social actors (nodes) and a collection of social relations that specify how these actors are relationally tied together.

Tabu Search: Single-solution based heuristic method that explores a neighborhood of a current solution by using memory structures that describe the visited solutions or user-provided sets of rules.

Chapter 11
Big Data at Scale for Digital Humanities:
An Architecture for the HathiTrust Research Center

Stacy T. Kowalczyk
Dominican University, USA

Craig Willis
University of Illinois, USA

Yiming Sun
Indiana University, USA

Jiaan Zeng
Indiana University, USA

Zong Peng
Indiana University, USA

Milinda Pathirage
Indiana University, USA

Beth Plale
Indiana University, USA

Samitha Liyanage
Indiana University, USA

Aaron Todd
Indiana University, USA

Guangchen Ruan
Indiana University, USA

Loretta Auvil
University of Illinois, USA

J. Stephen Downie
University of Illinois, USA

ABSTRACT

Big Data in the humanities is a new phenomenon that is expected to revolutionize the process of humanities research. The HathiTrust Research Center (HTRC) is a cyberinfrastructure to support humanities research on big humanities data. The HathiTrust Research Center has been designed to make the technology serve the researcher to make the content easy to find, to make the research tools efficient and effective, to allow researchers to customize their environment, to allow researchers to combine their own data with that of the HTRC, and to allow researchers to contribute tools. The architecture has multiple layers of abstraction providing a secure, scalable, extendable, and generalizable interface for both human and computational users.

DOI: 10.4018/978-1-4666-4699-5.ch011

INTRODUCTION

Big Data is big news. The data deluge of scientific research data, social media data, and financial/commercial data is now mainstream. It is discussed in the public press, studied in academic situations, and exploited by entrepreneurs (Press, 2013). Until very recently, the humanities have not been included in the digital data wave (Anderson, 2007). However, the state of humanities research is undergoing a major transformation (Drucker, 2009; Dunn & Blanke, 2009). Digitally-based research methodologies are becoming more widely used and accepted in the humanities (Borgman, 2009). Big data is just becoming available for humanists (Manovich, 2012).

The initial efforts at doing *in silico* humanities research were personal projects of forward-looking researchers (Dunn & Blanke, 2009). These initial efforts entailed digital scholarly editions (Newman, 2013; Walsh, 2013), specialized applications for specific research projects (Walsh & Hooper, 2012), and specialized applications for a specific research domain (Almas et al., 2011). Some of these initiatives evolved into community-based efforts to develop a set of standards for text encoding that became the focus of much of the digital humanities work for the past 10 years (Drucker, 2009). Institutional support for digital humanities includes the trend towards Digital Humanities Centers in colleges and universities. Many of these centers have not been as successful as initially expected due to the resource intensive nature of digital humanities projects such as text digitization and encoding or specialty applications development (Borgman, 2009). Cross-institutional activities, including funding agency initiatives to develop shared technical infrastructures, have had mixed results (Friedlander, 2009). All of these efforts have not provided the desired results. Infrastructure for digital humanities remains unavailable to many researchers (Borgman, 2009).

This chapter describes the research efforts to create a cyberinfrastructure to support Big Data for digital humanities. In the sections that follow, the need for this research is placed in the context of digital humanities and cyberinfrastructure research, the nature of data in the humanities is discussed, the HathiTrust Research Center (HTRC) is introduced, the cyberinfrastructure research is described, and the architecture is explicated.

BACKGROUND

Digital Libraries and Digital Humanities

Digital Humanities encompasses many types of research domains, methodologies, and data types (Manovich, 2012). However, much of the work in digital humanities deals with textual data (Crane, 2006; Drucker, 2009; Unsworth, Rosenzweig, Courant, Frasier & Henry, 2006). Until very recently, the biggest barrier to digital humanities was getting textual data in digital form; digitizing materials or negotiating for access to digital materials was the first step in most digital humanities projects (Cunningham, 2011; Pitti, 2004). With the advent of massive digitizing efforts by many libraries and by Google, digital data for researchers in the humanities is now becoming available (Cunningham, 2011; Svensson, 2010; Williford & Henry, 2012). These digital libraries offer services to researchers that include bibliographic and full text searching, results management, metadata, and text and image displays. In addition, some digital libraries can provide specialized or advanced functionality to specific communities of users within the scope and mission of the library (Candela et al., 2011).

Digital libraries vary in size and scope. Small and narrowly scoped collections may have begun as digital humanities projects. These digital research collections result in a resource that is indistinguishable from a digital library (Pitti, 2004). Two such projects are the Chymistry of Isaac Newton and the Perseus Digital Library.

The Chymistry of Isaac Newton is a tightly scoped collection of the Alchymical Notebooks of Isaac Newton that also provides a research environment for developing new insights into Newton's work and his impact on the history and philosophy of science (Newman, 2013; Walsh & Hooper, 2012). It is also a scholarly edition of these manuscripts, a set of reference works on early chemistry and alchymical work (Pastorino, Lopez & Walsh, 2008), and an interface for a Latent Semantic Analysis Tool[1] to analyze the relationships between the terms within the documents in the Newton Digital Library (Hooper, 2013). The Perseus Digital Library is another narrowly scoped digital library of approximately 3,000 digitized historic manuscripts with search tools and some analytics such as word statistics (word occurrence in the documents and the corpus) and cross references to other documents[2].

Before big data was a term in popular use (Press, 2013), Crane defined a set of dimensions to differentiate between typical digital libraries and massive digital libraries that could incorporate all print books. These dimensions are scale, heterogeneity of content, granularity of content, audience, and collections and distributors (2006). Crane proposes that massive digital libraries are very large (over 1,000,000 books) with a broad scope (similar to brick and mortar libraries) that can manage the data of each book more granularly than as a volume (providing structure at the section, page, or concept level) for a broad set of users and are available via a number of points of entry and interfaces (2006). Project Gutenberg and the Internet Archive are examples of well-known digital libraries (Manovich, 2012). Project Gutenberg has 42,556 volumes[3] in the collection available at the volume only. Project Gutenberg does not have multiple distribution channels. The content is heterogeneous and appeals to a broad audience (Project Gutenberg, 2013). The Internet Archive has 4,510,411 texts[4]. This collection is heterogeneous with broad appeal and available through multiple distribution channels. The data is only available at the volume level without other levels of granularity of content (Internet Archive, 2013). Using Crane's criteria, the Internet Archive would be considered a massive digital library, but Project Gutenberg would not.

The HathiTrust Digital Library, a shared and secured digital repository, is a partnership of major research libraries. It is one of the largest collections of digital books and documents available to researchers (Christianson, 2011). As of May 2013, the HathiTrust Digital Library collection included 10,728,728 total volumes, comprising 5,617,818 individual book titles and 278,481 serial titles for a total of 3,755,054,800 pages, totaling 481 terabytes of storage[5]. By all measures, the HathiTrust Digital Library fits Crane's criteria of a massive digital library. Nearly 11 million volumes prove scale, and the granularity of this collection is multi-dimensional. The data is available at the volume or the page as full text or PDF (when copyright allows). The HathiTrust Digital Library has a broad, comprehensive, and heterogeneous collection. The most common subjects are Language and Literature followed by History, Sociology, and Business & Economics (Piper, 2013), a broad audience, and multiple distribution channels.

From Digital Libraries to Big Data

Massive digital libraries with millions of digitized books can be considered Big Data for the humanities. Unlike Big Data in other domains such as purchasing data, telecommunications, sensors, satellites, or microarrays, humanities data consists of thoughts, ideas, concepts, words, language, events, time, voice, grammar, persons, identities, character, location, and place. All of which are in a totally unstructured format and most of which originate in books, journals, and documents. A significant characteristic of Big Data is dimensionality (Jacobs, 2009). Humanities textual data in general and the HathiTrust Digital Library data in particular are multidimensional. One dimension of this data is the logical structure of the document; access and understanding of this data can be at the volume, section, chapter, page, or word level. Another dimension of the data is conceptual; access and understanding of the concepts, ideas, and attitudes within the pages of the books. Another dimension is the language itself; access and understanding of this data can be the meaning of words, the structure of language, and the organization of thought through language. Yet another dimension is temporal; access and understanding of the data can be the time period of the author and the writing of the book or the time period of the subject of the book. The data could be used as a longitudinal survey of ideas, attitudes, word meanings, language structure, publishing trends, and so on. Williford and Henry assert that the underlying humanities data is just as heterogeneous, complex, and massive as big data in other domains. In addition, the research methods used in the humanities may produce a very large data output. Many scholars engaged in computationally intensive research see this output as more important than the original data (Williford & Henry, 2012).

By multiple measures, HathiTrust data is Big Data. If Big Data is to be defined as "data whose size forces us to look beyond the tried-and-true methods that are prevalent at that time" (Jacobs, 2009) or as "data [that] is too big, moves too fast, or doesn't fit the strictures of your (sic) database architectures [so to] gain value from this data, you must choose an alternative way to process it" (Dumbill, 2012), then the HathiTrust data is Big Data. If Big Data is defined by its network properties, its relationship to other data, and its value derived from patterns and connections between pieces of data (Boyd & Crawford, 2011), then again, HathiTrust data is Big Data.

Cyberinfrastructure for the Humanities

The availability of this new, huge corpus of material has lowered one of the major barriers to the wide adoption of digital humanities methodolo-

gies. However, this big data has presented a new set of challenges and barriers for humanities scholars access to computation platforms that can process the quantity of data available, the knowledge of algorithms and the ability to build appropriate applications, and the technical skills required to get the research results.

Digital library resources such as HathiTrust and Google Book Search that provide only traditional library functions such as searching and reading interfaces are not sufficient as infrastructure for humanities research (Borgman, 2009; Williford & Henry, 2012). The current model of digital humanities, a multi-disciplinary research group including humanities researchers and computer scientists supported by grant funding developing a resource or a tool, is unsustainable (Manovich, 2012). Developing cyberinfrastructure, "computing systems, data storage systems, advanced instruments and data repositories, visualization environments, and people, all linked together by software and high performance networks to improve research productivity and enable breakthroughs not otherwise possible" (Stewart et al., 2010, p. 1) will free humanities researchers to pursue their scholarly and intellectual interests using technology that they themselves did not need to develop (Unsworth et al., 2006).

A suitable cyberinfrastructure for digital humanities would be accessible and sustainable, could facilitate interoperability and collaboration, and would support experimentation (Unsworth et al., 2006). Multiple calls for developing cyberinfrastructure for the humanities have been issued (Svensson, 2011; Manovich, 2012; Unsworth et al., 2006; Williford & Henry, 2012). However, the response has been sparse. Only two projects are known to be developing broad, public cyberinfrastructure for the humanities – Project Bamboo and the HathiTrust Research Center (Christenson, 2011; Sieber, Wellen & Jin, 2011). The Andrew W. Mellon Foundation awarded a grant to the University of Chicago and the University of California, Berkeley to build a consortium of institutions to develop and sustain cyberinfrastructure for the arts and humanities (Greenbaum & Kainz, 2009). This project was begun in 2008 and ended in 2013. The project developed a registry, the Digital Research Tools website, to help humanities researchers locate tools, services and collections[6] (Adams & Gunn, 2012).

The HathiTrust Digital Library founding partner institutions determined that the data in their digital library "would serve as an extraordinary foundation for many forms of computing-intensive research", and thus commissioned a call for proposals to establish up to two research centers that would develop a cyberinfrastructure for the entire HathiTrust Digital Library corpus (Christenson, 2011). Indiana University and the University of Illinois developed a proposal to develop the HathiTrust Research Center which was accepted July 2011.

HATHITRUST RESEACH CENTER

It is important to delineate the structure of the HathiTrust Research Center (HTRC) with respect to the HathiTrust Digital Library itself. The HathiTrust Digital Library offers long-term preservation and access services, including bibliographic and full-text search and reading capabilities for public domain volumes and some copyrighted volumes. The HTRC on the other hand, provides computational research access to the HathiTrust Digital Library collection. Limited reading of materials will be possible in the Research Center to accommodate needs for reviewing results and so on, but the destination for reading-based research remains the HathiTrust Digital Library.

The HTRC is a distributed cyberinfrastructure that meets the specific needs of long-term secure research and analysis of the HathiTrust text corpus. The core goal of the cyberinfrastructure is to deliver optimal access and use of the HathiTrust corpus. The sheer size of the corpus, nearly 11 million digitized books with nearly 4 billion individual pages, demands innovative thinking about the architecture and the optimization at all levels of the software infrastructure from disk to tools. Research and development has focused on scalability by reducing reads, intelligent caching, and delivering maximum cycles at minimal costs; interoperability of algorithms and data by providing APIs and flexible parameter driven interfaces; accessibility by simplification of technologies for researchers who care about their theories but not the technology; and experimentation support by providing user contributed data and algorithms.

The corpus is a dynamic collection. As mentioned previously, the collection has 10,728,728 total volumes, comprising 5,617,818 individual book titles and 278,481 serial titles for a total of 3,755,054,800 pages, slightly over 30% (3,287,832 volumes) were in the public domain with the remaining volumes being under copyright protection. The first version of the HRTC will provide research access to the public domain materials.

An Architecture for Digital Humanities Cyberinfrastructure

In this section, we will describe the architecture for the HathiTrust Research Center (HTRC), which is designed to support a broad range of functions in a secured environment.

The HTRC supports six primary functions: data discovery, service discovery, data retrieval, job management, results management, and data management. Data discovery provides an interface for searching the HTRC collection for specific subsets of data to be processed as well as to create and save individualized subsets as sub-collections of the data for ongoing use. Service discovery allows researchers to find available algorithms for analyzing, visualizing, and processing the data with individualization of these algorithms via parameters. Job management is the processes of allocating computational resources, as well as submitting and monitoring algorithm execution. Results management allows for the persistent storage of the output of the research process. As noted above, the output of the algorithms (the data extracted, collated, annotated, and analyzed) is the research product (Williford & Henry, 2012). Data management includes data storage, data access, and ongoing maintenance of the data. The HTRC infrastructure includes a massive data store with secured programmatic retrieval via web service architecture. Access for data, services, and computation are controlled via a secured set of APIs.

The HTRC architecture was designed to support the functions developed above. Both conceptually and technically, the functions form three layers: Discovery and Access, Services Management, and Data Management (see Figure 1). The goal of this three-layered architecture is to provide multiple levels of abstraction, to protect the underlying data, to manage services and resources, and to provide a simple model for interoperability.

Sustainability is a major concern in cyberinfrastructure (Bietz, Ferro, & Lee, 2012; Mackie, 2007; Schopf, 2009; Stewart, Almes, & Wheeler, 2010). Sustainability includes funding, relationship management, and resource preservation (Bietz, Ferro, & Lee, 2012). Schopf contends that while funding is important, it is more important that the cyberinfrastructure culture change to embrace reuse of exiting code and software packages to enhance reliability and increase maintainability and sustainability (2009). Therefore, a major goal of the HTRC cyberinfrastructure architecture is long-term sustainability. The design is intended to be implemented with existing, well-known, and well-supported open source software to facilitate the ongoing maintenance and support of this software long after the research and development are completed. The HTRC was built using Apache, WS02, SEASR/Meandre infrastructure, and other open source projects.

Figure 1. HTRC Architecture

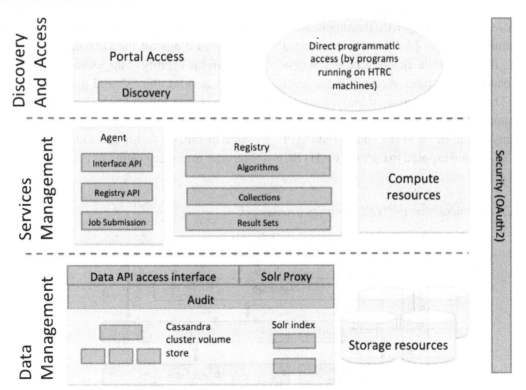

Access Management

With Big Data comes big security challenges such as appropriate access and privacy (Bryant, Katz, & Lazowska, 2008; Cloud Security Alliance Big Data Working Group, 2012; Manadhata, 2012; Rong, Nguyen, & Jaatun, 2013). Cyberinfrastructure security in a cloud environment has additional considerations for privacy that include managing user services and data dispersed across multiple clouds possibly in other legislative domains, protecting user data against unauthorized access from other users running processes on the same physical server, insuring that data is not modified without the owner's consent, and protecting logs that may contain sensitive infrastructure information, query terms, and results information (Rong et al., 2013). Security is applied throughout the HTRC infrastructure to ensure data and to protect privacy.

The HTRC follows a layered approach to security, where the lowest level ensures that data is securely and reliably stored with necessary network level security and replication for reliability (see Figure 2). The next layer, the data application programming interface (API), provides secured access to the data while ensuring proper access control based on user roles. Agent API, the level atop the Data API and computational resources, implements proper security measures for the algorithms deployed on HTRC data. Data API and Agent API are exposed to the user via HTRC

portal and discover service. Authentication and authorization across these layers are implemented based on OAuth2 (OAuth, 2012) protocol. A separate identity provider that supports OAuth2 is deployed to manage users including user profiles with the necessary access control metadata.

Access to the HTRC resources is secured using the OAuth2 token-based authentication protocol. Each request that comes to the Data API, the Agent API, or the Registry API must be accompanied by an access token issued by the HTRC identity provider. Applications or users who invoke HTRC APIs can acquire an access token by following standard OAuth2 protocols. The HTRC OAuth2 implementation uses the "Authorization code" as the authorization grant (Hardt, 2012). The benefits of this grant include such features as authorizing third party clients on behalf of users and managing user identities in a single location while eliminating the need to share credentials with any third party clients.

Upon receiving a request to the API endpoint, the security filter is invoked before passing the request to the actual business logic. This filter extracts the access token from the request and validates it against the OAuth2 provider, which returns the validity of the token to the filter. If the token is valid, the OAuth2 provider returns the authorization information that token represents such as user name and roles. This information is used by the API layers to decide whether the user has the necessary rights to access the resources

Figure 2. Implementation of HTRC Security Framework

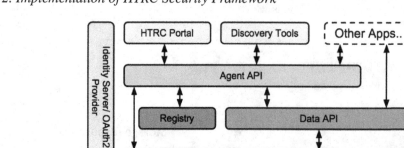

requested. In addition, this information will be used to log the API access history for audit purposes. One of the limitations of OAuth2 protocol is lack of support for authorization based on user attributes. The HTRC addresses this by utilizing role based access control mechanisms (Sandhu, Ferraiolo, & Kuhn, 2000) provided in WSO2 Identity Server (WS02, 2013), which is used as the OAuth2 provider in HTRC. This enables the handling of different types of users with varying levels of permissions.

DISCOVERY AND ACCESS

This layer is designed to provide access to the HTRC corpus. The goal is to simplify the interactions of technologies so that researchers who care about their theories but not the technology can use digital humanities methodologies to explore the data, to experiment with new ideas, and to develop new theories.

Discovery and Collection Building

Searching for data in the HathiTrust Research Center (HTRC) collection is an essential function and is the primary starting point for digital humanities research. Among many other criteria, researchers require the ability to find items from a certain region or period, by one or more known authors, that contain a specific set of concepts. Once identified, researchers also require the ability to store and modify collections of selected items. These collections serve as the foundation for the large-scale analysis supported by HTRC services.

For end user searching, the HTRC selected Blacklight, a widely used, open-source library catalog and discovery system designed to work with both bibliographic and full text data in SOLR indexes (Sadler, 2009). Using an established search interface helps with the HTRC's sustainability (Schopf, 2009). Blacklight is based on the "Ruby on Rails" web application framework and is easily customized or extended. As part of the HTRC

initial implementation, the Blacklight application was extended to support the creation of research collections for analysis. Once authenticated, researchers are able to search the indexes (described in following sections) and create new collections based on items selected or to modify previously saved collections. Users are also able to derive new collections from public sets created by others. In the initial implementation, collections consist of a set of HathiTrust volume identifiers along with collection metadata including the collection name, description, availability (public or private), and descriptive keywords. Once created, research collections are available for analysis.

The HTRC is currently exploring improvements to the discovery and collection building interfaces. Future enhancements will include greater user control over bibliographic and full-text searching, improved faceting, and more sophisticated collection building capabilities. While many questions remain open, the ability to define, gather, and preserve collections of items for analysis remains a central challenge for the HTRC project.

HTRC Portal

The HTRC portal serves as an entry point for the entire HTRC infrastructure. It provides a web interface for users to interact with the backend services. The simple web interface provides access to the digital humanities text analysis tools (algorithms), subsets of the public domain volumes (collections), and computational resources. In the portal, a researcher will select an algorithm, choose a collection to process, and submit the request. As an example, a researcher is interesting in creating a tag cloud of the words from the novels of Charles Dickens. The researcher decides that the tag cloud workflow that checks spelling and eliminates commonly used words called stop words (words such as "a", "and", "of", "the", etc.) would provide a more meaningful result. When the researcher chooses the algorithm, the portal requests the parameter information about this algorithm and dynamically builds the web form (see Figure 3). When the researcher has completed the request and clicks on submit, the portal sends the data to the agent to be processed.

The portal interacts with the HTRC services layer to verify the input data is correct, to allocate computing resources, and to submit a job to be processed. The portal provides an interface to monitor the progress of the process and provides status updates to the researcher. When the process is completed, the results are available to the researcher. The web interface allows the researcher to terminate a running algorithm if necessary. When ready to view the results, the researcher goes to the results tab, selects the job and can see and download the results (see Figure 4).

The HTRC web interface hides the backend services from the users as much as possible. The portal issues calls to the services layer to build all of the lists of services available such the collections that the research is allowed to process, the algorithms, the status of jobs submitted, and the results sets from both the current and previous sessions. To make the application easy to maintain, the HTRC web interface is implemented based on Apache Struts 2 framework and deployed in the Apache Tomcat container.

The HTRC anticipates that additional access methods to the HTRC data will be required. The HTRC is designed to allow other interfaces from other digital humanities services, systems, and cyberinfrastructure to securely access the data, the algorithms, and computational resources.

SERVICES MANAGEMENT

Managing the available services is the second major layer of the HTRC cyberinfrastructure. In this layer, the HTRC manages access control via

Figure 3. Dynamic Algorithm Submission Process

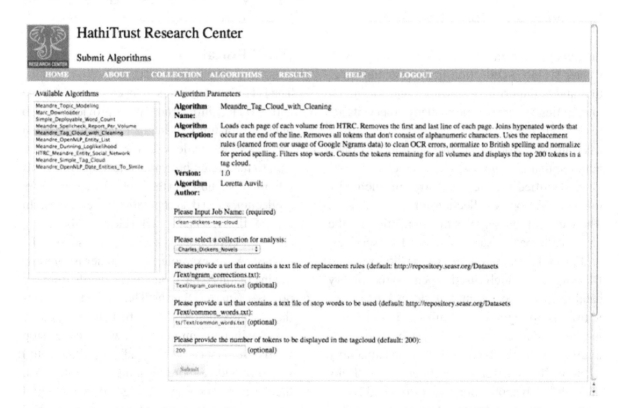

Figure 4. Results of the Tag Cloud Algorithm

authentication and authorization in a security module, provides access to data collections and digital humanities algorithms, manages the results, and allocates computing resources and jobs.

Agent Architecture

The architecture is designed with an agent/actor framework (Hewitt, Bishop, & Steiger, 1973). In this framework, a central program (the agent) manages individual requests for services by spawning and managing individual processes (actors) that fulfill the service requests. The agent/actor model helps to mitigate the problems associated with shared memory concurrency. An actor is a lightweight cooperative thread that serially receives messages, performs computation based on the message, and then suspends until the next message is available. These messages are the only way actors communicate, as they do not share memory. Actor systems are automatically parallel

since actors are executed on a parallel task pool and are not allowed to perform blocking operations. Actors are also very lightweight, on the order of 400 bytes. These features make them very scalable. The HTRC agent is written in Scala (École Polytechnique Fédérale de Lausanne, 2013) and uses the Akka library for the actors (Akka, 2012).

In the HTRC cyberinfrastructure, the service requests are always created via a program – either from an HTRC process such as the public portal interface or from an algorithmic program using HTRC resources. The service requests use the Representational State Transfer (REST) architecture (Fielding & Taylor, 2002). The agent framework allows for an abstracted and secured access to the services of the HTRC by controlling the access to the services via a set of "transactions" via a RESTful API. The RESTful API sends assignments to this internal actor, which will then perform the tasks and returns the results back to the requestor. The communication between the agent and the action uses asynchronous messaging to ensure no API call will block a user's actor process (see Figure 5). The agent receives a request and then forwards it to the actor representing that user. This actor then modifies the user's state and performs the specified action. In the case of a registry query, the user actor sends a message to the "registry proxy" actor. This actor contacts the registry, executes the query, and sends the response to the user actor. Once the user actor has the response it completes the original web request.

The user actor sends a message and then waits for a response, in what seems a violation of the actor model, as it would block the actor until the response arrived. An asynchronous process can mimic this synchronicity by use of the "Future" feature. When the user actor sends the message to the registry, rather than waiting for a response, it registers a callback. The user actor is then free to process new user requests. When the information from the registry is available, the web request is completed by the callback. To match this model, a non-blocking approach was used to present the REST API, as a blocking model would interact poorly with the asynchronous actors.

Job submissions are handled by having the user actor create a child actor to manage the job. This "compute child" retrieves data from the registry actor, combines it with the user input and launches a child actor representing the actual job. These job actors simply stage data via a secure copy (scp) and launch jobs via a secure shell (ssh). The job actors send status updates to the compute child. When a user queries job status, the corresponding actor queries its compute children, which are always available to respond with recent status information.

Governance Registry

Digital humanities services within the HTRC include such functions as creating sub-collections of the data, running analysis algorithms, and managing analysis results. These services are managed via the HTRC governance registry. The services offered through the HTRC are generic with specific instantiations; that is, the service itself is a general function with specific parameters, programs, and/or data that is unique to the execution. As a simple example, a tag cloud algorithm has a specific set of input parameters

Figure 5. Agent Interaction Model

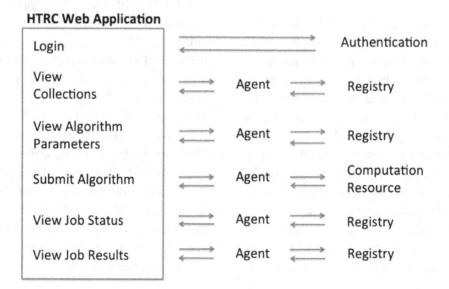

that must be provided for a successful run. These parameters include the identifier of the set of the collection to be processed, the number of words to be included in the tag cloud, a stop word list to remove the most common, unimportant words, and a dictionary for a spell checking function. These parameters are encoded in an XML schema (see Figure 6). The basic information such as name, version, description, and author is represented in the "info" element. The second component of the info element is the parameters element. Each

parameter specified is given a name, a type, a flag indicating if it is mandatory or optional, and a default value if appropriate (such as a generic stop word list or a general dictionary). A label for the portal user interface is also present, along with a description of purpose of the argument.

Defined registry services available via the agent include such general tasks as: listing all available collections, uploading a new collection, modifying a collection, listing all available algorithms, fetching the full properties of an algorithm,

Figure 6. Registry Algorithm XML for Tag Cloud with Data Cleaning

```xml
<algorithm>
  <info>
    <name>Meandre_Tag_Cloud_with_Cleaning</name>
    <version>1.0</version>
    <description>Loads each page of each volume from HTRC. Removes the first and last line
    </description>
    <authors>
      <author name="Loretta Auvil"/>
    </authors>
    <supportUrl>http://help.me/please</supportUrl>

    <parameters>
      <param
        name="input_collection"
        type="collection"
        required="true">
        <label>Please select a collection for analysis</label>
        <description>The collection containing the volume ids to be used for analysis.</de
      </param>
      <param
        name="replacement_rules_url"
        type="url"
        required="false">
        <label>Please provide a url that contains a text file of replacement rules (defaul
        <description>The replacement rules are used for cleaning and normalizing tokens.</
      </param>
      <param
        name="stopwords_list_english_url"
        type="url"
        required="false">
        <label>Please provide a url that contains a text file of stop words to be used (de
        <description>The stop words are removed from the list of tokens.</description>
      </param>
      <param
        name="n_top_tokens"
        type="int"
        required="false">
        <label>Please provide the number of tokens to be displayed in the tagcloud (defaul
        <description>The number of tokens to be displayed in tagcloud.</description>
      </param>
    </parameters>
  </info>

  <run_script>run_Meandre_Tag_Cloud_with_Cleaning.sh</run_script>
```

submitting jobs, fetching standard counsel error (strderr) and standard output console (stdout) for a job, querying for the status of a job. Specific digital humanities processes and algorithms available for the initial implementation include word counts, tag clouds, named entity extraction (characters, locations, and dates), concept modeling, bibliographic data download, and viewing results. Algorithms results are stored persistently and are accessible from the HTRC portal.

The text analysis algorithms in the HTRC cyberinfrastructure were available by integrating a well-known humanities workflow engine, Meandre, and analytics toolkits SEASR (Ács et al., 2010). With these tools, the HTRC has been able to demonstrate basic text processing such as word counts visualized as Tag Cloud (using d3.js) and data cleaning based on transformation rules that were created as part of the Mellon SEASR Services project (Searsmith, 2011). These transformation rules expose thousands of OCR error corrections and normalization of spellings. To demonstrate additional text analytics, the HTRC leveraged flows that extract entities such as dates and plot them on a Simile timeline or extract locations and plot them on a Google map and flows that perform the comparison of two collections of documents using Dunning Loglikelihood. Meandre flows were executed by running scripts, which encapsulate all the necessary dependencies. The integration of the Meandre flows into the HTRC tested the both the agent APIs, the actor model, the job submission process, and the registry data model. During a large-scale demonstration and test, 354 HTRC sessions with agent actors were initiated, 43 sub-collections were created, and 153 algorithms were successfully executed.

DATA MANAGEMENT

The final layer of the architecture is data management. At the heart of the HTRC is a corpus consisting of millions of volumes and billions of pages that will give digital humanities researchers access to data at an unprecedented scale and allow them to make new discoveries that would be unimaginable before. The types of data available at the HathiTrust Digital Library (HT) include the original scanned images, text from optical character recognition software (OCR), OCR coordinates data, structural metadata stored in the Metadata Encoding and Transmission Standard[7] (METS), and bibliography metadata in the MAchine Readable Cataloging[8] (MARC) metadata standard. The HT deposits and replicates the data at both the University of Michigan and Indiana University.

The HTRC acquires the data from the HT. Currently the HTRC only obtains a subset of the corpus, which consists of the raw OCR texts from 2.6 million volumes in public domain and their associated METS and MARC metadata documents. The total size of this subset amounts to only about 2.2TB on a file system. Initially, this does not appear to be impressive as the data can easily fit on a single disk. But the total file system size alone does not indicate the challenges that must be overcome in the ingestion, storage, and management of the data. The challenges are primarily due to the differences in data structures that each system needs to meet their individual goals: the HTRC, a digital humanities cyberinfrastructure that uses text both as index and as raw data for algorithmic processing, needs fast access to the individual text files while the HT, a digital library that uses the text as index and page images as display data, needs fast access to images and rarely uses the text files.

The HathiTrust Digital Library's data structure is designed for fast access to large volumes of data and to facilitate page reading. Each volume at the HT bears a unique identifier made up of a prefix and a string ID. The string ID is the original identifier assigned by the contributing institution of that volume. The format of this ID ranges from alphanumeric strings to handle URIs; the prefix is a short alphanumeric code identifying the contributing institution that essentially serves as a namespace qualifier to avoid potential collisions among the institution-specific string IDs. Each actual volume is an individual Zip file containing a number of text files where each text file corresponds to a single page of the volume. Accompanying each volume Zip file is an XML document containing the METS metadata for that volume. The HT uses the Pairtree hierarchical directory structure to store these files on their specialized hardware and file system (Kunze, Haye, Hetzner, Reyes, & Snavely, 2011). Each prefix has its own Pairtree. The string ID portion of a volume ID is first *cleaned* according to the Pairtree rules to replace characters that are not file system safe. Then the cleaned string is broken into a sequence of 2-character *shorties* and sometimes with a trailing 1-character *morty* (if the cleaned string contains an odd number of characters). The sequence is used to create a *ppath*, a nested list of directories starting from the Pairtree root where each directory name corresponds to a *shorty* or a

morty. At the end of each *ppath* are the volume Zip file and the associated METS XML file (see Figure 7). Advantages of the Pairtree structure include a well-balanced directory tree, and mutually referable *ppaths* and IDs (Kunze et al, 2011). However, this structure also introduces a lot of overhead because on average each volume Zip file is less than 1MB, yet accessing the file from the Pairtree requires reading many inodes and directory entries first resulting in a seek time that is much greater than the read time of the data itself. Storing a large number of small files directly on disk is also not efficient as the files are too small to leverage the advantages from modern high performance file systems which typically are optimized to use parallelization to achieve high throughput on large files (Borthakur, 2007; Schmuck & Haskin, 2002; Schwan, 2003). It becomes apparent that the HTRC must store and manage the corpus data in a more efficient way.

Figure 7. HTRC Simplified Pairtree Structure

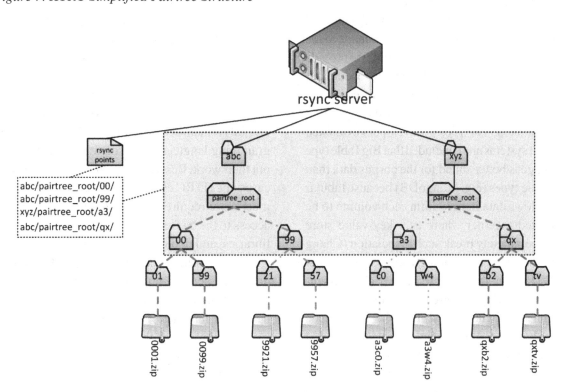

The most obvious data management solution is a relational database system (RDBMS). It is a very mature technology that has been a staple in data-centric systems for decades. However, as Big Data is becoming more pervasive, relational database is known to have limitations on its ability to scale well. A relational database also imposes a very rigid schema that is optimized for dense data but is not efficient for sparse data such as the HTRC corpus (Cattell, 2011). For the HTRC, an intuitive schema design would define each volume as a row in a table, and each page a column; however, since these volumes have different numbers of pages that could vary by several orders of magnitude, such a schema needs to have enough columns to accommodate the book with the most pages while the majority of the rows will be only partially filled. Therefore a relational database is quickly ruled out.

There is an abundance of alternative storage and data management solutions that all share the term "NoSQL" although they vary greatly in data models and data storage mechanisms (Han, Haihong, Le, & Du, 2011). One commonality is that some of the strong assertions found in typical relational database systems are relaxed in accordance to the CAP theorem (e.g. consistency) in order to provide better availability and scalability (Stonebraker, 2010). Since supporting large-scale research and analysis is a goal of the HTRC, a NoSQL solution was evaluated. The HTRC developers evaluated different systems and concluded that BigTable type of storage is better suited for the corpus data than key-value types (e.g. MongoDB) because tabular form allows data items within each volume to be associated together where as a key-value store would completely break such association (Chang et al., 2008). The specific NoSQL solution that the HTRC has implemented is Apache Cassandra as it is an open source and fully distributed column store (whereas a similar one, the Apache HBase has special nodes that could become single point of failure) (Hecht & Jablonski, 2011). The data model in Cassandra consists of *Keyspaces*, *Column Families*, *Rows*, and *Columns*, which at a high level are analogous to database terms such as *Databases*, *Tables*, *Rows* and *Columns*. Each row can have its own set of columns that can be entirely different from the columns in other rows. Cassandra is designed for scalability and is typically setup with multiple nodes to form a *ring*, and each node is assigned a token which controls the range of the data the node is in charge of, and the data is usually replicated across different nodes and the number of replica is controlled by a *replication factor*. Cassandra stores data onto the disk as *SSTables* and a *compaction* process can consolidate smaller *SSTables* into larger ones.

Data API

There are two competing requirements on how the HTRC corpus data should be served to the users: security and ease of use. Data security is a significant aspect of the HTRC cyberinfrastructure in order to keep the large repository of digitized books, both public domain and copyrighted, safe and free from unauthorized access. Logging access to each volume is a key requirement. Of course, the HTRC wants to simplify access to allow researchers to be able to find and process the data that they require without imposing a heavy programming burden and without a significant performance penalty. From a set of use cases, researchers in Digital Humanities work with a wide range of programming languages and software tools to carry out their work. Based on the requirements and use cases, the HTRC examined several approaches to meet these requirements including giving direct access to the backend data store, providing client libraries, and deploying a service.

Giving users direct access to the Cassandra data store seems to be the most straightforward approach. Cassandra servers use the Thrift interface definition language for communication, which would allow each of the algorithms in the HTRC to directly access the data store (Slee, Aditya & Kwiatkowski, 2007). However, giving direct access to the backend repository does not conform to either the security requirement or the ease of use requirement. Cassandra has implemented few security provisions and has no auditing functions. Neither the data itself nor any communication via the Thrift interface is encrypted (Okman, Gal-Oz, Gonen, Gudes, & Abramov, 2011). In addition, the Thrift communication interface to Cassandra is rather complex and presents a learning curve to the users. The approach of providing client libraries brings a middle layer between the backend store and user's client code. This approach is capable of presenting a simplified API to the users while hiding much of the backend detail. This middle layer also allows user activities to be audited and other necessary security measures to be enforced. However, in order to support the various languages, the HTRC developers would face the difficult task of developing and maintain a client library for each different programming language, making ongoing maintenance and long-term sustainability more difficult.

Using a simple, lightweight protocol for the Data API was determined to be the optimal choice. RESTful web service works over the standard HTTP protocol, and most modern programming languages come with libraries and methods for establishing communications over HTTP, so the HTRC only needs to maintain a single service (Pautasso, Zimmermann, & Leymann, 2008). Auditing can be done at the service level. Using HTTP over SSL (i.e. HTTPS) also protects the communication channel between the client and the service and keeps the data safe from eavesdroppers. The HTRC Data API needs to be able to deliver data at either the volume or the page level. As straightforward as it may seem, the Data API faces a few challenges associated with delivering multiple volumes.

The first challenge is maintaining the structures of multiple volumes with their pages while delivering the set through a single stream to the client as the HTTP protocol is designed to allow a single response stream. Using a Zip stream to encapsulate and deliver the data and metadata to the client worked in all of our use cases. Zip, a technology for aggregating and compressing data, is integrated into many modern programming languages via libraries. Other advantages of using Zip include its ability to reduce data size and its compatibility with both textual and binary data

Using Zip also provides a solution to the second challenge, conveying error messages to the client after the response stream is committed. By design, the HTTP protocol dictates that when a response is sent back to the client, it provides a status code to indicate whether the request succeeded or failed. In case of a failure, the status code provides some information about the error. While this design is sufficient for conventional HTTP use where one request typically asks for just one document, streaming a set of volumes or pages is inherently different because an error may occur after the initial success response code is sent and the Zip file has begun to stream. It would be impossible to change the status code or add other HTTP response headers once the stream has started. Failing silently is an unacceptable approach; not only would users be confused or frustrated by this lack of information but in a worse case scenario, if the algorithm did not realize the stream was interrupted, incorrect analysis could be produced. Fortunately, with Zip stream, error messages can be injected as a Zip entry just as other volume data. The HTRC Data API uses a specially named Zip entry "ERROR. err" to convey error messages to the client. This allows the client to check the presence of this entry to detect if any error occurred and to request the data again or to abort the process.

The initial implementation of the Data API was logically straightforward. A client sends a list of volume identifiers or page identifiers in the request. Upon receiving a request, the Data API service instantiates a handler for the request, parses the identifiers list to ensure their validity, and iterates through the list retrieving each one from Cassandra. The data is Zipped to be streamed back to the client. However, such a synchronized process between the retrieval from the data store and the data transmission process was unnecessarily slow.

After the initial testing, the Data API was redesigned using an asynchronous mechanism to fetch data from the Cassandra store. In this new implementation, requests from all clients are added to a common queue. A pool of threads work asynchronously by taking entries off of the queue, fetching the data from Cassandra, and notifying the corresponding handlers when some data is ready. Such an asynchronous approach provides synchronous data fetching, zipping and transmitting. The new Data API increased the average transfer rate from below 6MB/sec to about 20MB/sec. The asynchronous Data API employs a throttling mechanism to limit the number of entries each client may place in the queue at any given time, thus controlling the amount of data that can wait in memory. The data is stored as volumes (books) and pages. The API uses page as the throttling unit since the size volumes varies widely. If each throttling unit were defined to be 100 pages, an entry requesting for 200 pages would occupy 2 units. The throttling mechanism solves the problem of a single client monopolizing the queue because at any given time, the number of pages a single client can have in the queue is bounded, so that other requests will get resources as well. The Data API utilizes the Java WeakReference class to wrap client request entries before they are added to the queue, so that if a client drops before the request is complete, its queued entries will no longer be valid and therefore will not be processed. The throttling increased the transfer rate to 60MB/sec.

HTRC Indexing

Indexing is a key component to the HTRC cyberinfrastructure. As researchers may search in both the HathiTrust Digital Library as well as the HathiTrust Research Center, the HTRC decided to use the same indexing software and index

schema as the HathiTrust Digital Library. Both use Apache Solr, a lucene-based open source enterprise search platform, to index both bibliographic data (fielded data such as author, title, publisher, publication dates) and the unstructured OCR full text data. Solr, like most indexing tools, requires large amount of memory. The HTRC Solr index files for the public domain data described above are 1.8 TB. In the foreseeable future, the size will increase significantly as new data is processed. It is currently hosted in seven servers by using the Solr sharding technique. Solr sharding is a way to scale Solr horizontally by breaking a single Solr instance into multiple Solr instances, each with identical schema. The shards run independently and have no overlap with one another. Because each Solr shard runs on its dedicated machine, the distribution enables HTRC Solr to be able to utilize more resources, like CPU and memory, which improves search performance significantly (see Figure 8).

Solr sharding is not completely transparent. It requires specific knowledge of the access point of every single shard for each query. In addition, Solr does not have a strong security layer at either the document level or the communication level, meaning that it is possible to modify a Solr index freely when the access points of the shards are known. To solve these problems, we designed and implemented a proxy for the HTRC Solr indices. This proxy runs in front of HTRC Solr shards as an extra lightweight layer to protect the index files from being modified, to hide the details of distributed deployment of Solr shards, and to audit access. The proxy allows only the Solr search functionality and preserves all of the Solr query syntax. Queries are sent to the Solr proxy as if it were a single Solr instance. The Solr proxy logs all requests, including any prohibited commands. The head shard receives the queries and then distributes them to all shards including the head shard itself. The head shard then aggregates the query results and returns the aggregated results to the Solr proxy. Finally, the Solr proxy returns

Figure 8. Solr Shards

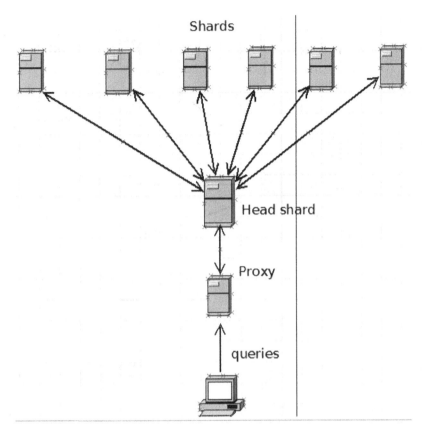

the result back to the requesting application. The proxy also provides extra RESTful calls for enhanced functionality such as downloading the MARC records for a set of volume IDs.

The HTRC is currently holding approximately 2.6 millions of volumes. To build an index efficiently against such a large corpus, the index building process needs to execute in parallel. We are now using seven machines, each with four cores and 16GB memory, to build full text index. Of the seven machines, six have Solr instances and are responsible for building index. The seven machine starts N threads, each responsible for 1/N of all volumes to index (see Figure 9). For each volume, the responsible thread gets the bibliographic information from the corresponding MARC record, extracts the text content from the pairtree, prepares SolrInputDocument by adding all bibliographic fields and OCR files into SolrInputDocument object, and finally commits it to one of the six Solr servers. We track the index shard for each volume in this distributed environment to make debugging and data management easier. Although the process of building index is generally considered a one time effort, a complete reindex can be required periodically for such reasons as schema changes and performance enhancements and thus, our efforts to create an efficient process.

Data Ingest Process

The ingest of the HT data into the HTRC is done using rsync, which is a tool available on many Linux distributions that allows data to be synchronized between a source and a destination by transmitting only the differences. The HT hosts

Figure 9. HTRC Solr Instances

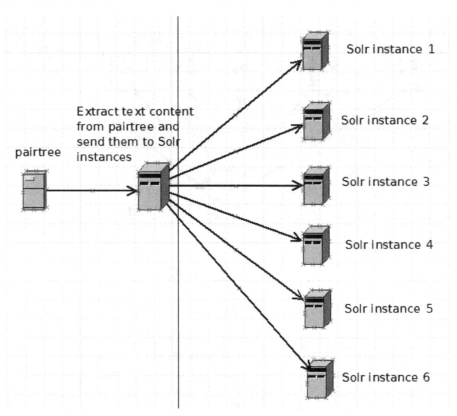

an rsync server that points to a directory containing Pairtrees from all prefixes (see Figure 7). An rsync client at the HTRC can retrieve and store a mirror copy of the entire directory structure on the local disk. The data is parsed and loaded into the Cassandra NoSQL server. After rsync finishes updating the Pairtrees on disk, the ingest process uses the output from the rsync process to determine what updates and deletions there are and modifies the data in the Cassandra ring accordingly.

Cassandra is a fully distributed data store; however the initial tests of the HTRC ingest service showed a bottleneck in the process caused by the single rsync point. The early version of the ingest service ran on one machine, which launched a single rsync command to transfer the Pairtrees. This process proved to be very slow. Testing showed that while the rsync server exposes a single entry point at the root directory, it

does not prevent rsync clients from specifying a path pointing directly to a deeper level under the rsync root. Taking advantage of this capability, a method to allow multiple rsync to transfer the data was devised. At the source end, the HT runs a Linux command such as "tree" to list all the paths with a fixed depth into these Pairtrees and store these paths in a file (referred to as the rsync points file) at the root level on the rsync server. At the destination site, the HTRC's ingest service receives the rsync points file. The ingest service then opens the file to retrieve the list of paths and creates these directories as if they were new. Meanwhile, the paths in the rsync points file are also added to a common queue. After all directories are available on the disk, multiple threads issue rsync commands with a specific path as the entry point. This effectively changes from transferring one single tree with a single rsync to transferring multiple subtrees with multiple rsync commands.

To further improve performance, the rsync processes are distributed across all Cassandra nodes. Each ingest service instance is assigned a unique number between *0* and *(n -1)* where *n* is the total number of nodes with the ingest service. Each ingest service instance first transfers its own copy of the rsync points file from the HT, but rather than processing and creating directories for all paths in the file, the ingest service computes the modulo hash value of each path. If the hash value matches the unique number assigned to this ingest instance, it processes the subtree under this path. This allows all nodes to participate in the rsync process of the source Pairtree. This is a more scalable and efficient model distributing the workload and data across all current and future nodes.

Research Contributions

The HathiTrust Research Center is a research project to develop a cyberinfrastructure research environment using the HathiTrust Digital Library corpus for humanities researchers. This cyberinfrastructure offers a simple way to subset a huge collection of millions of books with billions of pages, allows researchers to choose and execute algorithms without having to manipulate the data to fit the algorithm, and view and save results with the ultimate goal of helping researchers create new knowledge.

This research effort has contributed to the general understanding of developing cyberinfrastructure with open source components without compromising a sound logical architecture. Using open source software to build robust cyberinfrastructure has a number of benefits; it allows for rapid development; it provides a solid code base for basic features; and it allows for efficient use of resources. We were able to build a distributed data synchronization process using simple tools

that processed a billion files. This innovative approach can be a model for big data systems with massive amounts of data to be transferred.

The HTRC cyberinfrastructure allows, indeed encourages, users to contribute their algorithms for analyzing the millions of books in the corpus. These user-contributed algorithms need access to the HTRC data and indexes to perform their work. Balancing security for the data and with ease of use for the users and their algorithms, we developed a layer of security over two popular open source tools – Cassandra and Solr. For Cassandra, we developed a RESTful Data API that allows algorithms to access data without exposing the underlying Cassandra schema. The API provides a simple mechanism to stream huge sets of data to the algorithms. In addition to providing a more secure interface, the Data API allows us to log access to understand usage of the materials and to provide copyright protections. Algorithms need access to the Solr indexes. With a proxy service, we are able to simplify access to the Solr shards, provide logging for access analysis, and to add a layer of security to the indexes. This work contributes towards a better understanding of the issues of data security when users need to execute their own programs in a cyberinfrastructure.

FUTURE RESEARCH DIRECTIONS

The HTRC has ongoing initiatives for security and increased access. In the next phase of the project as the HTRC prepares to receive the works still under copyright from the HathiTrust Digital Library, significant research on the non-consumptive research is in process; non-consumptive research is a legal term meaning that no action or set of actions on the part of users, either acting alone or in cooperation with other users over the duration of one or multiple sessions, can result in sufficient information gathered from the HathiTrust collection to reassemble pages from the collection.

Non-consumptive as a research challenge is approached through deeper study of the constraint and recommendations for tooling adaptations to satisfy it.

The HTRC production roll out includes scaling up to full operational capacity in both hardware and support mechanisms. This includes providing a Sandbox for algorithm developers to test their code against the Data and Indexing APIs and scaling their code to the data. In the future, the HTRC will allow for the ability of end users to contribute algorithms, data, and notations, and metadata improvements. Research is underway to determine the data structures, interfaces and relationships that must be created to support this new and important functionality.

Big data in the humanities, and the tools that provide access to them, have the potential to revolutionize the process of humanities research methodologies as well as the outcomes of that research (Boyd, & Crawford, 2011). As the work of humanists change and evolve, the HTRC will evolve and change as well. Future work will focus on the new requirements of humanities researchers.

CONCLUSION

The HathiTrust Research Center has been designed to make the technology serve the researcher – to make the content easy to find, to make the research tools efficient and effective, to allow researchers to customize their environment, to allow researchers to combine their own data with that of the HTRC, and to allow researchers to contribute tools. The architecture has multiple layers of abstraction providing a secure, scalable, extendable, and generalizable interface for both human and computational users.

REFERENCES

Ács, B., Llorà, X., Auvil, L., Capitanu, B., Tcheng, D., Haberman, M., & Welge, M. (2010). A general approach to data-intensive computing using the Meandre component-based framework. In *Proceedings of the 1st International Workshop on Workflow Approaches to New Data-Centric Science*. IEEE.

Adams, J. L., & Gunn, K. B. (2012). Digital humanities: Where to start. *College & Research Libraries News, 73*(9), 536–569.

Akka. (2012). *Akka documentation*. Retrieved from http://akka.io/docs/

Almas, B., Babeu, A., Bamman, D., & Boschetti, F. Cerrato, L., Crane, G., … Smith, D. (2011). *What did we do with a million books: Rediscovering the Greco-ancient world and reinventing the humanities* (White Paper). Washington, DC: National Endowment for the Humanities.

Anderson, S. (2007). *The arts and humanities and e-Science: Scoping survey report and findings*. Retrieved from http://www.ahessc.ac.uk/scoping-survey

Bietz, M. J., Ferro, T., & Lee, C. P. (2012). Sustaining the development of cyberinfrastructure: An organization adapting to change. In *Proceedings of the ACM 2012 conference on Computer Supported Cooperative Work* (pp. 901-910). ACM. Retrieved from http://dx.doi.org.ezproxy.lib.indiana.edu/10.1145/2145204.2145339

Borgman, C.L. (2009). The digital future is now: A call to action for the humanities. *Digital Humanities Quarterly, 4*(1).

Borthakur, D. (2007). *The Hadoop distributed file system: Architecture and design.* Apache Software Foundation. Boyd, d., & Crawford, K. (2011). Six provocations for big data. In *A Decade in Internet Time: Symposium on the Dynamics of the Internet and Society.* Academic Press.

Bryant, R. E., Katz, R. H., & Lazowska, E. D. (2008). Big-data computing: Creating revolutionary breakthroughs in commerce, science, and society. In *Computing Research Initiatives for the 21st Century.* Computing Research Association. Retrieved from www.cra.org/ccc/docs/init/Big_Data.pdf

Candela, L., Athanasopoulos, G., Castelli, D., El Raheb, K., Innocenti, P., & Ioannidis, Y. ... Ross, S. (2011). *The digital library reference model.* Retrieved from http://bscw.research-infrastructures.eu/pub/bscw.cgi/d222816/D3.2b Digital Library Reference Model.pdf

Cattell, R. (2011). Scalable SQL and NoSQL data stores. *SIGMOD Record, 39*(4), 12–27. doi:10.1145/1978915.1978919.

Chang, F., Dean, J., Ghemawat, S., Hsieh, W. C., Wallach, D. A., Burrows, M., & Gruber, R. E. (2008). Bigtable: A distributed storage system for structured data. *ACM Transactions on Computer Systems, 26*(2), 4. doi:10.1145/1365815.1365816.

Christianson, H. (2011). HathiTrust. *Library Resources & Technical Services, 55*(2), 93–102. doi:10.5860/lrts.55n2.93.

Cloud Security Alliance Big Data Working Group. (2012). *Top 10 big data security and privacy challenges.* Cloud Security Alliance. Retrieved from https://cloudsecurityalliance.org/research/big-data/#_downloads

Crane, G. (2006). What do you do with a million books? *D-Lib Magazine, 12*(3). Retrieved from http://www.dlib.org/dlib/march06/crane/03crane.html doi:10.1045/march2006-crane.

Cunningham, L. (2011). The librarian as digital humanist: The collaborative role of the research library in digital humanities projects. *Faculty of Information Quarterly, 2*(1). Retrieved from http://fiq.ischool.utoronto.ca/index.php/fiq/article/view/15409/12438

Drucker, J. (2009, April 3). Blind spots: Humanists must plan their digital future. *The Chronicle of Higher Education.*

Dumbill, E. (2012, November). Making sense of big data. *Big Data.*

Dunn, S., & Blanke, T. (2009). Digital humanities quarterly special cluster on arts and humanities e-science. *Digital Humanities Quarterly, 3*(4).

École Polytechnique Fédérale de Lausanne. (2013). *Scala.* Retrieved from http://www.scala-lang.org/

Fielding, R. T., & Taylor, R. N. (2002). Principled design of the modern web architecture. *ACM Transactions on Internet Technology, 2*(2), 115–150. doi:10.1145/514183.514185.

Friedlander, A. (2009). Asking questions and building a research agenda for digital scholarship. In *Working Together or Apart: Promoting the Next Generation of Digital Scholarship.* Academic Press.

Greenbaum, D. A., & Kainz, C. (2009). *Report from the bamboo planning project.* Coalition for Networked Information. Retrieved from http://www.cni.org/topics/ci/report-from-the-bamboo-planning-project/

Han, J., Haihong, E., Le, G., & Du, J. (2011). Survey on NOSQL database. In *Proceedings of the 6th International Conference on Pervasive Computing and Applications (ICPCA),* (pp. 363-366). ICPCA.

Hardt, D. (2012). *The OAuth 2.0 authorization framework, draft-ietf-oauth-v2-31.* Retrieved from http://tools.ietf.org/html/draft-ietf-oauth-v2-31

HathiTrust. (n.d.). *Call for proposal to develop a hathitrust research center.* Retrieved from www.hathitrust.org/documents/hathitrust -research-center-rfp.pdf

Hecht, R., & Jablonski, S. (2011). NoSQL evaluation: A use case oriented survey. In Cloud and Service Computing (CSC), (pp. 336-341). IEEE.

Hewitt, C., Bishop, P., & Steiger, R. (1973). A universal modular ACTOR formalism for artificial intelligence. In *Proceedings of the 3rd International Joint Conference on Artificial Intelligence (IJCAI'73)*, (pp. 235-245). IJCAI.

Hooper, W. (2013). *About latent semantic analysis.* Retrieved from http://webapp1.dlib.indiana.edu/newton/lsa/help/hs20.html

Internet Archive. (2013). Retrieved from http://archive.org/index.php

Jacobs, A. (2009). The pathologies of big data. *Communications of the ACM, 52*(8), 36–44. doi:10.1145/1536616.1536632.

Kunze, J., Haye, M., Hetzner, E., Reyes, M., & Snavely, C. (2011). Pairtrees *for collection storage (V0.1).* Retrieved from https://wiki.ucop.edu/download/attachments/14254128/PairtreeSpec.pdf

Mackie, C. J. (2007). Cyberinfrastructure, institutions, and sustainability. *First Monday, 12*, 6–4. doi:10.5210/fm.v12i6.1908.

Manadhata, P. K. (2012). Big data for security: Challenges, opportunities, and examples. In *Proceedings of the 2012 ACM Workshop on Building Analysis Datasets and Gathering Experience Returns for Security* (pp. 3-4). ACM. Retrieved from http://dl.acm.org/citation.cfm?id=2382420

Manovich, L. (2012). Trending: The promises and the challenges of big social data. In M. K. Gold (Ed.), *Debates in the Digital Humanities*. Minneapolis, MN: The University of Minnesota Press. Retrieved from http://lab.softwarestudies.com/2011/04/new-article-by-lev-manovich-trending.html

Newman, W. R. (2013). *Chymistry of Isaac Newton.* Retrieved from http://www.dlib.indiana.edu/collections/newton/

OAuth. (2012). *Documentation.* Retrieved from http://oauth.net/documentation/

Okman, L., Gal-Oz, N., Gonen, Y., Gudes, E., & Abramov, J. (2011). Security issues in NOSQL databases. In Proceedings of Trust, Security and Privacy in Computing and Communications (TrustCom), (pp. 541-547). IEEE.

Pastorino, C., Lopez, T., & Walsh, J. A. (2008). The digital index chemicus: Toward a digital tool for studying Isaac Newton's index chemicus. *Body, Space & Technology Journal, 7*(20).

Pautasso, C., Zimmermann, O., & Leymann, F. (2008). Restful web services vs. big web services: Making the right architectural decision. In *Proceedings of the 17th International Conference on World Wide Web* (pp. 805-814). ACM.

Piper, P. S. (2013). *HathiTrust and digital public library of America as the future.* Retrieved from http://www.infotoday.com/OnlineSearcher/Articles/Features/HathiTrust-and-Digital-Public-Library-of-America-as-the-future-88089.shtml

Pitti, D. V. (2004). Designing sustainable projects and publications. In S. Schreibman, R. Siemens, & J. Unsworth (Eds.), *A Companion to Digital Humanities*. Oxford, UK: Blackwell. doi:10.1002/9780470999875.ch31.

Press, G. (2013). A very short history of big data. *Forbes*. Retrieved from http://www.forbes.com/sites/gilpress/2013/05/09/a-very-short-history-of-big-data/

Project Gutenberg. (2013). Retrieved from http://www.gutenberg.org/ebooks/

Rong, C., Nguyen, S. T., & Jaatun, M. G. (2012). Beyond lightning: A survey on security challenges in cloud computing. *Computers & Electrical Engineering*. Retrieved from http://www.sciencedirect.com/science/article/pii/S0045790612000870

Sadler, E. (2009). Project blacklight: A next generation library catalog at a first generation university. *Library Hi Tech, 27*(1), 57–67. doi:10.1108/07378830910942919.

Sandhu, R., Ferraiolo, D., & Kuhn, R. (2000). The NIST model for role-based access control: Towards a unified standard. In *Proceedings of the Fifth ACM Workshop on Role-Based Access Control,* (pp. 47-63). ACM.

Schmuck, F., & Haskin, R. (2002). GPFS: A shared-disk file system for large computing clusters. In *Proceedings of the First USENIX Conference on File and Storage Technologies,* (pp. 231-244). USENIX.

Schopf, J. M. (2009). Sustainability and the office of cyberinfrastructure. In *Proceedings of Network Computing and Applications.* IEEE.

Schwan, P. (2003). Lustre: Building a file system for 1000-node clusters. In *Proceedings of the 2003 Linux Symposium.* Linux.

Searsmith, K. (2011). *Making progress: SEASR at the Andrew W. Mellon research in information technology retreat.* Retrieved from http://seasr.org/blog/2008/02/28/making-progress-seasr-at-the-andrew-w-mellon-research-in-information-technology-retreat/

Sieber, R. E., Wellen, C. C., & Jin, Y. (2011). *Spatial cyberinfrastructures, ontologies, and the humanities.* Retrieved from http://www.pnas.org/citmgr?gca=pnas,108/14/5504

Slee, M., Aditya, A., & Kwiatkowski, M. (2007, January). *Thrift: Scalable cross-language services implementation.* Facebook.

Stewart, C. A., Almes, G. T., & Wheeler, B. C. (2010). *Cyberinfrastructure software sustainability and reusability: Report from an NSF-funded workshop.* Retrieved from http://hdl.handle.net/2022/6701

Stewart, C. A., Simms, S., Plale, B., Link, M., Hancock, D., & Fox, G. C. (2010). What is cyberinfrastructure? Norfolk, VA: Association for Computing Machinery (ACM). doi:doi:10.1145/1878335.1878347.

Stonebraker, M. (2010). Errors in database systems, eventual consistency, and the CAP theorem. *Communications of the ACM, 5.*

Svensson, P. (2010). The landscape of digital humanities. *Digital Humanities Quarterly, 4*(1).

Svensson, P. (2011). From optical fiber to conceptual cyberinfrastructure. *Digital Humanities Quarterly, 5*(1).

Unsworth, J., Rosenzweig, R., Courant, P., Frasier, S. E., & Henry, C. (2006). *Our cultural commonwealth: The report of the American council of learned societies commission on cyberinfrastructure for the humanities and social sciences.* New York: American Council of Learned Societies. Retrieved from http://www.acls.org/programs/Default.aspx?id=644

Walsh, J. A. (2013). *The Algernon Charles Swinburne project text collection.* Retrieved from http://www.swinburneproject.org/

Walsh, J. A., & Hooper, E. W. (2012). The liberty of invention: Alchemical discourse and information technology standardization. *Literary and Linguistic Computing, 27,* 55–79. doi:10.1093/llc/fqr038.

Williford, C., & Henry, C. (2012). *One culture.* Council on Library and Information Resources. Retrieved from http://www.clir.org/pubs/reports/pub151

WSO2. (2013). *WSO2 identity server - Identity & entitlement management.* Retrieved from http://wso2.com/products/identity-server/

ENDNOTES

1   http://webapp1.dlib.indiana.edu/newton/lsa/index.php

2   http://www.perseus.tufts.edu/hopper/collections

3   As of May 9, 2013 at http://www.gutenberg.org/ebooks/

4   As of May 9, 2013 at http://archive.org/index.php

5   May 10, 2013 at http://www.hathitrust.org/about

6   http://dirt.projectbamboo.org/

7   http://www.loc.gov/standards/mets/

8   http://www.loc.gov/marc/

Chapter 12
GeoBase:
Indexing NetCDF Files for Large–Scale Data Analysis

Tanu Malik
University of Chicago, USA

ABSTRACT

Data-rich scientific disciplines increasingly need end-to-end systems that ingest large volumes of data, make it quickly available, and enable processing and exploratory data analysis in a scalable manner. Key-value stores have attracted attention, since they offer highly available data storage, but must be engineered further for end-to-end support. In particular, key-value stores have minimal support for scientific data that resides in self-describing, array-based binary file formats and do not natively support scientific queries on multi-dimensional data. In this chapter, the authors describe GeoBase, which enables querying over scientific data by improving end-to-end support through two integrated, native components: a linearization-based index to enable rich scientific querying on multi-dimensional data and a plugin that interfaces key-value stores with array-based binary file formats. Experiments show that this end-to-end key-value store retains the features of availability and scalability of key-value stores and substantially improves the performance of scientific queries.

INTRODUCTION

Advances in remote sensing technology have significantly lowered the cost of data acquisition via satellites and aircrafts. Well-known satellites, such as GOES (NOAA), Landsat (NASA), and Aqua/Terra (NASA) continuously stream 20-60 GB of remotely sensed image datasets to receiving stations per day. To use these datasets for analysis, scientists typically determine relevant datasets through a metadata search. Given the large data volumes, a metadata search, however, is increasingly becoming insufficient in retrieving datasets of interest. Content-based searches, such

DOI: 10.4018/978-1-4666-4699-5.ch012

as determining ranges of pressure or temperature within the data files, can improve retrieval. To conduct these searches, however, currently scientists have to download datasets, and perform data management tasks, such as format conversions, pre-process the datasets, index, and visualize, and then subset the content. It is not uncommon for scientists to work with many different systems to perform the entire data management task, Alternatively, it is desirable to have an *end-to-end* system that ingests datasets in their native format, indexes them as part of the ingestion process, and provides a simple API for content-based searches.

We are interested in designing such an end-to-end system for geoscience datasets. In several sub-domains of geosciences, end-to-end issues are addressed through data access libraries. For instance most geoscience datasets are stored in self-describing formats, such as NetCDF (Rew 1990), and HDF5 (Folk 1999), and are made available for exploration and analysis through the NetCDF-Java API or HDF5 API. These libraries address some end-to-end issues in that they hide the nitty-gritty details specific to their format. They, however, do not address other end-to-end issues. In particular, the libraries do not provide a mechanism for indexing the datasets or the ability to conduct content-based analysis on multiple datasets in parallel.

Another alternative is to explore data through parallel file systems tailored for NetCDF files (Li 2003), but these file systems introduce other end-to-end issues, namely, communication between high-level data analysis operators that must be controlled by the programmer (Buck 2011). Datasets can also be explored by using geospatial databases, such as PostGIS Raster and MySQL. Most database systems, however, require datasets resident in a file system to be imported into their native format. For instance, raster images can be ingested into the databases through the Geospatial Data Abstraction Library (GDAL), but bulk loading of large volumes of data is known to be slow. For analysis, the storage model in these traditional databases is row-oriented, i.e., they store multi-dimensional array data as a single record. They do not leverage the performance benefit derived from a column-oriented design, which has shown to provide orders of magnitude of performance improvement (Abadi 2008).

For geoscience applications, a useful alternative is distributed key-value stores, e.g., BigTable (Chang 2008) and their open-source counterparts, e.g., HBase (Apache 2010) that are built on a parallel storage framework and have shown to scale to millions of updates while being fault-tolerant and highly available. Key-value stores, however, do not address all end-to-end issues in data exploration of geoscience datasets. In particular, key-value stores do not natively support files in self-describing formats, which are commonly used in geoscience disciplines. They also do not provide for efficient exploration of multi-dimensional datasets. Lack of support for self-describing files leads to format transformation, and lack of support for multi-dimensional data leads to inefficient indexing, and additional data management that soon become too cumber- some given the size of common scientific data sets.

In this chapter, we present GeoBase an end-to-end system that enables efficient exploratory data analysis on geoscience datasets without incurring any additional data transformation costs. To achieve this vital goal, GeoBase uses space-filling curves to store multi-dimensional spatio-temporal data in a one-dimensional key-value store. In adopting space-filling curves as an indexing technique, GeoBase does not introduce any data transformation costs that are often implicit in the linearization process. GeoBase intercepts requests for the sub-queries on the space-filling curve and corresponds them to contiguous, low-level byte extents at the physical level. Through this modification, data can continue to reside in thousands of files without the need to transform and/or transport them to another system. Our work makes the following technical contributions:

1. The multi-dimensional index enables efficient data exploration through array operations, such as multi dimensional range queries and aggregation queries.
2. The underlying key-value store provides the ability to sustain large number of data files coming at a fast rate, ensuring fault-tolerance and high availability, but more importantly multi-dimensional exploration on spatial, time, and other dimensions.
3. The system can retain the original file formats and need not transform into alternate formats and/or make coordinate transformations. These formats are not legacy formats but chosen and widely adopted by the geoscience community as space efficient formats for describing data.
4. We conduct and present a thorough experimental study of our solution.

The rest of the chapter is organized as follows: In *Background*, we cover related work. We then describe the problems in designing an end-to-end system for geoscience applications in *Problems in End-to-End Analysis*. We then introduce an end-to-end key-value store for geoscience, the architecture of GeoBase and focuses on the storage layer and the indexing method. Our solution discusses optimization issues that arise in an end-to-end system and provides solutions for the same. In *Experiments* we describe a full evaluation of GeoBase through experiments done on thousands of NetCDF files taken from the climate modeling studies and using HBase as our key-value store.

BACKGROUND

In this section, we review some recent works that address aspects of end-to-end data management.

In general, relational data processing improves end-to-end data processing by bringing analysis closer to storage. This is often achieved by abstracting the storage layer for analysis. Several early works abstracted data in the storage layer as multi-dimensional arrays and examined query-processing techniques (Libkin 1996, Marathe 1997). Baumann explored these abstractions on raster image data (Baumann 1999). More recently Howe and Maier proposed a logical grid abstraction by separating the topology of the grid from its geometry, which is encoded in the data files (Howe 2007). SciDB also improves end-to-end processing by natively enabling a variety of relational operators on multi-dimensional data (Stonebraker 2009). While these works improve end-to-end processing, none of them provide the scalability, ease-of-use and availability of key-value systems.

End-to-end issues have also been explored in key-value systems. In Zhao (Zhao 2010), the authors enable basic NetCDF processing via Hadoop but first require the data be converted into text. There has been work towards extending the NetCDF operator library to support parallel processing of NetCDF files to reduce data movement and transformation costs (Wang 2008), but does not address issues of efficient access. SciHadoop (Buck 2011) addresses fault tolerance issues and native access to scientific file formats but does not address multi-attribute analysis. Reducing the input space, i.e., using indexes in Hadoop systems has been investigated in HadoopDB (Abouzeid 2009) and in (Lu 2010). In both works, data must be ingested into the underlying database, thereby incurring extra data movement and preventing the use of scientific file formats, which are more commonly used.

Since scientific data is mostly read-only, another useful method for preserving locality is to construct bitmap indexes. FastBit, a multi-dimensional bit index, is built over NetCDF files (Wu 2009). Bit indexes, however, provide secondary, non-clustered index over the base data. Since geospatial data is multidimensional, an end-to-end system would benefit from spatial clustering, especially for range queries. Therefore, in this chapter we adopt space-filling curves (SFC) (Jagadish 1997) to cluster the data. We do not consider bitmap indexes but they can, in principle, be built over the clustered data. The size of the compressed bitmaps, in this case, will be smaller since clustering increases the average run length by storing tuples with equal values near to each other.

SFCs have recently been used to improve performance (Jensen 2004, Tao 2009), but must scale to large volumes of data. In this regard, a work closely related to ours is the one by Nishimura et al. (Nishimura 2011) on scalable multidimensional data infrastructure for location-aware services, such as location-aware social networking services or gaming services. However, our work differs from theirs in two primary respects. First, they primarily focus on object-based spatio-temporal data (point objects), whereas our approach exclusively focuses on field-based spatio-temporal data, in particular satellite imagery and its specific operators. Second, their linearization scheme requires data to be ingested in HBase, while we use Z-regions (Fenk 2002), a variant of Z-curve to provide native access to NetCDF files.

PROBLEMS IN END-TO-END ANALYSIS

We define an end-to-end system as a system that incurs minimal data transformation costs from the time it ingests data in a native format to the time data is available for exploratory analysis. Data transformation costs primarily arise due to differing choice of formats within the storage, intermediate, and analysis layers. Further, transformation costs may either correspond to one-time extract, transform, load (ETL) costs, which itself may be significant if the data comes in real-time and/or may correspond to repeated costs, especially if the same data is downloaded several times in a given format to be analyzed in a different format later. In this section, we describe a typical data ingestion system for geosciences, popular types of analysis operations, and problems in conducting end-to-end analysis.

In geosciences, the data ingestion system is typically a file system storing datasets generated during an experiment, an observation or while simulating geophysical phenomena. Each dataset is a collection of data files, in which each file records multiple physical variables in self-describing, portable formats. Each variable is described as a multi-dimensional array and its data laid out in the file in a specified order. Figure 1 illustrates a data ingestion system.

Two common exploratory analysis operations are:

- **Data Reduction:** A data reduction operation subsets multiple geophysical regions in space and time. An example two-region query is "Project temperature and precipitation attributes for the selected region R1 and project solar radiation for the selected region R2 between a common time frame of 26th of June, 1990 and 26th of June, 2000." Typically there will be thousands of selected regions. For an analysis system a data reduction query corresponds to several multi-dimensional range queries.

- **Data Condensation:** Condensation operations are data reduction operations followed by aggregation operations. The complexity of the aggregation operation varies from computing a simple maximum, minimum, or median to filter kernels, in which a new value for the array cell is determined by combining each old value plus its neighborhood. For the analysis system, condensation operation can be represented as a function f applied to a data reduction

Figure 1. Measurement of sea surface temperature and pressure variables on Earth. The continuous phenomenon is discretized into a regular grid; each grid cell records the values of the physical variables under its spatial extent, and is manifested into a file, based on a chosen format, such as NetCDF, HDF5, GRIB.

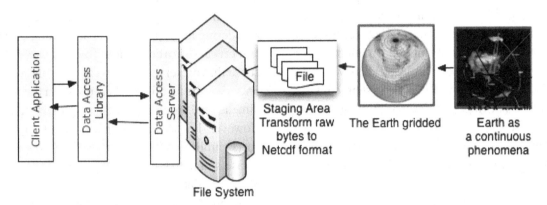

set S, yielding a result R, which is either scalar or composed of output of arrays r R. Thus,

$$f: (s_1, s_2, ...) \leftarrow (r_1, r_2, ...) \qquad (1)$$

A data access library, such as the NetCDF API (Unidata) combined with data protocols, such as OPeNDAP (OPeNDAP) and Pomengranate (NASA) enable reduction operations over a data ingestion system and thus enable an end-to-end system. However, this end-to-end system does not scale for analysis over large number of files. We realized a modest end-to-end system with NetCDF API and OPeNDAP with datasets hosted in a Linux ext3 file system. Figure 2 shows the

Figure 2. End-to-end system performance of data ingestion system

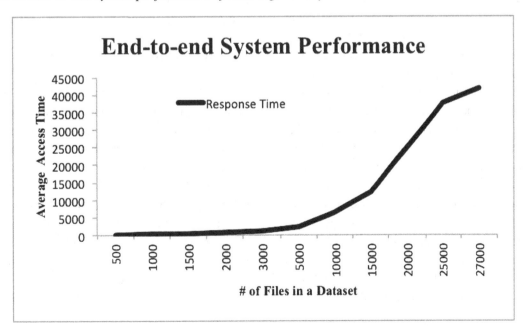

average total time it takes to execute 100 data reduction queries when the size of the dataset is increased from 500 to 27,000 NetCDF files. Each query asks for a subset of data by specifying a region over all files. The time to access increases non-linearly as in addition to serial execution on files, a large amount of state information is kept in memory. This strictly limits efficiency of data access, especially when the file system consists of millions of files or if the resolution of the file is increased.

Our objective is to build an end-to-end system on key-value stores that provides scalable, distributed access to data and thus improve performance. A vanilla key-value store currently does not lead to an end-to-end system. Most key-value systems support binary sequence file formats, which are different from self-describing formats of geoscience datasets. Thus data has to either translate into text or a custom translator needs to be written. Further, data reduction analysis operation is limited to one of the attributes (for e.g. one of the spatial dimensions) onto the key space of the key-value stores (Hill 2011). So analysis operations such as data reduction and condensation cannot be performed efficiently on the same system where data is stored.

In this chapter, we determine if a more efficient end-to-end system can be designed that does not incur data transformation costs during the ingestion phase and also enables multi-attribute access so that reduction and condensation operations can be conducted on the data system itself and not by downloading datasets. Towards this, in this chapter, we explore enabling a native interface to self-describing datasets and a linearization technique as an indexing mechanism for multi-attribute access to build a more efficient end-to-end system. While a native interface reduces data transformation costs, linearization does not.

Linearization (Samet 2005) is a common technique to transform multi- dimensional data points to a single dimension and allows for effi-

cient multi-attribute access in database systems. A space-filling curve (Jagadish 1997) is one of the most popular approaches for linearization, in which the curve visits all points in the multi-dimensional space in a systematic order. Hilbert curves and Z-ordering are examples of space-filling curves. Hilbert curve is a continuous fractal space-filling curve that preserves locality. Z-ordering loosely preserves the locality of data-points in the multi-dimensional space and is also easy to implement. However, linearization imposes data translation costs similar to those imposed by importing datasets in native format. In particular, to create linearized data all data values must be read from each individual file and reordered according the order of the curve.

Linearization also reduces data dimensionality to one and allows data to be searched in $log(n)$ complexity. However, there is loss of information, often leading to false-positives. It is often possible that objects far away in the original dimension are close together in the reduced dimension. The converse is also true, *i.e.* objects near to each other in the original dimension may be further away in the reduced dimension. While several alternatives are suggested in literature (Jagadish 1997, Samet 2005), it is important that the chosen method is compliant with the native file system interface.

An End-to-End System

We address the shortcomings of key-value stores, described in the previous section, by introducing two capabilities in GeoBase: (A) a native interface for accessing datasets in self-describing formats, and (B) efficient multi-attribute access over the datasets. The addition of these features improves upon the much needed end-to-end functionality in key-value systems in that they provide efficient analysis over self-describing datasets, while continuing to provide high scalability and availability as new datasets are inserted. In this section, we first provide background on some technologies that are used in GeoBase. We then describe improvisations to the technologies and optimizations schemes in GeoBase.

Background

GeoBase relies on *(i)* NetCDF, the self-describing data formats widely used in geosciences, *(ii)* HBase, the open-source key-value store, and *(iii)* Z-curves, a simple and efficient linearization technique.

Self-Describing Formats

There are a variety of available formats in the geosciences, such as NetCDF, HDF5, GRIBB, Fast, etc. Amongst these formats NetCDF remains a widely adopted and popular format because of its simple data format and easy-to-use API. Consequently, in GeoBase we use NetCDF as the governing format.

The NetCDF file format divides a given dataset file, physically, into two parts: file header and array data. The file header is the metadata defining *(i)* dimensions, *(ii)* global attributes, and *(iii)* variables. Dimensions such as spatial extents and time define shape of the variables in the dataset. One dimension can be unlimited and is considered the record dimension for growing-size variables. The header for the variables define its name, shape, named attributes, data type, array size, and data offset. The data part of the file, contains arrays of variable values (or raw data), and lays fixed-size arrays before laying out variable-sized arrays.

Figure 3. NetCDF File Format. (Source: Li, Liao, Choudhary, et. al (Li 2003))

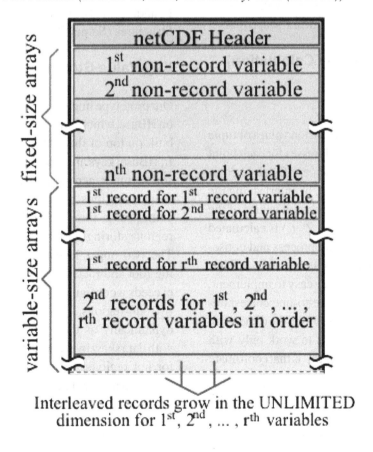

Each array is laid out in row-major order. This ordering, as we show later, influences our choice of linearization.

An important characteristic of the geo-scientific data is that it is often skewed spatially. Skew may lead to certain regions being absent, which are handled as null values, and certain spatial extents being present at high resolutions.

An important characteristic of the geo-scientific data is that it is often skewed spatially. Skew may lead to certain regions being absent, which are handled as null values, and certain spatial extents being present at high resolutions.

Linearization

Z-ordering loosely preserves the locality of data points in a multi-dimensional space.

Functionally, $Z(p)$ is a bijective function that computes for every tuple p its equivalent Z- address, which is a position on a linear Z shaped curve.

Definition (Z-Curve by Calculation)

$Z(p) = \text{bitinterleave}(p_1, ..., p_d)$,

in which $p_1, ..., p_d$ are d dimension values of tuple p. Figure 4 presents the Z-addresses for each point in a 4×4 grid. Z-addresses are efficiently computed by bit-interleaving, i.e., by interleaving the bit-representation of the dimension values of the tuple p. The inverse function $Z^{-1}(.)$ is calculated by reversing the interleaving process and consequently it has the same complexity as $Z(.)$. Thus the Z-ordering scheme is very easy to implement.

It is to be noted that a one-to-one correspondence of bits in the address to bits in the dimension values allows for algorithms to work only with addresses. An implication of this is that coordinate comparisons can be performed solely on addresses. Bit-interleaving is very useful for on geospatial files because it extends easily to any

Figure 4. Bit interleaving using Z-order for 4X4 universe

	00	01	10	11
11	0101	0111	1101	1111
10	0100	0110	1100	1110
01	0001	0011	1001	1011
00	0000	0010	1000	1010

number of dimensions, and dimensions with differing cardinalities by considering only those dimensions for bit-interleaving that have bits left for interleaving, i.e., if all bits of a dimension are exhausted it will not be considered for the interleaving process anymore. The Z-curve and the bit interleaving process are explained in-depth in Foundations of Multidimensional and Metric Data Structures (Samet 2005).

Key-Value Stores

Our prototype implementation of GeoBase is done on HBase, which is an open-source key-value store built on top of the Hadoop file system (HDFS). In HBase, keys are stored in byte-lexicographical sorted order across distributed regions, which range partitions the key space. Its architecture comprises a three layer B+ tree structure; the regions storing data constitute the lowest level. The two upper levels are special regions storing root and meta information. If a region's size exceeds a configurable limit, HBase splits it into two sub-regions. This allows the system to grow dynamically as data is inserted, while dealing with data skew by creating finer grained partitions for hot regions. In its data model, HBase uses the concept of column families, which is a set of columns within a row that are typically accessed together. All the values of a specific column-family are stored sequentially together on the disk. Such a data layout results in fast sequential scans on the consecutive rows, and also on the adjacent columns within a column family in a row.

HBase relies on HDFS for durability. Each key-value pair is multi-versioned and an update to a key-value pair is appends data in the file system. Updates are first written onto memory buffers, and flushed periodically to the disk. As a result writes are faster than reads. HBase can typically handle hundreds of thousands of inserts per second while efficiently processing range queries in real- time with response times as low as hundreds of milliseconds (George 2008). In a vanilla use of key-value stores for multi-dimensional data, Z-value of the dimensions being indexed; for instance the location and timestamp become the key and the values correspond to the data values at these indexed positions. As described in the next section, this mapping of keys to Z-values imposes significant data translation costs.

GEOBASE

We describe the architecture of GeoBase that enables end-to-end analysis, a few optimization issues that arise in its implementation, and finally describe our query algorithms.

Architecture

The key idea in GeoBase is to cluster regions of space, in- stead of individual data values, to preserve spatial proximity, and interface with the native file system. A region of space corresponds to a space covered by an interval on the Z-curve, more commonly called as the Z-region (Fenk 2002). The Z-region has a linear and spatial interpretation, as shown in the Figure 5, which shows a linear region 'G: [4:20]' and a spatial extent of the Z-region. Since the Z–region corresponds to the first and last Z-values of tuples in a spatial extent; Z-regions can themselves be calculated based on

Figure 5. A Z-region [α:β] is the space covered by an interval of Z-curve and is defined by two Z-addresses α and β. The letters denote a single contiguous region.

10

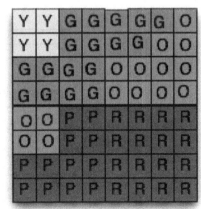

Z-region [4:20]

Z-regions: Y: [0:3], G: [4:20],
O: [21:35], P: [36:47],
R: [48:63]

bit interleaving, which is the most efficient means to calculate a Z-value. In GeoBase indexing based on Z-regions preserves spatial proximity though not at a point level, but only at the block level. Thus, neighboring blocks are spatially close with high probability (Fenk 2002).

To realize this clustering GeoBase implements a data storage layer and an index layer. The data storage layers maps one more file blocks to a physical storage abstraction termed file bucket. The overlaid index layer consists of key-value pairs, in which each key corresponds to a region of space, and value maps to blocks in the file bucket. Since the key-value pairs are sorted, the index imposes an ordering over the region space. The mapping between a region in the index layer and a file bucket in the data storage layer can be one-to-one, many-to-one, or many-to-many depending on the implementation and requirements of the application.

Figure 6 shows the interaction between index layer and storage layer. In this figure, space is partitioned into 4 disjoint Z-regions. The region marked 'G' and 'P' consists of two disconnected parts, but as we see the index layers maintains

the spatial proximity of the two regions by mapping neigh- boring Z-regions to file buckets and keeping them together. In addition, for Z-ordering regardless of the dimensionality of the Z-ordered space (i.e., not only for 2d) the number of not connected parts of a Z-region is at most two. It is to be noted that HBase internally stores key-value pairs as a B+tree and Z-regions can be stored in a B+tree by storing the upper limit of the Z-value.

Optimization Issues

Partitioning

The data storage layer is built over HDFS, which offers default partitioning. However, the default partitioning ignores file layout knowledge encoded in NetCDF files, and thus effectively disables any automatic optimizations that rely on such knowledge. We know that a NetCDF file is divided into metadata and data sections as described in Section 4.1.1. In addition, the metadata may occur at any place in the file. This occurrence of metadata often does not lead to even partitioning of the multi-dimensional space into blocks. Thus some

Figure 6. GeoBase Architecture. The letters denote Z–regions

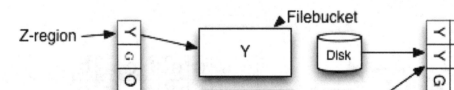

blocks will have more data values and some more metadata. In addition a single time dimension may get split across blocks.

We adopt three optimizations with respect to partitioning a NetCDF file. In the first optimization, file data is partitioned into blocks based on logical array data model. Thus, a NetCDF file with a variable v is partitioned into n blocks, each equal in the size of the array. Practically, this scheme translates to unequal data distribution because of presence of metadata. In the second optimization, we partition the file based on the actual distribution of data and metadata. So for each file we calculate the bytes occupied by the meta- data and data and partition each block into equal byte sized regions. Finally, our last partitioning scheme is to split files such that all metadata is copied to one block, and data is split based on the logical level. This scheme requires some data rearranging and processing prior to reading the input splits.

Load Balancing

Some load balancing is built into HBase as HDFS distributes the blocks randomly among data nodes. In addition the index layer is B+tree, which is also balanced. However, since HBase follows a range-partitioning scheme on the key-space, and, given skew in the data, certain regions become hot while querying. One alternative is to use other key-value stores, such as MongoDB and Voldemort, which support a hash-partitioning scheme, but would require implementing another index layer to support simple range queries.

To improve load balancing, a simple optimization heuristic is that a node attempts to shed its load whenever its load increases by a factor δ, and attempts to gain load when it drops by the same factor. In GeoBase this corresponds to moving file buckets from one physical node to another. But since HDFS provides some level of replication, in practice no data needs to be moved, only the index layer randomly chooses from the many mappings of the index element to the file

buckets. This strategy as we show in experiments increases the response time of query, but not in a significant way.

GeoBase can be used to answer point queries and range queries. Determining the Z-region to which a point belongs forms the basis for point queries. Since the index layer comprises a sorted list of Z-region names, determining the region to which a point belongs is efficient. Recall that the region name determines the bounds of the region. To answer a point query, we first lookup the Z-region that corresponds to the Z-value of the point. The point is then queried in the bucket to which the Z-region maps.

In the range query, first calculate the start and the end Z-values of the query box coordinates ql and qh. We calculate the set of candidate Z-regions that will satisfy the range. All those regions within the query box are candidate regions, which can be pipelined for further processing. Note that any false positives are eliminated by a scan of the index. As the region name only is enough to determine the boundary of the region enclosed by the subspace, points in a region are scanned only if the range of the subspace intersects with the query range.

Nearest neighbor queries are also an important primitive operation for geoscience applications, but are currently a work in progress in GeoBase. The index layer is a sorted sequence of subspace names. Since the subspace names encode the boundaries, the index layer essentially imposes an order between the subspaces. In our prior discussion, we represented the index layer as a monolithic layer of sorted subspace names. A single partition index is enough for many application needs. Assume each bucket can hold about 10^6 data points. Each row in the index layer stores very little information: the subspace name, the mapping to the corresponding bucket, and some additional metadata for query processing. Therefore, 100 bytes per index table row is a good estimate. The underlying key-value store partitions its data across multiple partitions. Considering the typical size of a partition in key-value stores is about 100 MB, the index partition can maintain a mapping of about 10^6 subspaces. This translates to about 10^{12} data points using a single index partition. This estimate might vary depending on the implementation or the configurations used. But, it provides a reasonable estimate of the size.

The data storage layer is implemented in which we allocate a table per bucket. The data storage layer therefore consists of multiple HBase tables. This model provides flexibility in mapping subspaces to buckets and allows greater parallelism by allowing operations on different tables to be dispatched in parallel.

Partitioning and placement of data is implemented using low-level customizations to HDFS default partitioning and placement that targets text-based formats. Hadoop's *FileInputFormat* class, performs chunking and grouping which result in a set of partitions, each related to a host on which the partition should be processed. A partition in the *InputSplit* class represents a subset of the total logical input space. Each *InputSplit* and associated partition is placed transparently by HDFS using higher-level policies such as load balancing. The data storage layer indexes via the *InputSplit* class by reading the associated logical space from the underlying file system. The reading capability is built into Hadoop's RecordReader class that utilizes the NetCDF-Java library to access data specified at the logical level.

In order to support logical-to-physical translation, we extended the NetCDF-Java library to expose mapping information. The translation mechanism is exposed via a function that takes as input a set of logical coordinates, and produces a set of physical byte stream offsets corresponding to each coordinate. Internally this is implemented as a simulation of the actual request that NetCDF would perform, but does not complete the read to the underlying file system, and instead responds with the offset of the request.

Additional software layers also had to be created to allow NetCDF-Java to interoperate with HDFS. NetCDF-Java is tightly integrated with the standard POSIX interface to reading files. Unfortunately, HDFS (the distributed file system built for Hadoop), does not expose its interface via standard POSIX system calls. To accommodate this API mismatch we built an HDFS connector, which translated POSIX calls issued by NetCDF-Java into calls to the HDFS library.

EXPERIMENTS

We conducted an experimental study to measure the performance of GeoBase on representative queries and data.

The setup consists of a cluster ranging from 10 to 15 small instance nodes, provisioned on Amazon EC2. The cluster is homogeneous in that each node consists of 1 virtual core, 1.7GB memory, 160 GB HDD, and 64bit Ubuntu 10.10. The deployed version of Hadoop is 0.22 and HBase 0.20.6. The Hadoop cluster is configured with 1 master node and the remaining HDFS and HBase nodes.

Methodology

Our datasets consist of 24 weather variables that are of high importance to crop models and coordinate and time attributes. There are 27,000 files in the system. Each files stores daily values of each variable over a grid that spans a land mass and the water region. Our queries are generated synthetically. Each query is either a data reduction query or a data condensation query. A data reduction query selects 5-40 distinct regions from the grid, and a data condensation query selects from computing on a max, min or median. A total of 10,000 queries are executed over a period of two hours with varying arrival times. The query workload that specifies the weather variables and the set of ranges is generated synthetically, but closely corresponds to queries that come for data over standard crop model simulations.

The primary end-to-end metrics used in evaluating GeoBase is the time to make an incoming file interface with the analysis system and then the runtime of the query. In addition, we also look into throughput, CPU utilization, and HDFS Local Reads. The latter is a measurement of the fraction of the input to the range query that was read from a local disk managed by HDFS.

Results

In Section 3, we demonstrated the performance of an end-to-end system with access enabled through data access libraries (DA). We also showed performance results when large amounts of data in NetCDF format is first transformed into text format and then accessed through 1-dimensional ordering, where the one dimension is one of the spatial coordinates (1D). We consider two other baseline end-to-end implementations: First, transforming every incoming file's input value into z-order and then inserting the Z-order values with using z-ordering for linearization (ZO) without any specialized index. Our other baseline implementation uses the plugin for NetCDF in Hadoop to run MapReduce style data reduction and condensation queries. Thus the queries are implemented in Map Reduce to evaluate the performance of a MapReduce system (MR) performing a full parallel scan of the data. Finally, we run the queries over the GeoBase system (GB).

To conduct the experiment we inserted 27000 files, in batches of multiples of 1000 files into the data ingestion system, and then queries corresponding to the time inserted so far were run on the ingested files. On the y-axis we report the total end-to-end time for the data ingestion and query execution (Figure 7). The experiment over increasing number of cluster nodes shows that the performance of GB scales linearly and continues to outperform ZO and MR, with DA and 1D being poor choices. In fact, MR performs better than the ZO showing that the cost of translating every data value into ZO is very large. But then full scans in MR are not particular useful. The average query selectivity is 50% over the entire dataset so most nodes conduct the scan but lead to low actual yields for the reduction operator. In GeoBase (GB) files do not incur any data transformation costs but are available immediately. The Z-region

Figure 7. All end-to-end systems compared (on log scale)

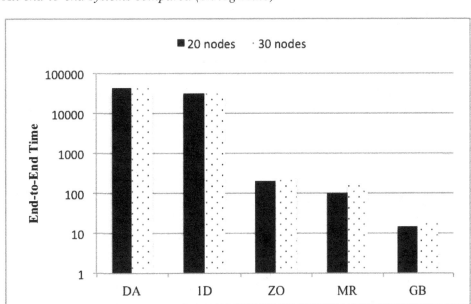

is indexed within the indexing layer with very low overhead, and each inserted file is incrementally indexed with some processing overhead.

Query Performance

We now evaluate range query performance using the different implementations of the index structures and the storage layer and compare performance with ZO and MR. The MR system filters out points matching the queried range and reports aggregate statistics on the matched data points. In GeoBase we choose the no-load-balancing scheme and file data is partitioned based on the first scheme in which data and second scheme in which a file data and metadata is partitioned based on logical model and the number of bytes in each partition, respectively. We then choose load balancing with second partitioning scheme.

Figure 8 plots the range query response times for the different designs as a function of the varying selectivity. As is evident from Figure 8, GeoBase with its design choices outperform the baseline systems. In particular, for highly selective queries where our designs show a one to two orders of magnitude improvement over the baseline imple-

mentations using simple ZO or MR. Moreover, the query response time of our proposed designs is proportional to the selectivity, which asserts the gains from the index layer when compared to brute force parallel scan of the entire data set as in the MR implementation whose response times are the worst amongst the alternatives considered and is independent of the query selectivity. In the design using just Z-ordering (ZO), the system scans between the minimum and the maximum Z-value of the queried region and filters out points that do not intersect the queried ranges. If the scanned range spans several buckets, the system parallelizes the scans per bucket. ZO response time is almost ten times worse when compared to our proposed approaches, especially for queries with high selectivity. The main reason for the inferior performance of the ZO is the false positive scans resulting from the distortion in the mapping of the points introduced by linearization.

File Insert Throughput

We describe the performance of inserts of file batches into the GeoBase. Figure 9 shows the near-constant performance over increasing num-

Figure 8. Response times for range query as function of selectivity

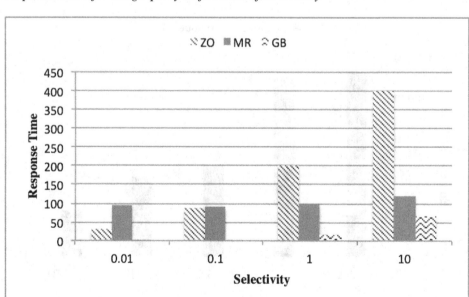

Figure 9. Throughput of file inserts

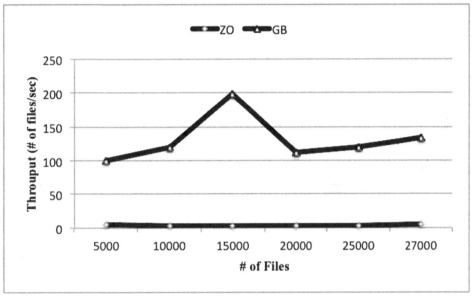

ber of files, which demonstrates the scalability of the files. The performance is due to the fact that GeoBase incurs no data transformation costs while inserting files. It is to be noted that when a file is inserted it is simply written onto the file system. The insertion of the file notifies the storage layer, and the corresponding Z-regions on the file are computed, which are then indexed by the index layer. Sometimes, a file bucket has to split or an index has to split. Thus we see some cost increasing with the number of files, but it is not hugely significant. Also the system block other operations until the bucket split completes. In our experiments, this required about 30 to 40 seconds to split a bucket.

Optimizations

We consider file partitioning optimization and load balancing. File partitioning optimization has significant impact on the end-to-end performance of GeoBase. Figure 10 shows the end-to-end time for the three schemes as described in Section 4.2.2. While the third partitioning scheme performs the best it also has an additional data transformation cost, which is 1.5x more than the cost incurred by other schemes. Though, the scheme achieves the best data locality, achieving close to 90% local reads. The other schemes also show good data locality with experiments going from 9% local reads to 80% local.

HBase employs automatic and dynamic load balancing scheme onto the region to scale the system. For instance, if each region is configured to account for 100MB of data, the region will split into 2 regions with each of them accounts for 50MB of data when this threshold (i.e. 100MB) is exceeded. We instrumented the dynamic load-balancing scheme in HBase to conduct region splits when the threshold exceeds δ times, in which delta is varied from 1 to 2. We used a synthetic spatially skewed data set using a Zipfian distribution with a Zipfian factor of 1.0 representing moderately skewed data. Using a Zipfian distribution allows us to control the skew while allowing quick generation of large data sets. Figure 11 shows when load is moved and GeoBase performance under the variation. The system is compared with ZO and MR and GeoBase has better performance under all load variations.

Figure 10. Partitioning Schemes compared

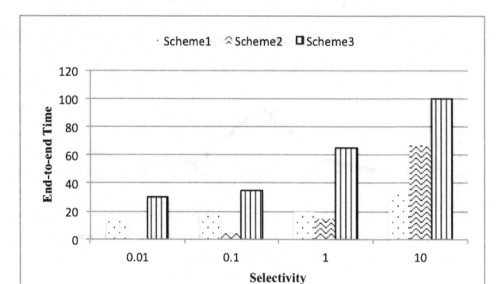

Figure 11. Load Balancing

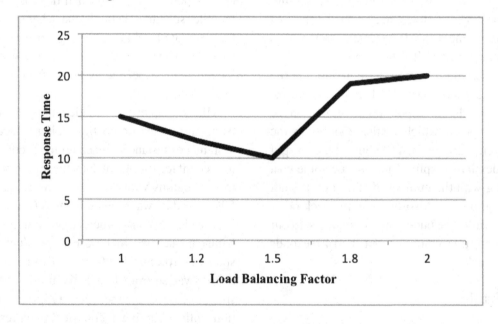

FUTURE RESEARCH DIRECTIONS

Scientists are increasingly facing big data issues but are not equipped with appropriate tools to manage it. In the case of geosciences, large amounts of data are now available, but its analysis is limited by non-scalable access methods that affect analysis and visualization methods. There is an emerging need to reduce scientists' data management tasks, especially scientists' directing single-investigator laboratories, comprising of a few graduate students and technicians, and yet striving to make their data available to other community members for sharing. Such scientists need end-to-end systems and services that are efficient, robust, and scalable. GeoBase, is a step in that direction, interfacing directly with files and providing a scalable querying service.

Our immediate future research directions is to explore such an end-to-end approach for log-structured merge trees (O'Neil 1996), which will be more suitable for rapidly streaming multidimensional data that arises from simulation experiments.

CONCLUSION

In a data-centric approach, scientists typically first explore data using standard statistical analysis tools and visualization, and then perform sophisticated data mining to extract deeper information and create knowledge. Given ever-increasing data volumes, scientists often find themselves conducting more data storage and management tasks rather than entirely focusing on data exploration and data mining. Most providers of large datasets provide simple mechanisms for data exploration, such as search based on metadata. Consequently, scientists have to first download large volumes of data, learn about storage management and data organization, and do so in a scalable way given the sheer size of data, before undertaking any meaningful data exploration and data mining.

In this chapter, we have presented GeoBase, a parallel data access system for scalable analysis that is based on open-source HBase. A vanilla installation of HBase is not sufficient for Geoscience applications since it neither provides interface to commonly used self-describing formats nor multi-attribute access, essential to for accessing data from spatio-temporal datasets. GeoBase provides an end-to-end solution by natively incorporating support for both.

REFERENCES

Abadi, D., Madden, S., & Hachem, N. (2008). Column-stores vs. row-stores: How different are they really? In *Proceedings of the 2008 ACM SIGMOD International Conference on Management of Data*. ACM.

Abouzeid, A., Bajda-Pawlikowski, K., Abadi, D., Silberschatz, A., & Rasin, A. (2009). HadoopDB: An architectural hybrid of MapReduce and DBMS technologies for analytical workloads. *Proceedings of the VLDB Endowment*, 2(1), 922–933.

Apache. (2010). *HBase: Bigtable-like structured storage for Hadoop HDFS*. Retrieved from http://hadoop.apache.org/hbase/

Baumann, P. (1999). A database array algebra for spatio-temporal data and beyond. In *Proceedings of the Workshop on Next Generation Information Technologies and Systems*. IEEE.

Buck, J., Watkins, N., LeFevre, J., Ioannidou, K., Maltzahn, C., Polyzotis, N., & Brandt, S. (2011). *SciHadoop: Array-based query processing in Hadoop*. Supercomputing.

Chang, F., Dean, J., Ghemawat, S., Hsieh, W., Wallach, D., & Burrows, M. et al. (2008). BigTable: A distributed storage system for structured data. *ACM Transactions on Computer Systems*, 26(2). doi:10.1145/1365815.1365816.

Fenk, R., Markl, V., & Bayer, R. (2002). Interval processing with the UB-tree. In *Proceedings of the Database Engineering and Applications Symposium*. IEEE.

Folk, M., Cheng, A., & Yates, K. (1999). *HDF5: A file format and I/O library for high performance computing applications*. Supercomputing.

George, L. (2008). *HBase: The definitive Guide*. Sebastopol, CA: O'Reilly Media.

Hill, D., & Werpy, J. (2011). Satellite imagery production and processing using Apache Hadoop. In *Proceedings of the American Geophysical Union Fall Meeting*. AGU.

Howe, B. (2007). *GridFields: Model-driven data transformation in the physical sciences*. (PhD, Dissertation). Portland State University, Portland, OR.

Jagadish, H. (1997). Analysis of hilbert curve for representing 2-dimensional space. *Information Processing Letters*, *62*(1), 17–22. doi:10.1016/S0020-0190(97)00014-8.

Jensen, C., Lin, D., & Ooi, B. (2004). Query and update efficient B+-tree based indexing of moving objects. In *Proceedings of the Thirtieth International Conference on Very Large Data Bases*. IEEE.

Li, J., Liao, W., Choudhary, A., Ross, R., Thakur, R., Gropp, W., … Zingale, M. (2003). Parallel NetCDF: A high performance scientific I/O interface. *Supercomputing*.

Libkin, L., Machlin, R., & Wong, L. (1996). A query language for multidimensional arrays: Design, implementation, and optimization techniques. *SIGMOD Record*, *25*(2), 228–239. doi:10.1145/235968.233335.

Lu, M., & Zwaenepoel, W. (2010). HadoopToSQL: A MapReduce query optimizer. In *Proceedings of the European Conference on Computer Systems*. IEEE.

NASA. (n.d.a). *AQUA*. Retrieved from http://aqua.nasa.gov/

NASA. (n.d.b). *Landsat 7*. Retrieved from http://landsat.gsfc.nasa.gov

NASA. (n.d.c). *Pomegranate*. Retrieved from http://pomegranate.nasa.gov/

Nishimura, S., Das, S., Agrawal, D., & Abbadi, A. (2011). MD-HBase: A scalable multi-dimensional data infrastructure for location aware services. In *Proceedings of the 12th IEEE International Conference on Mobile Data Management*. IEEE.

NOAA. (n.d.). *Geostationary satellite server*. Retrieved from http://www.goes.noaa.gov/

O'Neil, P., Cheng, E., Gawlick, D., & O'Neil, E. (1996). The log-structured merge-tree (LSM-tree). *Acta Informatica*, *33*(4).

OPeNDAP. (n.d.). Retrieved from http://opendap.org/

Rew, R., & Davis, G. (1990). NetCDF: An interface for scientific data access. *IEEE Computer Graphics and Applications*, *10*(4). doi:10.1109/38.56302.

Samet, H. (2005). *Foundations of multidimensional and metric data structures*. San Francisco, CA: Morgan Kaufmann Publishers Inc..

Stonebraker, M., Becla, J., Dewitt, D., Lim, K., Maier, D., Ratzesberger, O., & Zdonik, S. (2009). Requirements for science databases and SciDB. In *Proceedings of the Conference on Innovative Database Research*. IEEE.

Tao, Y., Yi, K., Sheng, C., & Kalnis, P. (2009). Quality and efficiency in high dimensional nearest neighbor search. In *Proceedings of the 35th SIGMOD International Conference on Management of Data*. ACM.

Unidata. (n.d.). *NetCDF Java API*. Retrieved from http://http://www.unidata.ucar.edu/software/netcdf-java/

Wang, D., Zender, C., & Jenks, S. (2008). Clustered workflow execution of retargeted data analysis scripts. In *Proceedings of the 8th IEEE International Symposium on Cluster Computing and the Grid*. IEEE.

Wu, K., Ahern, S., Bethel, E., Chen, J., Childs, H., & Cormier-Michel, E. et al. (2009). FastBit: Interactively Searching massive data. *Journal of Physics*, *180*(2).

Zhao, H., Ai, S., Lv, Z., & Li, B. (2010). *Parallel accessing massive NetCDF data based on MapReduce*. Berlin: Springer. doi:10.1007/978-3-642-16515-3_53.

Silberschatz, A., Korth, H. F., & Sudarshan, S. (1997). *Database system concepts* (Vol. 4). Hightstown, NJ: McGraw-Hill.

Vora, M. N. (2011). Hadoop-HBase for large-scale data. [ICCSNT]. *Proceedings of Computer Science and Network Technology*, *1*, 601–605.

White, T. (2012). *Hadoop: The definitive guide*. Sebastopol, CA: O'Reilly.

ADDITIONAL READING

Egenhofer, M. J. (1994). Spatial SQL: A query and presentation language. *IEEE Transactions on Knowledge and Data Engineering*, *6*(1), 86–95. doi:10.1109/69.273029.

George, L. (2011). *HBase: The definitive guide*. Sebastopol, CA: O'Reilly Media, Inc..

Hjaltason, G. R., & Samet, H. (2003). Index-driven similarity search in metric spaces. *ACM Transactions on Database Systems*, *28*(4), 517–580. doi:10.1145/958942.958948.

Lam, C. (2010). *Hadoop in action*. Manning Publications Co..

Lin, J., & Dyer, C. (2010). Data-intensive text processing with MapReduce. *Synthesis Lectures on Human Language Technologies*, *3*(1), 1–177. doi:10.2200/S00274ED1V01Y201006HLT007.

Miller, M. (2008). *Cloud computing: Web-based applications that change the way you work and collaborate online*. Que Publishing.

Rew, R., Davis, G., Emmerson, S., Davies, H., & Hartnett, E. (1993). *NetCDF user's guide*. Boulder, CO: Unidata Program Center.

Samet, H. (1990). *The design and analysis of spatial data structures*. Reading, MA: Addison-Wesley.

KEY TERMS AND DEFINITIONS

Data-Intensive Computing: Is a class of parallel computing applications which use a data parallel approach to processing large volumes of data typically terabytes or petabytes in size and typically referred to as Big Data.

File Format: A standard way that information is encoded for storage in a computer file.

MapReduce: Is a programming model for processing large data sets with a parallel, distributed algorithm on a cluster.

Multidimensional Structure: Is defined as "a variation of the relational model that uses multidimensional structures to organize data and express the relationships between data".

NetCDF: (Network Common Data Form): A set of software libraries and self-describing, machine-independent data formats that support the creation, access, and sharing of array-oriented scientific data.

NoSQL: Database: Provides a mechanism for storage and retrieval of data that uses looser consistency models rather than traditional relational databases.

Space-Filling Curve: A curve whose range contains the entire 2-dimensional unit square (or more generally an n-dimensional hypercube).

Z-Order: A function, which maps multidimensional data to one dimension while preserving locality of the data points.

Chapter 13

Large–Scale Sensor Network Analysis:
Applications in Structural Health Monitoring

Joaquin Vanschoren
University of Leiden, The Netherlands

Marvin Meeng
University of Leiden, The Netherlands

Ugo Vespier
University of Leiden, The Netherlands

Ricardo Cachucho
University of Leiden, The Netherlands

Shengfa Miao
University of Leiden, The Netherlands

Arno Knobbe
University of Leiden, The Netherlands

ABSTRACT

Sensors are increasingly being used to monitor the world around us. They measure movements of structures such as bridges, windmills, and plane wings, human's vital signs, atmospheric conditions, and fluctuations in power and water networks. In many cases, this results in large networks with different types of sensors, generating impressive amounts of data. As the volume and complexity of data increases, their effective use becomes more challenging, and novel solutions are needed both on a technical as well as a scientific level. Founded on several real-world applications, this chapter discusses the challenges involved in large-scale sensor data analysis and describes practical solutions to address them. Due to the sheer size of the data and the large amount of computation involved, these are clearly "Big Data" applications.

DOI: 10.4018/978-1-4666-4699-5.ch013

1. INTRODUCTION

Sensors are increasingly being used to monitor the world around us. They measure movements of structures such as bridges, windmills and plane wings, vital signals of humans, atmospheric conditions, and fluctuations in power and water networks. In many cases, this results in large networks with different types of sensors, generating impressive amounts of data. In this chapter, we look at a specific case in considerable detail - a sensor network attached to a large highway bridge - and demonstrate what generic techniques may be required to analyze this data (Knobbe et al., 2010; Vespier et al., 2011).

1.1 Bridge Monitoring

Structural health monitoring, i.e. the monitoring of the behavior of man-made structures such as bridges, tunnels and buildings, is an important case for large-scale sensor data analysis (Knobbe et al., 2010). Many existing structures are now past their design lifetime, and complex degradation processes such as corrosion and excessive load cycles can sometimes cause unpredictable behavior (ASCE, 1990). Monitoring their dynamic behavior is key in understanding how fast they are degrading and predicting when critical maintenance, or even replacement, is needed. This requires the infrastructure to be equipped with a network of sensors, continuously measuring and collecting various structural and climate features such as vibration, strain and weather conditions. This continuous measuring process generates a massive amount of streaming data which must be analyzed over large time intervals.

One such structure is the 'Hollandse Brug' (Holland Bridge), one of the busiest highway bridges in the Netherlands. The bridge was opened on June 1969, but on April 2007 inspection measurements showed that the bridge did not meet quality and security requirements. Subsequently, it was closed in both directions to freight traf-fic, and most of the bridge deck has since been replaced. To monitor the bridge's behavior, and avoid such abrupt bridge closures in the future, a sensor network was installed to learn how the bridge, and many other bridges like it, degrades over time and to use this data to plan future maintenance more accurately.

The monitoring system comprises 145 sensors that measure how the bridge responds to external forces, at several locations along its span (see Figure 1 for an illustration). The following types of sensors are employed:

- 34 'geo-phones' (vibration sensors) that measure the vertical movement of the bottom of the road-deck as well as the supporting columns.
- 16 strain-gauges embedded in the concrete, measuring horizontal longitudinal stress, and an additional 34 gauges attached to the outside.
- 28 strain-gauges embedded in the concrete, measuring horizontal stress perpendicular to the first 16 strain-gauges, and an additional 13 gauges attached to the outside.
- 10 thermometers embedded in the concrete, and 10 attached on the outside.

These sensors measure at 100 Hz, yielding about 4 GB of data per day, or well over a terabyte of data per year. In addition, a weather station measures wind speeds, rainfall and solar radiation, and a video camera provides a live stream of the traffic on the bridge. This system creates a constant influx of high-throughput data. While manageable over short intervals, this data needs to be collected over many years for detailed analysis, quickly turning this fast data into big data. It may be clear that this requires a radical departure from current field-testing approaches that rely of spreadsheets and proprietary data-acquisition software with capacity limitations.

A small 1-minute sample of the strain and vibration data is shown in Figure 2. One can easily

Figure 1. Cross-section of the bridge with sensor placement

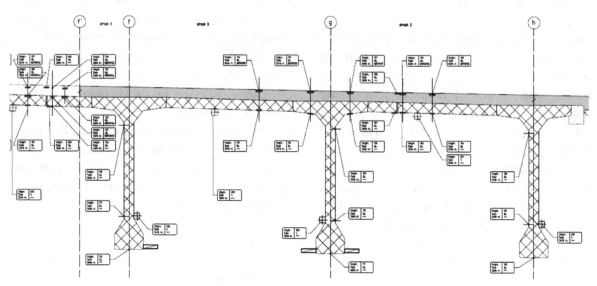

Figure 2. Short sample of strain (top) and vibration (bottom) sensor data

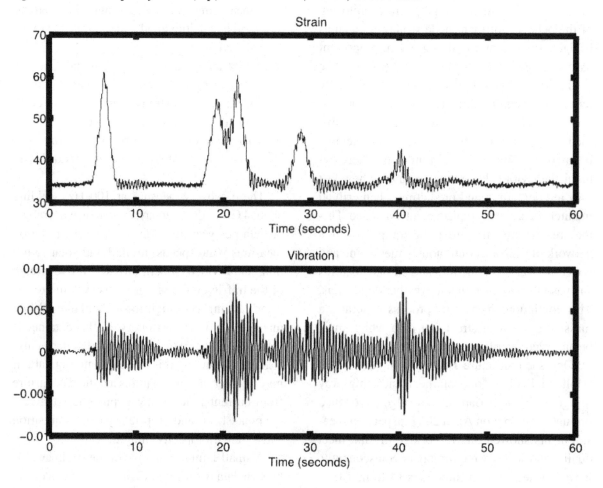

distinguish the 'bumps' caused by passing traffic and the resulting oscillation of the bridge deck.

Analyzing such large, real-world data is wrought with difficulty. For instance, Figure 3 shows the output of one single strain sensor over the course of an entire day. One can easily distinguish events occurring on different time scales. First, narrow, sharp peaks are caused by passing vehicles of different weights: a detailed peak is shown in Figure 3 (right). Second, prolonged increases in strain are caused by traffic congestion during rush hours (9:00 and 14:00). Mini-traffic jams, lasting only a few minutes, also occur. Third, there is a subtle, gradual change in strain over the course of the day caused by changes in the outside temperature, which influences the stiffness of the concrete and hence the strain measurements. On even longer time scales (weeks and months), one will also see the effects of seasonal changes and atmospheric conditions. In Section 4, we will use *scale-space* filtering (Lindeberg, 1990; Witkin, 1983) to decompose this signal into k sub-signals corresponding to events occurring at different time scales, as shown in Figure 4. We can also build models by first labeling each interval of the strain data by the type of traffic that is passing over the sensor location at that time. In Section 3, we will use clustering to identify the different types of traffic on the bridge (e.g., car, truck, or heavy truck) and then label each part of the signal accordingly.

Moreover, these signals are measured per support girder and deck element, and they influence each other indirectly. For instance, in Figure 3 one can see peaks during traffic congestion. This is caused by traffic passing in one direction, whilst there is traffic congestion in the other direction, thus on the other side of the bridge. As such, we

Figure 3. (left) One day of strain measurements. The multiple external factors affecting the bridge are visible at different time scales. (right) A detail of the left plot showing one of the peaks caused by a passing vehicle.

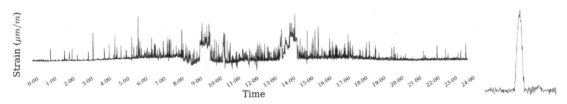

Figure 4. (left) Signal (top) and top-ranked scale decomposition, respectively showing traffic, congestion, and temperature-related baseline shifts. (right) Strain readings plotted against temperature readings over the course of two days (different colors).

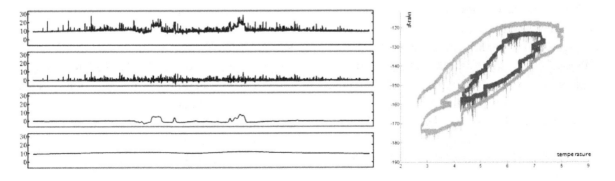

need to model the dependencies between signals measured at different locations. Moreover, we also need to model the dependencies between signals generated by different types of sensors. For instance, Figure 3 (left) shows the effect of temperature on the strain data. This shows that the effect of temperature on the strain in the bridge is not linear, otherwise it would vary along a straight line, Instead, there exists a delay between a temperature change and a change in (average) strain. This can be modeled accurately using a exponential decay function, as will be discussed in Section 5.

1.2 Large-Scale Sensor Data Analysis

It will be clear that these different types of analysis require substantial computation. While some analyses build on fairly standard techniques from Digital Signal Processing, such as signal convolution or Fourier transforms, they become extremely challenging on data of the size we are dealing with in this context. To be able to support the kinds of computations described here, we reimplemented many time series analysis operations in the MapReduce framework using Hadoop (White, 2009). This allows us to parallelize the necessary disk reads over many different computing nodes, map the required data points together, and run computations over them as if all data were read by the same node. These implementations scale linearly with the amount of data, and can be speeded up by simply adding more nodes to the cluster. Moreover, such a cluster can be constructed using traditional data storage and processing hardware, making it cost-effective, and is extremely fault-tolerant (White, 2009). Compared the other 'Big Data' applications, we are facing many of the same challenges (Giangarra, Metrovich, Schwitters, & Semple, 2011; Agrawal, Das, & El Abbadi, 2011). One major challenge is the recording and organization of large data streams, easily leading to terabytes of storage needs in a short amount of time.

This requires advanced database technology that supports scalable, distributed, and structured data storage, as well as scalable software architectures (Agrawal et al., 2011; Brantner, Florescu, Graf, Kossmann, & Kraska, 2008; Dean & Ghemawat, 2008; Lars, 2011). Scalability is an especially important requirement in applications such as these. With the ever-increasing deployment and falling cost of sensors, one can easily envisage applications with thousands of sensors. Also, one may want to monitor many structures (e.g., bridges) at the same time, which again requires a scalable solution.

Hadoop has been employed in many Big Data applications, including e-commerce (Jiang, Lu, Zhang, & Long, 2011), social network analysis (Borthakur et al., 2011), and bio-informatics (Taylor, 2012). It is also increasingly being employed in applications that involve sensor data (Jardak et al., 2010). An interesting comparison between Hadoop and relational database systems for large-scale data analysis in terms of performance, ease-of-use and robustness can be found in (Pavlo et al., 2009).

Secondly, many data-rich environments motivate the need to relate various streams of data to one another in a hierarchical manner based on criteria with can be spatial, temporal, as well as functional in nature. For instance, sensors may be embedded in different locations in a structure, providing different types of readings, may be measuring at different rates (or even intermittently), and may measure functionally different variables such as temperature and strain which need to be associated rather than analyzed independently. This entails that data should be stored in a coherent and consistent format. In some cases, the data may even originate from different data-acquisition systems, requiring complex communication systems to ensure that all data is transmitted, normalized and stored consistently (Giangarra et al., 2011).

A third challenge is capturing and analyzing the data in real time. In many cases it is necessary to provide access to live data streams that can provide immediate warning of impending danger, e.g., when sensor readings go beyond the normal operating range or when baselines shift abruptly. To perform real-time analysis, and issue alarms when something is out of the ordinary, we built a workflow system that processes the data from its raw form to the key indicators we wish to observe. It is specifically designed for streaming data, allowing individual readings from many sensors to flow through the system, be processed and combined (Reutemann & Vanschoren, 2012). Furthermore, data analysis should be able to produce timely prognostics (e.g., of the future performance of a structure) to allow proper decision making. This again requires scalable data storage and software implementations (Agrawal et al., 2011).

Finally, many Big Data applications require advanced visualizations of data, and analytics performed on that data, so that it can be interpreted with minimal effort. Visualizations of live events, as well as trends revealed by analyzing large amounts of data are often crucial to quickly and confidently understanding what is happening and make proper decisions (Cox & Ellsworth, 1997).

In the remainder of this chapter, we will first introduce the basic concepts needed to formalize our methods in Section 2. Afterwards, we discuss different types of analysis performed on this data, including Clustering (Section 3), Multi-Scale Analysis (Section 4) and modeling the interaction between various types of sensor data (Section 5). Section 6 concludes.

2. PRELIMINARIES

In this section we introduce notation and basic definitions for operations needed throughout this chapter. Since we are analyzing sensor data, we deal with finite sequences of numerical measurements (samples), collected by observing some property of a system with a sensor, and represented in the form of time series as defined.

Definition 1: A **time series** of length n is a finite sequence of values $x = x[1],...,x[n]$ of finite precision.[1] A subsequence x[a: b] of x is defined as follows:

$$x\big[a:b\big] = \big(x\big[a\big],x\big[a+1\big],...,x\big[b\big]\big), a < b$$

We also assume that all the considered time series have no missing values and that their sampling rate is constant.

2.1 Convolution

A fundamental operation for analyzing time series data is the convolution:

Definition 2: Given a signal **x** of length N and a response function (kernel) **h** of length M, the result of the **convolution x ∗ h** is the signal **y** of length N, defined as:

$$y\big[t\big] = \sum_{j=-\frac{M}{2}+1}^{\frac{M}{2}} x\big[t-j\big]h\big[j\big]$$

For most of our analysis, **h** is a Gaussian kernel with mean $\mu=0$, standard deviation σ, area under the curve equal to 1, discretized into M values.[2] Also, since **x** is finite, **x**[$t-j$] may be undefined. To account for these boundary effects, **x** is padded with $M/2$ zeros before and after its defined range. A complete overview on how to compute the Gaussian convolutions for discrete signals can be found in Lindeberg (1990).

The convolution acts as a smoothing filter which smooths each value **x**[t] based on its surrounding values. The amount of removed detail is directly proportional to the standard deviation σ (and thus M), from now on referred to as the scale parameter. This is illustrated in Figure 5. It shows the calibrated, but still noisy sensor data, and the result of two convolutions with Gaussian kernels of different widths. The wider kernel (k1)

Figure 5. An example of convolution with two kernels, k1 and k2, of different widths

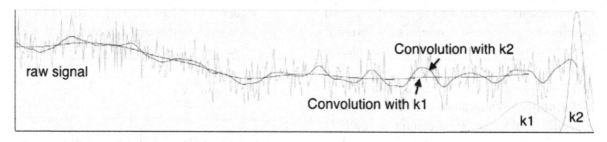

removes a lot of detail, only preserving large bumps, while the narrow kernel (k2) removes noise but still preserves small oscillations in the signal. In the limit, when, $\sigma \to \infty$, the result of the Gaussian convolution converges to the mean of the signal **x**.

2.2 Discrete Fourier Transform

Definition 3: Given a signal **x** of length N, the discrete Fourier Transform (DFT) is a series of N complex numbers X_k, each describing a sine function of given frequency:

$$X\big[k\big] = \sum_{n=0}^{N-1} x\big[k\big] e^{-2\pi i k n/N}$$

Conversely, the inverse Fourier transform (DFT^{-1}) is defined by:

$$x\big[n\big] = \frac{1}{N} \sum_{k=0}^{N-1} X[k] e^{2\pi i k n/N}$$

The Fourier transform converts a signal from the time domain into the *frequency domain*, representing the data as a sum of sine functions with different frequencies and amplitudes, as shown in Figure 6. The Fourier transform has several useful applications. For instance, we can filter out noise by removing high- and/or low frequency components (i.e., dropping some of the sine functions), and taking the inverse Fourier transform to get us back to the time domain.

Figure 6. Discrete Fourier transform (right) of the vibration and strain data (left). The large peak in (b) corresponds to the eigenfrequency of the bridge.

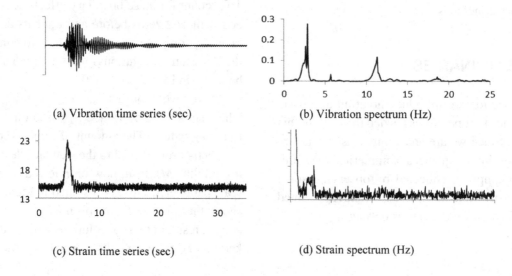

The Fourier transform proves very useful to detect and remove baseline shifts in sensor data. In the frequency domain, the baseline is usually treated as a low frequency signal, and filtering out low frequency components in the signal spectrum helps to remove the baseline. The question remains which frequencies must be filtered out, i.e. do we only want to remove very gradual changes, or also spurious events such as traffic jams? There also exist very useful methods to remove baselines in the time domain (Schulze et al., 2005), some of which will be discussed later.

2.3 MapReduce

When working with terabytes of data, loading all data in memory, e.g. to compute a Fourier transform, is out of the question, and reading the data from disk becomes a major bottleneck. For instance, reading 4TB of data at 50MB/s takes almost an entire day. However, using the MapReduce framework (Dean & Ghemawat, 2008), and it's open-source implementation Hadoop (White, 2009), we can parallelize our processes (and disk reads) over an arbitrary number of computing nodes[3]. For a good understanding of our methods, we include a short, high-level introduction here.

In the MapReduce framework, data is processed in two stages, as depicted in Figure 7. The first phase, the *Map phase*, reads the input data from a distributed file system, into a set of *M splits* (input partitions) of typically 16 to 64MB. Each split is assigned to a worker node, a *Mapper*. Each mapper reads the contents of the input split,

Figure 7. The MapReduce model (Source: University of Washington)

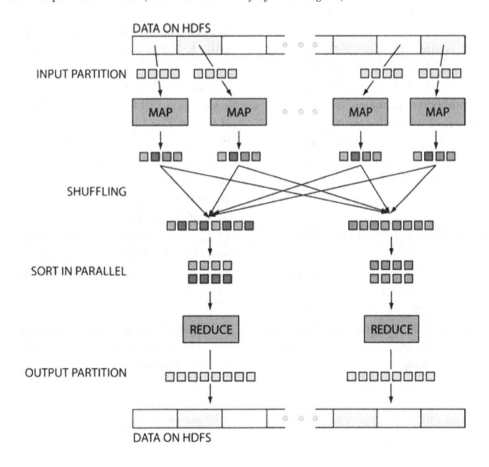

parses key/value pairs out of the input data (e.g. line numbers and a line of text, or a timestamp and sensor readings), and passes each pair to a user-defined *Map* function. The latter processes this data and emits new, *intermediate* key-value pairs, which are then partitioned into R partitions using a *partition function* (e.g., *hash(key)* mod R) and stored on local disk. Optionally, a *Combiner* function can be written that combines intermediate key-value pairs with the same key into a new key-value pair in which the value is a combination of the initial values. This reduces traffic between the mappers and the reducers.

In the *Reduce phase*, a set of worker nodes called *Reducers* collects all partitions (from all mappers) that are assigned to them, sorts the key-value pairs based on the intermediate keys, and passes each key and the corresponding set of intermediate data to a user-defined *Reduce* function. Finally, each Reduce function emits output key-value pairs which are appended to output files.

Programs written in this framework, by implementing the Map and Reduce functions, are automatically parallelized and executed on a large cluster of commodity machines. The run-time system takes care of scheduling the program's execution across a set of machines, handling machine failures, and managing the required inter-machine communication (Dean & Ghemawat, 2008).

3. SUBSEQUENCE CLUSTERING

In this section, we focus on one specific type of sensor: the strain measurements such as shown in Figure 3. This data can be used to identify the type of traffic that is passing over the bridge at each point in time. While we could impose a number of classes manually, such as 'car', and 'truck', it is usually better to infer such categories from the data itself using *subsequence clustering* (SSC) (Höppner, 2002; E. Keogh & Lin, 2005;

Fujimaki, Hirose, & Nakata, 2008; Idé, 2006): we first employ a sliding window technique to split the data stream in individual subsequences (observations), which can then be clustered, and labeled with the cluster they belong to.

Definition 4: (Subsequence) A subsequence $S_{p,w}$ of a time series $X = x_1,...,x_m$ is the sequence of values $x_p,...,x_{p+w-1}$ such that $1 \leq p \leq m-w+1$ and the window length $w < m$.

Definition 5: (Subsequences Set) The subsequences set $D(X, w) = \{S_{i,w} \mid 1 \leq i \leq m - w + 1\}$ is the set of all the subsequences extracted by sliding a window of length w over the time series X.

The subsequences set $D(X,w)$ contains all possible subsequences of length w of a time series X. The aim of *subsequence clustering* is discovering groups of similar subsequences in $D(X,w)$.

3.1 Subsequence Clustering with k-Means

The clustering method typically used for SSC is k-Means, a well known method that, given a set of vectors $D = \{x_1, ..., x_n\}$ aims to find a partition $P = \{C_1, ..., C_k\}$ and a set of centroids $C = \{c_1, ..., c_k\}$ such that the sum of the squared distances between each x_i and its associated centroid c_j is minimized. In this case, the set D is the set of subsequences $D(X,w)$.

The classic k-Means heuristic implementation looks for a local minimum by iteratively refining an initial random partition. The algorithm involves four steps:

1. **Initialization:** Randomly choose k initial cluster prototypes $c_1, ..., c_k$ in D.
2. **Assignment:** Assign every vector $x_i \in D$ to its nearest prototype c_j according to a distance measure. The classic k-Means uses the Euclidean distance.

3. **Recalculation:** Recalculate the new prototypes c_1, ..., c_k by computing the means of all the assigned vectors.

4. Stop if the prototypes did not change more than a predefined threshold or when a maximum number of iterations has been reached, otherwise go back to step 2.

The intuition in SSC is that, if there are repeated similar subsequences in X, e.g. bumps of a specific shape, they will be grouped in a cluster and eventually become associated to an actual event of the application domain, such as a passing truck.

3.2 Subsequence Clustering vs. Event Detection

However, this intuition does not always translate into good results. It has been shown that SSC with k-Means is prone to a number of undesirable behaviors that make it unsuitable for the task at hand (E. Keogh & Lin, 2005; Idé, 2006; Fujimaki et al., 2008). Most notably, the cluster prototypes, constructed by averaging the subsequences in each cluster, do not always resemble the subsequences themselves: smooth, sinusoid-like prototypes emerge even when the original data was extremely noisy and angular. Also, differ-

ent random initializations were shown to lead to completely different results.

This unintuitive behavior of SSC can be understood by considering the nature of the subsequence set $D(X,w)$ that is the outcome of the initial sliding window step. Each member of $D(X,w)$ forms a point in a Euclidean w-dimensional space, which we will refer to as w-space, illustrated in Figure 8. As each subsequence is fairly similar to its successor, the associated points in w-space will be quite close, and the members of $D(X,w)$ form a trajectory in w-space. Figure 8 shows an example of a (smoothed) fragment of strain data, and its associated trajectory in w-space (only two dimensions shown). Individual prototypes correspond to points in w-space, and the task of SSC is to find k representative points in w-space to succinctly describe the set of subsequences, in other words, the trajectory. Figure 8 (right) also shows an example of a run of k-Means on this data. As the example demonstrates, the prototypes do not necessarily lie along the trajectory, as they often represent an (averaged) curved segment of it.

While most of these issues do not occur in our sensor data (see Vespier et al. (2011) for a detailed analysis), the clustering does indeed result in multiple representations of what is intuitively one single event, as shown in Figure 9. Indeed, each

Figure 8. Two plots of the same data, showing the original data as a function of time (left), and a projection on two selected dimensions in w-space and the four prototypes generated by k-Means (red circles). Clearly, the sliding window technique creates a trajectory in w-space, where each loop corresponds to a bump in the original signal.

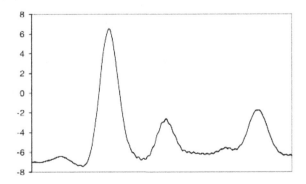
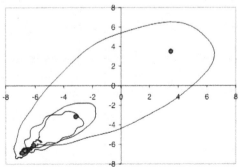

of the two bump-shaped prototypes resembles only a fraction of the visible bump in the strain data. In other words, our notion of traffic event does not coincide with the Euclidean distance used in *k*-Means, which assigns a large distance to essentially quite similar subsequences.

3.3 The Snapping Distance

To resolve this issue, we introduced a novel distance function that explicitly takes the local context of a subsequence into account. Given a time series X and two subsequences $S_{p,w} \in X$ and S_{fixed} of length w, we consider not only the Euclidean distance between S_{fixed} and $S_{p,w}$, but also between S_{fixed} and the neighboring subsequences, to the left and to the right, of $S_{p,w}$. The minimum Euclidean distance encountered is taken as the final distance value between $S_{p,w}$ and S_{fixed}.

Formally, given a shift factor f and a number of shift steps s, we define the neighbor subsequences indexes of as:

$$NS = \left\{ p + \frac{fw}{s} \cdot i \mid -s \le i \le s \right\}$$

The extent of data analyzed to the left and to the right of $S_{p,w}$ is determined by the shift factor while the number of subsequences considered in the interval is limited by the shift steps parameter. The *Snapping* distance is defined as:

$$\begin{aligned} Snapping&\left(S_{p,w}, S_{fixed}\right) \\ &= \min\{Euclidean(S_{i,w}, S_{fixed}) \mid i \in NS\} \end{aligned} \quad (1)$$

Figure 10 illustrates the intuition behind the *Snapping* distance measure in the context of *k*-Means clustering. When measuring the distance between each cluster centroid and the subsequence $S_{p,w}$, in the *assignment* step of the *k*-Means algorithm, the snapping distance looks beyond the edges of the subsequence window to match the bump in the sensor data to the centroid, thus avoiding boundary effects. Moreover, we force the initialization step to choose the random subsequences such that they do not overlap in the original time series.

3.4 Scalable Implementation

Given the amount of data generated by the sensor network, it is important to have a very scalable implementation of our clustering method. As in

Figure 9. Multiple representation of events. The left plot shows the prototypes computed by the classic k-Means. The right plot shows, in black, the portion of the data assigned to the two bump-shaped prototypes: the top sequence corresponds to the left prototype, the bottom sequence to the right prototype.

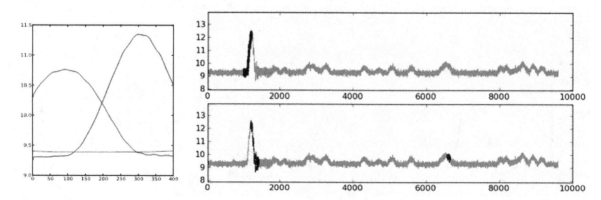

Figure 10. A subsequence $S_{p,w}$ *is compared against the centroid* C_k. *The snapping distance between* C_k *and* $S_{p,w}$ *corresponds to the minimum distance measured as we move* C_k *over all neighbor subsequences of* $S_{p,w}$, *including itself. Here, the best match is outlined in gray.*

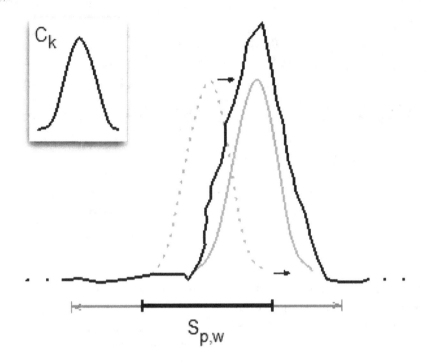

most clustering applications, the main computational bottleneck lies in calculating the (snapping) distances between every subsequence and the cluster centroids. Indeed, the snapping distance further increases the computational complexity since it also needs to take the neighborhood of each subsequence into account, depending on the shift factor and shift steps parameters. Furthermore, since the data stream is too large to load into memory, repeated disk reads will be necessary.

This type of I/O-intensive operation calls for a MapReduce approach, so we can distribute the data reads over a cluster of machines. The resulting system, implemented in the Hadoop (White, 2009) framework, is a chain of two Map-Reduce phases/jobs.

In the first phase, we prepare the data for the clustering phase, as shown in Figure 11. The data is stored on disk in flat files with a timestamp and the sensor readings of the 145 sensors on each line. For faster reading, data can be reformatted

to SequenceFiles, consisting of binary key/value pairs. Each mapper reads a data split, selects the sensor(s) of interest[4], and links each sensor reading to $(1+f)w$ subsequences, marked by the initial timestamp t_s. Remember that f is the shift factor used for the snapping distance and w is the window length. The reducers collect the data points belonging to a given timestamp key and emit the whole subsequence as an array, including the correct lead-in and lead-out necessary to compute the snapping distances. Optionally, additional processing can be done in the reducers, such as data segmentation to reduce the number of individual readings in the subsamples, and thus speed up future computations.

One important implementation detail here is the choice of key. Using the time in milliseconds results in a poor partitioning since the 100Hz data only has a reading every 10 milliseconds. This means that the hash function will not distribute keys evenly over the reducers, and at least half of

Figure 11. The data preparation phase: sensor readings are read from file and emitted as subsequences with lead-ins and lead-outs according to the shift factor f of the used snapping distance

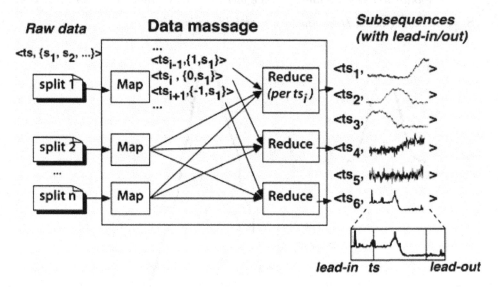

them will not receive any key-value pairs, thus sitting idle. A much better distribution can be obtained using a string key or, in this case, by dividing the time in milliseconds by 10.

As soon as the subsequences are emitted, the clustering phase can start, as shown in Figure 12. First, *k* non-overlapping subsequences are randomly chosen as initial cluster centroids. Each

mapper then reads in part of the subsequences, measures the snapping distance to each of the cluster centroids, and emits a key-value pair consisting of the nearest centroid and the subsequence. Optionally, a combiner can be used that counts and computes the partial vector sum of all subsequences emitted by the same mapper and mapped to the same centroid. Next, each reducer

Figure 12. The k-Means clustering phase: after choosing k non-overlapping subsequences as initial cluster centroids, all subsequences are clustered and new cluster centroids are computed until convergence

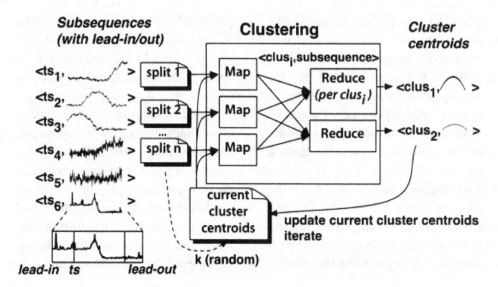

receives all the subsequences mapped to a specific cluster, and emits the new cluster centroid, i.e., the average of all received subsequences. This map-reduce cycle is repeated n times or until the clusters converge.

We were able to build upon the k-Means implementation present in the Mahout library[5], though extended to support the more complex snapping distance.

We evaluated this implementation on two Hadoop clusters: a small cluster with 6 nodes and larger one with 66 compute nodes. The runtimes are plotted in Figure 13. This shows that the runtime scales linearly with the amount of data, and that adding more compute nodes linearly reduces the required time to compute the clusters.

3.5 Experimental Evaluation

To evaluate the quality of the clustering, we first need to fix a number of parameters. First, the window length w has been set at 4 seconds, given that the bridge spans are 50 meters long, and at a maximum speed of 100 km/h, a typical vehicle takes in the order of 2.5 seconds to cross the span. 4 seconds thus allows to capture a complete 'bump' in strain data. The shift factor f and shift step s were experimentally determined at values 0.5 and 10, respectively.

Figure 14 depicts the results obtained by applying the k-Means SSC based on the *Snapping* distance on the same data used previously to illustrate the effect of the classic (Euclidean) k-Means approach in Figure 9. Comparing both figures, it is clear that this time, the clustering correctly converges to a single bump-shaped peak, caused by a heavy passing vehicle, as well as smaller prototypes for a lighter passing vehicles and the strain baseline. On the top right, the intervals are highlighted corresponding to the small peak (light vehicles), and on the bottom right, intervals are highlighted corresponding to the big peak (heavy truck).

Using more data results in even nicer cluster prototypes, as shown in Figure 15. On longer time series, more clusters are needed to match the higher variability caused by temperature variations, more varied traffic, and traffic jams. We

Figure 13. Runtimes of the clustering implementation on datasets of increasing size and and two different Hadoop clusters

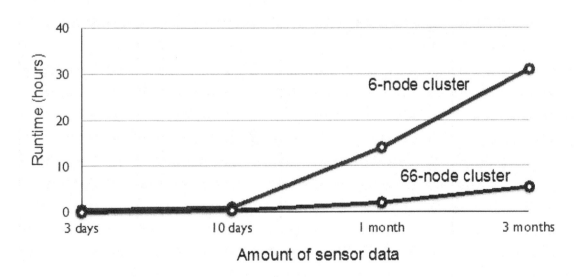

Figure 14. Improved results using the Snapping distance (see Figure 9)

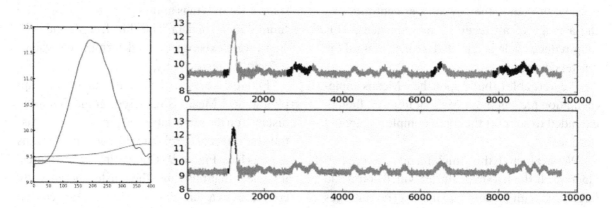

found $k=10$ to be large enough to account for most of the interesting variations in the time series, though we also show the result with $k=4$ for comparison. The third image in Figure 15 shows that, again, the classic k-Means SSC introduces double representations of the same logical events. This is avoided by using the snapping distance (right image), which captures much better different 'states' of the bridge, corresponding to different events. From bottom to top: the key baselines, light vehicles, heavy vehicles, traffic jam baseline and light and heavy vehicles passing during traffic jams (in the opposite direction).

4. MULTI-SCALE ANALYSIS

As briefly discussed in the introduction, and also apparent in the clusters generated in the previous section, different 'events' on the bridge occur at

Figure 15. Prototypes produced by applying k-Means respectively with Euclidean and Snapping distance on the FullWeekDay data, for both k=4 (left) and k=10 (right)

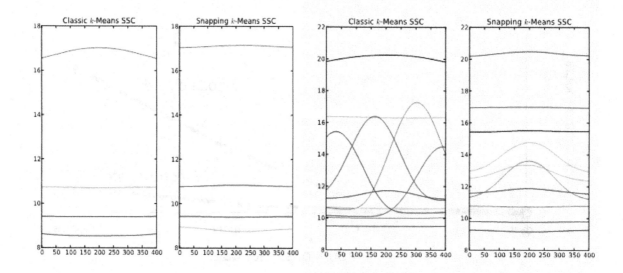

different time scales: passing vehicles rush by in seconds, while traffic jams can take minutes or hours, and temperature gradually changes over the course of an entire day. In order to understand the various changes in the sensor signal, one would benefit substantially from separating out the events at various scales. The analysis of time scales in time series data is often approached from a *scale-space* perspective, which involves convolution of the original signal with Gaussian kernels of increasing size (Witkin, 1983) to remove information at smaller scales. By subtracting carefully selected components of the scale-space, we can effectively cut up the scale space into *k* ranges.

4.1 The Scale-Space Image

The *scale-space image* (Witkin, 1983) is a scale parameterization technique for one-dimensional signals based on the operation of convolution, discussed in Section 2.1.

Given a signal **x**, the family of σ-smoothed signals Φ_x over scale parameter σ is defined as follows:

$$\Phi_x(\sigma) = x * g_\sigma, \sigma > 0$$

where g_σ is a Gaussian kernel having standard deviation σ, and $\Phi_x(0)=\mathbf{x}$.

The signals in Φ_x define a surface in the time-scale plane (t,σ) known in the literature as the *scale-space image* (Lindeberg, 1990; Witkin, 1983). This visualization gives a complete description of the scale properties of a signal in terms of Gaussian smoothing. Moreover, it has other properties useful for segmentation, as we will see later in the paper.

For practical purposes, the scale-space image is quantized across the scale dimension by computing the convolutions only for a finite number of scale parameters. More formally, for a given signal **x**, we fix a set of scale parameters

$$S = \{2^i \mid 0 \leq i \leq \sigma_{max} \wedge i \in \mathbb{N}\}$$

and we compute $\Phi_x(\sigma)$ only for $\sigma \in S$ where σ_{max} is such that $\Phi_x(\sigma)$ is approximately equal to the mean signal of **x**.

Figure 16. Scale-space image of an artificially generated signal totaling 259200 points

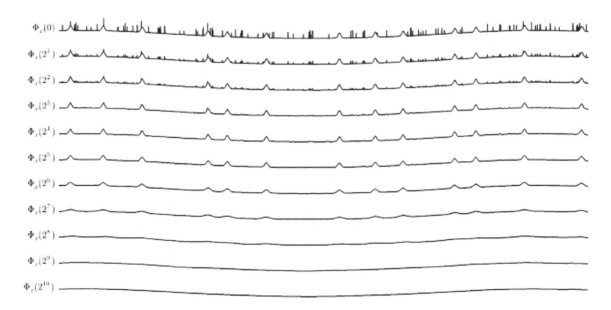

As an example, Figure 16 shows the scale-space image of an artificially generated signal. The topmost plot represents the original signal, constructed by three components at different temporal scales: a slowly changing and slightly curved baseline, medium term events (bumps) and short term events (peaks). It is easy to visually verify that, by increasing the scale parameter, a larger amount of detail is removed. In particular, the peaks are smoothed out at scales greater than $\sigma=2^4$, and the bumps are smoothed out at scales greater than $\sigma=2^8$, after which only the baseline remains.

Figure 17 shows the scale-space created by convoluting the strain signal of a single sensor with Gaussian kernels of sizes ranging from $\sigma=2^1$ to $\sigma=2^9$. At the smallest scales, all detail in preserved, even the noise in the data. At slightly larger scales, noise is smoothed out, but the signal still follows the effect of a truck's suspension on the bridge (resulting in oscillations in the large

bump itself), as well as the oscillation of the bridge after the truck has passed. At larger scales, those oscillations are smoothed out so that only the bump remains, and at the very largest scales even the bump will diminish until it is also smoothed out and only the baseline remains.

In the next section, we show how to manipulate the scale-space image to filter out the effects of transient events in a specific range of scales. This will lead to the definition of a signal decomposition scheme.

4.2 Scale-Space Decomposition

Along the scale dimension of the scale-space image, short-time transient events in the signal will be smoothed away sooner than longer ones. In other words, we can associate to each event a maximum scale σ_{cut} such that, for $\sigma>\sigma_{cut}$, the transient event is no longer present in $\Phi_x(\sigma_{cut})$. This fact leads to the following two observations:

Figure 17. Scale-space convolutions overlapping with strain sensor data

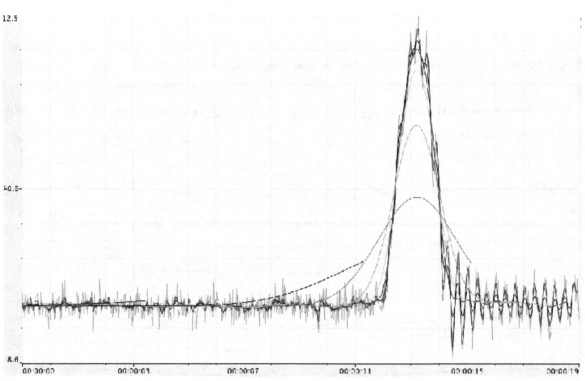

- Given a signal scale-space image Φ_x, the signal $\Phi_x(\sigma)$ is only affected by the transient events at scales greater than σ. This is conceptually equivalent to a *low-pass filter* in signal processing.

- Given a signal scale-space image Φ_x and two scales $\sigma_1 < \sigma_2$, the signal $\Phi_x(\sigma_1) - \Phi_x(\sigma_2)$ is mostly affected by those transient events present in the range of scales (σ_1, σ_2). This is similar to a *band-pass filter* in signal processing.

As an example, reconsider the signal **x** and its scale-space image Φ_x of Figure 16. Figure 18 shows (from top to bottom):

- The signal $\Phi_x(0) - \Phi_x(2^2)$, which is the result of a high-pass filtering; this feature represents the short-term events (peaks),

- The signal $\Phi_x(2^4) - \Phi_x(2^{10})$, which is the result of a band-pass filtering; this feature represents the medium-term events (bumps),

- The signal $\Phi_x(2^{10})$, which is the result of a low-pass filtering; this feature represents the long-term trend.

Generalizing the example in Figure 18, we can define a decomposition scheme of a signal **x** by considering adjacent ranges of scales of the signal scale-space image. We formalize this idea below.

Definition 6: Given a signal **x** and a set of $k-1$ scale parameters $C = \{\sigma_1, \ldots, \sigma_{k-1}\}$ (called the cut-points set) such that $\sigma_1 < \ldots < \sigma_{k-1}$, the scale decomposition of **x** is given by the set of component signals $D_x(C) = \{x_1, \ldots, x_k\}$, defined as follows:

$$x_i = \begin{cases} \Phi_x(0) - \Phi_x(\sigma_1) & if \ i = 1 \\ \Phi_x(\sigma_{i-1}) - \Phi_x(\sigma_i) & if \ 1 < i < k \\ \Phi_x(\sigma_{k-1}) & if \ i = k \end{cases}$$

Note that for k components we require $k-1$ cut-points. This decomposition has several elegant properties:

- x_k can be seen as the baseline of the signal, as obtained by a low-pass filter;

- x_i for $1 \leq i < k$ are signals as obtained by a band-pass filter, and can be used to identify transient events;

- $\sum_{i=1}^{k} x_i = x$, i.e., the original signal can be recovered from the decomposition.

4.3 Convolution in MapReduce

Computing the scale-space image and the scale-space decompositions are quite expensive operations when dealing with terabytes of sensor data. Moreover, our data streams are too large to fit in memory, so we will need to break them up into data splits and convolve each split separately. Again, the bottleneck will be the disk reads, so we again resort to the MapReduce framework for comput-

Figure 18. Examples of signal decomposition obtained from the scale-space image in Figure 16

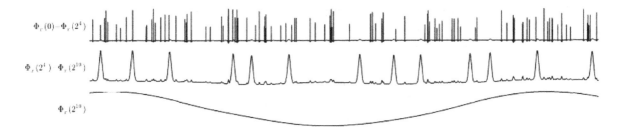

ing the convolutions and scale-space images. To simplify things, we start with convolution by itself.

In its simplest form, each mapper could just read a data split, do the convolution and output the convolved data (the reducer being simply an identity reducer). However, this will not be correct, because at both ends of each data split, we don't have the necessary data to calculate the convolution. This is also called the *wrap-around problem*, and is illustrated in Figure 19. Indeed, at the borders of the data split, the Gaussian kernel $\mathbf{g}_\sigma$ does not overlap the signal completely. While we could wrap the kernel around the edge, and take a portion of the right side of the signal while we are convoluting the very left side, this will result in a section of spoiled data.

To compute the convolution in practice, we will cut off the Gaussian kernel $\mathbf{g}_\sigma$ at some point, e.g. at 3σ on each side. That means that the first and the last $\frac{3}{2}\sigma$ points of the convolution will be spoiled. If we use very wide Gaussians, e.g. to establish the baseline component, this will result in a *lot* of spoiled data.

A simple solution is to pad the signal with zeros on both ends, as shown in Figure 20. The resulting convolution will still include spoiled intervals, but now they correspond to the zero-padded intervals, so we can safely ignore them.

While this works for the very beginning and end of our sensor data, it is not correct for most data splits: indeed, the beginning and end of each split should be influenced by the previous and

Figure 19. The wrap-around problem with convolution

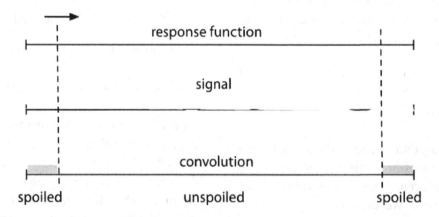

Figure 20. Solving the wrap-around problem with zero-padding

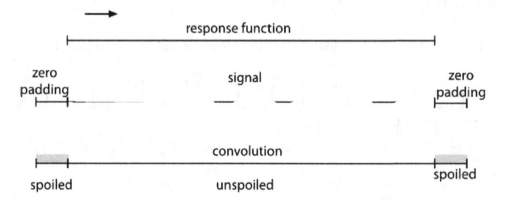

next split, respectively, not by zeros. Thus, these data points should somehow be appended to each data split. One solution would be to write a custom Hadoop InputFormat to generate data splits in such a way that they overlap. This is indeed a (nontrivial) solution, but what if the data is physically stored in separate files, or even on different machines?

Another solution is to activate our idle reducers. This is illustrated in Figure 21. The mappers each read a data split, and output it in as an array, again using the first timestamp of the split as the key. However, for the first and last $\frac{3}{2}\sigma$ points, it

will also emit them to the previous and next data split, respectively. An additional indicator will be sent with the data to indicate whether it is a head, body, or tail section of the enlarged split. The reducers thus receive the 3 components, can compute the convolution, and only emit the unspoiled 'body' part of each split. At the very beginning and end of the signal, we still use zero padding.

However, zero-padding can also be used in a different way, illustrated in Figure 22. Here, the mappers read their data split, append zero's at the beginning and each of it, and emit the *entire*

Figure 21. Convolution in MapReduce with Overlap-Convolute

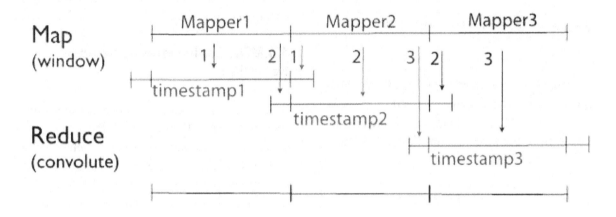

Figure 22. Convolution in MapReduce with Convolute-Add

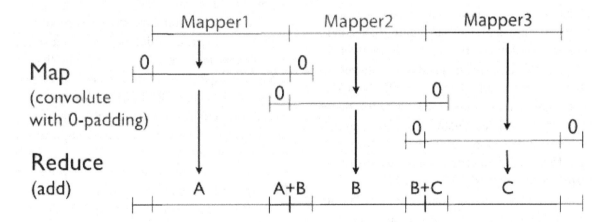

convolution. This will obviously result in 'spoiled' regions. However, if you have carefully zero-padded both ends, there is no ambiguity and you can reconstruct the convolution in that region by simply adding the convoluted values of both mappers in the reducer. Each mapper has effectively computed part of the convolution.

There is another, faster method to compute the convolution: the Fast Fourier Transform. This is a result of the *discrete convolution theorem*: if a signal x is periodic with period N, so that it is completely determined by the N values x_0, ..., x_{N-1}, then its discrete convolution with a response function h of *finite duration N* can be obtained as the inverse DFT of the product of the individual transforms:

$$x * h = \sum_{k=-\frac{N}{2}+1}^{\frac{N}{2}} x_{t-k} h_k = DFT^{-1}\left\{X_n H_n\right\}$$

Here, X_n ($n = 0,...,N-1$) is the discrete Fourier transform of the signal x_t ($t = 0,...,N-1$), while H_n($n = 0,..., N-1$) is the discrete Fourier transform of the response function h_t ($t = 0,..., N-1$). Thus, in simple terms,

$$x * h = DFT^{-1}\left\{DFT(x)DFT(h)\right\}$$

Because our data is not periodic, we face the same wrap-around problem, but we can work around this problem by using the zero-padding discussed above and shown in Figure 20. Second, our response function g_σ is much shorter than N, but again this is solved by padding it with zeros. All this is interesting because, while both the direct convolution and the DFT are $O(n^2)$, there exist several implementations for the parallel Fast Fourier Transform (FFT) that take $O(n\log n)$ time. However, their efficient implementation in MapReduce is non-trivial (Sze, 2011).

In our experiments, doing the convolution directly using MapReduce turned out to be suf-

ficient. Indeed, our response function g_σ is often much smaller than N, approaching $\log n$. Moreover, when computing the scale space image, we can compute multiple convolutions in parallel. Each mapper can compute g_σ for several or all values of σ, as long as it employs the exact amount of zero-padding for each convolution, and emits the results using a key that includes the value of σ used, so that the reduces can combine the correct partial convolutions.

Efficiently implemented, our MapReduce implementation of the direct convolution can smooth 3 months of data in only a few minutes. In fact, writing the results to disk takes longer that the actual computations. The time to compute large scale spaces also grows linearly in the length of the time series and the size of the longest considered time scale.

4.4 MDL Scale Decomposition Selection

In order to construct a scale-space decomposition, such as shown in Figure 4 (left), that can be used to adequately model the bridge's behavior, we still need to choose several key parameters: the appropriate scales at which to model the components, and the optimal number of components. More formally, we need to find a good subset of cut-points C such that the resulting k components of the decomposition $D_x(C)$ optimally capture the effect of transient events at different scales.

The rationale behind the scale decomposition is that it is easier to model the effect of a single class of transient events at a given scale than to model the superimposition of many, interacting transient events at multiple scales. We thus need to trade off the added complexity of having to represent multiple components for the complexity of the representations themselves. A good approach for establishing this trade-off is the Minimum Description Length (MDL) principle.

The Minimum Description Length (Grünwald, 2007) is an information-theoretic model selection framework that selects the best model according to its ability to *compress* the given data. In our context, the two-part MDL principle states that the best model M to describe the signal x is the one that minimizes the sum $L(M) + L(\mathbf{x} \mid M)$, where:

- $L(M)$ is the length, in bits, of the description of the model,
- $L(\mathbf{x} \mid M)$ is the length, in bits, of the description of the signal when encoded with the help of the model M.

In order to apply the MDL principle, we need to define a model $M_{D_\mathbf{x}(C)}$ for a given scale decomposition $D_\mathbf{x}(C)$ and, consequently, how to compute both $L(M_{D_\mathbf{x}(C)})$ and $L(\mathbf{x} \mid M_{D_\mathbf{x}(C)})$. The latter term is the length in bits of the information lost by the model, i.e., the residual signal $\mathbf{x} - M_{D_\mathbf{x}(C)}$.

4.4.1 Time Series Values Discretization

In order to use the MDL principle we need to work with a quantized input signal and scale-space image. Because of this, we assume that the values v of both the input signal $\mathbf{x}$ and $\Phi_\mathbf{x}(\sigma)$, for each considered σ, have been quantized to a finite number of symbols by employing the function defined below:

$$Q(v) = \frac{v - \min(x)}{\max(x) - \min(x)} l - \frac{l}{2}$$

where l, assumed to be even, is the number of bins to use in the discretization while $\min(\mathbf{x})$ and $\max(\mathbf{x})$ are respectively the minimum and maximum value in $\mathbf{x}$. Throughout the rest of the paper, we assume $l=256$. A similar approach is described in (Hu et al., 2011). All the subsequent operations, from the computations of the scale decompositions to the encoding of the components, are kept in this quantized space.

4.4.2 Component Modeling

Next, we also need a model to describe each of the decomposition components and calculate the length $L(M)$ of the model. In the next paragraphs we introduce two such methods, illustrated in Figure 23: the first is based on discretization, the second on segmentation.

Discretization-Based Representation

A desirable encoding would give short codes to long stretches of baseline and the commonly occurring amplitudes. Unfortunately, our original discretization is too fine-grained to capture regular occurrences of similar amplitudes. Hence, we consider a more coarse-grained discretization by discretizing each value v in a component to a value

Figure 23. Example of discretization-based encoding (left) and segmentation-based encoding with first degree polynomial approximations (the markers show the zero-crossings) (right)

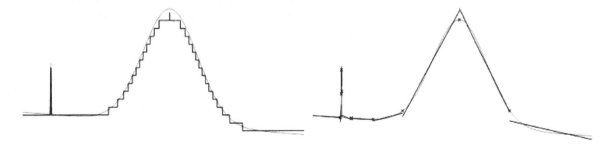

$\lfloor Q(v)/2_i \rfloor$, where several values for i are considered for each component, typically $i \in \{2,4,6\}$. By doing so, similar values will be grouped together in the same bin. The resulting sequence of integers is compacted further by performing run-length encoding, resulting in a string of (v,l) pairs, where l represents the number of times value v is repeated consecutively. This string is finally encoded using a Shannon-Fano or Huffman code (see Section 4.4.3).

Segmentation-Based Representation

The main assumption on which we base this method is that a clear transient event can be accurately represented by a simple function, such as a polynomial of a bounded degree. Hence, if a signal contains a number of clear transient events, it should be possible to accurately represent this signal with a number of segments, each of which represented by a simple function.

Given a component $\mathbf{x}_i$ of length n, let

$$z\left(\mathbf{x}_i\right) = \left\{t_1, t_2, \ldots, t_m\right\}, 1 < t_1 \le n$$

be a set of indexes of the segment boundaries.

Let $fit(\mathbf{x}_i\left[a:b\right], d_1)$ be the approximation of $\mathbf{x}_i\left[a:b\right]$ obtained by fitting a polynomial of degree d_i. Then, we represent each component $\mathbf{x}_i$ with the approximation $\hat{\mathbf{x}}_i$, such that:

$$\hat{\mathbf{x}}_i\left[0:z_1\right] = fit\left(\mathbf{x}_i\left[0:z_1\right], d_i\right)$$

$$\hat{\mathbf{x}}_i\left[z_i:z_{i+1}\right] = fit\left(\mathbf{x}_i\left[z_i:z_{i+1}\right], d_i\right), 1 \le i < m$$

$$\hat{\mathbf{x}}_i\left[z_m:n\right] = fit\left(\mathbf{x}_i\left[z_m:n\right], d_i\right)$$

Note that approximation $\hat{\mathbf{x}}_i$, is quantized again by reapplying the function Q to each of its values.

For a given k-components scale decomposition $D_\mathbf{x}(C)$ and a fixed polynomial degree for each of its components, we calculate the complexity in bits of the model $M_{D_\mathbf{x}(C)}$, based on this representation scheme, as follows. Each approximated component $\hat{\mathbf{x}}_i$ consists of $\left|z\left(\mathbf{x}_i\right)\right| + 1$ segments. For each segment, we need to represent its length and the $d_i + 1$ coefficients of the fitted polynomial. The length ls_i of the longest segment in $\hat{\mathbf{x}}_i$ is given by

$$ls_i = \max\left(z_1 \bigcup \left\{z_{i+1} - z_i \mid 0 < i \le m\right\}\right)$$

We therefore use $\log_2(ls_i)$ bits to represent the segment lengths, while for the coefficients of the polynomials we employ floating point numbers of fixed[6] bit complexity c. The MDL model cost is thus defined as:

$$L\left(M_{D_x(c)}\right) = \sum\nolimits_{i=1}^{k}\left(\left|z\left(\mathbf{x}_i\right)\right| + 1\right)$$
$$\left(\log_2\left(ls_i\right) + c(d_i + 1)\right)$$

So far we assumed to have a set of boundaries $z(\mathbf{x}_i)$, but we did not specify how to compute them. A desirable property for our segmentation would be that a segmentation at a coarser scale does not contain more segments than a segmentation at a finer scale.

The scale space theory assures that there are fewer zero-crossing of the derivatives of a signal at coarser scales (Witkin, 1983). In our segmentation we use the zero-crossings of the first and second derivatives. These can be computed efficiently, because the derivative of the convolution of a signal $\mathbf{x}$ is the same as the convolution of $\mathbf{x}$ with the derivative of the response function $\mathbf{g}_\sigma$.

More formally, we define the segmentation boundaries of a component $\mathbf{x}_i$ to be

$$z\left(x_i\right) = \left\{ t \in \mathbb{R} \mid \frac{d\boldsymbol{x}_i}{dt}\left(t\right) = 0 \right\}$$
$$\cup \left\{ t \in \mathbb{R} \mid \frac{d^2\boldsymbol{x}_i}{dt}\left(t\right) = 0 \right\}$$

Figure 23 (right) shows an example of segmentation obtained as above using fitted polynomials of degree 1. However, many other segmentation algorithms are known in the literature (E. Keogh, Chu, Hart, & Pazzani, 1993; E. J. Keogh, Chu, Hart, & Pazzani, 2001) and all of them can be interchangeably employed in this context.

4.4.3 Residual Encoding

Given a model $M_{D_x(C)}$, its residual $r = x - \sum_{i=1}^{k}\hat{\boldsymbol{x}}_i$, computed over the components approximations, represents the information of **x** not captured by the model. Having already defined the model cost for the two proposed encoding schemes, we only need to define $L(\boldsymbol{x} \mid M_{D_x(C)})$, i.e., a bit complexity $L(\mathbf{r})$ for the residual **r**.

Here, we exploit the fact that we operate in a quantized space; we encode each bin in the quantized space with a code that uses approximately $-\log(P(x))$ bits, where $P(x)$ is the frequency of the xth bin in our data. The main justification for this encoding is that we expect that the errors are normally distributed around 0. Hence, the bins that reflect a low error will have the highest frequency of occurrences; we will give these the shortest codes. We use Huffman coding in our experiments, as in Hu et al. (2011).

4.4.4 Model Selection

We can now define the MDL score that we are optimizing as follows:

Definition 7: Given a model $M_{D_x(C)}$, its MDL score is defined as:

$$L\left(M_{D_x(c)}\right) + L(\boldsymbol{r})$$

In the case of discretization-based encoding, the MDL score is affected by the cardinality used to encode each component. In the case of segmentation-based encoding the MDL score depends on the boundaries of the segments and the degrees of the polynomials in the representation. In both cases, also the cut-points of the considered decomposition affect the final score.

The simplest way to find the model that minimizes this score is to enumerate, encode and compute the MDL score for every possible scale-space decomposition and all possible encoding parameters. As we shall now show, this brute-force approach is practically feasible.

The number of possible scale decompositions depends on the total number of cut-points sets we can build from the computed scale parameters in Φ_x. We fix the maximum number of cut-points in a candidate set to some value c_{max}. This also means that we limit our search to those scale decompositions having $c_{max}+1$ components or less. Moreover, given our wish to consider only simple approximations of the signals, we can also assume a reasonably low limit d_{max} (in practice, $d_{max}=2$) on the degree of the polynomials that approximate the segments of each given component.

Computing the MDL score for each encoded scale decomposition, obtained by ranging over all the possible configurations of cut-points $C_1,\ldots,C_{k-1}$, and all the possible configurations of polynomial degrees $d_1,\ldots,d_k$ hence requires calculating MDL scores for

$$\sum_{k=2}^{c_{max}+1} \binom{\mid \boldsymbol{S} \mid}{k-1} d_{max}^k$$

scale decompositions. This turns out to be a reasonable number in most practical cases we consider, and hence we use an exhaustive approach in our experiments.

4.5 Experiments

In this section, we experimentally evaluate this method on real-world sensor data. For a more detailed analysis of the MDL-based approach on artificial data, see Vespier et al. (2012).

Figure 24 shows strain data from a single sensor, and the resulting decomposition into three scale-space components. We evaluated all the possible decompositions up to three components (two cut-points) allowing both the discretisation and segmentation representation schemes. In the case of the discretization-based representations, we limit the possible cardinalities to 4, 16 and 64.

The top-ranked decomposition results in 3 components as shown in the last three plots in Figure 24. The selected cut-points appear at scales $2^6=64$ and $2^{11}=2048$. All three components are represented with the discretization-based scheme, with a cardinality of respectively 4, 16, and 16 symbols. The decomposition has an MDL-score of 344,276, where $L(M)=19,457$ and $L(D|M)=324,818$. The found components accurately correspond to physical events on the bridge. The first component, covering scales lower than 2^6, reflects the short-term influence caused by passing vehicles and represented as peaks in the signal. Note that the cardinality selected for this component is the lowest admissible in our setting (4). This is reasonable considering that the relatively simple dynamic behavior occurring at these scales, mostly the presence or not of a peak over a flat baseline, can be cheaply described with 4 or fewer states without incurring a too large error. The middle component, covering scales between 2^6 and 2^{11}, reflects the medium-term effects caused by traffic jams. As in the artificial data, the first component is slightly influenced by the second one, especially at the start and ending points of a traffic jam. Finally, the third component captures all the scales greater than 2^{11}, here representing the effect of temperature during a whole day. To sum up, the top-ranked decomposition successfully reflects the real physical phenomena affecting the data. The decompositions with rank 8 or less all present similar configurations of cut-points and cardinalities, resulting in comparable components where the conclusions above still hold. The first 2-component decomposition appears at rank 10 with the cut-point placed at scale 2^6, which separates the short-term peaks from all the rest of the signal (traffic jams and baseline mixed together). These facts make the result pretty stable as most of the good decompositions are ranked first.

Figure 24. Signal (top) and top-ranked scale decomposition for the sensor data

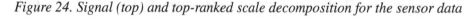

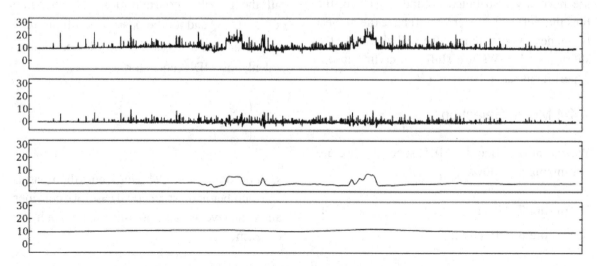

5. MODELING DEPENDENCIES

When dealing with multiple sensors measuring a physical system, each individual sensor will be sensitive to some aspects of the system, based on the specific characteristics of the type of sensor and on which part of the system the sensor is placed. This is clearly the case for sensors of different types (such as vibration and temperature sensors), but also for identical sensors attached differently to the system. In this section, we focus on modeling dependencies between different types of sensors on high volumes of data.

5.1 Strain and Temperature

First, we study the relationship between strain and temperature sensors. Figure 25 (left) shows the absolute correlation coefficients between strain and temperature readings, varying from 0 to 0.97. For these sensor pairs with high correlation coefficients, we can simply employ a linear model that assumes the measured strain is directly influenced by the temperature of one of the temperature sensors:

$$S = a \cdot T + b$$

In this model, the coefficients a and b translate between the temperature scale (in Celsius) and the micro-strain scale (in $\mu m/m$), and can be obtained through linear regression over a significant portion of the data streams of both sensors. Figure 26(left) shows the accuracy of this model for two sensor time series that are only moderately related, with $a=-3.288$ and $b=27.547$. The correlation coefficient for this example is $r=0.776$, which indicates that the selected pair of sensors are moderately correlated. This mismatch is caused by the fact that the bridge does not immediately react to a change in the outside temperature, but rather does so in a delayed fashion.

The amount of delay depends on the size and material of the structure, with larger structures (such as the bridge in question) being less sensitive to sudden changes of outside temperature. In other words, a large concrete bridge has a large capacity to store heat, which is mirrored in a slow response of the strain signal.

In the systems analysis field, systems with a capacity are often modeled as a *Linear Time-Invariant* system (Hespanha, 2009). *Time-invariant* systems do not change over time, which is a reasonable assumption for a bridge, if subtle deterioration of the structure is ignored. LTI systems are *linear* because their 'output' is a linear combination of the 'inputs'. In this case, the temperature of the bridge is modeled as a linear combination of the outside temperature over a certain period of time (typically the recent temperature history):

Figure 25. Correlation matrices for Strain-Temperature (left), Strain-Vibration (middle) and Strain-Vibration after band-pass filtering (right, see Section 5.2). The numbers on the axes indicate the sensor number

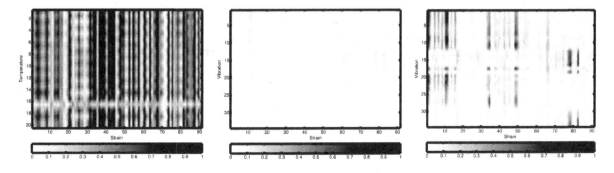

Figure 26. The linear (left) and exponential decay model (right) between strain and temperature

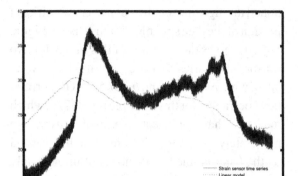
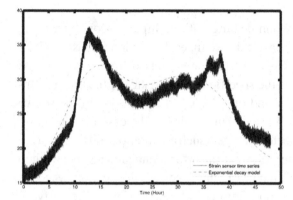

$$T_{bridge}\left(t\right) = \sum_{m=0}^{\infty} h\left(m\right) T(t-m)$$

where $T_{bridge}(t)$ is the internal temperature and h is an impulse response (to be defined below). Note that this is a special case of *convolution*, which means we can reuse our methods for computing convolution over large amounts of data.

Of the many impulse response functions h, which include for example the well-known moving average operation, we decide to model the delayed effect of the outside temperature using the exponential decay function $h_e(m)=e^{-\lambda m}$ (for $m \geq 0$). In this function, λ is the decay factor, which determines how quickly the effect of past values reduces with time. Note that the resulting equation:

$$S = a.h_e * T + b, where\, h_e\left(m\right) = e^{-\lambda m} \qquad (2)$$

is the solution to a linear differential equation that is known as *Newton's law of cooling*, which states that the change in temperature of the bridge is proportional to the difference between the temperature of the bridge and its environment:

$$\frac{dT_{bridge}}{dt} = -r.\left(T_{bridge}\left(t\right) - T(t)\right)$$

This is a somewhat simplified representation of reality, in that it assumes that the systems consists of two 'lumps', the bridge and the environment, and that within each lump the distribution of heat is instantaneous. Although in reality this is clearly not the case, this model performs fairly well in practice.

For a given pair of sensors and the associated data, we will have to choose optimal values for a,b and λ. It turns out that λ behaves very decently, with only a single optimum for given a and b, such that simple greedy optimization will produce the desired result.

Figure 26 (right) shows the fitted model using Equation 2, which clearly demonstrates that the exponential decay model has removed the apparent delay in the data. The fitted coefficients were $a = -12.147$, $b = 30.463$, and $\lambda = 3 \cdot 10^{-5}$, yielding a correlation coefficient $r = 0.867$. Considering every possible pair of strain-temperature sensors, we find that the correlation coefficients of 47.4% of sensor pairs are improved by the exponential decay model.

5.2 Strain and Vibration

As illustrated in Figure 25 (middle), the correlations between strain and vibration sensor pairs are quite weak, the highest one for this data being

Figure 27. Strain and Vibration signal

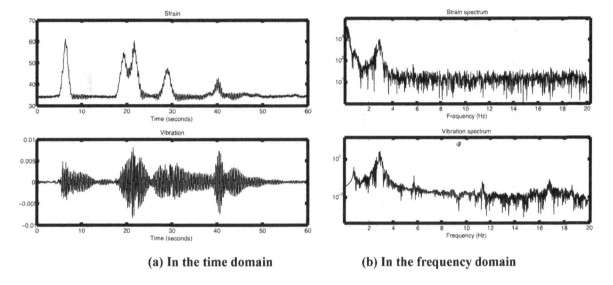

(a) In the time domain   **(b) In the frequency domain**

0.1557. A sensor pair with moderate correlation coefficient is shown in Figure 27. The graphs show that the vibration sensor is a symmetric signal, while the strain sensor time series is not. However, the peaks in both occur consistently, which indicates that they are related. A simple correlation will however not be able to capture this similarity.

In order to extract the amplitude of the vibration signal, which should correspond to the magnitude of the strain on the bridge, we apply an *envelope* operation. We approximate the envelope by detecting peaks (using zero-crossings as discussed in Section 4.4.2) and interpolating between them. For negative peaks, we simply take the absolute value. The peaks are then interpolated with a piece-wise linear approximation. The result is demonstrated in Figure 28.

Figure 27b features the spectra obtained for the two signals by means of a Discrete Fourier Transform (Stranneby & Walker, 2004), showing that despite a lack of a direct relation in the time domain, the signals are actually fairly similar in parts of the spectrum, notably on frequencies above 1 Hz. Note the big peak around 2.8 Hz in both spectra. In fact, what is missing in the vibra-

tion spectrum are the lower frequencies, which correspond to slower bridge movements. In other words, the vibration sensors are not sensitive to gradual changes in the deflection of the bridge, as the sensors themselves simply move along with the bridge. The strain gauges, on the other hand, *are* sensitive even to the slowest changes in bridge deflection. However, both sensors measure shaking of the bridge (frequencies above 1 Hz) in a similar fashion.

Based on these observations, an obvious way to relate strain to vibration is to focus on a fairly specific range of frequencies. As we have done in the previous section, we can apply a *band-pass filter* (BPF) to remove all components of the signal outside the range 2.0–3.2 Hz. The linear model between the strain and vibration time series then becomes:

$$BPF_{2-3.2}\left(S\right) = a.BPF_{2-3.2}\left(V\right) + b$$

After applying the band-pass filter operation to both strain and vibration data, the correlation coefficient improves from 0.10 to 0.94.

The model we achieved through the band-pass filter operation works well for a small selection of

Figure 28. The strain signal compared to the envelope-based model

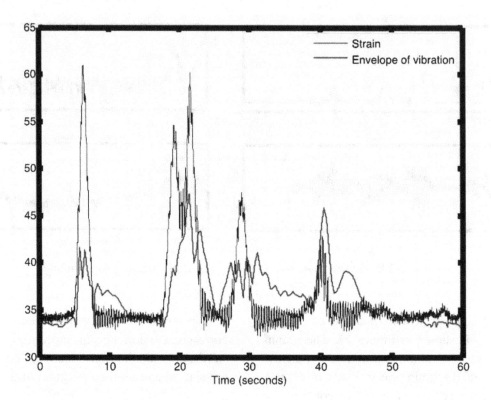

sensor pairs. In Figure 25 on the right, information is displayed on which sensor pairs specifically gain from this operation. Note that some strain gauges correspond well to most of the vibration sensors (dark columns in the matrix). These sensors are primarily located on the right side of the bridge. The few exceptions (St78, St79 and St83) are located on the girder entirely on the other side of the bridge. We look into such observations in more detail later.

5.3 Vibration and Temperature

As mentioned in the previous section, the vibration spectrum shows little activity in the range below 1 Hz, which happens to be where all of the temperature changes occur (for example due to the daily difference between day and night). For this reason, we do not expect significant dependencies between the sensors from Vi and Te. However,

the vibration of the bridge does depend on the temperature. It is well known that bridges tend to oscillate at specific frequencies, and that these frequencies are determined by the stiffness of the structure, which in turn is influenced by changes in the temperature of the material. In a simplified model of a span of the bridge, an Euler-Bernoulli beam (Yang & Chang, 2009), the *natural frequency* of the span is computed as follows:

$$f_n = \frac{1}{2\pi}\sqrt{\frac{k}{m}}$$

In this equation, m refers to the mass of the bridge (including the possible load on the bridge), and k is a stiffness coefficient that depends on several factors such as material, humidity, corrosion, etc., but also on temperature. Note that an increasing temperature leads to a decreasing stiffness k, and hence a decrease in frequency, such that we expect a negative relationship between vibration and temperature sensors.

The effect of temperature on natural frequencies is widely studied Song & Dyke, 2006; Xia, Hao, Zanardo, & Deeks, 2006). After external excitation, for example traffic or wind, a bridge can vibrate in different *modes* (Reynolds & Pavic, 2001). Each mode stands for one way of vibration, which can be vertical, horizontal, torsional or more complicated combinations thereof, and there is one natural frequency corresponding to each.

Figure 29a shows the modes corresponding to free vibration of the bridge (when no traffic is present). We can easily detect several interesting modes, summarized in Table 1. A mode 'occurs' in a given spectrum (corresponding to a traffic-free section of vibration data) if there is at least one peak with amplitude bigger than the average. Mode 2 (2.69 Hz) and mode 3 (2.88 Hz) are the principal modes of the bridge, which occur in every event. Mode 4 and mode 5 are also important modes, which have strong amplitude and happen in most events. Mode 1 and mode 8 have modest occurrence, but their amplitudes are relatively weak. Mode 6 and mode 7 are so weak that they can be ignored in most cases.

Table 1. Statistics of modes

Mode	Frequency (Hz)	Occurrence
mode 1	0.73-0.93	71.8%
mode 2	2.69	100%
mode 3	2.88	100%
mode 4	5.61-5.77	97.3%
mode 5	11.22-11.43	98.7%
mode 6	15.35-15.55	12.1%
mode 7	16.55-16.90	10.7%
mode 8	18.30-18.70	48.3%

For a short period, we can assume the stiffness of the bridge as a constant. The only factor influencing the natural frequencies is the mass of the bridge. When the truck is on the bridge, the mass of the bridge increases, and the natural frequencies should decrease. From Figure 29b, we can see that mode 2, mode 3, mode 4 and mode 5 indeed show a left shift of the peaks. Furthermore, the spectrum for passing trucks contains more peaks than that of free vibration, which can be explained by the complex interaction between the trucks' suspension systems and the bridge. Further details can be found in (Miao et. al, 2013).

Figure 29. The spectra of the bridge during free vibration and passing trucks

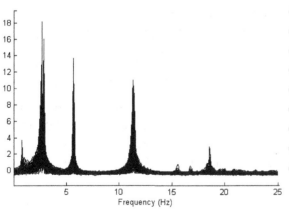

(a) The free vibration modes of the bridge

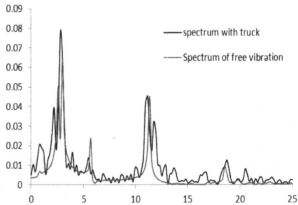

(b) The spectra during free vibration plus the spectra during truck passings

6. CONCLUSION

In this chapter, we have introduced novel techniques for large-scale sensor network analysis. We have especially focused on subsequence clustering, multi-scale analysis, scale-space decomposition, and modeling the interaction between various types of sensors in a network. For these methods we have offered scalable, MapReduce-based implementations, typically by focusing on the key underlying types of processing such as convolution, smoothing, computing derivatives and Fourier transforms. We also presented improvements on subsequence clustering techniques that are useful for all unlabeled time series applications, and introduced novel methods to automatically decompose complex sensor signals into subcomponents that correspond to events occurring on different temporal scales.

While we focused on a specific application, a sensor network attached to a major highway bridge, these techniques will likely be useful in many other large-scale time series applications, as they often depend on the same basic building blocks such as convolution, segmentation, clustering and classification. On the other hand, some aspects are also of specific use to structural health monitoring, such as modeling physical interactions between temperature, vibration and strain, and monitoring key structural aspects such as vibration modes over long periods of time.

REFERENCES

Agrawal, D., Das, S., & El Abbadi, A. (2011). Big data and cloud computing: Current state and future opportunities. In *Proceedings of the 14th International Conference on Extending Database Technology* (pp. 530–533). New York, NY: ACM.

ASCE. (2009). *Report card for americas infrastructure*. Retrieved from http://apps.asce.org/reportcard/2009/grades.cfm

Borthakur, D., Muthukkaruppan, K., Ranganathan, K., Rash, S., Sen Sarma, J., Spiegelberg, N., et al. (2011). Apache hadoop goes realtime at Facebook. In *Proceedings of SIGMOD 2011*. ACM.

Brantner, M., Florescu, D., Graf, D., Kossmann, D., & Kraska, T. (2008). Building a database on S3. In *Proceedings of the 2008 ACM SIGMOD International Conference on Management of Data* (pp. 251–264). New York, NY: ACM.

Cox, M., & Ellsworth, D. (1997). Managing big data for scientific visualization. In *Proceedings of ACM SIGGRAPH* (Vol. 97). ACM.

Dean, J., & Ghemawat, S. (2008). MapReduce: Simplified data processing on large clusters. *Communications of the ACM, 51*(1), 107–113. doi:10.1145/1327452.1327492.

Fujimaki, R., Hirose, S., & Nakata, T. (2008). Theoretical analysis of sub- sequence time-series clustering from a frequency-analysis viewpoint. In *Proceedings of SDM 2008* (pp. 506–517). SDM.

George, L. (2011). *HBase: The definitive guide*. Sebastopol, CA: O'Reilly Media.

Giangarra, P., Metrovich, B., Schwitters, M., & Semple, B. (2011). Smarter bridges through advanced structural health monitoring. *IBM Journal of Research and Development, 5*(1-2).

Grünwald, P. D. (2007). *The minimum description length principle*. Cambridge, MA: The MIT Press.

Hespanha, J. (2009). *Linear system theory*. Princeton, NJ: Princeton University Press.

Höppner, F. (2002). Time series abstraction methods - A survey. In Proceedings of Informatik bewegt: Informatik 2002 - 32. jahrestagung der gesellschaft für informatik e.v. (gi) (pp. 777–786). GI.

Hu, B., Rakthanmanon, T., Hao, Y., Evans, S., Lonardi, S., & Keogh, E. (2011). Discovering the intrinsic cardinality and dimensionality of time series using mdl. [ICDM.]. *Proceedings of ICDM, 2011*, 1086–1091.

Idé, T. (2006). Why does subsequence time-series clustering produce sine waves? In *Proceedings of ECML PKDD 2006* (pp. 211–222). ECML.

Jardak, C., Riihijärvi, J., Oldewurtel, F., & Mähönen, P. (2010). Parallel processing of data from very large-scale wireless sensor networks. In *Proceedings of the 19th ACM International Symposium on High Performance Distributed Computing* (pp. 787–794). New York, NY: ACM.

Jiang, J., Lu, J., Zhang, G., & Long, G. (2011). Scaling-up item-based collaborative filtering recommendation algorithm based on Hadoop. In *Proceedings of the 2011 IEEE World Congress on Services* (pp. 490-497). IEEE.

Keogh, E., Chu, S., Hart, D., & Pazzani, M. (1993). Segmenting time series: A survey and novel approach. In Data mining in time series databases (pp. 1–22).

Keogh, E., Chu, S., Hart, D., & Pazzani, M. J. (2001). An online algorithm for segmenting time series. [ICDM.]. *Proceedings of ICDM, 2001*, 289–296.

Keogh, E., & Lin, J. (2005). Clustering of time-series subsequences is meaningless: Implications for previous and future research. *Knowledge and Information Systems, 8*(2), 154–177. doi:10.1007/s10115-004-0172-7.

Knobbe, A., Blockeel, H., Koopman, A., Calders, T., Obladen, B., Bosma, C., et al. (2010). InfraWatch: Data management of large systems for monitoring infrastructural performance. In *Proceedings IDA 2010* (pp. 91–102). IDA.

Lindeberg, T. (1990). Scale-space for discrete signals. *IEEE Transactions on Pattern Analysis and Machine Intelligence, 12*(3), 234–254. doi:10.1109/34.49051.

Miao, S., Knobbe, A., Koenders, E., & Bosma, C. (2013). Analysis of traffic events on a Dutch highway bridge. In *Proceedings of the Conference of the International Association for Bridge and Structural Engineers* (IABSE). IABSE.

Pavlo, A., Paulson, E., Rasin, A., Abadi, D. J., DeWitt, D. J., Madden, S., et al. (2009). A comparison of approaches to large-scale data analysis. In *Proceedings of the 2009 ACM SIGMOD International Conference on Management of Data* (pp. 165–178). New York, NY: ACM.

Reutemann, P., & Vanschoren, J. (2012). Scientific workflow management with ADAMS. *Proceedings of ECMLPKDD, 2012*, 833–837.

Reynolds, P., & Pavic, A. (2001). Comparison of forced and ambient vibration measurements on a bridge. In *Proceedings of the International Modal Analysis Conference*. IMAC. 846-851.

Scrakthhulze, G., Jirasec, A., Yu, M., Lim, A., Tumer, R., & Blades, M. (2005). Investigation of selected baseline removal techniques as candidates for automated implementation. *Applied Spectroscopy, 59*(5), 545–574. doi:10.1366/0003702053945985 PMID:15969801.

Song, W., & Dyke, S. (2006). Ambient vibration based modal identification of the Emerson bridge considering temperature effects. In The 4th world conference on structural control and monitoring.

Stranneby, D., & Walker, W. (2004). *Digital signal processing and applications*. London: Elsevier.

Sze, T.-W. (2011). Schönhage-strassen algorithm with MapReduce for multiplying terabit integers. In *Proceedings of the 2011 International Workshop on Symbolic-Numeric Computation* (pp. 54-62). IEEE.

Taylor, R. (2012). An overview of the Hadoop/MapReduce/HBase framework and its current applications in bioinformatics. *BMC Bioinformatics, 11*(12). PMID:21210976.

Vespier, U., Knobbe, A., Nijssen, S., & Vanschoren, J. (2012). MDL-based analysis of time series at multiple time-scales. In *Proceedings of ECML-PKDD 2012* (pp. 371-386). ECML.

Vespier, U., Knobbe, A., Vanschoren, J., Miao, S., Koopman, A., Obladen, B., et al. (2011). Traffic events modeling for structural health monitoring. In *Proceedings of Advances in Intelligent Data Analysis* (IDA 2011), (pp. 376-387). IDA.

White, T. (2009). *Hadoop: The definite guide*. Sebastopol, CA: O'Reilly.

Witkin, A. P. (1983). Scale-space filtering. [San Francisco, CA: IJCAI.]. *Proceedings of IJCAI, 1983*, 1019–1022.

Xia, Y., Hao, H., Zanardo, G., & Deeks, A. (2006). Long term vibration monitoring of an RC slab: temperature and humidity effect. In Engineering structures (pp. 441–452).

Yang, Y., & Chang, K. (2009). Extracting the bridge frequencies indirectly from a passing vehicle: Parametric study. *Engineering Structures*, *31*(10), 2448–2459. doi:10.1016/j.engstruct.2009.06.001.

ADDITIONAL READING

Chang, D., Banack, C. D., & Sirish, L. S. (2007). Robust baseline correction algorithm for signal dense NMR spectra. *Journal of Magnetic Resonance (San Diego, Calif.)*, *187*(2), 288–292. doi:10.1016/j.jmr.2007.05.008 PMID:17562374.

Chen, J. R. (2005). Making subsequence time series clustering meaningful. In *Proceedings ICDM 2005*. ICDM.

Dejori, M., Malik, H. H., Moerchen, F., Tas, N. C., & Neubauer, C. (2009). Development of data infrastructure for the long term bridge performance program. In *Proceedings of Structures '09*. Austin, TX: Structures. doi:10.1061/41031(341)46.

Doupal, E., & Calderara, R. (2004). Weigh-in-motion. In *Proceedings of First International Conference on Virtual and Remote Weigh Stations*. Orlando, FL: IEEE.

Friedrichs, M. S. (1995). A model-free algorithm for the removal of baseline artifacts. *Journal of Biomolecular NMR*, *5*(2), 147–153. doi:10.1007/BF00208805 PMID:22911463.

Karoumi, R., Wiberg, J., & Liljencrantz, A. (2005). Monitoring traffic loads and dynamic effects using an instrumented railway bridge. *Engineering Structures*, *27*(12), 1813–1819. doi:10.1016/j.engstruct.2005.04.022.

Kaur, M., Singh, B., & Seema. (2011). Comparisons of different approaches for removal of baseline wander from ECG signal. In *Proceedings on International Conference and Workshop on Emerging Trends in Technology* (ICWET). IJCAI.

Li, W. L. (2000). Free vibration of beams with general boundary conditions. *Journal of Sound and Vibration*, *237*(4), 709–725. doi:10.1006/jsvi.2000.3150.

Papadimitriou, S., & Yu, P. (2006). Optimal multi-scale patterns in time series streams. In *Proceedings SIGMOD 2006*, (pp. 647-658). ACM.

Press, W.H., Teukolsky, S.A., Vetterling, W.T., & Flannerly, B.P. (2007). *Numerical recipes: The art of scientific computing*. Cambridge, UK: Cambridge University Press.

Schulze, G., Jirasek, A., Yu, M. M. L., Lim, A., Turner, R. F. B., & Blades, M. W. (2005). Investigation of selected baseline removal techniques as candidates for automated implementation. *Applied Spectroscopy*, *59*(5). doi:10.1366/0003702053945985 PMID:15969801.

Tanaka, Y., Iwamoto, K., & Uehara, K. (2005). Discovery of time-series motif from multi-dimensional data based on MDL principle. *Journal of Machine Learning*, *58*(2-3), 269–300. doi:10.1007/s10994-005-5829-2.

van Leeuwen, M., & Siebes, A. (2008). Stream-Krimp: Detecting change in data streams. In *Proceedings of ECML-PKDD 2008*, (pp. 672-687). ECML.

Zhu, X. Q., & Law, S. S. (2006). Moving load identification on multi-span continuous bridges with elastic bearings. *Mechanical Systems and Signal Processing, 20*(7), 1759–1782. doi:10.1016/j.ymssp.2005.06.004.

KEY TERMS AND DEFINITIONS

Clustering: The task of grouping a set of objects or events into clusters in such a way that the objects or events within each cluster are more similar to each other than to those in other clusters.

Discrete Fourier Transform: A transformation that converts a finite list of equally spaced samples (e.g. sensor readings), the time domain, into a finite combination of complex sinusoids ordered by their frequencies, the frequency domain. Naturally occurring oscillations in the time domain will result in sharp peaks at the frequencies of that oscillation.

Hadoop: An open-source software framework implementing the MapReduce paradigm. MapReduce applications divide data-intensive processes into many small fragments of work, each executed on any node of a computing cluster, making them robust and scalable.

Minimum Description Length: A principle stating that the best model or hypothesis for a given set of data is the one that leads to best compression of the data. The description length of a model is the amount of bits needed to describe the model plus the amount of additional bits needed to reconstruct the original data given the model.

Sensor Network: Network of autonomous sensors, typically attached or embedded in a structure, to monitor physical or environmental conditions, such as temperature, vibration and strain, and send their readings to a central location.

Structural Health Monitoring: The process in which the structural integrity of a structure (e.g., a building or a bridge) is monitored over time by continuously measuring key geometric properties, and analyzing the measurement to determine the current or future state of system health.

Subsequence Clustering: The clustering of segments of a time series (subsequences) into clusters that represent a certain type of event. Events within each cluster have certain characteristics that distinguish them from other events occurring in the time series.

Time Series Analysis: Methods for analyzing time series data in order to extract meaningful statistics and patterns. Time series data is any sequence of data points, typically measurements are uniform intervals, such as sensor readings.

ENDNOTES

[1] 32-bit floating point values in our experiments.
[2] To capture almost all non-zero values, we define $M = \lfloor 6\sigma \rfloor$.
[3] For instance, in our setup, we use a cluster with 66 DataNode, each with 4 disks.
[4] When processing multiple sensors in parallel, extra care must be taken to distinguish the subsequences of different sensors, e.g., by adding the sensor id to the keys.
[5] Mahout - Scalable Machine Learning Library. http://mahout.apache.org
[6] In our experiments $c = 32$.

Section 4
Big Data and Computer Systems and Big Data Benchmarks

Chapter 14

Accelerating Large-Scale Genome-Wide Association Studies with Graphics Processors

Mian Lu
Institute of High Performance Computing, A*STAR, Singapore

Qiong Luo
Hong Kong University of Science and Technology, Hong Kong

ABSTRACT

Large-scale Genome-Wide Association Studies (GWAS) are a Big Data application due to the great amount of data to process and high computation intensity. Furthermore, numerical issues (e.g., floating point underflow) limit the data scale in some applications. Graphics Processors (GPUs) have been used to accelerate genomic data analytics, such as sequence alignment, single-Nucleotide Polymorphism (SNP) detection, and Minor Allele Frequency (MAF) computation. As MAF computation is the most time-consuming task in GWAS, the authors discuss in detail their techniques of accelerating this task using the GPU. They first present a reduction-based algorithm that better matches the GPU's data-parallelism feature than the original algorithm implemented in the CPU-based tool. Then they implement this algorithm on the GPU efficiently by carefully optimizing local memory utilization and avoiding user-level synchronization. As the MAF computation suffers from floating point underflow, the authors transform the computation to logarithm space. In addition to the MAF computation, they briefly introduce the GPU-accelerated sequence alignment and SNP detection. The experimental results show that the GPU-based GWAS implementations can accelerate state-of-the-art CPU-based tools by up to an order of magnitude.

DOI: 10.4018/978-1-4666-4699-5.ch014

INTRODUCTION

Nowadays, with the rapid progress of DNA sequencing techniques, large-scale genome-wide association studies (GWAS) have become practical. The research focuses on investigating DNA variation among a group of individuals to identify causes of complex traits (Johnson & O'Donnell, 2009). GWAS covers various applications for different uses. In this chapter, we focus on three fundamental tasks, which are sequence alignment, single-nucleotide polymorphism (SNP) detection, and minor allele frequency (MAF) computation.

To perform GWAS, a large number of short *reads* (sequence fragments generated from a Next-Generation Sequencing device) are first matched against a reference sequence (sequence alignment). Then the SNP information is calculated for every individual using a Bayesian model (SNP detection). Finally, based on the multiple individuals' SNP detection results, MAF is calculated by a probabilistic model (MAF computation). The results of MAF can be used to study the association between genes and traits, such as diseases (Manolio, 2010).

With the high throughput of modern DNA sequencing devices, a great amount of sequence data is generated on a daily basis at sequencing centers. For example, in BGI-Shenzhen, which is the largest sequencing center in the world, TBs of sequence data are generated per day. In this chapter, we identify two major challenges for large-scale GWAS.

- First, due to the large amount of data to process and high intensity of computation, the genome data analysis usually takes an excessively long running time using existing tools. For example, it takes several days for a commodity CPU server to perform sequence alignment and SNP detec-

tion on the data of a single individual. If MAF computation is applied to the data set of thousands of individuals, it will take months or even years to complete the analysis. Therefore, developing high-speed, scalable analysis tools is crucial for large-scale GWAS.

- Second, the computation may suffer from numerical issues due to the limit of floating point number representation in machines. In this chapter, we will show a floating point underflow issue in the MAF computation. It occurs when applying multiplications to a large number of small probability values from different individuals. The program will crash when the floating point underflow occurs.

As a result, due to the high computation intensity and high precision requirement, so far the state-of-the-art MAF results reported by genomists are based on the data set of up to hundreds of individuals (Kim et al., 2011; Li et al., 2010; Yi et al., 2010). To enable the study for data sets of up to thousands of individuals, these two challenges must be addressed.

Nowadays, the GPU has become a mainstream many-core hardware architecture to accelerate various scientific applications (Owens et al., 2007). However, applications can fully utilize the powerful GPU hardware resource only when their algorithm features match the GPU's architecture features, e.g., massive data parallelism and the coalesced memory access pattern. In practice, many algorithms do not expose sufficient data parallelism and have random memory accesses, including many algorithms in GWAS. Therefore, in this chapter, we show that careful design and optimization techniques are necessary in order to achieve the efficiency on the GPU. On the other hand, GPUs employ a similar numerical system as that of the CPUs. The floating point underflow issue needs to be addressed for GPU-based implementations as well. In this chapter, we will cover three topics for high-performance GWAS with GPU acceleration.

1. We will present the high-performance GPU-accelerated MAF computation in detail. Accelerating MAF computation on the GPU is non-trivial. The original algorithm is difficult to exploit the small cached *shared memory* on the GPU. To implement the algorithm efficiently on the GPU, we propose an equivalent parallel reduction algorithm to better utilize the GPU hardware resource.
2. To address the underflow issue, we transform the computation to logarithm space. Compared with a straightforward solution using existing extended precision libraries, our solution is more efficient. Our solution is applicable to other applications suffering from similar numerical issues.
3. Finally, we briefly introduce the GPU acceleration for two other important tasks, which are the sequence alignment and SNP detection. We show that the acceleration on the GPU is achieved through specific optimization techniques. In particular, we propose a filtering-verification framework for sequence alignment in order to improve the memory access pattern. For the SNP detection, we use a sparse data representation format to reduce the total memory accesses.

In the reminder of this chapter, we will first introduce the background of GWAS. Then we will present major optimization techniques for GPU-accelerated GWAS tasks as well as their experimental results. Next, we will discuss related future research directions. We finally conclude this chapter.

BACKGROUND

Genome-Wide Association Studies and Big Data

We first introduce basic concepts of DNA sequences and analysis. A DNA sequence is a double-stranded structure consisting of two strings of characters *A*, *T*, *C*, and *G*. Each of these characters represents a nucleotide base (or base). Base A complements T, and C does G. The number of base pairs (*bp*) is used to measure the length of a DNA sequence. For example, short reads generated by the current generation sequencing devices are usually tens of *bp* long. A position on a sequence storing a base pair is called a site. The human genome has around three billion sites (or *bp*). In this chapter, we focus on the data scale for human genomes.

A large number of short reads (mostly tens of *bp*) are first generated by sequencing machines based on biological samples. These short reads are stored as plain text files with a typical size of tens of GBs for one individual's sequence data. There are two common formats for sequence data storage, which are FASTA and FASTQ. In the FASTA format, each read corresponds to two lines in text, which are the description line and the content of the read respectively. In FASTQ, in addition to the description line and the content line, each read has a third line recording the sequencing score of the read.

Based on these short reads, three tasks of GWAS - sequence alignment, SNP detection, and MAF computation are performed in order. We first briefly introduce these three tasks and then focus on the MAF computation.

- **Sequence Alignment:** For a given reference sequence and a large number of reads, sequence alignment matches each read with the reference sequence. The input of sequence alignment is a FASTA or FASTQ file produced from sequencing, containing all reads of an individual's genome data. The input and output data sizes of such one run of sequence alignment are both around 100 GB. Mismatches are allowed for the alignment, e.g., typically up to two mismatches per read. Sequence alignment for short reads usually utilizes indexing techniques to accelerate the processing speed, such as Burrows-Wheeler transform (BWT) (Lam et al., 2008) or hashing (Li, Terrell & Patel, 2011) based indexing techniques.

- **SNP Detection:** SNP detection finds DNA sequence variations for a single nucleotide between the reference sequence and an individual. Specifically, after the sequence alignment, on each site (base) of the reference sequence there are multiple aligned reads, and SNP detection finds whether the site with different aligned bases is a SNP. The input of SNP detection is the results of sequence alignment for one individual. The input and output data sizes for such one run of SNP detection are both hundreds of GBs. State-of-the-art SNP detection algorithms for short reads are based on a Bayesian model (Li et al., 2009).

- **MAF Computation:** For diploid creatures, e.g., human, there are two almost identical copies for each chromosome (known as homologous chromosomes). However, if a SNP occurs on one of the paired homologous chromosomes, then the same site on two homologous chromosomes have different bases. For a given population with N individuals, there are $2N$ bases in total for each site. Then the less common allele is called a *minor allele*, otherwise a *major allele*. The frequency of minor allele occurring in the given population is called *minor allele frequency* (MAF). The input of MAF

computation is the results of SNP detection from multiple individuals. The total size of input files for the MAF computation can be hundreds of TBs. Existing tools for MAF computation essentially employ a Bayesian model (Thorfinn, 2012).

Figure 1 shows the workflow between the three tasks - sequence alignment, SNP detection, and MAF computation. In this workflow, the input are sequence data from n individuals, and the output is the MAF information calculated based on all n individuals. Specifically, before the workflow, sequencing devices generate DNA fragments from input biological samples, which are stored in plain text files. Based on the generated sequence data, the sequence alignment is the first step to process short reads. Based on the result of sequence alignment, the SNP detection calculates the SNP information for every site for an individual. After that, based on the results of SNP detection from multiple individuals, the MAF computation is performed. In this chapter, we will present the MAF computation in detail, and introduce the other two tasks briefly.

The three genome data analysis tasks are Big Data applications. A common definition of Big Data (Laney, 2001) is by the 3 "V"s - volume, velocity and variety. As shown in Figure 1, a GWAS task for one individual takes hundreds of GBs or even larger input and output data. In a sequencing center, thousands of such tasks can be executed concurrently day and night. This data size is of a big volume. Furthermore, sequencing devices generate sequence data at a very high throughput, and thousands of sequencing devices may be used concurrently in a sequencing center. For example, at BGI-Shenzhen, which is the largest sequencing center in the world, around 10 TB of sequence data are generated per day on average. Finally, though the raw sequence data are usually stored in similar formats, after a certain number of processing rounds, there are various data formats used for different GWAS tasks. Additionally,

Figure 1. The workflow between three GWAS tasks: sequence alignment, SNP detection and MAF computation

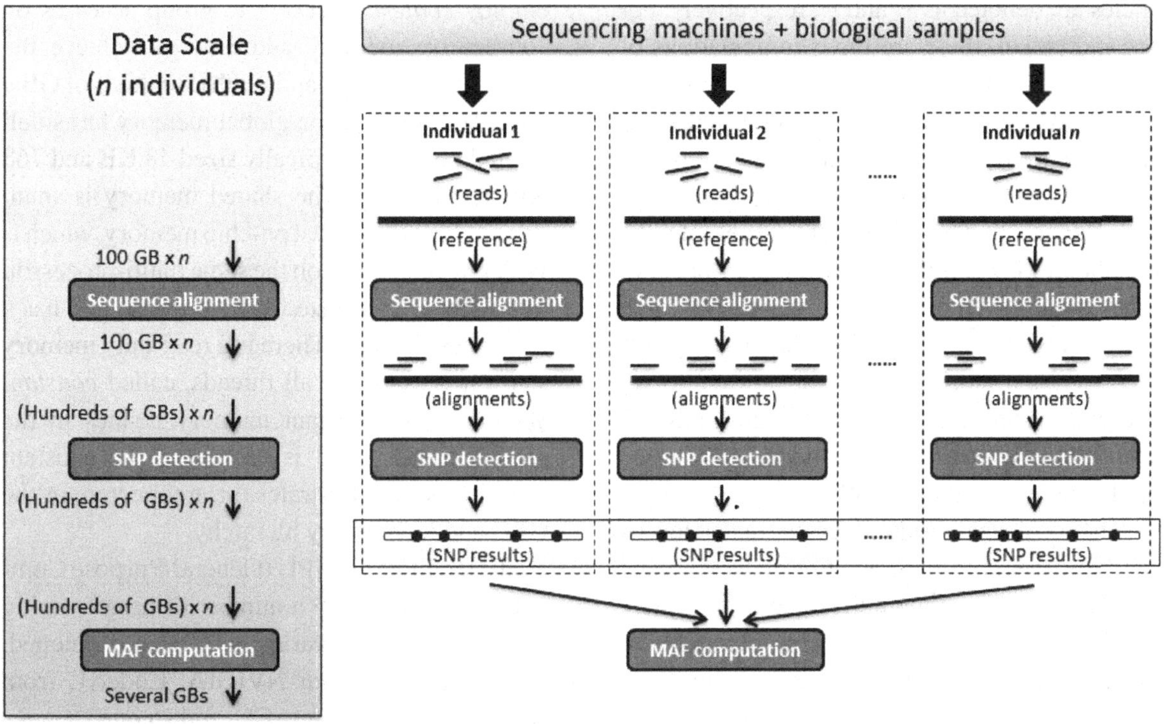

sequencing centers often develop their own GWAS tools in house with customized data formats. As a result, GWAS tasks process a big variety of genome data formats. In this study, we present the GPU acceleration for GWAS applications, with a focus on addressing the aspects of volume and velocity. With large amounts of data to process and high data generation throughput of sequencing devices, developing efficient data processing tools is a must. We show how the GPU can be used to accelerate the GWAS applications on a single GPU as well as multiple nodes/GPUs.

Minor Allele Frequency and Site Frequency Spectrum

We introduce the MAF computation algorithm implemented in realSFS (Thorfinn, 2012), which is a state-of-the-art MAF computation tool (Nielsen, Paul, Albrechtsen, & Song, 2011). Overall, the

same processing algorithm is applied to every site independently. There are four major steps when processing a site, which are SNP calling, site frequency spectrum (SFS) construction, normalization and post-processing. Particularly, the performance bottleneck is the SFS construction, and the floating point underflow occurs in the normalization. Therefore, we will focus on these two steps for detailed description. Throughput the four steps, the in-memory computation with the time complexity $O(n^2)$ dominates the overall performance taking more than 85% of the overall time for a thousand individuals. Therefore, we focus on the optimization techniques for in-memory computation rather than disk I/O in this chapter.

SFS construction is to build a set of vectors h. For a given population with N individuals (N will represent the number of individuals for the MAF computation throughout the chapter), for each site, we define a vector h. $h[i]$ stores the likelihood for when the MAF is equal to *i* for this site. For example, for a given site, the major and minor alleles are denoted as *M* and *m*, respectively. For one individual, there are three combinations of bases in homologous chromosomes, which are {*MM*}, {*Mm*}, and {*mm*}. Then for two individuals, there are five combinations of alleles, which are {*MMMM*}, {*mMMM*}, {*mmMM*}, {*mmmM*}, and {*mmmm*}. Therefore, *h[i]* represents the likelihood of when the minor allele *m* occurs *i* times in the given population. As a result, for *N* individuals, the size of the likelihood vector *h* is (*2N + 1*) for a site. The set of all *h* vectors for all sites is called the site frequency spectrum (SFS). The SFS construction is to build the SFS based on the input SNP data for all sites.

The normalization introduces the underflow issue due to the finite representation of the exponent in computers. The minimum value of a positive 64-bit double precision floating point number to represent is around 10^{-308}. However, when there are more than around 400 individuals, the result of an exponent function will be less than this value, which causes floating point underflow. The underflow will eventually cause the application to crash due to a subsequent *division by zero* error.

We will introduce the detailed algorithm of SFS construction and normalization in corresponding design sections.

Graphics Processing Units (GPUs)

We use GPUs as hardware accelerators to improve the in-memory computation performance for GWAS. The GPU architecture consists of multiple multi-processors, or Streaming Multiprocessors (*SMs*) from NVIDIA, and it can run thousands of concurrent threads in the *SIMT* (*Single-Instruction, Multiple-Thread*) style. Each SM is a SIMD-style processor and consists of tens of SIMD cores. The GPU memory hierarchy consists of global memory, shared memory and registers. The global memory is several gigabytes, which is accessible for all threads. The access latency of

the global memory is high, e.g., 400-600 cycles. However, threads within a multiprocessor can employ *coalesced access* to group accesses on consecutive memory addresses to achieve the high GPU memory bandwidth (hundreds of GBs/sec). Additionally, the global memory has small L1 and L2 caches typically sized 48 KB and 768 KB, respectively. The shared memory is small (tens of KBs) but is fast on-chip memory, which is visible to all threads on the same multi-processor. The register is private for each thread and has a low access latency. There is a read-only memory space accessible by all threads, called *constant memory*. The constant memory resides in the global memory and is cached in the constant cache. Figure 2 illustrates the architecture of the GPU and its memory hierarchy.

To facilitate GPGPU (General-Purpose Computing on the GPU), a number of programming frameworks and libraries have been developed, such as CUDA from NVIDIA, CodeXL from AMD, OpenCL, OpenACC, and so on.

We briefly introduce NVIDIA's CUDA (Compute Unified Device Architecture), which is one of the most popular GPGPU programming platforms. In CUDA, the piece of code executed by the GPU is called a *kernel,* which is launched by a CPU thread. A kernel usually consists of hundreds of *thread blocks*, and each thread block further contains hundreds of *threads*. All threads can access the global and constant memory. Threads in the same thread block share the shared memory, and each thread has its own private registers.

When a CUDA program is executed on a GPU, the thread blocks are distributed across SMs, and one SM can execute multiple thread blocks concurrently. Specifically, every consecutive 32 threads are grouped as a *warp*, which is the unit of creating, managing, scheduling and executing threads on a SM. When multiple thread blocks are mapped to one SM, thread blocks are first partitioned into warps and then scheduled by a *warp scheduler* for execution. The warp scheduler selects a warp with threads that are ready to execute

Figure 2. The GPU architecture and memory hierarchy

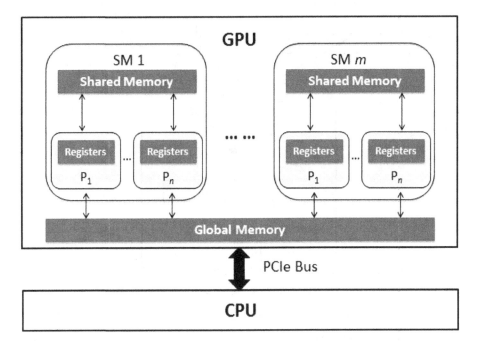

its next instruction and then issues instructions to those threads. The number of warps that can be executed (the *active warps*) concurrently on a SM depends on available hardware resource, e.g., the amount of vacancy in shared memory and registers. Additionally, threads of the same warp are automatically synchronized by the hardware. When branch divergence occurs within a warp, the different execution paths have to be serialized, increasing the total number of instructions for the warp. The instructions of a SM are pipelined to leverage instruction-level parallelism within a single thread, as well as thread-level parallelism through simultaneous hardware multithreading.

Figure 3 illustrates an example of the mapping between a CUDA program and the GPU architecture. In this example, two thread blocks are mapped to the same SM, and each thread block is partitioned into four warps. Five warps are executed concurrently at the time, and the other three are inactive.

In general, there are three main strategies for achieving high performance on GPUs. First, we should expose sufficient data parallelism in the application for high thread concurrency on the GPU. Second, the high GPU memory bandwidth can be fully utilized through coalesced memory accesses. Third, the program should take advantage of the small but low latency cached memory, such as the shared memory. In this chapter, we mainly show how to optimize a GPU program to benefit from the shared memory as well as keep the high concurrency.

Related Work

High-performance GWAS tools have attracted much attention from both industry or academic communities. For CPU-based sequence alignment tools, most implementations are based on the BWT index and can take advantages of multi-cores, such as 2BWT (Lam et al., 2009), Bowtie (Langmead,

Figure 3. The mapping between the CUDA program and GPU architecture

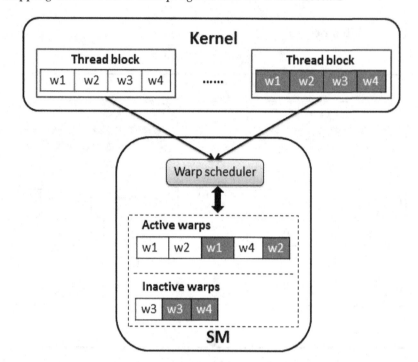

Trapnell, Pop, & Salzberg, 2009), BWA (Li, & Durbin, 2009) and SOAP2 (Li et al., 2009). Additionally, WHAM (Li, Terrell, & Patel, 2011) is another multi-threaded sequence alignment tool but based on hashing. In general, the BWT based implementations are more efficient to find all valid alignments and consume less memory than the hashing based implementations. However, the hashing based implementation is more efficient when the number of alignments is small. When the number of alignments increases, the search space increases linearly, and more hashing conflicts arise. In addition to sequence alignment tools, SOAPsnp (Li, 2009) and realSFS (Thorfinn, 2012) are state-of-the-art CPU-based SNP detection and MAF computation tools, respectively.

There are also a few studies on GPU-accelerated GWAS tools for short reads. Specifically, SOAP3 (Liu et al., 2012) is a GPU-accelerated version of SOAP2, which adopts the same BWT algorithm but employs the GPU acceleration. The experimental results show it is at least 7.5 and 20

times faster than BWA and Bowtie, respectively. Another GPU-accelerated implementation G-Aligner (Lu, Tan, Bai, & Luo, 2012) further improves the performance by 1.8-3.5 times compared with SOAP3 by employing a filtering-verification framework. Additionally, BarraCUDA (Klus et al., 2012) is another GPU-based sequence alignment tool, which shows the performance speedup of around 6X over the CPU-based sequential BWA. For the SNP detection, the GPU-accelerated GSNP (Lu et al., 2011) implements the same algorithm as SOAPsnp, but can achieve the overall performance speedup of 42-50X. Additionally, GAMA (Lu, Zhao, Luo, & Wang, 2012) implements the same MAF computation model as realSFS with the GPU acceleration. It outperforms the single-threaded optimized realSFS by around 47 times.

Most existing state-of-the-art GPU-accelerated GWAS tools are developed for a single node with a single GPU card. The main reason is that so far the focus of the genomics community has been on improving the performance on data that fits in one node. When using multiple GPUs/nodes in a distributed environment, disk I/O and network communication may dominate the overall performance. BGI-Shenzhen (Wang, 2013) has extended a single GPU-accelerated MAF computation implementation into multiple nodes and GPUs on a supercomputer Tianhe-1A. They demonstrate that the scalability essentially is limited by the IO and communication. Nevertheless, with the rapid increase of data volume and growth of computational expertise of genomists, we expect that distributed computing on multiple GPU-equipped nodes will be further utilized to improve the performance of GWAS tasks.

In addition to the performance improvement for a single task, there are also a few platforms offering systematic optimization for multiple GWAS tasks. Crossbow (Langmead, Schatz, Lin, Pop, & Salzberg, 2009) is a CPU-based system that is built on Bowtie and SOAPsnp to perform the genomic sequence analysis in cloud computing. Similar work (Kienzler, Bruggmann, Ranganathan, & Tatbul, 2012) is an incremental sequence analysis platform in cloud computing by Kienzler et al.. Their platform also adopts Bowtie and SOAPsnp for sequence alignment and SNP detection. To improve the I/O speed, they adopt an in-memory file system using very large main memory to avoid writing intermediate data into the disk. Furthermore, Lu, Tan, Zhao, Bai, & Luo (2012) propose tight integration techniques for GPU-accelerated sequence alignment and SNP detection tools, which is able to reduce the overall I/O cost significantly.

DESIGN AND IMPLEMENTATION

In this section, we first focus on the major step of MAF computation, which is the SFS construction. Specifically, we first present a baseline implementation and discuss its performance issues. Then we present an optimized reduction based SFS construction algorithm and its GPU-based implementation. After that, we describe two solutions to address the floating point underflow issue, which are using extended precision and transforming computation to logarithm space. All these techniques have been implemented in the MAF computation tool GAMA (Lu, Zhao, Luo, & Wang, 2012). GAMA is the first MAF computation tool that can handle the data set of one thousand individuals successfully. Finally, we briefly introduce the GPU acceleration for another two GWAS tasks. We present the design of G-Aligner (Lu, Tan, Bai, & Luo, 2012) and GSNP (Lu et al., 2011) as representative sequence alignment and SNP detection tools, respectively.

A Baseline Implementation of SFS Construction: Per-Thread-Per-Site

The original SFS construction implemented in realSFS is based on an iterative-update approach. Specifically, the same algorithm is applied to every site. For every site, there are three arrays P_{MM}, P_{Mm}, and P_{mm}, which store initial likelihoods of three MAF for every individual. These three arrays are the input of the SFS construction. Additionally, for every site, there is an output array h (the SFS for a site) storing $(2N + 1)$ double precision floating point numbers. The output array h is iteratively updated by scanning every individual. Algorithm 1 outlines such a SFS construction algorithm for one site, with the iterative updates performed in line 9-10.

A straightforward approach to parallelize the SFS construction is to make one thread handle one site. Thousands of sites can be processed in parallel on the GPU. However, the major performance bottleneck of such an implementation is the large number of memory accesses on the output array h. The memory access pattern on h is non-coalesced. A natural optimization is to utilize the shared memory to hold the array h. However, if we directly use the shared memory, it will reduce the level of parallelism. In particular, due to the small size of the shared memory,

Algorithm 1. The iterative-update SFS construction algorithm for one site

```
INPUT:
N: the number of individuals
P_MM, P_Mm, P_mm: three arrays, each of which has N double-
precision numbers
OUTPUT:
h: the array with (2N + 1) doubles
1  h ← 0
2  for i ← 0 to N do {
3    p_MM = P_MM[i - 1]; p_Mm = P_Mm[i - 1]; p_mm = P_mm[i - 1];
4    if i = 1 then
5      h[0] = p_MM; h[1] = p_Mm; h[2] = p_mm;
6    else
7      h[2i] = p_MM • h[2i - 2];
8      h[2i - 1] = p_MM • h[2i - 3] + p_Mm • h[2i - 2];
9      for j ← 2i – 2 to 2 do
10       h[j] = p_MM • h[j - 2] + p_Mm • h[j - 1] + p_mm • h[j];
11     h[1] = p_Mm • h[0] + p_mm • h[1];
12     h[0] = p_mm • h[0];
13 }
```

the concurrency level will be very low if the *h* array is entirely stored in the shared memory. Suppose there are *N* individuals. The size of *h* for one site is $8 \times (2N + 1)$ bytes (*h* is double precision). However, the size of cached shared memory on each multiprocessor of the GPU is up to 48 KB on our platforms. Therefore, if we store *h* using the shared memory, when N = 1,000, the number of active threads on each multiprocessor is only three, out of 1,536 concurrent threads on NVIDIA GPUs that are supported per GPU multiprocessor. Such low concurrency under-utilizes the GPU hardware resource. Therefore, such a straightforward implementation cannot directly take advantage from the fast but small shared memory on the GPU effectively. A new design of the algorithm is required to take advantage from the shared memory as well as keep high data parallelism.

An Improved Implementation of SFS Construction: A Reduction Based Algorithm

In the last section, we have shown that the straightforward implementation cannot effectively utilize the shared memory on the GPU to hide the global

memory access latency. In this section, we present a novel reduction based algorithm to solve this issue (Lu, Zhao, Luo, & Wang, 2012). The basic idea is to use multiple threads to process one site. This way, the small shared memory can be effectively utilized and the high concurrency is able to be maintained as well.

The challenge of utilizing multiple threads to process one site is that the original SFS construction algorithm (Algorithm 1) does not explicitly expose data-parallelism. Instead, it implements the algorithm in an iterative-update style, which may have data dependency among iterations. Therefore, the first problem to tackle is to prove the iterative-update on *h* (line 4 to 12 in Algorithm 1) is parallelizable.

To help the presentation, we first define a *super-band matrix* particularly for this implementation:

Definition 1: Super-band matrix. Given an $n \times n$ lower triangular band matrix and an integer C, where $n \geq C \geq 1$, the matrix is a super-band matrix iff: (1). For each integer k, where $0 \geq k > C$, cells at positions (i, i-k), where $N > i \geq k$, have the same value. (2). All other cells are zeros.

In Definition 1, the parameter *C* is called the *cardinality* for the super-band matrix. By definition, a super-band matrix has the following two properties: (1) The number of unique non-zero values is up to *C*; (2) Each of the first n-C+1 columns contains unique non-zero values. Furthermore, we have the following two observations on the multiplication of two $(n \times n)$ super-band matrices with the same cardinality C ($n \geq 2C - 1$),:

Lemma 1: The result matrix of the multiplication is a super-band matrix.

Lemma 2: The cardinality of the result matrix is $(2C - 1)$.

We can prove these two lemmas through directly generating the result matrix following the definition of matrix multiplication. These observations are useful when removing computation redundancy in our algorithm.

To simplify the presentation, in the remainder of this section, the *matrix multiplication* specifically refers to the multiplication on two $(n \times n)$ super-band matrices with the same cardinality C ($n \geq 2C - 1$), unless otherwise specified.

For a given site, for the i-th individual (i starts from 1), suppose the likelihoods of three initial MAF for this individual are denoted as p_{mm}^i, p_{Mm}^i and p_{MM}^i. We can define a super-band matrix F_i with the size of $(2N+1) \times (2N+1)$ and the cardinality of 3 for this i-th individual, which is illustrated as follows in Box 1.

Based on such a representation, for a given site, suppose the computation for the first $(k-1)$ individuals has been done, then the computation of iterative-update on h for the k-th individual (line 7 to 12 in Algorithm 1) can be equivalently represented as a matrix-vector multiplication (the vector size is $(2N+1)$):

$$F_k \times \begin{pmatrix} h_{k-1}[0] \\ h_{k-1}[1] \\ \vdots \\ h_{k-1}[2k-2] \\ 0 \\ 0 \\ \vdots \\ 0 \end{pmatrix}_{(2N+1)} = \begin{pmatrix} h_k[0] \\ h_k[1] \\ \vdots \\ h_k[2k-2] \\ h_k[2k-1] \\ h_k[2k] \\ \vdots \\ 0 \end{pmatrix}_{(2N+1)}$$

Note that the input (h_{k-1}) and output vectors (h_k) are actually the same vector. However, we represent them separately as h_{k-1} and h_k in the matrix-vector multiplication for clarity of presentation. Now for N individuals, we can expand such a representation as:

$$h_N = F_N \cdot h_{N-1} = F_N \cdot F_{N-1} \cdot h_{N-2} = F_N \cdot F_{N-1} \cdot F_{N-2} h_{N-3}$$
$$= \dots\dots = F_N \cdot F_{N-1} \cdot F_{N-2} \dots h_1$$

$$(1)$$

Table 1. Speedup of different steps and the overall speedup of GSNP over SOAPsnp

	Cal_p.	Read.	Count.	Likelihood	Post.	Output	Recycle	Total
Ch. 1	1X	5X	4X	204X	7X	13X	2738X	42X
Ch. 21	1X	4X	4X	231X	6X	15X	1603X	50X

Box 1.

$$F_i = \begin{pmatrix} p_{mm}^i & 0 & 0 & 0 & 0 & \dots & 0 \\ p_{Mm}^i & p_{mm}^i & 0 & 0 & 0 & \dots & 0 \\ p_{MM}^i & p_{Mm}^i & p_{mm}^i & 0 & 0 & \dots & 0 \\ 0 & p_{MM}^i & p_{Mm}^i & p_{mm}^i & 0 & \dots & 0 \\ 0 & 0 & p_{MM}^i & p_{Mm}^i & p_{mm}^i & \dots & 0 \\ \vdots & \vdots & \ddots & \ddots & \ddots & \ddots & 0 \\ 0 & 0 & \dots & p_{MM}^i & p_{Mm}^i & p_{mm}^i & 0 \\ 0 & 0 & 0 & \dots & p_{MM}^i & p_{Mm}^i & p_{mm}^i \end{pmatrix}_{(2N+1) \times (2N+1)}$$

where h_N is the final result h based on all N individuals. Note that as the matrix multiplication is associative, we have removed the original association among matrices (the original association is from right to left). Such a representation confirms that the original iterative-update SFS construction algorithm for a single site is parallelizable due to the matrix multiplication representation. However, if we directly implement the matrix multiplication for the SFS construction, the performance is pool due to a large amount of redundant computation.

The redundant computation for matrix multiplication is due to the characteristics of super-band matrices. Figure 4 illustrates an example of multiplication on two super-band matrixes when $N = 4$. This example shows that the number of unique values in the result matrix is only five. According to Lemma 1 and 2 for the super-band matrix multiplication, we can eliminate the redundancy. This is because the unique values of a super-band matrix all appear in the first column.

Now we can simplify the representation of the result matrix of matrix multiplication using a vector. Recall that for a super-band matrix, the first column stores all unique values. Therefore, the first column of result matrix can be represented using the elements from the first columns of two input super-band matrixes. This way, the computation and storage redundancy can be eliminated. Suppose a and b are the first columns of two input super-band matrices A and B respectively, then the first column c of the result matrix can be represented as follows.

$$
c = \begin{pmatrix}
a_{[0]}b_{[0]} \\
a_{[0]}b_{[1]} + a_{[1]}b_{[0]} \\
a_{[0]}b_{[2]} + a_{[1]}b_{[1]} + a_{[2]}b_{[0]} \\
\vdots \\
\sum_{i=0}^{C-2} a_{[i]}b_{[C-2-i]} \\
\sum_{i=0}^{C-1} a_{[i]}b_{[C-1-i]} \\
\sum_{i=1}^{C-1} a_{[i]}b_{[C-i]} \\
\sum_{i=2}^{C-1} a_{[i]}b_{[C+1-i]} \\
\vdots \\
a_{[C-3]}b_{[C-1]} + a_{[C-2]}b_{[C-2]} + a_{[C-1]}b_{[C-3]} \\
a_{[C-2]}b_{[C-1]} + a_{[C-1]}b_{[C-2]} \\
a_{[C-1]}b_{[C-1]} \\
0 \\
\vdots \\
0
\end{pmatrix} \quad (2)
$$

Note that, the vector is obtained by replacing the element not in the first column of matrix A or B using the corresponding element with the same value in the first column of A or B. For example, the second element in the above vector in fact is $A_{[1][0]}B_{[0][0]} + A_{[1][1]}B_{[1][0]}$. Since $A_{[1][1]} = A_{[0][0]}$, the result is represented as $(a_{[0]}b_{[1]} + a_{[1]}b_{[0]})$ using all elements from the first columns of A and B.

Figure 4. Multiplication of two super-band matrixes when N=4. Different patterns indicate different non-zero values.

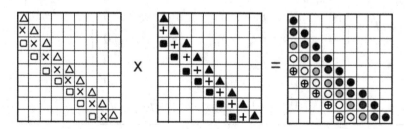

Algorithm 2. The definition of operator ⊗

```
INPUT:
a: an array with the size of n
b: an array with the size of m
OUTPUT:
c: an array with the size of (m + n - 1)
1 c ← 0
2 for i ← 0 to n − 1 do
3   for j ← 0 to m − 1 do
4     c[i + j] += a[i] × b[j]
```

Now we further abstract the above vector-based representation c (Equation 2) using an operator $\otimes$ defined in Algorithm 2. We can prove that the output array c generate by Algorithm 2 is equivalent to the vector-based representation c shown above (Equation 2). In other words, the original matrix multiplication based representation (Equation 1) can be simplified by using the operator $\otimes$. Such an operator is nested-loop computation, which can easily employ massive data parallelism on the GPU. Additionally, the defined operator is associative, and is part of the matrix multiplication.

Now we are ready to introduce the reduction SFS construction algorithm for a single site (the same algorithm is applied to every site). Overall, the matrix multiplication based representation (Equation 1) can be converted to a reduction algorithm based on the operator $\otimes$. Specifically, for every individual, there is an initial vector (denoted as v_i for the i-th individual) holding three elements storing its p_{mm}, p_{Mm} and p_{MM}. Then we perform a vector-based reduction on all vectors to generate the result vector h:

$$h = v_1 \otimes v_2 \otimes ... \otimes v_N \qquad (3)$$

where h is the final SFS with $(2N + 1)$ elements for the specific site. The operator $\otimes$ is the reduction operator for this formula. Compared with the original SFS construction algorithm as shown in Algorithm 1, the reduction based algorithm has eliminated the data dependency among individu-

als and allows potential high concurrency. In the next section, we show that this reduction-based algorithm can be naturally mapped to the GPU architecture efficiently. Massive data parallelism as well as the small shared memory can be exploited effectively.

Furthermore, the nested-loop computation for the operator $\otimes$ (Algorithm 2) has an additional advantage. As long as an element in the outer input array ($a[i]$ at line 4 in Algorithm 2) is zero, the entire scan on the inner input array (line 3 to 4 in Algorithm 2) for that element is unnecessary. Such an optimization is difficult to be adopted by the original iterative-update construction. In practice, this improvement is able to save the computation workload significantly due to the characteristics of real-world data sets. Therefore, before each $\otimes$ operation, we scan the two input arrays once, and make the one with more zeros as the outer input array.

GPU-Accelerated Reduction-Based SFS Construction

Now we present the GPU-based implementation for the optimized reduction-based SFS construction algorithm (Equation 3). We first define a primitive *binaryMerge* to process multiple $\otimes$ operators in parallel. The primitive is illustrated in Figure 5, in which all input arrays have the same length L. Then each two consecutive input arrays are merged into an output array with the size of $(2L - 1)$ using the reduction operator $\otimes$. With such a primitive, it is straightforward to implement the new reduction based SFS construction as shown in Equation 3 on the GPU. Note that to fully utilize the hardware resource, multiple sites are processed in parallel, which also can be done based on the primitive. Therefore, we focus on the implementation and optimization techniques for this primitive *binaryMerge*.

To implement the primitive *binaryMerge* on the GPU efficiently, multiple threads are used to

Figure 5. The primitive binaryMerge. The size of each input and output array are L and (2L-1), respectively.

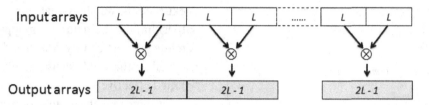

handle one $\otimes$ operator for data parallelism. Furthermore, multiple $\otimes$ operators are processed in parallel as well to increase the concurrency. We focus on how to use multiple threads to handle an $\otimes$ operator. It is straightforward to parallelize multiple $\otimes$ operators as they have the same operations.

The basic strategy to parallelize an $\otimes$ operator is to take advantage of the nested-loop computation (line 2 to 4 in Algorithm 2). Specifically, each thread first holds an element from the outer array a, and then scans the entire inner array b sequentially to perform the computation. There are two major optimization techniques adopted, which are shared memory utilization and the automatic thread warp based synchronization.

Shared Memory Utilization

To reduce the global memory access latency using the shared memory, we implement Algorithm 2 in a block nested-loop scheme. There are two data buffers in the shared memory, which are used to hold the inner input array b (denoted as buf_b) and output array c (denoted as buf_c) block by block. The inner array b is loaded into the shared memory block by block. For each block of b, there are several computation stages, and each stage will access a fixed number of elements in a to do the nested-loop computation. Within a stage, the output results are stored in buf_c. Suppose buf_b and buf_c can hold n_b and n_c elements respectively, then the number of elements accessed for a in each stage is $(n_c - n_b + 1)$. Note that for the nested-loop computation on a block of b, each

element of a stored in the global memory is just accessed once by a thread, as a is the outer input array. The purpose of accessing the input array a through multiple stages is to utilize the small shared memory for buf_c to hold output elements.

Figure 6 illustrates an example of block nested-loop computation employing the shared memory. Suppose the lengths of two input arrays are both 6, and the block size for the input array b and output array c are 3 and 5, respectively. Then the number of elements in a accessed for each stage is 3. In the first step, the elements $b[0]$, $b[1]$, $b[2]$ are buffered in the shared memory. Then for the first stage, elements $a[0]$, $a[1]$, $a[2]$ are accessed, and each of which accesses $b[0]$, $b[1]$, $b[2]$ that are stored in the shared memory to perform the computation. The output position on c of this stage is from 0 to 4. Therefore, the elements $c[0]$, $c[1]$, ..., $c[4]$ are buffered in the shared memory. Next, in the second stage of step one, $a[3]$, $a[4]$, and $a[5]$ are accessed, and $c[3]$, $c[4]$, ..., $c[7]$ are buffered in the shared memory. The second step will perform the similar operations with the second block of b buffered in the shared memory. Note that, since there is overlap of the output elements buffered between different stages or steps, the data transfer between the global and shared memory for the output array is unnecessary for the elements that are already in the buffer

Warp Based Implementation

Recall that we make each thread fetch one element of the outer array a, and then access all elements sequentially in the inner array b to perform the

Figure 6.The shared memory usage for one $\otimes$ operator implemented on the GPU

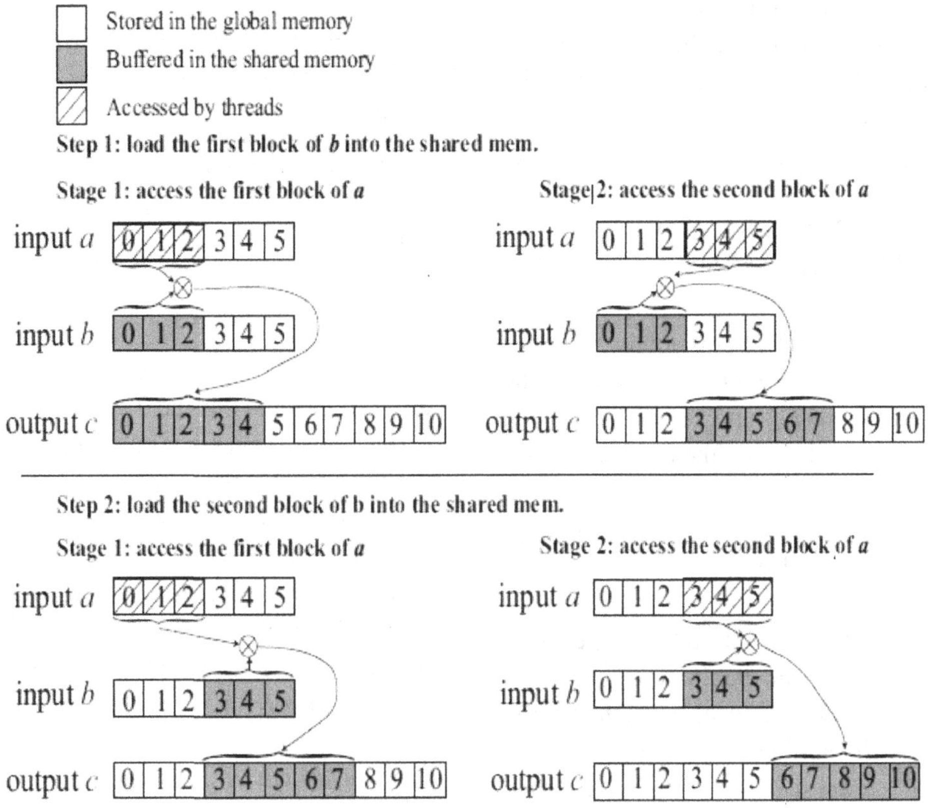

nested-loop computation. For the computation on i-th element in a and j-th element in b, the output position on c is $(i + j)$ (line 4 in Algorithm 2). There may be write conflict among threads without synchronization. For example, for the first thread, suppose $i = 0$ and $j = 3$, then its output position is $c = 3$. For the second thread, suppose $i = 1$ and $j = 2$, then its output position is $c = 3$, too. If these two threads access this output element at the same time, there will be write conflicts. With the synchronization for every step, due to the sequential scan on the inner input array, it ensures the write positions among different threads to be different. For the same example, when the first thread holds $i = 0$ and $j = 3$ (the output position is 3), the second thread must holds $i = 1$ and $j = 3$ (the output position is 4) at the same time due to the synchronization. This way, the write conflict is avoided.

However, a large number of synchronization operations will introduce considerable overhead. As threads in the same warp are automatically synchronized by the GPU, we use one warp to handle one $\otimes$ operator. This is equivalent to issuing synchronization before every write. This way, the write conflict is solved without user-level overhead.

Discussion on the Reduction-Based Algorithm

Compared with the basic per-thread-per-site parallel implementation, the new reduction-based algorithm takes advantage of both the fast shared memory and the massive data parallelism. Specifically, this algorithm well utilizes the memory hierarchy on the GPU, in particular the fast shared memory. Furthermore, taking advantage of the properties of the $\otimes$ operator, the nested-loop computation is done through a high amount of thread parallelism. As a result, the new algorithm can exploit the small shared memory effectively as well as maintain high thread concurrency for massive data parallelism.

Numerical Optimization for Floating Point Underflow

In this section, we present two solutions to address the floating point underflow issue in the normalization: (1) using an extended precision library and (2) transforming the computation to logarithm space.

Normalization Algorithm

The third step (SFS normalization) in the MAF computation suffers from the floating point number underflow issue. Algorithm 3 shows the major steps of the normalization algorithm for a site, where t, g, p are scalars storing intermediate results. Specifically, at line 3 of Algorithm 3, when the number of individuals is greater than 400, t will be less than -800. As a result, the result of $exp(t)$ will be less than 10^{-308}, which will be treated as 0 in computers (double precision) due to the finite representation of the exponent. Therefore, all elements in the array a (line 3 in Algorithm 3) may become 0 when t is sufficiently small. In such a case, the variable h_sum at line 4 in Algorithm 3 also becomes 0. Furthermore, at line 5 in Algorithm 3, if g is also 0, b will become 0. As a result, the program will crash due to the *division by zero* error at line 7 of Algorithm 3.

Therefore, the key to avoid the underflow is to represent small numbers correctly rather than treat them as zeros. There are two solutions proposed: using extended precision and the logarithm transformation. Note that implementations using the two different approaches may produce slightly

Algorithm 3. The SFS normalization algorithm for a site

```
1 ......
2 for i ← 0 to 2N do
3 a[i] = h[i] × exp(t);
4 h_sum = sum(a, 2N + 1);
5 b = p × h_sum + (1 - p) × g
6 for i ← 0 to 2N do
7 h[i] = (p × a[i]) / b
8 ......
```

different results. For the data-scale that does not suffer from the underflow, both methods can produce exactly the same result as the original implementation without any numerical optimizations. When the underflow occurs, as both methods are reasonable and no reference result is available (since existing software cannot handle the underflow), the result from either solution is considered correct.

Computation with Extended Precision

There are extended precision libraries on both CPUs (GMP 2012; David 2012) and GPUs (Lu, He, & Luo, 2010). Most extended precision formats can extend the exponent component of floating point numbers. Specifically, GAPREC (Lu, He, & Luo, 2010) is adopted to support the MAF computation with extended precision. The advantage of using extended precision libraries is the saved coding effort. However, we should be careful when applying extended precision as they usually introduce significant computation overhead.

We first make the exponential function $exp(t)$ (line 3 of Algorithm 3) use the extended precision in order to avoid the underflow. Then the extended precision is adopted in the computation from line 4 to 7 in Algorithm 3. Finally the extended precision result of the division at line 7 is converted back to the native precision and stored in h. However, such a direct adoption of extended precision is inefficient due to the expensive exponent function. Since our purpose of using the extended precision for floating point numbers is to extend the representation scope of the exponent rather than increase the accuracy of the fractional part, we can further optimize this solution to avoid the exponent function.

For a given positive floating point number f (a negative number is handled in a similar way), it can be naturally represented as:

$$f = m + C_1 \times 10 + C_2 \times 100 + ... + C_n \times 10^n$$

where m is a decimal number that is less than 10, and $C_1, C_2, ... C_n$ are integers, each of which is in the range of [0, 9]. Therefore, the exponent of f can be represented as:

$$exp(f) = exp(m) \times exp(C_1 \times 10) \times ... \times exp(C_n \times 10^n)$$

For each C_i, there are only nine possible values. Thus we can build a lookup table to store all possible results for $exp(C_1 \times 10)$, $exp(C_2 \times 100)$, ..., $exp(C_n \times 10^n)$. Note that the table is calculated using the extended precision. It is sufficient for the current application to build the table for up to $n = 10$, which makes the lookup table store 90 elements. For the decimal number m, the exponential function with native precision is applied at runtime. This way, the expensive exponential function employing extended precision is replaced with several relatively inexpensive multiplications with extended precision and an exponential function with native precision. In practice, this improvement is able to double the speed of exponential computation directly with extended precision either on the GPU or CPU.

Computation with Logarithm Transformation

Though the solution using extended precision is simple and has minor source code modification, the computation overhead introduced may slow down the overall performance. A more efficient solution is to transform computation to logarithm space. This way, very small numbers can be converted to normal numbers, which can be represented by native precision correctly.

Algorithm 4 and 5 show the new normalization algorithm with the logarithm transformation. Note that the function *addProtect* (Algorithm 5) essentially performs the following computation:

$$addProtect(log(x) + log(y), log(z)$$
$$+ log(w)) = log(xy + zw)$$

Algorithm 4. The new normalization algorithm with logarithm transformation for a site

```
1 ......
2 for i ← 0 to 2N do
3   a[i] = log(h[i]);
4 for i ← 0 to 2N do
5   a[i] = h[i] + t;
6 h_max = max(a);
7 h_sum = 0.0;
8 for i ← 0 to 2N do
9   h_sum += exp(a[i] – h_max);
10 h_sum = log(h_sum) + h_max;
11 b = addProtect(log(p) + h_sum, log(1 – p) + log(g));
12 for i ← 0 to 2N do
13   h[i] = exp(a[i] + log(p) – b);
14 ......
```

Algorithm 5. addProtect

```
1 m = max(a, b);
2 s = exp(a – m) + exp(b – m);
3 return log(s) + m;
```

Additionally, the purpose of the *max* operation in line 6 of Algorithm 4 and line 1 of Algorithm 5 is to further avoid the underflow.

From evaluations based on real-world data sets, the implementation employing this logarithm transformation is around three times faster than that employing the extended precision library.

High-Performance GPU-Accelerated Sequence Alignment and SNP Detection

Now we briefly introduce the other two tasks in GWAS with the GPU acceleration, which are sequence alignment and SNP detection. We only introduce the major techniques adopted in these two tasks. For more details, we refer readers to the related papers for GPU-accelerated sequence alignment (Lu, Tan, Bai, & Luo, 2012) and SNP detection (Lu et al., 2011).

GPU-Accelerated Sequence Alignment

There are two major categories of indexing techniques for sequence alignment, which are based on Burrows-Wheeler transform (BWT) and hashing. The major consideration to choose the BWT rather than hashing based indexing for the GPU-based sequence alignment is the memory consumption. With the limited GPU memory size (up to 6 GBs for GPUs in the market), the hashing index files (tens of GBs) cannot fit into the GPU memory. In this chapter, we will introduce the optimization techniques adopted in G-Aligner (Lu, Tan, Bai, & Luo, 2012).

The BWT index consists of a suffix array (SA) and a few occurrence arrays. An element in SA records the matched position of a sequence (or subsequence) on the reference sequence. In general, the BWT search works backward on a given input read. It starts from the suffix with size 1. Then each step increases the suffix by 1 and calculates a new SA pair (denoted as $<l, u>$, where $l \leq u$) for the new suffix. The SA pair indicates

that the matched positions for the corresponding suffix are SA[l], SA[$l + 1$], ... SA[$u - 1$]. The exact BWT search for a *n-bp* short read has the time complexity $O(n)$.

Since the BWT search for each short read is independent but the search algorithm is inherently sequential, the basic strategy is to make one thread handle one read. The major performance issue of such an implementation is that it has a large number of random memory accesses. To calculate an SA pair, the memory accesses on the occurrence arrays are highly random. The random memory access pattern dramatically hurts the performance of GPU-based applications. For example, the peak memory bandwidth of an NVIDIA Tesla C2070 GPU is 144 GB/sec. However, the random memory access pattern can reach only several GBs per second. Furthermore, the search algorithm may also introduce many branch divergences among threads. However, due to the algorithmic features of BWT search, it is difficult to change the memory access pattern and avoid branch divergences. Therefore, it is challenging to optimize the BWT search on the GPU.

A filtering-verification framework can be adopted to improve the GPU resource utilization. The basic idea is that we do not perform the complete BWT search. Instead, we stop the BWT search for a suffix when some conditions are satisfied (filtering). Then we use another algorithm employing massive data-parallelism to finish the remaining work (verification). Note that the verification algorithm may have a higher time complexity than the BWT search. However, it better matches the GPU's architecture features. The verification turns out to be more efficient than the BWT search on the GPU to finish the remaining work. Note that due to the higher time complexity of the verification, filtering is still important to help reduce the candidates.

The filtering-verification framework is based on the following property. Suppose the set of matched positions for a given read (we use the matched position of the last base of the read indicates the matched position for the entire read) is A, and the set of matched positions for its suffix is B, we have $A \subseteq B$. We call the matched positions in B the candidates. Based on this property, we design two phases of our framework as follows.

- **Filtering:** There is a threshold t for the filtering phase. For a given suffix generated in the BWT search, if its corresponding SA pair satisfies $(u - l) < t$, we stop the BWT search and mark the matched positions in the current SA pair as the candidates. This way, for each read, it generates up to t candidates per read. The threshold t is fixed to 10 by default, which can generate good performance in most cases.

- **Verification:** With candidates generated in the filtering phase, we directly compare the original read corresponding to each candidate to the reference sequence one base by one base. As this direct matching employs massive data parallelism, it can fully benefit from the high GPU memory bandwidth.

To simplify the presentation, we illustrate an example for exact match. Figure 7 illustrates an example of filtering-verification framework. After the filtering, the matched positions are {4, 8} for the suffix *TC* (they are also the candidates). Then the original read *ATTC* is directly compared to the reference based on the positions of 4 and 8. As a result, the candidate position 4 is a matched position for the input read and 8 not. Note that the BWT search algorithms with mismatches are more complex. However, our framework is applicable as well. The only difference is to consider the mismatch in the verification phase.

This filtering-verification framework can be implemented efficiently on the GPU. The filtering phase is difficult to be highly optimized on the GPU due to the algorithmic features as introduced before. However, various GPU-specific techniques have been investigated. Some techniques can help improve the performance significantly, such as lock-free multi-pass output, one-layer occurrence array and large kernel split. Some techniques have moderate performance improvement, including 16-byte word accesses, ordered reads and large L1 cache configuration. Furthermore, some techniques hurt the performance due to the side effect, such as shared memory for intermediate data, binding index to texture memory and kernel concurrent execution. On the other hand, the verification phase can be implemented efficiently on the GPU. A GPU thread warp is used to handle one read to avoid user-level synchronization. The small shared memory is exploited as well to further reduce the memory access latency.

GPU-Accelerated SNP Detection

We introduce the design of GPU-accelerated SNP detection tool GSNP (Lu et al., 2011), which is based on the same computation model implemented in the CPU-based SOAPsnp (Li et al., 2009). Overall, the same processing algorithm is applied to every site. Therefore, the GPU can be efficiently exploited by massive data parallelism. However, there are two major technical challenges:

Figure 7. An example of filtering-verification framework

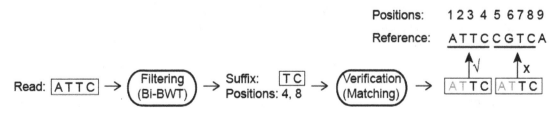

1. For every site, a core data structure is to store aligned bases (denoted as *base_occ*) for five pieces of information. SOAPsnp adopts an array with a dense data representation format. However, in practice, the percentage of non-zero elements in this array is very low (usually lower than 0.1%). Additionally, computation is only performed on non-zero elements. Such a low non-zero element percentage introduces a large number of unnecessary memory accesses as well as branch divergence due to the uneven distribution of non-zero elements.

2. Modern GPUs support IEEE-compliant floating point numbers as CPUs. However, several mathematical functions, e.g., *exp* and *log*, may not produce exactly the same result on the GPU and CPU due to different implementation details (NVIDIA, 2012a). As a result, a direct implementation on the GPU produces around 0.1% different results compared with the CPU implementation. Such inconsistent results are unacceptable for genomics research.

We first introduce the dense data representation format for aligned bases (*base_occ*), which is adopted in the CPU-based SOAPsnp. Specifically, for one site, every aligned base needs to store five pieces of information, which are the base character, the sequencing quality score, the position on the read, the strand and the number of occurrences corresponding to the first four attributes. Moreover, a follow-up step needs to access the number of occurrences in a canonical order based on the first four attributes. SOAPsnp adopts a dense representation format. Specifically, the first four attributes are encoded into the array's index, and every cell value stores the number of occurrences corresponding to four attributes encoded in its index. The advantage of such a representation format is the canonical order is naturally kept. However, there are a large number of zero elements, which are useless for computation.

The sparse representation format is proposed to avoid unnecessary memory accesses. It encodes the first four attributes as a 32-bit word. Then these words are packed together and stored in an array (denoted as *base_word*). If the number of occurrences is greater than one, we store two identical words. Figure 8 illustrates an example of the dense and sparse representation formats for aligned bases. The issue of the sparse representation format is that the canonical order is not naturally preserved anymore. Words stored in *base_word* follow the observation order. Therefore, an additional sorting step is required to order aligned bases for every site. However, the benefit of adopting the sparse representation format is much more than the overhead introduced by the sorting.

To address the inconsistency of GPU and CPU results, a special technique using a look-up table is adopted. Through further study, we observe that the only mathematical function producing inconsistent results is a base-10 logarithm on sequencing quality scores. Fortunately, the score is an integer between 0 and 64. Therefore, we pre-calculate the results of logarithm functions for all scores on the CPU, and store them in a look-up table. The lookup table is stored in the GPU's *constant memory*, which supports fast read.

GWAS using Large Data Sets

So far, we introduce the GPU acceleration for in-memory computation only. However, due to the limited GPU memory size (up to several GBs), for GWAS applications, it is very common that a large data set cannot fit into the GPU memory. Therefore, we next discuss techniques of handling large data sets in order to utilize GPUs for real-world sequence data. Note that these techniques of handling large data sets for GPUs are also applicable to CPUs.

All state-of-the-art GWAS tools have been able to handle large data sets that cannot fit into the GPU or CPU memory. A common method to handle very large data sets for GWAS applications is to

Figure 8. Dense and sparse data representation formats of aligned bases for a site

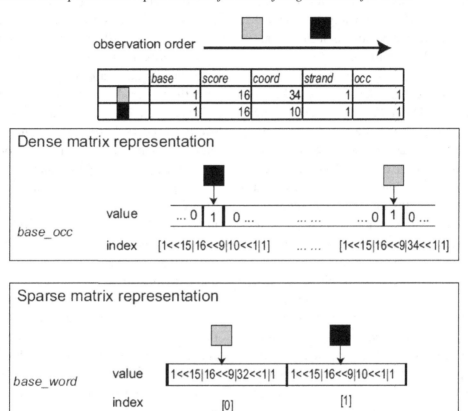

partition input data. Through application-specific data partitioning, there is no dependency among different partitions. Then the data processing is done in rounds on the partitioned data. For each round, one data partition that fits into the GPU memory is processed on the GPU.

Overall, there are two ways for data partitioning, which are read-based and site-based partitioning. For a given data set of N reads in total, the read-based partitioning splits all reads into several disjoint read chunks. The chunk size depends on the GPU memory capacity. For example, suppose a chunk contains m reads, which is the largest number of reads that can be processed on the GPU for one run. Then round i will process reads $[i \times m, (I + 1) \times m)$ on the GPU. Sequence alignment

tools employ such read-based data partitioning for large data sets.

Different from read-based partitioning, SNP detection and the MAF computation should adopt the site-based data partitioning. This different partitioning strategy is because for such kind of applications, the computation among sites is independent from each other. Specifically, in the site-based partitioning, a data set is split into several chunks according to their aligned positions (sites) on a reference sequence. In particular, we define a window size on the reference sequence. For each round, all reads (as well as other information) aligned to the positions that are in the given window are loaded to the GPU memory and processed. However, the site-based partitioning does introduce significant overhead in some cases.

For example, before the SNP detection, external sorting should be performed on aligned reads according to their aligned positions. Such external sorting may introduce significant overhead due to the slow disk I/O, especially when the in-memory computation has been accelerated by the GPU.

In order to address the performance issue of external sorting in the site-based data partitioning, integration techniques are proposed to systematically optimize the overall performance. Lu, Tan, Zhao, Bai, & Luo (2012) have proposed a technique to tightly integrate the sequence alignment and SNP detection into one system. In their system, when outputting alignments by the sequence alignment component, it maintains a fixed-size in-memory buffer to hold partitioned alignments. When the buffer is full, all alignments are flushed to the disk. The data written on disk by one flush is called a *data block*. Then within a data block, alignments are partitioned. In order to fetch alignments of the same partition across different data blocks, a linked list is maintained for each partition. This way, the external sorting is eliminated, and the overall performance is improved by reducing the disk I/O overhead. Such techniques are useful if different GWAS programs are performed in a pipeline.

GWAS on Multi-GPUs in Distributed Computing

We have introduced the optimization techniques for GWAS employing a single GPU and handling large data sets. However, a single GPU solution is not sufficient today. Particularly, as a typical area of big data for scientific computing, a solution that is able to scale up to a large number of compute nodes and GPUs is expected. In this section, we present state-of-the-art work using multiple GPUs for GWAS.

The data partitioning technique presented in the last section can be used to extend the single-GPU solution to multiple GPUs. Specifically, it divides input data into multiple partitions, and

then distributes partitions to different GPUs for processing. BarraCUDA (Klus et al., 2012) can support multiple-GPUs on a single server using data partitioning for sequence alignment. Such data partitioning is applicable to multiple GPUs on different servers in distributed or cloud computing as well. However, we need to consider the overhead of data shuffling among nodes. We take the MAF computation in distributed computing as an example, which requires multiple input files.

We present the MAF computation using multiple GPUs and nodes in distributed computing in detail. Recall that the input of MAF computation is the output of SNP detection for multiple individuals. The major result of SNP detection for one individual is stored in one file. Therefore if the MAF computation is performed based on M individuals, there are M input files. In a cluster, those M input files may be stored in different nodes. As mentioned, the MAF computation adopts the site-based partitioning. However, one input file contains all sites for one individual. As a result, in order to access the corresponding partition for a given GPU, it needs to access all input files to collect the required data, which results in data shuffling among nodes.

To efficiently perform the data shuffling, BGI-Shenzhen presents a solution using a distributed file system (Wang, 2013), extending the single GPU-accelerated implementation presented before in this chapter to multiple GPUs in distributed computing. Specifically, they use the Lustre file system on the Tianhe-1A supercomputer to perform the MAF computation employing multiple nodes and GPUs. Before the start of MAF computation on each node, all-to-all data exchange is performed for all nodes to collect their required data from all input files.

Figure 9 illustrates the data shuffling between nodes. There are M individuals (input files) distributed across N different nodes. Each input file is evenly partitioned into N chunks. Before the processing, each node collects its corresponding chunks from all M input files through all-to-all

Figure 9. Communication for the MAF computation in distributed computing

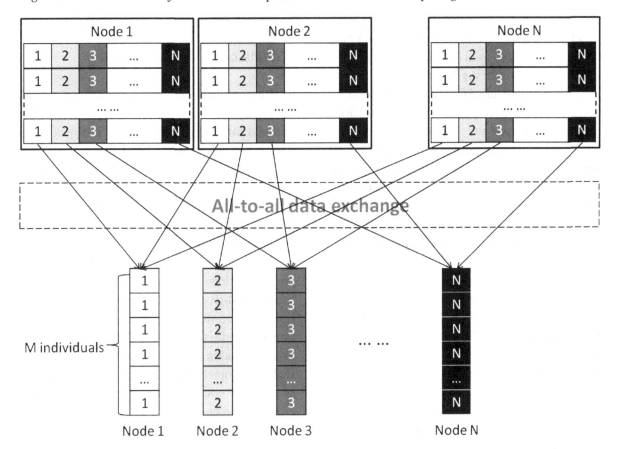

communication. In order to reduce the data shuffling overhead, data is compressed. Through tuning the stripe count and stripe size in Lustre, the I/O throughput can be significantly improved compared with the default configuration.

To evaluate the performance of distributed MAF computation, BGI-Shenzhen deploys their solution on 256 nodes (each node has an NVIDIA Tesla M2050 GPU) in Tianhe-1A. Thanhe-1A uses high speed InfiniBand (160Gbit/s) for node interconnection. Based on the human data set for 1,024 individuals, they find that the best performance (around 32X speedup over single-node performance) is achieved when there are 64 nodes. The poor scalability is mainly due to the non-computation overhead, e.g., disk I/O and network communication. The in-memory computation can

be accelerated by the GPUs significantly, which can achieve the speedup of an order of magnitude over the CPU counterpart. As a result, the disk I/O and network communication become the performance bottleneck.

From this distributed GPU-accelerated MAF computation implementation, we can see that the in-memory computation can be accelerated by the GPU significantly. As a result, the non-computation components, i.e., disk I/O and communication among nodes, may dominate the overall performance. Therefore, to design a high-performance GWAS system for distributed computing, in addition to the acceleration for the in-memory computation, the implementation should be optimized systematically. Specifically, the disk I/O and data communication should be carefully designed, which are most likely to be the performance bottleneck.

On the other hand, nowadays, cloud computing services are usually used to handle big data applications. For example, the Amazon cloud not only provides many standard CPU cores but also GPU cores. The GPU-accelerated GWAS applications can be deployed on the Amazon using multiple GPUs. The data partitioning approach can be applicable to the cloud computing. It is feasible for a researcher to transfer the data to Amazon for computation and storage. However, whether such transfer is reasonable and efficient depends on the relative computation capacity the researcher owns locally versus the cost of such transfer at Amazon. Similar to distributed computing, the disk I/O and data communication also can be performance bottleneck in cloud computing for GPU-accelerated GWAS applications.

Performance Results

In this section, we present the performance results of GPU-accelerated GWAS tools, including GAMA (Lu, Zhao, Luo, & Wang, 2012), G-Aligner (Lu, Tan, Bai, & Luo, 2012) and GSNP (Lu et al., 2011), to demonstrate the efficiency of GPU-accelerated MAF computation, sequence

alignment, and SNP detection, respectively. These tools are developed for a single GPU.

Results on MAF Computation

The experiments are conducted on a server equipped with an NVIDIA Tesla C2070 GPU and two Intel Xeon E5520 2.27 GHz quad-core CPUs. The server has 32 GB memory. CUDA 4.0 is used for testing. We use a real-world human genome data set based on 1,024 individuals. There are around 2.7 million sites in total (around 0.1% of the whole human genome). We report the in-memory computation time only, which is more expensive than the I/O cost. We show performance numbers of three implementations: the single-threaded realSFS (Thorfinn, 2012), an optimized 16-threaded CPU-based implementation (denoted as GAMA-CPU) and the GPU-based implementation (denoted as GAMA). Note that the realSFS adopted in the experiments has already been highly optimized by removing unnecessary computation and integrating the numerical optimization. GAMA-CPU adopts the same algorithm as GAMA except it is executed on the multi-core CPU (16-threaded).

Figure 10 shows the overall performance comparison between the GPU-accelerated GAMA and

Figure 10. Computation performance comparison among realSFS, GAMA-CPU and GPU-accelerated GAMA. (a) Different steps. (b) Overall performance comparison.

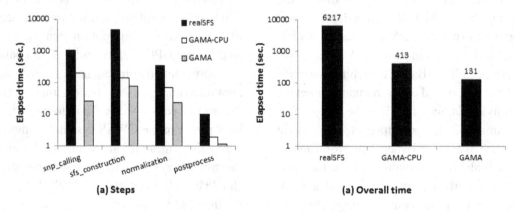

the optimized realSFS. Particularly, Figure 10(a) shows the time of different steps in the MAF computation. Compared with the optimized realSFS, GAMA accelerates different steps by up to 60X. Additionally, compared with the 16-threaded GAMA-CPU, the GPU-based GAMA can achieve a speedup of 1.7-7.7X for different steps. For the end-to-end performance comparison, Figure 10(b) shows GAMA outperforms the optimized realSFS and 16-threaded GAMA-CPU by 47.4X and 3.2X, respectively.

Results on Sequence Alignment

The evaluation of sequence alignment is conducted on the same platform as the MAF computation experiment. Three real-world data sets with various lengths (51-*bp*, 67-*bp* and 100-*bp*) are used, and each has 1 million reads. We compare G-Aligner to 2BWT (Lam et al., 2009) with both a single and 16 CPU threads, and another Bi-BWT based GPU-accelerated sequence alignment tool SOAP3 (Liu et al., 2012). Additionally, we show performance for two result reporting schemes, which are reporting all valid matches (*all-valid*) and reporting only one best match (with fewest mismatches) per read (*random-best*).

Figure 11 shows the performance comparison among G-Aligner, 2BWT and SOAP3. Figure 11(a) and (b) show that the optimized G-Aligner outperforms other tools for the all-valid and random-best reporting schemes by 1.3-7.8X and 1.2-9.4X, respectively. Particularly, compared with another GPU-accelerated SOAP3, G-Aligner is 1.8-3.5X faster.

Results on SNP Detection

The SNP detection tools are evaluated on a server equipped with an NVIDIA Tesla M2050 GPU and Intel Xeon E5630 2.53 GHz CPUs. The server has 64 GB memory and CUDA 3.2 is installed. We use two real-world date sets for evaluations, which are short reads aligned to human chromosome 1 and 21 (denoted as *Ch. 1* and *Ch. 21*). We compare GSNP with the CPU-based SOAPsnp (Li et al., 2009). SOAPsnp is a single-threaded program. The whole process of SNP detection is decomposed into 7 different steps.

Table 1 shows the speedup for different steps as well as the total speedup of GPU-accelerated GSNP over the CPU-based SOAPsnp. Since the likelihood computation and memory recycle directly benefit from the sparse representation

Figure 11. Performance comparison among G-Aligner, 2BWT and SOAP3

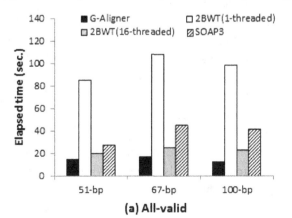

(a) All-valid

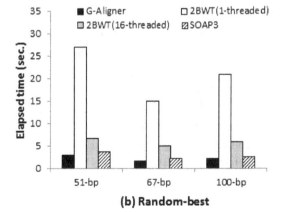

(b) Random-best

format, the speedups from GSNP are up to two and three orders of magnitude compared with SOAPsnp for the likelihood computation and memory recycle, respectively. Additionally, GSNP accelerates the overall performance of SOAPsnp by 42-50X.

FUTURE RESEARCH DIRECTIONS

Now we identify a few potential future research directions. The suggestions are mainly for the modern genome-wide association study with big genome data.

First, high-performance GWAS tools employing modern processors continue to attract research interests from either bioinformatics or computer science communities. In this chapter, we have demonstrated that it is non-trivial to adopt the GPU to accelerate existing GWAS algorithms. Careful design and specific optimization techniques are necessary to fully utilize the GPU hardware resource. Furthermore, in order to build a complete system, e.g., in cloud or distributed computing, employing the GPU acceleration, we should particularly pay attention to two issues. First, we should optimize the performance systematically. This is because after the GPU acceleration for the in-memory computation, other components, such as disk I/O and network communication, may dominate the performance. Second, numerical optimization is important for some applications. For example, we have demonstrated the floating-point underflow in the MAF computation and inconsistent results of floating point computation on the GPU and CPU in the SNP detection. These issues must be addressed for real-world applications.

Second, the DNA sequencing technique also evolves fast, which directly affects the design of GWAS tools. The GWAS algorithms presented in this chapter are for the data generated by the second generation sequencing devices, which produce very short reads at a high throughput. However, the third generation sequencing tech-

nique is already on the way and may be available in the market in the near future (Schadt, Turner, & Kasarskis, 2010). The major impacts for the algorithm design from the third generation sequencing data are longer reads and more sequencing errors. Therefore, new high-performance GWAS tools should be ready when the third generation sequencing technique is widely used at sequencing centers. Specifically, the impact of the third generation sequencing technique will be mainly on the tools that directly process raw sequence data, such as sequence alignment. Due to the different characteristics of the data (e.g., more errors), the current sequence alignment algorithm should be enhanced. For tools such as the SNP detection and MAF computation, which are based on the output of sequence alignment, existing algorithms (including performance optimization and numerical optimization techniques) should be directly applicable to the third generation sequencing data.

Third, hardware also keeps progressing. For example, the new NVIDIA Kepler GPU architecture has been available in the market recently (NVIDIA, 2012b). It introduces a few new useful features to help programs better exploit the GPU hardware resource, such as dynamic parallelism and Hyper-Q. With such new techniques, existing GPU-based implementations may be revisited. On the other hand, other emerging hardware architectures also should be explored. Some platforms, such as FPGAs, have already been studied for genomics applications (Oliver, Schmidt, Nathan, Clemens, & Maskell, 2005). Instead, there is no related work yet for a few new hardware architectures for GWAS applications, such as AMD APU (AMD, 2012) and the newly released Intel Xeon Phi processor (Intel 2012). Different hardware platforms may be suitable for different workloads. Together with these different platforms, heterogeneous computing is a promising direction to accelerate various GWAS tools.

Fourth, integration techniques for GWAS tasks are necessary. In this chapter, we describe three tasks of sequence alignment, SNP detection, and

GAMA separately. However, there is dependency among these three tools as shown in Figure 1. As a genome data analysis workflow, the overall performance can be further improved if integration techniques are adopted for separate software packages. For example, as mentioned, a previous study has shown that the sequence alignment and SNP detection can be tightly integrated in order to reduce the I/O overhead storing intermediate results (Lu, Tan, Zhao, Bai, & Luo, 2012). We expect exploring more integration techniques for more GWAS tasks in the future. The ultimate goal is to provide a platform with automatic workflow optimization for various GWAS tasks.

CONCLUSION

GWAS has become an important research direction for genomists. However, efficient and accurate genomics data processing is challenging due to the high computation intensity and numerical issues, e.g., floating point underflow, from particular applications. These two issues become more crucial for large-scale genome data analysis. In this chapter, we present state-of-the-art techniques to solve these two problems. We focus on three fundamental GWAS tasks, which are sequence alignment, SNP detection and MAF computation. Specifically, to accelerate the data processing, GPUs are adopted as hardware accelerators. However, we have demonstrated that to achieve the high performance on the GPU, careful algorithm designs and optimization techniques are necessary. For example, the major technical contributions presented in the chapter for GPU-accelerated GWAS tools include a novel reduction based SFS construction algorithm for the MAF computation, a filtering-verification framework for sequence alignment and a sparse data representation format for SNP detection.

On the other hand, to address the floating point underflow issue, the computation is transformed to logarithm space. As a result, with the GPU acceleration, the performance of GPU-accelerated GWAS tools (GAMA, G-Aligner and GSNP) can outperform their CPU-based counterparts by up to an order of magnitude. Furthermore, with the numerical optimization (transforming computation to logarithm space), GAMA can handle the data set of 1,024 individuals for MAF computation, which cannot be processed correctly by the previous tool. We believe these techniques are useful for the genomics research community to develop high-performance and numerically optimized tools for large-scale GWAS in the future. Additionally, these techniques may also inspire solutions for similar problems arising from other fields of big data analysis.

REFERENCES

AMD. (2012). AMD fusion family of APUs: Enabling a superior, immersive PC experience. *AMD Fusion Whitepaper*. Retrieved January 24, 2013, from http://www.amd.com/us/Documents/48423_fusion_whitepaper_WEB.pdf

David, H. B. (2012). ARPREC: C++/Fortran-90 arbitrary precision package. *High-Precision Software Directory*. Retrieved January 24, 2013, from http://crd-legacy.lbl.gov/~dhbailey/mpdist/

GMP. (2012). GMP. *The GNU Multiple Precision Arithmetic Library*. Retrieved January 24, 2013, from http://gmplib.org/

Intel. (2012). Intel Xeon Phi coprocessor 5110P. *Intel Website*. Retrieved January 24, 2013, from http://www.intel.com/content/www/us/en/processors/xeon/xeon-phi-detail.html

Johnson, A., & O'Donnell, C. (2009). An open access database of genome-wide association results. *BMC Medical Genetics*, *10*(1), 6. doi:10.1186/1471-2350-10-6 PMID:19161620.

Kienzler, R., Bruggmann, R., Ranganathan, A., & Tatbul, N. (2012). Incremental DNA sequence analysis in the cloud. In *Scientific and Statistical Database Management* (pp. 640–645). Berlin: Springer. doi:10.1007/978-3-642-31235-9_50.

Kim, S. Y., Lohmueller, K. E., Albrechtsen, A., Li, Y., Korneliussen, T., Tian, G., & Nielsen, R. (2011). Estimation of allele frequency and association mapping using next-generation sequencing data. *BMC Bioinformatics*, *12*(1), 231. doi:10.1186/1471-2105-12-231 PMID:21663684.

Klus, P., Lam, S., Lyberg, D., Cheung, M. S., Pullan, G., McFarlane, I., & Lam, B. Y. (2012). BarraCUDA-A fast short read sequence aligner using graphics processing units. *BMC Research Notes*, *5*(1), 27. doi:10.1186/1756-0500-5-27 PMID:22244497.

Lam, T. W., Li, R., Tam, A., Wong, S., Wu, E., & Yiu, S. M. (2009). High throughput short read alignment via bi-directional BWT. In *Proceedings of the IEEE International Conference on Bioinformatics and Biomedicine,* (pp. 31-36). Los Alamitos, CA: IEEE Computer Society.

Laney, D. (2001). 3D data management: Controlling data volume, velocity, and variety. *Application Delivery Strategies*. Retrieved May 1, 2013, from http://blogs.gartner.com/doug-laney/files/2012/01/ad949-3D-Data-Management-Controlling-Data-Volume-Velocity-and-Variety.pdf

Langmead, B., Schatz, M. C., Lin, J., Pop, M., & Salzberg, S. L. (2009). Searching for SNPs with cloud computing. *Genome Biology*, *10*(11), R134. doi:10.1186/gb-2009-10-11-r134 PMID:19930550.

Langmead, B., Trapnell, C., Pop, M., & Salzberg, S. L. (2009). Ultrafast and memory-efficient alignment of short DNA sequences to the human genome. *Genome Biology*, *10*(3), R25. doi:10.1186/gb-2009-10-3-r25 PMID:19261174.

Li, H., & Durbin, R. (2009). Fast and accurate short read alignment with Burrows–Wheeler transform. *Bioinformatics (Oxford, England)*, *25*(14), 1754–1760. doi:10.1093/bioinformatics/btp324 PMID:19451168.

Li, R., Li, Y., Fang, X., Yang, H., Wang, J., Kristiansen, K., & Wang, J. (2009). SNP detection for massively parallel whole-genome resequencing. *Genome Research*, *19*(6), 1124–1132. doi:10.1101/gr.088013.108 PMID:19420381.

Li, R., Yu, C., Li, Y., Lam, T. W., Yiu, S. M., Kristiansen, K., & Wang, J. (2009). SOAP2: An improved ultrafast tool for short read alignment. *Bioinformatics (Oxford, England)*, *25*(15), 1966–1967. doi:10.1093/bioinformatics/btp336 PMID:19497933.

Li, Y., Terrell, A., & Patel, J. M. (2011). Wham: A high-throughput sequence alignment method. In *Proceedings of the 2011 ACM SIGMOD International Conference on Management of Data* (pp. 445-456). New York: ACM.

Li, Y., Vinckenbosch, N., Tian, G., Huerta-Sanchez, E., Jiang, T., Jiang, H., & Wang, J. (2010). Resequencing of 200 human exomes identifies an excess of low-frequency non-synonymous coding variants. *Nature Genetics*, *42*(11), 969–972. doi:10.1038/ng.680 PMID:20890277.

Liu, C. M., Wong, T., Wu, E., Luo, R., Yiu, S. M., Li, Y., & Lam, T. W. (2012). SOAP3: Ultrafast GPU-based parallel alignment tool for short reads. *Bioinformatics (Oxford, England)*, *28*(6), 878–879. doi:10.1093/bioinformatics/bts061 PMID:22285832.

Lu, M., He, B., & Luo, Q. (2010). Supporting extended precision on graphics processors. In *Proceedings of the Sixth International Workshop on Data Management on New Hardware* (pp. 19-26). New York: ACM.

Lu, M., Tan, Y., Bai, G., & Luo, Q. (2012). High-performance short sequence alignment with GPU acceleration. *Distributed and Parallel Databases*, 1–15.

Lu, M., Tan, Y., Zhao, J., Bai, G., & Luo, Q. (2012). Integrating GPU-accelerated sequence alignment and SNP detection for genome resequencing analysis. In *Scientific and Statistical Database Management* (pp. 124–140). Berlin: Springer. doi:10.1007/978-3-642-31235-9_8.

Lu, M., Zhao, J., Luo, Q., & Wang, B. (2012). Accelerating minor allele frequency computation with graphics processors. In *Proceedings of the 1st International Workshop on Big Data, Streams and Heterogeneous Source Mining: Algorithms, Systems, Programming Models and Applications* (pp. 85-92). New York: ACM.

Lu, M., Zhao, J., Luo, Q., Wang, B., Fu, S., & Lin, Z. (2011). GSNP: A DNA single-nucleotide polymorphism detection system with GPU acceleration. In *Proceedings of the 2011 International Conference on Parallel Processing (ICPP)* (pp. 592-601). Los Alamitos, CA: IEEE Computer Society.

Manolio, T. A. (2010). Genome-wide association studies and assessment of the risk of disease. *The New England Journal of Medicine*, *363*(2), 166–176. doi:10.1056/NEJMra0905980 PMID:20647212.

Nielsen, R., Paul, J. S., Albrechtsen, A., & Song, Y. S. (2011). Genotype and SNP calling from next-generation sequencing data. *Nature Reviews. Genetics*, *12*(6), 443–451. doi:10.1038/nrg2986 PMID:21587300.

NVIDIA. (2012a). Mathematical functions. In *CUDA C Programming Guide*. NVIDIA.

NVIDIA. (2012b). NVIIDA's next generation CUDA compute architecture: Kepler GK110. *NVIDIA Kepler GK110 Architecture White Paper*. Retrieved January 24, 2013, from http://www.nvidia.com/content/PDF/kepler/NVIDIA-Kepler-GK110-Architecture-Whitepaper.pdf

Oliver, T., Schmidt, B., Nathan, D., Clemens, R., & Maskell, D. (2005). Multiple sequence alignment on an FPGA. In *Proceedings of the 11th International Conference on Parallel and Distributed Systems,* (Vol. 2, pp. 326-330). Los Alamitos, CA: IEEE Computer Society.

Owens, J. D., Luebke, D., Govindaraju, N., Harris, M., Krüger, J., Lefohn, A. E., & Purcell, T. J. (2007). A survey of general-purpose computation on graphics hardware. *Computer Graphics Forum*, *26*(1), 80–113. doi:10.1111/j.1467-8659.2007.01012.x.

Schadt, E. E., Turner, S., & Kasarskis, A. (2010). A window into third-generation sequencing. *Human Molecular Genetics*, *19*(R2), R227–R240. doi:10.1093/hmg/ddq416 PMID:20858600.

Thorfinn, S. (2012). realSFS. *The Bioinformatics Centre University of Copenhagen*. Retrieved January 24, 2013, from http://128.32.118.212/thorfinn/realSFS/

Wang, B. (2013). GPU accelerated MAF estimation on tianhe-1A. In *Proceedings of Parallel Programming Model for the Masses (PPMM 2013)*. Shenzhen, China: PPMM.

Yi, X., Liang, Y., Huerta-Sanchez, E., Jin, X., Cuo, Z. X. P., Pool, J. E., & Cao, Z. (2010). Sequencing of 50 human exomes reveals adaptation to high altitude. *Science Signaling*, *329*(5987), 75. PMID:20595611.

ADDITIONAL READING

Aji, A. M., Zhang, L., & Feng, W. C. (2010). GPU-RMAP: Accelerating short-read mapping on graphics processors. In *Proceedings of the 2010 IEEE 13th International Conference on Computational Science and Engineering* (pp. 168-175). Los Alamitos, CA: IEEE Computer Society.

Davis, N. A., Pandey, A., & McKinney, B. A. (2011). Real-world comparison of CPU and GPU implementations of SNPrank: A network analysis tool for GWAS. *Bioinformatics (Oxford, England)*, *27*(2), 284–285. doi:10.1093/bioinformatics/btq638 PMID:21115438.

Hemani, G., Theocharidis, A., Wei, W., & Haley, C. (2011). EpiGPU: Exhaustive pairwise epistasis scans parallelized on consumer level graphics cards. *Bioinformatics (Oxford, England)*, *27*(11), 1462–1465. doi:10.1093/bioinformatics/btr172 PMID:21471009.

Hu, X., Liu, Q., Zhang, Z., Li, Z., Wang, S., He, L., & Shi, Y. (2010). SHEsisEpi: A GPU-enhanced genome-wide SNP-SNP interaction scanning algorithm, efficiently reveals the risk genetic epistasis in bipolar disorder. *Cell Research*, *20*(7), 854–857. doi:10.1038/cr.2010.68 PMID:20502444.

Jia, P., Xuan, L., Liu, L., & Wei, C. (2011). MetaBinG: Using GPUs to accelerate metagenomic sequence classification. *PLoS ONE*, *6*(11), e25353. doi:10.1371/journal.pone.0025353 PMID:22132069.

Jiang, R., Zeng, F., Zhang, W., Wu, X., & Yu, Z. (2009). Accelerating genome-wide association studies using cuda compatible graphics processing units. In *Proceedings of the International Joint Conference on Bioinformatics, Systems Biology and Intelligent Computing,* (pp. 70-76). Los Alamitos, CA: IEEE Computer Society.

Khajeh-Saeed, A., Poole, S., & Blair Perot, J. (2010). Acceleration of the Smith–Waterman algorithm using single and multiple graphics processors. *Journal of Computational Physics*, *229*(11), 4247–4258. doi:10.1016/j.jcp.2010.02.009.

Lee, S., Kwon, M. S., Huh, I. S., & Park, T. (2011). CUDA-LR: CUDA-accelerated logistic regression analysis tool for gene-gene interaction for genome-wide association study. In *Proceedings of the 2011 IEEE International Conference on Bioinformatics and Biomedicine Workshops* (pp. 691-695). Los Alamitos, CA: IEEE Computer Society.

Ligowski, L., & Rudnicki, W. (2009). An efficient implementation of Smith-Waterman algorithm on GPU using CUDA, for massively parallel scanning of sequence databases. In *Proceedings of the IEEE International Symposium on Parallel & Distributed Processing,* (pp. 1-8). Los Alamitos, CA: IEEE Computer Society.

Ling, C., Benkrid, K., & Hamada, T. (2009). A parameterisable and scalable Smith-Waterman algorithm implementation on CUDA-compatible GPUs. In *Proceedings of the IEEE 7th Symposium on Application Specific Processors,* (pp. 94-100). Los Alamitos, CA: IEEE Computer Society.

Mahmood, S. F., & Rangwala, H. (2011). GPU-euler: Sequence assembly using GPGPU. In *Proceedings of the 2011 IEEE 13th International Conference on High Performance Computing and Communications* (pp. 153-160). Los Alamitos, CA: IEEE Computer Society.

Manavski, S. A., & Valle, G. (2008). CUDA compatible GPU cards as efficient hardware accelerators for Smith-Waterman sequence alignment. *BMC Bioinformatics*, 9(Suppl 2), S10. doi:10.1186/1471-2105-9-S2-S10 PMID:18387198.

Meng, Z., Li, J., Zhou, Y., Liu, Q., Liu, Y., & Cao, W. (2011). bCloudBLAST: An efficient mapreduce program for bioinformatics applications. In *Proceedings of the 2011 4th International Conference on Biomedical Engineering and Informatics* (Vol. 4, pp. 2072-2076). Los Alamitos, CA: IEEE Computer Society.

Munekawa, Y., Ino, F., & Hagihara, K. (2008). Design and implementation of the Smith-Waterman algorithm on the CUDA-compatible GPU. In *Proceedings of the 8th IEEE International Conference on BioInformatics and BioEngineering,* (pp. 1-6). Los Alamitos, CA: IEEE Computer Society.

Pang, B., Zhao, N., Becchi, M., Korkin, D., & Shyu, C. R. (2012). Accelerating large-scale protein structure alignments with graphics processing units. *BMC Research Notes*, 5(1), 116. doi:10.1186/1756-0500-5-116 PMID:22357132.

Psychiatric, G. W. A. S., Cichon, S., Craddock, N., Daly, M., Faraone, S. V., Gejman, P. V., & Sullivan, P. F. (2009). Genomewide association studies: History, rationale, and prospects for psychiatric disorders. *The American Journal of Psychiatry*, 166(5), 540. doi:10.1176/appi.ajp.2008.08091354 PMID:19339359.

Sandes, E. F. O., & de Melo, A. C. (2010). CUDAlign: Using GPU to accelerate the comparison of megabase genomic sequences. *ACM Sigplan Notices*, 45(5), 137–146. doi:10.1145/1837853.1693473.

Schatz, M. C., Trapnell, C., Delcher, A. L., & Varshney, A. (2007). High-throughput sequence alignment using graphics processing units. *BMC Bioinformatics*, 8(1), 474. doi:10.1186/1471-2105-8-474 PMID:18070356.

Shi, H., Schmidt, B., Liu, W., & Muller-Wittig, W. (2009). Accelerating error correction in high-throughput short-read DNA sequencing data with CUDA. In *Proceedings of the IEEE International Symposium on Parallel & Distributed Processing,* (pp. 1-8). Los Alamitos, CA: IEEE Computer Society.

Sinnott-Armstrong, N. A., Greene, C. S., & Moore, J. H. (2010). Fast genome-wide epistasis analysis using ant colony optimization for multifactor dimensionality reduction analysis on graphics processing units. In *Proceedings of the 12th Annual Conference on Genetic and Evolutionary Computation* (pp. 215-216). New York: ACM.

Su, X., Xu, J., & Ning, K. (2011). Parallel-META: A high-performance computational pipeline for metagenomic data analysis. In *Proceedings of the 2011 IEEE International Conference on Systems Biology* (pp. 173-178). IEEE.

Suzuki, S., Ishida, T., Kurokawa, K., & Akiyama, Y. (2012). GHOSTM: A GPU-accelerated homology search tool for metagenomics. *PLoS ONE*, 7(5), e36060. doi:10.1371/journal.pone.0036060 PMID:22574135.

Vouzis, P. D., & Sahinidis, N. V. (2011). GPU-BLAST: Using graphics processors to accelerate protein sequence alignment. *Bioinformatics (Oxford, England)*, 27(2), 182–188. doi:10.1093/bioinformatics/btq644 PMID:21088027.

Wei, G., Ma, C., Pei, S., & Wu, B. (2009). The accelerating implementation of BLAST with stream processor. In *Proceedings of the IEEE 10th International Conference on Computer-Aided Industrial Design & Conceptual Design*, (pp. 2245-2250). Los Alamitos, CA: IEEE Computer Society.

Xiao, S., Lin, H., & Feng, W. C. (2011). Accelerating protein sequence search in a heterogeneous computing system. In *Proceedings of the 2011 IEEE International Parallel & Distributed Processing Symposium* (pp. 1212-1222). Los Alamitos, CA: IEEE Computer Society.

Yung, L. S., Yang, C., Wan, X., & Yu, W. (2011). GBOOST: A GPU-based tool for detecting gene–gene interactions in genome–wide case control studies. *Bioinformatics (Oxford, England)*, 27(9), 1309–1310. doi:10.1093/bioinformatics/btr114 PMID:21372087.

KEY TERMS AND DEFINITIONS

Genome Sequence Analysis: A process that analyzes genome sequence data and outputs useful information for further studies for genomists. Major genome sequence analysis applications include sequence alignment, SNP detection and MAF computation.

Genome-Wide Association Study (GWAS): A study on the association between genetic variants and traits.

GPGPU: Using the GPU for general-purpose computing applications.

MAF Computation: The calculation of the likelihood of minor allele frequency for multiple individuals of the same species on every site of the reference sequence.

Parallel Computing: A computing paradigm in which a task is executed on multiple computing nodes concurrently.

Performance Optimization: The process of improving the speed.

Sequence Alignment: The process of matching a sequence fragment against a reference sequence, with mismatches possibly allowed.

SNP Detection: The discovery of the variation of one individual's DNA from that of a reference on every site of the reference sequence.

Chapter 15
The Need to Consider Hardware Selection when Designing Big Data Applications Supported by Metadata

Nathan Regola
University of Notre Dame, USA

David A. Cieslak
Aunalytics, Inc., USA

Nitesh V. Chawla
University of Notre Dame, USA

ABSTRACT

The selection of hardware to support big data systems is complex. Even defining the term "big data" is difficult. "Big data" can mean a large volume of data in a database, a MapReduce cluster that processes data, analytics and reporting applications that must access large datasets to operate, algorithms that can effectively operate on large datasets, or even basic scripts that produce a needed resulted by leveraging data. Big data systems can be composed of many component systems. For these reasons, it appears difficult to create a universal, representative benchmark that approximates a "big data" workload. Along with the trend to utilize large datasets and sophisticated tools to analyze data, the trend of cloud computing has emerged as an effective method of leasing compute time. This chapter explores some of the issues at the intersection of virtualized computing (since cloud computing often uses virtual machines), metadata stores, and big data. Metadata is important because it enables many applications and users to access datasets and effectively use them without relying on extensive knowledge from humans about the data.

DOI: 10.4018/978-1-4666-4699-5.ch015

INTRODUCTION

Big data systems have emerged as a set of hardware and software solutions to allow organizations to obtain value from the increasing volume and complexity of data that is captured. Web sites are one example of leveraging big data systems and data to improve key business metrics. For example, large organizations often have a portal site that is a vital part of their business operations, whether it a private extranet, a public site for news, or an e-commerce site. While major public portal sites often appear that they are one seamless site, they are often built from many separate applications. For example, a news site may have an application that lists the top ten most popular news articles or an ecommerce site may recommend products for a user. Increasingly, these applications or components are driven by big data systems. Major portal sites are essentially large distributed systems that appear as a seamless site. This approach allows the operators of the site to experiment with new applications and deploy new applications without impacting existing functionality. It also importantly enables the workflow of each application to be distinct and supported by the necessary hardware and application level redundancy that is appropriate for that specific application. An e-commerce site would likely invest substantial resources to ensure that the "shopping cart" application was available with an uptime of 100%, while the "recommended products" application may have a target uptime of 99.9%. Likewise, a news site may decide that the front page should be accessible with a target uptime of 100%, even during periods of extreme load such as on a national election day. The news site may decide that the "most popular articles" application should have a target uptime of 99.99%. For example, a small pool of servers may present the content for display that is produced by each application, but each application may have its own internal database servers, Hadoop cluster, or caching layer.

News Site Use Case

Assume that a news site began their "most popular articles application" by ranking the frequency of news article displays. The intent of the "most popular articles application" on a news site is often to increase the length of a site visit and this is naturally linked to the business objectives of an organization. If the news site is revenue driven then increasing the length of a site visit increases the likelihood that the user will click on advertisements that generate revenue for the owner. Given this background, assume that in the initial version of the "most popular articles" application, users in the southern United States caused the most popular article to be an article that discussed an impending hurricane that might hit the southern United States. Users in the central United States may only rarely read this "most popular article" since it is not relevant to users in the central United States. Calculating the most popular articles on a news site is relatively easy, assuming that a well designed database of activity exists. However, this simple calculation isn't necessarily optimal from a business metric standpoint. The user should be presented the "most popular articles" that are actually relevant or are likely to be clicked on, since the goal is to increase traffic, not just present a ranking of the most read articles to the user. Perhaps the data scientist discovers that weather articles are generally sought out by users that are aware of impending weather events or are rarely read outside of the immediate geographic area of the weather event. The data scientist may decide to utilize information concerning the type of the article and the geographic area discussed by an article to determine whether it should be present in a "most popular articles list." Both enhancements require more complex data and a more complex query. For example, in the simplest revision of the "most popular articles" application, articles must be tagged with the type of article: "weather" or "non-weather" and the geographic area discussed in the article. These tags can likely be created by the article author. When a user visits the site, each user's geographic location must be approximated so that they can be mapped to a "geographic area" that the news site recognizes. The type of article and the geographic area discussed in the article also need to be retrieved, and the algorithm can determine which articles will be the "most popular articles" for that user, considering the type of each article and the geographic area of the user and article.

The article's tags (metadata) and any information that is utilized to approximate the location should be available for rapid retrieval. This requirement is often imposed because the "most popular articles" application will need to calculate the result quickly so that the web page can be generated and displayed within a fraction of a second. An operational data store may be utilized to store and recall the data that is needed for the application. An operational data store could be implemented as an in-memory database to provide low latency responses to the "top articles" application. The hardware to support the in-memory database may be a machine with a high speed bus connecting the CPU, memory, and network card.

The results of user behavior (e.g. user X read article Y or user X viewed advertisement Z) may be captured in the data warehouse for longer term analysis to develop improved algorithms, measure advertisement revenue, and monitor site traffic over time. The hardware to support a data warehouse is often a large volume of storage and compute capacity. Storage can be implemented as a storage area network, Hadoop file system, or directly attached local storage.

The site and its applications will likely change over time. For example, the "top articles application" may have begun with five articles for all users but is later changed to display ten articles to all users. A metadata store could track the number of articles that the top articles application displayed during a given date range. Analytics and reporting applications would utilize the metadata store and the data warehouse to explore the relationship between the number of articles displayed through the "top articles application" and the number of articles that users read, including information about their geographic area.

BACKGROUND

The performance of the application is often the ultimate concern of the big data system designer. Business managers are not concerned with which components are utilized, but merely that the system will achieve its performance targets such as precision, recall, and "response to application within .1 seconds." Therefore, the system designer's job is to determine which components and hardware can reach the desired performance targets when coupled with an appropriate algorithm. Obviously, the capabilities of current hardware technologies are useful in order to determine the latency and throughput that is achievable for a given budget. For example, system designers could implement an operational data store to create near real-time response rates. However, an operational data store would be cost prohibitive for an archived dataset where all of the data did not have to be close to the applications as memory and solid state (or flash) storage has traditionally been more costly per gigabyte than a magnetic disk. Ultimately, the applications that will execute on the hardware need to be considered as part of the decision to ensure that the application will be able to meet its performance targets when implementation is complete as various implementations of algorithms will result in differing performance results.

Background in Virtualization

The use of a virtualized environment (such as most cloud providers) presents additional complexity to the big data system architect, due to the fact that virtualization adds an additional source of overhead to the system that must be factored into the hardware and software selection process. Virtualization also enables fault tolerance when the hardware is experiencing a failure (such as degraded network connectivity because one network card in a team has failed or a disk has failed in a RAID array) and the operator wishes to move the workload to another piece of hardware while the repairs are occurring. Obviously, many modern applications that are intended to execute in distributed environments have some support for fault-tolerance, but some applications are not designed to handle hardware failures. Alternatively, it may be more efficient to relocate a workload rather than restart the execution of the workload (MPI jobs without check-pointing are one situation where the ability to migrate a workload from one failing node to a new node may save significant computational time over restarting a job). Virtualization has been utilized for this type of fault-tolerance (when hardware errors are detected on a node) with MPI jobs without MPI checkpointing (Nagarajan, Mueller, Engelmann, & Scott, 2007).

Types of Virtualization Overhead

The type of overhead present in a virtual machine can be classified into two main categories for purposes of discussion--CPU virtualization overhead and I/O virtualization overhead. I/O virtualization has an overheard that is above 0% (an ideal virtualized environment would be 100% efficient, thus having an overhead of 0%) and may affect the efficiency of a cluster to the point that adding additional nodes does not speedup the application. CPU virtualization overhead will affect the runtime of applications, especially for applications that result in a workload that is memory access intensive. These two types of overheads are useful to think about in the context of building large systems that span multiple nodes. A single node, N_1 will be efficient at task T if its CPU efficiency is high (assuming that the task is not bottlenecked by I/O constraints). Expanding

beyond one node, high I/O efficiency allows the task T to scale efficiently across multiple nodes (assuming that the application is designed to be distributed across multiple nodes).

To determine the CPU efficiency, it may be prudent to benchmark a single virtualized node and compare the performance to performance on the same operating system on the same hardware. This will allow the benchmarking process to establish the CPU overhead on a given node and rule out issues resulting from significant overhead from a workload with specific patterns of memory accesses that stress the page table mapping strategies. For example, the hypervisor may not take advantage of the Intel EPT (Extended Page Tables) or AMD RVI (Rapid Virtualization Indexing) capability or the capability may not be enabled in the BIOS. VMWare ESX implemented support for these technologies in version 3.5 and demonstrated performance increases of up to 42% for benchmarks that stress the memory management unit (Bhatia, 2009).

One strategy to determine if there are any CPU or memory management bottlenecks in the virtual machine is to run the target application (or benchmark) on one machine, first utilizing one core, and scaling up the application to N cores, where N is the number of cores in the server on the native hardware, and then in the virtualized operating system. The only caveat to this approach (discussed in more depth below) is to ensure that there is not significant unintended I/O activity.

CPU virtualization overhead can be approximated by running a given application in a virtual machine and running the same application on the same native hardware that powered the virtual machine. The best method of setting up the experiment is not quite as easy as it may appear. The same conditions should exist when the application is executed in the virtual machine and when the application is executing in the native operating system. Establishing these "conditions" is perhaps largely a problem of defining the comparison. For example, should the virtual machine be running so that the virtualized operating system kernel is consuming some RAM during the test on native hardware since the underlying operating system and the virtualized operating system were running during the benchmark of the virtualized operating system? Should this virtualized operating system also have an application running to ensure that some memory is being actively used to force the hypervisor to deal with frequent memory accesses and page table mappings from both the virtual machine and the "native" operating system? Whether an experimenter should create an experiment that allows the virtual machine to run while the benchmark application is executing on the native hardware (since utilizing the native operating system for a task does not strictly require a virtual machine to be running since the virtual machine does not contribute to the work being completed in the native operating system, while a benchmark executing in the virtualized operating system requires both the hypervisor or native operating system and the virtual operating system to be executing) is perhaps a question of semantics and the goal of the experiment.

The major CPU manufacturers have been introducing additional hardware support to improve the performance of memory accesses in virtualized (or guest) operating systems for some time. A 2010 study found that the maximum CPU overhead when executing the NASA Parallel Benchmark Suite was approximately 5% (Regola & Ducom, 2010). The loss in efficiency may be palpable to consumers of cloud resources if they intend to accomplish a given task within a required elapsed time. To compensate for the loss of efficiency (if there are more strict timing requirements that require higher efficiency in the virtualized operating system), a consumer could lease more CPU capacity (either by leasing a more powerful processor, or if that is not possible, an additional machine). The efficiency of CPU virtualization will likely increase as CPU manufacturers incorporate additional hardware features to support virtualization.

Hardware enhancements to support efficient CPU virtualization enabled lower cost cloud computing and allow more servers to be consolidated on a single physical server. Low I/O efficiency is problematic because if I/O overhead is too high, it can drastically reduce the size of a cluster that can be efficiently operated in a virtualized environment. For example, a 32 core MPI cluster (each node had 8 cores) with a one gigabit Ethernet connection resulted in an average speedup across various "benchmark kernels" (workloads) in the NASA Parallel Benchmark Suite of 1.01 when the ideal speedup would be 4 (Regola & Ducom, 2010). However, an InfiniBand connection (20Gbps and lower latency) resulted in an average speedup of 3.05 when the ideal speedup would be 4 (Regola & Ducom, 2010). This demonstrates the problem introduced above; suboptimal network performance can limit the ability to efficiently add nodes to a cluster of machines and this is exacerbated in a virtualized environment where the I/O overhead can be significant.

Relationship of Big Data to I/O Virtualization Efficiency

I/O virtualization is problematic for big data problems because big data applications often require a cluster of nodes that communicate in some manner. When dealing with big data problems, typically a large volume of data is transferred through network connections (whether intentionally or as a result of requests to local storage that is actually not "local" to the node and is funneled through network connections). Even in paradigms such as MapReduce that attempt to keep data close to the processors that will ultimately analyze the segment of data stored "locally", the data must be loaded to the nodes, and data is often replicated to other nodes in the cluster for fault tolerance, even if it is locally accessible for analysis. This point demonstrates that is often important to be concerned with other operations that occur in distributed systems, such as data replication, when using virtual machines since the performance of various steps could drastically alter the performance of the overall system depending on the frequency of data loading, replication, backups, etc.

Virtualized environments, such as Amazon's EC2 offering, typically utilize complex storage systems that are not physically a part of the servers containing the virtualized nodes. These storage systems are often accessed through network connections. Depending on the design of the cloud environment and choices of the user, the network bandwidth available for a MapReduce "application" could be shared with the network bandwidth that is also being used for the "local disk" since the storage blocks may actually be located on a remote system. Often, major cloud providers place "local storage" disk blocks on remote systems for scalability, performance and redundancy. Even though the MapReduce/Hadoop node (this describes the situation where a user builds their own MapReduce/Hadoop node and does not utilize the Amazon Hadoop service) believes that that disk is local, the disk blocks are actually stored on a remote system and disk requests generate network traffic when data is needed. This conflicts with the design assumptions of Hadoop and MapReduce that a node's data is actually stored locally.

In the case of allowing the Hadoop file system to store its data on an EBS volume, MapReduce is actually accessing the "local" data through a network request. One metric that is often used to describe I/O performance (especially in relation to solid state disks) is IOPS, or input/output operations per second. For example, Amazon allows users to provision a standard EBS volume (EBS volumes appear as "local disks" in Amazon's EC2 product) with a target IOPS of 100 or an enhanced volume with a user specified IOPS rate up to a maximum of 2000 IOPS per EC2 instance (Amazon Web Services, Inc.). The enhanced EBS volume includes dedicated bandwidth for communication to the EBS volume that is distinct from the bandwidth that is allocated to the customer's operating system's network connection. Amazon also supports multiple EBS volumes per instance, but the underlying bandwidth dedicated to EBS volumes ranges from 500Mbps to 1000Mbps depending on the instance type. Larger instances, such as the cluster compute nodes, utilize a 10Gbps network connection that appears to be shared with network requests that are directed to EBS volumes (Amazon Web Services, Inc.).

I/O is not always 100% efficient and in some cases the virtualization layer inhibits scalability. Fortunately, ongoing improvements are occurring in virtualized I/O performance with the introduction of technology such as PCI-SIG Single Root I/O Virtualization (PCI-SIG Industry, 2010) that allows the partitioning of a single Ethernet adapter port into multiple virtual functions. It is apparent that big data systems often have several components, each with distinct hardware requirements. The interaction of the hardware components has an impact on the performance of the applications.

Business Rules and Metadata Stores

The concept of metadata in a data warehouse is not new. Metadata that is complete and allows analysts to understand the context of the raw data will likely lead to higher success rates with data mining projects (Inmon, 1996). Likewise, allowing applications to understand the data quality of data that they are utilizing will allow report creation tools to tag the appropriate reports with confidence metrics based on the data quality. The metadata can also serve to track the progress of data ingestion and data cleaning jobs. For example, data may only be available for use after it has passed through X steps in a data cleaning pipeline. The value of X can also be stored as a business rule, and applications (or a data access layer) can utilize this rule to determine when they can access data. It is conceivable that metadata may need to be shared between organizations and systems. Vetterli et al. (Vetterli, Vaduva, & Staudt, 2000) provides an overview of two industry standards for metadata models, the Open Information Model (OIM) and the Common Warehouse Metamodel (CWM). Metadata can also be utilized to support security policies (Katic, Quirchmay, Schiefer, Stolba, & Tjoa, 1998) in data warehouses. Metadata of all types forms the basis of the organization's business rules. Ideally, there should be one model to generically represent all types of business rules (Perkins, 2000). Perkins also notes that the business rule process facilitates data sharing because the institutional knowledge is accessible to any application or analyst. Kaula discusses an implementation of a business rule framework in Oracle PL/SQL (Kaula, 2009).

BUSINESS RULES AND METADATA STORES

Businesses are increasingly using data for analysis purposes and revisiting old data sources, such as click-stream data, for integration with other enterprise data sources. The promised benefit of integration is that new insights will emerge from an integrated view of data. Providing more data to decision support algorithms will allow the algorithms to select the most "relevant" attributes from a larger set of attributes for a classification task. Ideally, this will enable the algorithm to build more sophisticated models since data from other data sources may enable discovery of trends that were not discernible in a smaller dataset. For clustering algorithms, click-stream data from multiple websites would potentially enable finer clusters of users to be established. For example, if one website is a foreign policy blog, and another website is a technology blog, correlating data from both sources would ideally allow clustering algorithms to determine finer grained clusters. Perhaps those that read both blogs regularly form one cluster, while another cluster is composed of casual readers of the technology blog, and a third cluster contains casual readers of the foreign policy blog.

Data integration may appear to be a straightforward and obvious task, and indeed it is obvious from a theoretical perspective. Clearly, one major requirement is to ensure that the appropriate data can always be correctly correlated. Revisiting the example above, this integration would require that a common user identity is available across both websites, or at least that it is possible to identify the same unique user in both data sets. Assume for a moment, that the foreign policy blog was created by a political science professor, and the technology blog was created by a technology hobbyist, and both blogs were later acquired by a media company. It is unlikely that both blogs contain a common user identity platform and the media company must attempt to use email addresses, or other proxy attributes for user identity (of course, internet users can have multiple email identities, and therefore this process would likely introduce errors). This idea of correlation may appear to be an obvious and trivial requirement, but in practice, it is a major concern. Based on experiences at several organizations, it is clear that projects are often created and managed within a silo, without regard for enterprise wide integration. Years after the initial systems were designed there is an interest in correlating data across many sources. Each system typically has its own user identity management system, or perhaps even generic group accounts that are utilized by web applications or external organizations. Obviously, discerning user identity mappings between sources within this type of framework may be quite error prone. One approach that could partially alleviate this problem is if each data source provides an interface for other applications or data sources. This interface could be provided by a service or consist of a metadata repository that was easily accessible to other applications.

One trend that was observed across a variety of industries is the need for metadata (or an interface to access other data sources). Many current data warehouse designs resemble the design of databases. Essentially, they contain schemas to describe related objects. The primary assumption, which appears to be false in a dynamic business environment, is that the relationships are static and attribute sets (to represent objects) are static. For example, the assumption that a specific query Q that is executed in year X covering a set of attributes A will also be correct in year Y (where Y is after X), because the business will still have a set of attributes A that map to the same object(s) in the real world. A simple example to illustrate why the same attributes do not often represent objects at later times is below.

Simple Case Study Outlining the Need for Metadata

A university creates a student information system in 1985 and decides to utilize social security numbers to uniquely identify a student. Sometime later, perhaps in the year 2000, when identify theft becomes popular, the university realizes that social security numbers are not ideal identifiers since they may lead to identity theft if the system is compromised or reports are shown to disreputable individuals. They decide to implement a ten digit student identifier, composed of a monotonically increasing integer. Student records from 1985 through 2000 have primary keys of social security numbers. They could generate a student identifier for previous students, but these students may not have any documentation to uniquely identify their records, since they were never assigned a "student identifier" during their time at the university. They may decide to keep the social security number in another table, and allow privileged applications and users to access this data for specific purposes, such as former student records. Various systems within the university may need updated to expect a ten digit identifier, instead of a nine digit social security number for the primary student identification number. The rules to validate a social security number (some area identifiers are not issued and it is impossible to have a social security number

containing an unissued area number) are distinct from those that validate a student identifier. In this example, the social security number would be used to lookup records in other tables, such as a student grade table, in the data warehouse that used the social security number as a key from the years 1985-2000. And, the student identifier would be used to lookup records in the student grade table after the year 2000.

Metadata

The benefits of an integrated enterprise business rule (or metadata) repository are significant. The challenge is to determine how to build a general and hierarchical business rule repository that will support a wide variety of applications. The system should be hierarchical (from a logical perspective) because the business will likely have high level rules that will span a variety of lower level rules. For example, if data is missing from a given website for a specific period of time, then the first level rule may be the dataset, followed by a second level rule stating the data quality requirement of a date range, a third level rule noting the date range, and a fourth level rule with a data range. A figure of such a structure is demonstrated in Figure 1.

The advantage of a general and hierarchical business rule framework is that it should be able to support a dynamic business environment without changes to the repository structure. Several rule engines are implemented as in memory systems and can be integrated with other software packages through an API or used as SOA endpoint. Two examples are Drools (The JBoss Drools Team, 2012) and Jess (Friedman-Hill, 2008).

There are several challenges to implementing a business rule repository. For example, how does the need to query the repository along with querying the data warehouse affect the response time for the data warehouse applications? How does the repository designer ensure that the business rule repository is general enough from a structural standpoint? How does the designer preserve the

Figure 1. Diagram showing data path when benchmarking with an operating system running on native hardware compared to benchmarking with a guest operating system and a host operating system (the lines show the data path to illustrate the longer data path in a virtualized system where additional overhead can be introduced)

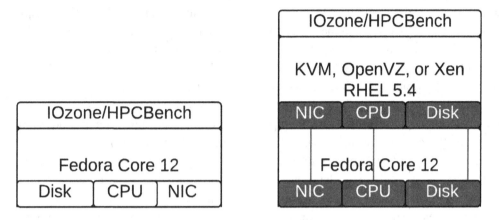

Figure 2. Shows a logical view of a rule that describes data quality

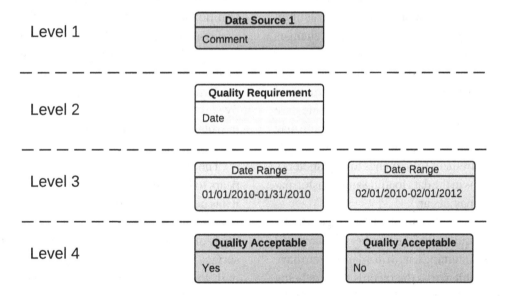

history of rule changes as applied to various sets of data (i.e. apply the 2011 data quality rules to data in 2012 to compare data quality in 2012 to the data quality that was presented in a report in 2011)? Additionally, the mapping of "business rules" to a hierarchical structure has sparse treatment in the literature. The challenge is to build a framework that is general enough to support the dynamic nature of business needs yet also yields

appropriate performance. Several rule engines exist that can be incorporated into existing software through API calls or SOA requests.

Metadata Benchmarking Techniques

Determining the appropriate rule engine for a big data project should start with an understanding of the system's architecture. For example, does a lookup in a rule engine need to occur for each row of data that is retrieved? Secondly, do the time constraints permit a SOA procedure call to a remote system? If the time constraints do not permit a lookup, the rule engine may be able to be integrated into the software, data may need to be tagged with rules (of course, tagging data and introducing additional code into the MapReduce job will increase the computation time necessary to process the data and the rules) or the rules engine may be completely separate from the big data system. In the case of the later, the rules may only be consulted as a post processing step to answer ad-hoc questions about the data source.

Big data systems introduce interesting considerations since they are often separate pieces of software that are not extensively integrated with databases and other enterprise middleware such as rule engines. Unstructured and semi-structured data often varies in its quality over time as changes are made to the software generating data, bugs are discovered and corrected, or the data loading and transformation workflow breaks down. Structured data can also change over time as attributes are added or removed, the meaning of an attribute may change (for example, a customer may change the unit of measurement from inches to centimeters), or breakdowns in the data loading and transformation system may occur.

For example, calculating the "average length" of a widget requires that the numbers contained in an attribute containing length in a data system have a consistent unit across the records that are being used to calculate "average length." As part of the data loading process, data could be converted to a standard unit of length at the time of data load or converted during computation if a rule engine could be consulted and the conversion, if any, could be applied. In this simple case, the organization may decide to correct the data at the time of data loading. However, situations arise when it is necessary to retain original data from customers in a data warehouse and transform the raw data into clean data in a data mart or when data is lost.

In situations such as these, it may be necessary to know that data is missing or not available for computation so that correct results are computed. For example, if 10% of a click behavior data feed is missing for a given day X then simply counting these records in the data mart would not allow a comparison of the actual traffic for days X & Y.

The benchmarking of a Rete algorithm based rule engine, such as Jess or Drools, should be performed with actual rules and data since the runtime of the algorithm depends on the specific rules and data used (Friedman-Hill, 2008). The performance of a rule engine based on database records and stored procedures would depend on the layout of the tables, attributes, indexing structure and the algorithm for the rule checking. In memory databases may prove useful if the goal is provide a lower response time than a database based on traditional magnetic disks or solid state disks.

Given the apparent lack of accepted big data benchmarking methodologies, rules engines add to the complexity of constructing a benchmark for modern big data systems. If possible, representative tasks and data should be used to determine if the rules engine or metadata repository can satisfy the requirements.

The use of metadata in data warehouses appears to be a novel idea in practice (theoretically, it has been recognized for some time). Additional research needs to be carried out to categorize the types of workloads that modern data warehouses service so that appropriate benchmarks can be built that consider metadata. Regrettably, since data warehouses contain organizations' sensitive data, organizations are often reluctant to release any information about the data warehouse or its architecture. Perhaps a more important problem is that design standards for data warehouse metadata don't appear to be adopted in practice.

Benchmarking

Big data systems are unique for several reasons. First, they typically transfer a large volume of data in large chunks and do so for an extended period of time (i.e. a large MapReduce job processing several TB of data). Secondly, production big data systems, such as a MapReduce cluster, are typically purpose built and not shared with general purpose computing workloads. I/O performance becomes critically important when building big data systems. To maximize the I/O throughput, the motherboard and chipset should support adequate dedicated PCI-Express bandwidth for hardware peripherals such as network and storage devices. The chipset should also support adequate bandwidth between the PCI-Express bus and the CPU and memory. Some motherboard manufacturers make this information available in their manuals. When performing benchmarks of storage or network devices, the benchmark parameters should be selected carefully. Benchmarks of network devices should include a range of packet sizes around the packet size that is typically used in the target application workload. This will ensure that the desired throughput and latency is achievable at the packet size that is used in the target workload. Benchmarks of storage systems should include read and write patterns that closely mirror the workload of the target application. The goal of these benchmarks is to establish an upper bound on the performance of the hardware under ideal conditions. As an added benefit, benchmarks of hardware devices may expose stability issues with drivers or incompatibilities with the motherboard or other hardware components.

After this phase is complete, an application level benchmark should be completed to ensure that the operating system, CPU, and memory can effectively achieve the desired performance while performing extensive I/O activity. Various benchmarks are available for specific big data applications such as MapReduce. If virtualized compute nodes are utilized, it would be appropriate to perform hardware micro-benchmarks and application benchmarks at the native operating system level and then repeat this process in the virtualized environment. The benchmarks at the native operating system level establish an upper bound on performance. The benchmarks in the virtualized environment will allow the designer to determine the level of overhead that is present as a result of the virtualized environment.

Storage systems often need to be highly stable under prolonged periods of load in big data systems. Therefore, the selection of a stable yet high performance storage controller is an important consideration if the system will rely on local storage. Additionally, network controllers are likely to be utilized extensively for applications such as a Hadoop file system. If the storage for the big data application is accessed over a network, it is advisable to ensure that if only one network controller is used, it can support the bandwidth necessary to read data from a network file system, and perform the network communication that is necessary for the big data application. Some designers may decide to create a network for network based storage and another network for cluster communication and devote a team of network ports or even a controller to each network. If the big data application is running in a virtualized environment, PCI-Passthrough (Jones, 2009) and PCI-SIG SR-IOV (PCI-SIG Industry, 2010) enables the allocation of devices or virtualized devices (at the hardware level), respectively, to virtual machines.

Benchmarking Case Study

A car manufacture wants to predict the failure of products in the field using data from component vendors, repair shops, and internal manufacturing databases. The internal databases allow the manufacturer to determine which components were used to create each product. The data warehouse will need to continuously load data from these sources. The benchmarking strategy should begin with an estimation of the volume of data that needs loaded in a given time frame and the estimated storage volume of the data warehouse. Then, the system designer should consider whether a cloud environment (private or public) or a traditional operating system installed in a local data center is appropriate. Considerations such as cost, fault-tolerance, and network bandwidth and network reliability will influence the decision of whether to utilize an existing local data center or utilize a public or private cloud.

Cloud implementations utilize virtualization to achieve cost efficiency (by placing numerous virtual machines on one physical server or enabling virtual machines to be quickly provisioned on a physical server) but the I/O efficiency of virtual environments is lower than an application executing on an operating system executing directly on the hardware. If a cloud implementation is utilized, then the I/O virtualization overhead should be evaluated, especially for storage and networking devices, and the data warehouse product should be evaluated to ensure that it is certified by the vendor for use in a virtualized environment. Then, testing of the data warehouse application can be conducted. These tests should determine if the data warehouse can support the desired level of data loading performance and query performance (based on estimated use). If multiple nodes are required to achieve the target level of performance, then multiple nodes should be utilized in the test. If multiple nodes are utilized in a virtual environment, networking benchmarks between virtual nodes will give an approximation of the best-case scalability that can be achieved across multiple nodes. Basic fault-tolerance of the application can be tested by disconnecting the node from the network, halting the node, or removing disks from the storage system to ensure that the application can still function under a variety of hardware failure conditions. More detailed or advanced fault-tolerance testing could be carried out, but fault-tolerance testing in a cloud computing environment is not significantly theoretically distinct from fault-tolerance testing of other types of distributed systems. For example, Tannenbaum and Van Steen's book devotes a chapter to a comprehensive discussion of fault-tolerance in distributed systems (Tannenbaum & Van Steen, 2007).

FUTURE RESEARCH DIRECTIONS

The benchmarking of big data systems appears to be primarily focused on specific classes of systems, such as MapReduce clusters, databases, or distributed storage. While it is certainly important to understand the baseline performance of each component in a system, it is also important to understand how a system will behave in production when it is built from various components. An important opportunity for increased focus may be the classification of big data workloads to determine if there are common types of workloads. For example, are most batch analysis workloads similar irrespective of whether MapReduce or another tool is used? Do most reporting applications place similar demands on the data sources and metadata stores? What is the typical response time expected from a batch analysis system? What type of demands do big data applications, such as ecommerce sites, place on components? Answering these types of questions would allow a characterization of a "big data" workload in a modern organization and allow tool builders to determine which specific systems produce the optimal mix of performance and cost for a given workload. Is it possible to use one analysis tool, such as MapReduce, to support the workload, or must the big data system be composed of various components? While basic concepts suggests that algorithm X should be implemented in system Y, or system A can only scale to B terabytes, design of big data systems in the real world appears to be guided by heuristics rather than more formal scientific processes.

CONCLUSION

Big data systems can include data collection systems, data cleaning, data processing, data analysis, and applications for reporting. Big data systems typically process large amounts of data in a distributed fashion and may rely on accessing metadata to produce accurate results. Big data systems are composed of many components and each component often requires multiple nodes and extensive storage. Therefore, these types of systems are relatively costly to design and maintain, whether they are capital purchases or cloud computing based. The choice of utilizing applications in a native operating system environment or in a cloud computing environment will likely depend on the infrastructure capabilities of the organization, the respective costs, and the requirements of the project. Cloud computing is typically implemented with virtual machine technologies and the choice of a hypervisor has an impact on the performance of the system, especially in regard to I/O. Since big data systems often rely on I/O capacity, the performance of I/O subsystems is important. The chapter presents several issues that emerge when attempting to use metadata stores and cloud computing to support "big data" projects.

REFERENCES

Amazon Web Services, Inc. (n.d.). *Amazon EC2 instance types*. Retrieved January 19, 2013, from http://aws.amazon.com/ec2/instance-types/

Bhatia, N. (2009). *Performance evaluation of AMD RVI hardware assist*. VMWare, Inc.

Friedman-Hill, E. J. (2008, November 5). *Jess, the rule engine for the java platform - The rete algorithm*. Retrieved January 26, 2013, from http://www.jessrules.com/jess/docs/71/rete.html

Industry, P. C. I.-S. I. G. (2010, January). *Single root I/O virtualization and sharing 1.1 specification*. Retrieved November 2010, from http://www.pcisig.com/specifications/iov/single_root/

Inmon, W. H. (1996). The data warehouse and data mining. *Communications of the ACM*, 49–50. doi:10.1145/240455.240470.

Jones, T. (2009, October). *Linux virtualization and PCI passthrough*. Retrieved May 2012, from http://www.ibm.com/developerworks/linux/library/l-pci-passthrough/

Katic, N., Quirchmay, G., Schiefer, J., Stolba, M., & Tjoa, A. (1998). A prototype model for data warehouse security based on metadata. In *Proceedings of the Ninth International Workshop on Database and Expert Systems Applications,* (pp. 300-308). IEEE.

Kaula, R. (2009). Business rules for data warehouse. *International Journal of Information and Communication Engineering*, 359-367.

Nagarajan, A. B., Mueller, F., Engelmann, C., & Scott, S. L. (2007). Proactive fault tolerance for HPC with xen virtualization. In *Proceedings of the 21st Annual International Conference on Supercomputing* (pp. 23-32). Seattle, WA: ACM.

Perkins, A. (2000). Business rules=meta-data. In *Proceedings of the 34th International Conference on Technology of Object-Oriented Languages and Systems,* (pp. 285-294). IEEE.

Regola, N., & Ducom, J.-C. (2010). Recommendations for virtualization technologies in high performance computing. In *Proceedings of the IEEE International Conference on Cloud Computing Technology and Science* (pp. 409-416). Indianapolis, IN: IEEE.

Tannenbaum, A., & Van Steen, M. (2007). Fault tolerance. In A. Tannenbaum, & M. Van Steen (Eds.), *Distributed systems: Principles and paradigms* (pp. 321–375). Upper Saddle River, NJ: Pearson Education.

Vetterli, T., Vaduva, A., & Staudt, M. (2000). Metadata standards for data warehousing: open information model vs. common warehouse metadata. *SIGMOD Record*, 68–75. doi:10.1145/362084.362138.

ADDITIONAL READING

Bennett, C., Grossman, R. L., Locke, D., Seidman, J., & Vejcik, S. (2010). Malstone: towards a benchmark for analytics on large data clouds. In *Proceedings of the 16th ACM SIGKDD International Conference on Knowledge Discovery and Data Mining* (pp. 145-152). New York: ACM.

Chen, Y. (2012). We don't know enough to make a big data benchmark suite an academia-industry view. In *Proceedings of the Second Workshop on Big Data Benchmarking*. Pune, India: IEEE.

Chu, C.-T., Kim, S. K., Lin, Y.-A., Yu, Y., Bradski, G., & Ng, A. Y. et al. (2007). In B. Scholkopf, J. Platt, & T. Hoffman (Eds.), *Map-reduce for machine learning on multicore* (pp. 281–288). Advances in Neural Information Processing Systems Cambridge, MA: MIT Press.

Dean, J., & Ghemawat, S. (2004). Mapreduce: Simplified data processing on large clusters. In *Proceedings of the 6th Conference on Symposium on Opearting Systems Design & Implementation*. USENIX Association.

Figueiredo, R., Dinda, P. A., & Fortes, J. (2003). A case for grid computing on virtual machines. In *Proceedings of the 3rd International Conference on Distributed Computing Systems*. Washington, DC: IEEE Computer Society.

Grossman, R., & Gul, Y. (2008). Data mining using high performance data clouds: Experimental studies using sector and sphere. In *Proceedings of the 14th ACM SIGKDD International Conference on Knowledge Discovery and Data Mining,* (pp. 920-927). New York, NY: ACM.

Jian, Z., Xiaoyong, L., & Haibing, G. (2008). The optimization of Xen network virtualization. In *Proceedings of the 2008 International Conference on Computer Science and Software Engineering* (pp. 431-436). Washington, DC: IEEE Computer Society.

Juve, G., Deelman, E., Vahi, K., Mehta, G., Berriman, B., Berman, B., et al. (2009). Scientific workflow applications on Amazon EC2. In *Proceedings of the 2009 5th IEEE International Conference on E-Science Workshops* (pp. 59-66). IEEE.

Kontagora, M., & Gonzalez-Velez, H. (2010). Benchmarking a mapreduce environment on a full virtualisation platform. In *Proceedings of the 2010 International Conference on Complex, Intelligent and Software Intensive Systems* (pp. 433-438). Washington, DC: IEEE Computer Society.

Lee, S.-W., Moon, B., & Park, C. (2009). Advances in flash memory SSD technology for enterprise database applications. In *Proceedings of the 35th SIG-MOD International Conference on Management of Data* (pp. 863-870). New York: ACM.

Lee, S.-W., Moon, B., Park, C., Kim, J.-M., & Kim, S.-W. (2008). A case for flash memory ssd in enterprise database applications. In *Proceedings of the 2008 ACM SIGMOD International Conference on Management of Data* (pp. 1075-1086). New York: ACM.

Liu, J., Huang, W., Abali, B., & Panda, D. K. (2006). High performance VMM-bypass I/O in virtual machines. In *Proceedings of the Annual Conference on USENIX '06 Annual Technical Conference*. Berkeley, CA: USENIX Association.

Menon, A., Cox, A. L., & Zwaenepoel, W. (2006). Optimizing network virtualization in xen. In *Proceedings of the USENIX Annual Technical Conference* (pp. 15-28). USENIX.

Menon, A., Santos, J., Turner, Y., Janakiraman, G., & Zwaenepoel, W. (2005). Diagnosing performance overheads in the Xen virtual machine environment. In *Proceedings of the International Conference on Virtual Execution Environment*. IEEE. Armbrust, M., Fox, A., Griffith, R., Joseph, A. D., Katz, R., et al. (2010). A view of cloud computing. *Communications of ACM*, 50--58. Bailey, D., Harris, T., Saphir, W., Van Der Wijngaart, R., Woo, A., & Yarrow, M. (1995). *NAS parallel benchmarks 2.0*. NASA Ames Research Center.

Nagle, D., Serenyi, D., & Matthews, A. (2004). The panasas activescale storage cluster: Delivering scalable high bandwidth storage. In *Proceedings of the 2004 ACM/IEEE Conference on Supercomputing* (pp. 53). Washington, DC: IEEE Computer Society.

Nussbaum, L., Anhalt, F., Mornard, O., & Gelas, J.-P. (2009). Linux-based virtualization for HPC clusters. In *Proceedings of the Linux Symposium* (pp. 221-234). Linux.

Padala, P., Zhu, X., Wang, Z., Singhal, S., & Shin, K. G. (2007). *Performance evaluation of virtualization technologies for server consolidation*. HP Labs.

Pavlo, A., Paulson, E., Rasin, A., Abadi, D. J., DeWitt, D. J., Madden, S., et al. (2009). A comparison of approaches to large-scale data analysis. In *Proceedings of the 35th SIGMOD International Conference on Management of Data*, (pp. 165-178). New York: ACM.

Ranger, C., Raghuraman, R., Penmetsa, A., Bradski, G., & Kozyrakis, C. (2007). Evaluating mapreduce for multi-core and multiprocessor systems. In *Proceedings of the 13th International Symposium on High-Performance Computer Architecture* (pp. 13-24). IEEE Computer Society.

Wang, G., & Ng, T. (2010). The impact of virtualization on network performance of Amazon EC2 data center. In *Proceedings of the 2010 IEEE INFOCOM* (pp. 1-9). IEEE.

Wu, J., Ping, L., Ge, X., Wang, Y., & Fu, J. (2010). Cloud storage as the infrastructure of cloud computing. In *Proceedings of the 2010 International Conference on Intelligent Computing and Cognitive Informatics (ICICCI)* (pp. 380-383). IEEE.

Youseff, L., Wolski, R., Gorda, B., & Krintz, C. (2006). Evaluating the performance impact of Xen on MPI and process execution in HPC systems. In *Virtualization Technology in Distributed Computing*. Washington: IEEE Computer Society.

Zaharia, M., Konwinski, A., Joseph, A. D., Katz, R., & Stoica, I. (2008). Improving mapreduce performance in heterogeneous environments. In *Proceedings of the 8th USENIX Conference on Operating Systems Design and Implementation*, (pp. 29-42). Berkeley, CA: USENIX Association.

KEY TERMS AND DEFINITIONS

Benchmarking: An experimental method to determine the performance of a system for a range of operations (e.g. disk read, disk write, disk random read, and disk random write) or an application workflow.

Cloud Computing: A generic term utilized to describe leased computer resources including storage, networking, backup, application runtimes, and clusters.

Data Warehouse: A generic description of an enterprise data store that is utilized to store data that is utilized to operate a business.

MapReduce: A paradigm of data processing or the specific paper that introduced the implementation.

Microbenchmark: An experimental method to determine the performance of a specific type of hardware device or a specific operation (e.g. disk read).

Overhead: loss in efficiency as a result of an intermediate stage that is not present in the "maximally efficient" design.

Virtual Machine: A generic name to denote support for running guest operating systems, irrespective of the type of implementation.

Chapter 16
Excess Entropy in Computer Systems

Charles Loboz
Microsoft Corporation, USA

ABSTRACT

Modern data centers house tens of thousands of servers in complex layouts. That requires sophisticated reporting – turning available terabytes of data into information. The classical approach was introduced decades ago to handle a small number of lightly connected computers. Today, we also need to identify problematic groups of servers, strange patterns in load, and changes in composition with minimal human involvement. The authors show how, as a single concept, entropy can describe multiple aspects of system use. Entropy is well grounded in physics, used in economics, and the authors extend it to large computer systems.

INTRODUCTION

Complexity and scale of computer systems keeps growing. A modern server has over 2000 performance counters which are relevant to the description of its state and usage – that applies to both Windows and UNIX servers. For one server we can select a smaller subset of counters requiring monitoring, but if we have several servers running different applications the size of the monitoring set grows quickly. Modern data centers house tens of thousands of servers in complex layouts.

Global provision of services requires tens of datacenters - and many such data centers are required for global provisioning of services. That generates a large volume of data – but, more importantly, this data is both complex and not easily tractable by traditional methods.

The costs of the infrastructure so large run into hundreds of millions of dollars per data center and efficient use of that infrastructure requires sophisticated reporting management. That, in turn, requires turning available (terabytes) of data describing system use into information.

DOI: 10.4018/978-1-4666-4699-5.ch016

Computer system performance analysis and capacity planning started decades ago with a single mainframe. Then we have moved to multiple mainframes and groups of servers. That was followed by multiple virtual machines running on a single server. The current stage – cloud computing - is, in effect, an operating system controlling execution of processing on clusters of servers and cluster groups.

We need to consider both traditional system descriptors as well as the new ones arising from the handing server groups and virtualization. Examples of the need for new descriptors include effects of competition for disk bandwidth between multiple virtual machines running on the same server and sharing physical disks - or similar competition for network rack switches between virtual machines deployed to the same rack of servers.

Performance analysts and capacity planners have to deal with information explosion in two different dimensions. The first one is related to the scale of modern web services, when datacenters containing tens of thousands of servers are providing thousands of services – thus we have data from a single server multiplied. The second dimension is growing layering and complexity of the underlying data.

Most complexity in this dimension is coming from the number of servers. The second dimension is the virtualization and cloud artifacts – consideration of deployment strategy for virtual machines, consideration of migration options for virtual machines to other servers or clusters and management of whole clusters of servers. To manage such information explosion we need descriptors of overall system usage that are on higher conceptual level than direct performance counters, like processor utilization, number of disk operations, memory bytes used, packets transferred through a network and other performance counters of this type.

Classical methods of describing and analyzing the use of computer systems were introduced decades ago (Lazowska, 1984), (Jain, 1991) and

designed to handle a small number of lightly connected computers. Introduction of new methods is forced by the need to handle problems arising from the growing size and complexity of new systems – operations in such system require higher-level descriptors.

An example of such a higher-level descriptor is Performance Impact Factor (PIF) introduced in (Loboz, 2009). For servers the average processor utilization is frequently misleading, because a low daily average can hide occasional spikes during the day – and such spikes may create reduced response time with disastrous consequences to service level agreements. PIF was designed to summarize in one number existence of such spikes. That replaces the need for looking at daily load charts – clearly impractical even with thousands of servers. In effect PIF transforms the data from performance counter space to performance impact space. That simplifies analysis of a large number of servers, because PIF is a one-number summary and captures the information not easily discernible from the original counters. PIF does not replace the traditional utilization description – it augments it and aggregates it so handling of a very large number of servers becomes practical.

Another example of a scalable aggregating descriptor is Capacity Utilization Factor introduced in (Loboz, 2010). It allows comparison of usage levels between servers with different hardware and between groups of such servers.

Describing usage of a system consisting of tens of thousands of computers with classical descriptors, like utilization coefficients or response times, is still necessary. However, with at the current scale and complexity we need to do much more. We must identify problematic groups of servers, strange patterns in load, discover changes in composition of customers, classify historical use - and do that with minimal human involvement. That requires new descriptors and approaches.

This paper outlines an approach to describe many aspects of system use with one concept: entropy. The concept is well grounded in science (statistical physics) and also used in economics (distribution of wealth). Here we show how to describe aspects of use of large and small computer systems - aspects as varied as composition of customers, imbalance in disk usage, spikes in load, geographical differentiation in growth etc. Use of a single underlying concept, instead of a multitude of descriptors based on different approaches, reduces both learning and application overhead. In addition entropy-based descriptors have a vital advantage over many home-grown metrics – most complex systems are non-trivially hierarchical and entropy-based descriptors can describe systems composed of other systems. We can compose a descriptor for the total system from the constituent components – or decompose it.

We start with an example application of the concept of entropy to a simple system. Then we describe the theoretical grounding for entropy-based descriptor and show the application of the concept to various aspects of system use for larger systems.

BACKGROUND: ENTROPY, IMBALANCE AND CONCENTRATION

A single server with four disks is running a database application. If one disk is used more than others, the response time of that disk – and the whole application - will suffer. Database administrators spend considerable time balancing disk usage.

Diagnosing imbalance is intuitive if we have two disks – but it gets difficult if we have more disks. Consider three sets of disks with utilizations A=(0.5,0.1,0.7,0.3), B=(0.2,0.8,0.4,0.6), and C=(0.2,0.8,0.4,0.6,0.2,0.7). Is the imbalance of set A larger than set B? And how can we compare imbalance between sets A (with four disks) and C (with six disks)?

Imbalance is difficult to quantify – and quantification is necessary for comparison. Intuitive approach is of little use here. Analyzing servers by looking at utilization charts does not scale well

even for 100 servers, much less for 1000 servers. The entropy-based measure quantifies imbalance for sets A, B, and C being, respectively, 0.126, 0.077, and 0.070. Thus the quantitative descriptor allows (1) spotting relatively small differences in imbalance – almost invisible by chart inspection and (2) works for data sets with different cardinality.

Next we consider the theoretical background, properties and meanings of the measure of imbalance.

Entropy, Imbalance and Concentration of Resource Use

There is not one universal measure of imbalance. Attempts to quantify imbalance did occur in parallel in (at least) two different areas - physics and economics. In physics imbalance considerations originated in thermodynamics under the name of disorder and were measured by entropy – the concept introduced by Clausius in 19th century (Boltzmann 2011). In particular entropy describes how the system state is positioned among the all possible system states. That approach was later extended with use of entropy in information theory (Shannon 1948) (and see (Bais 2007) for an overview). In economics the analysis of income inequality and distribution of wealth in the society was, for decades, a large field of research. Many types of substantially different inequality measures were considered (see (Cowell, 1995) for an overview). The most popular inequality measure, the Gini Index (Gastwirth, 1972), is considered intuitive and still used in many papers in economics and elsewhere. Unfortunately its mathematical properties are weak, which makes it a bad candidate for general application.

Both streams of imbalance quantification came together with the introduction of the Theil index to measure economic inequality (Theil, 1967) (Sen, 1997). The Theil index describes the excess entropy in a system. For a data set x_i, $i=1..n$ the Theil index is given by:

$$T_{index} = \frac{1}{n} \sum_{i=1}^{n} \frac{x_i}{x_{avg}} * \ln(\frac{x_i}{x_{avg}})$$

where n is the number of elements in the data set and x_{avg} is the average value of all elements in the data set. Examining closer the formula above, we can derive several properties:

The ratio x_i / x_{avg} describes how much element i is above or below the average for the whole set. Thus excess entropy involves only the ratio of each element against the average of the sets, not the absolute values of the elements.

- Excess entropy is dimensionless – thus allows to compare imbalance between sets of substantially different quantities, for example when one set contains disk utilizations and another disk response times.
- The minimum value of excess entropy is zero - when all elements of the data set are identical. The maximum value is *log(n)* - when all elements but one are zero; the maximum depends on the set size and it can be normalized - allowing to compare imbalance between sets of different cardinality
- Excess entropy can be viewed as a description of how concentrated is the use of some resource – large values mean fewer users use most of the resource, small values mean more equal sharing (in this context imbalance is simply another word for concentration).
- Excess entropy does not assume any specific distribution of underlying values, so it bypasses the important problem of resource usage distributions being frequently asymmetric and sometimes fat-tailed (having infinite standard deviations) (Loboz, 2011, Loboz, 2012).
- Excess entropy does not involve computation of square of differences – unlike standard deviation; excess entropy attenu-

ates differences from the mean as it uses logarithm; standard deviation amplifies difference from the mean as it is squaring them – thus numerical properties of excess entropy are different than that of standard deviation; in particular excess entropy is much less sensitive to the large deviations from the mean

From the point of view of statistical physics the Theil index is the same as *excess entropy* (EE) – entropy in the system that is still available for modification. Excess entropy is always non-negative and larger values denote more concentration of the system mass in smaller number of its elements. (Entropy can be computed from excess entropy using $e = 1 - e^{-EE}$).

The terms *Theil index, excess entropy, imbalance coefficient, level of concentration* denote the same underlying concept: *excess entropy* and will be used interchangeably henceforth. We will frequently use the normalized version of excess entropy (*nEE*), as it is set-cardinality independent.

Example Application

We have three disk sets with utilizations A=(0.5,0.1,0.7,0.3), B=(0.2,0.8,0.4,0.6), and C=(0.2,0.8,0.2,0.4,0.6,0.2,0.7) over some relevant time period. Applying the EE formula to disk set A we get the normalized imbalance 1/4 * (0.279 + -0.347 + 0.979 + -0.216)/log(4) = 0.126

The components of the sum allow to quantify the input of each disk to the total imbalance of the whole set. This is different from the mean value – it gives the insight into the sizes of factors contributing to the imbalance. We see that *disk3* contributes the most: 0.979 while *disk1* contributes only 0.07.

An aside. The naive approach to quantity imbalance would be to use some measure only tangentially related to imbalance, for example standard deviation of utilizations. That creates a host of mathematical problems for further usage.

Among others, it does not differentiate well - for both sets A,B of utilizations the standard deviation is identical at 0.258 - yet the imbalance coefficients are quite different. So, at the minimum, excess entropy describes a different aspect of the system than standard deviation.

In the examples above we have used disk utilization to illustrate computations of imbalance - but we can use other bases, too. Selection of the base for imbalance computation depends on our goal. In some cases other (than utilization) disk characteristics may be more relevant to the overall system performance - the number of input/output operations, the number of bytes transferred, operation time, queuing time or disk response time. The goal may be to assure balance of, say, queuing times or normalized (for transaction type or size) response times rather than utilizations.

The same formula can be used for all such calculations but the resulting imbalance will differ when different bases are used – both in numerical value and in the meaning of the imbalance. For example using disk response times is likely to give larger imbalance values than when using disk utilizations – as response times grow disproportionately when utilization is high (and the range of utilizations vary from 0 to 1, while the range of response times varies from 1ms to seconds – much wider range).

The equivalent interpretation of the excess entropy is that of *the concentration of use*. High values mean that most of mass of the distribution is concentrated in the small number of elements. Low values mean that the distribution is spread more evenly. At the extremes, if only one disk has non-zero utilization, the excess entropy would have been equal to 1. If all disks have the same utilization the excess entropy is zero. The underlying mathematical apparatus is to keep the consistency in all intermediate situations.

Some Application Aspects of Excess Entropy

Excess entropy spots the imbalance even at low levels of load - thus giving an early warning signal that, if the load grows, the imbalance can impact performance. For example with two disks at utilization levels 0.05 and 0.4 the overall system performance is unlikely to be affected and such server may easily be overlooked during analysis. Were the load on this server to grow by a factor of two, the utilization levels may grow to 0.1 and 0.8 - and that level of utilization is likely to impact the performance of the second disk. Thus the imbalance coefficient works in a load-level-independent fashion and can be used as an early warning system.

That load-independence of excess entropy has its darker side. The practical use of imbalance coefficient must take into account the noise level in the data. For example with four disks with utilizations $(0.001, 0.001, 0.001, 0.009)$ we have high EE value of 0.4 - but at these load level the utilization will not affect performance - so there is little point in tuning effectively unused disks. At the same time, if the utilizations were like $(0.001, 0.001, 0.001, 0.1)$ – that is one disk was used in a non-trivial way – we could have had potential imbalance developing.

APPLICATION 1: IMBALANCE IN RESOURCE USE BY WINDOWS AZURE STORAGE ACCOUNTS

Excess entropy is a general concept and can be applied in multiple situations and contexts. In cloud computing we have hundreds and thousands of servers at various grouping levels: cluster, data center, geographical region. We also have tens of thousands of customer accounts with significantly different resource use profile profiles and dynamics using this server base. All that is resulting in a complex overall system. That complexity requires some constructive organizing views – traditional ones like utilization and response time are still valid but more is needed.

In this section we consider additional aspects and applications of excess entropy when applied in analysis of resource usage in Windows Azure storage clusters.

A storage cluster is a collection of servers providing storage function to Windows Azure customers. For the purpose of this chapter the internal architecture of a cluster is not important – we consider the cluster usage from the point of view of customers storing and retrieving data and a system administrator looking for unusual situation in cluster use. The resource use in Windows Azure is considered here as daily average use by a customer account – as reported by billing data (thus having high reliability and accuracy). We consider here also the number of 'active accounts' – not all accounts registered with Windows Azure but accounts which used some resource on given day.

We consider evolution of imbalance in time and how it differs for different resources. We also analyze what imbalance can tell us about underlying distributions and consequences of that. Finally we will consider if and how imbalance depends on the time scale at which the underlying data were collected.

Evolution of Excess Entropy in Time

For each day the important cluster descriptors are (1) the network transfer; (2) the number of active accounts; (3) excess entropy. We consider the network transfer (*NetTransfer*) - the amount used by each account on given day. We compute the excess entropy of the number of bytes transferred by each account. The most natural interpretation of excess entropy in this case is the concentration

of network use in few accounts. We consider also the number of storage transactions used by the accounts.

In the previous section we have considered excess entropy for a system at one point in time. Here we consider how excess entropy evolves with time – and how it is related to traditional system usage descriptors like resource use and number of accounts. The results are summarized in Figure 1, with the load descriptors normalized to (0..1) range. Figure 1 shows, for both resource types, the evolution in time for three descriptors. The values for load and number of accounts are normalized to fall between 0 and 1.

For *NetTransfer* resource we see steadily growing number of accounts (dashed line) and very jumpy growth of network transfers. We also have excess entropy around 0.5 with occasional spikes up to 0.7. About day 140 we have sudden growth in load coinciding with sudden growth in excess entropy – while the number of active accounts remains unchanged. The excess entropy growth means that growth in network use was caused by a small number of accounts. Were the network use growth caused by broadly based growth the excess entropy would fall down – or, at least, stay even. This application is important for forecasting – sudden growth caused by a small number of accounts is less likely to last than a broadly based growth. Another observation is that growths and drops in *NetTransfer* are somewhat correlated with growths and drops in excess entropy – suggesting that most variability in load comes from a small number of accounts.

The analysis above illustrates how combination of traditional descriptors (system load, number of customers) with excess entropy enables better understanding of system dynamics.

The right panel in Figure 2. shows the number of transactions in the same cluster, over much longer time span. The load in clusterA (black dashed line) is initially close to zero, then regularly grows to the maximum value over 300 days

Figure 1. Disk utilization for three disk sets - it is difficult to decide by visual inspection which set is the most imbalanced; the estimate of imbalance is especially difficult when disk sets have different number of disks

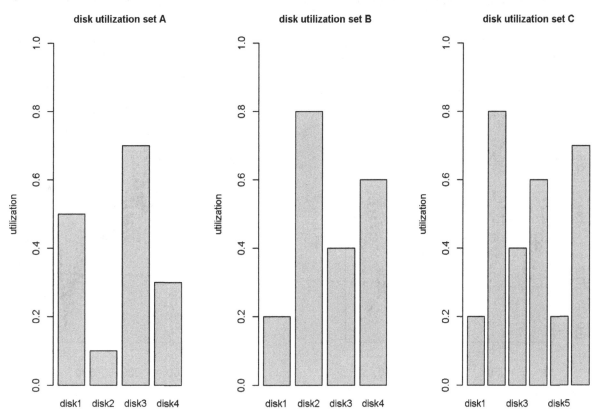

and after that falls off to 0.6 of the maximum. The number of accounts grows co-linearly with the load, but after 280 then number of accounts drops sharply without corresponding fall in load. Concentration evolves differently. Initially it is extremely high, because the number of accounts was very small so any one of them could dominate processing on any given day. With the number of accounts growing excess entropy settles down to around 0.5 – though that evolution took about 150 days. After 300 days we have sudden, large and irregular drop in load combined with gradual reduction in the number of accounts. Neither affects the imbalance, suggesting the changes are broadly based, affect similarly smaller and larger accounts. Were the excess entropy dropping we

would have had been losing larger accounts, were the excess entropy growing we would have been losing smaller accounts.

This shows how excess entropy can be used to gain additional insight into dynamics of large systems. A cluster houses thousands of accounts – analysis of each sudden jump in load is work-intensive. Large data centers contain multiple clusters each – and worldwide service provision requires multiple data centers. That amounts to hundreds or thousands of clusters - and plenty of management alerts on spikes. Combining excess entropy with existing traditional system descriptors allow for reduction of the number of false alerts – as well as better overall understanding of load dynamics.

Figure 2. Evolution of load for Network Transfer (left) and Storage Transactions (right); load (dotted), number of accounts (dashed), and excess entropy (solid gray)

clusterA descriptors NetTransfer

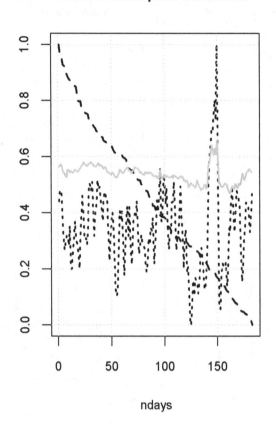

ndays

clusterA descriptors Tx

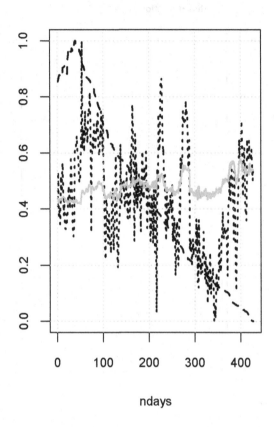

ndays

THE INTERPRETATION OF NORMALIZED EXCESS ENTROPY VALUES

So far we have compared excess entropy of resource usage for various characteristics of computer usage. The normalized excess entropy (nEE) values in our sample ranged from 0.4 to 1. What sort of information about the underlying data we can extract from the nEE value? In more general terms: what do values of excess entropy tell us about the distribution of the underlying data?

From the definition of nEE we know that, if – on given day - each account was using the same amount of resources, the nEE would be 0. Also, if only one account would be using all the resources the nEE would be 1. So nEE value is related to the distribution of resource use between the accounts at given time.

What sort of nEE values we could get for various distributions? This is of some interest, as there is enough anecdotal and published evidence that many distributions in computer systems are not normal (Gaussian) – they are asymmetric and many of them have so-called heavy-tails (Loboz, 2012) (see also the bibliography in there for an overview, especially (Clauset 2009) and (Newman 2006)).

If the underlying data has normal distribution we can expect that only one in 370 of all values will occur on the tail of the distribution, outside of the range of three standard deviations – and that goes down quickly to one in 16,000 for four standard deviations. For heavy tailed distributions such extreme values occur much more frequently – we can expect extreme values with reasonable probability. Such characteristic of the underlying distribution has consequences to capacity planning and performance evaluation – in fact it challenges most of our intuitions – average values do not describe the data well and standard deviations are meaningless. We would like to know if nEE can tell us something about the underlying distribution.

What sort of nEE values can we expect for some 'normal' (frequently used) distributions?

We assume that the underlying distribution of some resource usage between the accounts is uniform. In general the nEE will depend on the number of accounts. For 10 accounts nEE will be higher than for 100 accounts, with limit 0 for the infinite number of accounts. Simulations show that for number of accounts varying from 1000 to 10,000 with uniform distribution of resource usage the nEE ranges from 0.03 to 0.02. Similar simulations for normal distribution (with negative values removed) show that, for number of accounts varying from 1000 to 10,000, the nEE ranges from 0.05 to 0.03. Thus the ranges of nEE values for uniform and normal distributions are about order of magnitude smaller than the minimum nEE values we have observed in our data.

We consider now the log-normal distribution [a highly skewed distribution of v with $log(v)$ having normal distribution). The log-normal distribution is much closer approximation of the distributions of computer usage data than normal, exponential or uniform (but frequently the asymmetry of real data is higher than the asymmetry of log-normal distribution). The nEE value computed for such distribution depends on two main parameters: (1) the ratio of the standard deviation of v to the mean value of v in the sample (called henceforth coefficient of variation; $sd(v)/avg(v)$); and (2) the

number of data points in the sample. We want to assess what nEE tells us about the coefficient of variation in a sample with log-normal distribution.

As for other distributions, the nEE will depend on the number of elements in the sample. We simulate log-normal distributions with 100, 1000, and 10,000 elements. For each sample size the generation is repeated few thousand times to obtain the dependency between the nEE and the coefficient of variation.

Figure 3 shows that, for a sample size 1000 (dashed line), to obtain nEE value of 0.4 the standard deviation of the sample must be about *nine times greater than the average* – and all nEE values in our samples were at least that high. For nEE of 0.6 – fairly frequent value in our sample – the standard deviation of the data distribution must be twenty time greater than the average.

Even for a small sample size of 100 to obtain nEE=0.4 the standard deviation must be four times higher than average and for nEE=0.6 that goes up to eight times.

Thus the nEE found in cluster usage data is very high and, if the underlying distribution is log-normal, then its parameters must be extreme. That suggest that distributions in our data have heavier tails than the log-normal distribution.

Above comparison, through nEE measured and nEE obtained from a generated log-normal distribution, is yet another confirmation and illustration of heavy tails of underlying distributions of resource usage.

The tails are so heavy that a small percentage of accounts (less than 5%) are responsible for over 95% of resource usage.

These results also suggest that nEE can be (cautiously) used as a proxy for heavy tails of underlying distributions and for quantifying the degree of heavy tails. That is convenient as it saves us the use of special tests for power-law

Figure 3. Normalized excess entropy and the ratio standard deviation to average for log-normal distributions with sample sizes 100 (dotted), 1000 (dashed) and 10,000 (solid). Even for a small sample size of 100 the standard deviation has to be four times larger than average with nEE > 0.4

lognormal distribution and (normalized) excess entropy

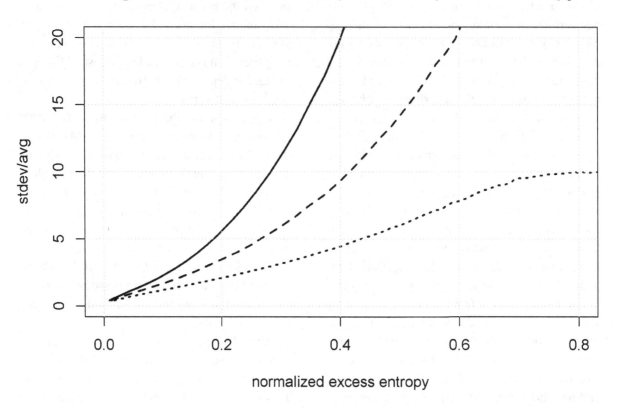

normalized excess entropy

distributions. Thus we can apply excess entropy to describe the level of 'heavy-tailness' in resource usage distribution – reducing the need for descriptors based on other concepts.

THE MEANING AND RAMIFICATIONS OF HIGH EXCESS ENTROPY VALUES

The high excess entropy values are frequently found in computer systems. This is a symptom of strongly non-normal distributions in computer system resource usage and has consequences for many traditional approaches and descriptors. Our earlier work (Loboz, 2012) found that statistical

distributions of resource usage in the cloud are heavy-tailed, with tails heavier than that of lognormal distribution – most of them even passing tests for power-law distribution.

In general standard deviation several times higher than average for a data set suggest that the classic approach to data analysis will not give sensible results – for example a data set c(1,1,1,1000) has an average of 334.6, which does not describe the set well. Such data set is an exaggerated version of a power-law distribution – most of the 'mass' is concentrated in a single element. Such distribution has serious volatility consequences for the resulting time series of use.

Consider for example a cluster with 1,000 customers, each using 1 terabyte of storage, with total cluster use of 1 petabyte. Going from day to day some customers will grow or drop their resource use by, say, 10%. The probability that all customers will drop 10% of storage from day to day is miniscule – so day-to-day changes in storage use in a cluster are likely to be well below 10%, mostly in a range of 1%. Now, assume a cluster with the same number of customers with the largest customer using 800Tb and the remaining customers using 200Tb. When the largest customer changes storage day-to-day by 10% the change in the whole cluster will be 8%. So, for highly imbalanced resource use, large day-to-day changes are much, much more likely than for balanced resource use. The time series of storage use in such imbalanced cluster will *not* be normally distributed – it will have large daily jumps and drops.

This non-normality of time series of resource use is caused by the underlying heavy-tailed usage distribution on any given day. It invalidates most of the traditional methods for system analysis and capacity planning. For example linear regression assumes normal distribution of the underlying time series – applying linear regression to the growth in resource use for imbalanced clusters will give wrong forecasts and wrong confidence intervals. Similarly, trying to test hypothesis that average load in two clusters is equal assumes statistics build on the assumption of normal distribution. Computation of most traditional statistics is based on least squares method – that amplifies large differences from average – and they are much more frequent and much larger when imbalance is high.

These considerations apply to all systems with high excess entropy – not only to computer systems. The heavy tails are usually not going away with the system growth - composition of heavy-tailed distributions does not result in a normal distribution – the central limit theorem does not apply to such distributions. Thus these considerations apply to systems with large variety of sizes.

COMPOSITE EXCESS ENTROPY: A SYSTEM AND ITS SUBSYSTEMS

So far computation of excess entropy was limited to a single subsystem. We have compared excess entropy between clusters – but that required only computing excess entropy for each cluster separately. For example, we did not consider excess entropy for the total data center consisting of three clusters. Most real-life situation require decomposition of the total system into subsystem – or combination of multiple subsystems into a larger system.

A good descriptor should allow consistent composition of subsystem descriptors into a system descriptor – as well as decomposition. Many inequality/imbalance descriptors proposed in the literature and used in economics do not allow for meaningful or consistent composition and decomposition (including the popular Gini index).

Entropy-based descriptors – like excess entropy - do allow composition and decomposition so they can be applied to hierarchical systems. Thus we are able to compute imbalance of a cluster load then compute the data center imbalance from cluster imbalances. We can extend that to compute imbalance of regions from data center imbalances and so on. That capability allows also to diagnose which clusters are creating most data center imbalance.

Composite Excess Entropy

We describe here how excess entropies for a set of subsystems can be combined to obtain excess entropy for the total system.

We have a system consisting of M subsystems and the subsystem m used fraction f_m of the total resource used by all subsystems. Also, avg_m is the average value of resource used by the subsystem m and avg_{tot} is the average value resources used across the total system. The formula for composite excess entropy (CEE) is (Cowell 1995):

$$CEE = \sum_{m=1}^{M} f_m * IC_m + \sum_{m=1}^{M} f_m * \ln\left(\frac{avg_m}{avg_{tot}}\right)$$

Thus the excess entropy of the whole group is the sum of (1) excess entropy within subsystem weighted by the fraction of resources used by that subsystem and (2) differences between averages in subsystems also weighted by the fraction of resources used by that subsystem. This formula allows us, for example, to compute the imbalance for the whole data center as a function of imbalance of individual clusters – and aggregate that further up to the region of data centers.

This approach allows us to decompose the imbalance of the total system into imbalances of its subsystems and identify which subsystems contribute most of the overall imbalance. In addition we can quantify whether contribution of a subsystem to overall imbalance is caused by internal imbalance within that subsystem or by the imbalance between that subsystem and other subsystems.

To illustrate the application we consider data transfer on individual disks in two sets of disks. The CEE formula takes the form

$$CEE_{sample} = f_1 * EE_1 + f_1 * \ln\left(\frac{avg_1}{avg_{tot}}\right)$$
$$+ f_2 * EE_2 + f_2 * \ln\left(\frac{avg_2}{avg_{tot}}\right)$$

This expression has four terms with a 'natural' interpretation. The first term is the contribution to the CEE due to internal imbalance of the first disk set. The second term is the contribution to the CEE from the ratio of the average value in that first set to the total average. (And third and fourth terms contain the same contributions for the second disk set). Both contributions are scaled by the fraction of the resources used by that set. That approach allows us to determine

whether CEE mostly caused by the differences between subsystems or by internal imbalance in the subsystem.

Assume we have two sets of disks with transfers values A=c(50,55,60); B = c(1,60,5);. The first set is obviously well balanced with nEE 0.003, the second set is strongly imbalanced with nEE 0.685. The total system imbalance is 0.00 + 0.25 + 0.22 + -0.16 = 0.31

Looking at the composition of the total imbalance we see that the first set contributes 0 from internal imbalance and all of its contribution is coming from the difference in averages between this set and the total (0.25). The second set contributes mostly through its internal imbalance (0.22). Note that the contributions coming from differences between averages(terms 2 and 4) add 0.25-0.16=0.09 to the total imbalance – so between-sets contribution is smaller than the contribution from internal imbalance of set B. (Note that the CEE computations are done on non-normalized excess entropy).

This example analysis demonstrates additional system understanding that can be derived from decomposition of a system into subsystems. The approach scales up large systems with much larger number of subsystems and multiple levels of subsystem nesting.

Evolution of Imbalance in Time

We now consider evolution in time of excess entropy for individual clusters and for the data center consisting of three clusters. Figure 4, left plot, shows the daily load in each cluster (scaled to the maximum load). Cluster1 (black line) has the load growing, Cluster2 (light gray) has very small load, close to 0. Cluster3 (dark gray) has very variable and decreasing load.

For each day we compute the normalized imbalance of resource use (*Network Transfer*) for each cluster. We also compute the normalized composite imbalance for the whole system con-

Figure 4. Evolution of resource use, imbalance and contributions to composite excess entropy for three clusters; The left plot shows (normalized) load with each cluster colored with different shade of grey; the middle plot shows imbalance for each cluster and composite imbalance (dotted line) for the total system; the right plot shows contributions to total system imbalance, solid lines denote contributions from internal cluster imbalance, dotted lines contributions from differences between average cluster values and total system average.

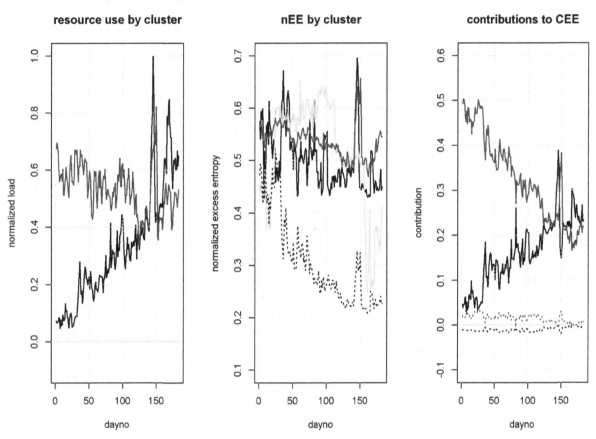

sisting of all three clusters. Figure 4, middle plot, shows the evolution of cluster's imbalance coefficients (solid lines, the same color coding as in the previous picture). Cluster imbalance levels are very variable but they stay mostly in 0.5-0.7 range. That means the imbalance inside clusters is very high – the network transfer is dominated by a small number of accounts. The imbalance of the total system, initially as high as cluster imbalance, drops later to the 0.2 level – that is not unusual, as resource use by large account in a single cluster is relatively smaller when considered against total resource use of in all clusters.

The comparison between load evolution and imbalance evolution for each cluster shows strong load growth around 140th day in clusters one and three – the co-temporal jump in imbalance suggests the growth is coming from a small number of accounts. Similar situations occur also at other days.

The system imbalance (dotted line) shows a jump around the day 140. This is a reflection of the jump in load in two clusters processing most of the system load. At the same time, after the day 150, Cluster2's imbalance (light gray line) is dropping heavily from 0.5 to 0.3 level – without affecting system imbalance. This is because the contribution to the system imbalance is weighted by the fraction of the load processed – and that fraction is extremely small for Cluster2.

Figure 4, right plot, shows the clusters' contributions to the composite imbalance from intra-cluster imbalance (solid lines) and inter-cluster differences of averages (dotted lines). Overall the system imbalance is dominated by internal imbalances of clusters 1 and 3 (black and dark-grey solid lines) – with all other components close to zero. The contribution pattern follows closely the pattern of resources used by the clusters (see Figure x). So we have relatively stable internal imbalance in clusters 1,3 and the contributions to system imbalance change only because of the relative distribution in load between these two clusters.

The analysis shown here was applied to a very specific set of real-world data to illustrate additional understanding that can be gained from adding excess entropy and composite excess entropy information to the traditional load description.

Excess Entropy for Categorizing Time Histories of Accounts

Previous sections considered the evolution of excess entropy in time – how did it change from day to day. This section deals with classifying patterns in time series using excess entropy – that is we take a time series of resource use and compute excess entropy of that time series.

Classification of accounts is vital to system management as well as account servicing. With large systems serving millions of accounts we need multiple methods of classification to describe different characteristics of account groups. One of such characteristics is the profile of resource use in time. Multiple traditional descriptors of time series are available – growth rate, volatility etc. However, typical time series metrics are not well suited to describe characteristics of resource use by a single account – an account may use a single virtual machine one day and 1000 of them

the next day – and it frequently does. Time series descriptors, like autocorrelation, volatility, and trend were designed for time series with normal (or reasonably close to normal) distributions – essentially for time series which are aggregations of a large number of elements, like GNP.

Many traditional descriptors are difficult to apply even to slightly non-normal time series, like stock price of a large company. In data centers the time series of resource use shows volatility several times higher than that of a stock market index. Going down to the level of individual accounts the real-world volatility of use is such that typical descriptors are insufficient.

This section applies excess entropy to classify certain patterns in account behavior in time. Each account has a daily history of use. Some accounts use similar amount of resources from day to day and some are more volatile than others. In practice that creates problems: how do you define a 'large' account? Consider two accounts: one using 100 VMs per day every day for a month and another using 12,000 VMs for six hours and nothing for the remainder of the month. Both accounts use the same number of VM hours, but the first account would not be considered large by most administrators while the second one will require some operational attention. The computation may cost the same in billing charges – but for the data center management the second account will cause a spike in load. The second account belongs to a special category of so-called 'bursty' accounts – the ones using resources in short bursts of high activity interspersed with irregular periods of very low use. Bursty accounts may use very small fraction of overall load on a longer timescale, but they add lots of volatility to the overall load. Since forecasting load depends on volatility reduction, bursty accounts need to be handled separately from the mainstream accounts.

Finding bursty accounts among hundreds of thousands of accounts in the datacenter requires some quantification of burstiness – and excess entropy can be used for that. We take the history of daily resource use by an account and compute excess entropy of resource use. For bursty accounts the excess entropy should be high – most of their processing is concentrated in a small number of days.

Figure 5 shows sample patterns of resource use. The left plot shows resource use over 600 days by an account with very low excess entropy of 0.025. We have reasonably regular growth from a single VM initially to tens of VMs. The middle plot shows history of resource use for an account with excess entropy of 0.30. We have a history of near-zero use interspersed with (very irregular) bursts of activity from hundreds to thousands of VMs. The right plot shows a history of an account with excess entropy of 0.53 – using mostly one VM with three days of using over 100 VMs.

That shows the utility of excess entropy to spot accounts with bursty profiles – accounts with excess entropy over 0.3 have clearly bursty profile. Using excess entropy we can identify bursty accounts quickly in a large population of accounts. Since the computation of the excess entropy is computationally trivial the descriptor is easy to compute even for large data sets. That allows classification by a degree of concentration in time of resources used by each account. We can categorize accounts in terms of the level of imbalance - both to spot extreme values and to separate in further analysis accounts with low and high values of imbalance.

Excess entropy should be usually combined with other descriptors. In this case it is advisable to ignore high values of excess entropy for accounts

Figure 5. Sample patterns of resource use with growing level of excess entropy (imbalance)

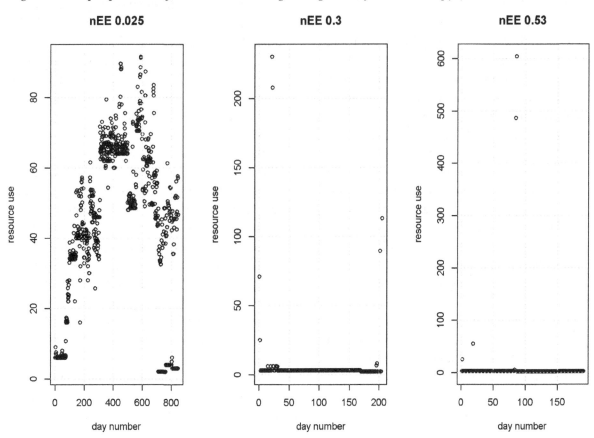

with trivial maximum resource use – an account using $(1,1,1,20)$ VMs would have very high excess entropy of 0.62, but is hardly influencing a data center or cluster utilization.

Other Considerations for Account Categorization

Excess entropy of an account can be used for multiple purposes, beyond identifying bursty accounts. But excess entropy is not a silver bullet and needs to be combined with other descriptors as well as understanding of the dynamics of the underlying system.

For example note that excess entropy of a history of use $(1,20,1,20,1,20)$ is the same as $(1,1,1,20,20,20)$. Both have value of 0.28 (so rather high), but they are not bursty – the pattern is regular. Excess entropy, when applied to a time series, describes the concentration of use in time regardless of the time ordering. To spot cyclical patterns in time series we should use traditional spectral analysis.

Forecasting demand is the fundamental activity in capacity planning – and reduction of volatility is critical to forecasting. We need to identify which accounts contribute most to the data center volatility on a longer timescale. Accounts with high maximum use and high excess entropy are prime candidates – but a combination of several smaller accounts with high excess entropy can also be volatility-inducing. Here excess entropy allows us to sort accounts in descending order of combination of excess entropy and size and try which subset of such accounts contributes most to the overall volatility.

The natural question here would be: wouldn't these bursty accounts average themselves out? No, they would not. Averaging out occurs due to Central Limit Theorem – it works if the underlying distributions are in the normal family of distributions. Unfortunately the distribution computer

resource usage between accounts in data centers is heavily skewed (more than log-normal distribution) and frequently has so-called heavy tails – for such distributions standard deviation does not make much sense and Central Limit Theorem is not applicable (see (Loboz, 2012) for reasoning and details). Hence volatility considerations in data center load require different approach than for classical systems.

SUMMARY

We have introduced the excess entropy (EE) as a way to describe various aspects of imbalance or concentration of resource use in computer systems, large and small. A variant of EE, normalized excess entropy (nEE) enables comparison of imbalance between different systems, even if these systems have different number of elements. Another variant, composite excess entropy (CEE), allows hierarchical composition and decomposition of imbalance in subsystems into imbalance in overall system. The CEE also allows discovery which subsystems contribute most to the overall imbalance – and in which fashion.

All variants of the excess entropy are dimensionless and their normalized versions exist. That allows for quantitative comparison of imbalance between different types of resources – for example imbalance of storage use can be compared with imbalance in network transfers, even though both resources are measured in different units.

Excess entropy of subsystems can be composed into an excess entropy of the total system and quantify how much each subsystem contributes to the overall imbalance and whether their contribution comes from high internal imbalance or difference from other subsystems – or both.

The normalized excess entropy can be used as an indicator that the underlying distributions are heavy-tailed. That also allows for comparison of the degree of heavy-tailness between different resources and systems – as well as for monitoring evolution in time of that degree.

Operationally, the formulas for computation of excess entropy are straightforward. They can be implemented trivially in a spreadsheet or a database and their computation time is trivial, even for large systems.

The useful operational interpretation of normalized excess entropy is that of *concentration of resource usage*. Higher nEE values imply resource use concentrated in a small number of accounts, lower nEE values indicate more even spread of resource use between accounts.

Excess entropy is not a silver bullet. It does not replace existing approaches to system description (like load, utilization, response time) - it adds to them and offers additional insights into the analyzed system. For example growth in load with growth in imbalance signals that only a small subset of accounts is getting more active. A growth in load with drop in imbalance signals broadly-based growth.

Imbalance describes only one aspect of the system – but this aspect has not been quantitatively analyzed earlier in computer systems (to the best of our knowledge).

The relevance of high or low imbalance in a system is heavily contextual. Depending on our goals and other aspects of the system under considerations high imbalance can be good, bad or irrelevant.

Imbalance between server usage in a group of servers managed by a load balancer is almost always a signal that something is wrong, so is imbalance in disk loads. However, when overall load is trivial then even high imbalance can be ignored – though we should check whether imbalance is growing with load or is independent of the load level. High imbalance in core usage for multicore servers may signal that affinity settings were used and a server working as intended – but it may also

signal that an application is serializing on some software element, therefore its implementation should be reviewed.

Other papers described application of excess entropy to analyze the resource use in Windows Azure storage clusters (Loboz, 2011a) and compute clusters (Loboz, 2011b). We found that imbalance is very high most of the time. We also found that the imbalance (and heavy tails) in cloud resource usage are not initial transients but persist even after months or years of system usage.

Composite normalized imbalance gave us additional insights into the structure of imbalances between the clusters and overall data center.

The few applications of quantitative imbalance shown here represent only a small subset of the potential applications of this method. For example we can consider relationships between imbalance of the hardware components of a server, a rack of servers, a cluster of servers, a datacenter, a region and the global datacenter set – thus composing the global from several hierarchical levels (instead of just two levels considered here). Another application would be analysis of imbalance at multiple time scales with detection at which time scale the imbalance picture starts to diverge – as this could be a signal of some underlying shift in the internal structure of usage and yield potentially useful information.

REFERENCES

Boltzmann, L. (2011). Lectures on gas theory. New York: Dover Publications. ISBN-10: 0486684555.

Clauset, A., Shalizi, C. R., & Newman, M. E. J. (2009). Power-law distributions in empirical data. *SIAM Review, 51*, 661–703.

Cowell, F. A. (1995). *Measuring inequality* (2nd ed.). Hemel Hampstead, UK: Harverster Wheatsheaf.

Gastwirth, J. L. (1972). The estimation of the Lorenz curve and Gini index. *The Review of Economics and Statistics*, *54*(3), 306–316. doi: doi:10.2307/1937992.

Jain, R. (1991). *The art of computer systems performance analysis: Techniques for experimental design, measurement, simulation, and modeling.* Hoboken, NJ: Wiley.

Lazowska, J., Zahorjan, J., Graham, G. S., & Sevcik, K. C. (1984). *Quantitative system performance: Computer system analysis using queueing network models.* Englewood Cliffs, NJ: Prentice-Hall.

Loboz, C. (2011a). Quantifying imbalance in computer systems. In *Proceedings of the Computer Measurement Group 2011 International Conference.* IEEE.

Loboz, C. (2011b). Describing multiple aspects of cloud usage with excess entropy. In *Proceedings of DataCloud-SC'11.* Seattle, WA: DataCloud-SC.

Loboz, C. (2012). Cloud resource usage – Heavy tailed distributions invalidating traditional capacity planning models. *Journal of Grid Computing*, *10*(1), 85–108. doi: doi:10.1007/s10723-012-9211-x.

Loboz, C., & Lee, S. (2010). Capacity, usage, computer work – And daily analysis of 100,000 servers. In *Proceedings of the Computer Measurement Group 2010 International Conference.* IEEE.

Loboz, C., Lee, S., & Yuan, J. (2009). How do you measure and analyze 100,000 servers. In *Proceedings of the Computer Measurement Group 2009 International Conference.* IEEE.

Newman, M. E. J. (2006). Power laws, Pareto distributions and Zipf's law. *Contemporary Physics*, *46*, 323–351.

R Project for Statistical Computing. (n.d.). Retrieved from www.r-project.org

Sen, A. (1997). *On economic inequality.* Oxford, UK: Clarendon Press.

Shannon, C. E. (1948). A mathematical theory of communication. *The Bell System Technical Journal*, *27*(3), 379–423.

Theil, H. (1967). *Economics and information theory.* Chicago: Rand McNally and Company.

KEY TERMS AND DEFINITIONS

Composite Excess Entropy: Combination of the Excess Entropy of individual subsystems into Excess Entropy of the overall system.

Excess Entropy: (also known as Theil Index) describes how concentrated is distribution of some resource among multiple agents; high values denote high concentration; multiple other interpretations are possible, but the formula to compute it stays the same across all interpretations.

Heavy-Tailed Distribution: There are multiple definitions in use; informally, for this chapter, we consider distribution to be heavy-tailed if it has heavier tail than log-normal distribution; such distributions have no (finite) variance and the average value does not describe them well – think (1,1,1,1000).

Large Computer Systems: For this chapter – computer ensembles with thousands, tens of thousands and hundreds of thousands servers; in other word: a modern, megawatt-scale datacenter.

Normalized Excess Entropy: Excess Entropy divided by logarithm of the number of agents using the resource, thus taking values in the [0,1] range – thus enabling comparison of degree of concentration between systems with different number of agents.

Chapter 17

A Review of System Benchmark Standards and a Look Ahead Towards an Industry Standard for Benchmarking Big Data Workloads

Raghunath Nambiar
Cisco Systems, Inc., USA

Meikel Poess
Oracle Corp., USA

ABSTRACT

Industry standard benchmarks have played, and continue to play, a crucial role in the advancement of the computing industry. Demands for them have existed since buyers were first confronted with the choice between purchasing one system over another. Over the years, industry standard benchmarks have proven critical to both buyers and vendors: buyers use benchmark results when evaluating new systems in terms of performance, price/performance, and energy efficiency; while vendors use benchmarks to demonstrate competitiveness of their products and to monitor release-to-release progress of their products under development. Historically, we have seen that industry standard benchmarks enable healthy competition that results in product improvements and the evolution of brand new technologies. Over the past quarter-century, industry standard bodies like the Transaction Processing Performance Council (TPC) and the Standard Performance Evaluation Corporation (SPEC) have developed several industry standards for performance benchmarking, which have been a significant driving force behind the development of faster, less expensive, and/or more energy efficient system configurations. The world has been in the midst of an extraordinary information explosion over the past decade, punctuated by

DOI: 10.4018/978-1-4666-4699-5.ch017

rapid growth in the use of the Internet and the number of connected devices worldwide. Today, we're seeing a rate of change faster than at any point throughout history, and both enterprise application data and machine generated data, known as Big Data, continue to grow exponentially, challenging industry experts and researchers to develop new innovative techniques to evaluate and benchmark hardware and software technologies and products. This chapter looks into techniques to measure the effectiveness of hardware and software platforms dealing with big data.

1. INTRODUCTION TO SYSTEM BENCHMARKS

System benchmarks have played, and continue to play, a crucial role in the advancement of the computing industry. Existing system benchmarks are critical to both buyers and vendors. Buyers use benchmark results when evaluating new systems in terms of performance, price/performance, and energy efficiency, while vendors use benchmarks to demonstrate the competitiveness of their products and to monitor release-to-release progress of their products under development. With no standard system benchmarks available for Big Data systems, today's situation is similar to that of the middle 1980s, when the lack of standard database benchmarks led many system vendors to practice what is now referred to as "benchmarketing," a practice in which organizations make performance claims based on self-designed, highly biased benchmarks. The goal of publishing results from such tailored benchmarks was to state marketing claims, regardless of the absence of relevant and verifiable technical merit. In essence, these benchmarks were designed as forgone conclusions to fit a pre-established marketing message. Similarly, vendors would create configurations, referred to as "benchmark specials," that were specifically designed to maximize performance against a specific benchmark with limited benefit to real-world applications.

As a direct consequence of the benchmarketing era, two benchmarking consortia emerged: the Transaction Processing Performance Council (TPC) and the Standard Performance Evaluation Corporation (SPEC). The TPC, founded in 1988, defines transaction processing and database benchmarks and disseminates objective, verifiable TPC performance data to the industry. While TPC benchmarks involve the measurement and evaluation of computer transactions, the TPC regards a transaction as it is commonly understood in the business world — as a commercial exchange of goods, services, or money. The TPC offers currently two benchmarks to measure On Line Transaction Processing (OLTP) systems, TPC-C and TPC-E, two others to measure decision support performance (TPC-H, TPC-DS), and one to measure virtualized databases. SPEC has been known mostly for their component-based benchmarks, such as SPEC CPU. It is a non-profit corporation formed to establish, maintain, and endorse a standardized set of relevant benchmarks that can be applied to the newest generation of high-performance computers, including processor-intensive benchmarks, benchmarks to measure graphics and workstation performance, high performance computing benchmarks, Java client/server benchmarks, mail server benchmarks, network file system benchmarks, and SPECpower_ssj2008, a benchmark focused on the relationship of power and performance.

While both consortia follow different methodologies in terms of benchmark development, benchmark dissemination, and benchmark compositions, they follow the same primary goal, namely to provide the industry and academia with realistic, verifiable, and fair means to compare performance.

Since the early days, other more specialized consortia arose, such as the Storage Performance Council (SPC), which is a non-profit corporation founded to define, standardize, and promote storage subsystem benchmarks and to disseminate objective, verifiable performance data to the computer industry and its customers. Since its founding in 1997, SPC has developed and publicized benchmarks and benchmark results focused on storage subsystems and the adapters, controllers, and storage area networks (SANs) that connect storage devices to computer systems. All major system and software vendors are members of these organizations. The TPC membership includes systems and database vendors. SPEC membership includes s universities and research institutions as associates. SPC membership includes systems and storage vendors.

System benchmarks can be classified into industry standard benchmarks, application benchmarks, and benchmarks based on synthetic workloads. Industry standard benchmarks are driven by industry standard consortia which are represented by vendors, customers, and research organizations. Industry standard consortia follow democratic procedures for all key decision making. Prominent industry standard consortia are the TPC, SPEC and SPC. Industry standard benchmarks enable the most fair comparison of technologies and are typically platform agnostic.

Application benchmarks are developed and administered by application vendors. The workloads employ actual applications that perform common functions from within a particular industry segment or a class of products. Examples are the SAP application benchmarks, designed and controlled by SAP AG, a global enterprise application software and service company based in Germany; the Oracle application benchmark, designed and controlled by Oracle Corporation, a global software company based in the United States specializing in the development of database, middleware, and application software that also providescloud services and manufacturing hardware systems; the VMark benchmark developed and controlled by U.S.-based VMware, which provides virtualization and virtualization-based

cloud infrastructure solutions. These application benchmarks enable customers to compare the performance of hardware platforms to run aparticular application. Application benchmarks are not designed to cross compare technologies or platforms, unlike industry standard benchmarks, and metrics like pricing and energy efficiencies are not included in the standards. Synthetic benchmarks don't consider the most important characteristics of an application domain. According to Twiki, "[they] simulate computer functions in proportions that yield an indicative measure of the performance capabilities of the system under test. These benchmarks try to match the average frequency of operations and operands." Synthetic benchmarks are based on the designer's experience and knowledge of an instruction mix. Examples of synthetic benchmarks are IOmeter, Dhrystone, and Whetstone.

Functions included in synthetic benchmarks are usually created artificially to match an average execution profile and this impairs their credibility. Synthetic benchmarks are component-level benchmarks and they evaluate a particular capability of a subsystem. For example, a disk subsystem performance benchmark may combine a series of basic seek, read, and write operations involving varying numbers of disk blocks of varying sizes.

1.1 Industry Landscape is Changing

The industry landscape has been changing rapidly and platforms that handle Big Data workloads have become mainstream. Big Data refers to data sets that are too large and too complex to store and process in a cost effectively and timely manner using traditional tools like scale-up systems and relational management systems.

Big Data was originally a Web 2.0 challenge. Solutions are now available to provision and manage these large workloads, including Hadoop and NoSQL. Big Data workloads can also be monetized using techniques such as sensitivity analysis, recommendation engines, etc. Enterprises see the value of Big Data and Big Data analytics across all major sectors, including health care, retail, education, and government, due to two main reasons:

- An increase in number of people connected to the Internet: The Internet revolution, which began started in the 1990s, has changed the technology and business landscape. About 33 percent of the world population has Internet access. Billions of users are connected though social media. Almost all businesses are conducted over the Internet. By year 2020, 50 percent of world population is expected to have Internet access.

- In 2011, over 15 billion devices were connected to the Internet: The Internet now includes communications via mobile phones, personal computers, IP cameras, sensors, enterprise systems, and many other types of devices. By year 2020 there will be 50 billion devices connected to the Internet, according to some estimates.

Hardware and software infrastructure technologies have also evolved from traditional scale-up and client/server systems to massive scale-out clusters and clouds. Hadoop and NoSQL systems have become cost–effective, scalable platforms for handling massive amounts of structured, semi structured and unstructured data. Many of these technologies were a contribution of Web 2.0-era companies. Enterprises are also considering the use of Hadoop and NoSQL, realizing that storing and mining large data sets can help optimize their business processes, improve the customer experience, uncover strategic and competitive opportunities, and thereby gain a competitive advantage. With this new Big Data landscape, and multiple technologies to choose from, there is a need for industry standards so users can see fair and unbiased comparisons of technologies and solutions. Open source workloads like Terasort, YCSB, and Gridmix are popular in this space at a

macro level but there is great demand for standards for measuring total system performance, total cost of ownership, and energy efficiency. Some of the benchmarks like TPC-H and TPC-DS can easily be extended for use in large structured datasets. (For example, current TPC-H and TPC-Ds benchmarks support scale factors of 100GB, 300B, 1TB, 3TB, 10TB and 30TB. This can be extended to larger scale factors like 100TB, 300GB, 1TB, 3PB and more, following the log scale, using existing data generation tools and queries.) There is work in progress to extend TPC-DS to handle unstructured data also (Ghazal 2013). There are initiatives like WBDB (Workshop on Big Data Benchmarking), which is intended developed brand new workloads. These two approaches are described on the following sections.

2. INDUSTRY STANDARD BENCHMARKS

Industry standard benchmarks are driven by industry standard consortia. Prominent bodies are the Transaction Processing Performance Council (TPC) and the Standard Performance Evaluation Corporation (SPEC) with a large variety of system benchmarks. There are also more specialized consortia such as the Storage Performance Council (SPC). The following sections give a detailed overview of these consortia with an emphasis on their benchmarks.

2.2 Transaction Processing Performance Council

The TPC is a non-profit corporation founded to define vendor-neutral transaction processing benchmarks and to disseminate objective, verifiable performance data to the industry. Omri Serlin and Tom Sawyer founded the TPC in 1988 as a response to the growing problem of "benchmarketing". Two of the first TPC benchmarks were the TP1 benchmark, originally developed by IBM, and the debit-credit benchmark, published by Jim Gray and 24 others from academia and industry titled "A Measure of Transaction Processing Power", that defined the debit-credit workload. The TP1 benchmark measured the performance of a system handling ATM transactions in batch mode without the network or user interaction (think-time) components of the system workload (similar in design to what later turned out to be TPC-B). Debit-credit included a price/performance metric which was quite novel at the time. In 1987, Jim Grey conceived and drove Tandem's "Top Gun" benchmark, which was named after the movie a year earlier, using the debit-credit workload, which, four years later, became TPC-A. TPC-A formalized the price model. Price/performance was a key differentiator for the TPC and has been included in every TPC benchmark ever since. Later, the TPC initiated a review process wherein each benchmark test had to be extensively documented and then carefully vetted by an independent auditor before it could be published as a formal TPC benchmark result.

Today, all published results of TPC benchmarks have been audited and verified by TPC certified auditors. In addition, TPC members have 60 days to peer review the result after the benchmark publication.

Over the past two decades, the TPC has had a significant impact on the industry and database centric benchmarks. Prior to the late 1980s, the industry lacked objective, verifiable benchmarks that were relevant to real-world computing. With their benchmarks, the TPC quickly raised the bar for the industry. TPC has developed benchmarks for many application domains, some of which were never released because support faded over time due to changes in the market while the benchmark was in development or because TPC's stringent release requirements were not met. We classify these as Aborted Benchmarks.

Figure 1 illustrates the benchmark development model of the TPC, which follows the traditional waterfall model of software development. Starting from a new idea, which might stem from within

Figure 1. Benchmark Development Model of the TPC

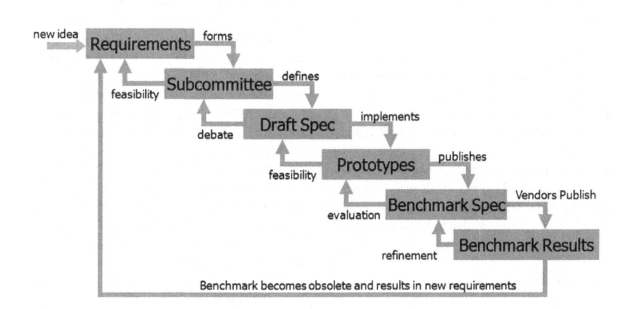

the TPC or from the outside, a list of requirements for the new benchmark is developed, usually by a small group of people called a Working Group. Once the requirements are defined, a subcommittee is formed to refine the requirements and start defining the benchmark specification. This results in a draft specification, which can be used to define a benchmark prototype. Using hands-on data from the prototype, the specification is further enhanced and then released as a benchmark specification. Once the benchmark is released, vendors can use it to produce benchmark results. During that process the TPC continuously maintains the benchmark. This is especially important because the TPC recognizes changes in technology and the way computer systems are used by corporations. It first tries to adapt existing benchmarks but if the changes are too intrusive, the TPC develops new benchmarks for the already existing application domain with the goal of ultimately replacing the older, outdated benchmark.

Once a new benchmark for an existing application domain is released, the old benchmark may be replaced or may coexist with the new benchmark. The following list shows current and retired benchmarks.

Retired Benchmarks:

- TPC-A evolved into TPC-B and was ultimately replaced by TPC-C standards for OLTP workloads.
- TPC-D was the first decision support benchmark, which evolved into TPC-H and TPC-R.
- The TPC also developed a web server benchmark, TPC-W, which was later replaced by TPC-App.
- TPC-R was retired due to lack of industry acceptance.

Current Benchmarks:

- TPC-E is a new OLTP benchmark with more complex schema and transactions which currently coexists with TPC-C.

- TPC-DS is the next generation decision support benchmark designed to overcome some of the limitations of TPC-H and is representative of modern decision support system.
- TPC-C continues to be the popular benchmark for OLTP workloads.
- TPC-H continues to be the popular benchmark for decision support workloads.

Figure 2 shows the TPC's roadmap of benchmarks. The TPC-C and TPC-H benchmarks continue to be popular yardsticks for comparing OLTP performance and decision support system performance, respectively. The main reasons for their popularity are the wide understanding of the workload and metric characteristics by the industry. The longevity of these benchmarks means that hundreds of results are publicly available over a wide variety of systems.

2.3 System Performance Evaluation Corporation

The Standard Performance Evaluation Corporation (SPEC) is a non-profit organization established in 1988, in same year the TPC was established. The objective of SPEC was to develop standards for system level performance measurements. SPEC has a history of developing relevant benchmarks to the industry in a timely manner. SPEC is represented by system and software vendors and a number of academic and research organizations.

Over that last few years the SPEC evolved into an umbrella organization encompassing four diverse groups - Graphics and Workstation Performance Group (GWPG), High Performance Group (HPG), Open Systems Group (OSG) and Research Group (RG).

SPEC provides the benchmark code written in a platform-neutral programming language, like C, Java or FORTRAN. The benchmark sponsors are not allowed to change the code but free to choose the compiler of their choice. In order

Figure 2. TPC Benchmark Roadmap

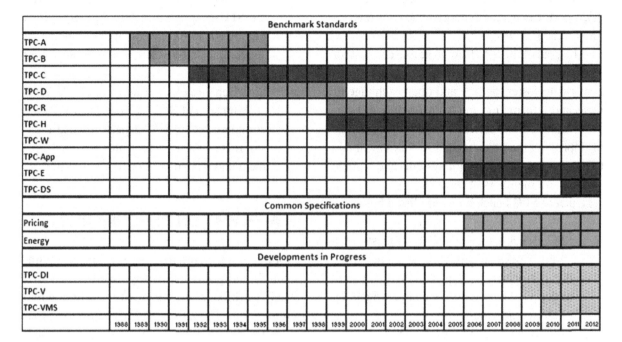

to use the SPEC benchmark, the sponsor has to purchase the license. Current SPEC benchmark standards include:

- SPEC CPU2006 isdesigned to measure the compute power of systems, contains two benchmark suites: CINT2006 for measuring and comparing compute-intensive integer performance, and CFP2006 for measuring and comparing compute-intensive floating point performance.
- SPEC MPI2007 is designed for evaluating MPI-parallel, floating point, and compute-intensive performance across a wide range of cluster and SMP hardware. The suite consists of the initial MPIM2007 suite and MPIL2007, which contains larger working sets and longer run times than MPIM2007.
- SPECjbb2013 measures server performance based on the Java application features by emulating a three-tier client/server system.
- SPECjEnterprise2010 measures system performance for Java Enterprise Edition

(Java EE) 5 or later application servers, databases, and supporting infrastructure.
- SPECsfs2008 is designed to evaluate the speed and request-handling capabilities of file servers utilizing the NFSv3 and CIFS protocols.
- SPECpower_ssj2008 evaluates the power and performance characteristics of volume server class computers.
- SPECvirt_sc2010 measures the end-to-end performance of all system components, including the hardware, virtualization platform, virtualized guest operating system, and application software.

2.4 Storage Performance Council (SPC)

The Storage Performance Council (SPC) is a vendor-neutral consortia established in 2000, focused on industry standards for storage system performance. Its first benchmark standard, SPC-1 was announced in 2001 (SPC 2013). Since then, the SPC has developed a robust methodology measuring, auditing, and publishing performance, price-performance, and energy-efficiency metrics for storage systems.

The goal of the SPC is to serve as a catalyst for performance improvement in storage subsystems. It works to foster the free and open exchange of ideas and information and to ensure fair and vigorous competition between vendors as a means of improving the products and services available to the general public. Major systems and storage vendors are members of the SPC.

Current SPC benchmarks are listed below:

- SPC Benchmark 1 (SPC-1) consists of a single workload designed to demonstrate the performance of a storage subsystem under OLTP workloads characterized by random reads and writes.
- SPC Benchmark 1/Energy (SPC-1/E) is an extension of SPC-1 that consists of the complete set of SPC-1 performance measurement and reporting plus the measurement and reporting of energy consumption.
- SPC Benchmark 2 (SPC-2) consists of three distinct workloads: large file processing, large database queries, and video on-demand simulating the concurrent large-scale sequential movement of data.
- SPC Benchmark 2/Energy (SPC-2/E) is extension of SPC-2 that consists of the complete set of SPC-2 performance measurement and reporting plus the measurement and reporting of energy consumption.
- SPC Benchmark 1C (SPC-1C) is based on SPC-1 for storage component products such as disk drives, host bus adapters, storage enclosures, and storage software stacks such as volume managers.
- SPC Benchmark 1C/Energy (SPC-1C/E) is an extension of SPEC-1C that consists of the complete set of SPC-1C performance measurements and reporting plus measurement and reporting of energy consumption.

- SPC Benchmark 2C (SPC-2C) is based on SPC-2, predominately by large I/Os organized into one or more concurrent sequential patterns for storage component products.
- SPC Benchmark 2C/Energy (SPC-2C/E) is an extension of SPC-2C that consists of the complete set of SPC-2 performance measurement and reporting plus the measurement and reporting of energy consumption.

3. APPLICATION BENCHMARKS

Application benchmarks are developed, administered, and published by application vendors. Their workloads are designed to mimic actual applications, (e.g., they perform common functions from within a particular industry segment or an array of products). Examples of application benchmarks are SAP application benchmarks, Oracle application benchmarks, and VMark from VMware. Because these benchmarks are application-specific and under the control of the application vendor, they are mostly used to compare the performance of the application software on different hardware platforms. All vendors providing such benchmark demonstrate their long-term public commitment to measuring and characterizing the performance of application performance.

3.1 SAP Standard Application Benchmarks

The SAP Standard Application Benchmarks was designed by the leading German application software provider, SAP AG, for its customers to evaluate hardware configurations and to find the appropriate hardware configuration for them. Hardware partners utilize results from SAP's Standard Application Benchmarks to position their products relative to their competitor's.

The SAP Standard Application Benchmarks test the hardware and database performance of SAP applications and their components while providing basic sizing recommendations. The tests, which can be conducted using two-tier and three-tier architectures, place a substantial load upon a system during the testing, thereby effectively stress-testing the system. During the benchmark an array of performance data, relevant to system, user, and business applications, is monitored. This data can be used to compare platforms.

3.2 Oracle Application Benchmark

Another application benchmark is Oracle's Application Benchmark, which ensures that Oracle applications perform to exceptional standards. Oracle is a leading provider of application software as well as database, middleware, and hardware products. Similar to the SAP Standard Application Benchmarks, the Oracle Applications Standard Benchmark is a standard workload which demonstrates the performance and scalability of Oracle applications and provides metrics for the comparison of different system configurations.

The Oracle Application Standard Benchmark can be run online and in batch, thereby measuring different modes customer of customer software usage. The online component measures the performance of the common UI flows most frequently used by customers while the batch flow measures the performance of the order management and payroll processes of a typical customer installation.

Oracle works with hardware companies, product development groups, and product line groups in a Applications Standard Benchmark Council to assure that the benchmark stays up-to-date with hardware and software developments and the needs of customers. These companies and groups have access to the latest marketing and technical information related to the Oracle Applications Standard Benchmark.

3.3 VMMark

VMmark® was developed by VMware a leading provider of virtualization software. VMware distributes VMmark® as a free tool to hardware vendors, virtualization software vendors, and other organizations so that they can measure the performance and scalability of applications running in virtualized environments. It was the virtualization platform benchmark for x86-based computers. Specifically, VMmark® allows the accurate and reliable measurement of virtual data center performance and the viewing and comparing of performance of different hardware and virtualization platforms

Over the years, VMmark® 2.x has established itself as the first standard methodology for comparing virtualized platforms. VMmark® 2.x generates a realistic measure of virtualization platform performance by incorporating a variety of platform-level workloads such as dynamic virtual machine (VM) relocation (vMotion) and dynamic datastore relocation (storage vMotion). These tests can be sub-categorized into "sub-tests" that are derived from commonly used load-generation tools and commonly initiated virtualization administration tasks. To increase the ease of benchmarking and to keep the benchmark flexible, it is organized into tiles. The total number of tiles that a platform can accommodate and the performance of each individual workload within the tile determine the overall benchmark score.

4. SYNTHETIC WORKLOADS

Synthetic benchmarks widely adapted in the industry and academic community. Synthetic benchmarks do not necessarily measure the performance of platforms under application workloads but instead simulate functions that yield an indicative measure of the performance capabilities of the system under test. Examples of synthetic benchmarks include IOmeter, Dhrystone, and Whetstone. Terasort, YCSB, and Gridmix are other synthetic benchmarks that are becoming popular in characterizing Big Data workloads.

4.1 Iometer

Iometer is an I/O subsystem measurement and characterization tool for. It was originally developed by the Intel Corporation and announced at the Intel Developers Forum (IDF) on February 17, 1998. Ever since it has been widely accepted within the industry. Iometer was released to the Open Source Development Lab (OSDL). Since February 2003, the project has been driven by an international group of individuals who are continuously improving, porting, and extending the product.

The tool (Iometer and Dynamo executable) is distributed under the terms of the Intel Open Source License. The iomtr_kstat kernel module, along with other future independent components, are distributed under the terms of the GNU Public License.

4.2 Terasort

Terasort is a benchmark that evolved from Jim Gray's Sort Benchmark from a paper titled "A Measure of Transaction Processing Power" (Gray 2009), originally published in *Datamation* April 1, 1985. The Apache Hadoop version of Terasort was written by Owen O'Malley, and resembles a common workload for measuring performance of Hadoop systems. It does considerable computation, networking, and storage I/O, and is often considered to be representative of real Hadoop workloads. It is split into three parts: generation, sorting, and validation. TeraGen creates random data. TeraSort does the actual sorting and writes sorted data. TeraValidate reads all the sorted data to verify that it is in order. For more details see (YCSB 2013).

4.3 Yahoo! Cloud Serving Benchmark

The Yahoo! Cloud Serving Benchmark (YCSB) project aims to develop a framework and common set of workloads for evaluating the performance of different key-value and cloud serving stores. The project includes:

- The YCSB Client, an extensible workload generator.
- The Core Workloads, a set of workload scenarios to be executed by the generator.

The workload allows read/write mix and reports latency and throughput. YCSB is a common workload to measure the performance of key-value store systems.

4.4 TextDFSIO

The TestDFSIO benchmark is a common workload to measure the performance of Hadoop File Systems (HDFS). There is a write test and read test, both of which measure the throughput and latency of underlying software and hardware.

5. CHANGING INDUSTRY LANDSCAPE

The Internet revolution of the 1990s and the following Web 2.0 revolution in early 2000s have significantly changed the world. As of 2011, 33 percent of the world population has Internet access and almost all business is conducted over the Internet, at least in developed countries. There are 15 billion devices connected to the Internet today, from mobile devices to enterprise computers. This equals more than two devices for every human being on the planet. If Facebook, was a country with over a billion unique users, it would be the third largest in the world after India and the United states. The volume of network data traversing the Internet is growing 40 percent per year, and will grow 44x between 2009 and 2020, when it is forecast to total more than 40 zettabytes. (IDC 2013)

The social media and Web 2.0 companies were the first to be challenged with the Big Data problem and they are the frontrunners in monetizing the analytics possibilities of mining the vast amount of data available today. For example, Hadoop was derived from Google's MapReduce and Google's File System (GFS) papers. Yahoo! Inc. launched what it claimed was the world's largest Hadoop production application in 2008. Over the years, Apache Hadoop has become the *de facto* platform for storing, processing, and managing massive sets of semi-structured and unstructured data. Big Data has become a critical priority for enterprises across all vertical industries yet no industry benchmarks that enable a fair comparison of performance and cost of ownership of underlying platforms exist.

5.1 Call for a New Standard

Though there are many innovations, a growing collection of new technologies, and new products in the Big Data space, enterprises are challenged with the influx of new data sources, new technologies, new products, and Big Data system performance claims. Industry standards are needed for the evaluation, comparison, and characterization of technologies, products, and workloads in terms of performance, cost of ownership, and energy efficiency.

Industry standards bodies like the TPC, SPEC, and SPC have been serving the industry capably with various standards. To address the challenges arising from Big Data, however, new standards need to be developed and existing standards need to be improved to complement the new standards.

The situation isn't much different from when the TPC was originally founded in 1998 in response to a growing trend in "benchmarketing," attempts by vendors to publish questionable

benchmark results in order to increase sales. The need for a vendor-neutral standard organization that is focused on creating and administering fair and comprehensive benchmark specifications to objectively evaluate Big Data systems under demanding but consistent and comparable workloads, is quickly becoming apparent.

Realizing the need for industry standards there are industry initiatives to develop and accelerate benchmark developments in new areas: SPEC Research, ICPE, TPCTC and WBDB.

SPEC Research

The SPEC Research Group (RG) is a new group within SPEC established to serve as a platform for collaborative research efforts in the area of quantitative system evaluation and analysis, fostering the interaction between industry and academia in the field.

The scope of the SPEC Research Group includes computer benchmarking, performance evaluation, and experimental system analysis considering both classical performance metrics such as response time, throughput, scalability and efficiency, and other non-functional system properties included under the category of dependability, (e.g., availability, reliability, and security). The research efforts span the design of metrics for system evaluation and the development of methodologies, techniques, and tools for measurement, load testing, profiling, workload characterization, dependability, and efficiency evaluation of computing systems.

TPC Technology Conference

TPC's Technology Conference Series (TPCTC) is intended to accelerate the development of relevant benchmark standards. The TPCTC provides industry experts and researchers with a forum to present and debate novel ideas and methodologies in performance evaluation, measurement, and characterization. Each of the four events held so far have advanced existing TPC benchmarks, sparked ideas for new TPC benchmarks or influenced the direction of the TPC.

The first TPCTC on Performance Evaluation and Benchmarking (TPCTC 2009) was held in conjunction with the 35th International Conference on Very Large Data Bases (VLDB 2009) in Lyon, France, from August 24-28, 2009 (Nambiar 2009).

The second TPCTCon Performance Evaluation and Benchmarking (TPCTC 2010) was held in conjunction with the 36th International Conference on Very Large Data Bases (VLDB 2010) in Singapore from September 13-17, 2010 (Nambiar 2010).

The third TPCTC on Performance Evaluation and Benchmarking (TPCTC 2011) was held in conjunction with the 37th International Conference on Very Large Data Bases (VLDB 2011) in in Seattle, Washington, from August 29-September 3, 2011 (Nambiar 2011).

The fourth TPCTC on Performance Evaluation and Benchmarking (TPCTC 2012), held in conjunction with the 38th International Conference on Very Large Data Bases (VLDB 2012) in Istanbul, Turkey, from August 27-31, 201 (Nambiar 2012).

The 5th TPCTC on Performance Evaluation and Benchmarking (TPCTC 2013) is scheduled to take place in Riva Del Garda, Italy, in conjunction with the 39th International Conference on Very Large Data Bases (VLDB 2012) in August 2013.

The Workshop Series on Big Data Benchmarking

The Workshop Series on Big Data Benchmarking (WBDB) is a first important step towards the development of a set of benchmarks for providing objective measures of the effectiveness of hardware and software systems dealing with Big Data applications. These benchmarks would facilitate evaluation of alternative solutions and provide for comparisons among different solution approaches.

The benchmarks need to characterize the new feature sets, enormous data sizes, large-scale and evolving system configurations, shifting loads, and heterogeneous technologies of Big Data and cloud platforms. There are new challenges and options in software for Big Data such as SQL, NoSQL, and the Hadoop software ecosystem; different modalities of Big Data, including graphs, streams, scientific data, and document collections, etc. The primary audience for the benchmark standards include hardware vendors, software vendors who want to showcase the performance of their products, and end user customers who are evaluating different technologies and products.

The WBDB 2012, held on May 8-9 in San Jose, California, served as an incubator for several promising approaches to define a Big Data benchmark standard for the industry. Through an open forum for discussions on a number of issues related to Big Data benchmarking — including definitions of Big Data terms, benchmark processes and auditing — the attendees were able to extend their own view of Big Data benchmarking and to communicate their own ideas, which ultimately led to the formation of small working groups to continue collaborative work. In this paper, we summarize the discussions and outcomes from this first workshop, which was attended by about 60 invitees representing 45 different organizations in industry and academia. Workshop attendees were selected based on their experience and expertise in the areas of Big Data management, database systems, performance benchmarking, and Big Data application development. There was consensus among participants about both the need and the opportunity for defining benchmarks to capture the end-to-end aspects of Big Data applications. Following the model of TPC benchmarks, it was felt that Big Data benchmarks should not only include metrics for performance but also price/performance along with a sound foundation for fair comparison through audit mechanisms. Additionally, the benchmarks should consider several costs relevant to Big Data systems, including total cost of acquisition, setup cost, and the total cost of ownership, including energy cost. The second WBDB will be held in December 2012 in Pune, India, and the third meeting is being planned for July 2013 in Xi'an, China.

Big Data 100

Beginning in late 2011, the Center for Large-scale Data Systems Research (CLDS) at the San Diego Supercomputer Center at the University of California, San Diego, in collaboration with several industry experts, initiated a community activity in Big Data benchmarking with the goal of defining reference benchmarks that capture the essence of Big Data application scenarios. The goal of this activity is to provide clear and objective information to help characterize and understand the hardware and system performance and price/performance of Big Data platforms. As previously mentioned, a workshop series on Big Data benchmarking (WBDB) was organized, sponsored by the National Science Foundation (http://clds. sdsc.edu/bdbc/workshops). The new Big Data benchmark should characterize the new feature sets, large data sizes, large-scale and evolving system configurations, shifting loads, and heterogeneous technologies of Big Data platforms. The first workshop, held on May 8–9, 2012, in San Jose, California, developed a number of initial ideas and was followed by subsequent meetings (see http://clds.sdsc.edu/events/nov-02-2012), and the second workshop was held on December 17–18, 2012, in Pune, India, (http://clds.sdsc.edu/ wbdb2012.in). These meetings substantiated the initial ideas for a Big Data benchmark, which will include definitions of the data along with a data-generation procedure; a workload representing common Big Data applications; and a set of metrics, run rules, and full-disclosure reports for fair comparisons of technologies and platforms. These results will be presented in the form of the Big Data Top 100 List, released on a regular basis at a predefined venue such as the Strata Conferences.

The Big Data Top 100 List will pursue a concurrent benchmarking model, where one version of the benchmark is implemented while the next revision is concurrently being developed, incorporating more features and feedback from the first round of benchmarking. While this will create different versions of the same benchmark, we believe that the community is sufficiently mature to be able to interpret benchmark results in proper context. Each release of the benchmark may also be accompanied by a set of issues under design consideration for the next release, so that the community is made fully aware of the benchmark development activity. Our goal is to pursue this open benchmark development process, soliciting input from the community at large, to be evaluated by a benchmark steering committee with representation from industry, academia, and other sectors.

In the final analysis, results from an industry-standard benchmark are only the first — though an important — step toward understanding system performance. A customer may then run their proprietary benchmarks to complement the open benchmark results.

Given the fast-moving nature of the field, it is likely that the execution criteria for the Big Data Top 100 List will evolve, especially early in the process as we receive and incorporate community input and make progress toward a more steady state. The list would be published for each revision of the benchmark specification, similar to the Sort Benchmark model (www.sortbench-mark.org). We are considering restrictions on the benchmark as follows:

First, the benchmark should include the cost of the overall systems, for example, the total system cost of hardware, software, and one year, 24/7 support. The vendors must guarantee the price for every priced component for one year from the date of publication. For example, if the total system cost is $100,000, then the benchmark sponsor must pick a configuration priced at $100,000 or less.

Second, the benchmarks would be run at specific "scale factors," that is, the size of the core dataset, similar to the scale factors in the TPC-H and TPC-DS benchmarks. To ensure data consistency, a cross-platform data-generation program and scripts would be provided for generating the reference dataset at the given scale factor. There are four key steps to executing the benchmark:

1. **System Setup:** Configure and install the system under test (SUT). This time is not included in the benchmark metric.
2. **Data Generation:** Generate the dataset that meets the benchmark specification. This time is not included in the benchmark metric.
3. **Data Load:** Load the data into the system. This time is included in the benchmark metric.
4. **Execute Application Workload:** Run the specified Big Data workload consisting of a set of queries and transactions. This time is included in the benchmark metric. The benchmark metric is often one of the most debated topics in the benchmark development process. The general consensus is to have a simple metric that can be recorded easily and that is also easily understood by the users of the benchmark. A simple metric is total time (i.e., the wall-clock time taken to complete Steps 3 and 4 above). The sponsor must run the benchmark three times to guarantee repeatability; the run-to-run variation must be within 2 percent — a number that is chosen arbitrarily; and the reported total time must be the slowest of the three runs. Results in the Big Data Top 100 List would then be ordered by total time, with efficiency reported as a secondary figure or metric. Thus, in this proposed approach, the system at the top of the Big Data Top 100 List would be the one that can process the representative Big Data workload on a dataset of fixed size in the least amount of total time (including initial data load time and application workload execution time) procured on a fixed budget, as specified by

the benchmark. The specified system cost could be revised with each revision of the benchmark specification.

The detailed run reports, including full-disclosure reports, would have to be submitted to a steering committee for peer review. The full-disclosure report would be required to include all steps to reproduce the benchmark and a corresponding price quote valid for one year from the date of publication. The Big Data Top 100 List would be maintained by this steering committee on behalf of the community." Source (Poess 2013).

Extending TPC-H and TPC-DS for Big Data

Building the foundation of a Big Data benchmark upon already established benchmarks has obvious advantages. The principles of these benchmarks are known, tools such as query and data generators are already developed and tested, and the ideas behind these benchmarks are already accepted in the industry. The TPC benchmarks TPC-H and TPC-DS are such benchmarks. In addition of being established, fully developed and accepted, they are well suited to provide the foundation of a Big Data benchmark because they fulfill most of the requirements already. They:

1. Scale up to very large volumes of data, (i.e., TPC-H and TPC-DS scale up to a raw data size of 100,000 GBytes, i.e. 100 TBytes).
2. Contain a diverse set of structured data.
3. Contain pricing requirements, which are demanded by customers.
4. Contain audit requirements that add significantly to the credibility of benchmark results.

The TPC Benchmark™H (TPC-H) is a decision support benchmark. It consists of a suite of business oriented *ad hoc* queries and concurrent data modifications. The queries and the data populating the database have been chosen based on broad industry-wide relevance while being easy to implement. This benchmark illustrates decision support systems that examine large volumes of data, execute queries with a high degree of complexity, and give answers to critical business questions.

The TPC Benchmark™DS (TPC-DS) is a decision support benchmark that models several generally applicable aspects of a decision support system, including queries and data maintenance. The benchmark provides a representative evaluation of the System Under Test's (SUT's) performance as a general purpose decision support system. This benchmark illustrates decision support systems that:

- Examine large volumes of data.
- Give answers to real-world business questions.
- Execute queries of various operational requirements and complexities (e.g., ad-hoc, reporting, iterative OLAP, data mining).
- Are characterized by high CPU and IO load.
- Are periodically synchronized with source OLTP databases through database maintenance functions.

Both TPC-H and TPC-DS only contain a diverse set of structured data and could easily be extended into a Big Data benchmark. One of the outcomes of the first workshop on Big Data Benchmarking is BigBench (Ghazal 2013). BigBench is an end-to-end Big Data benchmark proposal. It is based on TPC-DS. Hence, its underlying business model is a product retailer. In addition to TPC-DS it proposes a data model and synthetic data generator that address the variety, velocity and volume aspects of Big Data systems containing structured, semi-structured, and unstructured data. The structured part of BigBench's data model is adopted from TPC-DS. It is enriched with semi-structured and unstructured data components. The semi-structured part captures registered and guest user clicks on the retailer's web site.

The unstructured data captures product reviews submitted online. The data generator, which was designed for BigBench, provides scalable volumes of raw data based on a scale factor. BigBench's workload is designed around a set of queries against the data model. From a business prospective, the queries cover the different categories of Big Data analytics proposed by McKinsey. From a technical prospective, the queries are designed to span three different dimensions based on data sources, query processing types and analytic techniques. In the SIGMOD paper, the authors further illustrate the feasibility of BigBench by presenting an implementation on Teradata's Aster Database. The test includes generating and loading a 200 Gigabyte BigBench data set and testing the workload by executing the BigBench queries (written using Teradata Aster SQL-MR) and reporting their response times.

BigBench's data model focuses on volume, variety and velocity. The variety property of BigBench is illustrated in Figure 1. The structured portion of BigBench's data model is adapted directly from TPC-DS' data model, which also depicts a product retailer (Nambiar 2006) BigBench adds a table for prices from the retailer's competitors to the portion of TPC-DS' that contain store and online sales data. TPC-DS' structured part is enriched with semi-structured and un-structured data shown in the lower and right hand side of Figure 3. The semi-structured part is composed by clicks made by customers and guest users visiting the retailer's web site. The design assumes the semi-structured data to be in a key-value format similar to Apache's web server log format. The un-structured data in the new model is covered by product reviews that can be submitted by guest users or actual customers.

6. CONCLUSION

Big Data has become mainstream. The industry calls for standards for measuring the performance of platforms for Big Data. Some of the industry

Figure 3. Logical Data Model BigBench (Adapted from (Ghazal 2013)

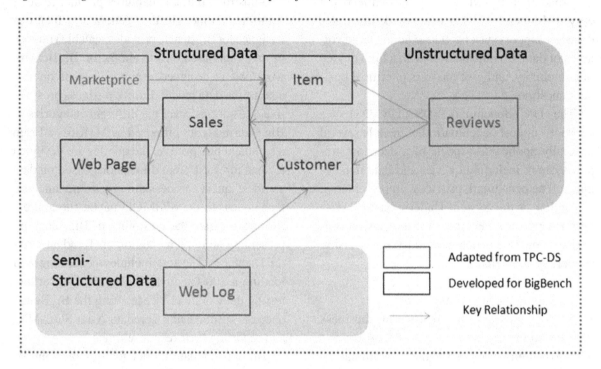

initiatives have been covered in this paper. The authors envision new standards evolving from initiatives like WBDB and enhancements to existing standards from standard bodies like the TPC. The authors, being members of both WBDB and TPC, plan to keep a close eye of the technology evaluations and drive the standards developments.

Historically we have seen that industry standard benchmarks enable healthy competition that results in product improvements and the evolution of brand new technologies. This has been a significant driving force behind the development of faster, less expensive, and/or more energy efficient system configurations.

The authors believes that the WBDB 2012 is a first important step towards the development of a benchmark standard that measures the effectiveness of hardware and software systems dealing with Big Data applications and will be used by vendors, researchers, and end users. From a vendor point of view, these standards define a level playing field with competitive comparisons and enable monitoring release-to-release progress of hard-

ware and software products. Like other industry standard benchmarks, these standards are expected to help customers to compare performance, cost of ownership, and the energy efficiency of Big Data platforms. Standardized workloads and metrics like these will also help researchers to develop and enhance relevant technologies for Big Data applications.

ACKNOWLEDGMENT

The authors thank Anakha and Monica for their support in writing this chapter.

REFERENCES

Anon, E. (1985). *A measure of transaction processing power*. Retrieved June 19, 2013 from http://research.microsoft.com/en-us/um/people/gray/papers/AMeasureOfTransactionProcessingPower.pdf

Ghazal, A., Rabl, T., Hu, M., Raab, F., Poess, M., Crolotte, A., & Jacobsen, H.-A. (2013). BigBench: Towards an industry standard benchmark for big data analytics. In *Proceedings of SIGMOD*. New York: ACM.

Gray, J. (2009). *Jim Gray – Industry leader*. Retrieved June 19, 2013 from http://www.tpc.org/information/who/gray.asp

IDC. (2013). *Big data in 2020*. Retrieved June 19, 2013 from http://www.emc.com/leadership/digital-universe/iview/big-data-2020.htm

Nambiar, R., & Poess, M. (2006). The making of TPC-DS. *VLDB*, 1049-1058.

(2009). In R. Nambiar, & M. Poess (Eds.). Lecture Notes in Computer Science: Vol. 5895. *Performance evaluation and benchmarking*.

(2010). In R. Nambiar, & M. Poess (Eds.). Lecture Notes in Computer Science: Vol. 6417. *Performance evaluation, measurement and characterization of complex systems*.

(2011). In R. Nambiar, & M. Poess (Eds.). Lecture Notes in Computer Science: Vol. 7144. *Topics in performance evaluation, measurement and characterization*. doi:10.1007/978-3-642-18206-8.

(2012). In R. Nambiar, & M. Poess (Eds.). Lecture Notes in Computer Science: Vol. 7755. *Selected topics in performance evaluation and benchmarking*.

Poess, M., Nambiar, R., Baru, C., Bhandarkar, M., & Raab, R. (2013). *Benchmarking big data systems and the big data top 100 list: Big data*. Mary Ann Liebert, Inc..

Poess, M., Nambiar, R., & Walrath, D. (2007). Why you should run TPC-DS: A workload analysis. *VLDB*, 1138-1149.

SAP. (2013). *SAP standard application benchmarks*. Retrieved June 19, 2013 from http://www.sap.com/campaigns/benchmark/index.epx

Shanley, K. (1998). *History and overview of the TPC*. Retrieved June 19, 2013 from http://www.tpc.org/information/about/history.asp

SPC. (2013). *SPC-1 and SPC-1/E benchmark results*. Retrieved June 19, 2013 from http://www.storageperformance.org/results/benchmark_results_spc1

Terasort. (2013). *org.apache.hadoop.examples.terasort*. Retrieved June 19, 2013 from http://hadoop.apache.org/docs/current/api/org/apache/hadoop/examples/terasort/package-summary.html

WBDB. (2012a). *First workshop on big data benchmarking*. Retrieved June 19, 2013 from http://clds.ucsd.edu/wbdb2012/

WBDB. (2012b). *Second workshop on big data benchmarking*. Retrieved June 19, 2013 from http://clds.ucsd.edu/wbdb2012.in

YCSB. (2013). Retrieved June 19, 2013 from http://research.yahoo.com/Web_Information_Management/YCSB

ADDITIONAL READING

J. Gray (Ed.). (1993). *The benchmark handbook for database and transaction systems*. San Francisco, CA: Morgan Kaufmann.

Gray, J., & Reuter, A. (1993). *Transaction processing: Concepts and techniques*. San Francisco, CA: Morgan Kaufmann.

Nambiar, R., & Poess, M. (2010). Transaction performance vs. Moore's law: Performance evaluation, measurement and characterization of complex systems. *Lecture Notes in Computer Science*, 6417.

Pavlo, A., Paulson, E., Rasin, A., Abadi, D., DeWitt, D., Madden, S., & Stonebraker, M. (2012). Comparison of approaches to large-scale data analysis. [ACM.]. *Proceedings of SIGMOD*, *2009*, 165–178.

Poess, M., & Nambiar, R. (2011). Power based performance and capacity estimation models for enterprise information systems. *A Quarterly Bulletin of the Computer Society of the IEEE Technical Committee on Data Engineering, 34*(1), 34–49.

KEY TERMS AND DEFINITIONS

Benchmark: A set of rules for running a specific workload using software and hardware in a controlled environment.

Benchmarking: The process of running a benchmark for the purpose of measuring the performance of software and hardware.

Big Data: Is a discipline in computer science that deal with the processing and analysis of extremely large and diverse data sets.

Databases: A collection of usually structured data set organized by database systems for fast update and retrieval of portions of the data.

Industry Standard Benchmark: A benchmark representing a workload of a specific industry segment. Usually the benchmark is accepted by a large number of companies active in this industry segment.

Non SQL Systems: Database systems not running the standard languages SQL (Structured Query Language).

Performance Analysis: Process of interpreting data collected during a benchmark run or performance run with the intent of understanding the performance characteristics of a system, both software and hardware, and identifying performance bottlenecks.

Compilation of References

(2009). In R. Nambiar, & M. Poess (Eds.). Lecture Notes in Computer Science: Vol. 5895. *Performance evaluation and benchmarking.*

(2010). In R. Nambiar, & M. Poess (Eds.). Lecture Notes in Computer Science: Vol. 6417. *Performance evaluation, measurement and characterization of complex systems.*

(2011). In R. Nambiar, & M. Poess (Eds.). Lecture Notes in Computer Science: Vol. 7144. *Topics in performance evaluation, measurement and characterization.* doi:10.1007/978-3-642-18206-8.

(2012). In R. Nambiar, & M. Poess (Eds.). Lecture Notes in Computer Science: Vol. 7755. *Selected topics in performance evaluation and benchmarking.*

Abadi, D., Madden, S., & Hachem, N. (2008). Column-stores vs. row-stores: How different are they really? In *Proceedings of the 2008 ACM SIGMOD International Conference on Management of Data.* ACM.

Abouzeid, A., Bajda-Pawlikowski, K., Abadi, D., Silberschatz, A., & Rasin, A. (2009). HadoopDB: An architectural hybrid of MapReduce and DBMS technologies for analytical workloads. In *Proceedings of VLDB 2009.* VLDB.

Abouzeid, A., Bajda-Pawlikowski, K., Abadi, D., Silberschatz, A., & Rasin, A. (2009). HadoopDB: An architectural hybrid of MapReduce and DBMS technologies for analytical workloads. *Proceedings of the VLDB Endowment, 2*(1), 922–933.

Abramowitz, M., & Stegun, I. A. (1964). *Handbook of mathematical functions with formulas, graphs, and mathematical tables* (9th ed.). New York: Dover.

Ács, B., Llorà, X., Auvil, L., Capitanu, B., Tcheng, D., Haberman, M., & Welge, M. (2010). A general approach to data-intensive computing using the Meandre component-based framework. In *Proceedings of the 1st International Workshop on Workflow Approaches to New Data-Centric Science.* IEEE.

Adamic, L. A., & Adar, E. (2005). How to search a social network. *Social Networks, 27*(3), 187–203. doi:10.1016/j.socnet.2005.01.007.

Adams, J. L., & Gunn, K. B. (2012). Digital humanities: Where to start. *College & Research Libraries News, 73*(9), 536–569.

Adar, E. Zhang, L. Adamic, L. A., & Lukose, R. M. (2004). Implicit structure and the dynamics of blogspace. *Workshop on the Weblogging Ecosystem, 13*(1).

Agrawal, D., Das, S., & Abbadi, A. E. (2011). Big data and cloud computing: Current state and future opportunities. In *Proceedings of the 14th International Conference on Extending Database Technology* (pp. 530-533). IEEE.

AH. (2011). *Apache Hadoop.* Retrieved from http://hadoop.apache.org/

AH. (2012). *Apache Hive.* Retrieved from http://hive.apache.org/

Ahuja, R. K., Magnanti, T. L., & Orlin, J. B. (1993). *Network flows*. Englewood Cliffs, NJ: Prentice Hall, Inc..

Akka. (2012). *Akka documentation*. Retrieved from http://akka.io/docs/

Albright, J. J., & Lyle, J. A. (2010). Data preservation through data archives. *PS: Political Science & Politics, 43*(1), 17–21. doi:10.1017/S1049096510990768.

Almas, B., Babeu, A., Bamman, D., & Boschetti, F. Cerrato, L., Crane, G., ... Smith, D. (2011). *What did we do with a million books: Rediscovering the Greco-ancient world and reinventing the humanities* (White Paper). Washington, DC: National Endowment for the Humanities.

Almuallim, H., & Dietterich, T. G. (1991). Learning with many irrelevant features. In *Proceedings of the Ninth National Conference on Artificial Intelligence (AAAI-91)*, (vol. 2, pp. 547–552). Anaheim, CA: AAAI Press.

Alumur, S., & Kara, B. Y. (2008). Network hub location problems: The state of the art. *European Journal of Operational Research, 190*(1), 1–21. doi:10.1016/j.ejor.2007.06.008.

Aluru, S., Prabhu, G. M., & Gustafson, J. (1992). A random number generator for parallel computers. *Parallel Computing, 18*(8), 839–847. doi:10.1016/0167-8191(92)90030-B.

Alves, D., Bizarro, P., & Marques, P. (2011). Deadline queries: Leveraging the cloud to produce on-time results. In *Proceedings of International Conference on Cloud Computing* (pp. 171–178). IEEE.

AM. (2012). *Apache Mahout*. Retrieved from http://mahout.apache.org/

Amazon Web Services, Inc. (n.d.). *Amazon EC2 instance types*. Retrieved January 19, 2013, from http://aws.amazon.com/ec2/instance-types/

AMD. (2012). AMD fusion family of APUs: Enabling a superior, immersive PC experience. *AMD Fusion Whitepaper*. Retrieved January 24, 2013, from http://www.amd.com/us/Documents/48423_fusion_whitepaper_WEB.pdf

American Council of Learned Society. (2006). *Our cultural commonwealth: The report of the American council of learned societies commission on cyberinfrastructure for the humanities and social sciences*. Retrieved from http://www.acls.org/cyberinfrastructure/ourculturalcommonwealth.pdf

Anderson, S. (2007). *The arts and humanities and e-Science: Scoping survey report and findings*. Retrieved from http://www.ahessc.ac.uk/scoping-survey

Anderson, C. (2006). *The long tail: Why the future of business is selling less of more*. New York: Hyperion.

Andreolini, M., Casolari, S., & Colajanni, M. (2008). Autonomic request management algorithms for geographically distributed internet-based systems. In *Proceedings of International Conference on Self-Adaptive and Self-Organizing Systems* (pp. 171–180). IEEE.

Anon, E. (1985). *A measure of transaction processing power*. Retrieved June 19, 2013 from http://research.microsoft.com/en-us/um/people/gray/papers/AMeasureOfTransactionProcessingPower.pdf

AP. (2012). *Apache Pig*. Retrieved from http://pig.apache.org/

Apache. (2010). *HBase: Bigtable-like structured storage for Hadoop HDFS*. Retrieved from http://hadoop.apache.org/hbase/

ASCE. (2009). *Report card for americas infrastructure*. Retrieved from http://apps.asce.org/reportcard/2009/grades.cfm

Avila-Garcia, M. S., Xiong, X., Trefethen, A. E., Crichton, C., Tsui, A., & Hu, P. (2011). A virtual research environment for cancer imaging research. In *Proceedings of the IEEE Seventh International Conference on eScience* (pp. 1-6). IEEE.

Badke, W. (2012). Big search, big data. *Online, 36*(3), 47–49.

Bakhtouchi, A., Bellatreche, L., & Ait-Ameur, Y. (2011). Ontologies and functional dependencies for data integration and reconciliation. In O. De Troyer, C. Bauzer Medeiros, R. Billen, P. Hallot, A. Simitsis, & H. Van Mingroot (Eds.), *Advances in Conceptual Modeling. Recent Developments and New Directions, (LNCS)* (Vol. 6999, pp. 98–107). Berlin: Springer. doi:10.1007/978-3-642-24574-9_13.

Bar-Ilan, J. (2005). Information hub blogs. *Journal of Information Science, 31*, 297–307. doi:10.1177/0165551505054175.

Barnett, T. (2011). Cisco visual networking index: The zettabyte era. *Cisco Systems Inc.* Retrieved August 2012 from http://www.cisco.com/en/US/solutions/collateral/ns341/ns525/ns537/ns705/ns827/VNI_Hyperconnectivity_WP.html

Bastian, M., Heymann, S., & Jacomy, M. (2009). Gephi: An open source software for exploring and manipulating networks. In *Proceedings of the 3rd International AAAI Conference on Weblogs and Social Media*. Retrieved January, 2013, from http://www.aaai.org/ocs/index.php/ICWSM/09/paper/view/154.

Baumann, P. (1999). A database array algebra for spatio-temporal data and beyond. In *Proceedings of the Workshop on Next Generation Information Technologies and Systems*. IEEE.

Beattie, R. (1970). ICPSR: Resources for the study of conflict resolution: The inter-university consortium for political and social research. *The Journal of Conflict Resolution, 23*(2), 337–345. doi:10.1177/0022002779 02300207.

Bekaert, J., & Sompel, V. (2006). *Augmenting interoperability across scholarly repositories*. Retrieved from http://msc.mellon.org/Meetings/Interop/FinalReport/

Berson, A., & Smith, S. J. (1997). *Data warehousing, data mining, and OLAP*. New York: McGraw-Hill, Inc..

Beyer, M. A., Lovelock, J.-D., Sommer, D., & Adrian, M. (2012, October 12). *Big data drives rapid changes in infrastructure and $232 billion in IT spending through 2016*. Retrieved June 12, 2013, from http://www.gartner.com/id=2195915

Bhatia, N. (2009). *Performance evaluation of AMD RVI hardware assist*. VMWare, Inc.

Bietz, M. J., Ferro, T., & Lee, C. P. (2012). Sustaining the development of cyberinfrastructure: An organization adapting to change. In *Proceedings of the ACM 2012 conference on Computer Supported Cooperative Work* (pp. 901-910). ACM. Retrieved from http://dx.doi.org.ezproxy.lib.indiana.edu/10.1145/2145204.2145339

Birney, E., Hudson, T. J., Green, E. D., Gunter, C., Eddy, S., & Rogers, J. et al. (2009). Prepublication of data sharing. *Nature, 461*, 168–170. doi:10.1038/461168a PMID:19741685.

Blanke, T., Dunn, S., & Dunning, A. (2006). Digital libraries in the arts and humanities – Current practices and future possibilities. In *Proceedings of the 2006 International Conference on Multidisciplinary Information Sciences and Technologies (INSciT 2006)*. INSciT.

Bollen, J., Mao, H., & Zeng, X. J. (2011). Twitter mood predicts the stock market. *Journal of Computational Science, 2*(1), 1–8. doi:10.1016/j.jocs.2010.12.007.

Bollier, D. (2010). *The promise and peril of big data*. Retrieved from http://www.thinkbiganalytics.com/uploads/Aspen-Big_Data.pdf

Boltzmann, L. (2011). Lectures on gas theory. New York: Dover Publications. ISBN-10: 0486684555.

Bonifati, A., Cattaneo, F., Ceri, S., Fuggetta, A., & Paraboschi, S. (2001). Designing data marts for data warehouses. *ACM Transactions on Software Engineering and Methodology, 10*, 452–483. doi:10.1145/384189.384190.

Borgman, C.L. (2009). The digital future is now: A call to action for the humanities. *Digital Humanities Quarterly, 4*(1).

Borgman, C. L. (2012). The conundrum of sharing research data. *Journal of the American Society for Information Science and Technology, 63*(6), 1059–1078. doi:10.1002/asi.22634.

Bornea, M. A., Deligiannakis, A., Kotidis, Y., & Vassalos, V. (2011). Semi-streamed index join for near-real time execution of ETL transformations. In *Proceedings of the IEEE 27th International Conference on Data Engineering (ICDE'11)* (pp. 159–170). IEEE. doi:10.1109/ICDE.2011.5767906

Borthakur, D. (2007). *The Hadoop distributed file system: Architecture and design*. Apache Software Foundation. boyd, d., & Crawford, K. (2011). Six provocations for big data. In *A Decade in Internet Time: Symposium on the Dynamics of the Internet and Society*. Academic Press.

Borthakur, D., Muthukkaruppan, K., Ranganathan, K., Rash, S., Sen Sarma, J., Spiegelberg, N., et al. (2011). Apache hadoop goes realtime at Facebook. In *Proceedings of SIGMOD 2011*. ACM.

Boulos, M. N. K., Sanfilippo, A. P., Corley, C. D., & Wheeler, S. (2010). Social web mining and exploitation for serious applications: Technosocial predictive analytics and related technologies for public health, environmental and national security surveillance. *Computer Methods and Programs in Biomedicine, 100*, 16–23. doi:10.1016/j.cmpb.2010.02.007 PMID:20236725.

Boupha, S., Grisso, A. D., Morris, J., Webb, L. M., & Zakeri, M. (2013). How college students display ethnic identity on Facebook. In R. A. Lind (Ed.), *Race/gender/media: Considering diversity across audiences, content, and producers* (3rd ed.), (pp. 107-112). Boston, MA: Pearson. boyd, d. (2010, April). *Privacy and publicity in the context of big data*. Retrieved from http://www.danah.org/papers/talks/2010/WWW2010.html

Box, G., Jenkins, G., & Reinsel, G. (1994). *Time series analysis: Forecasting and control*. Upper Saddle River, NJ: Prentice Hall.

Boyd, D., & Ellison, N. B. (2008). Social network sites: Definition, history, and scholarship. *Journal of Computer-Mediated Communication, 13*, 210–230. doi:10.1111/j.1083-6101.2007.00393.x.

Bradley, T., Toit, J. D., Tong, R., Giles, M., & Woodhams, P. (2011). Parallelization techniques for random number generators. In W. Hwu (Ed.), GPU Computing Gems Emerald Ed., (pp. 231–246). Boston: Morgan Kaufmann.

Brantner, M., Florescu, D., Graf, D., Kossmann, D., & Kraska, T. (2008). Building a database on S3. In *Proceedings of the 2008 ACM SIGMOD International Conference on Management of Data* (pp. 251–264). New York, NY: ACM.

Brunner, R. K., & Kale, L. V. (1999) Adapting to load on workstation clusters. In *Proceedings of the Symposium on the Frontiers of Massively Parallel Computation* (pp. 106–112). IEEE.

Brunner, R. J., Djorgovski, S. G., Prince, T. A., & Szalay, A. S. (2002). Massive datasets in astronomy. In J. Abello, P. Pardalos, & M. Resende (Eds.), *Handbook of massive data sets*. Norwell, MA: Kluwer Academic Publishers.

Bryant, R. E. (2007). *Data-intensive supercomputing: The case for DISC[R]* (CMU Technical Report CMU-CS-07-128). Pittsburgh, PA: Department of Computer Science, Carnegie Mellon University.

Bryant, R. E., Katz, R. H., & Lazowska, E. D. (2008). Big-data computing: Creating revolutionary breakthroughs in commerce, science, and society. In *Computing Research Initiatives for the 21st Century*. Computing Research Association. Retrieved from www.cra.org/ccc/docs/init/Big_Data.pdf

Buck, J. B., Watkins, N., LeFevre, J., Ioannidou, K., Maltzahn, C., Polyzotis, N., & Brandt, S. (2011). SciHadoop: Array-based query processing in Hadoop. In *Proceedings of 2011 International Conference for High Performance Computing, Networking, Storage and Analysis (SC '11)*. ACM.

Buck, J., Watkins, N., LeFevre, J., Ioannidou, K., Maltzahn, C., Polyzotis, N., & Brandt, S. (2011). *SciHadoop: Array-based query processing in Hadoop*. Supercomputing.

Burton, S., & Soboleva, A. (2011). Interactive or reactive? Marketing with Twitter. *Journal of Consumer Marketing, 28*(7), 491–499. doi:10.1108/07363761111181473.

Butler, B. J., & Chandler, C. J. (2012). Data management for the EVLA. In *Proceedings of SPIE Astronomical Telescopes+ Instrumentation* (pp. 84510A-84510A). International Society for Optics and Photonics.

Buyya, R. (1999). *High performance cluster computing: Architectures and systems* (Vol. 1). Upper Saddle River, NJ: Prentice Hall.

Caers, R., & Castelyns, V. (2011). LinkedIn and Facebook in Belgium: The influences and biases of social network sites in recruitment and selection procedures. *Social Science Computer Review, 29*, 437–448. doi:10.1177/0894439310386567.

Candela, L., Athanasopoulos, G., Castelli, D., El Raheb, K., Innocenti, P., & Ioannidis, Y. … Ross, S. (2011). *The digital library reference model*. Retrieved from http://bscw.research-infrastructures.eu/pub/bscw.cgi/d222816/D3.2b Digital Library Reference Model.pdf

Casavant, T. L., & Kuhl, J. G. (1994). A taxonomy of scheduling in general purpose distributed computing systems. *Transactions on Software Engineering, 14*(2), 141–153. doi:10.1109/32.4634.

Cattell, R. (2011). Scalable SQL and NoSQL data stores. *SIGMOD Record, 39*(4), 12–27. doi:10.1145/1978915.1978919.

Chakraborty, A., & Singh, A. (2009). A partition-based approach to support streaming updates over persistent data in an active datawarehouse. In *Proceedings of the 2009 IEEE International Symposium on Parallel & Distributed Processing* (pp. 1–11). Washington, DC: IEEE Computer Society. doi:http://dx.doi.org/10.1109/IPDPS.2009.5161064

Chakraborty, A., & Singh, A. (2010). A disk-based, adaptive approach to memory-limited computation of windowed stream joins. In *Proceedings of the 21st International Conference on Database and Expert Systems Applications: Part I* (pp. 251–260). Berlin: Springer-Verlag. Retrieved from http://portal.acm.org/citation.cfm?id=1881867.1881892

Chang, F., Dean, J., Ghemawat, S., Hsieh, W., Wallach, D., & Burrows, M. … Gruber, R. (2006). Bigtable: A distributed storage system for structured data. In *Proceeding of 7ᵗʰ Conference on Usenix Symposium on Operating System Design and Implementation*, (vol. 7). Usenix. Retrieved from http://citeseer.ist.psu.edu/viewdoc/summary?doi=10.1.1.101.9822

Chan, K.-P., & Fu, A. W.-C. (1999). Efficient time series matching by wavelets.[IEEE.]. *Proceedings of Data Engineering, 1999*, 126–133.

Chapman, B., Jost, G., & Ruud, R. V. D. P. (2007). *Using OpenMP: Portable shared memory parallel programming*. Cambridge, MA: The MIT Press.

Chen, Q., Hsu, M., & Zeller, H. (2011). Experience in continuous analytics as a service. In *Proceedings of International Conference on Extending Database Technology* (pp. 509-514). IEEE.

Cheng, J., Sun, A., Hu, D., & Zeng, D. (2011). An information diffusion-based recommendation framework for micro-blogging. *Journal of the Association for Information Systems, 12*, 463–486.

Chen, W. Y., Song, Y., Bai, H., Lin, C., & Chang, E. Y. (2011). Parallel spectral clustering in distributed systems. *IEEE Transactions on Pattern Analysis and Machine Intelligence, 33*(3), 568–586. doi:10.1109/TPAMI.2010.88 PMID:20421667.

Chen, Z. (2001). *Intelligent data warehousing: From data preparation to data mining*. Boca Raton, FL: CRC Press. doi:10.1201/9781420040616.

Chiba, R., & Sato-Ilic, M. (2012). Analysis of web survey data based on similarity of fuzzy clusters. In C. H. Dagli (Ed.), *Complex adaptive systems*. Procedia Computer Science. doi:10.1016/j.procs.2012.09.060.

Christianson, H. (2011). HathiTrust. *Library Resources & Technical Services*, *55*(2), 93–102. doi:10.5860/lrts.55n2.93.

Chtepen, M. (2005). Dynamic scheduling in grids system. In *Proceedings of the PhD Symposium*. Ghent, Belgium: Faculty of Engineering, Ghent University.

Cinquini, L., Crichton, D., Mattmann, C., Harney, J., Shipman, G., Wang, F., & Schweitzer, R. (2012). The earth system grid federation: An open infrastructure for access to distributed geospatial data. In *Proceedings of E-Science* (e-Science), (pp. 1-10). IEEE.

Clauset, A., Shalizi, C. R., & Newman, M. E. J. (2009). Power-law distributions in empirical data. *SIAM Review*, *51*, 661–703.

Cloud Security Alliance Big Data Working Group. (2012). *Top 10 big data security and privacy challenges*. Cloud Security Alliance. Retrieved from https://cloudsecurity-alliance.org/research/big-data/#_downloads

Cohen, J., Dolan, B., Dunlap, M., Hellerstein, J. M., & Welton, C. (2009). MAD skills: New analysis practices for big data. *Proccedings of VLDB 2009, 2*(2).

Cohen, J., Dolan, B., Dunlap, M., Hellerstein, J. M., & Welton, C. (2009). Mad skills: New analysis practices for big data. *Proceedings of the VLDB Endowment, 2*(2), 1481–1492.

Collier, K., & Highsmith, J. A. (2004). Agile data warehousing: Incorporating agile principles. Business Intelligence Advisory Service Executive Report, *4*(12).

Collins, D. W. (2004). US national oceanographic data center: Archival management practices and the open archival information system reference model. In *Proceedings of the 21st IEEE Conference on Mass Storage Systems and Technologies*. IEEE. Retrieved from http://storageconference.org/2004/Papers/39-Collins-a.pdf

Collins, D. W., & Rutz, S. B. (2005). The NODC archive management system: Archiving marine data for ocean exploration and beyond. In *Proceedings of MTS/IEEE Data of Conference*. IEEE. doi:10.1109/OCEANS.2005.1640202

Collins, D. W., Rutz, S. B., Dantzler, H. L., Ogata, E. J., Mitchell, F. J., Shirley, J., & Thailambal, T. (2003). Introducing the U.S. NODC archive management system: Stewardship of the nation's oceanographic data archive. *Earth System Monitor*, *14*(1). Retrieved from http://www.nodc.noaa.gov/media/pdf/esm/ESM_SEP2003vol14no1.pdf.

Cooper, B., Silberstein, A., Tam, E., Ramakrishnan, R., & Sears, S. (2010). Benchmarking cloud serving systems with YCSB. In *Proceedings of the ACM Symposium on Cloud Computing*. ACM. Retrieved January 2010 from http://research.yahoo.com/node/3202

Couper, M. P., & Miller, P. V. (2008). Web survey methods. *Public Opinion Quarterly*, *72*(5), 831–835. doi:10.1093/poq/nfn066.

Cowell, F. A. (1995). *Measuring inequality* (2nd ed.). Hemel Hampstead, UK: Harverster Wheatsheaf.

Cox, M., & Ellsworth, D. (1997). Managing big data for scientific visualization. In *Proceedings of ACM SIGGRAPH* (Vol. 97). ACM.

Crane, G. (2006). What do you do with a million books? *D-Lib Magazine*, *12*(3). Retrieved from http://www.dlib.org/dlib/march06/crane/03crane.html doi:10.1045/march2006-crane.

Crichton, D. J., Mattmann, C. A., Hughes, J. S., Kelly, S. C., & Hart, A. F. (2011). A multidisciplinary, model-driven, distributed science data system architecture. In *Guide to e-Science* (pp. 117–143). London: Springer. doi:10.1007/978-0-85729-439-5_5.

Crosas, M. (2011). The dataverse network: An open-source application for sharing, discovering and preserving data. *D-Lib Magazine*, *17*(1/2). Retrieved from http://www.dlib.org doi:10.1045/january2011-crosas.

Cunningham, L. (2011). The librarian as digital humanist: The collaborative role of the research library in digital humanities projects. *Faculty of Information Quarterly*, *2*(1). Retrieved from http://fiq.ischool.utoronto.ca/index.php/fiq/article/view/15409/12438

Cuzzocrea, A., Song, I. Y., & Davis, K. C. (2011). Analytics over large-scale multidimensional data: The big data revolution! In *Proceedings of DOLAP Conference*, (pp. 101-104). DOLAP.

Daniel, J. (2012). *Sampling essentials: Practical guidelines for making sampling choices.* Thousand Oaks, CA: Sage.

David, H. B. (2012). ARPREC: C++/Fortran-90 arbitrary precision package. *High-Precision Software Directory.* Retrieved January 24, 2013, from http://crd-legacy.lbl. gov/~dhbailey/mpdist/

de Matteis, A., & Pagnutti, S. (1990). A class of parallel random number generators. *Parallel Computing, 13*(2), 193–198. doi:10.1016/0167-8191(90)90146-Z.

De Roure, D., Goble, C., & Stevens, R. (2009). The design and realization of the myExperiment virtual research environment for social sharing of workflows. *Future Generation Computer Systems, 25,* 561–567. doi:10.1016/j. future.2008.06.010.

de Vos, M., Gunst, A. W., & Nijboer, R. (2009). The LO-FAR telescope: System architecture and signal processing. *Proceedings of the IEEE, 97*(8), 1431–1437. doi:10.1109/JPROC.2009.2020509.

Dean, J., & Ghemawat, S. (2004). MapReduce: Simplified data processing on large clusters. In *Proceedings of the Symposium on Operating System Design and Implementation* (pp. 107-113). ACM.

Dean, J., & Ghemawat, S. (2008). Mapreduce: Simplified data processing on large clusters. *Communications of the ACM, 51*(1), 107–113. doi:10.1145/1327452.1327492.

DeCandia, G., Hastorun, D., Jampani, M., Kakulapati, G., Lakshman, K., & Pilchin, A. ... Vogels, W. (2007). Dynamo: Amazon's highly available key-value store. In *Proceedings of 21st ACM SIGOPS Symposium on Operating Systems Principles,* (pp. 205-220). ACM. Retrieved December 2007 from http://dl.acm.org/citation. cfm?id=1294281

dell'Aquila, C., Di Tria, F., Lefons, E., & Tangorra, F. (2009). Dimensional fact model extension via predicate calculus. In *Proceedings of the 24th International Symposium on Computer and Information Sciences* (pp. 211-217). IEEE Press.

dell'Aquila, C., Di Tria, F., Lefons, E., & Tangorra, F. (2010). Logic programming for data warehouse conceptual schema validation. In T. B. Pedersen, M. K. Mohania, & A. M. Tjoa (Eds.), *Data Warehousing and Knowledge Discovery (LNCS)* (Vol. 6263, pp. 1–12). Berlin: Springer. doi:10.1007/978-3-642-15105-7_1.

Demirkan, H., & Delen, D. (2012). *Leveraging the capabilities of service-oriented decision support systems: Putting analytics and big data in cloud.* Decision Support Systems. Retrieved January, 2013, from http://dx.doi. org/10.1016/j.dss.2012.05.048.

Desai, N., Kommu, S., & Rapp, J. (2011). Big data in the enterprise: Network design considerations. *Cisco Systems Inc.* Retrieved November 2011 from http://www.cisco. com/en/US/prod/collateral/switches/ps9441/ps9670/ white_paper_c11-690561.html

Dhillon, I., Mallela, S., & Kumar, R. (2002). Enhanced word clustering for hierarchical text classification. In *Proceedings of the 8th ACM SIGKDD.* Edmonton, Canada: ACM.

Di Tria, F., Lefons, E., & Tangorra, F. (2011). GrHyMM: A graph-oriented hybrid multidimensional model. In O. De Troyer, C. Bauzer Medeiros, R. Billen, P. Hallot, A. Simitsis, & H. Van Mingroot (Eds.), *Advances in Conceptual Modeling. Recent Developments and New Directions (LNCS)* (Vol. 6999, pp. 86–97). Berlin: Springer. doi:10.1007/978-3-642-24574-9_12.

Di Tria, F., Lefons, E., & Tangorra, F. (2012). Hybrid methodology for data warehouse conceptual design by UML schemas. *Information and Software Technology, 54*(4), 360–379. doi:10.1016/j.infsof.2011.11.004.

Diebold, F. X. (2003). Big data dynamic factor models for macroeconomic measurement and forecasting: A discussion of the papers by Reichlin and Watson. In M. Dewatripont, L. P. Hansen, & S. Turnovsky (Eds.), *Advances in Economics and Econometrics: Theory and applications.* Cambridge, UK: Cambridge Press. doi:10.1017/CBO9780511610264.005.

Dimiduk, N., & Khurana, M. (2012). *HBase in action.* Shelter Island, NY: Manning Publication Inc..

Domingos, P., & Richardson, M. (2001). Mining the network value of customers. In *Proceedings of the Seventh ACM SIGKDD International Conference on Knowledge Discovery and Data Mining.* San Francisco, CA: ACM.

Douglas, C., & Tang, H. (2012). Gridmix3-emulating Apache workload for Apache Hadoop. *Yahoo Developer Network.* Retrieved April 2012 from http://developer.yahoo.com/blogs/Hadoop/posts/2010/04/gridmix3_emulating_production/

DP. (2012). *Disco project.* Retrieved from http://discoproject.org/

Drucker, J. (2009, April 3). Blind spots: Humanists must plan their digital future. *The Chronicle of Higher Education.*

Dryad Development Team. (2010). *Dryad metadata application profile, version 3.0.* Retrieved from http://wiki.datadryad.org/wg/dryad/images/8/8b/Dryad3.0.pdf

Dryad. (n.d.). *Dryad digital repository.* Retrieved from http://datadryad.org/

Dumbill, E. (2012, November). Making sense of big data. *Big Data.*

Dunn, S., & Blanke, T. (2009). Digital humanities quarterly special cluster on arts and humanities e-science. *Digital Humanities Quarterly, 3*(4).

École Polytechnique Fédérale de Lausanne. (2013). *Scala.* Retrieved from http://www.scala-lang.org/

Ekanayake, J., Gunarathne, T., Fox, G., Balkir, A. S., Poulain, C., Araujo, N., & Barga, R. (2009). Dryadlinq for scientific analyses. In *Proceedings of the Fifth IEEE International Conference on e-Science* (E-SCIENCE '09), (pp. 329–336). IEEE.

Ekanayake, J., Li, H., Zhang, B., Gunarathne, T., Bae, S., Qiu, J., & Fox, G. (2010). Twister: A runtime for iterative mapreduce. In *Proceedings of the 19th ACM International Symposium on High Performance Distributed Computing,* (pp. 810–818). ACM.

Elmasri, R., & Navathe, S. B. (2010). *Fundamentals of database systems* (6th ed.). Reading, MA: Addison-Wesley.

Empson, R. (2013). *DARPA-backed Ayasdi launches with $10m from Khosla, Floodgate to uncover hidden value in big data.* Retrieved from http://techcrunch.com/2013/01/16/darpa-backed-ayasdi-launches-with-10m-from-khosla-floodgate-to-uncover-the-hidden-value-in-big-data/

Enright, A., & Ouzounis, C. (2000). GeneRAGE: A robust algorithm for sequence clustering and domain detection. *Bioinformatics (Oxford, England), 16,* 451–457. doi:10.1093/bioinformatics/16.5.451 PMID:10871267.

EPL. (2012). *Erlang programming language.* Retrieved from http://www.erlang.org/

Facebook Now Has 30 000 Servers. (n.d.). Retrieved January, 2013, from http://www.datacenterknowledge.com/archives/2009/10/13/facebook-now-has-30000-servers/

Faloutsos, C., Ranganathan, M., & Manolopoulos, Y. (1994). Fast subsequence matching in time-series databases. *SIGMOD Record, 23*(2), 419–429. doi:10.1145/191843.191925.

Fan, P., Wang, J., Zheng, Z., & Lyu, M. (2011). Toward optimal deployment of communication-intensive cloud applications. In *Proceedings of International Conference on Cloud Computing* (pp. 460–467). IEEE.

Fayyad, F., Piatetsky-Shapiro, G., & Smyth, P. (1996). From data mining to knowledge discovery in databases. *AI Magazine, 17,* 37–54.

Fenk, R., Markl, V., & Bayer, R. (2002). Interval processing with the UB-tree. In *Proceedings of the Database Engineering and Applications Symposium.* IEEE.

Ferguson, D. A., & Greer, C. F. (2011). Local radio and microblogging: How radio stations in the U.S. are using Twitter. *Journal of Radio & Audio Media, 18,* 33–46. doi:10.1080/19376529.2011.558867.

Ferilli, S., Basile, T. M. A., Biba, M., Di Mauro, N., & Esposito, F. (2009). A general similarity framework for horn clause logic. *Fundamentals of Informatics, 90*(1-2), 43–66.

Fielding, R. T., & Taylor, R. N. (2002). Principled design of the modern web architecture. *ACM Transactions on Internet Technology, 2*(2), 115–150. doi:10.1145/514183.514185.

Fienberg, S. E. (1994). Sharing statistical data in the biomedical and health sciences: Ethical, institutional, legal, and professional dimensions. *Annual Review of Public Health*, *15*, 1–18. doi:10.1146/annurev. pu.15.050194.000245 PMID:8054076.

Filipović, V. (2003). Fine grained tournament selection operator in genetic algorithms. *Computing and Informatics*, *22*, 143–161.

Folk, M., Cheng, A., & Yates, K. (1999). *HDF5: A file format and I/O library for high performance computing applications*. Supercomputing.

Fortner, B. (1998). HDF: The hierarchical data format. *Dr Dobb's J Software Tools Prof Program*, *23*(5), 42.

Foster, I., Zhao, Y., Raicu, I., & Lu, S. (2008). Cloud computing and grid computing 360-degree compared. In *Proceedings of the Grid Computing Environments Workshop* (pp. 1-10). IEEE.

Foster, I. (2011). Globus online: Accelerating and democratizing science through cloud-based services. *IEEE Internet Computing*, *15*(3), 70–73. doi:10.1109/MIC.2011.64.

Foster, I., Kesselman, C., & Tuecke, S. (2001). The anatomy of the gird: Enabling scalable virtual organizations. *International Journal of High Performance Computing Applications*, *15*(3), 200–222. doi:10.1177/109434200101500302.

Foxvog, D. (2010). Cyc. In *Theory and Applications of Ontology: Computer Applications* (pp. 259–278). Berlin: Springer. doi:10.1007/978-90-481-8847-5_12.

Friedlander, A. (2009). Asking questions and building a research agenda for digital scholarship. In *Working Together or Apart: Promoting the Next Generation of Digital Scholarship*. Academic Press.

Friedman-Hill, E. J. (2008, November 5). *Jess, the rule engine for the java platform - The rete algorithm*. Retrieved January 26, 2013, from http://www.jessrules.com/jess/docs/71/rete.html

Fujimaki, R., Hirose, S., & Nakata, T. (2008). Theoretical analysis of sub- sequence time-series clustering from a frequency-analysis viewpoint. In *Proceedings of SDM 2008* (pp. 506–517). SDM.

Fullwood, C., Sheehan, N., & Nicholls, W. (2009). Blog function revisited: A content analysis of Myspace blogs. *CyberPsychology & Behavior*, *12*(6), 685-689. doi: 10. 1089/cpb.2009.0138

Gantz, J., & Reinsel, D. (2011). The 2011 digital universe study: Extracting value from chaos. *IDC iView Research*. Retrieved June 2011 from http://www.emc.com/collateral/analyst-reports/idc-extracting-value-from-chaos-ar.pdf

Gastwirth, J. L. (1972). The estimation of the Lorenz curve and Gini index. *The Review of Economics and Statistics*, *54*(3), 306–316. doi: doi:10.2307/1937992.

George, L. (2008). *HBase: The definitive Guide*. Sebastopol, CA: O'Reilly Media.

George, L. (2011). *HBase: The definitive guide*. Sebastopol, CA: O'Reilly Media.

Ghazal, A., Rabl, T., Hu, M., Raab, F., Poess, M., Crolotte, A., & Jacobsen, H.-A. (2013). BigBench: Towards an industry standard benchmark for big data analytics. In *Proceedings of SIGMOD*. New York: ACM.

Ghemawat, S., Gobioff, H., & Leung, H. (2003). The Google file systems. In *Proceedings of the 19th ACM Symposium on Operating Systems Principles*. ACM. Retrieved October 2003 from http://research.google.com/archive/gfs.html

Giangarra, P., Metrovich, B., Schwitters, M., & Semple, B. (2011). Smarter bridges through advanced structural health monitoring. *IBM Journal of Research and Development*, *5*(1-2).

Gilbert, E., Bergstrom, T., & Karahalios, K. (2009). Blogs are echo chambers: Blogs are echo chambers. In *Proceedings of the 42ⁿᵈ Hawaii International Conference on System Sciences*. IEEE. Retrieved http://comp.social.gatech.edu/papers/hicss09.echo.gilbert.pdf

Gilbert, S., & Lynch, N. (2002). Brewer's conjecture and the feasibility of consistent. *ACM SIGACT*, *33*(2), 51–59. doi:10.1145/564585.564601.

Gilpin, D. (2010). Organizational image construction in a fragmented online media environment. *Journal of Public Relations Research*, *22*, 265–287. doi:10.1080/10627261003614393.

Giorgini, P., Rizzi, S., & Garzetti, M. (2008). GRAnD: A goal-oriented approach to requirement analysis in data warehouses. *Decision Support Systems*, *45*, 4–21. doi:10.1016/j.dss.2006.12.001.

GMP. (2012). GMP. *The GNU Multiple Precision Arithmetic Library*. Retrieved January 24, 2013, from http://gmplib.org/

Golab, L., Johnson, T., Seidel, J. S., & Shkapenyuk, V. (2009). Stream warehousing with DataDepot. In *Proceedings of the 35th SIGMOD International Conference on Management of Data* (pp. 847–854). New York, NY: ACM. doi:http://doi.acm.org/10.1145/1559845.1559934

Golder, S. A., Wilkinson, D. M., & Huberman, B. A. (2007). Rhythms of social interaction: Messaging within a massive online network. In *Proceedings of 3rd International Conference on Communities and Technologies* (pp. 41-66). IEEE.

Golfarelli, M., & Rizzi, S. (2009). *Data warehouse design: Modern principles and methodologies*. New York: McGraw-Hill Osborne Media.

Gray, J. (2009). *Jim Gray – Industry leader*. Retrieved June 19, 2013 from http://www.tpc.org/information/who/gray.asp

Gray, J. (2009). Jim Gray on eScience: A transformed scientific method. In T. Hey, S. Tansley, & K. Tolle (Eds.), *The fourth paradigm: Data-intensive scientific discovery*. Redmond, WA: Microsoft Research.

Green, A. G., & Gutmann, M, P. (2007). Building partnerships among social science researchers, institution-based repositories and domain specific data archives. *OCLC Systems & Services*, *23*(1), 35–53. doi:10.1108/10650750710720757.

Greenbaum, D. A., & Kainz, C. (2009). *Report from the bamboo planning project*. Coalition for Networked Information. Retrieved from http://www.cni.org/topics/ci/report-from-the-bamboo-planning-project/

Greenberg, J. (2009). Theoretical considerations of lifecycle modeling: An analysis of the dryad repository demonstrating automatic metadata propagation, inheritance, and value system adoption. *Cataloging & Classification Quarterly*, *47*(3-4), 380–402. doi:10.1080/01639370902737547.

Greenberg, J., White, H., Carrier, S., & Scherle, R. (2009). A metadata best practice for a scientific data repository. *Journal of Library Metadata*, *9*(3/4), 194–212. doi:10.1080/19386380903405090.

Greer, C. F., & Ferguson, D. A. (2011). Using Twitter for promotion and branding: A content analysis of local television Twitter sites. *Journal of Broadcasting & Electronic Media*, *55*(2), 198–214. doi:10.1080/08838151.2011.570824.

Griffiths, A. (2009). The publication of research data: Researcher attitudes and behaviors. *International Journal of Digital Curation*, *4*(1), 46–56. doi:10.2218/ijdc.v4i1.77.

Gropp, W., Lusk, E., & Skjellum, A. (1999). *Using MPI: Portable parallel programming with the message-passing interface*. Cambridge, MA: MIT Press.

Grosu, D., & Chronopoulos, A. T. (2005). Noncooperative load balancing in distributed systems. *Journal of Parallel and Distributed Computing*, *65*(9), 1022–1034. doi:10.1016/j.jpdc.2005.05.001.

Gruhl, D., Guha, R., Liben-Nowell, D., & Tomkins, A. (2004). Information diffusion through blogspace. In *Proceedings of the 13th International Conference on World Wide Web*. New York: IEEE.

Grünwald, P. D. (2007). *The minimum description length principle*. Cambridge, MA: The MIT Press.

Guba, S., Rastogi, R., & Shim, K. (1998). Cure: An efficient clustering algorithm for large databases. In *Proceedings of the ACM SIGMOD International Conference on Management of Data*, (pp. 73–84). ACM.

Gutmann, M., Schürer, K., Donakowski, D., & Beedham, H. (2004). The selection, appraisal, and retention of digital social science data. *Data Science Journal*, *3*, 209–221. doi:10.2481/dsj.3.209.

Gu, Y., & Grossman, R. L. (2007). UDT: UDP-based data transfer for high-speed wide area networks. *Computer Networks*, *51*(7), 1777–1799. doi:10.1016/j.comnet.2006.11.009.

Hadoop MapReduce Tutorial. (n.d.). Retrieved January, 2013, from http://hadoop.apache.org/common/docs/r0.20.2/mapred_tutorial.html

Hakimpour, F., & Geppert, A. (2002). Global schema generation using formal ontologies. In S. Spaccapietra, S. T. March, & Y. Kambayashi (Eds.), *ER (LNCS)* (Vol. 2503, pp. 307–321). Berlin: Springer.

Hale, S. A. (2012). Net increase? Cross-lingual linking in the blogosphere. *Journal of Computer-Mediated Communication*, *17*, 135–151. doi:10.1111/j.1083-6101.2011.01568.x.

Hall, P. J. (2005). The square kilometre array: An international engineering perspective. In *The Square Kilometre Array: An Engineering Perspective* (pp. 5–16). Springer Netherlands. doi:10.1007/1-4020-3798-8_2.

Han, J., Haihong, E., Le, G., & Du, J. (2011). Survey on NOSQL database. In *Proceedings of the 6th International Conference on Pervasive Computing and Applications (ICPCA)*, (pp. 363-366). ICPCA.

Hanisch, R. J., Farris, A., Greisen, E. W., Pence, W. D., Schlesinger, B. M., Teuben, P. J., & Warnock, A. III. (2001). Definition of the flexible image transport system (FITS). *Astronomy & Astrophysics*, *376*(1), 359–380. doi:10.1051/0004-6361:20010923.

Han, J., & Kamber, M. (2006). *Data mining: Concepts and techniques*. San Francisco, CA: Morgan Kaufmann.

Hardt, D. (2012). *The OAuth 2.0 authorization framework, draft-ietf-oauth-v2-31*. Retrieved from http://tools.ietf.org/html/draft-ietf-oauth-v2-31

Harmon, L. D. (1973). The recognition of faces. *Scientific American*, *229*(5), 71–82. doi:10.1038/scientificamerican1173-70 PMID:4748120.

Harrison, G. (2012). Statistical analysis and R in the world of big data. *Data Trends & Applications*, *26*(3), 39.

Hassid, J. (2012). Safety valve or pressure cooker? Blogs in Chinese political life. *The Journal of Communication*, *62*, 212–230. doi:10.1111/j.1460-2466.2012.01634.x.

HathiTrust. (n.d.). *Call for proposal to develop a hathitrust research center*. Retrieved from www.hathitrust.org/documents/hathitrust -research-center-rfp.pdf

Hayes, M. T. (2011). Parenting children with autism online: Creating community and support online. In M. Moravec (Ed.), *Motherhood online: How online communities shape modern motherhood* (pp. 258–265). Newcastle upon Tyne, UK: Cambridge Scholars Publishing.

Hecht, R., & Jablonski, S. (2011). NoSQL evaluation: A use case oriented survey. In Cloud and Service Computing (CSC), (pp. 336-341). IEEE.

Hedberg, S. R. (1995). Parallelism speeds data mining. *IEEE Parallel & Distributed Technology Systems & Applications*, *3*(4), 3–6. doi:10.1109/88.473600.

Heim, K. M. (1982). Introduction. *Library Trends*, *30*(3), 321–325.

Helfert, M., & Von Maur, E. (2001). A strategy for managing data quality in data warehouse systems. In E. M. Pierce & R. Katz-Haas (Eds.), *Sixth Conference on Information Quality* (pp. 62-76). Cambridge, MA: MIT.

Herodotou, H., Lim, H., Luo, G., Borisov, N., Dong, L., Cetin, F.-B., & Babu, S. (2011). Starfish: A self-tuning system for big data analytics. In *Proceedings of the 5th Biennial Conference on Innovative Data Systems Research (CIDR 2011)*. Asilomar, CA: CIDR.

Hespanha, J. (2009). *Linear system theory*. Princeton, NJ: Princeton University Press.

Hewitt, C., Bishop, P., & Steiger, R. (1973). A universal modular ACTOR formalism for artificial intelligence. In *Proceedings of the 3rd International Joint Conference on Artificial Intelligence (IJCAI'73)*, (pp. 235-245). IJCAI.

Highfield, T., Kirchhoff, L., & Nicolai, T. (2011). Challenges of tracking topical discussion networks online. *Social Science Computer Review*, *29*(3), 340–353. doi:10.1177/0894439310382514.

Hill, D., & Werpy, J. (2011). Satellite imagery production and processing using Apache Hadoop. In *Proceedings of the American Geophysical Union Fall Meeting*. AGU.

HMR. (2011). *Hadoop MapReduce*. Retrieved form http://hadoop.apache.org/mapreduce/

Hookway, N. (2008). Entering the blogosphere: Some strategies for using blogs in social research. *Qualitative Research*, *8*, 91–113. doi:10.1177/1468794107085298.

Hooper, W. (2013). *About latent semantic analysis*. Retrieved from http://webapp1.dlib.indiana.edu/newton/lsa/help/hs20.html

Hopkins, B., & Evelson, B. (2011). *Expand your digital horizon with big data*. Washington, DC: Forrester Research, Inc..

Höppner, F. (2002). Time series abstraction methods - A survey. In Proceedings of Informatik bewegt: Informatik 2002 - 32. jahrestagung der gesellschaft für informatik e.v. (gi) (pp. 777–786). GI.

Houle, M., Symnovis, A., & Wood, D. (2002). Dimension-exchange algorithms for load balancing on trees. In *Proceedings of International Colloquium on Structural Information and Communication Complexity* (pp. 181–196). IEEE.

Howe, B. (2007). *GridFields: Model-driven data transformation in the physical sciences.* (PhD, Dissertation). Portland State University, Portland, OR.

Howe, D., Costanzo, M., Fey, P., Gojobori, T., Hannick, L., & Hide, W. et al. (2008). Big data: The future of biocuration. *Nature, 455*(7209), 47–50. doi:10.1038/455047a PMID:18769432.

Huang, Y., Ho, Y., Lu, C., & Fu, L. (2011). A cloud-based accessible architecture for large-scale ADL analysis services. In *Proceedings of International Conference on Cloud Computing* (pp. 646–653). IEEE.

Hu, B., Rakthanmanon, T., Hao, Y., Evans, S., Lonardi, S., & Keogh, E. (2011). Discovering the intrinsic cardinality and dimensionality of time series using mdl.[ICDM.]. *Proceedings of ICDM, 2011*, 1086–1091.

Huberman, B. A., Romero, D. M., & Wu, F. (2009). Social networks that matter: Twitter under the microscope. *First Monday*, 14.

Huedo, E., Montero, R. S., & Llorente, I. M. (2005). The GridWay framework for adaptive scheduling and execution on grids. *Scalable Computing: Practice and Experience, 6*, 1–8.

Huffaker, D. A., & Calvert, S. L. (2005). Gender, identity, and language use in teenage blogs. *Journal of Computer-Mediated Communication, 10*. Retrieved September 10, 2008, from http://www3.interscience.wiley.com/cgi-bin/fulltext/120837938/HTMLSTART

Huffmire, T., & Sherwood, T. (2006). Wavelet-based phase classification. In *Proceedings of the 15th International Conference on Parallel Architectures and Compilation Techniques* (pp. 95–104). New York, NY: ACM.

Ibrahim, S., Jin, H., Lu, L., Qi, L., Wu, S., & Shi, X. (2009). Evaluating mapreduce on virtual machines: The hadoop case. In *Proceedings of the 1st International Conference on Cloud Computing*, (vol. 5931, pp. 519-528). Berlin: Springer.

ICPSR. (2012). *Guide to social science data preparation and archiving: Best practice throughout the data life cycle* (5th ed.). Retrieved from http://www.icpsr.umich.edu/files/ICPSR/access/dataprep.pdf

ICPSR. (n.d.). Retrieved from https://www.icpsr.umich.edu

IDC. (2012, March 7). *IDC releases first worldwide big data technology and services market forecast, shows big data as the next essential capability and a foundation for the intelligent economy.* Retrieved May 4, 2013, from http://www.idc.com/getdoc.jsp?containerId=prUS23355112

IDC. (2013). *Big data in 2020.* Retrieved June 19, 2013 from http://www.emc.com/leadership/digital-universe/iview/big-data-2020.htm

Idé, T. (2006). Why does subsequence time-series clustering produce sine waves? In *Proceedings of ECML PKDD 2006* (pp. 211–222). ECML.

Ifukor, P. (2010). Elections or selections? Blogging and twittering the Nigerian 2007 general elections. *Bulletin of Science, Technology & Society, 30*(6), 398–414. doi:10.1177/0270467610380008.

Industry, P. C. I.-S. I. G. (2010, January). *Single root I/O virtualization and sharing 1.1 specification.* Retrieved November 2010, from http://www.pcisig.com/specifications/iov/single_root/

Inmon, W. H. (1996). The data warehouse and data mining. *Communications of the ACM*, 49–50. doi:10.1145/240455.240470.

Intel. (2012). Intel Xeon Phi coprocessor 5110P. *Intel Website.* Retrieved January 24, 2013, from http://www.intel.com/content/www/us/en/processors/xeon/xeon-phi-detail.html

Internet Archive. (2013). Retrieved from http://archive.org/index.php

Intille, S. S. (2012). Emerging technology for studying daily life. In M. R. Mehl, & T. S. Conner (Eds.), *Handbook of research methods for studying daily life* (pp. 267–283). New York, NY: Guilford Press.

IssueCrawler. (n.d.). Retrieved January, 2013, from http://www.issuecrawler.net/

Ives, Z. G., Florescu, D., Friedman, M., Levy, A., & Weld, D. S. (1999). An adaptive query execution system for data integration. *SIGMOD Record, 28*(2), 299–310. doi:http://doi.acm.org/10.1145/304181.304209

Jacobs, A. (2009). The pathologies of big data. *Communications of the ACM, 52*(8), 36–44. doi:10.1145/1536616.1536632.

Jagadish, H. (1997). Analysis of hilbert curve for representing 2-dimensional space. *Information Processing Letters, 62*(1), 17–22. doi:10.1016/S0020-0190(97)00014-8.

Jain, A. K., & Dubes, R. C. (1988). *Algorithms for clustering data*. Hoboken, NJ: Prentice Hall.

Jain, A., Murty, M., & Flynn, P. (1999). Data clustering: A review. *ACM Computing Surveys, 31*(3), 264–323. doi:10.1145/331499.331504.

Jain, A., & Zongker, D. (1997). Feature selection: Evaluation, application, and small sample performance. *IEEE Transactions on Pattern Analysis and Machine Intelligence, 19*(2), 153–158. doi:10.1109/34.574797.

Jain, R. (1991). *The art of computer systems performance analysis: Techniques for experimental design, measurement, simulation, and modeling*. Hoboken, NJ: Wiley.

Jansen, B. J., Zhang, M., Sobel, K., & Chowdury, A. (2009). Twitter power: Tweets as electronic word of mouth. *Journal of the American Society for Information Science and Technology, 60*(11), 2169–2188. doi:10.1002/asi.21149.

Jardak, C., Riihijärvi, J., Oldewurtel, F., & Mähönen, P. (2010). Parallel processing of data from very large-scale wireless sensor networks. In *Proceedings of the 19th ACM International Symposium on High Performance Distributed Computing* (pp. 787–794). New York, NY: ACM.

Jensen, C., Lin, D., & Ooi, B. (2004). Query and update efficient B+-tree based indexing of moving objects. In *Proceedings of the Thirtieth International Conference on Very Large Data Bases*. IEEE.

Jiang, J., Lu, J., Zhang, G., & Long, G. (2011). Scaling-up item-based collaborative filtering recommendation algorithm based on Hadoop. In *Proceedings of the 2011 IEEE World Congress on Services* (pp. 490-497). IEEE.

Jiang, L., Xu, J., Xu, B., & Cai, H. (2011). An automatic method of data warehouses multi-dimension modeling for distributed information systems. In W. Shen, J.-P. A. Barthès, J. Luo, P. G. Kropf, M. Pouly, J. Yong, Y. Xue, & M. Pires Ramos (Eds.), *Proceedings of the 2011 15th International Conference on Computer Supported Cooperative Work in Design* (pp. 9-16). IEEE.

Jiang, W., Ravi, V., & Agrawal, G. (2009). Comparing map-reduce and freeride for data-intensive applications. In *Proceedings of the IEEE International Conference on Cluster Computing and Workshops*, (pp. 1–10). IEEE.

Jin, R., Goswami, A., & Agrawal, G. (2006). Fast and exact out-of-core and distributed k-means clustering. *Knowledge and Information Systems, 10*(1), 17–40. doi:10.1007/s10115-005-0210-0.

Ji, P., & Lieber, P. S. (2008). Emotional disclosure and construction of the poetic other in a Chinese online dating site. *China Media Research, 4*(2), 32–42.

John, G. J., Kohavi, R., & Pfleger, K. (1994). Irrelevant features and the subset selection problem. In *Proceedings of the International Conference on Machine Learning* (pp. 121–129). IEEE.

Johnson, A., & Eschenfelder, K. (2011). *Managing access to and use of data collections: A preliminary report*. Retrieved from http://minds.wisconsin.edu/handle/1793/48205

Johnson, A., & O'Donnell, C. (2009). An open access database of genome-wide association results. *BMC Medical Genetics, 10*(1), 6. doi:10.1186/1471-2350-10-6 PMID:19161620.

Jonas, J. L. (2009). MeerKAT—The South African array with composite dishes and wide-band single pixel feeds. *Proceedings of the IEEE, 97*(8), 1522–1530. doi:10.1109/JPROC.2009.2020713.

Jones, T. (2009, October). *Linux virtualization and PCI passthrough*. Retrieved May 2012, from http://www.ibm.com/developerworks/linux/library/l-pci-passthrough/

Jung, G., Joshi, K., Hiltunen, M., Schlichting, R., & Pu, C. (2009). A cost sensitive adaptation engine for server consolidation of multi-tier applications. In *Proceedings of International Conference on Middleware* (pp. 163–183). ACM/IFIP/USENIX.

Kailasam, S., Gnanasambandam, N., Dharanipragada, J., & Sharma, N. (2010). Optimizing service level agreements for autonomic cloud bursting schedulers. In *Proceedings of International Conference on Parallel Processing Workshops* (pp. 285–294). IEEE.

Kalton, G. (1983). *Introduction to survey sampling.* Newbury Park, NJ: Sage.

Kamarunisha, M., Ranichandra, S., & Rajagopal, T.K.P. (2011). Recitation of load balancing algorithms in grid computing environment using policies and strategies an approach. *International Journal of Scientific & Engineering Research, 2.*

Karakasidis, A., Vassiliadis, P., & Pitoura, E. (2005). ETL queues for active data warehousing. In *Proceedings of the 2nd International Workshop on Information Quality in Information Systems* (pp. 28–39). New York, NY: ACM. doi:http://doi.acm.org/10.1145/1077501.1077509

Karunadasa, N. P., & Ranasinghe, D. N. (2009). Accelerating high performance applications with cuda and mpi. In *Proceedings of the Industrial and Information Systems (ICIIS),* (pp. 331–336). ICIIS.

Katic, N., Quirchmay, G., Schiefer, J., Stolba, M., & Tjoa, A. (1998). A prototype model for data warehouse security based on metadata. In *Proceedings of the Ninth International Workshop on Database and Expert Systems Applications,* (pp. 300-308). IEEE.

Kaula, R. (2009). Business rules for data warehouse. *International Journal of Information and Communication Engineering,* 359-367.

Keating, E., & Sunakawa, C. (2010). Participation cues: Coordinating activity and collaboration in complex on-line gaming worlds. *Language in Society, 39,* 331–356. doi:10.1017/S0047404510000217.

Kelly, J., Floyer, D., Vellante, D., & Miniman, S. (2013, April 17). *Big data vendor revenue and market forecast 2012-2017.* Retrieved May 22, 2013, from http://wikibon.org/wiki/v/Big_Data_Vendor_Revenue_and_Market_Forecast_2012-2017

Kempe, D., Kleinberg, J., & Tardos, É. (2003). Maximizing the spread of influence through a social network. In *Proceedings of the Ninth ACM SIGKDD International Conference on Knowledge Discovery and Data Mining.* Washington, DC: ACM.

Keogh, E., Chu, S., Hart, D., & Pazzani, M. J. (2001). An online algorithm for segmenting time series.[ICDM.]. *Proceedings of ICDM, 2001,* 289–296.

Keogh, E., & Lin, J. (2005). Clustering of time-series subsequences is meaningless: Implications for previous and future research. *Knowledge and Information Systems, 8*(2), 154–177. doi:10.1007/s10115-004-0172-7.

Kienzler, R., Bruggmann, R., Ranganathan, A., & Tatbul, N. (2012). Incremental DNA sequence analysis in the cloud. In *Scientific and Statistical Database Management* (pp. 640–645). Berlin: Springer. doi:10.1007/978-3-642-31235-9_50.

Kim, H., & Parashar, M. (2011). CometCloud: An autonomic cloud engine. In *Cloud Computing: Principles and Paradigms.* Hoboken, NJ: Wiley. doi:10.1002/9780470940105.ch10.

Kim, S. Y., Lohmueller, K. E., Albrechtsen, A., Li, Y., Korneliussen, T., Tian, G., & Nielsen, R. (2011). Estimation of allele frequency and association mapping using next-generation sequencing data. *BMC Bioinformatics, 12*(1), 231. doi:10.1186/1471-2105-12-231 PMID:21663684.

King, G. (2011). Ensuring the data-rich future of the social science. *Science, 331*(6018), 719–721. doi:10.1126/science.1197872 PMID:21311013.

Klus, P., Lam, S., Lyberg, D., Cheung, M. S., Pullan, G., McFarlane, I., & Lam, B. Y. (2012). BarraCUDA-A fast short read sequence aligner using graphics processing units. *BMC Research Notes, 5*(1), 27. doi:10.1186/1756-0500-5-27 PMID:22244497.

Knobbe, A., Blockeel, H., Koopman, A., Calders, T., Obladen, B., Bosma, C., et al. (2010). InfraWatch: Data management of large systems for monitoring infrastructural performance. In *Proceedings IDA 2010* (pp. 91–102). IDA.

Knuth, D. E. (1998). The art of computer programming: Vol. 3. *Sorting and searching* (2nd ed.). Redwood City, CA: Addison Wesley Longman Publishing Co., Inc..

Kratica, J., Milanović, M., Stanimirović, Z., & Tošić, D. (2011). An evolutionary-based approach for solving a capacitated hub location problem. *Applied Soft Computing*, *11*(2), 1858–1866. doi:10.1016/j.asoc.2010.05.035.

Kratica, J., & Stanimirović, Z. (2006). Solving the uncapacitated multiple allocation p-hub center problem by genetic algorithm. *Asia-Pacific Journal of Operational Research*, *23*(4), 425–437. doi:10.1142/S0217595906001042.

Kratica, J., Stanimirović, Z., Tošić, D., & Filipović, V. (2005). Genetic algorithm for solving uncapacitated multiple allocation hub location problem. *Computing and Informatics*, *24*(4), 415–426.

Kratica, J., Stanimirović, Z., Tošić, D., & Filipović, V. (2007). Two genetic algorithms for solving the uncapacitated single allocation p-hub median problem. *European Journal of Operational Research*, *182*, 15–28. doi:10.1016/j.ejor.2006.06.056.

Kumar, U.K. (2011). A dynamic load balancing algorithm in computational grid using fair scheduling. *International Journal of Computer Science Issues, 8*.

Kunze, J., Haye, M., Hetzner, E., Reyes, M., & Snavely, C. (2011). Pairtrees *for collection storage (V0.1)*. Retrieved from https://wiki.ucop.edu/download/attachments/14254128/PairtreeSpec.pdf

Kusnetzky, D. (2010). *What is big data?* Retrieved February 16, 2010, from http://blogs.zdnet.com/virtualization/?p=1708

Labio, W., & Garcia-Molina, H. (1996). Efficient snapshot differential algorithms in data warehousing. In *Proceedings of the 22th International Conference on Very Large Data Bases (VLDB '96)* (pp. 63–74). San Francisco, CA: Morgan Kaufmann Publishers Inc.

Labio, W., Yang, J., Cui, Y., Garcia-Molina, H., & Widom, J. (1999). Performance issues in incremental warehouse maintenance. In *Proceedings of the 26th International Conference on Very Large Data Bases (VLDB'00)*. Cairo, Egypt: VLDB.

Lacy, M., & Halstead, D. (n.d.). *NAASC memo 110: ALMA data rates and archiving at the NAASC*. Retrieved from https://science.nrao.edu/facilities/alma/naasc-memo-series/naasc-memos/110.naasc-data-rates

Lam, T. W., Li, R., Tam, A., Wong, S., Wu, E., & Yiu, S. M. (2009). High throughput short read alignment via bi-directional BWT. In *Proceedings of the IEEE International Conference on Bioinformatics and Biomedicine,* (pp. 31-36). Los Alamitos, CA: IEEE Computer Society.

Laney, D. (2001). 3D data management: Controlling data volume, velocity, and variety. *Application Delivery Strategies*. Retrieved May 1, 2013, from http://blogs.gartner.com/doug-laney/files/2012/01/ad949-3D-Data-Management-Controlling-Data-Volume-Velocity-and-Variety.pdf

Langmead, B., Schatz, M. C., Lin, J., Pop, M., & Salzberg, S. L. (2009). Searching for SNPs with cloud computing. *Genome Biology*, *10*(11), R134. doi:10.1186/gb-2009-10-11-r134 PMID:19930550.

Langmead, B., Trapnell, C., Pop, M., & Salzberg, S. L. (2009). Ultrafast and memory-efficient alignment of short DNA sequences to the human genome. *Genome Biology*, *10*(3), R25. doi:10.1186/gb-2009-10-3-r25 PMID:19261174.

Larose, D. T. (2005). *Discovering knowledge in data: An introduction to data mining*. Hoboken, NJ: Wiley. doi:10.1002/0471687545.

LaValle, S., Lesser, E., Shockley, R., Hopkins, M. S., & Kruschwitz, N. (2011). Big data, analytics and the path from insights to value. *MIT Sloan Management Review*, *52*(2), 21–32.

Lawrence, R. (2005). Early hash join: A configurable algorithm for the efficient and early production of join results. In *Proceedings of the 31st International Conference on Very Large Data Bases* (pp. 841–852). VLDB Endowment.

Lazowska, J., Zahorjan, J., Graham, G. S., & Sevcik, K. C. (1984). *Quantitative system performance: Computer system analysis using queueing network models*. Englewood Cliffs, NJ: Prentice-Hall.

Leibiusky, J., Eisbruch, G., & Simonassi, D. (2012). *Getting started with storm*. Sebastopol, CA: O'Reilly Media Inc..

Levine, J. (2009). *Flex & bison text processing tools*. Sebastopol, CA: O'Reilly Media.

Li, J., Liao, W., Choudhary, A., Ross, R., Thakur, R., Gropp, W., … Zingale, M. (2003). Parallel NetCDF: A high performance scientific I/O interface. *Supercomputing*.

Li, Y., Terrell, A., & Patel, J. M. (2011). Wham: A high-throughput sequence alignment method. In *Proceedings of the 2011 ACM SIGMOD International Conference on Management of Data* (pp. 445-456). New York: ACM.

Libkin, L., Machlin, R., & Wong, L. (1996). A query language for multidimensional arrays: Design, implementation, and optimization techniques. *SIGMOD Record*, *25*(2), 228–239. doi:10.1145/235968.233335.

Li, H., & Durbin, R. (2009). Fast and accurate short read alignment with Burrows–Wheeler transform. *Bioinformatics (Oxford, England)*, *25*(14), 1754–1760. doi:10.1093/bioinformatics/btp324 PMID:19451168.

Lin, F., & Cohen, W. W. (2010). Power iteration clustering. In *Proceedings of the 27th International Conference on Machine Learning*. Haifa, Israel: IEEE.

Lindeberg, T. (1990). Scale-space for discrete signals. *IEEE Transactions on Pattern Analysis and Machine Intelligence*, *12*(3), 234–254. doi:10.1109/34.49051.

Lintott, C. J., Schawinski, K., Slosar, A., Land, K., Bamford, S., Thomas, D., & Vandenberg, J. (2008). Galaxy zoo: Morphologies derived from visual inspection of galaxies from the Sloan digital sky survey. *Monthly Notices of the Royal Astronomical Society*, *389*(3), 1179–1189. doi:10.1111/j.1365-2966.2008.13689.x.

Li, R., Li, Y., Fang, X., Yang, H., Wang, J., Kristiansen, K., & Wang, J. (2009). SNP detection for massively parallel whole-genome resequencing. *Genome Research*, *19*(6), 1124–1132. doi:10.1101/gr.088013.108 PMID:19420381.

Li, R., Yu, C., Li, Y., Lam, T. W., Yiu, S. M., Kristiansen, K., & Wang, J. (2009). SOAP2: An improved ultrafast tool for short read alignment. *Bioinformatics (Oxford, England)*, *25*(15), 1966–1967. doi:10.1093/bioinformatics/btp336 PMID:19497933.

Liu, Z., Lin, M., Wierman, A., Low, S., & Andrew, L. (2011). Greening geographical load balancing. In *Proceedings of SIGMETRICS Joint Conference on Measurement and Modelling of Computer Systems* (pp. 233–244). ACM.

Liu, C. M., Wong, T., Wu, E., Luo, R., Yiu, S. M., Li, Y., & Lam, T. W. (2012). SOAP3: Ultra-fast GPU-based parallel alignment tool for short reads. *Bioinformatics (Oxford, England)*, *28*(6), 878–879. doi:10.1093/bioinformatics/bts061 PMID:22285832.

Liu, Y. et al. (2013). Hsim: A mapreduce simulator in enabling cloud computing. *Future Generation Computer Systems*, *29*(1), 300–308. doi:10.1016/j.future.2011.05.007.

Li, Y., & Lan, Z. (2005). A survey of load balancing in grid computing. *Computational and Information Science*, *3314*, 280–285. doi:10.1007/978-3-540-30497-5_44.

Li, Y., Vinckenbosch, N., Tian, G., Huerta-Sanchez, E., Jiang, T., Jiang, H., & Wang, J. (2010). Resequencing of 200 human exomes identifies an excess of low-frequency non-synonymous coding variants. *Nature Genetics*, *42*(11), 969–972. doi:10.1038/ng.680 PMID:20890277.

LLoyd, S. P. (1982). Least squares quantization in PCM. *IEEE Transactions on Information Theory*, *28*, 129–137. doi:10.1109/TIT.1982.1056489.

Loboz, C. (2011). Quantifying imbalance in computer systems. In *Proceedings of the Computer Measurement Group 2011 International Conference*. IEEE.

Loboz, C., & Lee, S. (2010). Capacity, usage, computer work – And daily analysis of 100,000 servers. In *Proceedings of the Computer Measurement Group 2010 International Conference*. IEEE.

Loboz, C., Lee, S., & Yuan, J. (2009). How do you measure and analyze 100,000 servers. In *Proceedings of the Computer Measurement Group 2009 International Conference*. IEEE.

Loboz, C. (2011). Describing multiple aspects of cloud usage with excess entropy. In *Proceedings of DataCloud-SC'11*. Seattle, WA: DataCloud-SC.

Loboz, C. (2012). Cloud resource usage – Heavy tailed distributions invalidating traditional capacity planning models. *Journal of Grid Computing, 10*(1), 85–108. doi: doi:10.1007/s10723-012-9211-x.

Lohr, S. L. (1999). *Sampling: Design and analysis*. Duxbury Press.

Loshin, D. (2010). *The Vertica analytic database technical overview white paper*. Vertica Systems Inc. Retrieved March 2010 from http://www.vertica.com/wp-content/uploads/2011/01/VerticaArchitectureWhitePaper.pdf

LSST. (2011). *Large synoptic survey telescope*. Retrieved from http://www.lsst.org/

Lu, M., & Zwaenepoel, W. (2010). HadoopToSQL: A MapReduce query optimizer. In *Proceedings of the European Conference on Computer Systems*. IEEE.

Lu, M., He, B., & Luo, Q. (2010). Supporting extended precision on graphics processors. In *Proceedings of the Sixth International Workshop on Data Management on New Hardware* (pp. 19-26). New York: ACM.

Lu, M., Zhao, J., Luo, Q., & Wang, B. (2012). Accelerating minor allele frequency computation with graphics processors. In *Proceedings of the 1st International Workshop on Big Data, Streams and Heterogeneous Source Mining: Algorithms, Systems, Programming Models and Applications* (pp. 85-92). New York: ACM.

Lu, M., Zhao, J., Luo, Q., Wang, B., Fu, S., & Lin, Z. (2011). GSNP: A DNA single-nucleotide polymorphism detection system with GPU acceleration. In *Proceedings of the 2011 International Conference on Parallel Processing (ICPP)* (pp. 592-601). Los Alamitos, CA: IEEE Computer Society.

Luca, R., Richer, J., Shepherd, D., Testi, L., Wright, M., & Wilson, C. (2004). *ALMA memo 501: Estimation of ALMA data rate*. National Radio Astronomy Observatory. Retrieved from https://science.nrao.edu/facilities/alma/aboutALMA/Technology/ALMA_Memo_Series/alma501/abs501

Lu, M., Tan, Y., Bai, G., & Luo, Q. (2012). High-performance short sequence alignment with GPU acceleration. *Distributed and Parallel Databases*, 1–15.

Lu, M., Tan, Y., Zhao, J., Bai, G., & Luo, Q. (2012). Integrating GPU-accelerated sequence alignment and SNP detection for genome resequencing analysis. In *Scientific and Statistical Database Management* (pp. 124–140). Berlin: Springer. doi:10.1007/978-3-642-31235-9_8.

Lynch, C. A. (2003). Institutional repositories: Essential infrastructure for scholarship in the digital age. *ARL: A Bimonthly Report, 226*. Retrieved from http://www.arl.org

Lynch, C. (2008). Big data: How do your data grow? *Nature, 455*(7209), 28–29. doi:10.1038/455028a PMID:18769419.

Lynch, C. (2008). How do your data grow? *Nature, 455*(7209), 28–29. doi:10.1038/455028a PMID:18769419.

Mackie, C. J. (2007). Cyberinfrastructure, institutions, and sustainability. *First Monday, 12*, 6–4. doi:10.5210/fm.v12i6.1908.

Madeira, S. C., & Oliveira, A. L. (2004). Biclustering algorithms for biological data analysis: A survey. *IEEE/ACM Transactions on Computational Biology and Bioinformatics, 1*, 24–45. doi:10.1109/TCBB.2004.2 PMID:17048406.

Maheswaran, M., Ali, S., Siegal, H., Hensgen, D., & Freund, R. (1999). Dynamic matching and scheduling of a class of independent tasks onto heterogeneous computing systems. In *Proceedings of Heterogeneous Computing Workshop* (pp. 30–44). IEEE.

Malik, T., Best, N., Elliott, J., Madduri, R., & Foster, I. (2011). Improving the efficiency of subset queries on raster images. In *Proceedings of the ACM SIGSPATIAL Second International Workshop on High Performance and Distributed Geographic Information Systems* (HPDGIS '11). ACM.

Malika, H., & Malik, A. S. (2011). Towards identifying the challenges associated with emerging large scale social networks. In *Proceedings of the 2nd International Conference on Ambient Systems, Networks and Technologies*. Niagara Falls, Canada: Procedia Computer Science.

Manadhata, P. K. (2012). Big data for security: Challenges, opportunities, and examples. In *Proceedings of the 2012 ACM Workshop on Building Analysis Datasets and Gathering Experience Returns for Security* (pp. 3-4). ACM. Retrieved from http://dl.acm.org/citation. cfm?id=2382420

Manfreda, K. L., Bosnjak, M., Berzelak, J., Haas, I., & Vehovar, V. (2008). Web surveys versus other survey modes: A meta-analysis comparin response rates. *International Journal of Market Research*, *50*(1), 79–104.

Manolio, T. A. (2010). Genome-wide association studies and assessment of the risk of disease. *The New England Journal of Medicine*, *363*(2), 166–176. doi:10.1056/ NEJMra0905980 PMID:20647212.

Manovich, L. (2012). Trending: The promises and the challenges of big social data. In M. K. Gold (Ed.), *Debates in the Digital Humanities*. Minneapolis, MN: The University of Minnesota Press. Retrieved from http:// lab.softwarestudies.com/2011/04/new-article-by-lev-manovich-trending.html

Marcial, L., & Hemminger, B. (2010). Scientific data repositories on the web: An initial survey. *Journal of the American Society for Information Science and Technology*, *61*(10), 2029–2048. doi:10.1002/asi.21339.

Matić, D., Filipović, V., Savić, A., & Staimirović, Z. (2011). A genetic algorithm for solving multiple warehouse layout problem. *Kragujevac Journal of Mathematics*, *35*(1), 119–138.

Mattmann, C. A., Crichton, D. J., Medvidovic, N., & Hughes, S. (2006). A software architecture-based framework for highly distributed and data intensive scientific applications. In *Proceedings of the 28th International Conference on Software Engineering* (pp. 721-730). ACM.

Mattmann, C. A., Crichton, D. J., Hart, A. F., Kelly, S. C., & Hughes, J. S. (2010). Experiments with storage and preservation of NASA's planetary data via the cloud. *IT Professional*, *12*(5), 28–35. doi:10.1109/MITP.2010.97.

Mattmann, C. A., Freeborn, D., Crichton, D., Foster, B., Hart, A., Woollard, D., & Miller, C. E. (2009). A reusable process control system framework for the orbiting carbon observatory and npp. sounder peate missions. In *Proceedings of Space Mission Challenges for Information Technology* (pp. 165–172). IEEE. doi:10.1109/ SMC-IT.2009.27.

Mattmann, C., & Zitting, J. (2011). *Tika in action*. Manning Publications Co..

Mazón, J. N., & Trujillo, J. (2009). A hybrid model driven development framework for the multidimensional modeling of data warehouses. *SIGMOD Record*, *38*, 12–17. doi:10.1145/1815918.1815920.

Mazón, J. N., Trujillo, J., & Lechtenbörger, J. (2007). Reconciling requirement-driven data warehouses with data sources via multidimensional normal forms. *Data & Knowledge Engineering*, *63*, 725–751. doi:10.1016/j. datak.2007.04.004.

Mazón, J. N., Trujillo, J., Serrano, M., & Piattini, M. (2005). Designing data warehouses: From business requirement analysis to multidimensional modeling. In K. Cox, E. Dubois, Y. Pigneur, S. J. Bleistein, J. Verner, A. M. Davis, & R. Wieringa (Eds.), *Requirements Engineering for Business Need and IT Alignment* (pp. 44–53). Wales Press.

McCallum, A., Nigam, K., & Ungar, L. H. (2000). Efficient clustering of high-dimensional data sets with application to reference matching. In *Proceedings of the ACM SIGKDD International Conference on Knowledge Discovery and Data Mining*, (pp. 169–178). ACM.

McMullin, J. P., Waters, B., Schiebel, D., Young, W., & Golap, K. (2007). CASA architecture and applications. In *Astronomical Data Analysis Software and Systems XVI* (Vol. 376, p. 127). ADASS.

McNeil, K., Brna, P. M., & Gordon, K. E. (2012). Epilepsy in the Twitter era: A need to re-tweet the way we think about seizures. *Epilepsy & Behavior*, *23*(2), 127–130. doi:10.1016/j.yebeh.2011.10.020 PMID:22134096.

Miao, S., Knobbe, A., Koenders, E., & Bosma, C. (2013). Analysis of traffic events on a Dutch highway bridge. In *Proceedings of the Conference of the International Association for Bridge and Structural Engineers* (IABSE). IABSE.

Michalewicz, Z. (1996). *Genetic algorithms + data structures = evolution programs* (3rd ed.). Berlin: Springer-Verlag. doi:10.1007/978-3-662-03315-9.

Miyoshi, T., Kise, K., Irie, H., & Yoshinaga, T. (2010). Codie: Continuation based overlapping data-transfers with instruction execution. In *Proceedings of International Conference on Networking and Computing* (pp. 71-77). IEEE.

Mokbel, M. F., Lu, M., & Aref, W. G. (2004). Hash-merge join: A non-blocking join algorithm for producing fast and early join results. In *Proceedings of the 20th International Conference on Data Engineering*. Washington, DC: IEEE Computer Society.

Mukhopadhyay, A., & Maulik, U. (2009). Unsupervised satellite image segmentation by combining sa based fuzzy clustering with support vector machine. In *Proceedings of the Advances in Pattern Recognition,* (pp. 381–384). IEEE.

Muñoz, L., Mazón, J. N., & Trujillo, J. (2009). Automatic generation of ETL processes from conceptual models. In I.-Y. Song & E. Zimànyi (Eds.), *DOLAP 2009, ACM 12th International Workshop on Data Warehousing and OLAP* (pp. 33-40). ACM.

MySpace Uses SQL Server Service Broker to Protect Integrity of 1 Petabyte of Data. (n.d.). Retrieved January, 2013, from http://www.techrepublic.com/whitepapers/myspace-uses-sql-server-service-broker-to-protect-integrity-of-1-petabyte-of-data/1097845

Naeem, M. A., Dobbie, G., & Weber, G. (2008). An event-based near real-time data integration architecture. In *Proceedings of the 2008 12th Enterprise Distributed Object Computing Conference Workshops* (pp. 401–404). Washington, DC: IEEE Computer Society. doi:http://dx.doi.org/10.1109/EDOCW.2008.14

Naeem, M. A., Dobbie, G., & Weber, G. (2011). X-HYBRIDJOIN for near-real-time data warehousing. In *Proceedings of the 28th British National Conference on Advances in Databases* (pp. 33–47). Berlin: Springer-Verlag. Retrieved from http://dl.acm.org/citation.cfm?id=2075914.2075919

Naeem, M. A., Dobbie, G., & Weber, G. (2012). Optimised X-HYBRIDJOIN for near-real-time data warehousing. In *Proceedings of the Twenty-Third Australasian Database Conference (ADC 2012)*. Melbourne, Australia: CRPIT.

Naeem, M. A., Dobbie, G., Weber, G., & Alam, S. (2010). R-MESHJOIN for near-real-time data warehousing. In *Proceedings of the ACM 13th International Workshop on Data Warehousing and OLAP*. Toronto, Canada: ACM. doi:http://dx.doi.org/10.1109/IPDPS.2009.5161064

Nagarajan, A. B., Mueller, F., Engelmann, C., & Scott, S. L. (2007). Proactive fault tolerance for HPC with xen virtualization. In *Proceedings of the 21st Annual International Conference on Supercomputing* (pp. 23-32). Seattle, WA: ACM.

Nambiar, R., & Poess, M. (2006). The making of TPC-DS. *VLDB,* 1049-1058.

Narendra, P. M., & Fukunaga, K. (1977). A branch and bound algorithm for feature subset selection. *IEEE Transactions on Computers, 26*(9), 917–922. doi:10.1109/TC.1977.1674939.

NASA Earth Science Office. (2011). *Interactive weather satallite imagery viewers.* Retrieved from http://weather.msfc.nasa.gov/GOES/goeseasthurrir.html

NASA. (n.d.a). *AQUA.* Retrieved from http://aqua.nasa.gov/

NASA. (n.d.b). *Landsat 7.* Retrieved from http://landsat.gsfc.nasa.gov

NASA. (n.d.c). *Pomegranate.* Retrieved from http://pomegranate.nasa.gov/

National Science and Technology Council. (2009). *Harnessing the power of digital data for science and society.* Retrieved from http://www.nitrd.gov/About/Harnessing_Power_Web.pdf

Neuroth, H., Lohmeier, F., & Smith, K. M. (2011). Text-Grid – Virtual research environment for the humanities. *The International Journal of Digital Curation, 2*(6), 222–231.

Newman, W. R. (2013). *Chymistry of Isaac Newton.* Retrieved from http://www.dlib.indiana.edu/collections/newton/

Newman, M. E. J. (2006). Power laws, Pareto distributions and Zipf's law. *Contemporary Physics, 46,* 323–351.

Nickolls, J., Buck, B., Garland, M., & Skadron, K. (2008). Scalable parallel programming with CUDA. *Queue, 6*(2), 40–53. doi:10.1145/1365490.1365500.

Nielsen, R., Paul, J. S., Albrechtsen, A., & Song, Y. S. (2011). Genotype and SNP calling from next-generation sequencing data. *Nature Reviews. Genetics, 12*(6), 443–451. doi:10.1038/nrg2986 PMID:21587300.

Nishimura, S., Das, S., Agrawal, D., & Abbadi, A. (2011). MD-HBase: A scalable multi-dimensional data infrastructure for location aware services. In *Proceedings of the 12th IEEE International Conference on Mobile Data Management.* IEEE.

NOAA. (n.d.). *Geostationary satellite server.* Retrieved from http://www.goes.noaa.gov/

NODC. (n.d.). Retrieved from http://www.nodc.noaa.gov

NVIDIA. (2012). Mathematical functions. In *CUDA C Programming Guide.* NVIDIA.

NVIDIA. (2012). NVIIDA's next generation CUDA compute architecture: Kepler GK110. *NVIDIA Kepler GK110 Architecture White Paper.* Retrieved January 24, 2013, from http://www.nvidia.com/content/PDF/kepler/NVIDIA-Kepler-GK110-Architecture-Whitepaper.pdf

O'Malley, O. (2008). TeraByte sort on Apache Hadoop. *Yahoo.* Retrieved May 2008 from http://sortbenchmark.org/YahooHadoop.pdf

O'Neil, P., Cheng, E., Gawlick, D., & O'Neil, E. (1996). The log-structured merge-tree (LSM-tree). *Acta Informatica, 33*(4).

OAuth. (2012). *Documentation.* Retrieved from http://oauth.net/documentation/

Okman, L., Gal-Oz, N., Gonen, Y., Gudes, E., & Abramov, J. (2011). Security issues in NOSQL databases. In Proceedings of Trust, Security and Privacy in Computing and Communications (TrustCom), (pp. 541-547). IEEE.

Oliver, T., Schmidt, B., Nathan, D., Clemens, R., & Maskell, D. (2005). Multiple sequence alignment on an FPGA. In *Proceedings of the 11th International Conference on Parallel and Distributed Systems,* (Vol. 2, pp. 326-330). Los Alamitos, CA: IEEE Computer Society.

OPeNDAP. (n.d.). Retrieved from http://opendap.org/

Owens, J. D., Luebke, D., Govindaraju, N., Harris, M., Krüger, J., Lefohn, A. E., & Purcell, T. J. (2007). A survey of general-purpose computation on graphics hardware. *Computer Graphics Forum, 26*(1), 80–113. doi:10.1111/j.1467-8659.2007.01012.x.

Pastorino, C., Lopez, T., & Walsh, J. A. (2008). The digital index chemicus: Toward a digital tool for studying Isaac Newton's index chemicus. *Body, Space & Technology Journal, 7*(20).

Patni, J. C., Aswal, M. S., Pal, O. P., & Gupta, A. (2011). Load balancing strategies for Grid computing. In *Proceedings of the International Conference on Electronics Computer Technology* (Vol. 3, pp. 239–243). IEEE.

Pautasso, C., Zimmermann, O., & Leymann, F. (2008). Restful web services vs. big web services: Making the right architectural decision. In *Proceedings of the 17th International Conference on World Wide Web* (pp. 805-814). ACM.

Pavlo, A., Paulson, E., Rasin, A., Abadi, D. J., DeWitt, D. J., Madden, S., et al. (2009). A comparison of approaches to large-scale data analysis. In *Proceedings of the 2009 ACM SIGMOD International Conference on Management of Data* (pp. 165–178). New York, NY: ACM.

Penmatsa, S., & Chronopoulos, A. T. (2005). Job allocation schemes in computational Grids based on cost optimization. In *Proceedings of 19th International Parallel and Distributed Processing Symposium.* IEEE.

Perkins, A. (2000). Business rules=meta-data. In *Proceedings of the 34th International Conference on Technology of Object-Oriented Languages and Systems,* (pp. 285-294). IEEE.

Perley, R. A., Chandler, C. J., Butler, B. J., & Wrobel, J. M. (2011). The expanded very large array: A new telescope for new science. *The Astrophysical Journal Letters, 739*(1), L1. doi:10.1088/2041-8205/739/1/L1.

P. Pertner (Ed.). (2007). *Advances in data mining: Theoritical aspects and applications.* Academic Press. doi:10.1007/978-3-540-73435-2.

Phipps, C., & Davis, K. C. (2002). Automating data warehouse conceptual schema design and evaluation. In L. V. S. Lakshmanan (Ed.), *DMDW: CEUR Workshop Proceedings, Design and Management of Data Warehouses* (pp. 23-32). CEUR.

Piper, P. S. (2013). *HathiTrust and digital public library of America as the future.* Retrieved from http://www.infotoday.com/OnlineSearcher/Articles/Features/HathiTrust-and-Digital-Public-Library-of-America-as-the-future-88089.shtml

Pitti, D. V. (2004). Designing sustainable projects and publications. In S. Schreibman, R. Siemens, & J. Unsworth (Eds.), *A Companion to Digital Humanities.* Oxford, UK: Blackwell. doi:10.1002/9780470999875.ch31.

Plattner, H. (2009). A common database approach for OLTP and OLAP using an in-memory column database. In *Proceedings of the SIGMOD Conference.* ACM.

Plattner, H., & Zeier, A. (2012). *In-memory data management: Technology and applications.* New York: Springer.

Poess, M., Nambiar, R., & Walrath, D. (2007). Why you should run TPC-DS: A workload analysis. *VLDB,* 1138-1149.

Poess, M., Nambiar, R., Baru, C., Bhandarkar, M., & Raab, R. (2013). *Benchmarking big data systems and the big data top 100 list: Big data.* Mary Ann Liebert, Inc..

Polyzotis, N., Skiadopoulos, S., Vassiliadis, P., Simitsis, A., & Frantzell, N. E. (2007). Supporting streaming updates in an active data warehouse. In *Proceedings of the 23rd International Conference on Data Engineering* (pp. 476–485). Istanbul, Turkey: IEEE.

Polyzotis, N., Skiadopoulos, S., Vassiliadis, P., Simitsis, A., & Frantzell, N. (2008). Meshing streaming updates with persistent data in an active data warehouse. *IEEE Transactions on Knowledge and Data Engineering, 20*(7), 976–991. doi:10.1109/TKDE.2008.27.

Popivanov, I., & Miller, R. J. (2002). Similarity search over time-series data using wavelets.[IEEE.]. *Proceedings of Data Engineering, 2002,* 212–221.

PPL. (2013). *Python programming language.* Retrieved from http://www.python.org/

Press, G. (2013). A very short history of big data. *Forbes.* Retrieved from http://www.forbes.com/sites/gilpress/2013/05/09/a-very-short-history-of-big-data/

Project Gutenberg. (2013). Retrieved from http://www.gutenberg.org/ebooks/

Pudil, P., & Novovičová, J. (1998). Novel methods for feature subset selection with respect to problem knowledge. In *Feature Extraction, Construction and Selection* (pp. 101–116). New York: Springer. doi:10.1007/978-1-4615-5725-8_7.

Pudil, P., Novovičová, J., & Kittler, J. (1994). Floating search methods in feature selection. *Pattern Recognition Letters, 15*(11), 1119–1125. doi:10.1016/0167-8655(94)90127-9.

Puerto, J., Tamir, A., Mesa, J. A., & Pérez-Brito, D. (2008). Center location problems on tree graphs with subtree-shaped customers. *Discrete Applied Mathematics, 156*(15), 2890–2910. doi:10.1016/j.dam.2007.11.022.

R Project for Statistical Computing. (n.d.). Retrieved from www.r-project.org

Reed, S. L., & Lenat, D. B. (2002). Mapping ontologies in Cyc. In *Proceedings of AAAI 2002 Conference Workshop on Ontologies for the Semantic Web.* Edmonton, Canada: AAAI.

Reese, S. D., Rutigliano, L., Hyun, K., & Jeong, J. (2007). Mapping the blogosphere: Professional and citizen-based media in the global news arena. *Journalism*, 8, 235–261. doi:10.1177/1464884907076459.

Regola, N., & Ducom, J.-C. (2010). Recommendations for virtualization technologies in high performance computing. In *Proceedings of the IEEE International Conference on Cloud Computing Technology and Science* (pp. 409-416). Indianapolis, IN: IEEE.

Reid, K., & Stumm, M. (2000). *Overlapping data transfer with application execution on clusters*. Paper presented at the meeting of Workshop on Cluster-based Computing. Santa Fe, NM.

Reutemann, P., & Vanschoren, J. (2012). Scientific workflow management with ADAMS.[ECML.]. *Proceedings of ECMLPKDD*, *2012*, 833–837.

ReVelle, C. S., & Eiselt, H. A. (2005). Location analysis: A synthesis and survey. *European Journal of Operational Research*, *16*, 1–19.

Rew, R., & Davis, G. (1990). NetCDF: An interface for scientific data access. *IEEE Computer Graphics and Applications*, *10*(4). doi:10.1109/38.56302.

Reynolds, P., & Pavic, A. (2001). Comparison of forced and ambient vibration measurements on a bridge. In *Proceedings of the International Modal Analysis Conference*. IMAC.

Rockwell, R. C. (1994). An integrated network interface between the researcher and social science data resources: In search of a practical vision. *Social Science Computer Review*, *12*(2), 202–214. doi:10.1177/089443939401200205.

Rogers, E. M., & Kincaid, D. L. (1981). *Communication networks: Toward a new paradigm for research*. New York: Free Press.

Romein, J. W., Broekema, P. C., van Meijeren, E., van der Schaaf, K., & Zwart, W. H. (2006). Astronomical real-time streaming signal processing on a blue gene/L supercomputer. In *Proceedings of the Eighteenth Annual ACM Symposium on Parallelism in Algorithms and Architectures* (pp. 59-66). ACM.

Romero, O., & Abelló, A. (2009). A survey of multidimensional modeling methodologies. *International Journal of Data Warehousing and Mining*, *5*, 1–23. doi:10.4018/jdwm.2009040101.

Romero, O., & Abelló, A. (2010). Automatic validation of requirements to support multidimensional design. *Data & Knowledge Engineering*, *69*(9), 917–942. doi:10.1016/j.datak.2010.03.006.

Romero, O., & Abelló, A. (2010). A framework for multidimensional design of data warehouses from ontologies. *Data & Knowledge Engineering*, *69*(11), 1138–1157. doi:10.1016/j.datak.2010.07.007.

Romero, O., Simitsis, A., & Abelló, A. (2011). GEM: Requirement-driven generation of ETL and multidimensional conceptual designs. In A. Cuzzocrea, & U. Dayal (Eds.), *Data Warehousing and Knowledge Discovery (LNCS)* (Vol. 6862, pp. 80–95). Berlin: Springer. doi:10.1007/978-3-642-23544-3_7.

Rong, C., Nguyen, S. T., & Jaatun, M. G. (2012). Beyond lightning: A survey on security challenges in cloud computing. *Computers & Electrical Engineering*. Retrieved from http://www.sciencedirect.com/science/article/pii/S0045790612000870

Rozsnyai, S., Slominski, A., & Doganata, Y. (2011). Large-scale distributed storage system for business provenance. In *Proceedings of International Conference on Cloud Computing* (pp. 516-524). IEEE.

Ryan, T., & Xenos, S. (2011). Who uses Facebook? An investigation into the relationship between the big five, shyness, narcissism, loneliness, and Facebook usage. *Computers in Human Behavior*, *27*, 1658–1664. doi:10.1016/j.chb.2011.02.004.

Sadler, E. (2009). Project blacklight: A next generation library catalog at a first generation university. *Library Hi Tech*, *27*(1), 57–67. doi:10.1108/07378830910942919.

Samet, H. (2005). *Foundations of multidimensional and metric data structures*. San Francisco, CA: Morgan Kaufmann Publishers Inc..

Sammer, E. (2012). *Hadoop operations*. Sebastopol, CA: O'Reilly Media Inc..

Sandhu, R., Ferraiolo, D., & Kuhn, R. (2000). The NIST model for role-based access control: Towards a unified standard. In *Proceedings of the Fifth ACM Workshop on Role-Based Access Control,* (pp. 47-63). ACM.

SAP. (2013). *SAP standard application benchmarks.* Retrieved June 19, 2013 from http://www.sap.com/campaigns/benchmark/index.epx

Sarood, O., Gupta, A., & Kale, L. V. (2012). Cloud friendly load balancing for HPC applications: Preliminary work. In *Proceedings of International Conference on Parallel Processing Workshops* (pp. 200–205). IEEE.

Savvas, I. K., & Kechadi, M. T. (2012). Mining on the cloud: K-means with MapReduce. In *Proceedings of the International Conference on Cloud Computing and Services Science* (CLOSER), (pp. 413–418). CLOSER.

Schadt, E. E., Turner, S., & Kasarskis, A. (2010). A window into third-generation sequencing. *Human Molecular Genetics, 19*(R2), R227–R240. doi:10.1093/hmg/ddq416 PMID:20858600.

Scheaffer, R. L., Mendenhall, W. III, Ott, R. L., & Gerow, K. G. (2012). *Elementary survey sampling* (7th ed.). Boston, MA: Brooks/Cole.

Scherle, R., Carrier, S., Greenberg, J., Lapp, H., Thompson, A., Vision, T., & White, H. (2008). Building support for a discipline-based data repository. In *Proceedings of the 2008 International Conference on Open Repositories.* Retrieved from http://pubs.or08.ecs.soton.ac.uk/35/1/submission_177.pdf

Schiffer, A. J. (2006). Blogs worms and press norms: News coverage of the Downing Street memo controversy. *Journalism & Mass Communication Quarterly, 83,* 494–510. doi:10.1177/107769900608300302.

Schilling, D. A., Jayaraman, V., & Barkhi, R. (1993). A review of covering problems in facility location. *Location Science, 1*(1), 25–55.

Schmuck, F., & Haskin, R. (2002). GPFS: A shared-disk file system for large computing clusters. In *Proceedings of the First USENIX Conference on File and Storage Technologies,* (pp. 231-244). USENIX.

Schönemannand, P. H., & Wang, M. M. (1979). An individual difference model for the multi-dimensional analysis of preference data. *Psychometrika, 37*(3), 275–309. doi:10.1007/BF02306784.

Schopf, J. M. (2009). Sustainability and the office of cyberinfrastructure. In *Proceedings of Network Computing and Applications.* IEEE.

Schwan, P. (2003). Lustre: Building a file system for 1000-node clusters. In *Proceedings of the 2003 Linux Symposium.* Linux.

Scott, S., Myers, S., & Momose, M. (2002). *Data rates for the ALMA archive and control system.* ALMA Science Software Requirements Committee. Retrieved from http://www.iram.fr/~lucas/almassr/report-2/DataRates.pdf

Scrakthhulze, G., Jirasec, A., Yu, M., Lim, A., Tumer, R., & Blades, M. (2005). Investigation of selected baseline removal techniques as candidates for automated implementation. *Applied Spectroscopy, 59*(5), 545–574. doi:10.1366/0003702053945985 PMID:15969801.

Searsmith, K. (2011). *Making progress: SEASR at the Andrew W. Mellon research in information technology retreat.* Retrieved from http://seasr.org/blog/2008/02/28/making-progress-seasr-at-the-andrew-w-mellon-research-in-information-technology-retreat/

Seibold, M., Wolke, A., Albutiu, M., Bichler, M., Kemper, A., & Setzer, T. (2012). Efficient deployment of main-memory DBMS in virtualized data centers. In *Proceedings of International Conference on Cloud Computing* (pp. 311-318). IEEE.

Sen, A. (1997). *On economic inequality.* Oxford, UK: Clarendon Press.

Shanley, K. (1998). *History and overview of the TPC.* Retrieved June 19, 2013 from http://www.tpc.org/information/about/history.asp

Shannon, C. E. (1948). A mathematical theory of communication. *The Bell System Technical Journal, 27*(3), 379–423.

Shapiro, L. G., & Stockman, G. C. (2001). *Computer vision.* Englewood Cliffs, NJ: Prentice Hall.

Sharma, S., & Gupta, R. K. (2010). Improved BSP clustering algorithm for social network analysis. *International Journal of Grid and Distributed Computing, 3*(3), 67–76.

Sheikholeslami, G., Chatterjee, S., & Zhang, A. (1998). Wavecluster: A multi-resolution clustering approach for very large spatial databases. In *Proceedings of the International Conference on Very Large Data Bases* (pp. 428-439). IEEE.

Sieber, R. E., Wellen, C. C., & Jin, Y. (2011). *Spatial cyberinfrastructures, ontologies, and the humanities.* Retrieved from http://www.pnas.org/citmgr?gca=pnas,108/14/5504

Sifuzzaman, M., Islam, M. R., & Ali, M. Z. (2009). Application of wavelet transform and its advantages compared to Fourier transform. *The Journal of Physiological Sciences; JPS, 13*, 121–134.

Singh, S., Kubica, J., Larsen, S., & Sorokina, D. (2009). Parallel large scale feature selection for logistic regression. In *Proceedings of the SIAM International Conference on Data Mining (SDM)*. SDM.

SKA. (2011). *Square kilometer array.* Retrieved from http://www.skatelescope.org/

Slee, M., Aditya, A., & Kwiatkowski, M. (2007, January). *Thrift: Scalable cross-language services implementation.* Facebook.

SocSciBot. (n.d.). *Web crawler and link analyzer for the social sciences.* Retrieved January 2013, from http://socscibot.wlv.ac.uk/

Somol, P., Pudil, P., Ferri, F. J., & Kittler, J. (2000). Fast branch & bound algorithm in feature selection. In B. Sanchez, M. J. Pineda, & J. Wolfmann, (Eds.), *Proceedings of SCI 2000: The 4th World Multiconference on Systemics, Cybernetics and Informatics* (pp. 646–651). Orlando, FL: IIIS.

Song, Z., & Roussopoulos, N. (2000). Using Hilbert curve in image storing and retrieving. In *Proceedings of the 2000 ACM Workshops on Multimedia* (MULTIMEDIA '00). ACM.

Space Telescope Science Institute. (2012). *HST publication statistics.* Retrieved from http://archive.stsci.edu/hst/bibliography/pubstat.html

SPC. (2013). *SPC-1 and SPC-1/E benchmark results.* Retrieved June 19, 2013 from http://www.storageperformance.org/results/benchmark_results_spc1

Srikant, R., & Agrawal, R. (1996). Mining sequential patterns: Generalizations and performance improvements. In *Proceedings of International Conference on Extending Database Technology* (pp. 3–17). IEEE.

Stanimirović, Z. (2008). An efficient genetic algorithm for the uncapacitated multiple allocation p-hub median problem. *Control and Cybernetics, 37*(3), 669–692.

Stanimirović, Z. (2010). A genetic algorithm approach for the capacitated single allocation p-hub median problem. *Computing and Informatics, 29*(1), 117–132.

Stanimirović, Z., Kratica, J., & Dugošija, D. (2007). Genetic algorithms for solving the discrete ordered median problem. *European Journal of Operational Research, 182*, 983–1001. doi:10.1016/j.ejor.2006.09.069.

Stearns, S. D. (1976). On selecting features for pattern classifiers. In *Proceedings of the 3rd International Conference on Pattern Recognition* (ICPR 1976) (pp. 71–75). Coronado, CA: ICPR.

Stein, L. D. (2008). Towards a cyberinfrastructure for the biological sciences: Progress, visions and challenges. *Nature Reviews. Genetics, 9*, 677–688. doi:10.1038/nrg2414 PMID:18714290.

Stewart, C. A., Almes, G. T., & Wheeler, B. C. (2010). *Cyberinfrastructure software sustainability and reusability: Report from an NSF-funded workshop.* Retrieved from http://hdl.handle.net/2022/6701

Stewart, C. A., Simms, S., Plale, B., Link, M., Hancock, D., & Fox, G. C. (2010). What is cyberinfrastructure? Norfolk, VA: Association for Computing Machinery (ACM). doi: doi:10.1145/1878335.1878347.

Stollnitz, E. J., DeRose, T. D., & Salesin, D. H. (1995). Wavelets for computer graphics: A primer, part 1. *IEEE Computer Graphics and Applications, 15*(3), 76–84. doi:10.1109/38.376616.

Stonebraker, M., Becla, J., Dewitt, D., Lim, K., Maier, D., Ratzesberger, O., & Zdonik, S. (2009). Requirements for science databases and SciDB. In *Proceedings of the Conference on Innovative Database Research.* IEEE.

Stonebraker, M. (2010). Errors in database systems, eventual consistency, and the CAP theorem. *Communications of the ACM, 5.*

Stranneby, D., & Walker, W. (2004). *Digital signal processing and applications.* London: Elsevier.

Subrahmanyam, K., Garcia, E. C., Harsono, L. S., Li, J. S., & Lipana, L. (2009). In their words: Connecting on-line weblogs to developmental processes. *The British Journal of Developmental Psychology, 27,* 219–245. doi:10.1348/026151008X345979 PMID:19972670.

Sumathi, S., & Esakkirajan, S. (2007). *Fundamentals of relational database management systems.* New York, NY: Springer. doi:10.1007/978-3-540-48399-1.

Surdeanu, M., Turmo, J., & Ageno, A. (2005). A hybrid unsupervised approach for document clustering. In *Proceedings of the Eleventh ACM SIGKDD International Conference on Knowledge Discovery in Data Mining* (pp. 685–690). New York, NY: ACM.

Sure, Y., Erdmann, M., Angele, J., Staab, S., Studer, R., & Wenke, D. (2002). OntoEdit: Collaborative ontology development for the semantic web. In I. Horrocks & J. A. Hendler (Eds.), *International Semantic Web Conference* (LNCS), (Vol. 2342, pp. 221-235). Berlin: Springer.

Svensson, P. (2010). The landscape of digital humanities. *Digital Humanities Quarterly, 4*(1).

Svensson, P. (2011). From optical fiber to conceptual cyberinfrastructure. *Digital Humanities Quarterly, 5*(1).

Sweetser Trammell, K. D. (2007). Candidate campaign blogs: Directly reaching out to the youth vote. *The American Behavioral Scientist, 50,* 1255–1263. doi:10.1177/0002764207300052.

Sze, T.-W. (2011). Schönhage-strassen algorithm with MapReduce for multiplying terabit integers. In *Proceedings of the 2011 International Workshop on Symbolic-Numeric Computation* (pp. 54-62). IEEE.

Tannenbaum, A., & Van Steen, M. (2007). Fault tolerance. In A. Tannenbaum, & M. Van Steen (Eds.), *Distributed systems: Principles and paradigms* (pp. 321–375). Upper Saddle River, NJ: Pearson Education.

Tao, Y., Yi, K., Sheng, C., & Kalnis, P. (2009). Quality and efficiency in high dimensional nearest neighbor search. In *Proceedings of the 35th SIGMOD International Conference on Management of Data.* ACM.

Taylor, I., Deelamn, E., Gannon, D., & Sheilds, M. (2006). *Workflows for e-science: Scientific workflows for grids.* London, UK: Springer-Verlag.

Taylor, R. (2012). An overview of the Hadoop/MapReduce/HBase framework and its current applications in bioinformatics. *BMC Bioinformatics, 11*(12). PMID:21210976.

Terasort. (2013). *org.apache.hadoop.examples.terasort.* Retrieved June 19, 2013 from http://hadoop.apache.org/docs/current/api/org/apache/hadoop/examples/terasort/package-summary.html

Theil, H. (1967). *Economics and information theory.* Chicago: Rand McNally and Company.

Thelwall, M., Buckley, K., & Paltoglou, G. (2011). Sentiment in Twitter events. *Journal of the American Society for Information Science and Technology, 62*(2), 406–418. doi:10.1002/asi.21462.

Thelwall, M., & Stuart, D. (2007). RUOK? Blogging communication technologies during crises. *Journal of Computer-Mediated Communication, 12,* 523–548. doi:10.1111/j.1083-6101.2007.00336.x.

Thenmozhi, M., & Vivekanandan, K. (2012). An ontology-based hybrid approach to derive multidimensional schema for data warehouse. *International Journal of Computers and Applications, 54*(8), 36–42. doi:10.5120/8590-2343.

Thessen, A. E., & Patterson, D. J. (2011). Data issues in the life sciences. *Zookeys, 150,* 15–51. doi:10.3897/zookeys.150.1766 PMID:22207805.

Thompson, S. K. (2012). *Sampling* (3rd ed.). Hoboken, NJ: Wiley. doi:10.1002/9781118162934.

Thorfinn, S. (2012). realSFS. *The Bioinformatics Centre University of Copenhagen.* Retrieved January 24, 2013, from http://128.32.118.212/thorfinn/realSFS/

Thoring, A. (2011). Corporate tweeting: Analysing the use of Twitter as a marketing tool by UK trade publishers. *Public Relations Quarterly*, *27*, 141–158. doi:10.1007/s12109-011-9214-7.

Thusoo, A., Sarma, J. S., Jain, N., Shao, Z., Chakka, P., Zhang, N., & Murthy, R. (2010). Hive-a petabyte scale data warehouse using hadoop. In Proceedings of Data Engineering (ICDE), (pp. 996-1005). IEEE.

Tian, F., & Chen, K. (2011). Towards optimal resource provisioning for running MapReduce programs in public clouds. In *Proceedings of International Conference on Cloud Computing* (pp. 155-162). IEEE.

Trammel, K. D. (2006). Blog offensive: An exploratory analysis of attacks published on campaign blog posts from a political public relations perspective. *Public Relations Review*, *32*, 402–406. doi:10.1016/j.pubrev.2006.09.008.

Trammel, K. D., Williams, A. P., Postelnicu, M., & Landreville, K. D. (2006). Evolution of online campaigning: Increasing interactivity in candidate web sites and blogs through text and technical features. *Mass Communication & Society*, *9*, 21–44. doi:10.1207/s15327825mcs0901_2.

Tran, J. J., Cinquini, L., Mattmann, C. A., Zimdars, P. A., Cuddy, D. T., Leung, K. S., & Freeborn, D. (2011). Evaluating cloud computing in the NASA DESDynI ground data system. In *Proceedings of the 2nd International Workshop on Software Engineering for Cloud Computing* (pp. 36-42). ACM.

Tremayne, M., Zheng, N., Lee, J. K., & Jeong, J. (2006). Issue publics on the web: Applying network theory to the war blogosphere. *Journal of Computer-Mediated Communication*, *12*, 290–310. doi:10.1111/j.1083-6101.2006.00326.x.

Troester, M. (2012). *Big data meets big data analytics: Three key technologies for extracting real-time business value from the big data that threatens to overwhelm traditional computing architectures*. SAS Institute. Retrieved from www.sas.com/resources/whitepaper/wp_46345.pdf

Tsafrir, D., Etsion, Y., & Feitelson, D. (2007). Backfilling using system generated predictions rather than user run-time estimates. *Transactions on Parallel and Distributed Systems*, *18*, 789–803. doi:10.1109/TPDS.2007.70606.

Tyson, J. A. (2002). Large synoptic survey telescope: overview. In *Astronomical Telescopes and Instrumentation* (pp. 10–20). International Society for Optics and Photonics.

Unidata. (n.d.). *NetCDF Java API*. Retrieved from http://http://www.unidata.ucar.edu/software/netcdf-java/

Unsworth, J., Rosenzweig, R., Courant, P., Frasier, S. E., & Henry, C. (2006). *Our cultural commonwealth: The report of the American council of learned societies commission on cyberinfrastructure for the humanities and social sciences*. New York: American Council of Learned Societies. Retrieved from http://www.acls.org/programs/Default.aspx?id=644

Urhan, T., & Franklin, M. J. (2000). XJoin: A reactively-scheduled pipelined join operator. *A Quarterly Bulletin of the Computer Society of the IEEE Technical Committee on Data Engineering*, *23*.

Vakharia, A. J., & Mahajan, J. (2000). Clustering of objects and attributes for manufacturing and marketing applications. *European Journal of Operational Research*, *123*(3), 640–651. doi:10.1016/S0377-2217(99)00103-4.

van Doorn, N., van Zoonen, L., & Wyatt, S. (2007). Writing from experience: Presentations of gender identity on weblogs. *European Journal of Women's Studies*, *14*, 143–159. doi:10.1177/1350506807075819.

Vardigan, M., & Whiteman, C. (2007). ICPSR meets OAIS: Applying the OAIS reference model to the social science archive context. *Archival Science*, *7*(1), 73–87. doi:10.1007/s10502-006-9037-z.

Verma, A., Cherkasova, L., & Campbell, R. H. (2012). *Two sides of a coin: Optimizing the schedule of MapReduce jobs to minimize their makespan and improve cluster performance*. Paper presented at 2012 IEEE 20th International Symposium on Modeling, Analysis and Simulation of Computer and Telecommunication System. Arlington, VA.

Vespier, U., Knobbe, A., Nijssen, S., & Vanschoren, J. (2012). MDL-based analysis of time series at multiple time-scales. In *Proceedings of ECML- PKDD 2012* (pp. 371-386). ECML.

Vespier, U., Knobbe, A., Vanschoren, J., Miao, S., Koopman, A., Obladen, B., et al. (2011). Traffic events modeling for structural health monitoring. In *Proceedings of Advances in Intelligent Data Analysis* (IDA 2011), (pp. 376-387). IDA.

Vetterli, T., Vaduva, A., & Staudt, M. (2000). Metadata standards for data warehousing: open information model vs. common warehouse metadata. *SIGMOD Record*, 68–75. doi:10.1145/362084.362138.

Viglas, S. D., Naughton, J. F., & Burger, J. (2003). Maximizing the output rate of multi-way join queries over streaming information sources. In *Proceedings of the 29th International Conference on Very Large Data Bases* (pp. 285–296). VLDB Endowment.

Vision, T. J. (2010). Open data and the social contract of scientific publishing. *Bioscience*, *60*(5), 330. doi:10.1525/bio.2010.60.5.2.

Walsh, J. A. (2013). *The Algernon Charles Swinburne project text collection*. Retrieved from http://www.swinburneproject.org/

Walsh, J. A., & Hooper, E. W. (2012). The liberty of invention: Alchemical discourse and information technology standardization. *Literary and Linguistic Computing*, *27*, 55–79. doi:10.1093/llc/fqr038.

Wang, B. (2013). GPU accelerated MAF estimation on tianhe-1A. In *Proceedings of Parallel Programming Model for the Masses (PPMM 2013)*. Shenzhen, China: PPMM.

Wang, D., Zender, C., & Jenks, S. (2008). Clustered workflow execution of retargeted data analysis scripts. In *Proceedings of the 8th IEEE International Symposium on Cluster Computing and the Grid*. IEEE.

Wang, D. L., Zender, C. S., & Jenks, S. F. (2007). Server-side parallel data reduction and analysis. *Advances in Grid and Pervasive Computing*, *4459*, 744–750. doi:10.1007/978-3-540-72360-8_67.

Wang, H. (2010). Privacy-preserving data sharing in cloud computing. *Journal of Computer Science and Technology*, *25*(3), 401–414. doi:10.1007/s11390-010-9333-1.

Wasserman, S., & Faust, K. (1994). *Social network analysis: methods and applications*. New York: Cambridge University Press. doi:10.1017/CBO9780511815478.

Wayth, R. B., Brisken, W. F., Deller, A. T., Majid, W. A., Thompson, D. R., Tingay, S. J., & Wagstaff, K. L. (2011). V-FASTR: The VLBA fast radio transients experiment. *The Astrophysical Journal*, *735*(2), 97. doi:10.1088/0004-637X/735/2/97.

WBDB. (2012). *First workshop on big data benchmarking*. Retrieved June 19, 2013 from http://clds.ucsd.edu/wbdb2012/

WBDB. (2012). *Second workshop on big data benchmarking*. Retrieved June 19, 2013 from http://clds.ucsd.edu/wbdb2012.in

Webb, L. M., Thompson-Hayes, M., Chang, H. C., & Smith, M. M. (2012). Taking the audience perspective: Online fan commentary about the brides of Mad Men and their weddings. In A. A. Ruggerio, (Ed.), Media depictions of brides, wives, and mothers (pp. 223-235). Lanham, MD: Lexington.

Webb, L. M., Wilson, M. L., Hodges, M., Smith, P. A., & Zakeri, M. (2012). Facebook: How college students work it. In H. S. Noor Al-Deen & J. A. Hendricks (Eds.), Social media: Usage and impact (pp. 3-22). Lanham, MD: Lexington.

Webb, L. M., Chang, H. C., Hayes, M. T., Smith, M. M., & Gibson, D. M. (2012). Mad men dot com: An analysis of commentary from online fan websites. In J. C. Dunn, J. Manning, & D. Stern (Eds.), *Lucky strikes and a three-martini lunch: Thinking about television's Mad Men* (pp. 226–238). Newcastle upon Tyne, UK: Cambridge Scholars Publishing.

Webb, L. M., Fields, T. E., Boupha, S., & Stell, M. N. (2012). U. S. political blogs: What channel characteristics contribute to popularity? In T. Dumova, & R. Fiordo (Eds.), *Blogging in the global society: Cultural, political, and geographic aspects* (pp. 179–199). Hershey, PA: IGI Global.

Webb, L. M., & Wang, Y. (2013). Techniques for analyzing blogs and micro-blogs. In N. Sappleton (Ed.), *Advancing research methods with new technologies*. Hershey, PA: IGI Global.

Wells, D. C. (1985). Nrao'S astronomical image processing system (AIPS). In *Data Analysis in Astronomy* (pp. 195–209). New York: Springer US. doi:10.1007/978-1-4615-9433-8_18.

White House. (2012, March 29). *Obama administration unveils "big data" initiative: Announces $200 million in new R&D investments*. Retrieved February 13, 2013, from http://www.whitehouse.gov/sites/default/files/microsites/ostp/big_data_press_release_final_2.pdf

White, T. (2009). *How to benchmark a Hadoop cluster*. O'Reilly Media Inc. Retrieved October 2009 from http://answers.oreilly.com/topic/460-how-to-benchmark-a-hadoop-cluster/

White, T. (2009). *Hadoop: The definite guide*. Sebastopol, CA: O'Reilly.

White, T. (2012). *Hadoop: The definitive guide* (3rd ed.). Sebastopol, CA: O'Reilly Media.

Whitney, A. W. (1971). A direct method of nonparametric measurement selection. *IEEE Transactions on Computers*, *20*(9), 1100–1103. doi:10.1109/T-C.1971.223410.

Wiles, R., Crow, G., & Pain, H. (2011). Innovation in qualitative research methods: A narrative review. *Qualitative Research*, *11*, 587–604. doi:10.1177/1468794111413227.

Williams, A. P., Trammell, K. P., Postelnicu, M., Landreville, K. D., & Martin, J. D. (2005). Blogging and hyperlinking: Use of the web to enhance viability during the 2004 US campaign. *Journalism Studies*, *6*, 177–186. doi:10.1080/14616700500057262.

Williford, C., & Henry, C. (2012). *One culture*. Council on Library and Information Resources. Retrieved from http://www.clir.org/pubs/reports/pub151

Wilschut, A. N., & Apers, P. M. G. (1990). Pipelining in query execution. In *Proceedings of the International Conference on Databases, Parallel Architectures and Their Applications (PARBASE 1990)*. Los Alamitos, CA: IEEE Computer Society Press.

Wilschut, A. N., & Apers, P. M. G. (1991). Dataflow query execution in a parallel main-memory environment. In *Proceedings of the first International Conference on Parallel and Distributed Information Systems* (pp. 68–77). Los Alamitos, CA: IEEE Computer Society Press.

Witkin, A. P. (1983). Scale-space filtering.[San Francisco, CA: IJCAI.]. *Proceedings of IJCAI*, *1983*, 1019–1022.

WSO2. (2013). *WSO2 identity server - Identity & entitlement management*. Retrieved from http://wso2.com/products/identity-server/

Wu, Y., Agrawal, D., & Abbadi, A. E. (2000). A comparison of DFT and DWT based similarity search in time-series databases. In *Proceedings of the Ninth International Conference on Information and Knowledge Management*, CIKM '00 (pp. 488–495). New York, NY: ACM.

Wu, K., Ahern, S., Bethel, E., Chen, J., Childs, H., & Cormier-Michel, E. et al. (2009). FastBit: Interactively Searching massive data. *Journal of Physics*, *180*(2).

Xenos, M. (2008). New mediated deliberation: Blog and press coverage of the Alito nomination. *Journal of Computer-Mediated Communication*, *13*, 485–503. doi:10.1111/j.1083-6101.2008.00406.x.

Xu, C. Z., & Lau, F. C. M. (1997). *Load balancing in parallel computers: Theory and practice*. Boston: Kluwer.

Yagoubi, B., & Slimani, Y. (2006). Dynamic load balancing strategy for grid computing. *Transactions on Engineering. Computing and Technology*, *13*, 260–265.

Yang, Y., & Chang, K. (2009). Extracting the bridge frequencies indirectly from a passing vehicle: Parametric study. *Engineering Structures*, *31*(10), 2448–2459. doi:10.1016/j.engstruct.2009.06.001.

Yan, W., Brahmakshatriya, U., Xue, Y., Gilder, M., & Wise, B. (2013). p-PIC: Parallel power iteration clustering for big data. *Journal of Parallel and Distributed Computing*, *73*(3), 352–359. doi:10.1016/j.jpdc.2012.06.009.

YCSB. (2013). Retrieved June 19, 2013 from http://research.yahoo.com/Web_Information_Management/YCSB

Yıldırım, A. A., & Özdoğan, C. (2011). Parallel Wave-Cluster: A linear scaling parallel clustering algorithm implementation with application to very large datasets. *Journal of Parallel and Distributed Computing*, *71*(7), 955–962. doi:10.1016/j.jpdc.2011.03.007.

Yıldırım, A. A., & Özdoğan, C. (2011). Parallel wavelet-based clustering algorithm on GPUs using CUDA. *Procedia Computer Science*, *3*, 396–400. doi:10.1016/j.procs.2010.12.066.

Yi, X., Liang, Y., Huerta-Sanchez, E., Jin, X., Cuo, Z. X. P., Pool, J. E., & Cao, Z. (2010). Sequencing of 50 human exomes reveals adaptation to high altitude. *Science Signaling*, *329*(5987), 75. PMID:20595611.

Zaharia, M., Konwinski, A., & Joseph, A. D. (2008). Improving MapReduce performance in heterogeneous environments. In *Proceedings of Symposium on Operating Systems Design and Implementation* (pp. 29-42). USENIX.

Zaki, M. J., Li, W., & Parthasarathy, S. (1996). Customized dynamic load balancing for a network of workstations. In *Proceedings of International Symposium on High Performance Parallel and Distributed Computing* (pp. 282–291). IEEE.

Zhang, X., & Rundensteiner, E. A. (2002). Integrating the maintenance and synchronization of data warehouses using a cooperative framework. *Information Systems*, *27*(4), 219–243. doi:10.1016/S0306-4379(01)00049-7.

Zhao, W., Ma, H., & He, Q. (2009). Parallel k-means clustering based on mapreduce. In *Proceedings of the 1st International Conference on Cloud Computing*, (vol. 5931, pp. 674-679). Berlin: Springer.

Zhao, H., Ai, S., Lv, Z., & Li, B. (2010). *Parallel accessing massive NetCDF data based on MapReduce*. Berlin: Springer. doi:10.1007/978-3-642-16515-3_53.

Zhuge, Y., García-Molina, H., Hammer, J., & Widom, J. (1995). View maintenance in a warehousing environment. In *Proceedings of the 1995 ACM SIGMOD International Conference on Management of Data* (pp. 316–327). New York, NY: ACM. doi:http://doi.acm.org/10.1145/223784.223848

About the Contributors

Wen-Chen Hu received a BE, an ME, an MS, and a PhD, all in Computer Science, from Tamkang University, Taiwan, the National Central University, Taiwan, the University of Iowa, and the University of Florida, in 1984, 1986, 1993, and 1998, respectively. He is currently an associate professor in the Department of Computer Science of the University of North Dakota. He is the Editor-in-Chief of the *International Journal of Handheld Computing Research* (IJHCR), and has served as editor and editorial advisory/review board members for over 20 international journals/books and chaired more than 20 tracks/sessions and program committees for international conferences. Dr. Hu has been teaching more than 10 years at the US universities and advised more than 50 graduate students. He has published over 100 articles in refereed journals, conference proceedings, books, and encyclopedias, edited five books and proceedings, and solely authored a book. His current research interests include handheld computing, electronic and mobile commerce systems, Web technologies, and databases.

Naima Kaabouch received her BS, MS, and PhD, all in Electrical Engineering, from the University of Paris 11 and the University of Paris 6, Paris, France, in 1982, 1986, and 1990, respectively. She is currently an associate professor and graduate program director, in the Department of Electrical Engineering, University of North Dakota. Dr. Kaabouch research interests include configurable computing, real time systems, and signal/image processing. She has published over 80 articles in refereed journals, proceedings, and books. In green computing field, she co-edited two books. In teaching, she developed and taught several courses in the field of configurable computing and real time systems involving microcontrollers and field programmable gate array-based devices. She is the recipient of several awards recognizing her teaching and work with the electrical engineering students.

* * *

Loretta Auvil works at the Illinois Informatics Institute (I3) at the University of Illinois at Urbana Champaign. She received a MS in Computer Science from Virginia Tech and a BS in Applied Mathematics and Computer Science from Alderson-Broaddus College. She has worked with a diverse set of application drivers to integrate machine learning and information visualization techniques to solve the needs of research partners. She has led software development and research projects for many years. Prior to working for I3, she spent many years at NCSA on machine learning and information visualization projects and several years creating tools for visualizing performance data of parallel computer programs at Rome Laboratory and Oak Ridge National Laboratory.

Kapil Bakshi works for Cisco Systems Inc. He is responsible for leading and driving technology & business architectures, including data center, big data, and cloud computing strategy and initiatives. Kapil has extensive experience in strategizing, architecting, managing, and delivering complex technology solutions. During his career, he has held several architectural, consulting, and managerial positions within the industry. Prior to Cisco, Kapil worked for Sun Microsystems, where he spent a decade working with US Government, Enterprise and Service Provider customers. Prior to SUN Microsystems, he worked for Hewlett-Packard and several government system integrators in consulting and product development roles. Kapil is a native of Washington D.C. and holds both a BS in electrical engineering and a BS in computer science from the University of Maryland, College Park, as well as an MS in electrical & computer engineering from Johns Hopkins University, and an MBA from the University of Maryland, College Park. He chairs and leads several industry forums. He also holds U.S. patents for data center and related solution sets.

Thomas Bennett is a senior software developer in the MeerKAT Science Processing Team. Mr. Bennett has led the development of the KAT-7 ingestion software pipeline, developing automated file ingestion and crawling software using the Apache OODT framework. Mr. Bennett has established a close partnership with Dr. Mattmann and with NASA JPL building out open source software. He is the main point of contact from the SKA South Africa project.

Bryan Butler is a staff scientist in Socorro, New Mexico, at the National Radio Astronomy Observatory, where he has been since 1994. He received his Ph.D. in Planetary Science from the California Institute of Technology. His scientific research interests involve radio emission from solar system objects. He was in charge of all aspects of software architecture, development, deployment, and maintenance for the Expanded Very Large Array construction project from 2006 to 2013, and is currently in charge of the Monitor and Control software for the Very Large Array and Very Long Baseline Array.

Ricardo Cachucho earned his Bachelor of Economics from Porto University in 2009. He received his Master of Science degree in Modeling, Data Analysis and Decision Support Systems in 2011 from the University of Porto. In 2011, he joined the data mining group from Leiden Institute for Advanced Computer Science (LIACS). Since Ricardo Cachucho joined LIACS he has been working as a data miner for a STW project called InfraWatch (http://infrawatch.liacs.nl/) funded with the purpose of getting insights of how infrastructure assets evolve over time. His research focus is on mining sensor systems data from a time series perspective.

Nitesh Chawla, PhD, is the Frank Freimann Collegiate Associate Professor in the Department of Computer Science and Engineering, Director of Data Inference Analysis and Learning Lab (DIAL), and Director of the Interdisciplinary Center for Network Science and Applications (iCeNSA). He started his tenure-track position at Notre Dame in 2007 and was promoted and tenured in 2011. His research is focused on machine learning, data mining, and network science. He is at the frontier of interdisciplinary applications with innovative work in healthcare informatics, social networks, analytics, and climate/environmental sciences. He is the recipient of multiple awards for research and teaching innovation including outstanding teacher awards (2007 and 2010), National Academy of Engineers New Faculty Fellowship, and number of best paper awards and nominations. He received the IBM Watson Faculty Award in 2012. He was the chair of the IEEE CIS Data Mining Technical Committee (2010-2012). He serves on editorial boards of a number of journals and organization/program committees of top-tier conferences.

David Cieslak, PhD, is the Senior Data Scientist at Aunalytics, Inc., a company focused on bringing Big Data solutions to small and mid-sized businesses in a variety of industries, such as health care, manufacturing, and finance. His work focuses on generalizing data science methodologies into a unique platform. His research focuses on machine learning and data mining. He has served as an adjunct faculty member at Notre Dame and taught several courses. He has published in top conferences and journals throughout his field and served on the program committee for several conference workshops.

Luca Cinquini is a senior software engineer at the NASA Jet Propulsion Laboratory, where he's involved in architecting and developing software components for management and analysis of Earth system data. His major activity is working at the Earth System Grid Foundation. He also collaborates with the National Oceanic and Atmospheric Administration to promote shared development and common infrastructure between the two agencies. Cinquini has a PhD in high-energy physics from the University of Colorado.

Gillian Dobbie is a Professor in the Department of Computer Science at The University of Auckland, New Zealand. She received a Ph.D. from the University of Melbourne, an M.Tech. (Hons) and B.Tech. (Hons) in Computer Science from Massey University. She has lectured at Massey University, the University of Melbourne, and Victoria University of Wellington, and held visiting research positions at Griffith University and the National University of Singapore. Her research interests include formal foundations for databases, object oriented databases, semi-structured databases, logic and databases, data warehousing, data mining, access control, e-commerce, and data modelling. She has published over 100 international refereed journal and conference papers.

J. Stephen Downie is Associate Dean for Research and a Professor at the Graduate School of Library and Information Science at the University of Illinois at Urbana-Champaign. Downie is the Illinois Co-Director of the HathiTrust Research Center (HTRC). He is also Director of the International Music Information Retrieval Systems Evaluation Laboratory (IMIRSEL) and founder and ongoing director of the Music Information Retrieval Evaluation eXchange (MIREX). He has been very active in the establishment of the Music Information Retrieval (MIR) community through his ongoing work with the International Society for Music Information Retrieval (ISMIR) conferences. He was ISMIR's founding President and now serves on the ISMIR board. Professor Downie holds a BA (Music Theory and Composition) along with a Master's and a PhD in Library and Information Science, all earned at the University of Western Ontario, London, Canada.

Brian Glendenning is the head of the Data Management and Software Department at the National Radio Astronomy Observatory (NRAO). Before that, he was head of the Atacama Large Millimeter/Submillimeter Array (ALMA) Computing Integrated Product Team, responsible for delivering all the custom software and COTS computing equipment for this major new astronomical facility under construction in the Atacama Desert in Chile. Before that he played an architectural/development role in the development of the astronomical data analysis package now known as Common Astronomy Software Applications (CASA). He has been at NRAO since 1990.

David Harland is a software developer at the National Radio Astronomy Observatory, and is currently the System Architect for the group responsible for user-facing software at the observatory. He received a Bachelor of Science degree in Chemistry from the Massachusetts Institute of Technology and is a Fellow of the Society of Actuaries.

Andrew F. Hart is a software engineer at the NASA Jet Propulsion Laboratory, where he participates in science data system efforts across many domains including radio astronomy, Earth science, and cancer biomarker research. His interests lie in Web development, user interface design, data modeling, and API development for Web services. Hart has an MS in computer science from the University of Southern California.

Dayton Jones is a Principal Scientist at the Jet Propulsion Laboratory, California Institute of Technology. He has been involved in studies of space-based low frequency array mission concepts for the past two decades, most recently concepts for a large lunar-based array to observe neutral hydrogen from early cosmic epochs. His research interests include high angular resolution imaging and high precision astrometry with very-long-baseline interferometry. He is an author on ~200 scientific publications. He has a BA in Physics from Carleton College, an MS in Scientific Instrumentation from the University of California, Santa Barbara, and MS and PhD degrees in Astronomy from Cornell University.

Gueyoung Jung is a research scientist in Xerox Research Center Webster. His research background is in Distributed Computing, Autonomic Computing, and Services Computing. In particular, his research interests are in designing systems and analytical modeling to predict and optimize QoS in large-scale, data-intensive distributed systems like Cloud and Grid. His research straddles both theory and practice, ranging from analytical techniques to model and reason about system behaviors under dynamic conditions, to online control systems that use the models to implement adaptive behaviors. He is also serving as an adjunct professor in University of Rochester. He received his Ph.D. in Computer Science from Georgia Institute of Technology. He has authored and co-authored numerous papers in prestigious conferences, journals, books, and science magazines. Before starting his graduate program, he was a system engineer at a large and a startup companies for five years.

M.-Tahar Kechadi was awarded PhD and Masters Degree in Computer Science from University of Lille 1, France. He worked as a post-doctoral researcher under TMR program at UCD. He joined UCD in 1999 as a permanent staff member of the School of Computer Science & Informatics (CSI). He is currently Professor of Computer Science at CSI, UCD. His research interests span the areas of Data Mining, distributed data mining heterogeneous distributed systems, Grid and Cloud Computing, and digital forensics and cyber-crime investigations. Prof Kechadi serves on the scientific committees for a number of international conferences. He is currently an editorial board member of the *Journal of Future Generation of Computer Systems*. He is a member of the *Communications of the ACM* journal and *IEEE Computer Society*.

Jeff Kern is team lead for the Common Astronomical Software Applications (CASA) project at the National Radio Astronomy Observatory in Socorro, New Mexico. He received a Ph.D. in astrophysics from the New Mexico Institute of Mining and Technology before joining NRAO to work on the software control system for the Atacama Large Millimeter/sub-millimeter Array. Currently he is leading efforts to produce an automated data reduction pipeline for radio astronomy data, and enable data analysis on high performance computing clusters.

Shakeh Khudikyan is a software engineer at the NASA Jet Propulsion Laboratory within the Data Management Systems and Technologies team. Her work involves design and development of Web applications tools for science data systems. She received her Bachelors of Arts degree in Mathematics from the University of Southern California.

Jeonghyun Kim is an assistant professor at the Department of Library and Information Sciences, College of Information, University of North Texas, Denton, TX. She earned her PhD at Rutgers University. She has various areas of research interest ranging from digital libraries, data curation, human computer interaction, to convergence issues surrounding libraries, archives, and museums. She has published numerous papers in journals including *Journal of the American Society for Information Science and Technology* and *International Journal of Digital Curation*.

Arno Knobbe is a senior researcher in the Data Mining Group at the LIACS (the Leiden Institute of Advanced Computer Science). Additionally, he is the owner of a Dutch Data Mining consulting company called Kiminkii. His research is focused on projects that revolve around large collections of data. In these projects, novel and scalable Data Mining techniques are employed to effectively unearth the useful knowledge in these rich sources of data. His activities include the development of new techniques for uncovering hidden knowledge from this data, and the development of new ways to apply existing techniques to "Big Data," essentially relying on new developments in High-Performance Computing.

Stacy T. Kowalczyk is an Assistant Professor in the Graduate School of Library and Information Science at Dominican University where she teaches courses on digital libraries, library systems, and digital curation. She has an MLIS from Dominican University and a Ph.D. from Indiana University. Her research focuses on the problems of research data, big data, and curation, specifically looking at the intersection of social and technical issues. In her current work, she is investigating the research practices of scholars, the lifecycle of research data including data reuse, and the antecedents, barriers, and threats to preservation of research data. Her work with the HathiTrust Research Center involves issues of data, metadata and access including issues of metadata usability, quality, and versioning.

Joseph Lazio is a Principal Scientist at the Jet Propulsion Laboratory and Visiting Associate at the California Institute of Technology. He received a Ph.D. in astronomy from Cornell University and was a staff member at the Naval Research Laboratory before joining JPL. While at NRL, he was awarded one of 15 "Emerging Investigator" awards as part of the Department of the Navy's Top Scientists and Engineers of the Year, in the inaugural year of the program.

Ezio Lefons received his degree in Mathematics from University of Pisa in 1973. He holds his didactic activity at the Department of Informatics of University of Bari, since 1975. Currently, he is Associate Professor of Informatics and teaches the "Data Bases" and "Advanced Data Bases" courses for the computer science curricula. He served as Director of the three-year Doctoral Course in "Science of the Human Relations" and has been coordinator of the "Administration of Databases and Distributed Systems" curricula of degrees in Informatics. His scientific research is relative to the field of databases, and his interests also included researches in human relational interactions models. The overall research is relative to original methods to organize and access very large data files using quick three-valued logic algorithms, and data structures based on the analytical/statistical properties of data. The latter also permits the distributive sorting of data, the direct data access, and the estimation of crucial parameters utilized to set up the DBMS query optimizers. Further researches are relative to general methods to fast access incomplete information data and database query systems based on finite multi-valued logic. These studies have led to obtain international patents. In the last years, the research has been oriented also to the statistical/analytical database models, decision support systems, and approximate query systems in data warehouse environments. He is author and/or co-author of over 90 papers published in international journals, books, and conferences.

Samitha Liyanage is a Software Engineer at Data to Insight Center of the Indiana University Pervasive Technology Institute. She holds a Bachelor of Science of Engineering degree from University of Moratuwa, Sri Lanka. She is interested in Web development and Web related security models. Before joining Data to Insight Center she worked as an Electrical Engineer and specialized in Energy Conservation. Her work with the HathiTrust Research Center involves implementing security related components.

Charles Loboz grew up in Poland and graduated with MSc in Nuclear Physics. After working for few years in the area of scientific computing, he obtained his PhD in Computer Science from the Australian National University. Dr. Loboz worked for UNISYS in the area of transaction processing systems authoring multiple patents architectural and performance analysis areas. After a brief episode with a start-up company, he joined Microsoft as a Principal Capacity Planning Engineer in Global Foundation Services division responsible for building and operating Microsoft data centres worldwide. Three years ago, Dr. Loboz moved to Windows Azure as a Principal Architect, Capacity Planning. He has published occasional papers in both scientific and industry conferences and currently holds 10 patents, with few more patent applications in processing.

Mian Lu is currently employed as a Scientist at Institute of High Performance Computing, Agency for Science, Technology, and Research (A*STAR), Singapore. He recently received his Ph.D. degree in Computer Sciences from the Hong Kong University of Science and Technology (2007-2012). Before that, he got the Bachelor degree in Huazhong University of Science and Technology, China (2003-2007). His research interests are in high performance computing and scientific data management, especially for bioinformatics applications. His current focus is on using modern hardware accelerators (GPUs and Intel Xeon Phi coprocessors) to build high performance systems for data analytics applications.

Qiong Luo is an Associate Professor at the Department of Computer Science and Engineering, Hong Kong University of Science and Technology (HKUST). Her research interests are in database systems, parallel and distributed systems, and scientific computing. Current focus is on data management on modern hardware, GPU acceleration for data analytics, and database support for e-science. Qiong received her Ph.D. in Computer Sciences from the University of Wisconsin-Madison in 2002, her M.S. and B.S. in Computer Sciences from Beijing (Peking) University, China in 1997 and 1992, respectively.

Tanu Malik is a Research Scientist at the Computation Institute, University of Chicago. Her research focuses on the management, performance and provenance of the scientific data lifecycle. Her recent work focuses on HPC systems and databases, distributed data provenance, and interactive publications. Prior to joining UChicago, Tanu was a Research Assistant Professor at the Cyber Center and the Indiana Center for Database Systems at Purdue University. She earned her PHD and MS in 2008 from the Department of Computer Science, Johns Hopkins University and a B. Tech in 1999 from the Indian Institute of Technology, Kanpur. She is a member of the ACM and the IEEE.

Chris A. Mattmann is a senior computer scientist at the NASA Jet Propulsion Laboratory, working on instrument and science data systems on Earth science missions and informatics tasks. His research interests are primarily software architecture and large-scale data-intensive systems. Mattmann received his PhD in computer science from the University of Southern California. He's a senior member of IEEE.

Marvin Meeng is a scientific programmer at the LIACS, under the supervision of Arno Knobbe. Though now mainly occupied with Data Mining, he obtained his MSc in Cognitive Artificial Intelligence at the Philosophy department of Utrecht University. Being oriented towards philosophical subjects related to the human mind initially, focus shifted towards more practical areas related to machine learning later on. Resulting in a thesis about a Dual Purkinje Image Eyetracker at the Experimental Psychology division first, and his current employment after that.

Shengfa Miao obtained his MSc in Computer Software and Theory from Lanzhou University in 2009. He is currently a PhD candidate at Leiden Institute of Advanced Computer Science (LIACS) in Leiden University, The Netherlands, and at the same time, he is also involved in a PhD program in Lanzhou University, China. His research interests lie in the areas of Data Mining, Search Engine, Network Security, and Structural Health Monitoring, with a particular focus on applying Data Mining techniques to diagnose structural health. He is working on Data Management for Monitoring Infrastructural Performance, the InfraWatch project, which employs monitoring and sensing systems on a highway bridge to extract actual information about its condition and performance.

Stefan Mišković, MSc, is a PhD student at the Department for Informatics and Computer Science, Faculty of Mathematics, University of Belgrade. At the same Faculty, he graduated as a Bachelor of Mathematics and Computer Science in 2010. He defended his master thesis in 2011. He is currently working as a Teaching Assistant at Faculty of Mathematics, Department for Informatics and Computer Science. He is also a part-time researcher on a scientific project at Institute of Mathematics, supported by Serbian Ministry for Education, Science and Technological Development. His research areas are: optimization, facility location, evolutionary algorithms, metaheuristic methods, and hybrid optimization techniques.

Tridib Mukherjee is a Research Scientist at Xerox Research Center India (XRCI). He received B.E. degree in computer science and engineering from Jadavpur University, Kolkata, India, and Ph.D degree in computer science from Arizona State University (ASU), Tempe, USA. He was a finalist of the IBM PhD fellowship award in 2007. He has also previously done research internship at Intel Labs. His research interests include Cloud Computing, Green (Sustainable) Computing, Distributed Systems, and Cyber-Physical Systems. He has published numerous articles in reputed journals and conferences, and given tutorials on safe and sustainable computing in multiple forums. He has also co-authored a book on safety, security, and sustainability of body-area networks published by the Cambridge press in 2013. He is a member of the IEEE and served in the technical program committee of numerous top conferences.

Muhammad Asif Naeem is presently a lecturer in School of Computing and Mathematical Sciences, Auckland University of Technology, Auckland, New Zealand. He received his PhD degree in Computer Science from The University of Auckland, New Zealand. He has been awarded a best PhD thesis award from The University of Auckland. Before that Asif has done his Master's degree with distinction in the area of Web Mining. He has about twelve years research, industrial and teaching experience. He has published over 30 research papers in peer-reviewed journals, conferences, and workshops including IEEE, ACM, and VLDB. His research interests include Databases, Data Warehousing, Data Stream Processing and Query Optimization.

Raghunath Nambiar is a Distinguished Engineer at Cisco's Data Center Business Group. He has 18 years of technical accomplishments with significant expertise in system architecture and performance engineering. His current responsibilities include emerging technologies and big data strategy for Cisco. He has served on several industry standard committees for performance evaluation and program committees of academic conferences. He is a member of the board of directors of the Transaction Processing Performance Council (TPC), founding chair of its International Conference Series on Performance Evaluation and Benchmarking, and member of the Board of directors of Big Data 100 consortia. Prior to joining Cisco, Raghu was an Architect at Hewlett-Packard. He has published 4 books and over 30 papers. Raghu holds master's degrees from University of Massachusetts and Goa University, and completed advanced management program from Stanford University.

Cem Ozdogan received his B.Sc., M.Sc. and Ph.D. degrees in Physics in 1994, 1996, and 2002, respectively, all from the Middle East Technical University, METU, Ankara, Turkey. He joined the faculty at Cankaya University in 2001 as an Assistant Professor of Computer Engineering Department. After spending ten years from 2001 to 2011 at the same department, he joined the faculty at same university as Acting Chair of Materials and Engineering Department. He is presently an associate professor in the same department. His research interests are generally in the areas of nanoscience, solid state physics and scientific computing. Specific interests include electronic structure calculations of clusters and periodic systems, molecular dynamics simulations, linear scaling computations of large systems and parallel computing.

Milinda Pathirage is a Ph. D. student at Indiana University. He is also a Research Associate at Data to Insight Center of the Indiana University Pervasive Technology Institute. His research focuses on the problems of Cloud Computing for Scientific Applications and Compiler Optimizations for High Level Languages targeting GPGPUs. His work with the HathiTrust Research Center involves design of security architecture. Before coming to Indiana University, he worked at WSO2 Inc. as the product manager for business process execution engine project.

Zong Peng is a Ph.D. candidate in Computer Science in the School of Informatics and Computing at Indiana University Bloomington. He earned his Bachelor in Network engineering in 2009 from Dalian University of Technology in China and his Master of Science degree in Computer Science in 2011 from Indiana University Bloomington. He is a Research Assistant in Data to Insight Center of the Indiana University Pervasive Technology Institute, under supervision of Professor Plale. His current research with the HTRC focuses mainly on the building, deploying and maintaining the index infrastructure for the entire HTRC collection providing security, auditing, and customized functions. He research interests includes in Big Data, NoSQL, Cloud Computing, HPC, and Information Retrieval.

Beth A. Plale is a professor of Computer Science as well as the Director of the Data to Insight Center of the Pervasive Technologies Institute and the Director of the Center for Data and Search Informatics at Indiana University. Plale is the Indiana Co-Director of the HathiTrust Research Center (HTRC). She has broad research and governance interest in long-term preservation and access to scientific data, and enabling computational access to large-scale data for broader groups of researchers. Her specific research interests are in tools for metadata and provenance capture, data repositories, cyberinfrastructure for large-scale data analysis, and workflow systems. Plale is deeply engaged in interdisciplinary research and education and has substantive experience in developing stable and useable scientific cyberinfrastructure.

Meikel Poess is a software developer in the Server Technologies Group at Oracle Corporation, which he joined in 1998. He is mainly responsible for analyzing and improving the performance of Oracle Database software stack (database, network, and storage). As a chairman in the Transaction Processing Performance Council, Meikel has made significant contributions to the developments of key industry standards for performance measurement including TPC-H, TPC-R, TPC-Energy, TPC-DS, and TPC-DI. Raghu and he are co-chairing TPC's International Conference Series on Performance Evaluation and Benchmarking (TPCTC). Meikel served on program committees of several industry/research conferences, such as VLDB, SIGMOD and ICPE. As an elected member of SPEC Research, he is driving the future of benchmark developments. He is a member of the Board of Directors of BigData100, an emerging consortia to measure the performance of BigData systems. He has also published many academic papers and is a frequent speaker at VLDB, IEEE, and ACM conferences.

Robert Preston is a JPL astronomer, and is the Chief Scientist of the Interplanetary Network Directorate. He previously held several other positions including manager of the JPL astrophysics research program, project scientist for the NASA's Space VLBI Project, supervisor of an JPL astronomical research group, and an adjunct faculty appointment at Caltech (astronomy and planetary science). He has been an investigator on several planetary missions including being U.S. scientific team leader for balloons that flew in the atmosphere of Venus and for (ill-fated) landers destined for the Martian moon Phobos. His personal research interests include active galactic nuclei, planetary dynamics, stellar astrometry, and archeology.

Nathan Regola, PhD, was a senior analytics engineer at a Fortune 500 before beginning law coursework to examine data privacy and data security issues in the context of a data driven culture. His broad technical research interest is the design of integrated enterprise-wide decision support systems. His previous work includes the benchmarking of high performance computing hardware and virtualization technologies for use in data intensive systems. His research interest in building systems that leverage metadata was motivated by the needs of organizations that he worked with at the Interdisciplinary Center for Network Science and Applications (iCeNSA) at Notre Dame.

James Robnett is a Linux and network system administrator in Socorro, New Mexico, at the National Radio Astronomy Observatory, and is currently Division Head for the Computing Infrastructure Division there. His primary focus is in HPC computing platform specification and performance tuning for EVLA data collection, EVLA and ALMA data post-processing clusters using CASA, and the VLBA DiFX software correlators.

Guangchen Ruan is currently working toward the Ph.D. degree in Computer Science in the School of Informatics and Computing at Indiana University Bloomington. He received a B.S. degree from Xi'an Jiaotong University, China, and M.S. degree from Peking University, China, both in Computer Science. He is a Research Assistant in Data to Insight Center of the Indiana University Pervasive Technology Institute, under supervision of Professor Plale. His research interests include big data analysis and management, distributed data intensive computing, data visualization, and data mining.

Ilias K. Savvas was awarded PhD from UCD, Ireland, in Computer Science, a Masters degree in Computer Science from University of Dundee, UK, and BSc in Mathematics from Aristotle University of Thessaloniki, Greece. He was appointed as lecturer at the Computer Science and Telecommunications (CST) Department of TEI of Larissa, Greece. He is currently Associate Professor at CST, TEI of Larissa. His research interests span the areas of Cloud Computing, Big Data, Parallel Computing, Distributed Data mining, heterogeneous distributed systems and Grid computing. Dr. Savvas has published over 30 research articles in refereed journals and conferences. He serves on the scientific committees for a number of international journals and conferences. He was the general chair of the WETICE-2010 IEEE conference and he is member of the steering committee of the International IEEE Track on Cooperative Knowledge Discovery & Data Mining – CKDD.

Georgia N. Sofianidou was awarded her BSc in Computer Science and Telecommunications Department from Technological Education Institute of Larissa, Greece. Her research interests span the areas of Cloud Computing, Big Data, E-learning, and heterogeneous distributed systems.

Zorica Stanimirović, PhD, is Assistant Professor at the Department for Numerical Mathematics and Optimization and Vice-Dean for Science and Research at Faculty of Mathematics, University of Belgrade. She received her PhD in Optimization from Faculty of Mathematics, Belgrade, in 2007. Since 2002, she is a part-time researcher at several scientific projects at Institute of Mathematics, supported by Serbian Ministry for Education, Science and Technological Development. She was involved in several scientific and educational projects funded by EU. She is a member of local editorial board of Zentralblatt Math and MathEduc. Her research interests are: Combinatorial Optimization, Mathematical Modeling, Facility location, Hub location problems, and Metaheuristic methods.

Yiming Sun is a Senior Software Architect of the HathiTrust Research Center project and works as a full-time staff at the Data to Insight Center of the Indiana University Pervasive Technology Institute. He has a M.S. degree of Computer Science from the School of Informatics and Computing at Indiana University and is currently a PhD candidate in the same school. His research interest is in the long-term preservation of scientific datasets.

Filippo Tangorra received the "Laurea" degree in Computer Science from University of Bari, Italy, in 1975. He is currently an associate professor at the Computer Science Department of the University of Bari, Italy, where he teaches courses of "computer architecture," "database systems," and "information systems" for the computer science curriculum. He has been working at the same department from 1980 to 1986 as Assistant Professor and from 1975 to 1976 as university researcher. His researches were initially in human relational interaction system modelling. Successively, his research activities have regarded decision support systems in research context, models of databases and statistical databases, data dictionary systems, and query optimization. Other the above topics, his current research interests in computer architecture have led to the definition of a processor simulation environment for teaching purpose and query approximate in data warehousing. He has published more than 100 papers on the above topics.

Aaron Todd is a Ph.D. candidate in School of Informatics and Computing at Indiana University Bloomington. He is a Research Assistant in Data to Insight Center of the Indiana University Pervasive Technology Institute, under supervision of Professor Plale. His research interests are broad but focus on applying programming language innovations in real applications. Topics of interest in programming languages include concurrency, parallelism, compilers, parallel runtime systems, logic programming, type systems and effect systems. In the context of the HathiTrust Research Center, this involved writing the agent component, which presents a Web service API for job submission.

Francesco Di Tria received his Laurea degree in Informatics from University of Bari "Aldo Moro" in 2007. In 2011, he received the PhD in Informatics from the same University. He is currently a research fellow in the Computer Science Department, where he teaches courses of "Databases," "Information Systems," and "Computer Network," for the computer science curriculum. His research interests are in data warehousing and business intelligence systems. In detail, his main activity regards the automation of processes for data warehouse modelling and the definition of metrics for data warehouse quality measurement. Since 2007, he works into several research projects for the valorisation of intangible cultural heritage and the improvement of the healthcare system of the Apulia region. He is author and/or co-author of over 20 papers published in international journals, books, and conferences.

Joaquin Vanschoren obtained his PhD at the KU Leuven, Belgium on the topic of meta-learning, understanding when and why learning algorithms work well on certain types of data. He created OpenML. org, an open science platform to share and organize the results of machine learning researchers around the world so they can be combined and reused to answer questions quickly and tackle ever-larger problems. Besides this, his research interests include large-scale machine learning, scalable algorithms, collaborative filtering, graph mining, ontologies, and algorithms for data mining in general.

Ugo Vespier earned his BSc degree in Computer Science from the University of Pisa in 2007. During his Master's studies, he was exchange student at the Vrij Universiteit Amsterdam and research intern at the Parc Cientific de Barcelona, where he has been awarded for the best project of the internship programme. In 2010, he received his MSc degree in Computer Science cum laude from the University of Pisa with an award-winning thesis on Web Mining and Computer Vision. At present, Ugo is PhD candidate at Leiden University where he works on data mining, machine learning and visualization methods for large time series data in the context of the InfraWatch project. His work has been presented at international conferences and workshops. In the past, Ugo has worked as freelance software developer and, since 2013, he is co-founder of a Web startup specializing in video advertising, social media and analytics.

Yuanxin Wang is a doctoral student at Temple University, USA. She holds a Master of Philosophy degree in Communication from Hong Kong Baptist University and a Master of Arts in International Journalism from University of Central Lancashire. Her research interests include new media and media effects.

Dan Watson is an associate professor and head of the Department of Computer Science at Utah State University. He holds a Ph.D. in Electrical Engineering from Purdue University. Dr. Watson's recent work includes the efficient parallel implementation of algorithms for hydrological analysis of large digital elevation maps. He is a member of the ACM.

Lynne M. Webb (PhD, University of Oregon, 1980) is Professor of Communication, University of Arkansas, and previously held tenured appointments at the University of Florida and the University of Memphis. Dr. Webb is best known as an applied scholar and groundbreaking researcher in three areas: social media, family communication, as well as communication and aging. In 2012, she was named a J. William Fulbright Master Researcher by the University of Arkansas College of Arts and Sciences. Dr. Webb has published over 70 essays including multiple theories, research reports, methodological essays, and pedagogical essays. Her work has appeared in *Journal of Applied Communication Research*, *Health Communication*, and the *Journal of Family Communication*. Her co-edited readers include *Computer-Mediated Communication in Personal Relationships*; her social media research focuses on Facebook and blogs.

Gerald Weber is Senior Lecturer in the Department of Computer Science at The University of Auckland. He joined The University of Auckland in 2003. Gerald holds a PhD from the FU Berlin. He is information director of the Proceedings of the VLDB Endowment, and he has been program chair of several conferences. He is co-author of the book *Form Oriented Analysis*, and of over 40 peer-reviewed publications. His research interests include Databases and Data Models, Human-Computer Interaction and Theory of Computation.

Craig Willis is currently pursuing his doctorate at the Graduate School of Library and Information Science (GSLIS) at the University of Illinois at Urbana-Champaign where he works as a research assistant for the HathiTrust Research Center (HTRC) and International Music Information Retrieval Systems Evaluation Laboratory (IMIRSEL). His research focuses on information seeking and retrieval in large collections of digital books and music. Prior to pursuing his MLS from the University of North Carolina at Chapel Hill, he worked as a software developer for companies including ProQuest/Serials Solutions and Sony Recording Media.

Ahmet Artu Yıldırım received his M.S. degree in Computer Engineering from Cankaya University, Ankara, Turkey in 2011. He is currently a Ph.D. student in the Department of Computer Science at Utah State University. His research interests include bioinformatics, parallel and distributed computing and data mining.

Jiaan Zeng is a Ph.D. candidate in School of Informatics and Computing at Indiana University Bloomington. He is a Research Assistant in Data to Insight Center of the Indiana University Pervasive Technology Institute, under supervision of Professor Plale. His research focuses on large scale distributed system and data management, specially looking at how to run data analysis on large data set. In his current work, he is investigating the research of optimization in MapReduce paradigm, non-consumptive protection for copyright data access, and cloud infrastructure for text analysis.

Index

A

Adaptive, Hash-partitioned Exact Window Join (AH-EWJ) 153
adaptive sampling 95, 105, 109
Apache Lucene 205, 213
Apache Software Foundation 197, 199, 203-205, 218, 220, 291
Application Programming Interface (API) 3, 276
articulated network 113
Atacama Large Millimeter Array (ALMA) 197-198
Australian Square Kilometre Array Precursor (ASKAP) 203
Australia Telescope National Facility (ATNF) 203
average length 390

B

band-pass filter (BPF) 341
behavioral network 113
benchmarketing 416, 418, 425
benchmarks 1, 12-14, 21, 155, 163, 178, 250, 255, 381, 384-385, 390-392, 394-395, 415-432
big data analytics 1-2, 12, 47-51, 54-55, 57, 63, 65-66, 107, 112, 223-224, 265, 268, 418, 429, 431
blog audience 114
blogosphere 110-112, 114
Burrows-Wheeler transform (BWT) 352, 366
bursty

C

Cache Join (CACHEJOIN) 150
Capacity Utilization Factor 398
Center for Large-scale Data Systems Research (CLDS) 427
Central Limit Theorem 407, 412
centroid 24-25, 31-33, 40-42, 322, 324-327
cluster sampling 102-103

combiner 4-5, 32, 34, 39, 42-43, 322, 326
Common Warehouse Metamodel (CWM) 387
Commonwealth Scientific and Industrial Research Organization (CSIRO) 203
Complex Event Processing (CEP) 10
composite excess entropy (CEE) 407, 412
conceptual representation 149
constant memory 354, 368
Content Standard for Digital Geospatial Metadata (CSDGM) 188
CPU virtualization 384-385
Creative Commons Zero (CC0) 184
cyberinfrastructure 190, 193, 270-271, 273-276, 278-279, 282, 284, 286, 289-290, 292-293

D

data access libraries (DA) 307
Data Condensation 298, 306
data dictionary 125-127, 137, 139
Data Documentation Initiative (DDI) 186, 189
datanode 26, 32, 347
Data Reduction 72-74, 77-82, 84, 88-89, 92-93, 215, 298, 300, 306-307
data warehouse 15, 19, 26, 115-119, 124-125, 128-129, 133, 135-136, 141-142, 144-151, 175, 204, 220, 383, 386-388, 390-393, 395
Digital Humanities 270-271, 273-274, 277-280, 282, 284, 290-293
Digital libraries 191, 270-272
Digital Signal Processing 318, 345
discrete convolution theorem 334
Discrete Fourier Transform (DFT) 79, 320
Discrete Wavelet Transform (DWT) 80
discretization 335
Distributed Memory System (DMS) 82, 92
Double Pipelined Hash Join (DPHJ) 153
Dryad 177, 183-184, 190-192, 194
DryadLINQ 25, 44

E

EA and a Tabu Search heuristic (EA-TS) 228, 244
Early Hash Join (EHJ) 153
Enterprise Data Warehouse (EDW) 19
eScience 179, 190, 192, 205
evolutionary algorithm (EA) 228
excess entropy (EE) 400, 412
Expanded Very Large Array (EVLA) 197-198, 200, 218, 220
Extract, Transform and Load (ETL) 19
extract, transform, load (ETL) 298

F

Fast Fourier Transform (FFT) 334
Federal Geographic Data Committee (FGDC) 188
federated cloud 54, 71
federation 50, 57, 61-62, 66, 208-209, 214, 218
Fine Grained Tournament Selection (FGTS) 240
Flexible Extensible Digital Object Repository Architecture 190
frequency domain 80, 320-321, 347

G

genome-wide association studies (GWAS) 349-350
GeoBase 295-297, 300-309, 311
Geospatial Data Abstraction Library (GDAL) 296
global conceptual schema 119, 126-127, 141
Google's File System (GFS) 425
Graphics and Workstation Performance Group (GWPG) 420
Graphics Processing Units (GPUs) 73, 354
GrHyMM 118, 146

H

Hadoop file system (HDFS) 302
Hash-Merge Join (HMJ) 153
HathiTrust Research Center (HTRC) 270-271, 274, 277
HBase 8-11, 20-21, 284, 296-298, 301-306, 309, 311, 313, 344-345
HFile 8
High Performance Computing (HPC) 107
High Performance Group (HPG) 420
Hilbert curves 92, 300, 312
hybrid approach 115, 124, 135, 147, 149, 241

I

Independent Publishers Guild (IPC) 100
In-Memory Database 17, 22
Intel Developers Forum (IDF) 424
Interuniversity Consortium for Political and Social Research (ICPSR) 177
iRODS 190, 212

J

JobTracker 3-4, 11

K

Karoo Array Telescope (KAT-7) 202
k-means 23-25, 31-33, 37-38, 40, 42-46, 322-324, 326-328

L

lexical analyzer (LA) 129
Linear Time-Invariant 339
load balancing 8, 49-56, 58, 64-65, 67-69, 71, 305-306, 308-310
Local Search (LS) 242
logical program 115, 118, 129-131, 134-135, 142, 149
low-end local worker (LLW) 62
low-frequency component 80-81, 87-89
low-pass filter 331

M

mapper 2-3, 11-12, 25, 27, 32, 41-43, 321-322, 325-326, 332-334
Map phase 4, 46, 321
Maximally Overlapped Bin-packing (MOB) 58, 64-65
Mesh Join (MESHJOIN) 150, 153
metaheuristic 222, 224, 228, 235, 242, 250-251, 255, 262, 269
Metaheuristic 222, 269
METAHEURISTIC 234
metaheuristics 228, 234-235, 250, 257, 262, 267-268
Metaheuristics 269
micro-blog 95, 109, 112, 114
mid-end remote worker (MRW) 62
Minimum Description Length (MDL) 334
minor allele frequency (MAF) 349-350, 352

N

namenode 26, 32
National Aeronautics and Space Administration (NASA) 182
National Climate Data Center (NCDC) 182
National Institutes of Health (NIH) 178
National Oceanographic Data Center (NODC) 177, 183
National Radio Astronomy Observatory (NRAO) 196-198, 200, 203, 206-207, 217
National Science Foundation (NSF) 178
NetCDF-Java library 306
Network Attached Storage (NAS) 17
Newton's law of cooling 340
Non Uniform Memory Architecture (NUMA) 17
normalized excess entropy (nEE) 404, 412
NoSQL 1-2, 7-10, 12-14, 21, 213, 284, 288, 291-292, 313, 417-418, 426

O

Object Oriented Data Technology 203, 220
Ocean Acidification Data Stewardship (OADS) 187
Ocean Acidification Program (OAP) 187
Ocean Archive System (OAS) 188
Online Analytics Processing (OLAP) 17
On Line Transaction Processing (OLTP) 416
ontological representation 126, 136, 149
Open Information Model (OIM) 386
Open Source Development Lab (OSDL) 424
Open Systems Group (OSG) 420
optical character recognition software (OCR) 282
Oracle Application Standard Benchmark 423
outcoming flow 229-230, 238

P

parallelization 47-49, 53, 56-60, 66, 71, 90, 283
parallel processing techniques 82, 89, 93
Performance Impact Factor (PIF) 398
power iteration clustering (PIC) 223
predicate calculus 118, 128, 146, 149
Project Gutenberg 272, 292
Project MUSE 180
Publishers Association (PA) 100
purposeful sampling 100, 103
Python 26, 28, 32, 44-46, 206

R

real-time data warehousing 150-151, 154
Reduce phase 43, 46, 322
reengineering process 115-116, 118, 145, 149
Relational Database Management System (RDBMS) 107
relational database system (RDBMS) 284
Remote Procedure Calls (RPC) 3
Representational State Transfer (REST) 279
Research Group (RG) 420, 4255

S

scale-space image 329-331, 335
schemas integration 145, 149
Script Workflow Analysis for MultiProcessing (SWAMP) 84
Semi-Streaming Index Join (SSIJ) 154
semi-structured data 107, 114, 149, 390, 429
sensor data analysis 314-315, 318
Shared Memory System (SMS) 82, 93
single-nucleotide polymorphism (SNP) 349-350
Single Program Multiple Data (SPMD) 24, 46
site frequency spectrum (SFS) 353-354
Solr 197, 199, 205-206, 211, 213-214, 216-218, 221, 277, 286-289
space-filling curves (SFC) 298
Space Telescope Science Institute (STScI) 182
Square Kilometre Array (SKA) 197-198, 202
Standard Performance Evaluation Corporation (SPEC) 415-416, 418, 420
Storage Area Network (SAN) 14, 17
storage area networks (SANs) 417
Storage Performance Council (SPC) 416, 418, 421
stratified sampling 75, 105-106
Streaming Multiprocessors (SMs) 354
stream processing 150-151, 159
structured data 8, 14, 16, 20, 83, 107, 114, 119, 137, 149, 181, 223, 291, 311, 318, 390, 428-429, 432
Structured Query Language (SQL) 3
subsequence clustering (SSC) 322
suffix array (SA) 366
super-band matrix 358-360
Symmetric Hash Join (SHJ) 153
Symmetric Multi Processing (SMP) 19
synchronization 55, 66, 71, 84, 176, 289, 349, 362-363, 367

syntactical analyzer (SA) 129
systematic sampling 74-75, 101-102
system under test (SUT) 428

T

TableMapper 9
TableReducer 9
Tabu Search heuristic (TS) 234
TaskTracker 3
Tika 197, 199, 205, 207-208, 211, 217-219, 221
Time-invariant 339
token 129-130, 276, 284
TPC's Technology Conference Series (TPCTC) 425
Transaction Processing Performance Council (TPC)
    415-416, 418

V

V-FASTR 208-210, 213-216, 220-221
virtual machine 384-385, 393, 395-396, 410, 423
Virtual Research Environment (VRE) 179, 194
VMmark® 423

W

warp scheduler 354
wavecluster algorithm 82, 85-87, 89-90
Web 2.0 114, 417, 424-425
Workshop Series on Big Data Benchmarking
    (WBDB) 426-427
wrap-around problem 332, 334

Y

Yahoo! Cloud Serving Benchmark (YCSB) 13, 424

Z

zipfian distribution 152, 163, 165-166, 173, 309
Z-ordering (ZO) 308
Z-regions 298, 303-305, 307